Everyman's
CLASSICAL DICTIONARY

A Volume in
EVERYMAN'S REFERENCE LIBRARY

Everyman's Reference Library

CLASSICAL DICTIONARY

CONCISE ENCYCLOPAEDIA OF ARCHITECTURE

DICTIONARY OF ABBREVIATIONS

DICTIONARY OF DATES

DICTIONARY OF ECONOMICS

DICTIONARY OF FICTIONAL CHARACTERS

DICTIONARY OF LITERARY BIOGRAPHY:
ENGLISH AND AMERICAN

DICTIONARY OF MUSIC

DICTIONARY OF NON-CLASSICAL MYTHOLOGY

DICTIONARY OF PICTORIAL ART (2 volumes)

DICTIONARY OF QUOTATIONS AND PROVERBS

DICTIONARY OF SHAKESPEARE QUOTATIONS

EVERYMAN'S ENCYCLOPAEDIA (12 volumes)

ENCYCLOPAEDIA OF GARDENING

ENGLISH PRONOUNCING DICTIONARY

THESAURUS OF ENGLISH WORDS AND PHRASES

Other volumes in preparation

Everyman's
CLASSICAL
DICTIONARY

800 B.C.—A.D. 337

by

JOHN WARRINGTON

J. M. DENT & SONS LTD
LONDON, MELBOURNE AND TORONTO

Made in Great Britain
at the
Aldine Press · Letchworth · Herts
for
J. M. DENT & SONS LTD
Aldine House · Albemarle Street · London
First published 1961
Second edition revised 1965
Third edition revised 1969
Reprinted 1970, 1978

ISBN: 0 460 03004 3

PREFACE

THE PRESENT work takes the place hitherto occupied in Everyman's Reference Library by *Smith's Smaller Classical Dictionary*. This latter volume had done good service for half a century, but had become outdated in scope, style and scholarship; two slight revisions made by me in 1952 and 1956 were no more than 'holding operations' against such time as some more thoroughgoing improvement could be undertaken.

Having agreed to prepare a completely new *Classical Dictionary* within strictly defined spatial limits, I had first to decide what years and what countries should be denoted by the term 'classical'. The needs of students, whom I have had particularly in mind, as well as of those many general readers who will use the book mainly for the understanding of 'classical' references in English literature, suggested that the period should begin with the commonly accepted date of Homer (late 8th century B.C.) and end with the death of Constantine (A.D. 337). The same considerations led me to confine myself to pagan Greece and Rome. Early Christian affairs are consequently outside the scope of this work, excepting occasional mention; while articles on persons, places, institutions and events of other civilizations—Egyptian, Persian and so forth—are supplied only when their subject-matter has a direct and contemporary bearing upon Greek and Roman history, literature, etc.

As to the nature of separate articles there could be little doubt. Experience has shown that patrons of Everyman's Reference Library much prefer short, highly compressed articles, plentifully cross-referenced, to more extensive and copious tracts, which contain a wealth of information but from which points of detail are not easily extracted. The method followed here is calculated to give maximum help to the reader without unnecessary repetition. The most famous legends, however—e.g. the Atreids, Thebes, Jason and Medea—are best told as continuous narrations, with cross-references from the names of their individual characters.

Hundreds of articles are supplied on persons and subjects ignored by the old volume. Special attention has been given to geographical and topographical items, for the benefit of readers who may take the book on their travels; and a list is included of more than one hundred modern place-names with their ancient equivalents as found in these pages. In this connection, also, Professor Oliver Thompson's new *Everyman's Classical Atlas* will be found invaluable, with its learned Introduction on ancient geography and notes on the principal battlefields of antiquity.

For the benefit of readers who may wish to discover at a glance what information the Dictionary offers on particular aspects of classical antiquity, the preliminary pages include a list of articles classified according to the main subjects into which the contents are divisible. They contain also an up-to-date classified bibliography of general works, but many of the articles themselves conclude with their own more specialized bibliographies.

A final problem concerned the spelling of Greek names. Here it seemed wisest to follow the dictates of common sense and steer a middle course by giving first the spelling in which my readers are most likely to find such names elsewhere, but to indicate in brackets (wholly or in part) the actual Greek spelling, transliterated according to the recommendations of the International Organization for Standardization (1959). Thus I print Aeschylus (Aiskhulos); Leucothea (Leuko-); Erebus (-os). Where a name can be transliterated as it stands, e.g. Xenophanēs, nothing more is required.

JOHN WARRINGTON.

1961.

For this third (1969) edition some of the articles have been rewritten to accord with the most recent views of historians and archaeologists. Bibliographies to separate articles have again been brought up to date.

J. W.

1969.

CONTENTS

	PAGE
Preface	vii
Modern Place-names with Ancient Equivalents . . .	xi
The Chief Philosophical Schools of Antiquity . . .	xiii
Genealogical Tables	xv
Select Bibliography	xvii
Systematic List of Entries	xxi
The Dictionary	I

MODERN PLACE-NAMES
WITH ANCIENT EQUIVALENTS

ADARNO, Adranon
AIX-EN-PROVENCE, Aquae Sextiae
ALBI, Alba Pompeia
ALEPPO, Beroea
ALTINO, Altinum
AMMAN, Philadelphia
ANAGNI, Anagnia
ANIENE, Anio
ANKARA, Ancyra
ANTAKYA, Antioch
AOSTA, Augusta Praetoria Salassorum
AQUINO, Aquinum
AREZZO, Arretium
ARLES, Arelate
ARPINO, Arpinum
ASCOLI, Asculum
ASHMOUNEIN, Hermopolis
ASSISI, Asisium
AVELLA VECCHIA, Abella

BAALBEK, Heliopolis
BAIA, Baiae
BATH, Aquae Sulis
BEHRAM, Aspendus
BEIRUT, Berytus
BENEVENTO, Beneventum
BEVAGNA, Mevania
BOLOGNA, Bononia
BRINDISI, Brundisium
BUDRUM, Halicarnassus

CAERLEON, Isca
CAGLIARI, Carales
CAIAZZO, Caiatia
CALAHORRA, Calagurris
CALVI, Cales
CANOSA, Canusium

CANTERBURY, Durovernum
CAPRI, Capreae
CARSOLI, Carseoli
CARTAGENE, Carthage Nova
CASTEL GANDOLFO, Alba Longa
CASTELLAMARE, Stabiae
CERVETRI, Caere
CHARTRES, Autricum
CHESTER, Deva
CHIUSI, Clusium
CIRENCESTER, Corinium
CIVITAVECCHIA, Centum Cellae
COLCHESTER, Camulodunum
COLOGNE, Colonia Agrippina
COMO, COMUM
CONSTANTINE, Cirta
CONSTANZA, Tomis
CORDOVA, Corduba
CORFU, Corcyra

DENDERA, Tentyra
DORCHESTER, Durnovaria

ERBIL, Arbela

FAENZA, Faventia
FANO, Fanum Fortunae
FERMO, Firmum Picenum
FONDI, Fundi
FORMIA, Formiae
FRASCATI, Tusculum

GENEVA, Genava
GENOA, Genua
GUBBIO, Iguvium

IESI, AESIS
INEBOLI, Abounoteichos

ISCHIA, Aenaria
ISERNIA, Aesernia
ISOLE EGADI, Aegates Insulae
ISTANBUL, Constantinople
IVREA, Eporedia

LAMTA, Leptis Parva
LEBDA, Leptis Magna
LEPANTO, Naupactus
LERIDA, Ilerda
LINCOLN, Lindum
LIPARI Is., Aeoline Insulae
LONDON, Londinium
LUCCA, Luca
LYONS, Lugdunum

MAINZ, Moguntiacum
MARSEILLES, Massalia
MATAPAN, Taenarum
MELUN, Meclosedum
MESSINA, Messana
MILAN, Mediolanum
MONACO, Monoeci Portus
MONT-AUXOIS, Alesia
MONTE CAVO, Albanus Mons

NARBONNE, Narbo
NARNI, Narnia
NÎMES, Nemausus

ORANGE, Arausio
OSIMO, Auximum

PADUA, Patavium
PALERMO, Panormus
PARIS, Lutetia
PERUGIA, Perusia
PESTRO, Paestum
PEVENSEY, Anderida
PIACENZA, Placentia
PISA, PISAE, 2
PORTO D'ANZIO, Antium
POZZUOLI, Puteoli
PRATICA, Lavinium
PUY D'ISSOLU, Uxellodunum

REGGIO DI CALABRIA, Regium
RICHBOROUGH, Rutupiae
RIETI, Reate
RIMINI, Ariminum
ROSETTA, Bolbitine
ROUEN, Rotomagus

SAGUNTO, Saguntum
SALONIKA, Thessalonica
SANTA MAURA, Leucadia
SANTIPONCE, Italica, 1
SEGNI, Signia
SESSA, Suessa Aurunca
SEVILLE, Hispalis
SHAHR, Comana, 1
SILCHESTER, Calleva Atrebatum
SOISSONS, Noviodunum
SORRENTO, Surrentum
SUBIACO, Sublaqueum
SULMONA, Sulmo
SUR, TYRE
SUSA (AFRICA), Hadrumetum
SUSA (ITALY), Segusio
SUTRI, Sutrium

TAORMINA, Tauromenium
TARANTO, Tarentum
TARRAGONA, Tarraco
TERNI, Interamna, 1
TERSEUS, Tarsus
TIVOLI, Tibur
TRABZON, Trapezus
TREPANI, Drepanum

URFA, Edessa

VIENNA, Vindobona
VOLTERRA, Volaterrae

WROXETER, Viroconium

YORK, Eburacum

ZANTE, Zacynthus
ZARAGOSA, Caesaraugusta

THE CHIEF PHILOSOPHICAL
SCHOOLS OF ANTIQUITY

SOME OF THEIR MOST DISTINGUISHED MEMBERS

THE IONIANS were mainly occupied with physical and cosmological speculations: Thales, Anaximenes, Anaximander, Heraclitus.

THE PYTHAGOREANS instituted the systematic study of numbers and taught metempsychosis: Pythagoras, Alcmaeon of Croton, 2, Archytas.

THE ELEATICS held monism as a common tenet: Parmenides, Zeno of Elea.

THE PLURALISTS were opposed to the monism of the Eleatics: Empedocles, Anaxagoras, Leucippus, Democritus.

THE SOPHISTS were itinerant teachers who professed to instruct their pupils in 'virtue' which amounted to the way to material prosperity: Protagoras, Gorgias, Hippias, 2.

SOCRATES inquired into the right conduct of life by critical dialetic. He was also the founder of formal logic.

THE MINOR SOCRATIC SCHOOLS:
- (a) *The Megarians* used the doctrine of the Eleatics to criticize other schools (*see* the article ERISTICS): Euclid of Megara, Diodorus Cronus.
- (b) *The Cyrenaics* taught that sensual pleasure is the end of life, they were forerunners of Epicureanism: Aristippus, Hegesias, 2, Anniceris.
- (c) *The Cynics* rejected all conventions, possessions and social relationships: Antisthenes, Diogenes, 2, Crates, 3.

THE ACADEMY held as its fundamental doctrine the Theory of Ideas. Particular attention was given to biology and mathematics: Plato, Speusippus, Xenocrates, Crantor, 2 (*see* the article ACADEMY).

THE PERIPATETICS were devoted to metaphysics and scientific research. They laid the foundations of all subsequent science: Aristotle, Theophrastus, Eudemus, Aristoxenus, Demetrius Phalereus.

THE SCEPTICS (drawn partly from the Latin Academy) denied the possibility to know the nature of things: Pyrrhon, Arcesilaus, Carneades, Clitomachus, Aenesidemus.

THE STOICS maintained that virtue must be practised for its own sake, that it raises its adherents above all passions: Zeno of Citium, Panaetius, Poseidonios, Seneca, Epictetus, Marcus Aurelius.

THE EPICUREANS believed, as against the Stoics, that virtue is desirable simply as a means to happiness or peace of mind: Epicurus, Metrodorus, 2, Polystratus.

THE NEOPLATONISTS added to a strong mystical tendency derived from Philo Judaeus a synthesis of elements Pythagorean, Platonic, Aristotelian and Stoic: Ammonius Saccas, Plotinus, Porphyrius, Iamblichus.

TABLE I

THE JULIAN HOUSE

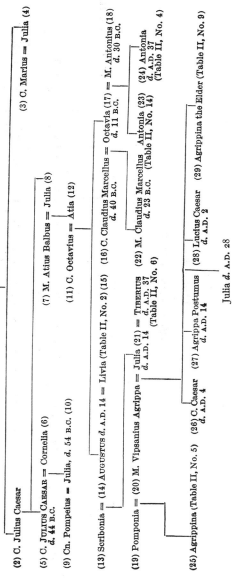

(1) Sextus Caesar, cos. 91 B.C.

(2) C. Julius Caesar

(3) C. Marius = Julia (4)

(5) C. JULIUS CAESAR = Cornelia (6)
d. 44 B.C.

(7) M. Atius Balbus = Julia (8)

(9) Cn. Pompeius = Julia, *d.* 54 B.C. (10)

(11) C. Octavius = Atia (12)

(13) Scribonia = (14) AUGUSTUS *d.* A.D. 14 = Livia (Table II, No. 2) (15)

(16) C. Claudius Marcellus = Octavia (17) = M. Antonius (18)
d. 40 B.C.   *d.* 11 B.C.   *d.* 30 B.C.

(19) Pomponia = (20) M. Vipsanius Agrippa = Julia (21) = TIBERIUS
     d. A.D. 14   *d.* A.D. 37
     (Table II, No. 6)

(22) M. Claudius Marcellus   Antonia (23)
     d. 23 B.C.   (Table II, No. 14)

(24) Antonia
d. A.D. 37
(Table II, No. 4)

(25) Agrippina (Table II, No. 5)   (26) C. Caesar   (27) Agrippa Postumus   (28) Lucius Caesar   (29) Agrippina the Elder (Table II, No. 9)
     d. A.D. 4   *d.* A.D. 14   *d.* A.D. 2

Julia *d.* A.D. 28

TABLE II

THE CLAUDIAN HOUSE

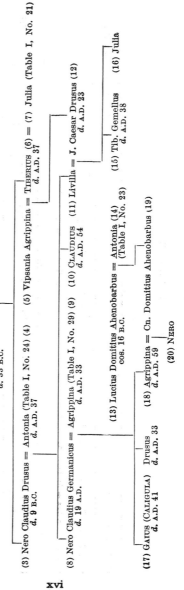

SELECT BIBLIOGRAPHY

1. History

T. MOMMSEN: *Provinces of the Roman Empire* (trans.), 1886.
The Cambridge Ancient History, 1923–7.
M. ROSTOVTZEFF: *A History of the Ancient World*, 1930.
J. B. BURY: *History of Greece*, 1913.
A. E. ZIMMERN: *The Greek Commonwealth*, 1931.
W. W. TARN: *Hellenistic Civilization*, 1929.
H. MICHELL: *The Economics of Ancient Greece*, 1940.
M. ROSTOVTZEFF: *Social and Economic History of the Hellenistic World*, 1941.
M. CARY: *History of Rome to the Reign of Constantine*, 1935.
W. E. HEITLAND: *The Roman Republic* (3 vols.), 1909.
M. P. NILSSON: *Imperial Rome*, 1926.
A. H. M. JONES: *Cities of the Eastern Roman Provinces*, 1937.
G. H. STEVENSON: *Roman Provincial Administration*, 1939.
SIR R. SYME: *The Roman Revolution*, 1939.
T. FRANK (ed.), *An Economic Survey of Ancient Rome* (5 vols.), 1933–40.
M. ROSTOVTZEFF: *Social and Economic History of the Roman Empire*, 2nd edition, revised by P. M. Fraser, 2 vols., 1957.
M. CARY: *Geographical Background of Greek and Roman History*, 1940.
K. FREEMAN: *Greek City States*, 1950.
H. MATTINGLY: *Roman Imperial Civilization*, 1957.
M. GRANT: *Roman History from Coins*, 1958; *The World of Rome*, 1960.
R. BLOCH: *The Origins of Rome*, 1960.
SIR M. WHEELER: *Rome beyond the Imperial Frontiers*, 1959.
C. G. STARR: *The Origins of Greek Civilizations*, 1962.

2. Philosophy

E. ZELLER: *History of Greek Philosophy*, 13th ed., 1931.
A. W. BENN: *The Greek Philosophers*, 2nd ed., 1914.
J. BURNET: *Early Greek Philosophy*, 4th ed., 1930.
T. GOMPERZ: *Greek Thinkers*, 1901–12.
W. JAEGER: *Theology of the Early Greek Philosophers*, 1947.
E. BARKER: *Greek Political Theory*, 3rd ed., 1947.
G. S. YORK and J. E. RAVEN: *The Pre-Socratic Philosophers*, 1951.
M. L. CLARKE: *The Roman Mind*, 1956.
A. H. ARMSTRONG: *An Introduction to Ancient Philosophy*, 1957.
W. K. C. GUTHRIE: *A History of Greek Philosophy*, 1962.

3. *Religion*

M. P. NILSSON: *History of Greek Religion*, 2nd ed., 1949.

L. R. FARNELL: *The Cults of the Greek States*, 1896–1909; *Greek Hero Cults and Ideas of Immortality*, 1921.

W. K. C. GUTHRIE: *The Greeks and their Gods*, 1950.

A. B. COOK: *Zeus: A Study in Ancient Religion* (3 vols.), 1914–40.

H. J. ROSE: *Handbook of Greek Mythology*, 1928.

F. ALTHEIM: *History of Roman Religion*, 1938.

F. CUMONT: *Oriental Religions in Roman Paganism*, 4th ed., 1929.

T. R. GLOVER: *Conflict of Religions in the Early Roman Empire*, 10th ed., 1923.

4. *Law*

R. J. BONNER and G. SMITH: *The Administration of Justice from Homer to Aristotle* (2 vols.), 1930–8.

H. F. JOLOWICZ: *Historical Introduction to the Study of Roman Law*, 1932

W. W. BUCKLAND: *Textbook of Roman Law*, 1932.

C. PHILLIPSON: *International Law and Custom of Ancient Greece and Rome*, 1911.

J. L. STRACHAN-DAVIDSON: *Problems of the Roman Criminal Law*, 1912.

G. M. CALHOUN: *Growth of Criminal Law in Ancient Greece*, 1927.

D. G. CRACKNELL: *Roman Law*, 1964.

5. *Literature*

G. MURRAY: *History of Ancient Greek Literature*, 1896; *The Rise of the Greek Epic*, 4th ed., 1934.

C. M. BOWRA: *Greek Lyric Poetry*, 1936.

A. W. PICKARD-CAMBRIDGE: *Dithyramb, Tragedy and Comedy*, revised by T. B. L. Webster, 1962.

G. NORWOOD: *Greek Comedy*, 1931.

T. B. L. WEBSTER: *Later Greek Comedy*, 1953.

H. D. F. KITTO: *Greek Tragedy*, 1939.

D. W. LUCAS: *The Greek Tragic Poets*, 1950.

A. W. PICKARD-CAMBRIDGE: *Dramatic Festivals at Athens*, 1953.

H. J. ROSE: *Handbook of Greek Literature*, 3rd ed., 1948.

E. E. SIKES: *Roman Poetry*, 1923.

J. W. DUFF: *A Literary History of Rome*, 1953.

J. W. H. ATKINS: *Literary Criticism in Antiquity*, 1934.

SIR J. E. SANDYS: *History of Classical Scholarship* (3 vols.), 1903–8.

SIR P. HARVEY (ed.): *Oxford Companions to Classical Literature*, 1946.

SIR C. M. BOWRA: *Landmarks in Greek Literature*, 1966.

6. *Art*

E. A. GARDNER: *The Art of Greece,* 1925.

P. GARDNER: *New Chapters in Greek Art,* 1926.

A. W. LAWRENCE: *Later Greek Sculpture,* 1927; *Classical Sculpture,* 1929.

H. B. WALTERS: *The Art of the Romans,* 1911.

E. STRONG: *Art in Ancient Rome,* 1929.

M. H. SWINDLER: *Ancient Painting,* 1929.

E. BUSCHOR: *Greek Vase Painting,* 1921.

W. J. ANDERSON: *The Architecture of Ancient Greece,* 1927; *The Architecture of Ancient Rome,* 1927.

D. S. ROBERTSON: *Greek and Roman Architecture,* 1943.

C. SACHS: *The Rise of Music in the Ancient World,* 1943.

J. BOARDMAN: *Greek Art,* 1964.

SIR M. WHEELER: *Roman Art and Architecture,* 1961.

J. BURCKHARDT: *History of Greek Culture* (trans.), 1964.

R. E. WYCHERLEY: *How the Greeks Built Cities,* 1962.

R. S. FOLSOM: *Handbook of Greek Pottery,* 1967.

W. DORIGO: *Late Roman Painting* (trans.), 1970.

7. *Science*

SIR T. L. HEATH: *History of Greek Mathematics,* 1921; *Greek Astronomy,* 1932.

H. F. TOZER: *History of Ancient Geography,* 1935.

W. E. HEITLAND: *Agricola,* 1921.

A. J. BROCK: *Greek Medicine,* 1929.

M. CLAGETT: *Greek Science in Antiquity,* 1957.

L. S. DE CAMP: *The Ancient Engineers,* 1964.

8. *Naval and Military*

C. TORR: *Ancient Ships,* 1894.

SIR R. PAYNE-GALLWEY: *Projectile-throwing Engines of the Ancients,* 1907.

H. J. ROSE: *The Mediterranean in the Ancient World,* 1933.

W. W. TARN: *Hellenistic Military and Naval Developments,* 1930.

F. W. CLARK: *Influence of Sea Power on the History of the Roman Republic,* 1915.

C. G. STARR: *The Roman Imperial Navy,* 1941.

H. M. D. PARKER: *The Roman Legions,* 1928.

G. L. CHEESMAN: *The Auxilia of the Roman Army,* 1914.

G. WEBSTER: *The Roman Army,* 1956.

9. *General*

The Oxford Classical Dictionary, 1949.

L. WHIBLEY (ed.): *Companion to Greek Studies*, 1905.

SIR R. W. LIVINGSTONE (ed.): *The Legacy of Greece*, 1921.

J. C. STOBART (ed.): *The Glory that was Greece*, revised ed., 1962.

SIR J. E. SANDYS (ed.): *Companion to Latin Studies*, 1910.

C. BAILEY (ed.): *The Legacy of Rome*, 1923.

J. C. STOBART (ed.): *The Grandeur that was Rome*, 3rd ed., 1934.

Everyman's Classical Atlas, 1961.

C. M. BOWRA: *The Greek Experience*, 1957.

A. A. M. VAN DER HEYDEN and H. H. SCULLARD, *Atlas of the Classical World*, 1959.

V. EHRENBERG: *Society and Civilization in Greece and Rome*, 1964.

M. GRANT (ed.): *The Birth of Western Civilization: Greece and Rome*, 1964.

SYSTEMATIC LIST OF ENTRIES

GEOGRAPHY AND TOPOGRAPHY

ABAE
ABDERA
ABELLA
ABILENE
ABONOUTEIKHOS
ABYDOS
ACARNANIA
ACHAEA
ACHARNAE
ACHELOÜS
ACHERON
ACHERUSIA PALUS
ACROCERAUNIA
ACROPOLIS
ACTE
ACTIUM
ADRANON
ADULIS
AECLANUM
AEGAE
AEGALEOS
AEGATES INSULAE
AEGEAN SEA
AEGINA
AEGIRA
AEGIROESSA
AEGOSPOTAMI
AELIA CAPITOLINA
AEMILIA, VIA
AENARIA
AEOLIAE INSULAE
AEOLIS
AESERNIA
AESIS
AETHIOPIA
AETNA
AETOLIA
AEXONE
AFRICA
AGANIPPE
AGEDINCUM
AGER FALERNUS
AGER GALLICUS
AGORA
AGRI DECUMATES

AGRIGENTUM
AGYRIUM
ALALIA
ALBA FUCENS
ALBA LONGA
ALBA POMPEIA
ALBANIA
ALBANUS, LACUS
ALBANUS MONS
ALBION
ALBIS
ALESIA
ALETRIUM
ALEXANDRIA
ALGIDUS MONS
ALLIA
ALLIFAE
ALPES
ALPHEUS
ALSIUM
ALTHIBUROS
ALTINUM
AMASIA
AMATHUS
AMBRACIA
AMERIA
AMISUS
AMITERNUM
AMORGOS
AMPHIPOLIS
AMPHISSA
AMPSANCTUS
AMYCLAE
ANAGNIA
ANCONA
ANCYRA
ANDERIDA
ANDROS
ANIO
ANTEMNAE
ANTICYRA
ANTIGONEA
ANTIOCH
ANTIUM
ANTONINE ITINERARY

ANTONINE WALL
AONIA
APAMEA
APENNINUS MONS
APHIDNAE
APOLLONIA
APPIA, VIA
APULIA
AQUAE CUTILIAE
AQUAE SEXTIAE
AQUAE SULIS
AQUILEIA
AQUINCUM
AQUINUM
AQUITANIA
ARABIA
ARAUSIO
ARCADIA
ARDEA
ARELATE
AREOPAGUS
ARGILETUM
ARGINUSAE
ARGOLIS
ARGOS
ARICIA
ARIMINUM
ARMENIA
ARMORICA
ARPI
ARPINUM
ARRETIUM
ARTAXATA
ARTEMISIUM
ASCALON
ASCRA
ASCULUM
ASIA
ASISIUM
ASOPUS
ASPENDUS
ASSOS
ASTACUS
ASTURA
ATELLA

ATHENS
ATRIA
ATROPATENE
ATTALIA
ATTICA
AUGUSTA
AULIS
AURELIA, VIA
AUSONIA
AUTRICUM
AUXIMUM
AVERNUS
BACTRIA
BAETICA
BAIAE
BALAGRAE
BALEARES
BARCA
BASSAE
BAULI
BENACUS, LACUS
BENEVENTUM
BERENICE
BEROEA
BERYTUS
BETRIACUM
BIBRACTE
BILBILIS
BITHYNIA
BOEOTIA
BOLBITINE
BONONIA
BORYSTHENES
BOSPORUS
BOVIANUM UNDECI-
    MANORUM
BOVILLAE
BRITAIN
BRUNDISIUM
BRUTTII
BUCEPHALA
BULLA REGIA
BYZANTIUM
CAECILIA, VIA
CAECUBUS AGER
CAERE
CAESARAUGUSTA
CAESAREA
CAIATIA
CAIETAE PORTUS
CALABRIA
CALAGURRIS
CALATIA
CALAURIA

CALCHEDON
CALEDONIA
CALES
CALLEVA
CALLIRRHOË
CALYDON
CAMARINA
CAMPANIA
CAMPI RAUDII
CAMPUS MARTIUS
CAMULODUNUM
CANNAE
CANOPUS
CANTABRIA
CANUSIUM
CAPENA
CAPERNAUM
CAPITOLIUM
CAPPADOCIA
CAPREAE
CAPUA
CARALES
CARIA
CARNUNTUM
CARRHAE
CARSEOLI
CARTHAGE
CARTHAGO NOVA
CARYAE
CASILINUM
CASINUM
CASSIA, VIA
CASSITERIDES
CASTALIA
CASTRUM MINERVAE
CASTULO
CATINA
CAUCASUS
CAUDIUM
CAULONIA
CELAENAE
CELTIBERIA
CENCHREAE
CENTUM CELLAE
CENTURIPAE
CEOS
CEPHALLENIA
CEPHISSUS
CERAMICUS
CERASUS
CHAERONEA
CHALCIDICE
CHALCIS
CHERSONESUS

CHIOS
CILICIA
CIMINIA, VIA
CIMOLUS
CIRCEII
CIRTA
CITHAERON
CITIUM
CLAUDIA NOVA, VIA
CLAZOMENAE
CLEITOR
CLITUMNUS
CLUSIUM
CNIDUS
COCYTUS
COELE-SYRIA
COLCHIS
COLLATIA
COLLYTUS
COLONIA AGRIPPINA
COLONUS
COLOPHON
COLOSSAE
COMANA
COMMAGENE
COMPSA
COMUM
CONCORDIA
CONOVIUM
CONSENTIA
CONSTANTINOPLE
COPAIS
CORA
CORCYRA
CORDUBA
CONFINIUM
CORINIUM
CORINTH
CORINTHIACUS ISTHMUS
CORNUS
CORONEIA
CORSICA
CORTONA
CORYCIAN CAVE
COS
COSA
COTTII REGNUM
CRATHIS
CREMERA
CREMONA
CRETE
CRISSA
CROMMYON
CROTON

CTESIPHON
CUMAE
CUNAXA
CURES
CYCLADES
CYDNUS
CYLLENE
CYNOSARGES
CYNOSCEPHALAE
CYNOSSEMA
CYPRUS
CYRENAICA
CYRENE
CYTHERA
CYZICUS
DACIA
DALMATIA
DAMASCUS
DANUBIUS
DAPHNAI
DAPHNE
DATUM
DEAD SEA
DECAPOLIS
DECELEA
DELIUM
DELOS
DELPHI
DEVA
DIOMEDEAE INSULAE
DODONA
DORIAN HEXAPOLIS
DORIS
DREPANUM
DURNOVARIA
DUROVERNUM
DYRRACHIUM
EBURA
EBURACUM
ECBATANA
ECNOMUS
EDESSA
EGNATIA, VIA
EGYPT
ELEUSIS
ELEUTHEROPOLIS
ELIS
EMERITA AUGUSTA
EMESA
EPHESUS
EPIDAURUS
EPIRUS
EPOREDIA
ERETRIA

ERYMANTHUS
ERYTHRAE
ERYX
ETRURIA
EUBOEA
EURYMEDON
EUTRESIS
EUXINUS
FAESULAE
FALERII
FALERNUS AGER
FANUM FORTUNAE
FAVENTIA
FERENTUM
FESCENNIA
FIDENAE
FIRMUM PICENUM
FLAMINIA, VIA
FLORENTIA
FORMIAE
FORUM
FOSSE WAY
FRETUM GADITANUM
FUCINUS, LACUS
FUNDI
GABII
GADARA
GAETULIA
GALATIA
GALLAECIA
GALLIA
GARGETTUS
GAUGAMELA
GAURUS, MONS
GAZA
GELA
GEMONIAE
GENAVA
GENUA
GERASA
GERGOVIA
GERMANIA
GORTYNA
GRANICUS
GREECE
GYARUS
GYTHIUM
HADRIAN'S WALL
HADRUMETUM
HALAESA
HALIARTUS
HALICARNASSUS
HELICON
HELIOPOLIS

HELLESPONT
HENNA
HERACLEA
HERCULANEUM
HERMOPOLIS
HIBERNIA
HIERAPOLIS
HIMERA
HIPPOCRENE
HISPALIS
HISPANIA
HYBLA
HYCCARA
HYDASPES
HYMETTUS
IAPYDIA
IBERIA
ICONIUM
IDA
IDUMAEA
IGUVIUM
ILERDA
ILIPA
ILLYRIA
ILLYRICUM
ILLYRICUS LIMES
ILVA
IMBROS
INDIA
INTERAMMA
INTERNUM MARE
IOLCUS
IONIA
IONIAN SEA
IPSUS
IRA
ISAURIA
ISCA
ISLANDS OF THE
    BLESSED
ISMARUS
ISSA
ISSUS
ISTRIA
ITALIA
ITALICA
ITHACA
ITHOME
ITIUS PORTUS
ITURAEA
JERUSALEM
JOPPA
JUDAEA
LACINIUM

LACONIA
LAMBAESIS
LAMPSACUS
LANUVIUM
LAODICEA
LARISA
LATINA, VIA
LATIUM
LATMOS
LAURIUM
LAVINIUM
LEBADEIA
LEMNOS
LEONTINI
LEPTIS
LERNE
LESBOS
LEUCADIA
LEUCTRA
LIBANOS
LIBURNIA
LIBYA
LIGURIA
LILYBAEUM
LIMES GERMANICUS
LINDUM
LINDUS
LITERNUM
LOCRI
LONDINIUM
LUCA
LUCANIA
LUCERIA
LUCRINUS, LACUS
LUGDUNUM
LUNA
LUTETIA
LYCAEUS
LYCAONIA
LYCEUM
LYCIA
LYCOSURA
LYDIA
MACEDONIA
MADAUROS
MAGNA GRAECIA
MAGNESIA
MANTINEA
MANTUA
MARATHON
MAREOTIS
MARPESSA
MASSALIA
MASSICUS, MONS

MAURETANIA
MECLOSEDUM
MEDIA
MEDIOLANUM
MEGALOPOLIS
MEGARA
MELAS
MELIBOEA
MELITA
MELITENE
MELOS
MENDE
MESEMBRIA
MESSANA
MESSENE
MESSENIA
METAPONTUM
METAURUS
METHONE
METHYMNA
MEVANIA
MIDEIA
MILETUS
MINTURNAE
MISENUM
MOESIA
MOGUNTIACUM
MONA
MONOECI PORTUS
MUNDA
MUNDUS
MUNYCHIA
MUSEUM
MUTINA
MYCALE
MYCENAE
MYLAE
MYSIA
MYTILENE
NAÏSUS
NARBO
NARNIA
NAUCRATIS
NAUPACTUS
NAXOS
NEAPOLIS
NEMAUSUS
NEMEA
NEMORENSIS, LACUS
NICAEA
NICOMEDIA
NICOPOLIS
NISYRUS
NOLA

NORICUM
NOVIODUNUM
NUMANTIA
NUMIDIA
OLBIA
OLYMPIA
OLYMPUS
OLYNTHUS
ORCADES
ORCHOMENUS
OROPUS
ORTYGIA
OSSA
OSTIA
OXYRHYNCHUS
PACTOLUS
PAEONIA
PAESTUM
PALMYRA
PAMPHYLIA
PANAENUS
PANNONIA
PANORMUS
PANTICAPAEUM
PAPHLAGONIA
PAPHOS
PARNASSUS
PAROS
PARTHENIUS
PARTHIA
PASARGADAE
PATAVIUM
PATRAE
PAXOS
PELION
PELLA
PELOPONNESUS
PENTAPOLIS
PENTELICUS
PERGA
PERGAMUM
PERINTHUS
PERSEPOLIS
PERSIS
PERUSIA
PESSINUS
PETRA
PHAROS
PHARSALUS
PHIGALEIA
PHILADELPHIA
PHILIPPI
PHOCAEA
PHOCIS

PHOENICIA
PHRYGIA
PHTHIOTIS
PICENUM
PISAE
PISIDIA
PISTORIAE
PLACENTIA
PLATAEA
PNYX
POLA
POMPEII
POMPTINAE PALUDES
PONTUS
POPILIA, VIA
POPULONIA
POSTUMIA, VIA
POTIDAEA
PRAENESTE
PRIENE
PROVINCES
PTOLEMAIS
PUTEOLI
PYDNA
PYLOS
PYRGI
RAVENNA
REATE
REGILLUS, LACUS
REGIUM
RHAETIA
RHAGAE
RHODES
ROME
ROSTRA
ROTOMAGUS
RUBICON
RUSELLAE
RUTUPIAE
SABRATHA
SACRA, VIA
SACRIPORTUS
SAGUNTUM
SALAMIS
SALARIA, VIA
SALONA
SAMARIA
SAMNIUM
SAMOS
SAMOSATA
SAMOTHRACE
SARDINIA
SARDIS
SARMATIA

SASSINA
SAXA RUBRA
SCAPTE HYLE
SCELERATUS CAMPUS
SCYROS
SCYTHIA
SEGESTA
SEGOVIA
SEGUSIO
SELEUCIA
SENTINUM
SERIPHOS
SETIA
SICILY
SICYON
SIDE
SIDON
SIGEUM
SIGNIA
SINOPE
SINUESSA
SIPHNOS
SIRENUSAE
SIRMIO
SMYRNA
SOLI
SORA
SORACTE
SPARTA
SPHACTERIA
SPORADES
STABIAE
STOA POIKILE
STROPHADES
STYMPHALUS
STYX
SUBLAQUEUM
SUBLICIUS, PONS
SUBURA
SUESSA AURUNCA
SUESSULA
SULMO
SUNIUM
SURRENTUM
SUTRIUM
SYBARIS
SYRACUSE
SYRIA
TABULARIUM
TAENARUM
TANAGRA
TARENTUM
TARQUINII
TARRACO

TARSUS
TARTESSUS
TAUROMENIUM
TAŸGETUS
TEGEA
TEMPE
TENEDOS
TENTYRA
THAMUGADI
THAPSUS
THASOS
THEBES
THERA
THERAPNAE
THERMOPYLAE
THESPIAE
THESSALONICA
THESSALY
THRACE
THULE
THURII
TIBER
TIBUR
TICINUS
TILPHUSIUM
TIRYNS
TOMIS
TRACHIS
TRAPEZOS
TRASIMENUS, LACUS
TREBIA
TROEZEN
TROY
TUSCULUM
TYRE
UMBRIA
UTICA
UXELLODUNUM
VADIMONIS, LACUS
VEII
VENTA BELGARUM
VENUSIA
VERULAMIUM
VESUVIUS
VETULONIA
VINDELICIA
VINDOBONA
VIROCONIUM
VOLATERRAE
VOLSINII
XANTHUS
ZACYNTHUS
ZAMA
ZELA

RACES AND TRIBES

ACHAEANS
AEDUI
AEQUI
AESTII
AETHIOPES
AGATHYRSI
ALAMANNI
ALLOBROGES
ANGLI
ARVERNI
ASTURES
AURUNCI
BASTARNAE
BATAVI
BELGAE
BELLOVACI
BISALTAE
BITURIGES
BOII
BRIGANTES
BRUCTERI
CARNUTES
CARPI
CELTAE
CENOMANI
CERRETANI
CHATTI
CHAUCI
CHERUSCI
CIMBRI
CIMMERII
CYNESII
DORIANS

ELYMI
FRENTANI
FRISII
GETAE
GOTONES
HELVETII
HERMUNDURI
HERNICI
HERULI
HIRPINI
ICENI
ICHTHYOPHAGI
INSUBRES
IONIANS
ISSEDONES
ITALIOTES
IYRCAE
LANGOBARDI
LATINI
LEUCOSYRI
LOCRI
LUGII
MANDUBII
MARCOMANNI
MARRUCINI
MARSI
MASSAGETAE
MENAPII
MESSAPII
MOLOSSI
MORINI
NABATAEI
ODRYSAE

PAELIGNI
PICTI
PYGMAEI
QUADI
REMI
RHOXOLANI
RUTULI
SABINI
SALYES
SAUROMATAE
SAXONES
SCENITAE
SCORDISCI
SCOTTI
SEMNONES
SENONES
SEQUANI
SERES
SICANI
SICULI
SILURES
SINAE
SUEBI
SUGAMBRI
TAURI
TENCTERI
TRIBOCI
UBII
VANDALI
VENETI
VOLSCI

GREEK HISTORY AND INSTITUTIONS

ACHAEAN LEAGUE
ACHAEMENIDAE
AETOLIAN LEAGUE
AGATHOCLES
AGESILAUS
AGIS
AGORANOMOI
ALCIBIADES
ALCMAEONIDAE
ALEUADAE
ALEXANDER
ALEXANDER THE PAPH-
  LAGONIAN

ALYATTES
AMPHICTYONIC
  LEAGUE
AMYNTAS
ANAXANDRIDES
ANTALCIDAS
ANTIGONIDAE
ANTIGONUS
ANTINOÜS
ANTIOCHUS
ANTIPATER, 1 and 2
ANYTUS
APELLA

ARATUS
ARCHELAUS, 1
ARCHIAS
ARCHIDAMUS
ARCHON
ARDASHIR
AREOPAGUS
ARIARATHES, 1–4
ARIOBARZANES OF
  PONTUS
ARISTAGORAS
ARISTEIDES, 1
ARRIA

ARSACES
ARSES
ARSINOË, 1–3
ARTABANUS
ARTABAZUS
ARTAPHERNES
ARTAXERXES
ARTAXIAS, 1
ASPASIA
ASTER
ASTYNOMI
ATTIC ORATORS
BAGOAS
BARSINE
BATTIADAE
BERENICE, 1–4
BESSUS
BOULE
BRASIDAS
BRENNUS, 2
CALLIAS
CALLICRATIDAS
CALLISTRATUS, 2
CAMBYSES
CASSANDER
CHABRIAS
CHARES, 1
CHARONDAS
CHIRISOPHUS
CIMON
CLEARCHUS
CLEISTHENES
CLEOMBROTUS, 1–3
CLEOMENES
CLEON
CLEOPATRA, 1
CLERUCHY
CLITUS
CLUBS
COINAGE
CONON, 1
CRATERUS
CRITIAS
CROESUS
CRYPTEIA
CYLON
CYPSELUS
CYRUS
DAMARATUS
DAMOCLES
DAMON AND PHINTIAS
DAREIOS
DATAMES
DELIAN LEAGUE

DEMADES
DEMETRIUS
DEMETRIUS PHALER-
EUS
DEMOCHARES
DEMOSTHENES
DIADOCHI
DICAST
DIODOTUS
DION
DIONYSIUS
DRACON
ECCLESIA
EPAMEINONDAS
EPHEBI
EPHIALTES
EPHOR
EPIMENIDES
EUCRATIDES
EUMENES (A) and (B), 1
EUPATRIDAE
EURYBATUS
EUTHYDEMUS
EVAGORAS
FOUR HUNDRED
GELON
GEROUSIA
GRYLLUS
GYLIPPUS
HARMODIUS
HARPALUS
HEGESIPPUS
HELOTS
HEPHAESTION, 1
HERACLIDES, 1
HERMEIAS
HERMOLAUS
HEROSTRATUS
HIERON, 1
HIERONYMUS
HIPPALUS
HIPPOMENES, 2
HIPPONICUS
HISTIAEUS
HOPLITES
HYPERBOLUS
HYPEREIDES
IPHICRATES
LAIS
LAMACHUS
LAMIAN WAR
LEITOURGIAI
LEONIDAS
LEOTYCHIDAS

LEPTINES
LYCURGUS
LYSANDER
LYSIMACHUS
MACHANIDAS
MARDONIUS
MAUSOLUS
MEGACLES
METIC
MILON
MILTIADES
MOTHONES
NABIS
NEARCHUS
NEODAMODES
NICIAS
NOMOTHETAI
OLYMPIAD
OLYMPIAS
ONOMACRITUS
OSTRACISM
PARIAN MARBLE
PARMENION
PAUSANIAS, 1 and 2
PEISISTRATUS
PELOPONNESIAN WAR
PELTASTS
PERDICCAS
PERIANDER
PERICLES
PERSIAN WARS
PHALANX
PHALARIS
PHARNABAZUS
PHAYLLUS
PHEIDIPPIDES
PHILIP
PHILOPOEMEN
PHILOTAS
PHOCION
PHORMION
PHRYNE
PITTACUS
POLYCRATES
POLYSPERCHON
PORUS
PROSTATES
PROXENOI
PTOLEMY I–IX
PYRRHUS
PYTHEAS
RHODOPIS
ROXANA
SACRED WARS

SELEUCUS
SISYGAMBIS
SOLON
STATEIRA
STRATEGOI
STRATONICE
TEN THOUSAND

THAÏS
THEMISTOCLES
THERAMENES
THERON
THIRTY TYRANTS, I
THRASYBULUS
THUCYDIDES, I

TIMOLEON
TIMON THE MISAN-
    THROPE
TISSAPHERNES
TYRANT
XANTHIPPUS
XERXES

GREEK LITERATURE

AELIANUS
AENEAS
AESCHINES, I
AESCHYLUS
AESOPUS
AGATHARCHIDES
AGATHON
ALCAEUS
ALCIDAMAS
ALCIPHRON
ALCMAEON, I
ALCMAN
ALEXANDER AETOLUS
ALEXANDER OF APHRO-
    DISIAS
ALEXIS
ALIMENTUS
AMEIPSIAS
AMMONIUS
ANACREON
ANDOCIDES
ANTHOLOGY, THE
    GREEK
ANTIGONUS OF CARYS-
    TUS
ANTIMACHUS
ANTIOCHUS OF SYRA-
    CUSE
ANTIPATER OF SIDON
ANTIPHANES
ANTIPHON
APICIUS
APION
APOLLODORUS, 2 and 3
APOLLONIUS, I, 2, 4
    and 5
APPIANUS
APULEIUS
ARATUS OF SOLI
ARCHILOCHUS
ARCTINUS
ARION

ARISTARCHUS, 2
ARISTEAS
ARISTEIDES, 2
ARISTEIDES, AELIUS
ARISTOBULUS, 3
ARISTOPHANES
ARRIANUS
ASCLEPIADES, 2
ASTYDAMAS
ATHENAEUS
ATHENODORUS, 2
BABRIUS
BACCHYLIDES
BAVIUS
BEROSSUS
BION, I
CAECILIUS
CALLIMACHUS, I
CALLINUS
CALLISTHENES
CALLISTRATUS, I and
    3-5
CHARITON
CHOERILUS
CONON, 2
CORINNA
CRATES, I
CRATINUS
CRATIPPUS, I
CREOPHYLUS
CTESIAS
DEINARCHUS
DEMOSTHENES, 2
DEXIPPUS
DIAGORAS
DIDYMUS
DIO CASSIUS
DIO CHRYSOSTOM
DIODORUS SICULUS
DIOGENES LAËRTIUS
DIONYSIUS OF HALI-
    CARNASSUS

DIONYSIUS PERIE-
    GETES
DIONYSIUS THRAX
DIPHYLUS
DURIS
EPHORUS
EPICHARMUS
EPIMENIDES
ERINNA
EUHEMERUS
EUPHORION
EUPOLIS
EURIPIDES
GORGIAS
HANNO, I
HARPOCRATION
HECATAEUS
HEGEMON OF THASOS
HEGESIAS, I
HEGESIPPUS
HELIODORUS
HEPHAESTION, 2
HERMESIANAX
HERMIPPUS
HERMOGENES
HERODAS
HERODIANUS
HERODOTUS
HESIOD
HIPPONAX
HOMER
HYPEREIDES
IBYCUS
ISAEUS
ISOCRATES
JOSEPHUS
LASUS
LEONIDAS OF TAREN-
    TUM
LONGUS
LUCIAN
LYCOPHRON

LYCURGUS
LYSIAS
MAXIMUS TYRIUS
MELEAGER OF GADARA
MENANDER
MIMNERMUS
MOSCHUS
NICANDER
NICOLAUS
OPPIANUS
PANYASIS
PARTHENIUS
PAUSANIAS, 3
PHILEMON
PHILETAS
PHILISTUS
PHILOSTRATUS

PHILOXENOS
PHRYNICUS
PINDAR
PLUTARCH
POLYAENUS
POLYBIUS
POSIDIPPUS
PRATINAS
QUINTUS CALABER
RHIANOS
SANNYRION
SAPPHO
SCHOLIA
SCYLAX
SIMONIDES
SKOLIA
SOPHOCLES

SOPHRON
SOSITHEUS
SOTADES
STESICHORUS
STRABO
SUSARION
TERPANDER
THEOCRITUS
THEOGNIS
THUCYDIDES, 2
TIMAEUS, 2
TIMOTHEUS
TYRTAEUS
XENOPHON
ZENODOTUS

GREEK LEGEND, MYTHOLOGY AND RELIGION

ACAMAS
ACARNAN
ACASTUS
ACHELOÜS
ACHILLES
ACIS
ACONTIUS
ACTAEON
ADMETUS
ADONIS
ADRASTUS
AEACUS
AEAEA
AËDON
AEGEUS
AEGIS
AENEAS
AEOLUS
AETHALIDES
AETHRA
AETOLUS
AGAMEDES
AGENOR
AGROTERAS THUSIA
AJAX
ALCATHOÜS
ALCINOÜS
ALCMENE
ALCYONE
ALOIDAE
AMALTHEIA
AMAZONS

AMBROSIA
AMMON
AMPHIARAÜS
AMPHILOCHUS
AMPHION AND ZETHUS
AMPHITRITE
AMPHITRYON
AMYCUS
ANAXARETE
ANCAEUS
ANDROCLUS
ANDROGEOS
ANDROMACHE
ANDROMEDA
ANTAEUS
ANTENOR
ANTHESTERIA
ANTICLEA
ANTIOPE
ANUBIS
APHAEA
APHRODITE
APOLLO
ARACHNE
ARCHEMORUS
ARCTOS
ARES
ARETHUSA
ARGONAUTS
ARGUS
ARIADNE
ARIMASPI

ARISTAEUS
ARISTODEMUS
ARISTOMENES
ARTEMIS
ASCALAPHUS
ASCLEPIUS
ASTERIA
ASTYANAX
ATALANTA
ATE
ATHAMAS
ATHENA
ATLAS
ATREIDS
ATTIS
AUGE
AUTOLYCUS
AUTOMEDON
AUTONOE
BACCHANALIA
BEBRYCES
BELLEROPHON
BELLONA
BITON
BOREAS
BRISEIS
BRITOMARTIS

CABEIRI
CADMUS
CALCHAS
CALLISTO

CALYPSO
CANEPHORAE
CAPANEUS
CARNEA
CASSANDRA
CASSIOPEIA
CECROPS
CELEUS
CENTAURS
CEPHALUS
CEPHEUS
CERBERUS
CERCOPES
CEYX
CHARITES
CHARON
CHIMAERA
CHIONE
CHIRON
CHRYSEIS
CIRCE
CISSEUS
CLYMENE
CLYTAEMNESTRA
COCALUS
CODRUS
CORYBANTES
COTYTTO
CRANTOR, I
CREUSA
CRIOBOLIUM
CRONUS
CURETES
CYCLOPES
CYDIPPE
DAEDALA
DAEDALUS
DANAÜS
DAPHNE
DAPHNIS
DARDANUS
DARES PHRYGIUS
DECELUS
DEIANEIRA
DEIPHOBUS
DELIA
DELPHINIA
DEMETER
DEMETRIA
DEMOPHON
DEUCALION
DICTYS CRETENSIS
DIOMEDES
DIONE

DIONYSIA
DIONYSUS
DIOSCURI
DRYOPE

ECHIDNA
ECHO
EILITHYIA
ELECTRA
ELPENOR
ELYSIUM
ENDYMION
EOS
EPIMETHEUS
EREBUS
ERECHTHEUS
ERIDANUS
ERINYES
ERIS
EROS
ERYSICHTHON
EUMENIDES
EUMOLPUS
EUROPA
EURYCLEA
GALEUS
GANYMEDES
GIGANTES
GLAUCE
GLAUCUS
GORDIUS
GORGON
GREAT MOTHER OF THE
    GODS
GRIFFIN
HADES
HALIRRHOTHIUS
HARMONIA
HARPIES
HARPOCRATES
HEBE
HECATE
HECTOR
HECUBA
HELENA
HELENUS
HELIOS
HELLEN
HEPHAESTUS
HERA
HERACLES
HERACLIDAE
HERMAPHRODITUS
HERMES

HERMIONE
HERO AND LEANDER
HESIONE
HESPERIDES
HESTIA
HIPPOLYTE
HIPPOLYTUS
HIPPOMENES, I
HORAE
HYACINTHUS
HYGIEIA
HYLAS
HYLLUS
HYMEN
HYPERBOREANS
HYPNOS
HYPSIPYLE
IACCHUS
ICARIUS
IDAS
IDOMENEUS
ILUS
IO
IOLAUS
ION
IPHICLES
IPHIGENEIA
IRENE
IRIS
ISIS
IXION
JASON AND MEDEA
KER
LAËRTES
LAESTRYGONES
LAMIA
LAOCOÖN
LAOMEDON
LAPITHAE
LELEGES
LETHE
LETO
LINOS
LYCAON
LYCOMEDES
MAIA
MARSYAS
MEDUSA
MELAMPUS
MELEAGER
MEMNON
MENELAUS
MENOECEUS
MENTOR, I

MEROPE
METIS
MIDAS
MINOS
MINOTAUR
MINYAE
MINYAS
MOIRAE
MOMUS
MOPSUS
MORPHEUS
MUSAEUS
MUSES
MYRMIDONS
MYRTILUS
MYSTERIES
NARCISSUS
NAUPLIUS
NAUSICAA
NELEUS
NEMESIS
NEOPTOLEMUS
NEREUS
NESTOR
NIKE
NOTOS
NYCTYMENE
NYMPH
NYX
OCEANUS
ODYSSEUS
OENEUS
OENOTROPAE
OGYGES
OILEUS
ORACLES
ORESTES
ORION
ORPHEUS
ORPHISM
ORTHIA
OSIRIS
OSSA (PHEME)
PAEAN
PALAEMON
PALAMEDES
PALICI
PALLADIUM
PAN
PANATHENAEA
PANDAREOS
PANDION
PANDORA
PANTHOUS

PARIS
PASIPHAË
PATROCLUS
PEGASUS
PELEUS
PELOPS
PENELOPE
PENTHESILEA
PENTHEUS
PERDIX
PERSE
PERSEPHONE
PERSES
PERSEUS
PHAEACIANS
PHAEDRA
PHAËTHON
PHARMAKOI
PHILAMMON
PHILEMON AND BAUCIS
PHILOCTETES
PHINEUS
PHLEGETHON
PHOEBE
PHOENIX
PHOLUS
PHOSPHOROS
PHRIXUS
PIRITHOUS
PLEIADES
POLYDORUS
POLYXENA
POSEIDON
PRIAM
PRIAPUS
PROCRUSTES
PROETUS
PROMETHEUS
PROTESILAUS
PROTEUS
PSYCHE
PYANEPSIA
PYGMALION
PYLADES
PYRAMUS AND THISBE
PYTHON
RHADAMANTHUS
RHEA
RHESUS
SABAZIUS
SALMONEUS
SARPEDON
SATYRS
SCIRON

SCYLLA AND CHARYBDIS
SELENE
SEMELE
SERAPIS
SILENUS
SINIS
SINON
SIRENS
SISYPHUS
SPHINX
STENTOR
STHENELUS
STYX
SYMPLEGADES
SYRIA DEA
SYRINX
TALOS
TALTHYBIUS
TANTALUS
TARTARUS
TECMESSA
TELAMON
TELEGONUS
TELEMACHUS
TELEPHUS
TETHYS
TEUCER
THAMYRIS
THARGELIA
THEBAN LEGEND
THEMIS
THERSITES
THESEUS
THESMOPHORIAE
THETIS
TIRESIAS
TITANS
TITHONUS
TITYUS
TLEPOLEMIS
TRITON
TROY
TWELVE LABOURS OF HERACLES
TYDEUS
TYNDAREUS
TYPHON
XUTHUS
ZEPHYRUS
ZETES AND CALAIS
ZEUS

ROMAN HISTORY AND INSTITUTIONS

ACTA
ACTA DIURNA
ACTA SENATUS
AEDILES
AEMILIANUS
AERARII
AERARIUM
AFRANIUS
AGRARIAN LAWS
AGRICOLA
AGRIPPA, HERODES
AGRIPPA, MARCUS VIP-
    SANIUS
AGRIPPINA
AHALA
AHENOBARBUS
ALA
ALBINUS
AMBIORIX AND CATU-
    VOLCUS
AMBITUS
ANDRISCUS
ANNONA
ANTIPATER, 3 and 4
ANTONIA
ANTONINUS PIUS
ANTONIUS
ARCHELAUS, 1–6
ARCHIAS, AULUS LI-
    CINIUS
ARETAS
ARIARATHES, 5–9
ARIES
ARIOBARZANES
ARIOVISTUS
ARISTOBULUS, 1
ARMINIUS
ARRIUS APER
ARTAVASDES
ARTAXIAS, 2 and 3
ASELLIO
ATIA
ATTALUS
AUGUSTUS
AURELIANUS
AUXILIA
AVIDIUS CASSIUS
BALBINUS
BALBUS
BALLISTA
BERENICE, 5–7

BESTIA
BIBULUS
BOCCHUS
BOMILCAR
BOUDICCA
BRENNUS, 1
BRITANNICUS
BRUTUS
BUCOLIC WAR
CAECILIUS, QUINTUS
CAECINA
CAEPIO
CAESAR
CAESARION
CALATINUS
CALIGULA
CALPURNIA
CALVINUS
CAMILLUS
CANDACE
CAPITO
CARACALLA
CARATACUS
CARAUSIUS
CARBO
CARINUS
CARUS
CASSIUS
CASSIVELLAUNUS
CATILINA
CATO, MARCUS POR-
    CIUS
CATO, MARCUS POR-
    CIUS (UTICENSIS)
CATULUS
CENSORS
CENTUMVIRI
CEREALIS
CETHEGUS
CHAEREA
CICERO
CIMBER
CINEAS
CINNA, LUCIUS COR-
    NELIUS
CIRCUMVALLATION
CIVILIS
CLAUDIUS
CLEOPATRA, 2
CLODIUS
CLUBS

CLUENTIUS
COINAGE
COLONIA
COMITIA
COMMENTARII
COMMIUS
COMMODUS
CONSTANTINE
CONSTANTIUS
CONSUL
CORBULO
CORNELIA
CORUNCANIUS
COTTA
COTTIUS
CRASSUS
CRUCIFIXION
CUNOBELIN
CURATOR
CURIO
CURSOR
CURSUS HONORUM
DECEBALUS
DECEMVIRI
DECIUS
DECURIO
DEIOTARUS
DELATOR
DENTATUS
DICTATOR
DIDIUS SALVIUS JULI-
    ANUS
DIOCESE
DIOCLETIAN
DOLABELLA
DOMITIANUS
DRUSILLA
DRUSUS
DUILIUS
DUUMVIRI
ELAGABALUS
EQUITES
EUMENES (B), 2
EUNUS
FABIUS AMBUSTUS
FABIUS MAXIMUS
FABIUS VIBULANUS
FABRICIUS
FASCES
FASTI
FAUSTINA

Felix
Festus, Porcius
Fimbria
Fiscus
Flaccus, Lucius Valerius, 1
Flaccus, Marcus Valerius
Flaccus, Quintus Fulvius
Flamininus
Flaminius
Florianus
Frontinus
Fulvia
Gabinius
Gaius
Gaius Caesar
Galba
Galerius
Gallienus
Gallio
Gallus
Germanicus
Geta
Glabrio
Gordianus
Gracchus
Hadrianus
Hamilcar
Hannibal
Hanno, 2
Hasdrubal
Helena
Helvidius Priscus
Herennius
Herodes
Herodes Atticus
Hiempsal
Hieron, 2
Hortensius, 1
Hyrcanus
Imperator
Infamia
Josephus
Juba
Jugurtha
Julia
Julian Calendar
Labarum
Labeo
Labienus
Laelius
Laenas

Latifundia
Latin League
Legion
Lentulus
Lepidus
Licinius
Lictors
Livia
Livia Drusilla
Livius Salinator
Locusta
Longinus
Lucullus
Macrinus
Maecenas
Maenius
Mago, 1
Mamurra
Manilius, Gaius
Manlius
Manumission
Marcellus
Marcus Aurelius
Marius
Maroboduus
Masinissa
Massa
Massiva
Mastanabal
Maxentius
Maximianus
Maximinus
Messala
Messalina
Metellus
Micipsa
Milo
Mithradates
Monumentum Ancyranum
Mummius
Municipium
Murena
Narcissus
Nero
Nerva
Nicomedes
Niger
Numerianus
Octavia
Octavianus
Octavius
Odaenathus
Opimius

Oppius
Optimates
Orodes
Otho
Ovation
Pacorus
Pallas
Pansa
Papinianus
Patria Potestas
Patricians and Plebeians
Paulinus
Paulus
Peculium
Perperna
Perseus
Pertinax
Petreius
Pharnaces
Philippus
Philo, Quintus Publius [lius
Phraates
Piso
Plautius
Polemon, 2
Pollio, Gaius Asinius
Pollio, Vedius
Pompeia
Pompeius
Pomponia
Pomponius
Pontius Pilatus
Poppaea Sabina
Porcia
Postumus
Praefectus
Praetor
Praetorian Guard
Praetorium
Primus
Probus, Marcus Aurelius
Proculus
Provocatio
Prusias
Ptolemy X–IV
Publicani
Punic Wars
Pupienus
Pyrrhus
Quaestor
Quintillus
Quirites

RABIRIUS
REGULUS
REX
ROMAN ARMY
ROSCIUS, SEXTUS
RUFUS
RUPILIUS
RUSTICUS
SABINA
SABINUS
SACRAMENTUM
SACRED MOUNT
SALLUSTIUS CRISPUS
SALVIUS JULIANUS
SAPOR
SASSANIDAE
SATURNINUS
SAXA, DECIDIUS
SCAEVOLA, PUBLIUS
  MUCIUS
SCAEVOLA, QUINTUS
SCAPULA
SCAURUS
SCIPIO
SCRIBONIA
SEJANUS

SELLA CURULIS
SENATE
SENECA, LUCIUS AN-
  NAEUS
SERTORIUS
SERVILE WARS
SERVILIA
SEVERUS
SITTIUS
SOCIAL WAR
SOPHONISBA
SOSIUS
SPARTACUS
SPOLIA OPIMA
SULLA
SULPICIUS RUFUS
SURENAS
SYPHAX
TACITUS, MARCUS
  CLAUDIUS
TERENTIA
TESTUDO
TETRICUS
THIRTY TYRANTS, 2
THRASEA PAETUS
TIBERIUS

TIGELLINUS
TIGRANES
TIRIDATES
TITUS
TORQUATUS
TRAIANUS
TREBONIUS
TRIBUNE
TRIUMPH
TRIUMVIRATE
TULLIA
TWELVE TABLES
TYRANNION
ULPIANUS
VALERIANUS
VARRO, GAIUS TEREN-
  TIUS
VARUS
VENTIDIUS
VERCINGETORIX
VERRES
VERUS
VIPSANIA AGRIPPINA
VIRIATHUS
VITELLIUS
ZENOBIA

LATIN LITERATURE

ACRON, HELENIUS
ACTIUS
AFER
ALBINOVANUS PEDO
ANDRONICUS, LIVIUS
ANTIPATER, LUCIUS
  CAELIUS
ATELLANAE FABULAE
AUFIDIUS BASSUS
BASSUS, CAESIUS
BASSUS, SALEIUS
BIBACULUS
CAECILIUS STATIUS
CAESAR, GAIUS JULIUS
CALPURNIUS SICULUS
CALVUS
CASSIUS PARMENSIS
CATO, MARCUS POR-
  CIUS
CATO, PUBLIUS VAL-
  ERIUS
CATULLUS

CATULUS, QUINTUS
  LUTATIUS, 1
CICERO, MARCUS TUL-
  LIUS, 1
CINNA, GAIUS HEL-
  VIUS
COLUMELLA
COMMODIANUS
CORDUS
CORNIFICIUS
CURTIUS RUFUS
ENNIUS
EUMENIUS
FABIUS PICTOR, QUIN-
  TUS
FENESTELLA
FESCENNINI VERSUS
FESTUS, SEXTUS POM-
  PEIUS
FIGULUS
FLACCUS, LUCIUS
  VALERIUS, 2

FLACCUS, MARCUS
  VERRIUS
FLORUS
FRONTINUS
FRONTO
GALLUS, CORNELIUS
GELLIUS, AULUS
GRATTIUS
HIRTIUS
HORACE
HORTENSIUS, 2
HOSTIUS
HYGINUS
JUSTINUS
JUVENAL
LABERIUS
LIVIUS
LUCANUS
LUCCEIUS
LUCILIUS
LUCRETIUS
LUPUS

MACER
MAECIANUS
MAGO, 2
MANILIUS
MARTIALIS
MELA
MESSALA
NAEVIUS
NEMESIANUS
NEPOS
NOVIUS
ORBILIUS PUPILLUS
OVIDIUS NASO
PACUVIUS
PATERCULUS
PEDIANUS
PERSIUS FLACCUS
PERVIGILIUM VENERIS

PETRONIUS
PHAEDRUS
PLAUTUS
PLINIUS SECUNDUS
PROBUS, MARCUS VAL-
    ERIUS
PROPERTIUS
PUBLILIUS SYRUS
QUADRIGARIUS
QUINTILIANUS
SALLUSTIUS CRISPUS
SCHOLIA
SCRIPTORES HISTORIAE
    AUGUSTAE
SENECA
SILIUS ITALICUS
SISENNA
SOLINUS

STATIUS
STILO PRAECONINUS
SUETONIUS TRANQUIL-
    LUS
SULPICIA
TACITUS, PUBLIUS
    CORNELIUS
TERENTIUS AFER
TIBERIANUS
TIBULLUS
TIRO
VALERIUS MAXIMUS
VARIUS RUFUS
VARRO, MARCUS
    TERENTIUS
VERGILIUS MARO
VERRIUS FLACCUS

ROMAN LEGEND, MYTHOLOGY AND RELIGION

ACCA LARENTIA
ACESTES
ACHATES
AEDICULA
AENEAS
AIUS LOCUTIUS
AMATA
AMBARVALIA
ANCHISES
ANCILE
ANCUS MARCIUS
ANNA PERENNA
ARVALES, FRATRES
ASCANIUS
AUGURES
BONA DEA
CACUS
CAMENAE
CARDEA
CARNA
CERES
CINCINNATUS
CLAUDIA
CLOELIA
COCLES
COLLATINUS
CONCORDIA
CONFARREATIO
CONSENTES DII
CONSUS
CORIOLANUS

CORVUS
CUPIDO
CURTIUS
DIANA
DIDO
EGERIA
EPONA
EVANDER
FAUNUS
FECIALES
FERONIA
FIDES PUBLICA
FIDIUS
FLAMEN
FLORA
FORTUNA
FURIAE
GENIUS
HARUSPICES
HONOS
HORATII

JANUS
JUNO
JUPITER
JUTURNA
KINGS OF ROME
LARES
LARUNDA
LATINUS
LAVERNA

LAVINIA
LECTISTERNIUM
LEMURES
LATONA
LIBER
LIBERTAS
LIBITINA
LUCRETIA
LUPERCALIA
MAELIUS
MAMILIUS
MANES
MARCIUS
MARS
MATRONALIA
MATUTA
MERCURIUS
MINERVA
MITHRAS
MONETA
NAVIUS
NEPTUNUS
NUMA POMPILIUS
NUMITOR
OPS
PALES
PALLADIUM
PAX
PENATES
PORSENA
PORTUNUS

PROCULUS, JULIUS
RHEA SYLVIA
ROBIGO
ROMULUS
SALACIA
SALII
SANCUS
SATURNALIA
SATURNUS
SCAEVOLA, GAIUS
　MUCIUS

SIBYL
SILVANUS
SPES
SUMMANUS
TAGES
TARPEIA
TARQUINIUS
TERMINUS
TOLUMNUS
TULLIUS, SERVIUS
TULLUS HOSTILIUS

TURNUS
VENUS
VERTUMNUS
VESTA
VESTALS
VICTORIA
VIRGINIA
VIRTUS
VULCAN

PHILOSOPHY AND SCIENCE

ACADEMY, THE
ACRON
AENESIDEMUS
AESCHINES, 2
AGATHODAIMON
ALCMAEON, 2
ALEXANDER AEGAEUS
AMMONIUS SACCAS
ANAXAGORAS
ANAXARCHUS
ANAXIMANDER
ANAXIMENES
ANDRONICUS OF
　RHODES
ANNICERIS
ANTIOCHUS OF ASCA-
　LON
ANTIPATER OF TARSUS
ANTISTHENES
APELLICON
APOLLONIUS, 3 and 7
ARCESILAUS
ARCHELAUS, 7
ARCHIMEDES
ARCHYTAS
ARISTARCHUS, I
ARISTIPPUS
ARISTOBULUS, 2
ARISTOTLE
ARISTOXENUS
ARTEMIODORUS
ASCLEPIADES, I
ATHENODORUS, I and 4
AUTOLYCUS
BIAS
BION, 2

CALLIPUS
CARNEADES
CENSORINUS
CHILON
CHRYSIPPUS
CICERO, MARCUS TUL-
　LIUS, I
CLEANTHES
CLEITOMACHUS
CLEOBULUS
CLEOMBROTUS, 4
CORNUTUS
CRANTOR, 2
CRATES, 2–4
CRATIPPUS, 2
CRITOLAUS
DEMETRIUS
DEMOCEDES
DEMOCRITUS
DICHAEARCHUS
DIODORUS CRONUS
DIOGENES
DIOPHANTUS
DIOSCORIDES
EMPEDOCLES
EPICTETUS, I
EPICURUS
ERASISTRATUS
ERATOSTHENES
ERISTICS
EUBULIDES
EUCLEIDES
EUCLID
EUDEMUS
EUDOXUS
FAVORINUS
GALEN
GARDEN

HEGESIAS, 2
HERACLIDES, 2
HERACLITUS
HERMETICA
HERON
HIPPARCHUS, 2
HIPPASUS
HIPPIAS, 2
HIPPOCRATES
HIPPON
IAMBLICHUS
LACYDES
LEUCIPPUS
LYCON
LYSIS
MENEDEMUS
MENIPPUS
METON
METRODORUS
PANAETIUS
PARMENIDES
PHAEDON
PHERECYDES, I
PHILO JUDAEUS
PHILODEMUS
PLATO
PLOTINUS
POLEMON, I
POLYSTRATUS
PORPHYRIUS
POSEIDONIOS
PROTAGORAS
PTOLEMAEUS
PYRRHON
PYTHAGORAS
SATYRUS
SERENUS
SEVEN SAGES

SEXTUS EMPIRICUS
SOCRATES
SOPHISTS
SORANUS
SOSIGENES

SPEUSIPPUS
STOA
STRATON
THALES
THEOPHRASTUS

TIMAEUS
XENOCRATES
XENOPHANES
ZENO

ART AND ARCHITECTURE

ABACUS, 2
AETION
AGASIAS
AGATHARCHUS
AGELADAS
AGESANDER
AGORACRITUS
ALCAMENES
ANTENOR
ANTIPHILUS
APELLES
APOLLODORUS, 1 and 4
APOLLONIUS, 6
AQUEDUCTS
ARISTEIDES, 3
ATHENODORUS, 5 and 6
BASILICA
BATHYCLES
BRYAXIS
BRYGUS
CALAMIS
CALLICRATES
CALLIMACHUS, 2
CEPHISODOTUS
CHARES, 2
CIMON OF CLEONAE

CLEOMENES (B)
COLOSSUS OF RHODES
COLUMNA ROSTRATA
CRESILAS
CRITIUS
DAMOPHON
DEINOCRATES
EPICTETUS, 2
ERECHTHEUM
EUPALINUS
EUPHRANOR
EUPHRONIUS
EUPOMPUS
EUTYCHIDES
EXEKIAS
FABIUS PICTOR
GAIUS
GLYCON
HERMAE
ICTINUS
LEOCHARES
LYSISTRATUS
MENTOR, 2
MICON
MNESICLES
MUS
MYRON

NICIAS
ONATAS
PANAENUS
PANTHEON
PARRASIOS
PARTHENON
PAUSON
PHAROS
PHEIDIAS
PHILON
PHILOXENUS, 2
POLYCLEITUS
POLYGNOTUS
PRAXIAS
PRAXITELES
PROTOGENES
PURGOTELES
PYTHIS
RHOECUS
SAMIAN WARE
SARCOPHAGUS
SCOPAS
SILANION
THERMAE
TIMOTHEUS, 2
VITRUVIUS POLLIO
ZEUXIS

SPORT, ENTERTAINMENT AND DOMESTIC

ABACUS, 1–3
ATHENODORUS, 3
BATHYLLUS
BULLA
CAESTUS
CHITON
CIRCUS
DIAULOS
EPHEBEUM
GLADIATORS

GYMNASIUM
HIPPODROME
IMAGINES
ISTHMIAN GAMES
LECYTHUS
LUDI APOLLINARES
LUDI MAGNI
LUDI MEGALENSES
LUDI SAECULARES
NAUMACHIA

NEMEAN GAMES
ODEUM
OLYMPIC GAMES
PARIS
PYTHIAN GAMES
ROSCIUS GALLUS
STADIUM
SYMPOSIUM
THEATRE
WINE

A

Abacus (Gk *abax*): 1. A counting-board. The Greek form was generally covered with sand or wax and marked with lines representing units, tens and hundreds, or different units of value. The Romans appear to have used also a table with grooves in which the counters could be made to slide.

2. In architecture, a flat padstone between the echinus and the architrave. The diminutive, *abacicus*, was applied to the squares of a tessellated pavement.

3. A Roman sideboard.

Abae (-ai), town of Phocis (q.v.), celebrated for its oracle of Apollo which was one of those consulted by Croesus (Herodotus, i. 46). The temple fell into decay after being sacked by the Persians in 480 B.C.; but according to Pausanias (*see* PAUSANIAS, 3) recourse was had to the oracle as late as 371 B.C., by the Thebans before Leuctra.

Abax, *see* ABACUS, I.

Abdēra: 1. Town on the coast of Thrace, near the mouth of the Nestos. It was colonized first from Clazomenae (q.v.) in the 7th century B.C., but its prosperity dates from 544 B.C. when most of the inhabitants of Teos migrated there to escape Persian rule (Herodotus, i. 168). Abdera was the birth-place of Democritus and Protagoras (qq.v.), but its inhabitants were traditionally dull witted.

2. Seaport town of Hispania Baetica (*see* HISPANIA), founded from Carthage. It was made a Roman colony (*see* COLONIA) by the emperor Tiberius.

Abella (mod. Avella Vecchia), city of Campania on the road from Nola. The region was celebrated for its apples and nuts, whence Horace calls it 'malifera'. There are ruins of walls and of an amphitheatre.

Abilēnē, tetrarchy of Syria. Originally a separate Iturean kingdom, it was given to Agrippa I (q.v.) by Caligula in A.D. 37, and to Agrippa II (q.v.) by Claudius in 52. The capital was Abila, on the road between Damascus and Heliopolis (Baalbek).

Abonouteikhos (mod. Inebolu), town on the north coast of Asia Minor, about 70 miles west of Sinope. It was the birth-place of Alexander the Paphlagonian (q.v.), who obtained leave from Marcus Aurelius to change its name to Ionopolis.

Abydos (Abudos), town of Mysia (q.v.) in Asia Minor, a colony of Miletus. From here Xerxes (q.v.) crossed the Hellespont on a bridge of boats in 480 B.C. In 200 B.C. it was besieged and captured by Philip V of Macedon after a desperate resistance. *See also* HERO AND LEANDER.

Abyla, a mountain of the Atlas range, opposite Calpe (q.v.), with which it formed the *Herculis Columnae* (Pillars of Hercules).

Academy, The (Gk Akadēmia), general name of the Platonic school (*see* PLATO) in its several periods or phases. The name was originally given to a public gymnasium about one mile north-west of Athens, the site of which was said to have belonged to Academus, a hero who assisted the Dioscuri (q.v.) when they invaded Attica. This place was walled by Hipparchus, adorned by Cimon, and (c. 398 B.C.) became the resort of Plato, who taught there for about fifty years. Cicero, among others, held (*de Orat.* iii. 18, etc.) that the history of the school justified no more than a twofold division, viz. the Old and the New Academy, the former of which was established by Plato and the latter by Carneades. Sextus Empiricus, however, states (*Outlines of Pyrrhonism*, i. 220) that there were commonly held to have been three Academies: the first or Old, under Plato, Speusippus and Xenocrates; the second or Middle, under Arcesilaus and Lacydes; and the third or New, under Carneades and Clitomachus. He also mentions a view according to which there were a fourth Academy, under Philo of Larissa and Charmadas, and a fifth, established by Antiochus of Ascalon. *See* articles on the philosophers mentioned above.

Acamas (Ak-), son of Theseus and grandson of Aethra (q.v.). He was the legendary founder of Soli in Cyprus (*see* Soli, 2).

Acarnan (Ak-), son of Alcmaeon (q.v.) by Callirrhoë, brother of Amphoterus and eponymous hero of Acarnania (q.v.). At the time of their father's murder they were very young; but Zeus enabled them to reach maturity at once, and they avenged Alcmaeon by putting to death Phegeus, together with his wife and two sons.

Acarnania (Ak-), most westerly district of Greece, supposed to have been colonized by Acarnan, son of Alcmaeon (q.v.) and Callirrhoë. It was bounded north by the Ambracian Gulf, west by the Ionian Sea, east and south by Mt Thyamus and the River Acheloüs. In the 7th century B.C. Corinth founded several towns on the coast, the chief of which was Stratos; but these were ruined in consequence of the Peloponnesian war, during which the Acarnanians first emerge from obscurity as allies of Athens. Owing to their geographical situation they were at that time a backward people; but Thucydides refers to them as expert slingers, and praises them for their courage and loyalty. Having passed successively under the control of Sparta, Thebes and Macedon, Acarnania became part of the Roman province of Macedonia (148 B.C.). Augustus transported most of the inhabitants to Nicopolis and Patrae (qq.v.).

Acastus (Akastos), son of Pelias, whom he succeeded on the throne of Iolcus (*see* Jason and Medea), and husband of Hippolyte (or Astydameia). For his relations with Peleus, by whom he was eventually murdered, *see* Peleus. Acastus was among the Argonauts (q.v.) and the Calydonian hunters (*see* Meleager). *See also* Protesilaus.

Acca Larentia, Italian earth-goddess of Etruscan origin. Her festival, the Larentalia, was celebrated on 23rd December. She became the heroine of two Roman legends. According to one, as wife of Faustulus she was nurse of Romulus (q.v.) and Remus. Another makes her the wife of Tarutius, a wealthy Etruscan, whose riches she inherited and bequeathed to the Roman people.

Accius, *see* Actius.

Ace (Akē), original name of Syrian Ptolemais.

Acesta, name used by Virgil for Segesta (q.v.).

Acestes (Akestēs), mythical king of Sicily, son of the river-god Crimisus by Egesta, a Trojan woman who had been sent to Sicily by her father to escape from a sea-monster that was ravaging Troy (*see* LAOMEDON). Acestes was afterwards considered founder of Segesta (q.v.). He welcomed Aeneas on the latter's arrival in Sicily.

Achaea (Akhaia): 1. District on the north coast of Peloponnesus. Bounded north by the Corinthian Gulf; west by Elis; east by Sicyon; south by Elis, Arcadia and Argolis. Twelve cities early formed a league for mutual defence with headquarters in the sanctuary of Poseidon at Helice, and from it developed the famous Achaean League (q.v.) of later times.

2. Roman province, formed in 146 B.C. It included all mainland Greece south of a line drawn from the Ambracian to the Maliac Gulf.

Achaea (Akhaia) Phthiōtis, district of southern Thessaly, west of the Gulf of Pagasae. Homer calls it Phthia and mentions a city of the same name, which was the home of Achilles (q.v.).

Achaean League. As explained in the article ACHAEA 1, twelve cities of Achaea in northern Peloponnesus early formed a league for mutual defence. They were Pellene, Aegira, Aegae, Bura, Helice, Aegium, Rhypae, Patrae, Pharae, Olenus, Dyme and Tritaea. During the 4th century B.C. the league fought in the wars between Thebes and Sparta, as well as against Philip II and Antipater of Macedon. It was dissolved by Antigonus Gonatas; but by 280 B.C. four towns had reunited, and before long all ten of those that survived had done the same. Thanks to the expansive policy of Aratus (q.v.), the league included in 228 Arcadia, Argolis, Corinth and Aegina. Between this date and 220 B.C., however, it lost much of its territory as a result of wars with Cleomenes III of Sparta (*see* ANTIGONUS, 3) and with the Aetolians, becoming in fact subject to Macedonia. Some ground was recovered under Philopoemen (q.v.); and in return for Achaean neutrality during the Macedonian war, T. Quinctius Flamininus restored all the league's former possessions and made it virtually supreme in Peloponnesus. But in 150 B.C. the Achaean League attacked Sparta in defiance of orders from Rome. Its army was defeated by L. Mummius near Corinth (146 B.C.), the league was finally dissolved and Greece was formed into the Roman province of Archaea. *See* M. Dubois, *Les Ligues achéenne et étolienne,* 1885.

Achaeans (Gk Akhaioi; Lat. Achaei), name given by modern archaeologists and historians to the second wave of hellenic invaders (*see* IONIANS), who entered Greece *c.* 1580 B.C. In Homer it is used generally of all Greek-speaking people, standing for those who enjoyed and propagated throughout the Mediterranean area what is called today Mycenaean civilization. The mention of 'Akhkhijawa' in Hittite tablets found at Boghaz Keui refers almost certainly to an independent 'Mycenaean' kingdom in Rhodes. It is also probable that the 'Ekwesh', described in an Egyptian inscription of *c.* 1225 B.C. as 'northerners' and 'peoples of the sea', included bands of 'Mycenaean' Greeks fleeing before the advance-guard of the Dorian invasion (*see* DORIANS).

Achaemenidae (Akhaimenidai), the Achaemenids, a dynasty of Persian kings, founded by Cyrus the Greek (q.v.). It ruled from 553 until 331 B.C., and was so called by the Greeks from a reputed ancestor of Cyrus, whose name (Hakhamanish) they rendered as Akhaimenēs. *See* ARSES; ARTAXERXES; DAREIOS; XERXES.

Acharnae (Akharnai), Attic deme, about 12 miles north of Athens. The Acharnians are used by Aristophanes as the chorus in his play of that name, the oldest surviving Greek comedy.

Achates, a companion of Aeneas (q.v.); the proverbial 'fidus Achates', a model of devoted loyalty in the *Aeneid*.

Acheloüs (Akheloos), name of several rivers in Greece. The most important (150 m.) rises in Mt Pindus and flows southward through a fertile plain to the Ionian Sea at the extreme south of Acarnania. The Acheloüs was the typical river-god of northern Greece (*see also* ALPHEUS), and was sometimes taken as representative of fresh water in general, whence Virgil's '*Acheloia pocula*.'

The god of this river is described as a son of Oceanus and Tethys. He fought with Heracles for the hand of Deianeira (q.v.), but had the worst of the contest. He then assumed the form of a bull, but was again overcome by Heracles, who deprived him of one horn. According to Ovid (*Metam*. ix. 87) this horn was changed by the naiads into the cornucopia. But *see* AMALTHEIA.

Acheron (Akherōn), name of several rivers which, on account of their black or bitter waters, were believed to be connected with the underworld. The best known was that in Epirus, flowing through the Acherusian swamps into the Ionian Sea. The name was also applied to an imaginary river of Hades itself (*see* CHARON; STYX).

Acherusia Palus (mod. Lago Fusaro), Italian lake near Baiae, separated from the sea on the west by a line of dunes. During the 1st century A.D. it was given an artificial outlet at its southern end in the shape of a tunnel driven through a hill on which stand remains of a villa once belonging to Servilius Vata and described by Seneca.

Achilles (Gk Akhilleus), son of Peleus and Thetis (qq.v.), the principal hero of the *Iliad*. According to Homer he was brought up by his mother at Phthia (*see* ACHAIA PHTHIOTIS), together with Patroclus (q.v.). Educated by Phoenix and Chiron (qq.v.), he led the Myrmidons (q.v.) in fifty ships to Troy, and during the first nine years of the war (*see* TROY) was responsible for the capture of twelve Trojan cities. In the tenth year Agamemnon, being compelled to surrender Chryseis (q.v.), made good his loss by depriving Achilles of a favourite slave-girl, Briseis. Achilles retired from active service to sulk in his tent, and the Greek were so hard pressed in consequence that they sent a deputation proposing to restore Briseis with additional rewards. Achilles would not accept their offer. At length, however, he agreed to lend his arms and armour to Patroclus, who was killed by Hector (q.v.) in the ensuing fight. Moved to fury by the death of his beloved friend, the hero made peace with Agamemnon, obtained new armour from Hephaestus (q.v.), and eventually slew Hector. We learn from the *Iliad* that Achilles was fated to die before the Scaean Gate of Troy, and in the *Odyssey* there is a reference to his funeral. The non-Homeric poems of the Trojan Cycle narrate several other legends of his life and death (see AJAX; LYCOMEDES; MEMNON; NEOPTOLEMUS; PARIS; PENTHESILEIA; THETIS); but these have no place in the Homeric text, and many bear the stamp of tales familiar in folklore everywhere. Achilles was worshipped in several places; but so far from his having been originally (as once suggested) a sun- or river-god, it is probable that a real man underlies the mass of legend. See L. R. Farnell, *Greek Hero Cults*, 1921; Sir J. Forsdyke, *Greece before Homer*, 1956.

Acis (Akis), in Greek mythology, son of Pan (q.v.) by the nymph Symaethis. He was a Sicilian shepherd and fell in love with the nereid Galatea (see NEREUS). The Cyclops Polyphemus (see CYCLOPS; POLYPHEMUS), who was likewise enamoured, crushed him with a rock, and the young shepherd's blood, gushing from beneath it, was changed by Galatea into the River Acis at the foot of Mt Aetna. See Ovid, *Metam.* xiii. 750; Silius Italicus, *Punica*, xiv. 221.

Acontius (Akontios), in Greek legend, a beautiful youth of Ceos (q.v.). While celebrating the festival of Artemis at Delos he fell in love with Cydippe, daughter of an Athenian noble. As she was sitting in the temple precinct he passed by and let fall an apple on which he had written: 'I swear by the sanctuary of Artemis to marry Acontius.' Her attendant picked it up and handed it to Cydippe, who read the words aloud. Her subsequent betrothals were frustrated by sickness, until the Delphic oracle revealed the breach of her vow, and she was married to Acontius. See Callimachus, *Aitia*, iii. 1. In 1910 a lost fragment of Callimachus describing the illness of Cydippe and its cure was discovered and published in Hunt's *Oxyrhynchus Papyri*, part vii.

Acragas, see AGRIGENTUM.

Acrisius (Akrisios), father of Danaë. See PERSEUS.

Acroceraunia (Akrok-), promontory of Epirus in the Ionian Sea. The coast was dangerous to shipping, whence Horace's '*infames scopulos Acrocerauniae.*'

Acron (Akrōn), 5th century B.C., Greek physician, born at Acragas. He is credited with having recommended some primitive and unsuccessful methods of fumigation during the great plague at Athens (430 B.C.).

Acron, Helenius (late 2nd century A.D.), Roman grammarian and commentator on Terence. Some extant scholia on Horace once attributed to him are spurious.

Acropolis (Akropolis, 'upper city'), a piece of high ground, generally a hill with steep sides, chosen by early settlers for purposes of defence. A site of this kind often became the hub of a larger city in the surrounding plain, e.g. at Argos, Athens, Corinth, Thebes (qq.v.). The word is now used most commonly of the Athenian Acropolis, for a description of which see ATHENS.

Acta : 1. Of the Roman magistrates or people, of their courts, or of the senate (see ACTA SENATUS), meaning (a) what was transacted before them, and (b) the records of such transactions.

2. Of the Roman emperors, meaning their official enactments, which, unless rescinded, successive rulers swore to observe.

Acta Diurna, a sort of daily gazette, was instituted at Rome by Julius Caesar during his first consulship (59 B.C.) and continued until the seat of empire was transferred to Constantinople (A.D. 330). Its contents were (1) official, e.g. court news, imperial decrees, etc.; (2) social, e.g. births, marriages and deaths. Written on a whitewashed board (*album*), the Acta were posted up daily in some prominent place. After removal they were stored with other public archives and were available for future reference. *See* G. Boissier, *Tacitus and other Studies* (trans.), 1906.

Acta Senatus, records of proceedings in the Roman senate. Julius Caesar ordered their publication (59 B.C.), before which time they had been issued unofficially and at irregular intervals. Augustus forbade publication, but arranged that full records should be deposited in the imperial archives and public libraries, where they might be inspected only by permission of the city prefect. *See also* AERARIUM, 1.

Actaeon (Aktaiōn), a Boeotian hero, son of Aristaeus and Autonoë (q.v.). Ovid relates (*Metam.* iii. 131) that while hunting on Mt Cithaeron he accidentally saw Artemis bathing; the goddess changed him into a stag, and he was torn to pieces by his fifty hounds. According to another version he suffered this fate for having claimed to excel Artemis as a hunter. The myth appears to represent the destruction of plant life during the fifty dog days, for statues of Actaeon were often set up in high places to ward off the evils of excessive heat.

Acte, most easterly of the three peninsulas projecting into the Aegean from Chalcidice in Macedonia and terminating in the promontory of Mt Athos (6,350 feet). On the isthmus, which is about one and a half miles across, there are traces of a canal cut by Xerxes in 480 B.C. Today the whole peninsula is called Athos; it is occupied entirely by monasteries, in the libraries of which, until about 150 years ago, there were important collections of classical manuscripts. Many of these were destroyed through the accidents of war and neglect; the remainder have been dispersed.

Actium, promontory of Acarnania at the mouth of the Ambracian Gulf. It was occupied by a town of the same name, with a temple of Apollo Actius. From the 7th to the 3rd centuries B.C., when it became Acarnanian territory, Actium belonged to the Corinthian colony of Anactorium, whose inhabitants probably established the worship of Apollo and instituted in his honour the quinquennial games which the Romans called *Ludi Actiaci*. It was off the promontory that Octavian's fleet, commanded by M. Vipsanius Agrippa (q.v.), defeated the combined navies of Mark Antony and Cleopatra, 2nd September 31 B.C., and thereby ended the civil war. To commemorate this victory Augustus enlarged the temple, revived the games and founded the city of Nicopolis (q.v.).

Actius, Accius or **Attius, Lucius**, Roman tragic poet, son of a freedman; born at Pisaurum, in Umbria, 170 B.C. Cicero and Horace both speak highly of his plays, most of which were adaptations of Greek originals; about 700 lines are extant. He also wrote in verse on the history of Greek and Latin poetry; but these works, together with his *Annales*, are lost. *See* W. Beare, *The Roman Stage*, 1950.

Admetus (Admētos), legendary king of Pherae, in Thessaly. He sued for the hand of Alcestis, daughter of Pelias, and the latter agreed on condition that he would come in a chariot drawn by lions and boars. This task Admetus performed with the help of Apollo, who had tended his flocks for nine years as a punishment (some said) for having killed the Cyclops. Learning that Admetus was soon to die, Apollo persuaded the Fates (*see* MOIRAE) to prolong his life if someone else would agree to die in his stead. His parents refusing, Alcestis consented to do so; but she was rescued by Heracles, who wrestled with Death and brought her back from the underworld. *See* Euripides, *Alcestis*.

Adōnis, in Greek legend, a beautiful youth favoured by Aphrodite. The story goes that Myrrha, daughter of the Syrian king Theias, was inspired by Aphrodite with incestuous love towards her father and tricked him into getting her with child. Theias, discovering the deceit, resolved to murder her; but the gods took pity and changed her into a tree, which in due course split open to release Adonis. Aphrodite, struck by his beauty, hid the child in a box and entrusted it for safe keeping to Persephone (q.v.). But when the time came for her to deliver up her charge Persephone would not do so. Zeus was therefore called upon to arbitrate: he ruled that Adonis should spend four months of every year with Aphrodite, four months with Persephone in the underworld, the remaining four being at his own disposal. Another version of the tale states that Adonis was killed by a boar, and that from his blood sprang the anemone; the grief of Aphrodite won from Zeus the above threefold division of his year.

Festivals called Adonia were held yearly at Byblus in Phoenicia, at Athens and elsewhere (from the 5th century B.C.), and later at Alexandria (*see* Theocritus, *Idylls*, xv). The ritual and history of this cult and the legend of Adonis, seem to justify the theory that his worship originated in Phoenicia, that his name derives from the Phoenician word *adon* (lord), and that he is identical with the Semitic deity Tammuz. He is therefore a spirit of vegetation in general or, perhaps, of the corn in particular. His association in legend and ritual with the boar and swine suggests that he was looked upon as incarnate in swine; nor does such a view conflict with that of a vegetation or corn spirit, which appears in various parts of Europe as a boar or sow. Cf. also the ritual of the Thesmophoria (q.v.). *See* L. R. Farnell, *Cults of the Greek States*, 1896–1906; Sir J. G. Frazer, *Attis, Adonis, Osiris*, 1907.

Adranon (mod. Adarno), town in Sicily, founded by Dionysius I, *c.* 400 B.C. It was called after a native deity, Adranos (identified by the Romans with Vulcan), whose temple was guarded by 1,000 dogs. Adranon was the first Sicilian town occupied by the Romans (263 B.C.). There are remains of the ancient wall.

Adrastus (-os): 1. Legendary son of Talaüs, King of Argos. Expelled from his throne by Amphiaraüs (q.v.), he fled to Polybus, King of Sicyon, whom he ultimately succeeded. He was later reconciled with Amphiaraüs and returned to the throne of Argos. For the part played by Adrastus in the expedition of the Seven against Thebes, and in the subsequent War of the Epigoni in which his son Aegialeus was killed, as well as for a notice of his death, *see* THEBAN LEGEND, 3 and 5. His daughters, Deipyle and Argia, were married respectively to Tydeus (q.v.) and Polynices.

2. Son of the Phrygian king Gordius (q.v.). Having unintentionally

killed his brother he took refuge with Croesus, King of Lydia, who purified him. While hunting he accidentally killed Atys, the son of Croesus, and took his own life in despair.

Adria, *see* ATRIA, I.

Adulis, city of Eritrea, on the Red Sea; founded, according to Pliny, by runaway slaves from Egypt. Here was discovered the *Monumentum Adulitanum*, listing the conquests of Ptolemy III Euergetes.

Aeacus (Aiakos), in Greek legend, son of Zeus by Aegina, daughter of the river-god Asopus (*see* ASOPUS). His mother was transported by Zeus to the island of Oenone, which was renamed after her (*see* AEGINA). The inhabitants were wiped out by a plague, but Zeus repeopled it by changing the ants (Gk *murmēkes*) into human beings, who were known as Myrmidons (q.v.). So impartially did Aeacus rule these his subjects that after his death he was appointed a judge of the underworld with Minos and Rhadamanthus (qq.v.). By his wife Endeis he was father of Peleus and Telamon (qq.v.).

Aeaea (Aiaia), legendary island in the River Oceanus. According to Homer it was the abode of Circe, and was afterwards identified with the promontory of Circeii (q.v.).

Aeclanum, Samnite town, an important road station on the Via Appia; capital of the Hirpini after 268 B.C. Captured by Sulla in 89 B.C., it was made a Roman colony (*see* COLONIA) by Hadrian. There are remains of walls, an aqueduct, baths and an amphitheatre.

Aedicula, a small house or temple, especially the Roman household shrine of the Lares and Penates (qq.v.).

Aediles, Roman magistrates. The office was instituted in 494 B.C. by the appointment of two plebeian aediles, whose name was derived from the *aedes* or temple of Ceres, the focus of the plebeian cult. With the appointment in 367 B.C. of two curule aediles of patrician rank the office became representative of the whole people. It was elective, though not an essential degree of the *cursus honorum* (q.v.), and its holders ranked next after praetors. The duties of aediles fell under two heads: (1) *cura urbis*, involving the supervision of temples, public buildings and markets; (2) *cura ludorum sollemnium*, i.e. care of the games. Until 45 B.C. the aediles also had charge of the city's corn supply; but in that year Julius Caesar, as dictator, appointed two *aediles cereales* to perform those duties, which were transferred by Augustus to the *praefectus annonae* (*see* PRAEFECTUS). *See* J. E. Sandys, *Companion to Latin Studies*, 1921.

Aēdōn, i.e. the 'Singer', wife of the Theban king Zethus and mother of Itylus. Envious of Niobe, wife of her brother-in-law Amphion (q.v.), who had numerous children, Aedon resolved to kill the eldest of Niobe's sons. By mistake, however, she slew her own son Itylus, and Zeus assuaged her grief by changing her into a nightingale.

Aedui or **Haedui,** Gallic tribe which in Caesar's time inhabited territory corresponding to the modern departments of Saône-et-Loire and Nevers and parts of Côte d'Or and Allier. Their capital was Bibracte (q.v.). In 123 B.C. they made a treaty with Rome, by whom they were styled 'friends and allies'. For many years, until Caesar's arrival in Gaul (58 B.C.), they were subject to Ariovistus (q.v.). Thereafter they proved themselves Caesar's most reliable supporters in Gaul; their defection to Vercingetorix (q.v.) in 52 B.C. was probably due more to intimidation than to choice, and they quickly returned to their allegiance. In imperial times the Aedui were a *civitas foederata,* and were the first Gallic tribe to be represented in the Roman senate.

Aeëtes (Aietēs), King of Colchis, father of Apsyrtus and Medea, *see* JASON AND MEDEA.

Aegae (Aigai): 1. One of the original twelve cities of Achaea (q.v.), on the River Crathis, with a temple of Poseidon.

2. City of Euboea, also with a temple of Poseidon (*see* AEGEUS and TRITON), who was hence called Aegaeus.

3. Otherwise Aegaeae, one of the twelve cities of Aeolis (q.v.), on the River Hyllus (*see* AEGEAN SEA).

4. Seaport town of Cilicia.

5. *See* EDESSA, 2.

Aegaleos (Aigaleōs), mountain of Attica (q.v.), opposite Salamis, from which Xerxes witnessed the destruction of his fleet (480 B.C.).

Aegates Insulae (mod. Isole Egadi), group of small islands off the west coast of Sicily, near which C. Lutatius Catulus (q.v.) defeated the Carthaginian fleet and thus terminated the first Punic war (241 B.C.).

Aegean Sea, part of the Mediterranean, bounded north by Macedonia and Thrace, west by Greece and east by Asia Minor. At the southern extremity are two groups of islands: the Cyclades (q.v.), separated from Attica and Peloponnesus by the Myrtoan Sea, and the Sporades (q.v.) in the Icarian Sea. The northern area, containing the islands of Thasos, Samothrace, Imbros and Lemnos, was sometimes known as the Thracian Sea. The name Aegean was supposed to derive from Aegae in Aeolis (*see* AEGAE, 3) or from Aegeus (q.v.).

Aegesta (Aig-), *see* EGESTA.

Aegeus (Ai-), in Greek legend, King of Athens, father of Theseus (q.v.). It should, however, be noted that Theseus is sometimes called son of Poseidon, which suggests that Aegeus was originally identical with Poseidon Aegaeus (*see* AEGAE, 2). *See also* ANDROGEOS.

Aegialeus (Aigialeus), son of Adrastus (*see* ADRASTUS, 1), *see* THEBAN LEGEND, 5.

Aegina (Aigina): 1. Island in the Saronic Gulf, about 24 miles from Peiraeus, supposed to have once been called Oeonone but to have been renamed after the mother of Aeacus (q.v.). Evidence of Bronze Age civilization has been found in the island, which appears also to have been a maritime power in the 2nd millennium B.C. Colonized from Epidaurus (q.v.), Aegina soon won its independence. Until the Persian Wars (q.v.) it was governed by an oligarchy and was perhaps the most flourishing state in the Greek world. This was due to naval strength and a busy trade with the Levant and elsewhere. Aegina was the first state of European Greece to coin money (*c.* 660 B.C.) (*see* COINAGE), and was one of the principal centres of Greek art during the 6th and early 5th centuries B.C. A war with Athens (506–481) terminated in favour of the Aeginetans, who also contributed to the victory of Salamis (q.v.). The next twenty years witnessed a steady decline owing to loss of trade consequent upon the

Persian wars, and renewed hostilities with Athens ended with the island's submission and reduction to the status of a subject ally (*c.* 456 B.C.). In 431 Athens occupied Aegina and expelled the inhabitants. Many of them settled in Thyreatis on the borders of Argolis and Laconica, but were massacred by an Athenian force under Nicias (424 B.C.).

2. Capital of the above situated in the north-west corner of the island; there are remains of the temple of Aphrodite. On a hill about seven miles to the east are the ruins of a temple dedicated to Aphaea (q.v.). The early 5th-century sculptures that adorned the sacred edifice were discovered in 1811 and are now in the Glypothek at Munich. *See* G. B. Grundy, *The Great Persian War*, 1901; A. Furtwängler and others, *Aegina, Heiligtum der Aphaia*, 1906.

Aegira (Aigira), one of the twelve cities of Achaea (*see* ACHAEA, 1), situated on a steep hill overlooking the Corinthian Gulf, about five miles from Aegae (*see* AEGAE, 1).

Aegiroessa (Ai-), one of the twelve cities of Aeolis (q.v.).

Aegis (Ai-), at first an emblem of Zeus, mentioned in the *Iliad*, where it is evidently the thunder cloud. In later art, from the 6th century B.C., the aegis is represented as a goatskin, adorned in the centre with Medusa's head (*see* GORGON), and covering the shoulders or hanging from the left arm of Athena. The Aegis in this form has a fringe of serpents, which may signify the ragged edges of the cloud; but it is commonly supposed that there was some confusion between cloud and skin owing to similarity between the Greek words *aigis* (goatskin) and *kataigis* (hurricane).

Aegisthus (Aigisthos), son of Pelopia by her father Thyestes, *see* ATREIDS, LEGEND OF THE.

Aegospotami (Aigospotamoi), a small creek on the Hellespont (q.v.), north-east of Sestos. Here, in 405 B.C., Lysander (q.v.) destroyed the last Athenian squadron in the Peloponnesian War (q.v.).

Aegyptus (Aiguptos), legendary King of Egypt, twin brother of Danaüs (q.v.).

Aelia Capitolina, name of the Roman *colonia* (q.v.) built by Hadrian in A.D. 135 on the site of Jerusalem (q.v.).

Aelianus, surnamed Tacticus (2nd century A.D.), Greek military writer who lived at Rome. His *Taktikē Theōria*, a handbook of Macedonian tactics, etc., exercised considerable influence down to the 16th century. *See* translation by Viscount Dillon, 1811.

Aelianus, Claudius (3rd century A.D.), author and rhetorician. His *De natura animalium* is a collection of animal stories; the fourteen books of his *Variae historiae* contain anecdotes of men and customs. He is also the reputed author of twenty *Peasant Letters*. His complete works were edited by Herscher, 1864–6.

Aemilia, Via, name of two Roman roads: 1. Built in 187 B.C. under the consul M. Aemilius Lepidus; a continuation of the Via Flaminia from Ariminum to Placentia, a distance of 176 miles. The stretch between Ariminum and the River Trebia was rebuilt by Augustus in 2 B.C., and the bridge over the Sillaro by Trajan in A.D. 100.

2. Built in 115 B.C. by the consul M. Aemilius Scaurus; an extension of the Aurelia Via from Vada Volaterrana to Dertona.

Aemilianus: 1. Son of L. Aemilius Paulus (*see* PAULUS, 2), was adopted by P. Cornelius Scipio Africanus the younger (*see* SCIPIO, 2) and thereafter known as P. Cornelius Scipio Aemilianus Africanus (q.v.).

2. Governor of Pannonia and Moesia under Gallus (*see* GALLUS, GAIUS VIBIUS TREBONIANUS). In A.D. 253 he was proclaimed emperor by his troops, who murdered him three months later.

Aenaria or **Inarime** (Gk Pithēkoussa; mod. Ischia), island about 62 miles north-west of Capreae (q.v.). On the north are hot springs where numerous votive offerings to Apollo and the Muses have been found, while the potter's clay of Aenaria supplied the factories of Cumae and Puteoli. The island was settled by Greek colonists from Chalcis and Eretria but was soon abandoned on account of frequent earthquakes. Later it came into the possession of Neapolis and passed with the latter to Rome in 326 B.C.

Aeneas (Aineias), in Greek and Roman legend, son of Anchises by Aphrodite. The *Iliad* (e.g. v. 311; xx. 308) shows him as a favourite of the gods, who more than once save his life because he is destined to rule the Trojans who survive the war. The story of his emigration is later and is told by Virgil in the *Aeneid*. After the fall of Troy, carrying his father and household gods on his back, and leading his son Ascanius (q.v.) by the hand, he managed to reach the coast, his wife Creusa being lost during the confusion of their flight. After voyaging to Thrace, Delos, Crete and Sicily (where Anchises died), he was driven to the coast of Africa by a storm. Here he stayed for some time as the guest and lover of Dido (q.v.), Queen of Carthage. At length, after seven years' wandering, he landed in Italy at the mouth of the Tiber, was hospitably received by Latinus, King of Latium, was betrothed to his daughter Lavinia, and founded a city (Lavinium, q.v.) named after her. Turnus, King of the Rutuli, a disappointed suitor for her hand, made war upon the Trojans, but was defeated and killed by the latter on the River Numicius. The *Aeneid* ends at this point; but according to Livy (I. i. 2) Aeneas reigned for a few years over Latium and then fell in battle against the Rutuli. His body could not be found, and was supposed to have been taken up to heaven. Subsequently deified, Aeneas was worshipped as *Iuppiter Indiges*. (*See* Dionysius of Halicarnassus, i. 64.)

Aeneas (Aineias) (4th century B.C.), Greek military writer. His *Poliorkētika*, on the defence of fortified positions, has survived. *See* the edition with translation by L. W. Hunter (revised by S. A. Handford), 1927.

Aenesidemus (Ainēsidēmos), 1st century B.C., sceptic philosopher, born at Knossos in Crete, and taught at Alexandria. An analysis of his *Pyrrhonian Principles* is contained in the *Myriobiblion* of Photius.

Aeoliae Insulae (Gk Aiolou nēsoi), the modern Lipari Islands, seven in number and named as follows: Lipara, Strongyle, Didyme, Phoenicusa, Ericusa, Hiera and Euonymus. One of them, probably Lipara, was the traditional home of Aeolus, ruler of the winds (*see* AEOLUS, 1). Beneath Strongyle (Gk Stroggule; mod. Stromboli, a constantly active volcano) was the legendary workshop of Hephaestus (q.v.).

Colonized from Cnidus and Rhodes between 580 and 577 B.C., the

islands were allied with Syracuse during the Peloponnesian war.
They served as a Carthaginian naval base in the first Punic war until
occupied by the Romans in 252 B.C.; and Sextus Pompeius (q.v.) used
them for the same purpose. Under the empire they were a place of
banishment.

Aeolis (Ai-), coastal district of Asia Minor, colonized at a very early
date by Aeolian Greeks. It extended from the River Hermus on the
south to the promontory of Lectum on the north. The twelve Aeolian
cities of the mainland were Cyme, Larissa, Neonteichos, Temnos,
Cilla, Notion, Aegiroessa, Pitane, Aegae, Myrina, Gryneia and
Smyrna (afterwards included in Ionia). There were other Aeolian
towns on the Troad coast, and several, including Mytilene, in the
island of Lesbos (*see* IONIANS).

Aeolus (Aiolos): 1. Ruler of the winds. According to Homer he was
son of Hippotes, and dwelt in a floating island named Aeolia (*see also*
AEOLIAE INSULAE). For his meeting with Odysseus see *Odyssey* x.
1 ff. He has been identified with Zeus, and his six sons and six
daughters with the twelve months of the year.

2. Legendary king of Thessaly and eponymous founder of the
Aeolic branch of the hellenic race. He was father of Athamas,
Cretheus, Salmoneus and Sisyphus.

Aequi, ancient Italian people, subdued by Rome in 302 B.C. Their
territory included the upper valleys of the Anio, Tolenus and Himella.

Aequi Falisci, *see* FALERII.

Aerarii (Lat. *aes*, poll tax), a class of Roman citizens who were
subject to a poll tax. Several different views have been put forward
as to who the Aerarii originally were. Under the later republic, however, they included: (1) inhabitants of conquered towns who, whatever their privileges, had no political rights; (2) Roman citizens subject to *infamia* (q.v.) in consequence of their occupation, or of their
conviction in the criminal courts; (3) Roman citizens branded by the
censor (q.v.) and thus deprived of the vote, qualification for office and
right to serve in the army. *See* J. E. Sandys, *Companion to Latin
Studies*, 1921; W. E. Heitland, *The Roman Republic*, 1923.

Aerarium: 1. Common treasury of republican Rome, containing
the state funds, public laws, decrees of the senate (*see* ACTA SENATUS),
and (in time of peace) the legionary standards. It was housed in the
temple of Saturn, in charge of the urban quaestors (*see* QUAESTOR) but
subject to the ultimate control of the senate. In 28 B.C. Octavian
(afterwards the emperor Augustus) substituted for the quaestors two
praefecti aerarii, who were supplanted five years later by two of the
praetors (*see* PRAETOR) chosen by lot and known as *praetores aerarii*.

2. *Aerarium Sanctum*, a special reserve fund for use in emergencies,
kept likewise in the temple of Saturn. It consisted at first of the spoils
of war, but was later maintained chiefly by a 5 per cent tax on the
value of manumitted slaves (*see* MANUMISSION).

Both the foregoing must be distinguished from the *Fiscus* (q.v.) or
imperial treasury established by Augustus, with which, however,
they were subsequently merged.

3. *Aerarium militare*, administered by three *praefecti*. It was
established by Augustus in A.D. 6 for the pensioning of discharged

soldiers. It was fed by a tax of 5 per cent on inheritances and of 1 per cent on auctions at Rome.

Aërope, wife of Atreus and mother of Agamemnon, *see* ATREIDS, LEGEND OF THE.

Aeschines (Aiskhinēs): 1. One of the ten Attic Orators (q.v.), the great antagonist of Demosthenes (*see* DEMOSTHENES, 2). He was born in 389 B.C., son of Atrometus, who had been impoverished owing to the Peloponnesian war and subsequently earned his living as a schoolmaster. In early life Aeschines is said to have helped his father run the school, and at some unknown period he worked as a tragic actor. He began his civilian career, *c.* 356, as a clerk first to the orator Aristophon of Collytus, and afterwards to Eubulus, an influential member of the democratic party. His contact with the latter, and a spell of military service under Phocion (q.v.), had already made him sympathetic towards their policy of conciliating Macedon when, in 346, he, together with Demosthenes and others, went on an embassy to Philip. Returning from a second mission to the same court, Aeschines was charged (probably on good grounds) by Timarchus of having accepted a bribe to promote Philip's ends. He saved himself by a counterattack on the morals of his accuser in the speech *Against Timarchus* (345 B.C.). Two years later Demosthenes resumed the charge, but Aeschines managed to secure his acquittal with his speech *On the Embassy*. In 339, by his celebrated appeal to the Delphians, he precipitated the Sacred War (q.v.), which resulted in Philip's victory at Chaeronea (338). In 337 Ctesiphon proposed that Demosthenes be rewarded with a golden crown for his services to the state. Aeschines thereupon accused Ctesiphon of unconstitutional procedure. The trial did not take place until 330, when, in reply to Aeschines's speech *Against Ctesiphon*, Demosthenes delivered his oration *On the Crown*. Aeschines, defeated, left Athens for Asia Minor, and later opened a school of declamation at Rhodes. He is said to have died in the island of Samos, in 314 B.C. There is an edition, with translation, of the three extant speeches (named above) by C. D. Adams and others, Loeb Library, 1919. *See also* J. F. Dobson, *The Greek Orators*, 1919.

2. Of Sphettos (5th–4th century B.C.), Greek philosopher and orator, disciple of Socrates. A bankrupt shopkeeper, he spent some time at the court of Dionysius II (q.v.). Three extant works are falsely attributed to him; but Cicero (*De inventione*, i. 31) quotes a genuine passage from one of his dialogues. The forensic speeches of Aeschines were celebrated for the purity of their style, but he appears to have earned the contempt of both Plato and Aristotle.

Aeschylus (Aiskhulos), 525–456 B.C., Greek tragic poet, born at Eleusis (q.v.). Son of Euphorion, a member of the Eupatridae (q.v.), he fought at Marathon (490), at Artemisium and Salamis (480), and at Plataea (479). His brother, Cynaegirus, is said to have died a hero's death in the first of these actions, and portraits of both were given places in a celebrated painting of the battle in the Stoa Poikile (q.v.). Aeschylus began his career as a dramatist in 499; he won the prize for tragedy first in 484 and at least twelve times thereafter. According to Suidas, Aeschylus wrote no fewer than ninety plays, of which only seven have survived, as follows: *Suppliants, c.* 490; *Persians* (which is said to have been performed again at Syracuse in the same year), 472; *Seven against Thebes*, 467; *Prometheus Bound*, *c.* 462; and the *Oresteia*, the only extant trilogy, which consisted of *Agamemnon*, *Choephorae* and *Eumenides*, 458. It is believed on the authority of Aristotle (*Nicomachaean Ethics*, iii. 2) that the poet was once accused, but acquitted by the Areopagus (q.v.), of having in one of his plays revealed the secrets of Demeter, i.e. of the Eleusinian Mysteries.

Aeschylus made two important contributions to the development of his art: (1) he introduced a second actor, restricted the choral parts and took the first steps in delineation of character; (2) by the profundity of his thought (influenced no doubt by his early associations with Eleusis) and the sublimity of his language he carried tragedy and tragic poetry far towards the realization of its full potentialities.

He visited the court of Hieron I (q.v.) at Syracuse *c.* 476 (*see* CATINA), and again *c.* 472, when the *Persians*, produced for the first time at Athens in that year, is said to have been repeated at Hieron's request. From a third visit to Sicily he did not return; dying at Gela (q.v.), he was buried there in a tomb which bore an epitaph attributed, with much probability, by Athenaeus and Pausanias to Aeschylus himself. Other stories that gathered round the poet's name are mere legend. *See* the edition of the extant plays by Gilbert Murray (Oxford Classical Texts), 1937; there is a complete verse translation by G. M. Cookson in Everyman's Library. *See also* Sir J. Sheppard, *Aeschylus and Sophocles*, 1927; G. G. A. Murray, *Aeschylus*, 1940; G. Thomson, *Aeschylus and Athens*, 1941; F. R. Earp, *The Style of Aeschylus*, 1948.

Aesculapius, Latin name of Asclepius (q.v.).

Aesernia (mod. Isernia), Samnite town, 58 miles north-east of Beneventum on the road to Corfinium. A Roman colony (*see* COLONIA) from 263 B.C., it became the headquarters of the Italian revolt after the loss of Corfinium during the Social war, and was recovered by Sulla in 80 B.C.

Aesis, an Italian town (mod. Iesi) on a river of the same name (mod. Esino), about 20 miles south-west of Ancona. From about 250 until about 82 B.C. the river formed the northern boundary of Italy proper; Augustus made it the boundary between his fifth and sixth regions (Picenum and Umbria; *see* ITALIA).

Aeson (Aisōn), father of Jason, *see* JASON AND MEDEA.

Aesopus (Aisōpos), Aesop, Greek fabulist, supposed to have lived *c.* 570 B.C. Originally the slave of one Iadmon of Samos, he was afterwards (*c.* 560) put to death for some unknown reason by the Delphians. Meanwhile, however, he must have been given his freedom; for Aristotle states (*Rhetoric*, ii. 20) that he once conducted the public defence of an Athenian demagogue. Other stories rest upon no cogent evidence, and involve some impossible chronology. The earliest surviving record of his traditional ugliness and deformity belongs to the 13th century A.D. Aesop never committed his fables to writing; but it is certain that prose fables bearing his name were popular at Athens, and Plato tells us that Socrates turned some of them into verse during his imprisonment. Those which have come down to us are derived mainly from Babrius and Phaedrus (qq.v.).

Aesopus, Clodius, Roman tragic actor, a friend of Cicero. He appeared in old age and for the last time at the dedication of Pompey's theatre (55 B.C.), when his voice failed and he was obliged to leave the stage.

Aestii, a Prussian or Esthonian people living in the coastlands at the mouth of the Vistula. For an account of their religion, language and customs, and of their trade in amber, *see* Tacitus, *Germania,* 45.

Aethalia (Ai-), Greek name for the island of Ilva (q.v.).

Aethalides (Aithalidēs), herald of the Argonauts (q.v.). His soul, like that of Panthoüs (q.v.), was said to have possessed the body of Pythagoras (q.v.).

Aethiopes (Ai-), name applied by the ancients (1) most generally to all black or dark races; (2) to all the inhabitants of inner Africa; and (3) most specifically to the inhabitants of the country immediately south of Egypt, which was called Aethiopia (q.v.), and to the nomad tribes dwelling south of Arabia on the Red Sea.

Aethiopia (Ai-), kingdom of north-east Africa, bounded on the north by Egypt and on the east by the Red Sea (*see* AETHIOPES). Under the Ptolemies (q.v.) Graeco-Egyptian colonies were established in Aethiopia, but the country was never subdued. In 24–23 B.C. Aethiopia was involved in war with Rome; it was invaded by C. Petronius, prefect of Egypt, who sacked Napata, the capital. Augustus, however, ordered an immediate evacuation; no tribute was imposed, but Roman troops were stationed at Hiera Sycaminus on the frontier. Christianity was introduced into Aethiopia at an early date, probably through the conversion of Queen Ameniremas's treasurer (Acts viii. 27) (*see* CANDACE).

Aethra (Ai-): 1. Daughter of Pittheus, King of Troezen, and mother of Theseus (q.v.). After the recovery of Helen by the Dioscuri (q.v.), Aethra was carried off by them to Sparta. There she became the slave of Helen, with whom she was taken to Troy. When that city was captured by the Greeks she was freed by one of her grandsons, Acamas or Demophon.

2. Daughter of Oceanus, by whom Atlas begot the Hyades, Pleiades and (according to some) Hesperides (qq.v.).

Aëtiōn or Eëtiōn (4th century B.C.), Greek painter, famous for his picture of the marriage of Alexander the Great and Roxana, which is described by Lucian (*Herodotus or Eetion,* 5).

Aetna (Ai-): 1. (mod. Etna). Volcano (10,758 feet) in the north-east of Sicily, between Tauromenium and Catina (qq.v.). There were several eruptions in antiquity. (*see also* GIGANTES). One occurred in 475 B.C., to which Aeschylus and Pindar probably allude; and another in 425 B.C., which Thucydides says was the third since the Greeks settled in Sicily. Roman remains have been found near the summit.

2. *See* CATINA.

Aetolia (Aitōlia), district of northern Greece (*see* AETOLUS), bounded north and east by the western spurs of Parnassus and Oeta, west by the River Acheloüs, south by the Corinthian Gulf. Among the principal towns were Thermon, Calydon and Pleuron. Aetolia appears first in classical history in 426 B.C., when it repelled an Athenian invasion. In 146 B.C. it was included in the Roman province of Achaea. For its intermediate history *see* AETOLIAN LEAGUE. *See also* W. J. Woodhouse, *Aetolia*, 1897.

Aetolian League, a league for mutual defence formed by the principal cities of Aetolia in the second half of the 4th century B.C. By 245 it controlled all central Greece, and soon afterwards extended its influence to Peloponnesus (*see* ACHAEAN LEAGUE) and the Aegean islands. Its territorial possessions, however, were gradually curtailed. After contributing to the Roman victory at Cynoscephalae (q.v.) in 197 B.C. the league wrought its final undoing by precipitating war between Rome and Antiochus III in 192. In 188 its authority was limited to Aetolia proper, after the inclusion of which in the Roman province of Achaea (146 B.C.) its functions became purely nominal. *See* M. Dubois, *Les Ligues achéenne et étolienne*, 1885.

Aetolus (Aitōlos), legendary king of Elis, was son of Endymion and husband of Promoë by whom he had two sons, Pleuron and Calydon. Having slain Apis, King of Argos, he fled to the country later called after him Aetolia, where his sons likewise gave their names to the cities of Pleuron and Calydon.

Aexone (Aixōnē), an Attic deme whose members had the reputation of scoffers and slanderers. Here was unearthed a cylindrical base bearing a choragic inscription which records the victories of plays by Ecphantides, Cratinus, Sophocles and an otherwise unknown tragedian named Timotheus. *See* J. U. Powell, *New Chapters in the History of Greek Literature*, 1933.

Afer, Domitius (1st century A.D.), Roman advocate, born at Nemausus (q.v.). Quintilian, once his pupil, calls Afer the greatest orator he had ever known, quotes some of his *bons mots* and mentions him as the author of two books *On Witnesses*. In the reign of Tiberius Afer turned informer and was responsible for the death of Claudia Pulchra, a cousin of Agrippina. He was consul in 39, superintendent of the water supply under Nero and died as a result of his intemperate habits in A.D. 60.

Afranius, Lucius : 1. (*fl. c.* 100 B.C.) Roman comic poet. Though he borrowed much from Menander and others, he was the first to abandon imitation of the Greeks by his representation of Roman middle-class life. About 400 lines of his work have survived. *See* O. Ribbeck, *Comicorum Romanorum Fragmenta*, 3rd ed., 1898; W. Beare, *The Roman Stage*, 1950.

2. Roman general; consul in 60 B.C. and governor of Cisalpine Gaul in the following year. When Pompey obtained the Spanish provinces (55 B.C.), Afranius and M. Petreius (q.v.) were sent to govern them as his legates. In 49 they were defeated by Caesar at Ilerda (q.v.). Their lives were spared on their promising to take no further part in the war. But Afranius joined Pompey at Dyrrachium, and at Pharsalus (48) had charge of his leader's camp. He fled to Africa, and was subsequently (46) present at Thapsus (q.v.). Attempting to escape into Mauretania he was captured by P. Sillius and delivered to Caesar, whose exasperated troops put him to death.

Africa : 1. General name given by Roman writers from the time of Ennius (q.v.) to all that was known of the present African continent, excepting Egypt and Aethiopia (qq.v.). The same region was called

Libya by the Greeks. The Phoenicians had established numerous colonies on the north coast of Africa long before the Greeks made their first settlement (c. 630 B.C.) at Cyrene (q.v.). At no time was the interior well known to the ancients; but Greek and Roman civilization exerted considerable influence between the Mediterranean and the desert. See AETHIOPIA; CARTHAGE; CYRENAICA; EGYPT; LIBYA; MAURETANIA; NUMIDIA. See Ptolemy, *Geographia* (ed. C. Müller), vol. i, 1883.

2. That part of north Africa which the Romans formed into a province after the third Punic war (*see* PUNIC WARS), and the boundaries of which varied during the period 146 B.C.–A.D. 25. *See* A. Graham, *Roman Africa*, 1902.

Africanus, *see* SCIPIO.

Agamēdēs, ruler of Orchomenus in Boeotia. He and his stepbrother Trophonius, who were skilled architects, built a treasury for another Boeotian king, Hyrieus, and contrived to lay one of the stones in such a way that it could be removed and replaced without detection. They then began systematic robbery of the treasure, until Hyrieus set snares to catch the thief. Agamedes was trapped; Trophonius at once decapitated his brother to conceal his identity, and made off with the head. He was swallowed up by the earth in the grove of Lebadeia, where he was afterwards worshipped and had a famous oracle in a nearby cave. A similar and most entertaining story is told by Herodotus (ii. 121) about the treasury of Rhampsinitus. Another tradition, mentioned by Cicero, states that Agamedes and Trophonius, having built the temple of Apollo at Delphi, asked him to reward them with what was best for men. The god promised to do so within seven days, at the end of which time they died.

Agamemnōn, *see* ATREIDS, LEGEND OF THE.

Aganippē, spring at the foot of Mt Helicon (q.v.). Sacred to the Muses, it was a reputed source of poetic inspiration.

Agasias, name of two Greek sculptors of the Ephesian school, who *fl. c.* 100 B.C.: 1. Son of Dositheus; he made the 'Borghese Warrior' now in the Louvre.

2. Son of Menophilus, whose figure of a warrior is in the museum at Athens. *See* E. A. Gardner, *Handbook of Greek Sculpture*, vol. ii, p. 475.

Agatharchides (-khidēs), 2nd century B.C., Greek historian and geographer, born at Cnidus. Extracts from his work *On the Red Sea* are preserved in Photius.

Agatharchus (-khos), 5th century B.C., Athenian painter, born at Samos. According to Vitruvius (q.v.) he was the first to paint stage scenery. He wrote a treatise on the subject, which is said to have inspired the investigations of Anaxagoras and Democritus (qq.v.) into the laws of perspective.

Agathocles (-klēs), 361–289 B.C., tyrant of Syracuse, born at Thermae Himeraeae (*see* HIMERA). Son of a potter, he served in the Syracusan army; married (333) the widow of his patron, Damas; and was later banished for endeavouring to overthrow the oligarchy. In 317 he returned at the head of an army, and was acknowledged as ruler of Syracuse. He was soon involved in hostilities with Carthage, which controlled the western half of the island. Besieged in his capital (310), he broke through the blockade and carried the war into Africa. After some initial successes he was decisively beaten (296) and escaped to Sicily. Having made peace with Carthage, he assumed the title of king and established his authority more firmly than ever over all the Greek cities of the island. Agathocles was an able and enlightened despot, but his last years were embittered by domestic feuds. There is no reliable evidence for the story that he died by poison.

Agathodaimōn (? 2nd century A.D.), Alexandrian map designer. Some manuscripts of Ptolemy's *Geographia* contain 27 maps said to have been made by him.

Agathōn (*c.* 448–400 B.C.), Athenian tragic poet. He won his first victory at the Lenaea in 416, an event commemorated in Plato's *Symposium.* He was the first to invent an original plot; but his effeminacy, reflected perhaps in the artificiality of his style, incurred the ridicule of Aristophanes. A few fragments survive.

Agathyrsi (-thursoi), a Thracian people originally inhabiting modern Transylvania, but subsequently driven farther north. Herodotus (iv. 104) speaks of their riches and their community of wives; Virgil (*Aen.* iv. 136) mentions their practice of tattooing the body; and the name Thyrsagetae given them by M. Verrius Flaccus (q.v.) suggests that they celebrated orgiastic rites.

Agave (Agauē), daughter of Cadmus and wife of Pentheus (qq.v.).

Agdistis, *see* ATTIS; RHEA.

Agedincum, Gallic town, capital of the Senones (q.v.), on the site of modern Sens, which preserves their name.

Ageladas or **Hagelaidas** (6th–5th century B.C.), Argive sculptor who was believed, upon no cogent evidence, to have taught Myron, Pheidias and Polycleitus (qq.v.).

Agēnōr, son of Poseidon, King of Tyre and father of Cadmus (q.v.). Virgil calls Carthage the city of Agenor because Dido (q.v.) was one of his descendants.

Ager Falernus, flat ground to the east and south-east of Mons Massicus (q.v.), in Campania (q.v.), where the celebrated Falernian wine was produced. *See* WINE.

Ager Gallicus, district of Italy stretching along the Adriatic coast between the rivers Aesis and Ariminus. It was so called from a branch of the Senones (q.v.), who settled there in 400 B.C. It included the towns of Caesena, Ravenna and Ariminum. In the organization of Italy by Augustus (*see* ITALIA) it formed part of the sixth *regio* with Umbria.

Ager Publicus, *see* AGRARIAN LAWS.

Agesander (Agēsandros), late 1st century B.C., Rhodian sculptor; joint author, with Polydorus and Athenodorus, of the Laocoön group (*see* LAOCOÖN).

Agesilaus (Agēsilāos) II, Eurypontid king of Sparta, son of Archidamus II (q.v.) and half-brother of Agis I (q.v.) whom he succeeded *c.* 401 B.C. From 396 until 394 he was in Asia Minor at the head of a successful expedition sent out to protect the Greek cities against Persia. In the latter year he was recalled to Greece on the outbreak of war between Sparta and a confederation of states, including Athens and Thebes. His pyrrhic victory at Coronea (394) obliged him to withdraw to Peloponnesus. In 378 hostilities were renewed with Thebes, culminating in the defeat of Cleombrotus (q.v.) at Leuctra (371) and the overthrow of Spartan supremacy in Greece. Agesilaus, however, twice again saved his city from total ruin when Epaminondas (q.v.) invaded Laconia. In 361 he led a force of mercenaries to Egypt in support of Tachos against the Persians, and died aged about eighty-four on his way home. Though small of stature and lame from birth, Agesilaus proved himself one of the best citizens and generals ever produced by Sparta. *See* lives by Xenophon, Cornelius Nepos and Plutarch.

Agis, name of three Eurypontid kings of Sparta: *Agis I*, son of Archidamus II and half-brother of Agesilaus II (q.v.), succeeded his father *c.* 427 B.C. From 425 until the end of the Peloponnesian war he was principal leader of the Spartan land forces. During the Peace of Nicias (421–416) he won several military successes against Argos. After the surrender of Athens (404) he invaded Elis, and, having dedicated spoils at Delphi, returned to Sparta where he died *c.* 401 B.C.

Agis II, son of Archidamus III (q.v.), whom he succeeded in 338 B.C. While Alexander was in Asia (333), Agis, with Persian support, led a revolt against Macedon, but was defeated and slain at Megalopolis (331).

Agis III, son of Eudamidas II, whom he succeeded *c.* 245 B.C. His attempts at reform won him powerful enemies who had him put to death, together with his mother and grandmother in 241 B.C.

Agora, originally an assembly of the people in a Greek city-state; hence the place where such meetings were held, and in classical times any open space for the transaction of official or commercial business (cf. the Roman *forum*). The most famous was the Athenian agora (*see* ATHENS); but others of even greater architectural interest existed, e.g. at Assos, Ephesus and Priene. *See* W. B. Dinsmoor (ed.), *Architecture of Ancient Greece*, 1927.

Agoracritus (-kritos), 5th century B.C., Athenian sculptor. Part of the head of his 'Nemesis' from Rhamnos is now in the British Museum.

Agoranomoi, Greek magistrates responsible for the proper conduct of markets and (in maritime cities) for the observance of shipping regulations and collection of harbour dues. At Athens they numbered ten—five for the upper city and five for the Peiraeus.

Agrarian Laws, bills submitted from time to time at Rome, with a view to giving the poorer classes a larger share in the distribution of the *ager publicus*, i.e. territory taken from a conquered enemy, which the patricians almost completely monopolized. Their passage and enforcement invariably gave rise to serious disorder.

The first of these laws is said to have been brought forward by Spurius Cassius; it passed, but a coalition of patricians and rich plebeians prevented it from being given effect. Cassius, accused of aspiring to be king, was condemned to death (485 B.C.). In 376 B.C. C. Licinius Calvus (*see* LICINIUS, 1) brought forward a new agrarian law, which provided that no one should hold more than 500 acres of

the *ager publicus*. Finally, in 133 B.C., Tiberius Gracchus (*see* GRAC-
CHUS, TIBERIUS SEMPRONIUS, 3), faced with the continual extension
of the great landed estates (*latifundia*), brought forward a law
intended to extend and enforce the provisions of the Licinian Rogations. He, his brother Gaius (*see* GRACCHUS, C.) and father-in-law,
Appius Claudius, were charged with its execution; but Tiberius was
assassinated (133 B.C.) in the Forum as the result of a reactionary
movement directed by Scipio Nasica. Twelve years later the same fate
overtook Gaius, who had attempted to revive his brother's projects.
Caesar, during his consulate (59 B.C.), was more successful and
managed to distribute large areas of the *ager publicus* in Campania
among plebeian fathers of three children.

Agri Decumates, part of Germany between the rivers Rhine, Main
and Danube. Originally occupied by Gallic adventurers (Tacitus,
Germania, 29), it was included in the Roman Empire from the late
1st century B.C. The word 'decumates' has nothing to do with tithes;
it is pre-Roman, and the name probably means land of ten cantons.

Agricola, Gnaeus Julius, born at Forum Julii on 13th June A.D. 40,
son of Julius Graecinus by Julia Procilla. He served first with the
army in Britain under Suetonius Paulinus (61); was quaestor in
Asia (64), governor of Aquitania (74–6), and consul (77). In 78 he
gave his daughter in marriage to the historian Tacitus (q.v.) and was
appointed governor of Britain (q.v.), an office which he held for seven
years, subduing the whole country except the highlands of Caledonia.
Jealousy caused Domitian to recall him in 85, after which he lived in
retirement until 93, when he died, some said by poison. *See* Tacitus,
Agricola.

Agrigentum (Gk Akragas), city on a hill near the south coast of
Sicily, one of the most splendid in the ancient world, and birth-place
of Empedocles. Founded from Gela in 582 B.C., it enjoyed its greatest
period of prosperity under Theron (q.v.). It was destroyed by the
Carthaginians in 405 B.C., and though rebuilt by Timoleon in 338,
it never regained its former prosperity. Agrigentum was thrice sacked,
alternately by the Romans and the Carthaginians, during the Punic
wars. *See* Phalaris.

Chief among ten temples on the southern slope, which date from
between *c.* 510 and 210 B.C., and of which some splendid ruins may be
seen, were those dedicated respectively to Zeus, Heracles and
Asclepius, together with two wrongly called 'of Hera' and 'of Concordia'. There are also remains of the ancient walls and of a gigantic
fishpond. *See* P. Marconi, *Agrigento*, 1929.

Agrippa, Herodes: 1. Commonly called Herod Agrippa I, born *c.*
10 B.C.; son of Aristobulus and Berenice, and grandson of Herod the
Great. Sent by the latter to Rome after the murder of his father, he
became intimate with Tiberius's son Drusus, upon whose death
(A.D. 23) he had to leave Rome, being heavily in debt. But he soon
returned and enjoyed the friendship of Gaius, the future emperor
Caligula. Imprisoned for a time by Tiberius, because of treasonable
words spoken in the hearing of a freedman, he was released on the
accession of Caligula (A.D. 37) and loaded with honours. He was given
the tetrarchies of Abilene, Batanaea, Trachonitis and Auranitis, to

which Claudius added the kingdom of Judaea. His government was popular among the Jews, especially because he opposed Caligula's desecration of the temple; and it was probably in order to increase this popularity that he had the apostle St James put to death and St Peter imprisoned (A.D. 44). The manner of his death, which took place at Caesarea in the same year, is related in Acts xii.

2. Commonly called Herod Agrippa II, son of the preceding, born c. A.D. 27. He received the kingdom of Chalcis after the death of his uncle Herod Antipas in A.D. 48, but was obliged to exchange it for other territories in 52. On the outbreak of the Jewish war he sided with the Romans, and after the capture of Jerusalem he went with his sister Berenice to Rome, where they lived together, not without suspicion of incest, until his death in A.D. 100. It was before Agrippa and Berenice that St Paul made his defence at Caesarea (Acts xxv–xxvi).

Agrippa, Marcus Vipsanius, Roman general and statesman, born of an obscure family c. 63 B.C. At the time of Caesar's murder he and Octavian were studying together at Apollonia in Illyricum, and it was Agrippa who advised the future emperor to hurry back to Rome. In 40 he played a leading part in the war against Lucius Antonius (q.v.), and he accepted the consulship in 37 as a mark of esteem for his successes in the previous year against the Aquitanians and some trans-Rhenane tribes. In 36 he planned and won the important naval victories of Mylae and Naulochus against Sextus Pompeius. As aedile in 33 he did much to improve and adorn the city of Rome. Consul for the second time, in 31, Agrippa was mainly responsible for the crowning glory of Actium. During his third consulship (27) he built the temple now represented by the Pantheon (q.v.) at Rome. Thereafter he was employed in various commands until his death, which took place in Campania in 12 B.C.

The many-sided genius of this extraordinary man is further illustrated by his supervision of the work, first conceived by Julius Caesar, of surveying the whole empire. On the basis of this survey and a geographical work (now lost) written by Agrippa himself, a map of the empire was subsequently engraved on marble and exhibited in the Porticus Vipsanius at Rome.

Agrippa married first Pomponia, daughter of Cicero's friend Atticus. She had either died or been divorced in 28 B.C., when Octavian honoured him with the hand of his niece Marcella. In 21, however, Augustus considered Agrippa as the man most fitted to succeed him, and accordingly made him divorce Marcella and marry her sister-in-law, the emperor's own daughter Julia. For his children and their marriages see Table I and separate articles.

Agrippina: 1. 'The Elder', daughter of M. Vipsanius Agrippa (q.v.) and of Julia, daughter of Augustus; married Germanicus (q.v.), by whom she had nine children, among them the emperor Caligula and Agrippina, the mother of Nero. She was distinguished for her virtues and heroism, and shared all the dangers of her husband's campaigns. On his death in A.D. 19 she returned to Italy; but the favour with which she was received by the people increased the hatred which Tiberius and his mother Livia had long entertained towards her. At length in A.D. 30 Tiberius banished her to the island of Pandataria, where she died three years afterwards, probably by voluntary starvation.

2. 'The Younger', daughter of Germanicus by the preceding, and mother of the emperor Nero, was born at Oppidum Ubiorum, afterwards called in honour of her Colonia Agrippina, now Cologne. She was beautiful and intelligent, but licentious, cruel and ambitious. She was first married to Cn. Domitius Ahenobarbus (A.D. 28), by whom she had a son, afterwards the emperor Nero; next to Crispus Passienus; and thirdly to the emperor Claudius (49), although she was his niece. In 50 she prevailed upon Claudius to adopt her son, to the prejudice of his own son Britannicus; and in order to secure the succession for Nero, she poisoned the emperor in 54. The young emperor soon became tired of the ascendancy of his mother, and after making several attempts to shake off her authority, he caused her to be assassinated in A.D. 59. *See* Tacitus, *Annals*, xii–xiv.

Agroteras Thusia, annual festival at Agrae in Attica, in honour of Artemis Agrotera. It was celebrated in fulfilment of a vow made by the inhabitants before the battle of Marathon, to sacrifice as many goats as there might be Persians left dead upon the field. The number, however, was so great that it was decided to offer 500 goats each year.

Aguieus, a title of Apollo as protector of streets, doors and public places.

Agyrium (Agurion), town of the Siculi (q.v.) in Sicily, 15 miles north-east of Henna. It was subject to native rulers until 399 B.C., when it was colonized by Greeks, and was the birth-place of the historian Diodorus Siculus (q.v.).

Ahala, Gaius Servilius, master of the horse (*magister equitum*) to Cincinnatus in 439 B.C. For his killing of Maelius (q.v.) he was brought to trial and escaped condemnation only by voluntary exile.

Ahenobarbus, 'brazen-beard', name of a Roman family belonging to the gens Domitia. According to legend they inherited this name from an ancestor to whom the Dioscuri (q.v.) announced the victory of Lake Regillus in 496, and, to confirm the truth of what they said, stroked his black beard which immediately became red.

1. Gnaeus Domitius Ahenobarbus was consul in 122 B.C., when he defeated the Allobroges (q.v.).

2. Gnaeus Domitius Ahenobarbus, tribune of the plebs in 104 B.C., brought forward the *Lex Domitia* which transferred the election of priests from the collegia to the people. He was afterwards pontifex maximus.

3. Lucius Domitius Ahenobarbus, consul in 54 B.C., married Porcia, sister of M. Porcius Cato. Soon after the outbreak of civil war (49 B.C.) his blundering greatly facilitated Caesar's bloodless conquest of Italy, and he was obliged by his own troops to surrender Corfinium. Though freed by Caesar, he then went to Massilia, after the fall of which he joined Pompey in Greece, and commanded the Pompeian left at Pharsalus (48), where he was killed, struck down, according to Cicero, by the hand of Mark Antony.

4. Gnaeus Domitius Ahenobarbus, son of the preceding, with whom he was taken prisoner, and freed, at Corfinium. He was present

at Pharsalus, but returned to Italy in 46 B.C., when he was pardoned by Caesar. He accompanied Antony on the Parthian campaign in 36, was consul in 32 and deserted to Octavian shortly before Actium.

5. Gnaeus Domitius Ahenobarbus married Agrippina the Younger (q.v.), daughter of Germanicus, and was father of the emperor Nero. *See also* ANTONIA, 1.

Aius Locutius, personification of the voice said to have been heard at Rome announcing the approach of the Gauls (390 B.C.). *See* Livy, v. 32.

Ajax (Gk Aias): 1. Son of Telamon, King of Salamis, and grandson of Aeacus. He sailed against Troy with twelve ships, and is represented in the *Iliad* as second only to Achilles in bravery. In the contest for the armour of Achilles he was conquered by Odysseus, and this, says Homer, was the cause of his death. Later poets (e.g. Sophocles) relate that his defeat threw him into a state of madness; that he slaughtered the sheep of the Greek army, fancying they were his enemies; and that at length he put an end to his own life. In Homer Ajax is spoken of as exceptionally tall and strong, but there is no evidence to prove the statement that he was originally regarded as a supernatural being.

2. Son of Oïleus, King of the Opuntian Locrians, called the lesser Ajax, sailed against Troy with forty ships. It is probable that he was an historical figure. He is described as small of stature, but skilled in throwing the spear, and, next to Achilles, the most swift-footed among the Greeks. On his return from Troy his vessel was wrecked; he himself got safe upon a rock through the assistance of Poseidon; but as he boasted that he would escape in defiance of the immortals, Poseidon split the rock, and Ajax was drowned. This is the account of Homer. Virgil tells us that the anger of Athena was excited against him, because, on the night of the capture of Troy, he violated Cassandra in the temple of the goddess.

Ala (Lat. *wing*), term applied until 90 B.C. to the contingent of allies on each flank of a Roman legion (q.v.). Thereafter it denoted a unit of cavalry, which numbered under Augustus 1,000 or 500 men, divided into *turmae* or squadrons.

Alalia or **Aleria**, town on the east coast of Corsica (q.v.). It was founded by the Phocaeans *c.* 560 B.C. Abandoned *c.* 535 B.C., it was centuries later the site of a Roman colony (*see* COLONIA) established by Sulla.

Alamanni or **Alemanni**, a confederacy of German tribes, first mentioned by Dio Cassius, and inhabiting an area between the rivers Rhine, Main and Danube. Caracalla assumed the title Alemannicus in honour of a pretended victory over them in A.D. 214, and from this time onwards they continually invaded Roman territory.

Alba Fucens, Italian town, a little north of the Fucine Lake (*see* FUCINUS, LACUS). Originally belonging to the Aequi, it became a Latin *colonia* (q.v.) in 303 B.C. Under the republic it was a place of detention for state prisoners, but its importance had ceased by imperial times. The extensive remains of its fortifications, which date from about 300 B.C., are of great architectural interest. See *Papers of the British School at Rome*, No. x, 1927.

Alba Longa (mod. Castel Gandolfo), traditionally the oldest city of Latium, situated on the western edge of the Alban Lake (*see* ALBANUS, LACUS), and supposed to have been founded by Ascanius, son of Aeneas. It was called 'Longa' because it stretched along a narrow ridge; 'Alba' probably means 'height', and not 'white'. Said to have been destroyed by Tullus Hostilius, it was never rebuilt; but in the immediate vicinity there are remains of an imperial villa (1st century A.D.) and of a camp, with baths, reservoir and amphitheatre, constructed by Septimius Severus. An ancient necropolis contains tombs of the 12th, 7th and 6th centuries B.C.

Alba Pompeia (mod. Albi), town of Liguria; birth-place of the emperor Pertinax. It was probably founded by the consul Pompeius Strabo in 89 B.C.

Albania, district of the eastern Caucasus. According to Strabo the inhabitants (Albani) were nomads; they worshipped the sun and moon, and honoured old age, but there was a taboo against speaking or even thinking of the dead. The Romans first became acquainted with them during the third Mithradatic war, when they are said to have opposed Pompey with an army of 80,000 men.

Albanus, Lacus (Alban Lake). It lies 12 miles south-east of Rome, in an extinct crater which is itself adjacent to that of Albanus Mons (q.v.). The lake derives its waters from subterranean springs; it is 560 feet deep, with banks towering 400 feet above water level. The *emissarium* which the Romans bored through the rock, to draw off the water during the siege of Veii (398–397 B.C.), is still in use; it is one mile long, 6 feet high and 4 feet wide.

Albanus Mons (mod. Monte Cavo), highest peak (3,115 feet) of the Alban Hills and an extinct volcano. On it stood the temple of Jupiter Latiaris, at which the annual festival of the Latin League (q.v.) was held. The ancient road from Aricia is still in good repair.

Albinovanus Pedo, Roman poet of the early 1st century A.D., author of epigrams and a *Theseid* (both now lost); also a poem on the exploits of Germanicus, of which a fragment is preserved in Seneca's *Suasoriae*, I. 15. Ovid addressed to him the *Epistles from Pontus* (iv. 10).

Albinus, Decimus Clodius, born at Hadrumetum; governor of Gaul and then of Britain under Commodus. Septimius Severus created him Caesar in 193, but declared war on him in 197. Albinus was defeated and killed near Lugdunum.

Albion (Gk Alouion), the most ancient name for England (*see* BRITAIN). It is first used in an anonymous *Periplus* of the 6th century B.C., and also in that of Pytheas of Massilia some two hundred years later. Though Celtic in origin, it was supposed by the Romans to be derived from *albus* (white), with reference to the chalk cliffs at Dover.

Albis (mod. Elbe). Augustus intended to make this river the north-east boundary of his empire, but abandoned the design after the disaster of the Saltus Teutoburgiensis (*see* VARUS).

Alcaeus (Alkaios), earliest of the Aeolian lyric poets, was born at Mytilene (Lesbos) in the last quarter of the 7th century B.C. During the war between Mytilene and Athens for the possession of Sigeum (606) he disgraced himself by turning tail and leaving his shield on the battlefield. Alcaeus and his brother Antemenidas, as members of the aristocracy, were driven into exile by the popular party. With other refugees they attempted to return by force of arms, but were prevented by Pittacus (q.v.).

The number of surviving fragments by Alcaeus has been increased by the discovery of papyri at Oxyrhynchus and Hermopolis (qq.v.) in Egypt. These recent finds express the keen ambition of the poet's political life rather than its convivial side, which is more marked in the remainder of his extant lines and in the imitations of Horace. *See* Lobel's complete edition of Alcaeus (1927). *See also* J. U. Powell, *New Chapters in the History of Greek Literature*, 1933.

Alcamenes (Alkamenēs), an Athenian sculptor who flourished 444–440 B.C. and may have been a pupil of Pheidias. An original group by him, 'Procne and Itys', has been discovered and is now at Athens. Its style has some affinity with that of the caryatids of the Erechtheum (q.v.), and it is thought that Alcamenes may have had a hand in the sculptures of that temple.

Alcathoüs (Alkathoos), son of Pelops by Hippodameia (qq.v.), and brother of Atreus, Thyestes and Chrysippus (*see* ATREIDS). By slaying the Cithaeronian lion, he won the hand of Euaechine, daughter of Megareus, whom he succeeded as King of Megara. He was said to have rebuilt the walls of that city with the aid of Apollo; and even in late times the stone upon which Apollo was supposed to have placed his lyre when at work was said to give forth, when struck, a sound similar to that of a lyre. Alcathoüs was the father of Periboea, second wife of Telamon (q.v.), and of Automedusa, wife of Iphicles (q.v.).

Alcestis (Alkēstis), *see* ADMETUS.

Alcibiades (-kibiadēs), son of Clinias and Dinomache, was born at Athens *c.* 450 B.C., and after the death of his father in 447 was brought up by his relation Pericles. He was handsome, able and wealthy; but his life was disgraced by debaucheries, and Socrates, who saw his capabilities, attempted to win him to virtue, but in vain. Their intimacy was strengthened by mutual services. At the battle of Potidaea (432) his life was saved by Socrates, and at that of Delium (424) he saved the life of Socrates. After the death of Cleon (422) he became the head of the war party in opposition to Nicias. In 415 he was appointed, along with Nicias and Lamachus, as commander of the expedition to Sicily. There then occurred the mysterious mutilation of the Hermae (q.v.), which the popular fears connected with an attempt to overthrow the Athenian constitution. Alcibiades was charged with being the ringleader in this attempt. He demanded an investigation before he set sail. This his enemies would not grant; but he had not been long in Sicily before he was recalled to stand his trial. On his return homewards he escaped at Thurii, and proceeded to Sparta, where he acted as the enemy of his country. The machinations of Agis I, however, induced him to abandon the Spartans and take refuge with Tissaphernes (412), whose favour he soon gained. Through his influence Tissaphernes deserted the Spartans and assisted the Athenians, who accordingly recalled Alciabades from banishment in 411. He remained abroad, however, for the next four years, during which the Athenians under his command gained the victories of Cynossema, Abydos and Cyzicus, and got possession of Chalcedon

and Byzantium. In 407 he returned to Athens, where he was received
with enthusiasm, and was appointed commander-in-chief by land and
sea. But the defeat of Notium, occasioned during his absence by the
imprudence of his lieutenant, Antiochus, encouraged his enemies, and
he was superseded in his command (406). He now went into voluntary
exile to his fortified domain at Bisanthe in the Thracian Chersonesus.
After the fall of Athens (404) he took refuge with Pharnabazus (q.v.)
in Phrygia. He was about to proceed to the court of Artaxerxes, when
one night his house was surrounded by armed men and set on fire. He
rushed out, sword in hand, but fell pierced with arrows (404 B.C.).

Alcidamas (Alki-), Greek sophist and rhetorician of the 4th century
B.C. A native of Elaea in Aeolis, he became a pupil of Gorgias and
afterwards taught at Athens. His only complete work to survive is a
treatise *On the Sophists* (ed. Blass, 1881).

Alcinoüs (Alkinoos), in Greek legend, King of the Phaeacians in the
island of Scheria. For his reception and entertainment of Odysseus see
Odyssey, vi, xii. Scheria is usually identified with Corcyra.

Alciphron (-kiphrōn), the most distinguished of the Greek epistolary
writers, was perhaps a contemporary of Lucian, *c.* A.D. 180. The
letters (118 in number) purport to have been written at Athens by
country folk, fishermen, prostitutes, etc. They are distinguished by
the purity and elegance of their style. *See* the text and translation in
Alciphron, Aelian and Philostratus (Loeb Library) by A. R. Benner
and F. H. Fobes; also translation by F. A. Wright, 1958.

Alcmaeon (Alkmaiōn): 1. Son of Amphiaraüs (q.v.) and brother of
Amphilochus (q.v.). After taking part in the War of the Epigoni (*see*
THEBAN LEGEND, 5), the two brothers slew Eriphyle, as commanded
by Amphiaraüs. For this crime Alcmaeon was pursued by the Erinyes
(q.v.). He fled to Psophis, where he was purified by King Phegeus and
married his daughter, Alphesiboea. To her he gave the *peplos* and
necklace of Harmonia, which had belonged to his mother by gift of
Polynices, to whom it had descended through the family of Cadmus
(q.v.). However, the land of Psophis ceased to bear fruit because of
the presence of a matricide; so Alcmaeon moved on to the country at
the mouth of the Acheloüs (q.v.), where the river-god of that name
gave him his daughter Callirrhoë in marriage. Callirrhoë being anxious
to possess the necklace and *peplos*, Alcmaeon returned to Psophis and
obtained them from Phegeus on the pretext of dedicating them at
Delphi; but when Phegeus learned that they were really wanted for
Callirrhoë he caused his sons to murder Alcmaeon. Alcmaeon's own
sons by Callirrhoë were Acarnan (q.v.) and Amphoterus.

2. Of Croton, physician, scientist and pupil of Pythagoras (q.v.).
He made a particular study of the eye, and is said to have been the
first to operate upon that organ.

Alcmaeonidae (Alkmaionidai), a powerful Athenian family claiming
descent from Alcmaeon, son of Nestor. In consequence of the treatment of Cylon (q.v.) and his fellow conspirators by the archon
Megacles, one of the family, in 632 B.C., the Alcmaeonidae incurred the
guilt of sacrilege and were expelled from Athens *c.* 596. They returned
c. 560. In 548 they contracted with the Amphictyonic Council to
rebuild the temple at Delphi and won great popularity throughout

Greece by executing the work with a degree of magnificence far in excess of their undertaking. Other distinguished members of the Alcmaeonidae were a second Megacles, his son Cleisthenes, Alcibiades and (through his mother) Pericles (qq.v.).

Alcman (Alk-), chief lyric poet of Sparta, a native of Messoa, *fl. c.* 630 B.C. The traditional story that he was a native of Sardis in Lydia and was brought to Sparta as a slave where he was emancipated by his master, who discovered his genius, has probably no foundation. The longest fragment of his poetry which survives is a *parthenion* or choir-song for maidens. The language of Alcman has elements of both Doric and Aeolic dialect. He is said, upon no reliable evidence, to have been the inventor of erotic poetry.

Alcmēnē (Alk-). Electryon, King of Mycenae, son of Perseus (q.v.) and Andromeda, had a daughter Alcmene who was married to her cousin Amphitryon (q.v.). Her husband having accidentally killed her father, Alcmene refused him intercourse until he should have avenged the death of her brothers who had been murdered by the sons of Pterelaus. Amphitryon agreed, and started out; but during his absence Alcmene was visited by Zeus disguised as her husband, who told her he had fulfilled his undertaking and described it in detail. Next day Amphitryon himself arrived, and in due time (at an interval of one day) Alcmene bore two sons: Heracles (q.v.) to Zeus, Iphicles (q.v.) to Amphitryon. She was the object of a religious cult at Thebes in Boeotia.

Alcyone (Alkuonē) or **Halcyone,** daughter of Aeolus (*see* AEOLUS, 1) and wife of Ceyx, King of Trachis. Her husband perished in a shipwreck, and Alcyone, grief-stricken, drowned herself in the sea. The gods, however, changed them both into kingfishers. These were imagined to build their nests upon the waters, which were always calm at their breeding time. Hence the phrase 'halcyon days' to denote the week before and after the winter solstice.

Alecto (Alektō), *see* ERINYES.

Aleria, *see* ALALIA.

Alesia (mod. Mont-Auxois), hill fortress of the Mandubii (q.v.). Remains of a Gallic and a Gallo-Roman site have been excavated. Here, in 52 B.C., Julius Caesar besieged and finally defeated Vercingetorix (q.v.). The Roman siege works, which included lines of contravallation (10 miles) and circumvallation, can still be traced. See *De Bello Gallico,* vii. 68–89.

Aletrium, town of the Hernici (q.v.). In the late 1st century B.C. and throughout imperial times it was a *municipium* (q.v.). There are some impressive remains of the fortifications, the outer circumference of which measured about two and a half miles.

Aleuadae (-ai), a family originating at Larissa in Thessaly, claiming to be descended from Aleuas, a reputed descendant of Heracles. They sided with the Persians in 480 B.C., but continued long afterwards predominant in Thessaly, where they supplied the 'tagos', or commander-in-chief, of the Thessalian levies until 369 B.C.

Aleus, King of Tegea in Arcadia, father of Auge (q.v.).

Alexander (Gk Alexandros). (A) *Kings of Epirus:* 1. Brother of Olympias, the mother of Alexander the Great; he was also son-in-law of Philip II of Macedon, whose daughter Cleopatra he married in 336 and who had made him King of Epirus *c.* 342 B.C. In 332 he crossed over to Italy to aid the Tarentines against the Samnites, Lucanians and Bruttii. After some initial successes, the Tarentines themselves became suspicious of his motives; his supporters dwindled, and he was ultimately defeated and killed near Pandosia *c.* 330 B.C.

2. Son of Pyrrhus, whom he succeeded in 272 B.C. Driven from his kingdom by Demetrius II, son of Antigonus Gonatas, he was later restored.

(B) *Kings of Macedonia:* 1. Son of Amyntas I, whom he succeeded *c.* 505 B.C., was obliged to submit to the Persians, and accompanied Xerxes in his invasion of Greece (480). He died in 450, when he was succeeded by Perdiccas II.

2. Son and successor of Amyntas II, reigned from 369 to 368 B.C.

3. Surnamed the Great, son of Philip II and Olympias, born in 356 B.C. at the Macedonian capital Pella (q.v.), where, from 342 until his accession in 336, Aristotle (q.v.) was his tutor.

Alexander first distinguished himself at the battle of Chaeronea (q.v.) in 338, which established Macedonian supremacy in Greece. On his accession, after the murder of Philip, he found himself surrounded by enemies. Having put down rebellion in his own kingdom, he marched into Greece, where his activity soon quietened opposition. Thebes (q.v.) opened its gates, and Alexander was chosen to lead the projected expedition against Persia. First, however, he thought it necessary to turn his arms against the northern barbarians, and crossed the Danube (335). A report reached Greece that he had been killed; whereupon the Thebans flew to arms. Alexander returned, descended upon the city, slew or enslaved most of the inhabitants and razed it to the ground, sparing only the temples and the house of Pindar.

It was now time to prepare for Asia. He made his preparations accordingly, and in the early spring of 334 B.C. crossed the Hellespont with about 40,000 men. He won his first victory over the Persians under Darius III, Codomannus, on the River Granicus in Mysia (May 334). In the following year he collected his army at Gordium in Phrygia, when he cut the famous knot (*see* GORDIUS). From there he marched to Issus, on the confines of Syria, and won his second great victory over Darius (333). The vanquished monarch escaped, but his mother, wife and children fell into Alexander's hands (*see* SISYGAMBIS; STATEIRA; BARSINE, 2).

The conqueror now turned to deal with the cities of Phoenicia. Most of them submitted, but Tyre was not taken until the middle of 332, after an obstinate siege of seven months. Alexander then marched into Egypt, which welcomed him as its deliverer from the Persian yoke. At the beginning of 331 he founded the city of Alexandria (q.v.) and visited the shrine of Ammon (q.v.). In the spring he set out once again to meet Darius, who had assembled an enormous host which was said to number more than a million men. The ensuing battle was fought near the village of Gaugamela, beyond the Tigris, about 50 miles north-west of Arbela (mod. Erbil). At this latter place Darius had deposited his harem and stores, whence the battle is often named after it. Gaugamela witnessed the final rout of Persia (October 331). Alexander then marched on Babylon, Susa and Persepolis, all of which submitted. He was master of Asia; but though his military genius did not desert him his character undoubtedly began to deteriorate. His adoption of oriental dress and manners may have been a sincere attempt to conciliate his new subjects, but little can be said for his destruction of Persepolis (q.v.).

After Gaugamela, Darius had been seized by Bessus (q.v.), satrap of Bactria, and at the beginning of 330 Alexander moved from Persepolis in pursuit, only to find, on reaching Parthia, that Darius had been murdered by his captor. In 329, therefore, Alexander crossed the Paropamisus (Hindu Kush) and entered Bactria. Here Bessus was delivered to him and put to death.

During the next two years he was engaged chiefly in the conquest of Bactria, and of Sogdiana (mod. Uzbekistan), east of the River Oxus. He also crossed the Jaxartes (Syr Darya) and defeated several Scythian tribes. It was at about this time (328) that he killed his friend Clitus (q.v.) in a drunken brawl. At about this time also, on the conquest of a mountain fortress, Roxana (q.v.) fell into his hands. He had previously (330) put to death his faithful friend Parmenion and the latter's son Philotas (qq.v.); and the year 327 was marked by the plot of Hermolaus (q.v.), in which Aristotle's nephew Callisthenes (q.v.) was alleged to have been involved.

It was in 327 also that Alexander invaded India and crossed the Indus, probably near the modern town of Attock. He met with no resistance until he reached the Hydaspes (Jhelum), where he defeated Porus (q.v.). On the banks of this river, too, he founded a city named Bucephala, in memory of his charger Bucephalus which died here after carrying him through so many victories. Next he penetrated to the Hyphasis (Sutlej), but this was journey's end. The Macedonians, worn out by long service, would go no farther, and Alexander was obliged to retrace his steps (326). He returned to the Hydaspes, and sailed downstream with a portion of his troops, while the remainder marched along the banks in two divisions. They reached the Indian Ocean about the middle of the year, and Nearchus (q.v.) was sent with the fleet to sail along the coast to the Persian Gulf. Alexander marched with the rest of his forces overland to Susa, which they reached early in 325. Here he allowed himself and his troops some rest from their labours, and, anxious to form his European and oriental subjects into one people, he assigned Asiatic wives to about eight of his generals and other senior officers, encouraging the rest to do likewise. He himself took a second wife in the person of Barsine, eldest daughter of Darius. Towards the end of the year he went to Ecbatana in Media, when he lost his favourite Hephaestion (q.v.). Thence he moved to Babylon, intending to make it the capital of his empire, as the best point of communication between his eastern and western dominions. Amid these grandiose schemes he was attacked by a fever, and he died after an illness of eleven days in the month of May or June 323 B.C. He appointed no one as his successor; but immediately before his death he gave his ring to Perdiccas (q.v.). But it mattered little; no sooner had he gone than the vast empire which was nominally his began to dissolve.

By his first wife, Roxana, Alexander was the father of Alexander Aegus (*see* 4 below). The second bore him a son named Heracles. *See* W. W. Tarn, *Alexander the Great*, 2 vols., 1948; J. F. C. Fuller, *The Generalship of Alexander the Great*, 1958.

4. Posthumous son of the preceding by Roxana (q.v.). He was acknowledged as partner in the empire with Philip Arrhidaeus, under the regency of Perdiccas, Antipater and Polysperchon successively. Alexander and his mother were imprisoned by Cassander (q.v.) in 316 and put to death in 310 B.C.

(C) *Syrian Pretenders:* 1. Surnamed Balas, a person of low origin who pretended to be the son of Antiochus IV, Epiphanes. He reigned 151–147 B.C., when he was defeated and dethroned by Demetrius II, Nicator.

2. Surnamed Zebina, a merchant, who was set up by Ptolemy VII, Physcon, of Egypt as a pretender to the Seleucid throne (128 B.C.). He was defeated and slain by Antiochus VIII, Grypus (122 B.C.).

Alexander Aegaeus (Alexandros Aigaios), Greek peripatetic philosopher, taught at Rome in the early 1st century A.D. and was tutor to the future emperor Nero.

Alexander Aetolus (Alexandros Aitōlos), Greek poet and man of letters, *fl. c.* 280 B.C. A native of Pleuron in Aetolia, he was entrusted by Ptolemy II, Philadelphus, with the arrangement of the tragedies and satyric dramas in the Alexandrian Library, but afterwards resided at the court of Antigonus Gonatas of Macedon. Fragments of his poetry have survived.

Alexander of Aphrodisias, the most celebrated of the ancient commentators upon Aristotle, a native of Aphrodisias in Caria. Coming to Athens about the end of the 2nd century A.D., he became head of the Lyceum. We possess his commentaries on *Analytica Priora*, i; *Topica*; *Meteorologica*; *De Sensu*; *Metaphysica*, i–v. Also extant are two treatises, *On Fate* and *On the Soul*; there is a text and translation of the first of these two works, entitled *On Destiny*, by A. Fitzgerald, 1931.

Alexander the Paphlagonian, famous impostor and oracle-monger, born at Abonouteikhos, in Paphlagonia, early in the 2nd century A.D. The account given of him in Lucian's *Alexander, or the False Prophet*, utterly fantastic as it may appear, is corroborated by reliable evidence from other sources.

Alexander began by establishing an oracle of Asclepius in his native place, and announced that the god was about to be born again. Such was the credulity of the people that he was able, by means of the most childish tricks, to convince them that Asclepius had indeed been reborn in the form of a serpent with the name Glycon. He now began to deliver his oracles seated in the newly built temple, draped with a large tame serpent (which wore a false human head) and employing all the sharp practices used by such people in every age to obtain advance information. Lucian himself undertook an investigation of these frauds; but an attempt was made to assassinate him, while Alexander went from one triumph to another, establishing an office at

Rome and instituting mysteries on the Eleusinian model from which Christians and Epicureans were banned. He died at the age of seventy and left a very large fortune. Besides Lucian's work mentioned above, *see* S. Dill, *Roman Society from Nero to Marcus Aurelius*, 1904.

Alexandria : 1. Ancient capital of Egypt, founded by Alexander the Great in 331 B.C. It was intended (*a*) to take the place of Naucratis (q.v.) as an hellenic centre for Egypt, (*b*) to serve as a naval base for operations against Persia and (*c*) to link Macedonia with the Nile valley. Within a hundred years of its foundation it had grown larger than Carthage. Its immense prosperity, which made it second only to Rome, was due to two main factors: (*a*) it inherited the commerce of Tyre (q.v.) and became the centre of a newly opened trade route between Europe and the East; (*b*) it quickly became the largest Jewish city in the world. Its cultural eminence was due in large measure to the Ptolemies, who created and fostered its celebrated university and library. During the 2nd century B.C. Alexandria came under the political influence of Rome. It passed formally under Roman jurisdiction by the will of Ptolemy X, Alexander (80 B.C.), and was incorporated in the Roman province of Egypt (q.v.) by Augustus. The city now reached the zenith of its glory; it is said by Diodorus to have contained 300,000 citizens, and there were probably at least an equal number of slaves. With the introduction of Christianity it became a centre of religious dispute. From the 3rd century A.D. it gradually declined.

TOPOGRAPHY. Building was begun under the supervision first of the architect Deinocrates and then of Alexander's viceroy, Cleomenes of Naucratis. It was virtually completed in the reign of Ptolemy II, Philadelphus (285–247 B.C.), but additions were made throughout the Ptolemaic and early Roman periods. Alexandria was situated on a narrow neck of land at the western end of the Nile Delta. It was bounded north by the Mediterranean; south by Lake Mareotis; west by the necropolis and its gardens; east by the Eleusinian road, near which stood the Hippodrome. The streets crossed one another at right angles, and beneath each of them ran a fresh-water channel feeding cisterns that were said to be capable of holding a year's supply for the entire population.

The Harbour Line. This commenced from the east with the peninsula of Lochias, which terminated seaward in a fort called Acro-Lochias; on it also stood the royal palaces, and the peninsula, together with the island of Antirrhodos, enclosed the Royal Harbour. Lochias has almost entirely subsided, and Antirrhodos has vanished altogether. West of the Royal Harbour was a promontory upon which stood the Poseideion (at the landward end) and the Timonium, a villa built by Mark Antony (at the northern extremity). Between Lochias and the mole called Heptastadion (see *Pharos* below) lay the Great Harbour; on the west side of the mole was the smaller port of Eunostos, connected by the Kibotos basin with a canal that led by one arm to Lake Mareotis (a wet dock and general haven for Nile shipping) and by another with the Canopic branch of the delta. Between the Poseideion and the Heptastadion the shore was lined with dockyards; on the western horn of Eunostos were public granaries.

Pharos. Fronting the city, at a distance of about a mile, lay the island of Pharos, connected with the mainland by a mole which was called, from its length, Heptastadion (7 stadia = ¾ mile). There were two gaps in the mole, to let the water through, in hope of avoiding the accumulation of silt; drawbridges were laid over these passages. Silting, however, has long since obliterated the Heptastadion. On the north-west of the island remains of a prehistoric port (probably Minoan) have been found. On an islet off the eastern point stood the celebrated lighthouse (*see* PHAROS), one of the Seven Wonders of the World (q.v.).

The Interior City. This was divided into three regions, corresponding to the original three elements of the population: (1) The Jewish region lay in the east; (2) the Brucheion (royal or Greek region) occupied the centre and included the peninsula and promontory mentioned above; (3) Rhakotis, the Egyptian region, lay in the west and was the first part of the mainland to be laid out by Deinocrates. In the reign of Augustus the Brucheion was formed into (*a*) the Greek and (*b*) the military and financial quarters. Buildings other than those already mentioned as included in the Brucheion were the Emporion (exchange), the Soma (royal mausoleum, where Alexander himself was buried), the Mouseion (university), the library, and, in Roman times, the Caesarium or temple of the Caesars. A stadium, a palaestra, a gymnasium and an amphitheatre provided exercise and amusement. The only building worthy of note in Rhakotis was the Serapeion, or temple of Serapis, which housed part of the library. Near by stood what has been known since the time of the crusades as Pompey's Pillar; it was erected *c.* A.D. 297 in honour of Diocletian. *See* E. M. Forster, *Alexandria*, 1922.

2. City of north Syria, founded to commemorate Alexander's victory at Issus (q.v.) in 333 B.C. The name, but probably not the exact site, is preserved in modern Alexandretta (Iskanderun).

3. Seaport town, built by Antigonus (*c.* 310 B.C.) a little south of Tenedos (q.v.) in the Troad. Called at first Antigoneia, its name was changed to Alexandria by Lysimachus (q.v.) in memory of Alexander the Great. From here St Paul started on his first journey to Europe. There are remains of the walls and of some Roman buildings.

Alexis (late 5th century B.C.), Greek poet of the Middle Comedy, born at Thurii in Magna Graecia, but was taken in childhood to Athens where he later received citizenship. According to Suidas he was Menander's uncle, and Plutarch says that he died at the age of 106 while being crowned on the stage. Alexis was the author of 245 plays, of which about 130 titles survive, together with fragments amounting to about 1,000 lines.

Algidus Mons, the eastern portion of that ridge which includes also Albanus Mons (q.v.). Through a narrow defile ran the Via Latina, in the vicinity of which was a temple of Diana.

Alimentus, Lucius Cincius, Roman senator and annalist, praetor in Sicily 209 B.C. He wrote in Greek a history of Rome to his own times which gave a valuable account of the second Punic war. He is to be distinguished from another writer of the same name, an antiquary and jurist, who wrote towards the end of the 1st century B.C.

Allia (mod. Fosso Bettina), small river flowing into the Tiber on its left bank, about 11 miles from Rome. Here in 390 B.C. the Romans were heavily defeated by the Gauls (*see* SENONES), who proceeded to occupy Rome; the disaster occurred on 18th July which was known thereafter as *dies Alliensis* and was an unlucky day in the republican calendar. *See* CELTAE.

Allifae (mod. Alife), Samnite town of which the site is unknown, though a Roman town of the same name and probably not far distant stood in the valley of the Vulturnus.

Allobroges, a Celtic tribe which inhabited territory between the Rhodanus, the Isara and the Alpes Graiae, in what was later called Gallia Narbonensis (*see* GALLIA). Their chief towns were Vienna (Vienne), Genava (Geneva) and Cularo (Grenoble). The Allobroges accompanied Hannibal on his invasion of Italy (218 B.C.). They were defeated by Cn. Domitius Ahenobarbus in 122, and subjugated by Quintus Fabius Maximus (Allobrogicus) in 121 B.C., but long continued hostile to Rome.

Aloidae (Alōidai). Aloeus, son of Poseidon, married Iphimide, daughter of Triops. Iphimede was seduced by Poseidon and bore him two sons, Otus and Ephialtes, who are called Aloidae after their putative father. At the early age of nine, being then nine fathoms tall and nine cubits broad, they threatened the gods with war by attempting to pile Ossa on Olympus and Pelion on Ossa. They would have succeeded, says Homer, had they been allowed to grow up; but Apollo destroyed them before their beards began to show. The Aloidae were also said to have put Ares in chains and to have kept him imprisoned for thirteen months. The episode of Ossa and Pelion is often associated with the war of the Gigantes (q.v.).

Alpes (the Alps), mountains forming the boundary of northern Italy. In imperial times the following main groups were distinguished: *Alpes Maritimae, Alpes Cottiae, Alpes Graiae,* and *Alpes Penninae,* dividing Italy from Gallia Narbonensis; *Alpes Rhaeticae,* the frontier between Italy and the province of Rhaetia; *Alpes Carnicae,* between Italy and Noricum; *Alpes Juliae,* between Italy and south-west Pannonia. The most frequented passes were Mont Genèvre in the Alpes Maritimae, and the Brenner in the Alpes Rhaeticae. *See* W. W. Hyde, *Roman Alpine Routes* (American Philosophical Society), 1936.

Alpheus (Alpheios; mod. Ruphea), chief river of Peloponnesus, flowing past Olympia into the Ionian Sea. Its source is in central Arcadia, but this was erroneously believed by the ancients to be the mere resurgence of a subterranean stream originating in the plain of Tegea. The principal tributaries are the Erymanthes and the Ladon, both of which join the Alpheus above Olympia. Alpheus was the typical river-god of Peloponnesus as was Acheloüs (q.v.) in northern Greece. His waters were said to run under the sea and reappear as the fountain of Arethusa (q.v.) at Syracuse. *See* W. Loring, *Journal of Hellenic Studies,* xv.

Alsium, an Etruscan town on the Via Aurelia, 22 miles from Rome. It was colonized by Rome in 247 B.C. There are extensive remains of villas, including those of Pompey and the Antonine emperors.

Althiburos (mod. Medeina), city of Numidia between Carthage and

Theveste. It was built (A.D. 123) by the emperor Hadrian, who granted it municipal rights. Excavations have revealed considerable remains. *See* A. Merlin, *Forum et Maisons d'Althiburos*, 1913.

Altinum (mod. Altino), town of Venetia. Originally a fishing village, it rose to some importance as the junction of the Via Postumia and the Via Popilia. From the time of Claudius it was the starting-point of yet another road (350 miles) leading to the Danubian provinces.

Alyattes (Aluattēs), King of Lydia 609–560 B.C., and father of Croesus (q.v.). He began his reign at war with Miletus, an inheritance from his father Sadyattes, but concluded a treaty of peace and alliance in 604. It was during a battle in his reign between the Lydians and the Medes that the solar eclipse took place (28th May 585) as predicted by Thales (q.v.). Alyattes drove the Cimmerii from Asia Minor, subdued the Carians and took a number of Greek cities. His tomb, near Lake Gygaea, north of Sardis, has a diameter of 281 yards, and is topped by a huge phallus about 9 feet thick.

Amaltheia, nurse of the infant Zeus in Crete, was according to some traditions the goat which suckled Zeus, and was rewarded by being placed among the stars. According to others Amaltheia was a nymph, who fed Zeus with the milk of a goat. When this goat broke off one of her horns, Amaltheia filled it with fresh herbs and gave it to Zeus, who placed it among the stars. According to other accounts Zeus himself broke off one of the horns of the goat, and endowed it with the power of becoming filled with whatever the possessor might wish, hence this horn was commonly called the Cornucopia (q.v.). *See*, however, ACHELOÜS.

Amasia, capital of the Pontic kings (*see* PONTUS); birth-place of Mithradates the Great and of the geographer Strabo. It was made a free city by Pompey in 65 B.C.

Amata, wife of Latinus and mother of Lavinia (qq.v.). Having already promised her daughter to Turnus, she opposed her marriage to Aeneas (q.v.). On hearing of Turnus's death she hanged herself.

Amathus (-os), city on the south coast of Cyprus, remains of which have been found dating from as early as 1000 B.C. A Phoenician foundation, it was a centre of the joint cult of Adonis and Aphrodite (qq.v.), and it was no doubt originally this cult whence arose the strange rite described by Plutarch as being an annual event at Amathus (*see* ARIADNE). Amathus owed its wealth to being situated in an extensive corn-growing area; there were also copper-mines in the neighbourhood.

Amazons, 'breastless', legendary race of female warriors said to have come from beyond the Caucasus and settled in Asia Minor. They were ruled by a queen, and according to some authorities the female children had their right breasts cut off in order to facilitate their use of the bow. The male children were exposed, and the race was continued by periodical unions with men of a different race. The Amazons occur frequently in Greek literature from Homer onwards, and were believed to have invaded Attica at a date corresponding to 1256 B.C. according to the Parian Marble (q.v.). In art they are sometimes represented with two breasts, but with the right one bared. The legend of the Amazons is probably connected with invasions of beardless nomads (Scythian and Mongolian) from the Russian steppe. *See* Sir J. Forsdyke, *Greece before Homer*, 1956.

Ambarvalia, an early Roman festival, celebrated annually in May, usually on the 29th, and intended to secure the growing crops against damage. Originally it was conducted by priests who led three victims (an ox, a sheep and a pig, called collectively *suovetaurilia*) around the *ager Romanus* with prayers to Ceres. But as this Roman territory was enlarged the rite became impossible, and individual farmers performed a similar lustration of their own land (*see* Virgil, *Georg.* i. 338 ff.; Cato, *De Re Rustica*, 141). *See* W. Warde Fowler, *Roman Festivals*, 1899.

Ambiorix and Catuvolcus, joint kings of the Eburones, who destroyed a legion of recruits and five veteran cohorts under Sabinus and Cotta (qq.v.) near Atuatuca in 54 B.C. *See* Caesar, *Bell. Gall.* v. 24–37.

Ambitus, the canvassing for office in republican Rome. It was open to many abuses; hence the word came to be used for the obtaining of any public appointment by illegal means, and the indictment therefore was *de ambitu*.

Ambracia (-kia), town of Epirus on the River Arachthus, about seven miles from the sea. Founded from Corinth *c.* 640 B.C., it soon discarded its original form of government by hereditary tyrants and became a strong democracy. It took a prominent part on the Spartan side in the Peloponnesian war until its forces were almost annihilated at Idomene (426 B.C.). Having surrendered to Philip of Macedon in 338 it enjoyed autonomy until 295, when it became the capital of Pyrrhus's kingdom. Ambracia joined the Aetolian League (q.v.), *c.* 210 B.C., and was captured by the Romans in 189. Thereafter it declined rapidly, and what remained of the population was transported to Nicopolis (q.v.) under Augustus.

Ambrosia, in Greek mythology, sometimes the food and sometimes the drink of the gods. The word is probably derived from *ambrosios*, meaning fragrant; and some authorities believe that both ambrosia and nectar (q.v.) were kinds of honey.

Ameipsias, Athenian poet of the Old Comedy. A contemporary of Aristophanes, he defeated his more famous rival in 423 B.C., when the *Clouds* was awarded third place, Ameipsias's *Connus* being placed second to the *Pytine* of Cratinus, and again in 414 when the *Revellers* was preferred to the *Birds*.

Ameria (mod. Amelia), town of Umbria, 65 miles north of Rome and 1,332 feet above sea level. It was the birth-place of Sextus Roscius (q.v.). There are remains of the wall and of a large Roman reservoir.

Amisus (-os), city on the coast of Pontus (q.v.). Founded in the 6th century B.C. from Phocaea or Miletus, it belonged to the Pontic kingdom by 250 B.C. Enlarged by Mithradates the Great, it enjoyed some measure of freedom and great wealth under Rome.

Amiternum, Sabine town in the upper valley of the Aternus, from which its name was derived; birth-place of Sallust. In imperial times it was extremely prosperous owing to the fact (1) that the neighbourhood was fertile, and (2) that it stood at the junction of the Via Caecilia, the Via Claudia Nova and the Via Salaria (qq.v.).

Ammōn, Egyptian divinity (*Amûn*), whom the Greeks identified with Zeus, and the Romans with Jupiter. He possessed a celebrated temple and oracle in the oasis of Ammonium (*Siwah*) in the Libyan desert. It was visited by Alexander the Great, some of whose coins show his head adorned with the curling ram's horns of the god.

Ammonius (Ammōnios), an Alexandrian scholar of the 2nd century B.C., pupil of Aristarchus of Samothrace. He wrote commentaries on Homer, Pindar and Aristophanes, but none of these has survived.

Ammonius Saccas (Ammōnios Sakkas), one of the founders of Neoplatonism, was born *c.* A.D. 160 and died in 242. Originally an Alexandrian porter of Christian parentage, he lapsed into paganism, taught himself philosophy and eventually attracted such pupils as Longinus, Origen and Plotinus. Ammonius left no writings; little or nothing is known about his doctrines, or even of his influence upon Plotinus (q.v.).

Amor, 'love', a mere translation of Eros (q.v.); the god of love had no place in Roman religion.

Amorgos, island of the Cyclades (q.v.), home of the iambic poet Semonides. Under the Roman Empire it was a place of banishment.

Amphiaraüs (-os), prophet and hero of Argos. He married Eriphyle, sister of Adrastus (*see* ADRASTUS, 1). At the instigation of his wife he took part in the expedition of the Seven against Thebes (*see* THEBAN LEGEND, 3), although he foresaw its fatal ending. But on setting out from Argos he enjoined his sons, Alcmaeon and Amphilochus (qq.v.), to punish their mother for his death. During the campaign he was swallowed up by the earth when fleeing from Periclymenus towards the River Ismenus. In historical times his cult included an oracle at Oropus, between Potniae and Thebes, famous for the interpretation of dreams.

Amphictyonic League, an association of Greek states for the maintenance of the temples and cults of Demeter at Thermopylae and Apollo at Delphi. It also enforced certain inter-state rights and laws arising from the Amphictyonic oath, and organized the Pythian games. The Council of the League met twice yearly, alternately at Delphi and Thermopylae; each member state had two votes, which appear to have been easily transferable. The league had political importance inasmuch as it could be used to promote the designs of its more powerful members. *See* SACRED WARS.

Amphilochus (-khos), son of Amphiaraüs and brother of Alcmaeon (qq.v.). He took part in the War of the Epigoni (*see* THEBAN LEGEND, 5), helped Alcmaeon in the murder of their mother—which, in his case, the Erinyes appear to have overlooked—and subsequently fought against Troy. Like his father, Amphilochus was a seer. He was killed by Mopsus (q.v.).

Amphiōn and Zēthos, twin sons of Zeus by Antiope (*see* ANTIOPE, 2). After avenging their mother they took possession of Thebes and fortified it with a wall. In this task they were greatly assisted by a lyre which Amphion had received from Hermes and upon which he played with such magic skill that the stones assembled of their own accord. Amphion then married Niobe, daughter of Tantalus, and Zethus Aedon (q.v.).

By Niobe Amphion begat seven sons and seven daughters. But Niobe was so proud of her numerous offspring that she deemed herself superior to Leto (q.v.), whose indignant children, Apollo and Artemis, killed all fourteen of them (another version says all but one). Zeus changed Niobe into a rock on Mt Sipylus in Lydia (*see* MAGNESIA AD SIPYLUM), which shed tears during the summer, and Amphion put an end to his own life.

Amphipolis, city of Macedonia on the east bank of the Strymon, about three miles from the sea. Its importance was due mainly to its command of a bridge over which passed all traffic between north Greece and the Hellespont. Originally a Thracian town called Ennea Hodoi ('Nine Roads'), it was colonized by Athenians and other Greeks under Hagnon (437 B.C.). During the Peloponnesian war (424) it surrendered to Brasidas (*see also* THUCYDIDES), and thereafter remained independent until 357 when it was occupied by Philip of Macedon. *See also* ROXANA.

Amphissa (mod. Salona), town of the Ozolian Locrians (*see* LOCRI), about 80 miles north-west of Athens. Its inhabitants having trespassed on the sacred lands of Delphi (q.v.), it was destroyed in 358 B.C. by the Delphic amphictyony, but was afterwards rebuilt. *See* AMPHICTYONIC LEAGUE; SACRED WARS.

Amphitheatre, a place of entertainment, originally for gladiatorial shows at Rome. The shape was elliptical, and the earlier specimens were temporary and constructed of wood. The first permanent stone amphitheatre was erected at Pompeii in 80 B.C. Among the most important ones of later date were the Colosseum (q.v.) at Rome and those at Verona, Nemausus (q.v.) and Arelate (q.v.).

Amphitritē, in Greek mythology, a sea-goddess, daughter of Nereus (or Oceanus) and wife of Poseidon, by whom she was the mother of Triton (q.v.).

Amphitryon (-truōn), son of Alcaeus and grandson of Perseus (q.v.), married his cousin Alcmene (q.v.). He was killed in a war against Erginna, King of the Minyae.

Amphora, earthenware vessel used by the Greeks and Romans, and having a handle on each side of the neck. It either rested on a base or ended in a point which was let into a hole in the ground. As a standard of liquid measurement the Greek amphora held about nine gallons, the Roman about six.

Ampsanctus or **Amsanctus**, small lake in the territory of the Hirpini, 10 miles south-east of Aeclanum. A nearby temple of the goddess Mephitis was adjacent to a cave from which arose poisonous (mephitic) vapours and which was consequently regarded as an entrance to the underworld.

Amyclae (Amuklai), town of Peloponnesus, on the Eurotas, $2\frac{1}{2}$ miles south-east of Sparta. It was originally an Achaean town, and retained its independence long after the Dorian invasion. Amyclae was the scene of an annual festival called Hyacinthia (*see* HYACINTHUS), and was also famous for a colossal statue of Apollo. *See* BATHYCLES.

Amycus (Amukos), son of Poseidon and King of the Bebryces in Bithynia, famous for his skill as a boxer. A challenge from him—and he challenged all strangers—meant certain death; but he was killed (or, according to Theocritus, knocked out) by Polydeuces (*see* DIOSCURI) when the Argonauts (q.v.) visited his territory.

Amyntas (Amun-), name of two kings of Macedonia:

1. Reigned from about 540 to 498 B.C. He made an alliance with the Peisistratids, and gave refuge to Hippias after the latter's expulsion from Athens in 510 B.C.

2. Succeeded to the throne in 389 B.C., after the 10 years of anarchy which followed the death of his cousin Archelaus. He was an admirer of Greek culture, maintained friendly relations with Athens and died in 369 B.C.

Anacreon (-kreōn), Greek lyric poet, born at Teos in Ionia *c.* 570 B.C. On the fall of Teos to the Persians he went to Abdera in Thrace, but afterwards lived at Samos under the patronage of Polycrates, who died in 522. Anacreon was then invited by Hipparchus to Athens, where he remained until his death (*c.* 485 B.C.). Only a few genuine fragments of his work have survived. The so-called *Anacreontica* date from about the 2nd century B.C.

Anagnia (mod. Anagni), chief town of the Hernici (q.v.), later a *municipium* and *colonia*. Cicero had an estate near by.

Anaxagoras, Greek philosopher of the Ionian school, born at Clazomenae *c.* 500 B.C. He gave up his property to his relations, and went to Athens *c.* 463; here he remained thirty years, and became the friend and teacher of Euripides and Pericles. He taught that an unlimited number of material elements constituted the universe, and combined to form bodies under the guidance of an independent Intelligence (*Nous*). He was also the first to attempt an explanation of eclipses, the nature of the heavenly bodies and other natural phenomena. Portions of his work *On Nature* survive. His doctrines offended the Athenians; and he was accused of impiety. It was only through the eloquence of Pericles that he was not put to death; but he was sentenced to pay a fine and to quit Athens (*c.* 433). He retired to Lampsacus, where he died in 428. *See* D. Gershenson and D. Greenberg, *Anaxagoras and the Birth of Physics*.

Anaxandridēs, Spartan king (*c.* 560–520 B.C.). Having a barren wife whom he would not divorce, the ephors obliged him to take a second, by whom he was father of Cleomenes I.

Anaxarchus (-khos), Greek philosopher of the school of Democritus, born at Abdera; a contemporary of Alexander the Great, whom he accompanied to Asia. Returning home after Alexander's death, he fell into the hands of Nicocreon, King of Cyprus, to whom he had given offence and who had him pounded to death in a stone mortar.

Anaxaretē, a maiden of Cyprus, who treated her lover Iphis with such haughty indifference that he most ungallantly hanged himself at her door. Even then she gazed upon the funeral so unmoved that Venus changed her into a stone statue (Ovid, *Metam.* xiv. 698 ff.).

Anaximander (Gk Anaximandros), philosopher of the Ionian school, born at Miletus *c.* 610 B.C. He taught that the primary source of all things is the Indeterminate and that the earth is a cylinder in equilibrium. He was also the first to speculate about the sizes and distances of the sun and moon, drew the first map of the inhabited world and hinted at a theory of evolution. He died in 546 B.C. His work *On Nature* has not survived. *See* C. H. Kahn, *Anaximander and the Origins of Greek Cosmology*, 1960.

Anaximenēs, Greek philosopher of the Ionian school, born at Miletus *c.* 584, and died some time between 528 and 524 B.C. He considered air to be the primary element of all things.

Ancaeus (Ankaios), King of the Leleges in Samos, son of Zeus or Poseidon, and helmsman of the Argo after the death of Tiphys. His legend is responsible for a well-known proverb. It relates that while planting a vineyard he was accosted by a soothsayer who told him he would never drink of its wine. Immediately the grapes ripened, Ancaeus squeezed their juice into a cup, and was just about to drink triumphantly when the soothsayer, happening to be present, said: 'There's many a slip between cup and lip.' Just then a messenger arrived with news that a wild boar was ravaging the countryside. Ancaeus put down the cup, went in pursuit and was killed by the boar.

Anchises (-khisēs), King of Dardanus on Mt Ida. He was loved by Aphrodite, and became by her the father of Aeneas (q.v.). Having boasted of his intercourse with the goddess, he was struck by lightning and blinded. On the capture of Troy, Aeneas carried him on his shoulders from the burning city (*see* Virgil, *Aen.* ii). Anchises died soon after the arrival of Aeneas in Sicily, and was buried on Mt Eryx.

Ancile, a sacred shield, said to have fallen from heaven in the reign of Numa. There was a prophecy that Rome's destiny was bound up with its safety; so, to avoid theft, eleven similar shields (*ancilia*) were made and placed in the temple of Mars Ultor in charge of the Salii (q.v.).

Ancona, town of Picenum, founded by refugees from Syracuse *c.* 390 B.C., in a bend (Gk *agkon,* elbow) of the Adriatic coast. Though subsequently a Roman *colonia* (q.v.), Ancona long remained an essentially Greek town. Under the empire it was a leading port; the harbour was enlarged by Trajan, in whose honour the surviving triumphal arch was erected (A.D. 115). *See* APOLLODORUS, 4.

Ancus Marcius, legendary fourth king of Rome 640–616 B.C., a grandson of Numa. He was said to have taken many Latin towns, to have settled their inhabitants on the Aventine, and thus to have formed the original Roman plebs. He was also credited with several public works, among them the Sublician Bridge and the port of Ostia.

Ancyra (Ankura; mod. Ankara), city of Galatia (q.v.). It was originally a Phrygian town, but became the capital of the Tectosages in the 3rd century B.C. From 65 to 25 B.C. Ancyra was governed by native rulers dependent on Rome, but in the latter year was made capital of the Roman province. It did not fully absorb Graeco-Roman culture until about the middle of the 2nd century A.D., and never became of much importance until the 4th century. Ancyra is famous chiefly on account of the *Monumentum Ancyranum* (q.v.).

Anderida (mod. Pevensey), Roman fort on the coast of what is now Sussex. It was built *c.* A.D. 300 as part of a defensive scheme against Saxon pirates. Though used by the Normans, the outer fortifications (repaired *c.* A.D. 400) are Roman and are in an excellent state of preservation.

Andocides (-kidēs), one of the ten Attic Orators (q.v.), born *c.* 440 B.C. In 415 he became involved in the affair of the mutilation of the Hermae (q.v.). He was imprisoned, but saved his life by denouncing the real or pretended perpetrators of the crime. Nevertheless he was deprived of certain civil rights, went into exile and lived as a merchant until 403 when he returned under the general amnesty that marked the restoration of the Athenian democracy. Three of his speeches are extant, notably *De Mysteriis*, the defence on a charge of having profaned the Eleusinian Mysteries. *See* R. C. Jebb, *Attic Orators*, vol. i, 1888.

Andraemon (-aimōn): 1. Son-in-law of Oeneus (q.v.), and father of Thoas (*see* THOAS, 1).

2. Son of Oxylus and husband of Dryope (q.v.).

Andriscus (-kos), a fuller of Adramyttium who, in 150 B.C., put himself forward as a son of Perseus, last king of Macedonia. In the following year he defeated a Roman army, overran Thessaly and allied himself with Carthage. In 148, however, he was defeated at Pydna by Q. Caecilius Metellus and subsequently put to death. Macedonia was then formed into a Roman province.

Androclus, usually but incorrectly **Androcles**, a Roman slave, presumably of Greek origin, who lived during the reign of Tiberius and whose story (for what it may be worth) is told in the *Noctes Atticae* (v. 14) of Aulus Gellius derived from the *Aegyptiaca* of Apion (q.v.). Androclus fled from the cruelty of his master, and took refuge in a cave in Africa. There he was accosted by a lion who offered him its swollen paw, from which he extracted a large thorn. Subsequently recaptured, he was thrown to the beasts in the arena, of which the lion happened to be one. The animal, instead of tearing him to pieces, fawned upon him, and he was set free by the emperor, who also made him a present of the lion.

Androgeos, son of Minos and Pasiphaë (qq.v.). According to legend he beat all his opponents in the Panathenaic games at Athens, thereby earning the jealousy of Aegeus (q.v.), who had him assassinated. Minos declared war on Athens, for the consequences of which *see* THESEUS. Androgeos was worshipped at Phalerum as a hero.

Andromache (-khē), wife of Hector (q.v.) and mother of Astyanax (or Scamandrius). At the fall of Troy the Greeks hurled her child from the walls, and she herself became the property of Neoptolemus (q.v.), son of Achilles. A later legend makes her subsequently the wife of Helenus (q.v.). *See* Euripides, *Andromache*.

Andromeda, daughter of Cepheus, King of Aethiopia, by Cassiopeia. Her mother having boasted that her daughter was more beautiful than the nereids (*see* NYMPHS), Poseidon sent a sea-monster to lay waste the country. The oracle of Ammon (q.v.) promised deliverance if Andromeda were surrendered to the beast, and Cepheus was obliged to chain his daughter to a rock. Here she was found and rescued by Perseus (q.v.), who obtained her as his wife. At the wedding, however, he was challenged by Phineus, brother of Cepheus, to whom she had been formerly promised. A fight ensued, during which Phineus was turned to stone by means of the Gorgon's head (*see* JOPPA).

Andronicus (-kos), **Livius**, the earliest Latin epic and dramatic poet. A Greek by birth, he was a freedman of M. Livius Salinator, whose gentile name he adopted on his emancipation. Andronicus wrote both tragedies and comedies, his first drama being acted in 240 B.C. He also translated the *Odyssey* into Saturnian verse. For text and translation of surviving fragments *see* E. H. Warmington, *Remains of Old Latin* (Loeb Library).

Andronicus (-kos) of Rhodes, became head of the Peripatetic school soon after 70 B.C. He edited the writings of Aristotle and Theophrastus, which had been brought to Rome by Sulla (q.v.), and his work forms the basis of our present texts.

Andros, an island of the Cyclades (q.v.), six miles south-east of Euboea. On the west coast may still be seen some ruins of its ancient capital, Palaeopolis. Andros was famous for its wine, and on that account was a centre of the worship of Dionysus (q.v.). During the 7th century B.C. it colonized several places in Chalcidice, notably Stageira. It supplied Xerxes with ships for the Salamis campaign (480 B.C.), and though subsequently a member of the Delian League (q.v.), it was never completely loyal to Athens. From 200 to 133 B.C. the island belonged to Pergamum (q.v.), and passed with that kingdom to Rome under the will of Attalus III.

Angli or Anglii, a Teutonic people who, late in the 1st century A.D., lived probably in the southern part of the Jutland peninsula. According to Tacitus (*Germania*, 40) they worshipped the goddess Nerthus (Mother Earth), whose sanctuary was 'on an island of the Ocean' (probably Zealand).

Anio (mod. Aniene), river of Italy, rising in the eastern borders of Latium and flowing 73 miles to join the Tiber, of which it is one of the main tributaries. Its waters supplied the Anio Vetus and the Anio Novus (*see* AQUEDUCTS), and form the beautiful falls at Tibur (Tivoli).

Anius (-os), priest of Apollo at Delos. By his wife Dryope he was father of three daughters known as the Oenotropae (q.v.).

Anna Perenna, an old Roman goddess of the circle of the year. Her festival, celebrated on 15th March in a grove at the first milestone on the Via Flaminia, was an occasion of unbridled revelry; the accompanying sacrifices were intended to secure her favour, that the year should come full circle without mishap.

Myths of the Augustan age make her the sister of Dido, after whose death she is supposed to have fled to Italy and been welcomed by Aeneas. Here she excited the jealousy of Lavinia; being warned in a dream by Dido she drowned herself in the River Numicia, of which stream she was thereafter considered as the nymph.

Anniceris (-keris), Greek philosopher of the Cyrenaic school, lived in the 3rd century B.C. He differed, however, from the majority of Cyrenaics in holding that the only wise man is he who has acquired a habit of wise conduct. *See* ARISTIPPUS.

Annona, a public service at Rome, responsible for the city's corn supply. Until the reign of Augustus it was managed by aediles (q.v.), and thereafter by the *praefectus annonae*.

Antaeus (-taios), a giant, son of Poseidon and Gē. He obliged all strangers to wrestle with him, and then slew them. Heracles defeated and slew him. According to a later version of the story, Antaeus was invincible so long as he remained in contact with his mother, Earth. Heracles therefore lifted him up and crushed him in the air.

Antalcidas (-kidas), Spartan soldier and diplomat. In 392 B.C. he was sent by his government to Sardis, in order to undermine the friendly relations then existing between Athens and Persia; and he would have succeeded but for the intervention of Artaxerxes II. In 388, however, while commanding the Spartan fleet, he managed to obtain Persian assistance against Athens. This formidable coalition was such that Athens accepted terms negotiated with Persia by Antalcidas and known to history as the Peace of Antalcidas (387 B.C.). By this treaty it was agreed that the whole of Asia Minor, together with the islands of Clazomenae and Cyprus, should be subject to Persia; that all other Greek cities not already under Persian rule should be independent, excepting Lemnos, Imbros and Scyros which should belong as previously to Athens. As the fortunes of Sparta declined after Leuctra (371), so did the influence of Antalcidas with Artaxerxes, and he is said to have starved himself to death (367 B.C.).

Antea or **Sthenoboea**, wife of Proetus (q.v.).

Antemnae, small town of Latium at the confluence of the Anio with the Tiber, about two miles north of Rome. According to legend it was taken by Romulus after the rape of the Sabines and supported the Tarquins after their expulsion. By the late 1st century B.C. it was a mere hamlet, though traces of earlier walls may still be seen.

Antēnōr, a Trojan. As husband of Theano, daughter of Cisseus (q.v.), he was brother-in-law of Hecuba (q.v.), and was sent by Priam to demand the return of Hesione (q.v.). He also received Menelaus and Odysseus when they in turn came to demand the return of Helen, and advised his fellow citizens to restore her to her husband. On the fall of Troy, therefore, he was spared by the Greeks.

Antēnōr (6th century B.C.), an Athenian sculptor. He made the group of Harmodius and Aristogeiton which was removed from the Acropolis by the Persians in 480 B.C. Two bases signed by him have been found on the Acropolis. *See* S. Casson, *The Technique of Early Greek Sculpture*, 1933.

Anthestēria, an Athenian festival in honour of Dionysus, celebrated each year on the 11th, 12th and 13th of the month Anthesterion (February–March). It was intended to mark the maturing of the wine stored at the previous vintage and the commencement of spring. On the second day there took place a kind of mystical marriage between the King-Archon's wife (*see* ARCHON) and Dionysus.

Anthology, The Greek. The first collection of Greek poems, *Stephanos* (garland), was made by Meleager of Gadara (q.v.). It included poems by forty-six poets, among them Sappho, and a few by the editor. This work was enlarged by succeeding editors, whose MSS have been lost, the earliest and fullest of the extant versions being that of Constantinus Cephalas, a grammarian of the mid-tenth century. It contained excerpts from more than 300 poets, and the poems ranged from the seventh century B.C. to the tenth A.D. Early in the fourteenth century Maximus Planudes clumsily revised this beautiful collection, abridging, re-arranging and even altering. For 300 years his was the only Greek Anthology known, but in 1606 Salmasius rediscovered the Anthology of Cephalas in the library of the counts palatine at Heidelberg, whence it is called the Palatine Anthology.

Anthropophagi, tribe of cannibals mentioned by Pliny as inhabiting a region near the Caspian Sea, and perhaps identical with the Androphagi mentioned by Herodotus (iv. 106). It was their custom to eat the flesh of their aged parents in order to preserve the ancestral soul from decay.

Anticlea (-kleia), daughter of Autolycus, wife of Laertes and mother of Odysseus. She died of grief at the long absence of her son.

Anticyra (-kura), name of three Greek cities:

1. In Phocis, on the Bay of Anticyra in the Corinthian Gulf. The town was celebrated for its black hellebore, a reputed remedy for madness; whence the saying ' Naviget Anticyram ' (' Let him sail to Ancyra ') when a person acted foolishly.

2. In Thessaly, on the right bank of the Spercheus near the head of the Maliac Gulf.

3. In Locris, near Naupactus.

Antigonē, daughter of Oedipus by Jocasta, *see* THEBAN LEGEND, 2 and 4.

Antigonea (-eia): 1. City of Syria, a few miles north of the Orontes. Founded by Antigonus I, Cyclops, in 307 B.C., it was afterwards used by Seleucus I as a quarry for the building of Antioch.

2. *See* ALEXANDRIA, 3.

Antigonidae, the Antigonids, a dynasty of kings in Asia and Macedonia, founded by Antigonus I, Cyclops. It lasted from 323 until 168 B.C. *See* ANTIGONUS; DEMETRIUS (B); PERSEUS; PHILIP V.

Antigonus (-os), name of three kings in Asia and Macedonia:

1. Surnamed Cyclops, ' One-eyed ', son of Philip of Elymiotis and a general of Alexander the Great. In the division of the empire after the death of the latter (323 B.C.), he received the provinces of Greater Phrygia, Lycia and Pamphylia. On the death of the regent Antipater in 319, he aspired to the sovereignty of Asia. In 316 he defeated Eumenes and put him to death, after a struggle of nearly three years. He afterwards carried on war, with varying success, against Seleucus, Ptolemy, Cassander and Lysimachus. After the defeat of Ptolemy's fleet in 306 Antigonus assumed the title of king, and his example was followed by Ptolemy, Lysimachus and Seleucus. Antigonus and his son Demetrius were at length defeated by Lysimachus at the decisive battle of Ipsus in Phrygia, in 301. Antigonus fell in the battle in the eighty-first year of his age.

2. Surnamed Gonatas, perhaps from Gonni in Thessaly, though the name may be a Macedonian word. He was the son and successor of Demetrius I, Poliorcetes. He assumed the title King of Macedonia after his father's death (283) and dissolved the Achaean League (q.v.), but he did not obtain possession of the throne until 277 B.C. Driven out by Pyrrhus in 272, he was restored in the following year and died in 239 B.C. Antigonus was a patron of learning and literature. *See* W. W. Tarn, *Antigonus Gonatas,* 1913.

3. Surnamed Dōsōn, because he was always ' going to give ' but never did, son of Demetrius of Cyrene, a younger brother of the preceding. On the death of Demetrius II in 229 B.C. Antigonus was

left guardian of the latter's son Philip (afterwards Philip V), but he married Demetrius's widow Phthia and became King of Macedonia himself. He supported Aratus (q.v.) and the Achaean League against Cleomenes III of Sparta, whom he defeated at Sellasia in 222 B.C. He died in the following year.

Antigonus (-os) of Carystus, in Euboea, Greek writer of the 3rd century B.C. He lived at the court of Attalus I of Pergamum. Fragments of his *Lives of Philosophers*, together with his *Wonderful Tales*, have survived. The latter has been edited by Keller in *Rerum Naturalium Scriptores Graeci Minores*, vol. i, 1877.

Antilibanos, *see* LIBANOS.

Antimachus (-khos), Greek epic and elegiac poet (late 5th century B.C.), author of a *Thebais*. Only fragments of his work survive. He also prepared an edition of Homer, remarkable as preceding by a century or more the work of the great Alexandrian scholars.

Antinoöpolis, *see* ANTINOÜS.

Antinoüs (-noös), a beautiful youth of Claudiopolis in Bithynia, was first a slave and afterwards the favourite of Hadrian, whom he accompanied in all his travels. Antinoüs was drowned at Besa on the Nile (there is insufficient evidence to prove the rumour of suicide) in A.D. 130. Hadrian enrolled him among the gods, built temples in his honour in Bithynia, Arcadia and Athens, and founded the city of Antinoöpolis in Egypt.

Antioch (Gk Antiokheia; mod. Antakya): 1. City of Syria, on the Orontes about 20 miles from the coast. It was founded in 300 B.C. by Seleucus I (*see also* ANTIGONEA) and named after his father Antiochus. The ground plan of the original city was modelled upon that of Alexandria (q.v.); but three other walled quarters were added (1) by Antiochus I (280–261 B.C.), (2) by Seleucus II (246–226 B.C.) and Antiochus III (223–187 B.C.), (3) by Antiochus IV (175–163 B.C.). Four miles to the west lay the pleasure resort of Daphne (q.v.) with a great temple of Pythian Apollo. Antioch passed to Rome, together with the rest of Syria, in 64 B.C., but was allowed the status of a free city (*civitas libera*). It was one of the most magnificent places in the ancient world (though frequently devastated by earthquakes), and one of the chief centres of trade. The emperors Augustus, Tiberius, Titus, Trajan, Antoninus Pius, Diocletian and Constantine helped to increase its splendour; Germanicus died and was cremated there; Commodus ordered the celebration of Olympic games. After the fall of Jerusalem (A.D. 70) Antioch became the metropolis of the infant Church, and here converts to the new faith were first called Christians. But the population as a whole, which in the 4th century A.D. numbered about 750,000, was noted throughout imperial times for its profligacy, and also for its political instability which led to constant turmoil. Excavations carried out since 1932 have brought to light substantial remains of the walls, baths, villas and other buildings, including one of the largest circuses in the world, capable of holding about 200,000 people. *See* G. Downey, *History of Antioch*, 1961.

2. City of Pisidia, founded by Seleucus I *c.* 282 B.C. Though in the heart of Asiatic territory and itself possessing a large Jewish population, it is proved by archaeological remains to have been hellenistic

in all essentials. Augustus made it a colony with the title Caesarea, and by the reign of Claudius (A.D. 41–54) it was the civil and military administrative centre of southern Galatia.

3. *See* EDESSA, I.

Antiochus (-khos). (A) Name of thirteen kings of the Seleucid dynasty:

1. *Antiochus I, Soter*, son and successor of Seleucus I, Nicator. He married his stepmother Stratonice (q.v.), succeeded his father in 280 and fell in battle against the Gauls in 261 B.C.

2. *Antiochus II, Theos*, son and successor of the preceding. His wars with Ptolemy II, Philadelphus, were concluded, towards the end of the latter's reign, by his putting away his wife Laodice and marrying Ptolemy's daughter Berenice. After Ptolemy's death (246 B.C.) he recalled Laodice, who, to revenge the insult done to her, caused Antiochus and Berenice to be murdered (246 B.C.).

3. *Antiochus III, the Great*, son of Seleucus II, Callinicus, and brother of Seleucus III, Ceraunos, whom he succeeded in 223 B.C. He carried on war against Ptolemy Philopator, King of Egypt, in order to obtain Coele-Syria, Phoenicia and Palestine, but was defeated at the battle of Raphia near Gaza, in 217. He was afterwards engaged for seven years (212–206) in an attempt to regain the eastern provinces of Asia, which had revolted during the reign of Antiochus II; but though he met with great success, he found it hopeless to effect the subjugation of the Parthian and Bactrian kingdoms, and accordingly concluded a peace with them. In 198 he conquered Palestine and Coele-Syria, which he afterwards gave as a dowry with his daughter Cleopatra upon her marriage with Ptolemy Epiphanes. Later he became involved in hostilities with the Romans, and was urged by Hannibal, who arrived at his court, to invade Italy without loss of time; but Antiochus did not follow his advice. In 192 he crossed over into Greece; and in 191 he was defeated by the Romans at Thermopylae, and compelled to return to Asia. In 190 he was again defeated by the Romans under L. Scipio, at Mt Sipylus, near Magnesia, and compelled to sue for peace, which was granted in 188, on condition of his ceding all his dominions west of Mt Taurus, and paying 15,000 Euboic talents. In order to raise the money he attacked a wealthy temple in Elymais, but was killed by the inhabitants (187).

4. *Antiochus IV, Epiphanes*, son of Antiochus III, succeeded his elder brother Seleucus IV, Philopator, in 175 B.C. He carried on war against Egypt (171–168) with great success, and he was preparing to lay siege to Alexandria in 168 when the Romans compelled him to retire. He endeavoured to root out the Jewish religion and to introduce the worship of the Greek divinities; but this attempt led to a rising of the Jewish people, under Mattathias and his heroic sons the Maccabees, which Antiochus was unable to put down. He attempted to plunder a temple in Elymais, in 164, but was repulsed, and died shortly afterwards in a state of raving madness, which the Jews and Greeks equally attributed to his sacrilegious crimes. His subjects gave him the name 'Epimanes', the Madman, as a parody of 'Epiphanes', the Glorious.

5. *Antiochus V, Eupator*, son and successor of the preceding, was

nine years old at his father's death. He was dethroned and put to death by Demetrius I, Soter (162 B.C.).

6. *Antiochus VI, Theos*, son of Alexander Balas (q.v.). He was put forward as a claimant to the crown (against Demetrius II, Nicator, q.v.) by Tryphon in 144 B.C. But he was murdered by Tryphon (142), who himself ascended the throne.

7. *Antiochus VII, Sidetes*, so called from Side in Pamphylia, where he was brought up. Younger son of Demetrius I, Soter, he succeeded Tryphon in 137, and was defeated and slain in battle by the Parthians, 129 B.C.

8. *Antiochus VIII, Grypus*, younger son of Demetrius II, Nicator, succeeded his brother Seleucus V in 125 B.C. He was at war for some years with his half-brother Antiochus IX, Cyzicenus, until 112 when they agreed to share the kingdom, Cyzicenus taking Coele-Syria and Phoenicia, Grypus the remainder of the provinces. Grypus was assassinated in 96 B.C.

9. *Antiochus IX, Cyzicenus*, so called from Cyzicus, where he was brought up. He pretended to reign as sole monarch from the death of Grypus until the following year (95), when he was killed in battle against Grypus's son Seleucus VI, Epiphanes. The last decades of Seleucid 'rule' present a picture of hopeless decadence and confusion.

10, 11, 12, 13. *Antiochus X, Eusebes*, son of the preceding. In 95 he routed Seleucus VI, who had defeated and slain his father in the same year; then he overwhelmed Seleucus's brother, who is styled *Antiochus XI* and called himself *Epiphanes*. The latter was drowned in the Orontes during his flight, and after his death his younger brother, calling himself *Dionysus* and known to history as *Antiochus XII*, took up the struggle against Eusebes, but was killed soon afterwards in battle against the Arabian king Aretas. The Syrians, worn out with civil strife, then offered the kingdom to Tigranes (q.v.) of Armenia, who united it to his own dominions and held it until his defeat by Lucullus in 69 B.C. Antiochus XIII, Asiaticus, then became King of Syria, but was deposed by Pompey in 65. The Seleucid dynasty was ended, and Syria became a Roman province.

(B) Name of four kings of Commagene (q.v.).

1. Ruled from about 69 to 34 B.C. In 64 he made an alliance with Rome; assisted Pompey with troops in 49, and was attacked by Antony in 38. Excavation of his temple-tomb, on the summit of Nimrud Dagh in eastern Turkey, began in 1953.

2. Succeeded Mithradates I, and was put to death by Augustus in 29 B.C.

3. Succeeded Mithradates II, and died in A.D. 17. Commagene then passed to Rome.

4. Surnamed Epiphanes, received back his kingdom from Caligula in 38. During the reigns of Nero and Vespasian he assisted Rome against the Parthians and the Jews respectively. In 72, however, being accused of conspiring with the Parthians, he was deprived of his crown and spent the remainder of his life in Rome. Commagene was included in the Roman province of Syria.

Antiochus (-khos) of Ascalon, founder of the fifth Academy and teacher of Cicero at Athens (79 B.C.).

Antiochus (-khos) of Syracuse, Greek historian, *fl. c.* 420 B.C. His *History of Sicily* down to 424 was used by Thucydides, and a work on the Greek colonization of Italy is quoted by Strabo. Some fragments of both survive.

Antiopē: 1. Sister of Hippolyte (q.v.) and wife of Theseus (q.v.), to whom she bore Hippolytus (q.v.).

2. Daughter of Nycteus and wife of Polydorus, King of Thebes (*see* THEBAN LEGEND, 1). Being left a widow soon after bearing Labdacus (q.v.), she was carried off by Epopeus, King of Sicyon. Nycteus gave chase but was slain in battle. The pursuit was taken up by his brother Lycus, who killed Epopeus and brought back Antiope to Thebes, where, together with his wife Dirce, he subjected her to brutal treatment. Meanwhile, however, Antiope had had intercourse with Zeus, who had come in the form of a satyr. To him she had born twin sons, Amphion (q.v.) and Zethus, who afterwards went to Thebes, where Lycus was ruling as regent for his great-grandnephew Laius. They avenged their mother by slaying both Lycus and Dirce, the latter of whom they tied to the horns of a maddened bull which tore her to pieces.

Antipas, *see* HEROD ANTIPAS.

Antipater: 1. A Macedonian officer in the service of Philip II and Alexander the Great, was left by Alexander regent of Macedonia when he departed for Asia (334 B.C.). After the monarch's death he defeated the allied Greeks at Crannon (*see* LAMIAN WAR), and died in 319, having appointed Polysperchon (q.v.) regent for Philip Arrhidaeus and Alexander Aegus. His son was Cassander (q.v.).

2. Second son of Cassander by Thessalonica, and grandson of the preceding. He and his brother Alexander quarrelled for the kingdom of Macedonia; but Demetrius I, Poliorcetes, obtained the throne and put them both to death (294 B.C.).

3. Father of Herod the Great, son of an Idumaean nobleman of the same name. He espoused the cause of Hyrcanus II against the latter's brother Aristobulus, was appointed procurator of Judaea by Caesar in 47 and died by poison in 43 B.C.

4. Eldest son of Herod the Great. He conspired against his father's life, and was executed five days before Herod's death (4 B.C.).

Antipater, Lucius Caelius, Roman historian of the 2nd century B.C., author of *Annales* which contained a valuable account of the second Punic war.

Antipater of Sidon (*fl. c.* 130 B.C.), Greek epigrammatist, represented by several epigrams in the Greek Anthology (*see* ANTHOLOGY, THE GREEK) and by another discovered more recently in a papyrus at Oxyrhynchus.

Antipater of Tarsus, Stoic philosopher of the 2nd century B.C., successor of Diogenes the Babylonian as head of the Stoa, and teacher of Panaetius (q.v.).

Antiphanēs, Greek poet of the Middle Comedy, of which, together with Alexis (q.v.), he was the most distinguished representative. He was a native of Rhodes, and died at Athens in 306 B.C. Many fragments of numerous comedies have been preserved. *See* Koch, *Comicorum Atticorum Fragmenta,* vol. ii, 1884.

Antiphatēs, king of the Laestrygones (q.v.) at the time of Odysseus's visit to that people.

Antiphilus (-os), Greek painter of the 4th century B.C. He was a rival of Apelles, and worked, as did the latter, for Alexander the Great.

Antiphōn, earliest of the ten Attic Orators (q.v.), born at Rhamnus in 480 B.C. He belonged to the oligarchical party at Athens, and played a leading part in the establishment of the Four Hundred (411 B.C.). On the restoration of the democracy he was accused of treason, condemned and executed. Of his fifteen surviving speeches only three were written for actual litigants; the remainder are mere exercises on imaginary lawsuits. *See* the edition by F. Blass, 1881; R. C. Jebb, *Attic Orators,* 1888.

Antisthenēs, Greek philosopher, founder of the Cynic school, born at Athens in 444 B.C. He served in the Peloponnesian war at the age of eighteen, and afterwards became a disciple of Socrates, with whom he remained until the latter's death in 399 B.C. Some time later he began to teach in the Cynosarges (q.v.), where Diogenes of Sinope (*see* DIOGENES, 2) was among his pupils. Antisthenes made the sovereign good to consist in virtue; and virtue, for him, consisted in contempt of riches, honours and enjoyment. It is said that while still a disciple of Socrates he adopted the beggar's wallet and staff as badges of philosophy, and that the master said: 'O Antisthenes, I see your pride through the holes in your cloak!' He died in 365 B.C. *See* R. Dudley, *A History of Cynicism,* 1937.

Antium (mod. Porto d'Anzio), town of Latium, 33 miles south of Rome; the original Volscian town, of which the fortifications can still be traced, stood at a somewhat higher level. Antium was taken by the Romans in 338 B.C.; six of its ships were captured, and their beaks (*rostra*) were used to decorate the orator's tribune (hence our word 'rostrum') in the Forum Romanum. From the 1st century B.C. the town was a favourite resort of the Roman aristocracy, and there are remains of several villas. The emperors Caligula and Nero were born here; and the latter not only established a colony of veteran soldiers, but also built a new harbour of which the moles survive. In the ruins of what is believed to have been Nero's villa was discovered the Apollo Belvedere (*see* APOLLO); and excavation of another building revealed the only known example of a pre-Julian calendar (*see* JULIAN CALENDAR), which was found painted on a wall.

Antonia: 1. Eldest daughter of Mark Antony by Octavia (*see* OCTAVIA, 1) and wife of L. Domitius Ahenobarbus, whose son, Cn. Domitius Ahenobarbus, was father of the emperor Nero.

2. Younger sister of the preceding. Married to Livius Drusus Claudianus (brother of the emperor Tiberius), she became the mother of Germanicus, Livia and Claudius. She died in A.D. 37.

3. Daughter of the emperor Claudius. She was put to death by Nero in A.D. 66 for having refused to marry him.

Antonine Itinerary, a register of stations and distances from Rome along the imperial roads and sea routes. The original edition may have been due to the emperor Caracalla (211–17), but the extant portion is believed to date from the reign of Diocletian (284–305). *See* edition by O. Cuntz in *Itineraria Romana,* vol. i, 1929.

Antonine Wall, earthen rampart and ditch, built *c.* A.D. 142 to strengthen the line of forts already laid down by Agricola (q.v.; *see also* BRITAIN). The mound (*vallum*) ran from Bo'ness on the Forth to West Kilpatrick on the Clyde, a distance of about 37 English miles. The width of the mound and ditch seems to have been about 25 yards; its depth from the top of the mound to the bottom of the ditch has been variously estimated at between 40 feet and 20 feet. There were between ten and twenty forts, and a military road ran at the back of the *vallum*. *See* A. S. Robertson, *The Antonine Wall,* 1963.

Antoninus Pius, Roman emperor A.D. 138–61. His full name was Titus Aurelius Fulvus Boionus Arrius Antoninus. He was born near Lanuvium in A.D. 86, the son of Aurelius Fulvus, whose family originated at Nemausus in Gaul. He served as consul in 120, and afterwards as governor of Asia. On 25th February 138 he was adopted by Hadrian as his successor, being himself obliged at the same time to adopt M. Annius Verus and L. Aelius Verus (afterwards the emperors Marcus Aurelius and L. Aelius Verus, qq.v.). Antoninus succeeded a few months later, and was surnamed Pius, 'dutifully affectionate', after he had appeared before the senate to ask that divine honours be conferred upon Hadrian. He was one of the best princes ever to mount a throne; and if his reign is almost a blank in history, that is due to the virtual suspension, if only for a time, of war and violence. All his thoughts and energies were devoted to the welfare and happiness of his subjects: they found expression in more humane legal reforms and in his care of orphans, as well as in his promotion of arts and sciences, in his buildings and in his improvement of the public services. He died at Lorium. *See* E. E. Bryant, *The Reign of Antoninus Pius,* 1895.

Antonius, Gaius: 1. Younger son of the orator (*see* ANTONIUS, MARCUS, 1) and uncle of Mark Antony, colleague of Cicero in the praetorship (66) and consulship (63). Though a partisan of Catiline, he deserted him when Cicero offered to resign the province of Macedonia in his (Antonius's) favour. Appointed to lead an army against Catiline, he was unwilling, when the day of action came, to command against his old friend. He therefore entrusted conduct of the battle to his legate M. Petreius (62 B.C.). Antonius then went to his province, plundered it and, on his return to Rome (59), was accused both of taking part in Catiline's conspiracy and of extortion in Macedonia. He was defended by Cicero, but was condemned and retired to the island of Cephallenia. Recalled, probably by Caesar, he was in Rome at the beginning of 41 B.C.

2. Brother of Mark Antony (*see* ANTONIUS, MARCUS, 3), served Caesar during the civil war, and was governor of Macedonia in 44 B.C. In 43 he fell into the hands of M. Junius Brutus, who put him to death in the following year, to revenge the murder of Cicero.

Antonius, Iullus, younger son of Mark Antony (*see* ANTONIUS, MARCUS, 3) by Fulvia (q.v.), was brought up by his stepmother Octavia at Rome, and received great marks of favour from Augustus. He was consul in 10 B.C., but was put to death eight years later because of his adultery with the emperor's daughter Julia (*see* JULIA, 5).

Antonius, Lucius, youngest brother of Mark Antony (*see* ANTONIUS,

MARCUS, 3), was consul in 41 B.C., when he made war upon Octavian at the instigation of his sister-in-law Fulvia (q.v.). He occupied Perusia, but surrendered in the following year and was granted his life by Octavian.

Antonius, Marcus: 1. Roman orator and magistrate, born 143 B.C.; quaestor, 113; praetor, 102, when he fought against the Cilician pirates; consul, 99; and censor 97 B.C. A member of Sulla's party, he was put to death when Marius and Cinna (qq.v.) entered Rome in 87 B.C. Cicero describes Antonius and L. Licinius Crassus as the most distinguished orators of their age, and introduces Antonius as one of the speakers in his *De Oratore*.

2. Surnamed Creticus, elder son of the preceding. As praetor in 74 B.C. he was given command against the Cilician pirates. His conduct of operations was an egregious failure, and on his death soon afterwards he was given the derisive surname Creticus.

3. Commonly known as MARK ANTONY, eldest son of the preceding by Julia, sister of L. Julius Caesar (consul 64 B.C.), was born in 83 B.C. His father died while he was young, and he was brought up in the house of his stepfather, P. Cornelius Lentulus Sura (q.v.). In 57 he served with distinction under Aulus Gabinius in Syria. In 54 he joined Caesar in Gaul, was elected quaestor through Caesar's influence, and was henceforth one of his most trusted officers and devoted adherents. As tribune of the plebs in 49, he fled to Caesar's camp in Cisalpine Gaul, after putting his veto on the senatorial decree which attempted to deprive Caesar of his command. Antony commanded the left wing at Pharsalus. In 44 he was consul with Caesar, and offered him the crown at the festival of Lupercalia. After Caesar's murder, on 15th March in that year, Antony entertained hopes of succeeding to his power. He pronounced the funeral oration, read Caesar's will to the people and also obtained possession of his papers and private property. [From this point the article should be read in conjunction with AUGUSTUS.] He found, however, a new and unexpected rival in the person of Gaius Julius Caesar Octavianus (Octavian), Caesar's great-nephew and adoptive son, who at first joined the senate in order to crush Antony. Towards the end of the year Antony set out for Cisalpine Gaul, which had been given him by the people; but Decimus Junius Brutus, to whom it had been promised by Caesar, threw himself into Mutina and was there besieged by Antony. The senate declared Antony a public enemy, and entrusted to Octavian the conduct of operations against him. Antony was defeated at Mutina in April 43, and was obliged to cross the Alps; but both consuls, Hirtius and Pansa, were killed in the battle, and the senate now began to show its jealousy of Octavian. Meanwhile Antony had been joined by Lepidus with a formidable army. Octavian therefore was reconciled to Antony, and the three men formed what is known as the Second Triumvirate, which was to last for five years. The enemies of each were proscribed, and among the most illustrious victims was Cicero, who had been detested by Antony since the execution of Lentulus in 63, and who had given the triumvir mortal offence by the *Philippic* orations. In 42 Antony and Octavian crushed the republican party at the battle of Philippi, in which Brutus and Cassius fell.

Antony then went to Asia, which he had received as his share of the Roman world. There, in Cilicia, he met Cleopatra (*see* CLEOPATRA, 2), and followed her to Egypt. In the following year Antony's wife Fulvia (q.v.) and his brother Lucius (*see* ANTONIUS, LUCIUS) declared war on Octavian in Italy. Antony prepared to assist his relatives; but before he could reach home the war was ended by the surrender of Lucius at Perusia in the first days of 40 B.C. The opportune death of Fulvia at this time facilitated the reconciliation of Antony and Octavian, which was cemented by the former's marriage with Octavia, sister of Octavian. Antony remained in Italy until 39, when the triumvirs made peace with Sextus Pompeius. He then returned to the East, where his general, P. Ventidius Bassus, inflicted a twofold defeat upon the Parthians (39 and 38 B.C.). Antony made one more journey to Italy—in 37 B.C. when the triumvirate was renewed for another five years. Back in Egypt, he sent Octavia to Italy and surrendered himself wholly to the charms of Cleopatra. In 36 he invaded Parthia, but was obliged to retreat. He was more successful in his invasion of Armenia (34), when he took prisoner the Armenian king Artavasdes (*see* ARTAVASDES, 1) and carried him to Alexandria. Antony now laid aside altogether the character of a Roman citizen, and assumed that of an oriental despot. His conduct, and the unbounded influence which Cleopatra had acquired over him, not to mention his formal repudiation of Octavia in 32, alienated many of his friends and supporters. Octavian saw that the time had come to settle the issue once and for all by crushing his rival. This was achieved at the naval battle of Actium (q.v.; *see also* AGRIPPA, MARCUS VIPSANIUS), 2nd September 31 B.C. Antony and Cleopatra fled to Alexandria, where he put an end to his own life when Octavian besieged the city (30 B.C.).

4. Elder son of the preceding by Fulvia (q.v.), was executed by order of Octavian after his father's suicide in 30 B.C.

Antony, Mark, *see* ANTONIUS, MARCUS, 3.

Anubis, an Egyptian deity worshipped in the form of a man with a jackal's head. Because he was the conductor of the dead, the Greeks identified him with Hermes. His worship was introduced at Rome in the late republican period.

Anytus (-utos), one of the democratic leaders at Athens, who, together with Thrasybulus, overthrew the thirty Tyrants (404 B.C.). Later he was the moving spirit in the prosecution of Socrates (399).

Aōnia, district of Boeotia. Among its natural features were the mountains of Helicon and Cithaeron (qq.v.), which made it sacred to the Muses.

Aornos, *see* AVERNUS.

Apamea (-eia): 1. City of Syria in the Orontes valley, founded by Seleucus I, who named it after his wife Apama. Here was a treasury and a stud farm of the Seleucid kings.

2. City of Phrygia near the headwaters of the Marsyas, founded by Antiochus I and called after his mother (*see* CELAENAE). Until the 3rd century A.D. it was important both as a strategic point and as a centre of trade. It was subsequently included in the kingdom of Pergamum, which passed to Rome in 133 B.C. (*see* ATTALUS III; PERGAMUM).

Apella, the Spartan popular assembly. It consisted of all male citizens over the age of thirty years. It met once a month, at first under the presidency of the kings, but later under that of the Ephors (*see* EPHOR). It could consider only such matters as were submitted to it by the Gerousia or the Ephors, merely voting upon questions debated in its hearing by them.

Apellēs, Greek painter of the 4th century B.C. A native of Ionia, he worked under Pamphilus in the famous Sicyonian school and became court painter to Alexander the Great. His improvements in technique and his sureness of line (which he practised every day) made him the greatest painter of antiquity. Among his most famous pictures were the portrait of Alexander wielding a thunderbolt, Aphrodite rising from the sea, the procession of the high priest of Artemis at Ephesus and an allegorical work entitled 'Calumny'.

Apellicon (-kōn), a native of Teos and a philosopher of the Peripatetic school at Athens. His valuable library, which included the originals of the works of Aristotle and Theophrastus, was taken to Rome by Sulla (84 B.C.).

Apenninus Mons, the Apennines, range of mountains (740 miles) forming the 'backbone' of Italy. A continuation of the Alpes Maritimae (*see* ALPES) it begins about five miles west of Savo (mod. Savona) and gives rise to most of the rivers of central and southern Italy. The highest peak is the Gran Sasso (9,560 feet). In Roman times there were large forests of pine, oak and beech; the fauna included wolves, bears and wild goats. Brigandage was common. The range, having traversed the whole peninsula from north to south, continues through Sicily, and thence by a line of submarine elevations to the mountains of North Africa.

Aper, praetorian prefect, *see* ARRIUS APER.

Aphaea (-aia), the indigenous goddess of Aegina (q.v.), identified by Pausanias with Britomartis (q.v.).

Aphidnae (-nai), an Attic deme not far from Decelea (q.v.). Here Theseus concealed Helen from her brothers Castor and Polydeuces.

Aphroditē, Greek goddess of love, beauty and fertility; frequently worshipped as the patroness of seafarers and of war. She probably reached Greece from Cyprus, a common meeting place of East and West; for she is undoubtedly related to the Semitic Ishtar and Astarte, and seems to have absorbed certain traits of pre-hellenic divinities (e.g. Ariadne). In classical Rome Aphrodite was identified with Venus. In the *Iliad* she is represented as the daughter of Zeus and Dione; but later poets frequently relate that she was sprung from the foam of the sea (*see* TITANS), whence they derive her name. She was the wife of Hephaestus; but she proved faithless, and was in love with Ares, the god of war. She also loved the gods Dionysus, Hermes and Poseidon, and the mortals Anchises and Adonis. She surpassed all the other goddesses in beauty, and hence received the prize of beauty from Paris. She likewise had the power of granting beauty and invincible charms to others, and whoever wore her magic girdle immediately became an object of love and desire. In the vegetable kingdom the myrtle, rose, apple, poppy, etc., were sacred to her. The animals sacred to her, which are often mentioned as drawing her chariot or serving as her messengers, are the sparrow, the dove, the swan and the swallow. She is generally represented in works of art with her son Eros. The principal places of her worship in Greece were the islands of Cyprus and Cythera. Her worship combined, with hellenic conceptions, many features of Eastern origin: she was often associated with Adonis. The most famous of her statues in ancient times was that by Praxitiles (copy at Munich), and the Melos statue, the original of which is at the Louvre. The painting by Apelles (q.v.) was renowned.

Apicius, name of three celebrated gluttons. The first lived early in the 1st century B.C. The second, M. Gabius Apicius, lived in the reign of Tiberius. Having squandered a fortune on the pleasures of the table he hanged himself. The third was a contemporary of Trajan, who, during his Parthian campaign (A.D. 115–16), received from Apicius some fresh oysters preserved by a skilful process of his own. The *De re coquinaria*, a work on cookery ascribed to Apicius, is much later. One of its recipes nearly killed Mme Dacier.

Apiōn (1st century A.D.), Greek grammarian and commentator on Homer, born in Libya. While head of the school at Alexandria he sent a deputation to the emperor Caligula complaining of the Jews. These complaints were opposed by the Jewish delegation led by Philo. They were also embodied in several works, to which Josephus replied (*Contra Apionem*). Apion later settled in Rome and taught rhetoric; he died in the reign of Claudius. His (lost) *Aegyptiaca* was the origin of the story of Androclus (q.v.).

Apollo (Gk Apollōn), in classical mythology, the son of Zeus and Leto; born with his twin sister Artemis in the island of Delos, whither Leto had fled from the jealousy of Hera. He stands for all in Greek character and life of which we think as civilization. Yet all scholars are agreed that in his origin Apollo is non-hellenic. Whence he was derived is uncertain: two main groups of scholars hold widely differing views. One, supported by Wilamowitz and Nilsson, maintain that he came from the interior of Asia Minor; they believe it probable that he may have derived from Apulunas, the Hittite gate god identified in 1936 by Professor Hrozny. Others, especially A. B. Cook and H. J. Rose, affirm that Apollo was originally a god of shepherds in the wild regions of the north, and they see in this character the origin of his office as patron of archery, music and medicine; his titles of *Nomius* (herdsman), *Lycaeus* (protector against wolves), *Sminthius* (guardian of farmers against mice). The last two, however, may refer to Lycia and Sminthia, both places of Apollo's worship. Whatever view is adopted, it must be remembered that the manifold characteristics of the classical god have been derived from many sources. The most striking and most important aspect of Apollo is his interest in all matters affecting law and order, as well in the physical and social as in the intellectual and moral spheres. He presides not only over the arts and all that manifests the well-springs of a man's conduct, but also over much of his public activity, such as the establishment of cities, constitutions, codes of law and their interpretation. The central function of Apollo's dominion in the realm of law is his jurisdiction in cases of homicide. Homicide involved the violation of social order and a divinely sanctioned code, and therefore required punishment at the hands of the divine archer. But it also involved pollution, which might extend to the whole community, through contact with the dead and their dark powers. It was Apollo *Catharsius* who granted purification; and from this office there were perhaps derived other titles of the god: *Apotropaeus*, protector of man and beast against every kind of harm, and *Agyieus*, guardian of gates. It is certain that in his double character of judge and ritual purifier Apollo forms a link between the hellenic religion and the more ancient cult of the chthonian gods. Many of his legislative and ritual powers were exercised through his oracles, especially at Delphi (q.v.). As Phoebus Apollo he was identified with the Sun in hellenistic and Roman imperial times, but on no good evidence.

The Romans made their first contact with Apollo partly through the Etruscans and partly through the Greek states of southern Italy. There was a temple of Apollo at Rome as early as 432, and in 212 B.C. the *Ludi Apollinares* were instituted in his honour. In republican times he was venerated chiefly as a god of healing and prophecy; but his status was greatly enhanced by the devotion of Augustus who erected magnificent temples of Apollo at Actium and on the Palatine. The famous statue, known as the Apollo Belvedere, in the Vatican does not represent the Greek conception in the strictly classical age; the latter is better illustrated by more ancient figures in the British Museum and elsewhere.

Apollodorus (-dōros): 1. Athenian painter, *fl.* 420 B.C., the first to depict light and shade.

2. A native of Carystus, in Euboea, and poet of the New Comedy. Fragments of his work survive.

3. Athenian grammarian and mythographer of the 2nd century B.C. The *Bibliothēkē* attributed to him (*see* text and translation by J. G. Frazer, Loeb Library) belongs probably to the early Christian era.

4. A native of Damascus; architect of Trajan's Forum, the Basilica Ulpiana, Hadrian's temple of Venus and Rome (all in the imperial capital), and the triumphal arch in honour of Trajan at Ancona (q.v.). His work *On Engines of War* has survived. Banished by Hadrian in 129 and later put to death.

Apollonia: 1. City of Illyria on the right bank of the Aoüs, founded by Corinthians and Corcyreans; important as a link between Brundisium and northern Greece, and subsequently as a terminus of the Via Egnatia (*see* EGNATIA, VIA). Towards the end of the 1st century B.C. Apollonia became a noted centre of learning, and here Octavian was studying when news reached him of Caesar's murder.

2. (Mod. Sizeboli), also called Apollonia Pontica, city of Thrace on the Euxine (Black Sea), colonized from Miletus. The colossal statue of Apollo by Calamis (q.v.) was removed to Rome by Lucullus in 72 B.C.

3. (Mod. Marsa Susa), town of Cyrenaica (q.v.) and harbour of Cyrene (q.v.), 12 miles north-east of the latter. It was the birth-place of Eratosthenes (q.v.).

Apollonius (-ōnios): 1. Surnamed Dyscolus, 'crabbed', Alexandrian grammarian of the 2nd century A.D., founder of scientific grammar. His four works, *On Syntax*, *On Pronouns*, *On conjunctions* and *On Adverbs* survive. The first was edited by Bekker in 1817, the other three by Schneider in 1878.

2. Surnamed Molon, a native of Alabanda, in Caria, and a rhetorician who taught at Rhodes. He went to Rome as an ambassador from the Rhodians in 81 B.C., and was heard by Cicero (q.v.), who afterwards attended his lectures at Rhodes (78 B.C.). He must be distinguished from his namesake, also of Alabanda, a rhetorician of the late 1st century B.C., among whose pupils was Mark Antony.

3. A native of Perga in Pamphylia (c. 265–190 B.C.), one of the greatest mathematicians of antiquity, commonly called 'the great geometer'. He was educated at Alexandria under the successors of Euclid (q.v.). Seven of the eight books of his *Conics* survive, four in Greek and three in an Arabic translation. *See* the edition by Sir T. Heath, 1896.

4. Surnamed the Rhodian (c. 295–c. 230 B.C.), Greek poet and grammarian, born at Alexandria. After studying under Callimachus (q.v.), with whom he afterwards quarrelled, Apollonius taught rhetoric at Rhodes with so much success that the Rhodians honoured him with their franchise, whence his surname 'the Rhodian'. After the death of Zenodotus (q.v.) he returned to Alexandria and succeeded him as head of the Library. *The Argonautica* of Apollonius, an epic poem on the adventures of the Argonauts (q.v.), is edited with a translation by R. C. Seaton in the Loeb Library.

5. Surnamed the Sophist, Alexandrian grammarian of the late 1st century A.D. His *Homeric Lexicon*, unique of its kind, has been edited by I. Bekker, 1833.

6. A native of Tralles in Caria, Greek sculptor of the 2nd century B.C. He and his brother Tauriscus executed the marble group known as the Farnese Bull, which represents Amphion and Zethus tying Dirce (q.v.) to the bull.

7. A native of Tyana in Cappadocia, neo-Pythagorean philosopher and occultist of the 1st century A.D. He obtained great influence by pretending to miraculous powers, which his biographer, Philostratus (*see* PHILOSTRATUS), attempted to offset against those of Christ. After travelling extensively he settled at Ephesus, where he opened a school, and died in 97.

Appia, Via, most famous of the Roman roads, begun in 312 B.C. by the censor Appius Claudius Caecus to consolidate the conquest of Samnite territory. This first stretch ran from the Porta Capena to Capua (132 miles), but by 244 B.C. the road had been extended to Beneventum, Venusia, Tarentum and Brundisium (234 miles). The original road was gravelled, but in 298 B.C. a paved footpath was laid from the starting-point to the temple of Mars (1 mile); three years later the road itself was paved from this temple to Bovillae; and the first mile was similarly treated in 191 B.C. The 19-mile stretch from Forum Appii (q.v.) through the Pomptine marshes (*see* POMPTINAE PALUDES) was paved, and its bridges repaired, by Nerva and Trajan. Under Trajan also the stretch between Beneventum and Brundisium (202 miles) was virtually superseded by the Via Traiana, which ran through Aequum Tuticum, Aecae, Herdoniae, Canusium, Barium and Gnatia. *See* EGNATIA, VIA.

Appianus (-os), commonly called Appian, Roman historian of the 2nd century A.D.; born at Alexandria. He wrote in Greek a history of

Rome (*Rhomaika*) in twenty-four books, of which only parts have survived. Though his style is clear and he supplies valuable information about the civil wars, he possesses few merits as an historian. *See* the edition with translation by H. White, 4 vols. (Loeb Library), 1912–13.

Appuleius, *see* APULEIUS.

Apsyrtus (Apsurtos), son of Aeëtes and brother of Medea, *see* JASON AND MEDEA.

Apuleius or **Appuleius, Lucius,** Platonic philosopher and rhetorician, born at Madaura in north Africa *c*. A.D. 124. Educated at Carthage and Athens, he travelled extensively in the East, in order to become an initiate of religious mysteries, and then practised for some time as an advocate at Rome. After returning to Africa he married a rich widow, Aemilia Pudentilla, whose family charged him with having won her by magic (*see* SABRATHA). His defence survives: *Apologia* or *De Magia* (ed. H. E. Butler and A. S. Owen, 1914). He was acquitted, and devoted the remainder of his life to philosophy and literature. By far the most important of his other works is *Metamorphoses* or *The Golden Ass*, an extremely entertaining story which includes the famous episode of Cupid and Psyche. With the exception of Petronius's (incomplete) *Satyricon*, it is the only surviving specimen of a Latin novel. *See* the edition, with translation by W. Aldington (revised by S. Gaselee), in the Loeb Library, 1915, and the unsurpassed version by Robert Graves (Penguin Classics), 1950.

Apulia, district of Italy, bounded east by the Adriatic, south-east by Calabria and the Tarentine Gulf, south and west by Lucania and Samnium. The most important towns were Teate (afterwards called Teanum Apulum), Luceria, and Canusium. The principal roads were the Via Appia and Via Traiana (*see* APPIA, VIA), and a coastal highway which ran from near Larinum to Barium, the chief port of Apulia. Together with Calabria, Apulia formed the second region of Augustus (*see* ITALIA). The country was famous for its wool, supporting at one time a million sheep. The shepherds were a constant source of trouble during the 2nd century B.C., and in 185 seven thousand of them were condemned to death.

Aquae Cutiliae, a mineral spring nine miles east of Reate. The nearby lake, which is called by classical writers the navel (*umbilicus*) of Italy, was celebrated for its floating islands. These were formed by the partial petrifaction of plants by mineral substances. The Roman bath was probably used by Vespasian and Titus, who both died at Aquae Cutiliae.

Aquae Sextiae (mod. Aix-en-Provence), a Roman colony in Provincia (afterwards called Gallia Narbonensis; *see* GALLIA). It was founded by Sextius Calvinus in 123–122 B.C. Its mineral waters were long celebrated. Near here, in 102 B.C., Marius (q.v.) defeated the Teutoni (q.v.). *See* SALYES.

Aquae Sulis (mod. Bath), Roman town of Britain, covering an area of only 25 acres but famous from the 1st century A.D. on account of its hot springs. There are splendid remains of the great bath, and fragments have been preserved from the temple of Sul Minerva.

Aqueducts, Greek and Roman. An aqueduct is an artificial channel for the conveyance of water, though the word is now generally applied to the bridge whereby such a channel is carried across a valley. The Greek aqueducts were in the form of tunnels. The two most remarkable are that which drained Lake Copais in Boeotia (it was driven from sixteen shafts) and that which the engineer Eupalinus constructed for Polycrates at Samos (q.v.). This latter, 8 feet by 8 feet in section, was driven clean through a hill for a distance of 4,200 feet. At Athens there were less spectacular works, until the reign of Hadrian, when a new tunnel, lined with brick and masonry, was constructed over a distance of 15 miles, with side galleries, etc., to tap intermediate sources.

The earliest Roman aqueduct, the Aqua Appia, was constructed in 312 B.C. by Appius Claudius Caecus, who also built the Via Appia. It consisted of a covered conduit, just over 10 miles in length, and entered the city on its eastern side. Other works of a similar nature soon followed. The first to be carried part of its length on arches was the Aqua Marcia (144 B.C.), which ran for about six and a half miles on masonry arches as it approached the city. By the end of the republic Rome was supplied by six aqueducts, and at the close of the 1st century by nine, as follows: Appia (312 B.C.), Anio Vetus (272 B.C.), Marcia (144 B.C.), Tepula (125 B.C.), Julia (33 B.C.), Virgo (19 B.C.), Alsietina (reign of Augustus), Claudia (A.D. 47) and Anio Novus (A.D. 52). For particulars of upkeep, etc., *see* the work of Frontinus (q.v.): *De Aqueductibus Urbis Romae*.

Some magnificent aqueducts were constructed in the provinces, particularly at Nemausus (Nîmes) and Segovia. They are remarkable for the wonderful bridges on which they were carried. The former, now called the Pont du Gard, rises to a height of 158 feet: it has three tiers of arches, the lowest 65 feet above the river, the second 65 feet above the first, and the third 28 feet above the second. It was built by M. Vipsanius Agrippa (q.v.) 16 B.C. The aqueduct bridge at Segovia is 2,700 feet long and 102 feet high; it has 109 arches in two tiers. *See* E. B. von Deman, *The Building of the Roman Aqueducts*, 1934; T. Ashby, *The Aqueducts of Ancient Rome*, 1935.

Aquileia, city founded by Rome in 181 B.C. as a bulwark against the northern barbarians. It was situated at the head of the Adriatic, six miles from the sea and 22 miles west-north-west of Tergeste; a canal led to the Adriatic at Grado where part of the Roman fleet was stationed. A place of great strategic importance, Aquileia was also a commercial centre: terminus of the Via Popilia, it was the starting-point of other roads to Illyria, Pannonia and Noricum. In imperial times its military associations made it one of the principal seats of Mithraism (*see* MITHRAS). In the reign of Hadrian its population numbered about half a million.

Aquincum, Roman town near modern Budapest; by A.D. 200 it was capital of Lower Pannonia. Extensive ruins have been excavated.

Aquinum (mod. Aquino), town of Latium on the Via Latina, six miles west of Casinum. Juvenal was probably born here, and it was the birth-place of Pescennius Niger.

Aquitania, country of the Aquitani, between the Garonne and the Pyrenees. Under Augustus it included the whole of Gaul south-west of the Loire and the Allier. In the 3rd century A.D. the whole area was divided into three: *Aquitania Prima, Secunda* and *Tertia. See* E. Desjardins, *Géographie historique et administrative de la Gaule romaine,* 1893.

Arabia. Classical writers from the 1st century A.D. divided Arabia as follows, according to political conditions then prevailing:

1. *Arabia Petraea* included the peninsula of Sinai and the country immediately north and north-east thereof. The chief city was Petra (q.v.). *See also* NABATAEI. Arabia Petraea was made a Roman province by Trajan (A.D. 106).

2. *Arabia Deserta* consisted of the Syrian desert and adjoining region of the Arabian peninsula. It was subject to Persia.

3. *Arabia Felix,* those parts of the Arabian peninsula not included in the above. The name was derived from the very fertile belt of land on the Red Sea coast and applied also to the interior by authors who were ignorant of its true nature.

Arachne (-khnē), 'spider', a Lydian girl, daughter of Idmon of Colophon, a famous dyer in purple. Arachne excelled in the art of weaving, and was so proud of her talent that she challenged Athena to compete with her. She produced a piece of cloth in which the amours of the gods were woven; but Athena, unable to find fault with it, tore the work to shreds. Arachne, in despair, hanged herself; Athena loosened the rope and saved her life, but the rope was changed into a cobweb and Arachne herself into a spider.

Aratus (-os), Greek general and statesman, born at Sicyon in 271 B.C., son of Clemias. His father was murdered when he was a child, and Aratus was brought up at Argos. In 251 he freed Sicyon from tyranny and brought it into the Achaean League (q.v.), of which he then became, as it were, the head and heart, and of which he was chosen general in alternate years. In 243 he took Corinth from Antigonus II, Gonatas, and the accession to the League of Megalopolis (234) and Argos (228) virtually freed the whole of Peloponnesus from Macedonian rule. At this stage, however, Aratus called in Antigonus Doson against his rival Cleomenes III of Sparta. Cleomenes was defeated at Sellasia (222), but the league itself thereby became subject to Macedonia. Aratus subsequently sought help from Philip V against the Aetolians; but dissensions arose between them, and Aratus died by poison in 213 B.C.

Aratus (-os) **of Soli,** in Cilicia, Greek didactic poet, born *c.* 315 B.C. He spent much of his life at the courts of Antigonus II, Gonatas, and Antiochus I, Soter, and died in Macedonia *c.* 245 B.C. His extant astronomical poem *Phaenomena,* criticized by Hipparchus, was a great favourite at Rome, where it was translated by Cicero. *See* the text and English translation by G. R. Mair (Loeb Library), 1921.

Arausio (mod. Orange), town of Gallia Transalpina, where the combined forces of the consul Maximus and the proconsul Q. Servilius Caepio (q.v.) were defeated by the Cimbri (q.v.) in 105 B.C. It was this disaster which inspired the military reforms of Marius (q.v.).

Arbela (mod. Erbil), *see* GAUGAMELA.

Arcadia (Ark-), central plateau of Peloponnesus, surrounded by high mountains and split up by subsidiary ranges. The inhabitants were mostly shepherds and hunters; they worshipped Pan and other nature-gods. Though difficult of access, the country was subjugated by Sparta in the 6th century B.C. After the battle of Leuctra (371 B.C.) the cities of Arcadia formed a league with Megalopolis (q.v.) as its capital. But this movement was rendered fruitless by a Spartan victory in 368 and a continuation of age-old feuds between the member-states, until Arcadia became part of the Roman province of Achaea in 146 B.C.

Arcesilaus (-kēsilaos), Greek philosopher, born at Pitane in Aeolis, 316 B.C. In 266 he succeeded Crates (*see* CRATES, 2) and founded the second or Middle Academy (*see* ACADEMY). He died in 241 B.C. The absolute scepticism of Arcesilaus, none of whose writings survive, is summed up in the cheerless phrase: 'We know nothing, not even our own ignorance.'

Archelaus (-khelaos): 1. King of Macedonia. An illegitimate son of Perdiccas II, he obtained the throne in 413 B.C. by the assassination of his half-brother and other relatives. Archelaus was a phil-hellene: his palace at Pella was adorned with paintings by Zeuxis, and Euripides, Agathon and others distinguished in the world of Greek letters resided at his court. His death in 399 B.C. was followed by ten years of anarchy, which ended in 389 with the accession of Amyntas II (q.v.).

2. General of Mithradates, by birth a Cappadocian; defeated by Sulla (q.v.) at Chaeronea and Orchomenus in Boeotia (86 B.C.). Five years later he deserted to Rome.

3. Son of the preceding, raised by Pompey to the priesthood of Comana (q.v.) in Pontus or Cappadocia (53 B.C.). In 56 he became ruler of Egypt as a result of his marriage with Berenice, daughter of Ptolemy XI, Auletes, who, after the expulsion of her father, had obtained the sovereignty. But in the following year he was defeated in battle and slain by Aulus Gabinius, who restored Ptolemy to the throne.

4. Son of the preceding and his successor in the priesthood of Comana, of which dignity, however, he was deprived by Caesar in 47 B.C.

5. Son of the preceding, received from Antony the kingdom of Cappadocia (41 or 34 B.C.), a favour for which he was indebted to the charms of his mother Glaphyra. He was deprived of his kingdom by Tiberius in A.D. 17, when Cappadocia was made a Roman province.

6. Son and successor of Herod the Great, received from Augustus Judaea, Samaria and Ituraea with the title of Ethnarch. In consequence of his tyrannical government, the same emperor banished him, in A.D. 7, to Vienna in Gaul, where he died.

7. Greek philosopher of the Ionian school, a native of Miletus or of Athens, and a pupil of Anaxagoras (q.v.).

Archemorus (Arkhēmoros), originally named **Opheltes**, baby son of Lycurgus, King of Nemea. When the Seven against Thebes (*see* THEBAN LEGEND) stopped at Nemea, the child's nurse, Hypsipyle (q.v.), left him for a while in order to do them some service. In her absence he was killed by a dragon, and Amphiaraüs, one of the heroes, saw in this an omen of disaster to himself and his companions, confirming his previous foresight (*see* AMPHIARAÜS). Accordingly they named the dead child Archemorus, 'Forerunner of Death', and instituted the Nemean games in memory of him. *See* NEMEAN GAMES.

Archias (-khias), tyrant of Thebes in Boeotia, imposed by Sparta upon the Thebans, who detested him for his cruelty and hatched a plot to destroy him (378 B.C.). During a banquet, at which the conspirators intended to assassinate him, Archias was handed a note and asked to read it without delay. 'Time enough for business tomorrow,' he replied, and slipped it under his cushion. It contained in fact a detailed warning of the plot; and a few moments later the conspirators, led by Pelopidas (q.v.), rushed in and slew him.

Archias, Aulus Licinius, Greek poet and grammarian, born at Antioch in Syria *c.* 120 B.C. He came to Rome in 102 and was received by the Luculli, in whose honour he assumed the gentile name Licinius. In 93 he was enrolled as a citizen of Heraclea in Lucania, and as that town was united with Rome by a *foedus*, he thereby obtained the Roman franchise in accordance with the Lex Plautia Papiria (89 B.C.). In 62 B.C. he was accused of having illegally assumed Roman citizenship, and was defended by Cicero, whose speech *Pro Archia* is extant; it secured his client's acquittal, and is also notable as containing a magnificent panegyric of literature.

Archidamus (-khidamos), name of five Eurypontid kings of Sparta between the 7th and late 3rd century B.C. The most famous was Archidamus II (476–427), who did his best to prevent the outbreak of the Peloponnesian war. Having been overruled by the war party, he led a Spartan force of 10,000 men into Attica (431) and conducted operations whose victims were commemorated in the celebrated funeral oration of Pericles (Thucydides ii. 34 et seq.). He carried out similar raids in 430 and 427, and died in 427 B.C.

Archilochus (Arkhilokhos), one of the earliest Greek lyric poets. A native of Paros, he flourished *c.* 700 B.C. and was famous for his lampoons in the iambic metre which he perfected. It is said that he went as a colonist to Thasos, but returned to Paros and died in battle against the Naxians. Many fragments of his work survive. To illustrate the power of his invective, a story was told that he was suitor to a lady named Neobule, one of the daughters of Lycambes, who first promised but afterwards refused to give his daughter in marriage to the poet. Enraged by this treatment Archilochus attacked the whole family in an iambic poem of such virulence that Neobule and her sisters hanged themselves for shame. *See* J. V. Powell, *New Chapters in the History of Greek Literature*, 1933.

Archimedes (-khimēdēs), Greek mathematician and inventor, born at Syracuse *c.* 287 B.C., son of Pheidias, an astronomer. He was a friend, if not a kinsman, of Hieron II and the latter's son Gelon. Having studied at Alexandria, where he probably invented the so-called Screw of Archimedes, he returned to spend the remainder of his life in mathematical studies. When Syracuse was captured by the army of M. Claudius Marcellus in 211 B.C., Archimedes was killed by a Roman soldier, despite the commander's order that the sage should go unharmed. He had not noticed the man's approach, being busy drawing a mathematical figure on the sand-board. Marcellus gave him

an honourable burial and cared for his surviving relatives. The tomb
had long since disappeared beneath a tangle of thorns when it was
discovered by Cicero during his Sicilian quaestorship (75 B.C.). It
was marked with a sphere inscribed in a cylinder, whose mutual
proportions constituted the discovery of which Archimedes was most
proud.

Other inventions of Archimedes were artillery, etc., for the defence
of Syracuse and one of the most important principles of hydrostatics.
The latter involves an old story which is often told wrongly and may
therefore be repeated. Hieron suspected that a golden crown which he
had ordered contained a certain amount of silver, and requested
Archimedes to discover the truth. One day, as he was stepping into a
bath-tub full of water, he noticed the overflow and realized that the
problem could be solved by putting the crown and equal weights of
gold and of silver into water and noting the differences in overflow.
Whereupon he ran naked from the bath-house through the city,
crying 'Heureka, Heureka' ('I have found it, I have found it'). Ten
works by Archimedes have survived. They have been edited by Sir
Thomas Heath (1897).

Archon (Arkhōn), 'ruler', title of the highest magistrate in several
Greek city-states. The emergence of this office corresponds with the
decay of absolute and comprehensive power once belonging to the
king. In the case of Athens, as we learn from Aristotle (*Ath. Con.* 3),
some of the kings had proved themselves inefficient on active service,
and their military duties were therefore taken over by an official
known thenceforward as the *Polemarch*. The king was next relieved of
his civil duties by an *Archon*; he was thus left with only his control of
the state religion and eventually became known as *Archon Basileus*
or King-Archon. At first these three officials held office for life; from
752 until some date before 683 B.C. it was held for ten years, and then
became annual. The Archon became the chief official, giving his
name to the year and hence being called Archon Eponymus. In 683
there were instituted six *Thesmothetae* whose duty it was to keep a
record of judicial decisions. From this date too all four offices became
annual, and from 487 B.C. their holders were chosen by lot. Meanwhile,
in the time of Solon they had begun to exercise collective responsibility, and were generally referred to as 'the Nine Archons'. For a
very detailed account of their selection and duties *see* Aristotle,
Athenian Constitution (Everyman's Library), 55–9; 63–6. *See also*
A. H. J. Greenidge, *Handbook of Greek Constitutional History*, 1895.

Archytas (-khutas), Greek general and philosopher of the Pythagor-
ian school, born *c.* 428 B.C. He was a close friend of Plato, and as
general of the Tarentine army he fought seven successful campaigns.
Only fragments of his works have survived; but he is known to have
propounded the first systematic theory of mechanics, to have distinguished harmonic from arithmetical and geometrical progressions, to
have solved the problem of duplicating the cube, and to have contributed to the theories of proportion, music and acoustics. Archytas
is said to have been drowned while sailing across the Adriatic, 347 B.C.

Arctinus (Arktinos), Greek cyclic poet, *fl. c.* 650 B.C. He is the
reputed author of (*a*) the *Aethiopis*, which began where the *Iliad* left

off, and ended with the death of Achilles; and (b) the *Sack of Troy*. Neither is extant.

Arctos (Ark-), the constellation of the Great Bear (*Ursa Major*) of which the ancient name was *Septem Triones* ('seven ploughing' oxen). The Lesser Bear (*Ursa Minor*) was called *Arctophylax* (Guardian of the Bear), of which the chief star was *Arcturus*, a name sometimes wrongly applied to the whole constellation. When the Great Bear was styled *The Wain*, the Lesser Bear was named *Boötes*, the Wagoner. These stars have been connected in mythology since Alexandrian times with Callisto (q.v.).

Ardashir, called in Greek Artaxerxes, Persian king and founder of the Sassanid dynasty. Having served with distinction in the army of Artabanus IV of Parthia (*see* ARTABANUS, 4), he was rewarded with ingratitude and revolted, claiming the throne of Persia on plea of descent from the Achaemenids. He won popular support by declaring himself a champion of the old popular religion, defeated Artabanus in A.D. 226, took the title King of Kings and immediately re-established Zoroastrianism. Ardashir next demanded from the Roman emperor Alexander Severus cession of all those parts of the empire which had belonged to Persia in the days of Darius and Xerxes. This meant the whole of Asia Minor and Egypt; war broke out, and lasted until the murder of Alexander in 235. Peace was then concluded on the understanding that each side should retain what it had possessed before the commencement of hostilities. (*See* Gibbon, *Decline and Fall*, ch. viii.) Ardashir died in A.D. 240 and was succeeded by his son Shapur (*see* SAPOR).

Ardea, chief town of the Rutuli, in Latium, 3 miles from the coast and 23 miles south of Rome on the Via Ardeatina. It was one of the most ancient places in Italy and the legendary capital of Turnus (q.v.). As a member of the Latin League (q.v.) Ardea controlled the shrine of Venus at Lavinium. The imperial elephants were kept in the neighbouring forests; but the place was unhealthy and it rapidly decayed. For an account of the ancient fortifications see *Archaeologia*, xlix (1885).

Arelate (mod. Arles), city of Gaul, on the left bank of the Rhône, near the head of the delta. Originally a Greek and later a Roman settlement, it was for some time residence of Constantine the Great. Roman remains include an amphitheatre which could hold 25,000 spectators; a theatre in which was discovered (1651) the Venus of Arles; the palace of Constantine; the forum, baths, ramparts, aqueducts; and a cemetery.

Aremorica, *see* ARMORICA.

Areopagus (Areiopagos), a rocky promontory to the west of the Acropolis in Athens (q.v.); the Hill of Ares (cf. Acts xvii). The name was also given to the council which met here to try cases of homicide, murderous wounding and arson. This council (which for the transaction of other business met in the Stoa Basileios) consisted of ex-archons under the presidency of the king-archon. Under the constitution of Solon the Areopagus had, besides judicial powers, a certain political importance. But that importance began to decline after sortition had been introduced for filling the archonship in

487 B.C., and by the laws of 461 it was deprived of all functions except the trial of homicides and certain religious cases.

Ares, Greek god of the warlike spirit, whom the Romans identified with Mars (q.v.). He was one of the great Olympian gods, and is called the son of Zeus and Hera. His savage and sanguinary character makes him hated by the other gods and by his own parents. He was wounded by Diomedes, who was assisted by Athena, and in his fall he roared like ten thousand warriors. The gigantic Aloidae had likewise conquered him, and kept him a prisoner for thirteen months, until he was delivered by Hermes. He was also conquered by Heracles, with whom he fought on account of his son Cycnus, and was obliged to return to Olympus. This fierce and gigantic, but withal handsome god, loved, and was beloved by, Aphrodite. According to a late tradition, Ares slew Halirrhothius (q.v.), the son of Poseidon, when he was offering violence to Alcippe, the daughter of Ares. Hereupon Poseidon accused Ares in the Areopagus, where the Olympian gods were assembled in court. Ares was acquitted, and this event was believed to have given rise to the name Areopagus. In Greece the worship of Ares was not very general. It was probably introduced from Thrace, possibly derived from very ancient war-magic.

Aretaeus (-aios), Greek doctor, 2nd cent. A.D. As a clinician he ranks next to Hippocrates, and gave the first clear account of diabetes. His extant works were translated by F. Adams, 1856.

Aretas, Greek form of the name Hāritha, born by several Nabataean kings. One of them invaded Judaea in 65 B.C. to support Hyrcanus against Aristobulus, but was driven off by the Romans. Another was father-in-law of Herod Antipas, who declared war upon and defeated the latter, because he had discarded his wife, Aretas's daughter, in favour of Herodias. This is the king Aretas mentioned in 2 Cor. xi. 32.

Arethusa (-thousa), one of the naiads (see NYMPHS), nymph of the fountain Arethusa at Syracuse (see ALPHEUS). Another legend makes her originally a nymph attendant upon Artemis who, while bathing in the Alpheus, was pursued by the river-god all the way to Syracuse, where, calling upon Artemis for help, she was changed into a spring.

Argiletum, district of Rome, extending from south of the Quirinal hill to the Capitol and Forum Romanum. It was the chief centre of the Roman book trade.

Arginusae (-ousai), group of small islands off the coast of Aeolis, opposite Mytilene in Lesbos. They are celebrated as the scene of Conon's naval victory over the Spartans under Callicratidas in 406 B.C. Towards the end of the battle a storm arose and the Athenian commanders ran for shelter without attempting to rescue the crews of twelve ships that were sinking; those of them who returned home were tried for dereliction of duty and put to death.

Argolis, also called **Argeia, Argos** and **Argolice,** district of Peloponnesus of which Argos (q.v.) was the capital. In the days of Greek independence Argeia consisted only of the sloping plain at the head of the Argive Gulf; but in Roman times Argolis (as it was then most commonly called) included the whole territory between the Sinus Saronicus, the Sinus Argolicus, Laconia, Arcadia and Corinthia.

Argonauts, The, 'sailors of the Argo', were the fifty heroes who sailed to Colchis (q.v.) with Jason in order to obtain the Golden Fleece (*see* JASON AND MEDEA; PHRIXUS). They travelled in a fifty-oared ship named *Argo* after its builder Argus, son of Phrixus, and included all the great heroes of the age. They arrived in due course at the mouth of the Phasis, and King Aeëtes promised to give up the fleece if Jason would yoke to a plough two fire-breathing oxen with brazen feet, and sow the dragon's teeth which had not been used by Cadmus (q.v.) at Thebes. Medea, the king's daughter and a sorceress, fell in love with Jason. Upon his promising to marry her, she furnished him with the means of resisting fire and steel, and sent to sleep the dragon which guarded the fleece. After Jason had secured the treasure, fled with Medea and eluded capture by Aeëtes, the Argonauts embarked by night and sailed away. On the return journey they were driven by a storm to the coast of Italy, and after wandering about the western Mediterranean they eventually reached Iolcus. The legend of the Argonauts is of great antiquity; Homer speaks as though it were universally familiar, and it may have some foundation in fact. *See* the *Argonautica* of Apollonius Rhodius (trans. R. C. Smeaton, 1912); J. R. Bacon, *Voyages of the Argonauts*, 1925.

Argos: 1. Town of Argolis (q.v.). Legend, history and archaeology alike bear witness to its great antiquity. In Homeric tradition its ruler was Diomedes, whose overlord, Agamemnon (*see* ATREIDS), had his capital at Mycenae. After the Dorian invasion, however, it regained its ancient ascendancy; and in the 8th or 7th century B.C. Argos controlled the entire eastern Peloponnesus. Thereafter its influence declined, and its power was weakened by wars with Sparta, hostility towards which caused it to take no part in the Persian wars. In the Peloponnesian war it sided with Athens after the Peace of Nicias, but gave very little help after the defeat of Mantinea (418). During the 4th century B.C. Argos continued to support the enemies of Sparta, but in 272 joined Sparta against Pyrrhus and afterwards became subject to the Macedonian kingdom of Antigonus Gonatas. In 229 B.C. it joined the Achaean League (q.v.), and on the conquest of the latter by Rome in 146 B.C. was included in the Roman province of Achaea. Argos was the seat of a famous school of bronze sculpture, among whose members were Ageladas and Polycleitus (qq.v.).

The Heraeum or temple of Hera lay in the foothills east of the Argive plain, about five miles from Argos, and three miles from Mycenae; it was maintained by both cities until the destruction of Mycenae by the Argives in 468 B.C. This shrine, the most important centre of Hera worship in the ancient world, was of great antiquity, the original foundation dating from *c.* 1750 B.C.; and the succession of priestesses was adopted at Argos and elsewhere as a chronological standard. In 423 B.C. the temple was burned down, and the Argives erected a magnificent new building to the designs of Eupolemus, which contained the chryselephantine statue of Hera by Polycleitus (*see* Pausanias ii. 17). The whole temple area, containing eleven separate buildings, was excavated by the American Archaeological Institute and School at Athens in 1892–5.

2. *See* ARGOLIS.

Argus (-os): 1. Son of King Inachus of Argos. He was surnamed

Panoptes, 'All-seeing', because he had a hundred eyes. Hera set him to watch Io, whom she had changed into a cow; but Hermes, at the command of Zeus, put him to sleep with the sweet sound of his flute, and then cut off his head. Hera transplanted the eyes to the tail of her favourite bird, the peacock. *See* ECHIDNA.

2. Son of Phrixus (q.v.) and builder of the ship *Argo* (*see* ARGO-NAUTS).

3. The faithful old dog of Odysseus, who alone recognized his master disguised in beggar's rags after an absence of twenty years, and died of joy (*Odyssey*, xvii. 292).

Argyripa (Argur-) or **Argyrippa**, *see* ARPI.

Ariadnē, in Greek legend, daughter of Minos and Pasiphaë, fell in love with Theseus (q.v.) when he came to Crete with the Athenian tribute, and gave him the clue of thread by means of which he found his way out of the Labyrinth. Theseus in return promised to marry her, and accordingly she left Crete with him; but on their arrival at the island of Naxos she was slain by Artemis. This is the Homeric account; but a more common tradition related that Ariadne was deserted by Theseus on Naxos, that Dionysus found her there, made her his wife and placed among the stars a crown which he gave her at their marriage. Plutarch relates a different story. He says that Ariadne was pregnant when abandoned on Naxos, and died in childbirth. He also states that each year at Amathus (q.v.), in Cyprus, her death was re-enacted by a youth who imitated a woman in labour. This strange rite suggests that Ariadne was originally a prehistoric deity. *See* APHRODITE.

Ariarathēs, name of several kings of Cappadocia:

1. Son of Ariamnes I; defeated by Perdiccas, and crucified, 322 B.C. Eumenes then obtained possession of Cappadocia.

2. Son of Holophernes, and nephew of Ariarathes I, recovered Cappadocia after the death of Eumenes, 315. He was succeeded by Ariamnes II.

3. Son of Ariamnes II, and grandson of the preceding, married Stratonice, daughter of Antiochus II, King of Syria.

4. Son of the preceding, reigned 220–162. He married Antiochis, daughter of Antiochus the Great, and assisted Antiochus against the Romans. After the defeat of Antiochus, Ariarathes sued for peace in 188, which he obtained on favourable terms.

5. Son of the preceding, surnamed Philopator, reigned 162–130. He assisted the Romans against Aristonicus of Pergamum, and fell in this war, 130.

6. Son of the preceding, reigned 130–96. He married Laodice, sister of Mithradates the Great of Pontus, and was put to death by Mithradates.

7. Son of the preceding, also murdered by Mithradates, who became king. The Cappadocians rebelled against Mithradates, and placed upon the throne.

8. Second son of No. 6; but he was speedily driven out of the kingdom by Mithradates, and died soon afterwards.

9. Son of Ariobarzanes III. He was deposed and put to death by Antony, who appointed Archelaus (No. 5).

Aricia, one of the oldest cities of Latium, on the Via Appia, 16 miles south-east of Rome. It was conquered by C. Maenius in 338 B.C. and received the Roman franchise soon afterwards. Aricia was famous for its wine and vegetables, but is now more celebrated for its cult of Diana (*see* NEMORENSIS, LACUS).

Aries, 'ram', Roman name for the ancient siege weapon, commonly called a battering ram. The earliest form was a long heavy beam having at its extremity a mass of iron shaped roughly like a ram's head. It was carried by a party of soldiers who simply thrust it with great force against the wall. A much more effective type consisted of a huge beam, sometimes as much as 120 feet in length, tipped as before with iron, but suspended from another beam supported by two posts (cf. Josephus, *Bell. Jud.* iii. 7, 19) and swung against the wall. The apparatus was shielded from enemy missiles by a penthouse (*vinea*), and was occasionally mounted on wheels.

Arimaspi (-oi), legendary people of north-eastern Scythia. According to Herodotus they were one-eyed. They also fought with griffins for the possession of gold which was guarded by the latter, a story no doubt based upon the real existence of gold-mines in that region.

Ariminum (mod. Rimini), Umbrian city on the Adriatic coast, 69 miles south-east of Bononia; but the harbour has now silted up. Founded in 268 B.C., it afterwards became a Latin *colonia* (q.v.), and was an important road centre. It was occupied by Caesar immediately after his crossing the Rubicon (49 B.C.). Twenty-two years later Augustus divided the city into seven *vici* (wards) named after those of Rome; he also repaired the Via Flaminia throughout its length from Rome to Ariminum. At the entrance to the city there stands a fine triumphal arch erected in honour of Augustus, and at the opposite end of the main street is a five-arched bridge over the Ariminus, built in the reigns of Augustus and Tiberius.

Ariobarzanēs, surnamed Philo-Romaeus, King of Cappadocia fro﹍ 93 to 63 B.C. Several times expelled from his throne by Mithradates th﹍ Great of Pontus, he was as often restored by the Romans and finally established in the kingdom by Pompey. He abdicated in favour of his son, also called Ariobarzanes and surnamed as his father, who was succeeded in turn (*c.* 51 B.C.) by his son Ariobarzanes Eusebes Philo-Romaeus. Though the latter had assisted Pompey in the civil war, he was pardoned and confirmed in his kingdom by Caesar. In 42 B.C. he was accused of conspiracy and put to death by order of Cassius.

Ariobarzanēs of Pontus, son of the satrap Mithradates, whom he succeeded in 363 B.C. In the following year he revolted from Artaxerxes, and founded the independent kingdom of Pontus. Both he and his three sons enjoyed the privilege of Athenian citizenship.

Ariōn, a native of Methymna in Lesbos, Greek lyric poet and player on the cithara, and the inventor of dithyrambic poetry. He lived *c.* 625 B.C. at the court of Periander, tyrant of Corinth. On one occasion, says Herodotus, Arion went to Sicily to take part in some musical contest. He won the prize, and, laden with presents, he embarked in a Corinthian ship homeward bound. The sailors coveted his treasures, and meditated his murder. After trying in vain to save his life, he at length obtained permission once more to play on the cithara, and as soon as he had invoked the gods in inspired strains, he threw himself into the sea. But many song-loving dolphins had assembled round the vessel, and one of them now took the bard on its back and carried him to Taenarus, from whence he returned to Corinth in safety, and related his adventure to Periander. Upon the arrival of the Corinthian vessel, Periander inquired of the sailors after Arion, who replied that he had remained behind at Tarentum; but when Arion came forward the sailors owned their guilt.

Ariovistus, a German chieftain who entered Gaul by invitation of the Arverni and Sequani in 71 B.C. and occupied large areas of the country. He was defeated and driven out by Caesar in 58 B.C. *See* Caesar, *Bell. Gall.* i. 31–53.

Aristaeus (-taios), son of Apollo by the nymph Cyrene (q.v.). He went from Libya to Thrace, and there fell in love with Eurydice, wife of Orpheus (q.v.). Fleeing from him, Eurydice perished by the bite of a snake, and the nymphs attendant upon her destroyed his bees. Aristaeus then consulted Proteus (q.v.), who advised him to sacrifice four bulls and as many heifers in order to appease the angry *manes* (q.v.) of Eurydice. This counsel worked wonders, for there immediately came forth from the entrails a new swarm of bees (*see* Virgil, *Georg.* iv). Aristaeus was worshipped as a protector of flocks and shepherds, of vine and olive plantations, and as having taught men to keep bees.

Aristagoras, brother-in-law and cousin of Histiaeus (q.v.), who left him as regent of Miletus during his absence at the Persian court. Having failed in an attack upon Naxos (500 B.C.), he found himself out of favour with the Persians and took occasion of a message from Histiaeus to raise the Ionian revolt (499). He obtained help from Athens, whose intervention led ultimately to the Persian Wars (q.v.). After the revolt had failed he emigrated to Thrace, where he was killed in an attack on Ennea Hodoi, a town of the Edoni, afterwards called Amphipolis.

Aristarchus (-khos): 1. Of Samos (*c.* 310–230 B.C.), Greek astronomer and mathematician at Alexandria, but included by Vitruvius among the few great men who possessed an equally profound knowledge of all branches of science. That Aristarchus actually put forward the heliocentric hypothesis is made certain by no less a person than Archimedes (*Psammites,* i. 1–10); it is supported by Sextus Empiricus (*Adv. math.* x. 174), and also by Plutarch (*De facie in orbe lunae,* 6) who adds that it was part of Aristarchus's scheme that the earth rotates about its own axis. Of the writings of Aristarchus only one survives: *On the Sizes and Distances of the Sun and Moon,* which has been edited with translation and commentary by Sir Thomas Heath (1913). *See* Sir T. L. Heath, *Greek Astronomy,* 1932.

2. Of Samothrace (2nd century B.C.), Greek grammarian and the greatest critic of antiquity. A pupil of Aristophanes of Byzantium (q.v.), he founded at Alexandria a grammatical and critical school, at the same time acting as tutor to the sons of Ptolemy VI, Philometor. He is said to have retired to Cyprus at the age of about seventy-two, and there starved himself to death because he was suffering from incurable dropsy. Aristarchus became the type of a severe but

enlightened critic. He published an edition of Homer, which has formed the basis of the text from his time to the present day, and which first divided the *Iliad* and *Odyssey* into twenty-four books each. Nothing of his work survives. *See* the Appendix to D. B. Monro's edition of the *Odyssey*, 1901.

Aristeas, the writer of a celebrated 'letter' professing to give a contemporary account of the translation of the Pentateuch into Greek in the time of Ptolemy Philadelphus (285–246 B.C.). The writer poses as a courtier in the service of that king, who is interested in Jewish antiquities. But the letter is not contemporary with the events described, and its later date may be put at about 100 B.C. Text in Swete's *Introduction to the Old Testament in Greek*, 2nd ed., 1902. *See also* H. G. Meecham, *The Letter of Aristeas*, 1935.

Aristeidēs: 1. An Athenian, son of Lysimachus, surnamed 'the Just', was of an ancient but not wealthy family. He fought at the battle of Marathon, 490 B.C.; and next year, 489, he was archon. He was the great rival of Themistocles, and it was through the influence of the latter that he suffered ostracism some time between 485 and 482 B.C. He was still in exile in 480 at the battle of Salamis, where he did good service by dislodging the enemy, with a band raised and armed by himself, from the islet of Psyttalea. Recalled from banishment after the battle, he was appointed general (479), and commanded the Athenians at Plataea. In 477, when the allies had become disgusted with Pausanias and the Spartans, he and his colleague Cimon obtained for Athens the command of the maritime confederacy known as the Delian League (q.v.), drew up its laws and fixed the contributions, as well as shaping home policy. He died in 468 B.C., so poor that his daughters, and even much later descendants, were pensioned by the state.

2. A native of Miletus (*c.* 150–100 B.C.), author of six books of erotic *Milesian Tales*, which were translated into Latin by L. Cornelius Sisenna (q.v.). Only fragments survive.

3. A native of Thebes in Boeotia, celebrated Greek military painter, *fl. c.* 305 B.C. His pictures are said to have fetched enormous prices.

Aristeides, Aelius, surnamed Theodorus, Greek rhetorician and sophist of the 2nd century A.D. A resident of Smyrna, he addressed a memorial to Marcus Aurelius after the earthquake in 178, and persuaded him to rebuild the city. We possess two small rhetorical treatises and fifty-five declamations upon a variety of topics. The latest edition is that of :Dindorf (1929).

Aristippus (-os), Greek philosopher and founder of the Cyrenaic school. He was born at Cyrene *c.* 435 B.C. Early in life he went to Athens and became a pupil of Socrates. After the latter's death in 399 he visited many Greek cities and then returned to Cyrene, where he founded his school. The Cyrenaics made the sovereign good to consist in pleasure, in a manner that seems to anticipate the modern Hedonists. Aristippus himself indulged in luxury, and the Cyrenaic teaching, forerunner of Epicureanism, was transmitted through his daughter and her son Aristippus to Theodorus and Anniceris.

Aristobulus (-boulos): 1. Name of several Jewish princes, of whom the best known was brother of John Hyrcanus II (q.v.).

2. Of Paneas, Jewish philosopher of the Peripatetic school, *fl. c.* 160 B.C., but his date is much disputed. His commentaries on the Pentateuch (of which only small fragments have survived) represented the first attempt to reconcile Jewish religion with Greek philosophy.

3. Of Cassandreia, Greek historian who accompanied Alexander the Great into Asia. His account of that journey (mainly geographical) was one of the sources used by Arrian (q.v.).

Aristodemus (-dēmos), semi-legendary king of Messenia (q.v.) during the first Messenian war. Having sacrificed his own daughter, in fulfilment of a vow, for the safety of his country, his efforts proved fruitless against the determination of Sparta, and he put an end to his own life upon that daughter's tomb (724 B.C.).

Aristomenēs, hero of the second Messenian war (*see* MESSENIA). Like that of Aristodemus (q.v.), his story belongs to legend rather than to fact. After the defeat of the Messenians in the third year of the war, Aristomenes retreated to the mountain fortress of Ira and there continued hostilities, constantly ravaging Spartan territory. During one of these expeditions he and fifty of his men were taken prisoner. They were carried to Sparta and thrown into a pit where condemned criminals awaited execution. His companions perished; but Aristomenes was caught as he fell, and was guided by a fox to safety. Ira was captured, the Spartans were once again masters of Messenia (666) and Aristomenes settled as an exile at Ialysus in Rhodes.

Aristonicus (-kos), illegitimate son of Eumenes II of Pergamum (*see* EUMENES (B)). On the death of Attalus III (q.v.), in 133 B.C., Aristonicus claimed the throne. Having defeated the Roman consul P. Licinius Crassus in 131, he was himself defeated and taken prisoner in the following year by the consul M. Perperna, and executed at Rome in 128 B.C.

Aristophanēs, Greek poet of the Old Comedy, born *c.* 445 B.C., probably at Athens. His father Philippus had possessions in Aegina, and may originally have come from that island; whence a question arose whether Aristophanes was a genuine Athenian citizen, Cleon (q.v.) attempting to deprive him of his civic rights. He had three sons, Philippus, Araros and Nicostratus; of his private history we know nothing. He died *c.* 380 B.C., having won four first prizes. The comedies of Aristophanes are of the highest historical interest, containing caricatures on the leading men of the day. The first evil against which he inveighs is the Peloponnesian war, to which he ascribes the influence of demagogues like Cleon at Athens. (*See* Gilbert Murray, *Aristophanes and the War Party*, 1919). Another object of his indignation was the educational system introduced by the Sophists, which he attacks in the *Clouds*, making Socrates the representative of them. Another feature of the times was the excessive love for litigation at Athens, which he ridicules in the *Wasps*. Eleven of his plays have come down to us: *The Archarnians* (425), *The Knights* (424), *The Clouds* (423), *The Wasps* (422), *The Peace* (421), *The Birds* (414), *Lysistrata* (411), *Thesmophoriazusae* (410), *The Frogs* (405), *Eccle-*

siazusae (393), *Plutus* (388). Aristophanes was a complete master of the Attic dialect, which appears in his works in its greatest perfection. If, as some think, his plots and characters are weak, the beauty of his chorus is unsurpassed. *See* complete edition by M. Hadas, 1962; V. Ehrenberg, *The People of Aristophanes*, 1962.

Aristophanēs of Byzantium (*c.* 257–*c.* 183 B.C.), Greek scholar; studied at Alexandria under Zenodotus and Callimachus, and was appointed head of the Library *c.* 187. His works included editions of Homer and other poets; his arguments to the plays of Aristophanes and the tragedians are mostly extant. He did valuable work as a lexicographer and grammarian, and introduced the tonic accent. *See* edition of surviving fragments by A. Nauck, 1848; *also* J. E. Sandys, *History of Classical Scholarship*, vol. i. ch. viii (3rd ed.), 1921.

Aristotelēs, called in English **Aristotle**, was born at Stageira (q.v.) in Chalcidice, 384 B.C., son of Nicomachus, who had been physician to Amyntas II of Macedonia, father of Philip II. By descent he was an Ionian Greek, for Stageira had been colonized from Chalcis in Euboea, which was also the birth-place of his mother Phaestis.

In 367, at the age of seventeen, he went to Athens and became a member of the Academy (q.v.). Here he so distinguished himself, first as a pupil and later as a research student and lecturer, that Plato (q.v.) nicknamed him 'the mind of the school'. There never was, as is sometimes alleged, any deep rift between his own thought and that of Plato, of whom he remained a close follower and devoted admirer until the end. Nevertheless, long before the master's death he had begun to lose sympathy with Academic theories as interpreted by some other members of the Academy, notably Speusippus (q.v.), who was designated to succeed Plato as its head. Accordingly, in 347, after the master's death, Aristotle and Xenocrates (q.v.) left Athens and settled at Assos in the southern Troad, where two former pupils of the Academy, Erastus and Coriscus, were living under the patronage of Hermeias (q.v.), ruler of the nearby city of Atarneus, whom they had interested in the Platonic doctrines. The four men were joined by Theophrastus (q.v.), and Aristotle opened a school. At this period he certainly regarded himself as a Platonist; but his subsequent thought led him farther from the traditions which had formed his earlier background, and in his later criticisms of Plato he sometimes appears to misinterpret the latter in a way that is not altogether fair. At all events, in about 344, probably at the suggestion of Theophrastus, Aristotle moved to Mitylene in Lesbos, and devoted the next two years chiefly to the study of natural history and of marine biology in particular. Meanwhile, during his residence at Assos, he had married Pythias, niece and adopted daughter of Hermeias, and had made contact with the more practical problems of politics; then, in 342, he accepted an invitation from Philip II of Macedon to go to the court of Pella and act as tutor to Philip's son Alexander.

After the accession of Alexander (336), Aristotle returned to Athens and opened his most famous school in the Lyceum, a gymnasium in the grove of Apollo Lyceius, from whose covered walks (*peripatoi*) the school derived its name, Peripatetic. It was during this second Athenian residence that Aristotle wrote or completed by far the greater part of his surviving works. These cover an enormous field and are a measure of their author's genius: metaphysics, psychology, biology, logic, ethics, politics and literary criticism.

Misfortune now overtook him. News was received of Alexander's death at Babylon (323); a strong nationalist party was momentarily in the ascendant, and since Aristotle was known to be a supporter of the Macedonian supremacy, not to mention his close personal friendship with Antipater (who was absent in the East), his position and even his life were endangered. He therefore fled to Chalcis, where he died in the following year at the age of sixty-two. His will is preserved by Diogenes Laertius (q.v.).

The genuine extant writings of Aristotle as usually cited are as follows: *Organon* (comprising *Categoriae, De Interpretatione, Analytica Priora, Analytica Posteriora, Topica* and *Sophistici Elenchi*); *Physics*; *De Caelo*; *De Generatione et Corruptione*; *Meteorologica*; *De Anima*; *Parva Naturalia* (comprising *De Sensu et Sensibili, De Memoria et Reminiscentia, De Somno, De Somniis, De Divinatione per Somnum, De Longitudine et Brevitate Vitae, De Vita et Morte* and *De Respiratione*); *Historia Animalium*; *De Motu Animalium*; *De Incessu Animalium*; *De Generatione Animalium*; *Metaphysics*; *Eudemian Ethics*; *Nicomachaean Ethics*; *Politics*; *The Athenian Constitution*; *Rhetoric*; *Poetics*: the standard edition of the works (excluding the *Athenian Constitution*, which was not recovered until 1890) is that of I. Bekker, 5 vols., Berlin, 1831–70. See also *The Works of Aristotle Translated into English*, edited by J. A. Smith and W. D. Ross, 1908–31. There are translations of the *Metaphysics*, *Politics* (with *Athenian Constitution*), *Nicomachaean Ethics* and *Poetics* in Everyman's Library.

The lost works included: (1) Some dialogues, of which the most important were *Protrepticus* (partly preserved in a work of the same name by Iamblichus) and *De Philosophia*; (2) an essay *On Monarchy*; (3) *Alexander, or On Colonies*; (4) accounts of 158 *Constitutions* (of which that on the Athenian alone survives); (5) *Customs of the Barbarians*; (6) *Cases of Constitutional Law*; (6) a list of victors in the Pythian and Olympic games; (7) a list of successful dramas produced at Athens.

See W. D. Ross, *Aristotle*, 2nd ed., 1930; E. Zeller, *History of Greek Philosophy*, 13th ed., 1931; G. R. G. Mure, *Aristotle*, 1932; W. W. Jaeger, *Aristotle* (trans.), 1934; D. J. Allan, *The Philosophy of Aristotle*, 1952; M. Gene, *A Portrait of Aristotle*, 1963.

Aristoxenus (-os), Greek philosopher of the Peripatetic school and a musician, *fl. c.* 318 B.C. His work on *Harmonics* is extant; *see* the text and translation by H. S. Macran, 1902.

Armenia, a country of somewhat indeterminate boundaries, lay between the Euxine and the Caspian. In Roman times it was divided into two unequal parts: *Armenia Major* east of the Euphrates, and *Armenia Minor* west of that river. The first was to all intents and purposes an independent kingdom, though sometimes formally acknowledging the sovereignty of Rome (*see* ARTAVASDES; ARTAXIAS; TIGRANES); the second was made a province of the empire by Trajan.

Arminius (latinized form of *Hermann*), chief of the Cherusci (q.v.). He was born in 18 B.C., and in youth led his people as auxiliaries of

the Roman legions in Germany, where he learnt the Roman language,
was given Roman citizenship and enrolled among the equites. In
A.D. 9 Arminius persuaded his countrymen to rise against the Romans,
who were now masters of this part of Germany. His attempt was
crowned with success. Quintilius Varus (q.v.), with three legions,
was defeated; and the Romans relinquished all their possessions
beyond the Rhine. In 14 Arminius had to defend his country against
Germanicus. At first he was successful; but Germanicus made good
his retreat to the Rhine, and it was in the course of this campaign
that the wife of Arminius fell into Roman hands. In 16 he was
defeated by Germanicus, and his country was probably saved from
subjection only by the jealousy of Tiberius, who recalled Germanicus
in the following year. At length Arminius aimed at absolute power,
and was in consequence cut off by his own relations in the thirty-fifth
year of his age, A.D. 17.

Armorica or **Aremorica** (Celtic *ar*, on; *mor*, the sea), Roman name
for the Gallic territory now roughly comprised by the peninsula of
Brittany. The principal tribe was the Veneti, whom Caesar practically annihilated in 56 B.C. (*Bell. Gall.* iii. 7–16). The region subsequently formed part of Gallia Lugdunensis (*see* GALLIA).

Arpi (Gk Arguripa or Argurippa), city of Apulia, 20 miles from the
Adriatic coast. Traditionally founded by Diomedes, King of Argos, it
was in early times famous for horse breeding. Long a faithful ally of
Rome, Arpi went over to Hannibal after Cannae (216 B.C.), but was
captured three years later by Q. Fabius Maximus. It never regained
its old prosperity, but the great circuit of its walls suggested to Strabo
that it had once been among the greatest cities of the peninsula.

Arpinum (mod. Arpino), town of Latium; part of a Volscian town
which afterwards belonged to the Samnites and was taken from them
by the Romans in 305 B.C. In the nearby valley of the Liris, on a site
now covered by the church of San Domenico, stood the villa in which
Cicero was born.

Arretium (mod. Arezzo), Etruscan city, 50 miles south-east of
Florence, famous for the exceptional strength of its brick walls and
also for its red pottery. It was an important Roman base during the
second Punic war; sided with Marius against Sulla, who probably
destroyed the fortifications in 81; and assisted Catiline in 62 B.C.
Roman remains include an amphitheatre; here too was discovered the
splendid bronze Chimaera now at Florence.

Arrhidaeus (Arrhidaios), *see* PHILIP ARRHIDAEUS.

Arria, wife of Caecina Paetus. When her husband was ordered by
the emperor Claudius to put an end to his life, A.D. 42, and hesitated
to do so, Arria stabbed herself, handed the dagger to her husband, and
said: 'Paetus, it does not hurt.'

Arrianus, Flavius, commonly called **Arrian**, Greek historian and
philosopher, was born at Nicomedia in Bithynia, *c.* A.D. 96. He was a
pupil and friend of Epictetus, whose lectures he published at Athens.
In 124 he received from Hadrian the Roman citizenship, and from
that time used the name Flavius. In 135 he was appointed prefect of
Cappadocia, which was invaded in the following year by the Alani or
Massagetae, whom he defeated. Under Antoninus Pius, in 146, he was

consul; he died at an advanced age in the reign of M. Aurelius. Arrian was a close imitator of Xenophon both in the subjects of his works and in the style in which they were written. The most important of them is the *Anabasis*, a history of the expedition of Alexander the Great, in seven books; the *Indica*, a supplement to the latter; and *Periplus of the Euxine*. The *Anabasis* and *Indica* have been edited with translation by E. I. Robson (Loeb Library), 2 vols.

Arrius Aper, Roman praetorian prefect, father-in-law of the emperor Numerianus (q.v.) whom he is said to have murdered (*see also* CARUS). He was put to death by Diocletian (A.D. 284).

Arsaces, chieftain of the Parni, a nomad Scythian tribe dwelling east of the Caspian. In about 250 B.C. he invaded Parthia, a province of the Seleucid empire, and became nominal founder of the Arsacid dynasty which ruled in Parthia until A.D. 226, a title which more truthfully belongs to his brother and successor Tiridates.

Arsacidae, the Arsacids, a dynasty of Parthian kings founded by Arsaces (q.v.). It lasted from 248 B.C. until conquered by the Sassanid kings of Persia in A.D. 226. *See also* ARTABANUS; ORODES; PACORUS; PHRAATES.

Arsēs, King of Persia, younger son and successor (338 B.C.) of Artaxerxes III, Ochus (q.v.). Like his father and brothers he was poisoned by Bagoas (q.v.) in the third year of his reign.

Arsinoë, name of several women of the family of Ptolemy:

1. A former concubine of Philip II of Macedon; married Lagos, by whom she was the mother of Ptolemy I, Soter.

2. Daughter of Ptolemy I by Berenice. She was married first to Lysimachus (298); secondly (275) to her half-brother Ptolemy Ceraunos, who murdered the sons she had borne to Lysimachus; thirdly, in the same year, to her own brother Ptolemy II, Philadelphus. Though she bore him no children, Philadelphus was devoted to Arsinoë: he gave her name to several cities, called a district of Egypt Arsinoïtes after her and honoured her memory in many other ways.

3. Daughter of Lysimachus, wife to Ptolemy II, Philadelphus, before his accession, and mother by him of Ptolemy III, Euergetes, and of Berenice, wife of Antiochus II.

4. Daughter of Ptolemy XI, Auletes, carried to Rome after the capture of Alexandria by Caesar, and led in triumph by him.(46 B.C.). She afterwards returned to Egypt, but in 41 B.C. her sister Cleopatra persuaded Mark Antony to have her put to death.

Artabanus (-os). (A) Name of several Persian princes and officials:

1. Brother of Darius I, and a trusted adviser of Xerxes.

2. Vizier of Xerxes, whom he killed in 465 B.C., together with his son Darius. He was all-powerful during the first seven months of the reign of Artaxerxes I, who then discovered the truth about the deaths of his father and brother, and put Artabanus and his sons to death.

3. Satrap of Bactria who rebelled against Artaxerxes I and was defeated in two battles.

(B) Name of four Parthian kings of the Arsacid dynasty:

1. Uncle and successor (*c.* 127 B.C.) of Phraates I, died in battle against Mongolian invaders after a brief reign.

2. An outsider, though of Parthian royal blood on his mother's side. He was chosen *c.* A.D. 10 by the nobles to succeed Vonones I, whom he defeated only after a long struggle. Tiberius then withdrew support from Vonones and concluded a treaty with Artabanus. The new king began his reign by murdering all possible rivals, and his invasion of Armenia in 35 brought him to the brink of war with Rome. His enemies, however, appealed to Tiberius for a new king who should be of the house of Arsaces. This was Tiridates III, who was established on the throne by L. Vitellius, father of the future emperor. But the Roman element in these proceedings caused new troubles, and Artabanus was restored, only to be twice again driven out and brought back. He died in A.D. 40.

3. Was on the throne in A.D. 80, but gave way to Pacorus II.

4. The last king of Parthia (209–226 B.C.), younger son of Vologaeses IV. He rebelled against his brother Vologaeses V, and the ensuing civil strife gave the emperor Carcalla an excuse for a campaign of conquest in the East (216). This ended in miserable failure, following the murder of Caracalla and defeat of Macrinus (217). Meanwhile, however, the Sassanid dynasty of Persia had begun its conquests (*see* ARDASHIR), and although the struggle was prolonged for some years, it ended with the defeat and death of Artabanus IV in A.D. 226.

Artabazus, a general of Darius III, Codomannus, whose daughter Barsine was married to Alexander the Great. He is to be distinguished from another Persian general of the same name who served under Mardonius at the battle of Plataea (479 B.C.).

Artaphernēs: 1. Brother of Darius I; he was satrap of Sardis at the time of the Ionian revolt (499 B.C.).

2. Son of the preceding. Together with Datis he commanded the Persian army at Marathon (490 B.C.), and subsequently led the Lydian and Mysian forces during the invasion of Greece by Xerxes (480 B.C.).

Artavasdēs: 1. King of Armenia Major (q.v.), succeeded his father Tigranes in 36 B.C. In that year also he betrayed Mark Antony in his expedition against the Parthians. Antony therefore invaded Armenia in 34, took Artavasdes prisoner and carried him to Alexandria, where he was put to death by order of Cleopatra after the battle of Actium, 31 B.C.

2. Grandson of the preceding, was placed upon the throne of Armenia by Augustus, but was deposed by his subjects not long afterwards.

Artaxata, city of Armenia Major (*see* ARMENIA), of which it subsequently became the capital. It was burned by Corbulo (q.v.) in A.D. 58, but was restored by Tiridates and called Neroniana.

Artaxerxēs: (A) Greek form of the name Artakhshatra, being that of three Persian kings of the Achaemenid dynasty:

1. Surnamed in Greek 'Macrocheir' and in Latin 'Longimanus', because his right hand was longer than his left. He succeeded his father Xerxes in 465 B.C. (*see* ARTABANUS (A) 2). It was during his reign that Athens supported an Egyptian revolt (460–454). He also sanctioned the Jewish religion in Jerusalem by the firman addressed

(458 B.C.) to Ezra (1 Esdras vii. 11–16) and by appointing (445) as governor of Judaea his cup-bearer Nehemiah. He died, 425 or 424 B.C.

2. Surnamed Mnēmōn because of his good memory, son and successor (404) of Darius II. For the rebellion of his younger brother Cyrus in 401 B.C. *see* CYRUS, 2. He was at war with Sparta, 399–394, and from the Peace of Antalcidas (*see* ANTALCIDAS) until 380 with Evagoras (q.v.), King of Salamis in Cyprus. His attempts to recover Egypt came to nothing; but elsewhere the disorder resulting from numerous other rebellions had been suppressed when Artaxerxes II died in 359 B.C.

3. Surnamed Ochus, son and successor of the preceding, obtained the throne by contriving the deaths of his three elder brothers. With the help of Greek generals and mercenary troops he quelled revolts in Phoenicia and Egypt. Throughout his reign, however, the real power lay with a eunuch named Bagoas (q.v.), who poisoned the king and his elder sons in 338 B.C.

(B) Greek form of the Persian name Ardashir (q.v.).

Artaxias, Greek form of the name (Artashes) of three kings of Armenia:

1. Founder of the kingdom, was a general of Antiochus III, the Great, but revolted and made himself an independent sovereign (191 B.C.). He was defeated and made prisoner by Antiochus IV, Epiphanes, *c.* 165.

2. Son of Artavasdes II. He was put to death by his subjects in 20 B.C., when Augustus placed Tigranes on the throne.

3. Son of Polemon, King of Pontus, was made King of Armenia by Germanicus in A.D. 18. He died *c.* 35.

Artemidorus (-tēmidōros) : 1. Greek geographer of the late 2nd century B.C. His works, eleven books on general geography, have not survived; but they were used by Strabo, and some fragments have been preserved.

2. Surnamed Daldianos, Greek soothsayer and oneirocritic, *fl.* A.D. 138–160. His valuable *Oneirokritika*, on the interpretation of dreams, is extant.

Artemis, Greek goddess, in mythology daughter of Zeus and Leto, and twin sister of Apollo. Originally she was, like Apollo, non-hellenic, but had no connection with him. She was worshipped in pre-hellenic Greece, Asia Minor and Crete as 'an earth-goddess associated chiefly with the wild life and growth of the field and with human birth' (Farnell; *see* HIPPOLYTUS). Her care extended specially over the young of every living species. Under the influence of the Homeric religion her character as a universal mother was largely obscured, and she became rather the virgin huntress, patroness of chastity. Yet much of her earlier character remained. Thus she was always a goddess of childbirth, whence her title *Locheia*; she was identified with Ilithyia (q.v.); and at Ephesus her distinctive position as a universal mother persisted and was exemplified in the many-breasted figure in the great temple of Ephesian Artemis. The myth of Callisto (q.v.) shows that nymph to have been originally identical with the Arcadian *Artemis Calliste*, a pre-hellenic divinity. It has been suggested that this title (*Calliste* = Fairest) was applied euphemistically to the goddess in the form of a bear. If this is so, a connection is established with *Artemis Brauronia* who, though traditionally brought to Greece from the Tauric Chersonese (*see* IPHIGENEIA), was worshipped at Brauron in Attica with ritual suggesting the cult of a bear-goddess (*see* Aristophanes, *Lysistrata*). Artemis, like Hecate and Selene, with whom she was sometimes identified, was associated with the moon because of its supposed influence upon erotic and organic life. She was also identified with the Dorian goddess Orthia who was worshipped at Sparta as Artemis Orthia. *See* HIPPOLYTUS; ORION.

Artemisia, queen of Halicarnassus (353–350 B.C.), *see* HALICARNASSUS; MAUSOLUS.

Artemisium (-on), promontory on the north coast of Euboea, with a temple of Artemis. On the approach of the Persian invaders in 480 B.C. the Greek fleet concentrated at Artemisium (Herodotus, vii. 177; viii. 1). The subsequent naval action was indecisive.

Arvales, Fratres, the Arval Brothers, a college of twelve priests at Rome, whose duty was to offer public sacrifice for the fertility of the land. Of high antiquity, it had almost ceased to exist by the end of the republic, but was revived by Augustus and always thereafter included the emperor. The principal festival at which the Arval Brothers officiated was that of an anonymous corn deity, Dea Dia, who may have been identified with Ceres. Celebrated in the month of May, it lasted for three days, on the first and third of which the ceremonies took place at Rome, but on the second in a grove sacred to the Dea Dia about five miles outside the city walls. Here took place a ritual dance, accompanied by a hymn so ancient that it was unintelligible in the time of Augustus (*see* text and translation in Mommsen, *History of Rome*, bk I, ch. xiv). Here also were discovered ninety-six records of the brotherhood, dating from between A.D. 14 and 241. *See* the edition by J. H. W. Heuzen, 1874.

Arverni, a Gallic people inhabiting what is now called Auvergne. In 52 B.C. their capital, Gergovia (q.v.), was successfully defended against Caesar by Vercingetorix (q.v.). After their defeat at Alesia (q.v.), in the same year, they were quickly romanized; even their tribal deity, the god of the mountain (Puy de Dôme), was renamed Mercurius Dumias, part of whose temple has been excavated.

Ascalaphus (Askalaphos): 1. Son of Ares and leader, with his brother Ialmenus, of the Minyans from Boeotian Orchomenus against Troy (*see* MINYAE). He was killed by Deiphobus (q.v.).

2. Son of Acheron. When Pluto allowed Persephone (q.v.) to return to earth provided she had eaten nothing, Ascalaphus declared that she had eaten part of a pomegranate. Persephone, in revenge, changed him into an owl by sprinkling him with water from the River Phlegethon.

Ascalon, Philistine city on the coast of what in classical times was Syria. Though dating from about 1810 B.C., it does not belong to the subject-matter of this work until its conquest by Alexander the Great (333 B.C.), after which it was hellenized and was tributary in turn to the Seleucids and the Ptolemies. During the Roman period it was a free city (from 104 B.C.) and centre of hellenic scholarship. Ascalon was the birth-place of Herod the Great, who erected many fine buildings. Excavations were carried out between 1920 and 1923 by the Palestine Exploration Fund.

Ascanius or **Iulus**, in Roman legend, son of Aeneas (q.v.) by Creusa. He accompanied his father to Italy, founded Alba Longa (q.v.) and was succeeded by his son Silvius. From him the Julian *gens* at Rome claimed to derive its name, and through him it traced its descent from Venus (q.v.; *see also* ANCHISES).

Asclepiades (Asklēpiadēs): 1. Greek physician (124–56 B.C.), born in Bithynia. In 91 he set up in Rome as a rhetorician, but resumed his former profession and enjoyed considerable success.

2. Greek lyric poet, a contemporary and friend of Theocritus (*c.* 270 B.C.), was born at Samos and was the first in a long line of erotic and convivial epigrammatists. Many of his poems are in the *Greek Anthology*.

Asclepius (Asklēpios), Latin **Aesculapius**, Greek god of medicine, though in Homer he is simply the 'blameless physician' whose sons, Machaon and Podalirus, were surgeons in the army. According to later legend Asclepius was son of Apollo and was instructed by Chiron (q.v.) in the art of healing. His proficiency was such that he not only cured the sick, but even raised men from the dead. Zeus, therefore, fearing that man might thus learn the way to immortality, killed him with a thunderbolt. The worship of Asclepius was centred at Epidaurus (q.v.). It was introduced at Athens in 420 and at Rome in 293 B.C. *See also* HYGIEIA. The serpent was sacred to Asclepius, both as a symbol of renovation and as being supposed to have power of discovering medicinal herbs. Cocks were sacrificed in his honour. *See* E. J. and L. Edelstein, *Asclepios*, 1945.

Ascra (-kra), town of Boeotia on Mt Helicon, home of the poet Hesiod (q.v.).

Asculum: 1. (mod. Ascoli di Satriano), town of Apulia, the scene of Pyrrhus's victory over the Romans in 279 B.C.

2. (Mod. Ascoli Piceno), town and capital of Picenum, on the south bank of the Truentus, 120 miles north-east of Rome on the Via Salaria. In 268 B.C. it was taken by the Romans, against whom it played an important part during the Social War (q.v.) until its capture, after a long siege, by Pompeius Strabo in 89 B.C. It was occupied by Caesar in 49 B.C. In 301 it was made capital of Picenum Suburbicarium. Roman remains include two bridges, which are still in use; while in the museum there are preserved numerous lead *glandes* (acorn-shaped missiles), which were used by slingers during the siege in 90–89 B.C.

Asellio, Publius Sempronius (2nd century B.C.), Roman historian. Having served under Scipio before Numantia (q.v.), he wrote a history of Rome from the Punic wars to the time of the Gracchi.

Asia: 1. Name given by ancient writers to one of the two parts into which they divided the land mass—Europe and Asia, this last including Libya, i.e. Africa (q.v.). Herodotus treats Libya as distinct from Asia. *See* ALEXANDER THE GREAT; INDIA; SERES; SINAE.

2. Roman province, the first one east of the Aegean. It was formed from the kingdom of Pergamum (q.v.), which in 133 B.C. was bequeathed to the Roman people by Attalus III, and consisted at first

of Mysia, Lydia, Caria and Phrygia. From 80 to 50 B.C. the upper valley of the Maeander and most of Phrygia were severed and included in the province of Cilicia. In 27 B.C. Asia became a senatorial province under a pro-consul. It was the richest of all the Roman provinces, and the benefits it derived from the peace re-established by Augustus led the provincials to introduce a religious cult of the emperor, which was quickly associated with that of Ephesian Artemis. Under Diocletian (A.D. 287) Asia was split up into a number of smaller provinces (*see* DIOCESE), one of which, with its capital at Ephesus, retained the original name.

Asisium (mod. Assisi), town of Umbria, about 15 miles east-south-east of Perusia; birth-place of Propertius (q.v.).

Asopus (Asōpos), river of Sicyon (q.v.) flowing into the Corinthian Gulf. Its god was a son of Oceanus and Tethys, and father of Aegina by whom Zeus was in turn the father of Aeacus (q.v.). There were two other rivers of the same name, one in Boeotia and another in Thessaly.

Aspasia, daughter of Axiochus and the most celebrated of the Greek *hetairai*. Born at Miletus, she came to Athens and won the affection of Pericles (q.v.), who, having parted from his wife, lived with her until his death in 429 B.C. Her house was the meeting-place of the best literary and philosophical society of Athens, and was frequented even by Socrates. The enemies of Pericles accused Aspasia of impiety (*see* HERMIPPUS), and all his personal influence was needed to secure her acquittal. After his death, according to one story, she attached herself to a cattle-dealer named Lysicles and made him by her instruction a first-rate orator.

Aspendus (-os), city of Pamphylia, on a hill above the right bank of the Eurymedon. Once quite close to the sea, it is now about seven miles inland. Of pre-hellenic origin, Aspendus had become by the 5th century B.C. a city of great wealth, due to its thriving trade in salt, oil and wool. Occupied by Alexander the Great in 333 B.C., it subsequently belonged to the kingdom of Pergamum (q.v.), and after 133 B.C. to Rome. There are fine remains of the city, but they are eclipsed by the wonderful Roman theatre on the north-east slope of the hill, which is the best preserved of any in the world. According to an inscription *in situ* the theatre was built in honour of the emperors Marcus Aurelius and Lucius Verus by the heirs of a local Roman citizen, and was designed by the architect Zeno. The auditorium could hold 7,500 spectators; it has forty tiers of seats (virtually intact) crowned by an arcade of somewhat later date. The structure that once supported a wooden stage is undamaged, as also is the *scena* wall except for its decoration. There are enormous vaults beneath the auditorium. *See* D. G. Hogarth, *Accidents of an Antiquary's Life*, 1910.

Assos (mod. Behram), Greek city and seaport of the Troad, magnificently situated on a series of lofty natural terraces overlooking the Adramyttian Gulf. On the summit was a temple of Athena. Assos is said to have been founded from Methymna in Lesbos between 1000 and 900 B.C. Subject in turn to the kings of Lydia, Persia and Pergamum, it passed under the will of Attalus III to Rome in 133 B.C. From 347 to *c.* 344 Aristotle (q.v.) lived here, at which time Assos, together with Atarneus, was under the immediate rule of Hermeias (q.v.). *See* J. T. Clarke, *Assos*, 2 vols., 1882, 1898 (Papers of the Archaeological Institute of America).

Astacus (-kos), Greek city of Bithynia, situated on a bay of the same name in the Propontis. Founded from Megara, it afterwards received other settlers from Athens, and was destroyed by Lysimachus (q.v.).

Astēr of Amphipolis, an archer of legendary skill. He offered his services to Philip II of Macedon with the boast that he never missed his mark. 'Good!' replied the king. 'I'll employ you when I make war on the starlings.' Angered by this mockery, Aster made his way into the town of Methone, which was besieged by Philip, and fired an arrow on which was written 'To Philip's right eye'. He had not exaggerated his prowess, for the arrow hit its mark. Philip had it returned to the archer with this inscription: 'If Philip takes the town, Aster will be hanged.' And so he was.

Asteria (-iē), daughter of the Titans Coeus and Phoebe (*see* TITANS), and sister of Leto (q.v.). She was the wife of Perses, son of Helios and mother of Hecate (q.v.). In order to escape the embraces of Zeus, she took the form of a quail (*ortyx*) and threw herself from heaven into the sea. Here she was metamorphosed into the island Asteria (which had fallen 'like a star') or Ortygia, which was afterwards called Delos.

Astraeus (-aios), one of the Titans (q.v.), husband of Eos (q.v.).

Astura, peninsula (formerly an island) on the coast of Latium, 39 miles south-east of Rome. Here Cicero had a villa to which he retired after the death of his daughter Tullia (45 B.C.). The place was frequented by Augustus and Tiberius, each of whom, according to Suetonius, here contracted his last illness.

Astures, a people inhabiting the mountains of north-west Spain (mod. Asturias). They were not subdued by Rome until the reign of Augustus.

Astyanax (Astu-) or **Scamandrius (Skamandrios)**, baby son of Hector and Andromache (qq.v.). The second of these names was said to have been given him by his parents, while the people of Troy conferred the other as a kind of honorary title because his father was 'protector of the city'. For his fate *see* ANDROMACHE.

Astydamas (Astu-), name of two Greek tragedians, father and son, of the 4th century B.C. Nothing of their works survives.

Astynomi (Astunomoi), 'city commissioners', Greek officials whose main functions were care of the streets and, in some states, supervision of the harbour and markets. At Athens, in the time of Aristotle, they were ten in number, five for Peiraeus and five for the upper city. They were chosen annually by lot, and the *Constitution of Athens* (50) lists their duties as follows: to supervise the hiring of female instrumentalists; to see that no sewage collector dumped any of his filth within ten stadia of the city walls; to prevent people encroaching on the streets with buildings, and from endangering passers-by with projecting balconies, overhead drainpipes or windows that opened outwards; to provide for the removal and burial of those who dropped dead in the streets.'

Atalanta or **Atalantē**, in Greek legend, daughter of the Arcadian

Iasus by his wife Clymene. Exposed at birth, she was suckled by a she-bear, the symbol of Artemis. She took part in the Calydonian hunt (*see* MELEAGER), and was later recognized by her father, and when he desired her to marry she required that every suitor should contend with her in the foot-race; she would wed the first man who outstripped her, but unsuccessful competitors would be put to death. She was eventually defeated by Meilanion: Aphrodite gave him three of the golden apples of the Hesperides (q.v.), which he dropped one after another during the race and which Atalanta stopped to pick up. She accordingly married him and became the mother of Parthenopaeus, one of the Seven against Thebes. Both she and Meilanion afterwards incurred the wrath of Aphrodite, and the goddess caused them to cohabit in a shrine sacred to Cybele, who turned them into lions.

In the Boeotian version of this legend the same stories are told, except that the scene is laid in Boeotia, Atalanta's father is named Schoenus, and her husband Hippomenes.

Atē, in Greek mythology, daughter of Zeus or of Eris (strife). She personifies infatuation or criminal folly, leading both gods and men astray. In later legend she is the avenger of sin.

Atella, Oscan town of Campania, nine miles south of Capua, of which it was a dependant. Having sided with Hannibal in the second Punic war it was captured by the Romans in 211 B.C., not, however, before the population had removed to Thurii. The town is famous chiefly as the place where *Atellanae Fabulae* (q.v.) are said to have been first produced.

Atellanae Fabulae, popular farces of Oscan origin, said to have been brought to Rome from Atella (q.v.). They were improvised burlesques from low life; but during the last century B.C. it became fashionable to present them after the performance of tragedies, and for this purpose they were given literary form by L. Pomponius and others. Certain stock characters appeared, e.g. Maccus the glutton, Bucco the fool, Pagus (Pantaloon) and Dossenus (Punch). *Atellanae fabulae* were gradually superseded by the mime and disappeared about the time of Tiberius. *See* O. Ribbeck, *Comicorum Romanorum Fragmenta,* 3rd ed., 1898; G. E. Duckworth, *The Nature of Roman Comedy,* 1952. *See* NOVIUS, QUINTUS.

Athamas, legendary king of Orchomenus in Boeotia, son of Aeolus, and brother of Salmoneus and Sisyphus (qq.v.). By command of Hera he wedded Nephele, who bore him Phrixus (q.v.) and Helle; but he was secretly in love with Ino, daughter of Cadmus (q.v.), by whom he begot Learchus and Melicertes. Having incurred the wrath of Hera, Athamas was driven mad and killed Learchus. Ino threw herself with the infant Melicertes into the sea, where both were changed into marine deities—Ino as Leucothea, Melicertes as Palaemon. The body of Melicertes, however, was carried by a dolphin to the Isthmus of Corinth. It was found by Sisyphus, who, in obedience to an order from the nereids, transferred it to Corinth and instituted the Isthmian games in his memory. Palaemon was sometimes identified at Rome with Portunus (q.v.), Leucothea with Mater Matuta (q.v.). Athamas, as murderer of his son, was obliged to flee from Boeotia, and settled in Thessaly.

Athēna or **Athēnē**, one of the great divinities of the Greeks. She is frequently called Pallas Athena, or simply Pallas. She was the daughter of Zeus and Metis (= wise counsel). Before her birth Zeus swallowed her mother; and Athena afterwards sprang forth from the head of Zeus in complete armour. The theory of her origin now generally accepted is that of Nilsson. She was the pre-hellenic patroness of Minoan and Mycenaean princes in their fortress-palaces, and her later association with the snake and the olive-tree is derived from the ancient worship of a snake-goddess and the tree-cults of Minoan-Mycenaean religion. The Athenian Acropolis was the site of a Mycenean palace, and the invading Greeks adopted the goddess with the conquered citadel. It is possible that they identified her with a warlike virgin goddess of their own from whom the name Pallas was derived. The chief characteristics of Athena may be summarized thus: (1) Under the titles *Polias* and *Poliuchos* she was patroness and defender of the Athenian state, a natural consequence of her status in Mycenaean days. (2) She was the personification of wisdom, expressed in the myth of her birth from the head of Zeus. From pre-hellenic times she was probably thought of as protecting and guiding the handicrafts carried on in the royal palace: with the increasing industrialization of Athens her functions tended to embrace every kind of skill, and lastly the purely intellectual activity of her citizens. (3) She was a virgin goddess, despising love and marriage: yet as guardian of the state she was concerned for the fertility of animal and vegetable life. (4) She was a goddess of war, a position due almost entirely to the Greek invaders and the fusion of Athena with their national goddess. Her principal festival at Athens was the Panathenaea (q.v.), and her temple, the Parthenon (q.v.), the most celebrated in the world.

Athenaeum (Athēnaion), in general, a building or other place sacred to Athena (q.v.); but used more particularly of a literary and scientific school founded at Rome by Hadrian in A.D. 133, also called *Schola Romana*, for courses in law, rhetoric and philosophy.

Athenaeus (Athēnaios), Greek grammarian, *fl. c.* A.D. 200. Born at Naucratis in Egypt, he lived first at Alexandria and afterwards at Rome. His *Deipnosophistai* (Scholars at Dinner) consists of anecdotes, extracts from ancient writers and discussions on various subjects, especially gastronomy. Fifteen of 30 books survive. *See* edition with translation by C. B. Gulick, 7 vols., 1927–41.

Athenodorus (Athēnodōros): 1. Stoic philosopher of Tarsus, born *c.* 74 B.C. at Canana near that city and thence surnamed Cananites. A pupil of Poseidonius (q.v.) at Rhodes, he afterwards taught for a while at Tarsus and then at Apollonia in Illyricum, where Octavian (later the emperor Augustus) was among his pupils at the time of Caesar's murder in 44 B.C. He accompanied Octavian to Rome in that year and exercised a permanent influence over him, but afterwards returned to Tarsus, for which he drew up a new constitution, and died in A.D. 7.

2. Surnamed Cordylion, *fl. c.* 65 B.C. After serving as head of the library at Pergamum he settled in Rome, where he died at an advanced age in the house of Cato some time after 47 B.C.

3. A musician of Teos, who played the cithara at the wedding of Alexander the Great and Stateira at Susa (324 B.C.).

4. Greek physician of the 1st century A.D. His work on epidemics has not survived.

5. Greek sculptor who made the statues of Zeus and Apollo dedicated by the Spartans at Delphi in thanksgiving for their victory at Aegospotami (405 B.C.).

6. One of the three sculptors of the Laocoön group. *See* AGE-SANDER; LAOCOÖN.

Athens (Gk Athēnai; Lat. Athenae) is situated on the Attic plain (*see* ATTICA) about four and a half miles from the harbour town of Peiraeus. The plain slopes gradually south-west to the Saronic Gulf. It is bounded east by Mt Hymettus (3,369 feet), famous for honey and marble; north-east by Pentelicus (3,635 feet), from which marble for the Parthenon and many other buildings was obtained; north-west by Parnes (4,636 feet), which formed the boundary between Boeotia and Attica; and west by Aegaleos (q.v.), which rises to a height of 1,532 feet. Through the centre of the plain there runs a ridge terminating in Mt Lycabettus (1,112 feet), which overlooked the ancient city though not included in its walls, and separating the valleys of the Cephissus (q.v.) and Ilissus. A little to the south-west of Lycabettus is the Acropolis (507 feet), with the hill of Areopagus to the north-west, and the Hill of the Nymphs and the Pnyx respectively west and south-east. Museum Hill lies south-west of the Acropolis.

The geographical situation, climate and natural resources assured to Athens her political and cultural greatness. Archaeological discoveries prove that the place was inhabited in neolithic times; in the late bronze age there was a palace-fort on the Acropolis (*see* ATHENA), and the city soon extended to the plain below.

The Acropolis forms a sharply defined plateau with precipitous sides, except at the western extremity which in early times was strengthened by an outer wall known as the Pelargicon or (from its nine gates) as Enneapylon. This, together with the cyclopean wall already mentioned, was strong enough to defy the Spartans when the Peisistratids took refuge in the Acropolis; but after the expulsion of the tyrants (510 B C.) they were partly dismantled, and what little was left of them, together with the old shrine of Athena and other buildings on the Acropolis, was destroyed by the Persians in 480 B.C. With the return of peace work began on rebuilding the walls of the Acropolis. The north wall was partly erected by Themistocles; it incorporated numerous fragments of buildings ruined by the Persians. The walls on the south and east were built by Cimon soon after 468 B.C.; they extend some distance beyond the original circuit, the intervening space being filled with debris of ruined buildings. Cimon also completed the north wall at both ends; and an ancient bastion at the south-west corner was made into a rectangular base for the temple of Athena Nike. The top of the Acropolis now measured about 1,000 feet from east to west and about 500 feet from north to south. For a detailed account of the three principal monuments on the Acropolis *see* ERECHTHEUM; PARTHENON; PROPYLAEA. The temple of Nike, designed by Callicrates, was built in Pentelic marble at about the same time as the Propylaea. Its plan is amphiprostyle tetrastyle; that is to say it has two porticoes (facing east and west) each with four columns, which in this case are of the Ionic order and 13 feet high. The temple measures 26 feet 10 inches by 17 feet 8 inches. From the apex of the pediment to the bottom of the stylobate of three steps the distance was 23 feet. The frieze, which is 85 feet 6 inches long, shows on the east a series of gods, on the north and south Greeks fighting Persians, and on the west Greeks fighting Greeks. The altar was situated before the east portico. Inside was a statue of the goddess holding a pomegranate in her right hand and a helmet in her left. Among the several shrines, altars and other works of art that adorned the Acropolis the most famous was the colossal bronze statue of Athena Promachos, which stood just inside the Propylaea. It was the work of Pheidias, 30 feet high, and visible to sailors off Cape Sunium. At the south-east corner of the Acropolis is now a museum, among the finest treasures of which are works of archaic art discovered among the rubble of buildings destroyed by the Persians.

 The Agora, lying north-west of the Acropolis, was the centre of public life. It has been excavated at vast expense and with infinite care by the American School of Classical Studies (1930–55). Here were the various administrative buildings (*see* BOULE). The area was surrounded by stoas, shed-like buildings, often containing shops, with deep porches in front that afforded both sun and shade. On the west side was the Stoa of Zeus, which Socrates frequented; on the north side the Stoa Poikile (q.v.), from which the Stoics derived their name. On the east side was the Stoa of Attalus which has now been restored and is used as a museum, housing more than 65,000 objects of every period found during the excavation of the Agora. It was built *c.* 158 B.C. by Attalus II of Pergamum. Towards the centre of the Agora, in Roman times, stood the Odeum built by M. Vipsanius Agrippa, *c.* 15 B.C. It was partially rebuilt after a fall of the roof in the 2nd century A.D., at which date also was constructed the Library of Pantaenus, south of the Stoa of Attalus.

On some rising ground called Agoraeus Colonos, facing the western end of the Agora, is the so-called Theseum. This, the best-preserved Greek temple in the world, was actually a temple of Hephaestus. It was built at about the same time as the Parthenon and mostly of Pentelic marble, though the bottom step of the stylobate and the frieze of the *cella* (labours of Heracles and deeds of Theseus) are respectively of Peiraic stone and Parian marble. The style is Doric and the plan peripteral hexastyle *in antis* with 13 columns each side; length 104 feet; width 45 feet 6 inches; height from bottom of stylobate to apex of pediment 33 feet 6 inches.

East of the Agora and below the northern slopes of the Acropolis are the remains of the *Roman Market* (1st century B.C.) with those of a vast enclosure built by Hadrian a little to the north-east. Immediately to the east of the Roman Market is the *Horologium*, commonly called the Tower of the Winds. Built in the 2nd or 1st century B.C. by Andronicus of Cyrrhus in Macedonia, it is a marble octagon with a diameter of 26 feet 8 inches and a height, including the stepped base, of 41 feet 7 inches. The frieze consists of poorly carved reliefs showing the eight winds; below it on the sides facing the sun are marks for the sundials. Inside was a water clock, and the structure was crowned by a bronze Triton which served as a weather-vane.

Below the south-east corner of the Acropolis stands the *choragic monument of Lysicrates* dating from the year 335–334 B.C. It is the only survivor of many which, lining the Street of Tripods from the city to the Theatre of Dionysus, bore the tripods awarded to success-ful choragoi at the Dionysiac festival. The monument of Lysicrates is a cylindrical structure of Pentelic marble, 21 feet 2 inches high and about 9 feet diameter, with six engaged columns of the Corinthian order; it stands on a rectangular base of Peiraic stone. The frieze illustrates the legend of Dionysus turning the Tyrrhenian pirates into dolphins. The roof, a single convex block of marble, originally bore the tripod.

Theatre of Dionysus and Odeum of Herodes Atticus. At the end of the Street of Tripods, below the eastern extremity of the south side of the Acropolis and in the sacred Precinct of Dionysus Eleuthereus, is the Theatre of Dionysus. The earliest Athenian theatre was in the Agora; the site now under discussion was chosen in 490 B.C., and it was here that the plays of Aeschylus, Sophocles, Euripides and Aristophanes were first performed. In their time, however, the audi-torium was of wood with the seating in straight lines; both actors and chorus used the orchestra except when circumstances required the erection of a temporary stage. Between 338 and 326 B.C. the orator Lycurgus (*see* LYCURGUS, 2) rebuilt the entire theatre in stone, with a permanent stage and a semicircular auditorium hollowed out in the slope. But the stage and orchestra were later modified, first under Nero and subsequently under Hadrian. The auditorium in its final form had 78 tiers divided into three sections and could seat between 14,000 and 17,000 spectators. The front row consisted of 67 marble thrones which were occupied by the Priest of Dionysus and other distinguished persons. The theatre was later used also for meetings of the Ecclesia (q.v.), which had formerly taken place on the Pnyx (*see* below).

East of the theatre was the Odeum of Pericles, which was restored and improved by King Ariobarzanes I of Cappadocia after its destruction by Sulla in 86 B.C. Immediately west of the theatre was a precinct and temple of Asclepius, westward from which ran a Doric colonnade 162 feet long.

Below the south-west corner of the Acropolis are the massive and well-preserved ruins of the Odeum built by Herodes Atticus (q.v.) soon after A.D. 161 in memory of his wife Appia Annia Regilla. At its eastern end it adjoined the stoa (about 250 yards) erected by Eumenes II of Pergamum (197–159 B.C.), which led, at its eastern extremity, to the theatre a little south of the above-mentioned Doric colonnade.

City Walls, Streets, etc. The sites and buildings mentioned above were all contained within the wall erected by Themistocles immedi-ately after the Persian withdrawal, reconstructed by Conon in 393 and again by Lycurgus about 333 B.C. It included four quarters: Collytos on the north, Melite on the west, Limnae on the south, and Diomeia on the east. The most important gate in this circuit was the

Dipylon, on the north-west, where the Sacred Way to Eleusis was joined by other roads to Peiraeus, Megara and Thebes. Just outside was the Ceramicus (q.v.), the main burial ground of the city, where many fine monuments of the fifth and fourth centuries B.C. have been discovered. On the east, between the Hill of the Nymphs and the Pnyx, was the Melitan gate, leading via the Long Walls to Peiraeus (see *Peiraeus and the Long Walls* below). On the south the road to Phaleron issued from the Itonian gate. In the city itself the Sacred Way wound through the Agora up to the western end of the Acropolis. From north of the Acropolis two roads curved round the eastern declivity: one, the Street of the Tripods (already mentioned), led to the Theatre of Dionysus and continued along the southern side to meet roads encircling the Areopagus; another ran in a much wider sweep to the Olympieion or temple of Olympian Zeus outside the wall. This enormous structure of Pentelic marble, begun by Hippias, was continued by the architect Cossutius for Antiochus IV of Syria in 175–164 B.C., and completed by Hadrian who dedicated it in A.D. 132. The plan was octostyle; length 318 feet, breadth 132 feet. Of the 104 Corinthian columns, 56 feet high, 24 were arranged in triple rows at each end and 28 in double rows at each side. Only 15 are now standing.

Hadrian also enlarged the circuit of the walls on the eastern side to form an area known as Hadrianopolis or Novae Athenae, which he embellished with beautiful gardens, buildings, and other works of art. The new wall began on the south a little north-east of the Itonian gate, ran in the same direction to include the Olympieion, and eventually turned north-west and west, rejoining the Themistoclean wall.

Finally, outside the wall of Hadrian, was the Stadium in which the Panathenaic games were held. Erected by Lycurgus about 330 B.C. on the left bank of the Ilissus, it was reconstructed in Pentelic marble about A.D. 143 by Herodes Atticus and restored in the latter part of the 19th century. Its shape was that of an elongated horseshoe, 670 feet in length and 109 feet in width; the tiered seats could accommodate 44,000 spectators.

Peiraeus and the Long Walls. The original harbour of Athens was in the north-east corner of Phaleron Bay: but Themistocles, seeing the advantages of Peiraeus both as a strategic and as a commercial centre, began to fortify it during his archonship (493 B.C.). After rebuilding the city walls he set to work again on the defences of Peiraeus, which included the western harbour of Cantharos (modified by Conon) and the two eastern harbours of Zea and Munychia, omitting only the high south-eastern extremity of the peninsula. The town was laid out by Hippodamus of Miletus under Pericles. Cantharos was the commercial port with the Emporium and state corn depot; in Zea and Munychia were the naval dockyards, some remarkable vestiges of which can still be seen. Among several temples the most noteworthy was that of Zeus Soter, patron god of sailors.

The Long Walls connecting Athens with Peiraeus were three: the North Wall, the Middle or South Wall, and the Phaleric Wall. The first and third were probably begun by Cimon and finished about 457 B.C., the second was constructed about 445 B.C. The north wall started in Athens from the north-eastern corner of the Hill of the Nymphs, the south wall from the Melitan gate; they gradually converged and ran parallel at a distance of 550 feet, widening out again as they approached Peiraeus. The course of the Phaleric wall is uncertain; it was found to be useless and was abandoned towards the end of the Peloponnesian war. Like the North and South walls, it was destroyed when Athens surrendered in 404 B.C.; but unlike them it was not rebuilt by Conon in 393. The two parallel walls were finally destroyed by Sulla.

The Pnyx, an ancient sanctuary of Zeus, was also the meeting-place of the Ecclesia (q.v.) until this was removed to the Theatre of Dionysus. On the north-east slope of the hills is a double terrace measuring 395 feet by 212 feet. The upper part is rock-hewn, the lower is supported by a huge semicircular retaining wall of the 4th century. This wall was originally much higher and carried tiers of seats or steps which sloped towards the upper terrace. From the chord of the semicircle projects a cube of rock 11 feet square and 5 feet high approached on each side by steps; this was the *bema* or orators' platform.

See ATTICA; CLEISTHENES; CYLON; DRACON; PEISISTRATUS; PELOPONNESIAN WAR; PERICLES; PERSIAN WARS; SOLON; THEMISTOCLES. For government see ARCHON; AREOPAGUS; BOULE; ECCLESIA; EUPATRIDAE. *See also* Sir J. G. Frazer (trans.), *Pausanias*, 6 vols., 1898; E. A. Gardner, *Ancient Athens*, 1902; A. E. Haigh, *The Attic Theatre*, 1907; M. L. D'Ooge, *Acropolis of Athens*, 1909; C. H. Weller, *The Monuments of Athens*, 1913; *Journal of the American School of Classical Studies at Athens*, 1932 onwards; L. T. Hill, *The Ancient City of Athens*, 1953; M. Hürlimann, *Athens* (superb photography with introductory text by Rex Warner), 1956.

Athos, see ACTE.

Atia, daughter of M. Atius Balbus by his wife Julia (sister of Julius Caesar), and mother of the emperor Augustus (q.v.).

Atlas, 'the Bearer', legendary king of Mauretania, son of the Titan Iapetus by Clymene, daughter of Oceanus. Having refused hospitality to Perseus (q.v.), he was changed into Mt Atlas by the latter, who showed him the head of Medusa, and condemned him to bear the heavens on his head and hands (*see also* TWELVE LABOURS OF HERACLES, 11). By Aethra, Atlas was father of the Hyades, the Pleiades (q.v.) and (according to some) the Hesperides (q.v.).

In hellenistic architecture the colossal statues used sometimes instead of columns were called Atlantes.

Atreids, Legend of the. Atreus and Thyestes, sons of Pelops (q.v.), King of Pisa in Elis, murdered their half-brother Chrysippus with the connivance of their mother Hippodameia. They then took refuge with Eurystheus, King of Mycenae, whom Atreus succeeded on the throne, having begotten by Aeropë two sons, Agamemnon and Menelaus, and a daughter Anaxibia. Thyestes now seduced Aeropë, and was driven into exile by his brother. Some time afterwards, pretending to be reconciled, Atreus recalled Thyestes, killed the latter's two sons and served up their flesh to him at a banquet. The sun turned back in horror, Thyestes fled, and the gods cursed the house of Atreus.

Mycenae was consequently visited by famine, and Atreus was advised by an oracle to bring back his brother. Going in search of him, he reached the court of King Thesprotus, and there married a lady named Pelopia, believing her to be the king's daughter. She was in fact none other than the daughter of Thyestes, and was already pregnant by her own father. In due time the son of this incestuous union, Aegisthus, slew Atreus and placed Thyestes on the throne of Mycenae. There are later variants of the genealogy up to this point, and elaborations of the story involving further incest, murder and intrigue.

After the murder of their father, Agamemnon and Menelaus fled to Sparta. They were hospitably received by King Tyndareus (q.v.), whose daughters Clytaemnestra and Helen (q.v.) they respectively married. By Clytaemnestra Agamemnon had a son, Orestes, and three daughters, Iphigeneia, Electra and Chrysothemis. Helped by Menelaus, who had succeeded Tyndareus, he drove Aegisthus and Thyestes from Mycenae, recovered his father's throne and established his authority over the whole of Argos. (For the rest of the story of Menelaus *see* MENELAUS). When Paris (q.v.) carried off Helen, Agamemnon visited the courts of various princes and persuaded them to unite in a war of revenge against the Trojans. He himself provided 100 ships and was chosen to lead the expedition. After two years of preparation a great fleet of 1,200 ships assembled at Aulis in Boeotia, where Agamemnon killed a stag sacred to Artemis. The goddess retaliated with a period of adverse weather, and the seer Calchas (q.v.) announced that her wrath could be appeased only by the sacrifice of Iphigeneia (q.v.). On his return home he was murdered by Clytaemnestra at the instigation of Aegisthus (*see* Aeschylus, *Agamemnon*). Agamemnon was worshipped at Sparta in hellenistic times (*see* J. R. Farnell, *Greek Hero Cults*, 1921), and it is not unlikely that behind the legend we have in him an historical figure. For the avenging of Agamemnon's death *see* ORESTES.

Atreus, son of Pelops, brother of Thyestes and father of Agamemnon, *see* ATREIDS, LEGEND OF THE.

Atria : 1. (Often but incorrectly **Adria** or **Hadria**.) Italian town situated about 13 miles from the sea between the mouths of the Athesis (Adige) and Padus (Po); once an Etruscan harbour, which gave its name to the Adriatic Sea. According to Aristotle it was noted for a breed of fowls. Being difficult of access owing to river silt, it was connected with the sea by a canal which was dug by order of Philistus (q.v.).

2. Town of Picenum, the modern Atri. *See* HADRIANUS.

Atropatēnē, an independent kingdom formed from the northern parts of Media (q.v.) after the death of Alexander the Great, and named after its first ruler, Atropates, satrap of Media (q.v.). The capital was Gazaca. The kings of Atropatene later became dependent first upon Parthia, then upon Tigranes (q.v.), and then upon Rome. Finally it became a province of the Parthian Empire, which was conquered (A.D. 226) by the Sassanid monarch Ardashir (q.v.).

Attalia (-eia), seaport city of Pamphylia, named after Attalus II of Pergamum. In the first centuries A.D. it superseded Perga (q.v.) as the Pamphylian capital. Its prosperity was due to its being the nearest point of export for the products of south-west Phrygia and of embarkation for travellers from Central Asia Minor to Syria and Egypt. It was also the beginning of a sea-land route from the eastern Mediterranean to Ephesus and Smyrna.

Attalus (-os), name of three kings of Pergamum:

1. *Attalus I*, 241–197 B.C., cousin and successor of Eumenes I (*see* EUMENES (B)). Thanks to his alliance with Rome and his support of the republic against Philip V of Macedon, Pergamum became the political and cultural capital of an enlarged territory. In order to commemorate a victory over the Gauls (*see* GALATIA) in 230, Attalus adorned the city with a number of statues, among which was the 'Dying Gaul', immortalized by Byron and now at Rome. Attalus was the first ruler of Pergamum to assume the kingly title.

2. *Attalus II*, surnamed Philadelphus, 159–138 B.C., brother and successor of Eumenes II (*see* EUMENES (B)). Like his two predecessors he was an ally of Rome. It was Attalus II who built the recently restored Stoa of Attalus (*see* ATHENS, *The Agora*).

3. *Attalus III*, surnamed Philometer, 138–133 B.C.; son of Eumenes II, nephew and successor of Attalus II. Being childless, he bequeathed his kingdom to Rome (*see* ARISTONICUS; PERGAMUM).

See E. V. Hanson, *The Attalids of Pergamum*, 1947.

Attic Orators, The ten: Antiphon, Andocides, Lysias, Isocrates, Isaeus, Lycurgus, Aeschines, Demosthenes, Hypereides, Deinarchus (qq.v.).

Attica, a division of Greece with an area of about 1,000 square miles, has the form of a triangle with its base in the mountains of Parnes and Cithaeron, which separated it from Boeotia, and its apex at Cape Sunium; the two remaining sides were washed by the Aegean Sea. The soil was not very fertile, except for the production of figs and olives; these grew in great abundance, and in the legendary dispute between Poseidon and Athena for the possession of Attica the god was obliged to yield to the giver of the olive. The country is mountainous, but several plains, notably those of Eleusis and Athens, lie between the ranges. The chief river is the Cephissus (q.v.). Marble was obtained from the quarries of Pentelicus and Hymettus, silver from the mines at Laurium (q.v.).

According to legend Ion, the grandson of Hellen, divided the people into four tribes. Theseus, to whom is attributed the fusion (synoecism) of the twelve independent states of Attica, with Athens as the capital, is supposed to have again divided the population into three classes— Eupatridae (q.v.), Geomori and Demiurgi. Historically this fusion seems to have been a slow process, not completed until the 7th century B.C. Cleisthenes (q.v.) abolished the old tribes and created ten new ones, which were subdivided into 174 demoi or townships.

Atticus, *see* POMPONIUS ATTICUS.

Attis or **Atys,** paramour of Agdistis (Cybele). There are variants of this, as of most ancient myths, but the following is the most ancient version. Agdistis, originally androgynous, was castrated by the gods. From the severed genitals there grew an almond-tree, by the fruit of which Nana, daughter of the river-god Sangarius, conceived and bore

Attis. Agdistis, having fallen in love with the youth and being jealous at his desire to marry another woman, drove him to frenzy, in which he castrated himself. From his blood the violets sprang, and Zeus thereupon turned him into a pine-tree.

In the rites commemorating his death (*see also* CRIBOLIUM) the corpse was represented by a felled pine wrapped with a shroud and adorned with wreaths. Attis was no doubt in origin a vegetation-god, whose death and resurrection were commemorated at the spring equinox. His worship was rare in Greece proper; but at Rome, under Claudius, he was granted official status and was regarded as a supreme solar deity. See H. Hepding, *Attis,* 1903; Sir J. G. Frazer, *Attis, Adonis, Osiris,* 1907.

Attius, *see* ACTIUS.

Atys, *see* ATTIS.

Aufidius Bassus, Roman historian of the 1st century A.D. Besides his lost *Bellum Germanicum,* an account of Tiberius's German campaigns, he wrote a history covering the period 44 B.C.–A.D. 50. This work was of high authority, but only fragments have survived.

Augē, daughter of Aleus, King of Tegea, and mother of Telephus (q.v.) by Heracles. She was afterwards married to Teuthras.

Augures, augurs, a college of priests at Rome, whose business it was to observe and interpret the signs (*auspicia*) of divine approval or otherwise on all important occasions. These signs most usually took the form of celestial and meteorological phenomena, the flight, song or feeding of birds, or accidental occurrences (*see* HARUSPICES).

Augusta, title of several Roman cities founded by Augustus. Among them were *Augusta Taurinorum* (Turin), *Augusta Treverorum* (Trier), *Augusta Emerita* (Mérida) and *Augusta Vindelicorum* (Augsburg). **By far** the most important, however, was *Augusta Praetoria Salassorum* (q.v.).

Augusta Praetoria Salassorum (mod. Aosta), town of Gallia Cisalpina (Transpadana), in the territory of the Salassi, a tribe subdued in 25 B.C. by Varro Murena. In the following year, and on the site of Murena's camp, Augustus founded this town, where he settled 3,000 praetorians. Its geographical situation, at the confluence of two rivers and on one of the main roads into Gaul, which bisected the town, made it of great strategic importance. The Roman walls, with 20 towers, enclosed an area of more than 100 acres; the streets, crossing one another at right angles, formed sixteen *insulae.* Roman remains have been discovered, but the most interesting survival is a one-arched bridge some five miles west of the town. This has a covered passage lighted by windows and an open path of the same width (3 feet 6 inches) above. See F. Haverfield, *Ancient Town Planning,* 1913.

Augustus (Gk Sebastos), meaning 'venerable' or 'majestic', a title conferred by the senate upon the first Roman emperor and borne by all his successors. (For events between 44 and 30 B.C. this article should be read in conjunction with ANTONIUS, MARCUS, 3.)

Gaius Octavius, son of Gaius Octavius by Atia, niece of Julius Caesar, was born at Rome on 23rd September 63 B.C. His father died in 58; his mother remarried, and Octavius passed into the household of his stepfather L. Marcius Philippus. At the age of fifteen or sixteen he was elected to the college of pontiffs, and in 46 took part in Caesar's triumph. In 45 he was sent by the latter to study at Apollonia in Illyricum, where the Stoic Athenodorus was among his teachers (*see* ATHENODORUS, 1), and M. Vipsanius Agrippa (q.v.) one of his companions. On receiving news of his great-uncle's assassination (44), he returned to Rome and found that Caesar had made him his heir. His correct name was now Gaius Julius Caesar Octavianus, and he is called in English, from this date until 27 B.C., Octavian. No one at the time thought him of the slightest consequence.

Octavian began by allying himself with the senatorial party in order to crush Mark Antony, whom, with the assistance of the two consuls, Hirtius and Pansa, he defeated at Mutina (43). But the death of both consuls in this action gave Octavian command of all their troops, who compelled the senate to give him the consulship. He could now afford a reconciliation with Antony. The latter had been joined by M. Aemilius Lepidus, and towards the end of that year (27 Nov.) the three formed a five-year coalition, known to history as the Second Triumvirate, dividing among themselves the western provinces and leaving Brutus and Cassius in possession of the East for the time being. Proscriptions followed, in which more than 200 knights and senators (among them Cicero) perished. What was left of the republican party joined Brutus and Cassius, or Sextus Pompeius (q.v.) whose fleet controlled the Mediterranean sea routes. In 42 Octavian and Antony defeated Brutus and Cassius at Philippi. Octavian returned to Italy, where, in 41, he defeated Antony's brother Lucius, and in the next year was reconciled anew with Antony and a fresh distribution of the provinces was made, Octavian taking the West, Antony the East and Lepidus (a slight unmeritable man) Africa. The alliance was cemented by a marriage between Antony and Octavian's sister Octavia. With the help of Agrippa, Octavian then turned his arms against Sextus Pompeius, who was defeated in 36 B.C. and put to death soon afterwards. Lepidus (q.v.) was also deprived of his authority, and only one obstacle remained—Mark Antony.

Octavian had married Livia in 38 (*see* SCRIBONIA), and with her assistance and that of Agrippa he proceeded to establish his own strength, to win public favour and to strengthen public confidence in his administration. In 31 the excesses of Antony, and the discovery of evidence proving the Egyptian queen's dangerous ambitions, led the senate to declare war on Cleopatra. On 21st December 31 B.C. Octavian's fleet, commanded by Agrippa, encountered the enemy off Actium (q.v.) in Acarnania. Antony's fleet was annihilated and his land forces surrendered. Alexandria was captured on 1st August 30, when Antony and Cleopatra committed suicide. Octavian returned to Italy in the summer of 29, celebrated a triumph, and was hailed by all classes as the saviour of Rome and the restorer of peace after sixty years of war and civil strife.

It is usual to describe the system of government now inaugurated by Octavian as the 'principate'. The old republican forms were restored in their entirety, but his was in fact the controlling hand. When he next left Rome, late in 27 B.C., he enjoyed the title of

Augustus (conferred by the senate on 17th January in that year), the tribunician power, the certainty of continuous re-election to the consulship and, above all, a ten years' *imperium* which gave him control of the frontier provinces, sole command of all the armed forces and the right to determine foreign relations.

From the end of 27 until the autumn of 19 B.C. Augustus was absent from Rome pacifying and reorganizing the provinces, first in the West and then in the East. In 18 B.C. his *imperium* was renewed for five years, in which his son-in-law Agrippa was his colleague. The next two years were spent in domestic reforms; but from 16 to 13 he was again absent, dealing with matters arising from the necessity of strengthening and extending the northern frontiers (*see also* DRUSUS, 4; TIBERIUS). Immediately on his return his *imperium* was renewed for yet another five years, and after the death of Lepidus in 12 B.C. he was elected pontifex maximus. Those five years witnessed the deaths of Agrippa, Drusus and Maecenas (q.v.).

For the problem of succession which occupied Augustus from 13 until A.D. 4 *see* GAIUS CAESAR; TIBERIUS.

The outstanding events of his last ten years were the great insurrection in Pannonia and Dalmatia (qq.v.), A.D. 6 (*see also* GERMANICUS; TIBERIUS), which was not finally put down until A.D. 9, and the defeat of Varus (q.v.) in the latter year.

Augustus died at Nola on 19th August A.D. 14 in the arms of Livia, exhorting her to 'live mindful of our wedded life'. He was seventy-six. *See* HORACE; LIVIUS; MONUMENTUM ANCYRANUM; OVID; VIRGIL. *See also* M. Hammond, *The Augustan Principate*, 1933; J. Buchan, *Augustus Caesar*, 1937; M. Grant, *From Imperium to Auctoritas*, 1946; G. W. Bowersock, *Augustus and the Greek World*, 1965.

Aulis, town of Boeotia on the Euripus, about three miles south of Chalcis. It is the traditional starting-place of the Greek fleet before the Trojan war and of the sacrifice of Iphigeneia (q.v.).

Aurelia, Via, Roman road of uncertain date. It ran north-west from Rome to Alsium, and thence along the coast to Cosa and Vada Volaterrana. From this last place it was extended in 109 via Genua to Dertona (*see* AEMILIA, VIA, 2). In the Antonine Itinerary (q.v.) the name Via Aurelia includes these extensions and even the further prolongation to Arelate (q.v.).

Aurelianus, Lucius Domitius, called in English **Aurelian**, Roman emperor A.D. 270-5, born at Sirmium, was successor of Claudius II. He defeated the Goths and Vandals, who had crossed the Danube, and the Germans, who had invaded Italy. He next turned his arms against Zenobia (q.v.), whom he defeated. He then recovered Gaul, Britain and Spain, which were in the hands of the usurper Tetricus. On his return to Rome he began a new line of walls (*see also* PROBUS). He abandoned Dacia, which had been first conquered by Trajan, and made the right bank of the Danube, as in the time of Augustus, the boundary of the empire. He was killed by some of his officers, while preparing to march against the Persians. Though a man of strong character and great military and administrative ability, he too readily followed the way of extreme severity.

Aurora, *see* EOS.

Aurunca or Ausona, *see* SUESSA AURUNCA.

Aurunci, name given by the Romans to a tribe who in the 4th century B.C. called themselves Ausones and were related to the Volsci (q.v.). In historical times they inhabited a narrow coastal strip between the rivers Liris and Volturnus, on the borders of Latium and Campania (*see* AUSONIA; SUESSA AURUNCA). They resisted the Roman advance from 340 to 295 B.C., when they were finally subdued.

Ausona or Aurunca, *see* SUESSA AURUNCA.

Ausonia, name given by Greek writers to the whole of Latium and Campania (*see* AURUNCI), and sometimes by the Augustan poets to the whole of Italy.

Auster, Latin name for the south-west wind (Gk Notos). It frequently brought fog and rain; but at certain seasons it was a dry sultry wind, the sirocco of modern Italy.

Autolycus (-lukos), son of Hermes by Chione, daughter of Daedalion. He dwelt on Mt Parnassus, and was the master-thief of Greek legend. His daughter Anticlea was wife of Laertes and mother of Odysseus.

Autolycus (-lukos), Greek astronomer of the 4th century B.C., a native of Pitane in Aeolis. He wrote *On the Moving Sphere*, the earliest complete Greek mathematical treatise that has survived. *See* the edition by H. Hultsch, 1885.

Automedon, the charioteer of Achilles, and, after the latter's death, the companion of his son Neoptolemus. Hence the name is used generally of a charioteer (cf. Juvenal, i. 61).

Autonoë, daughter of Cadmus and Harmonia (qq.v.), sister of Agave and Ino (*see* PENTHEUS). She was married to Aristaeus (not the son of Apollo and Cyrene) and became the mother of Actaeon (q.v.).

Autricum (mod. Chartres), capital of the Carnutes (q.v.) until its place was taken by Cenabum (Orleans) in A.D. 275.

Auxilia, the auxiliary Roman army created by Augustus on the basis of cavalry and light infantry forces, which for two hundred years had been raised outside Italy. The auxilia, recruited from unenfranchised provincials, were attached to individual legions and also employed as provincial garrisons. The cavalry contingents were known as *alae*, each commanded by an equestrian *praefectus*, while the infantry cohorts were under *tribuni*. Pay was lower than that of the legions, but the auxiliaries were granted the franchise at the end of their service. Some of these units preserved their native weapons, e.g. the oriental archers and Balearic slingers. *See* ROMAN ARMY. *See also* G. L. Cheesman, *The Auxilia of the Imperial Roman Army*, 1914.

Auximum (mod. Osimo), fortress town of Picenum, on a hill eight miles from the Adriatic. It overlooked the road from Ancona to Nuceria, and was built to protect Roman settlements in that area. The walls, dating from 174 B.C., survive.

Avernus (Gk Aornos), lake of Campania, about two miles from Baiae. Lying in the crater of an extinct volcano, it is 213 feet deep, though only 3½ feet above sea level. In ancient times it was surrounded by a forest sacred to Hecate (q.v.), and in order to explain the Greek name, which means 'birdless', the waters were said to exhale lethal vapours. A nearby cavern was one of the traditional entrances to the underworld. In 37 B.C. Agrippa made the lake a naval harbour (Portus Iulius), joining it to the Lacus Lucrinus (q.v.) by a canal which connected with the open sea. On the east side of Avernus are remains of baths. On the south side is a rock-hewn passage with vertical apertures for ventilation; known as the Grotto of the Cumaean Sibyl, it probably formed part of the harbour works.

Avidius Cassius, general of Marcus Aurelius and a native of Syria. In the Parthian war of A.D. 162–5 he commanded the army under Verus (q.v.), and was afterwards appointed governor of all the eastern provinces. In 175 he proclaimed himself emperor, but was murdered by his own officers (*see* MARCUS AURELIUS).

B

Baalbek, *see* HELIOPOLIS.

Babrius (-os), Greek poet, probably of the 2nd century A.D., versified the fables then current under the name of Aesop. The work was discovered in a monastery on Mt Athos in 1844. *See* the edition by W. G. Rutherford, 1883.

Bacchanalia, Latin name for the secret orgiastic rites of Bacchus (*see* DIONYSUS). They were introduced at Rome during the 3rd century B.C. Originally attended only by women on three days of the year, they were afterwards thrown open to men and celebrated five times in each month. The excesses with which they were accompanied, and the opportunities they afforded for political conspiracy, led to a senatorial decree banning them in Italy except in particular circumstances (186 B.C.). Despite severe penalties, however, they long continued to be celebrated.

Bacchylides (Bakkhulidēs), Greek lyric poet of the early 5th century B.C.; born at Iulis in the island of Ceos, he was a nephew of Simonides (*see* SIMONIDES, 2), and lived for a while at the court of Hieron I, at Syracuse, with Simonides and Pindar. Nothing was known of his poetry until the discovery at Oxyrhynchus (q.v.) of a papyrus containing the *Odes*. These were published very soon afterwards by Sir F. Kenyon (1897), and again by R. C. Jebb, with commentary and prose translation (1905), and were rendered into verse by A. S. Way (1929). More recently, the *Odes* have been supplemented by considerable fragments of five *Skolia* (q.v.), discovered likewise at Oxyrhyncus. *See* J. U. Powell, *New Chapters in the History of Greek Literature*, 1933; B. Snell, *Bacchylides*, 1949.

Bactria, a province of the Persian Empire, which was afterwards conquered by Alexander the Great. From the time of his death it was included in the territories of the Seleucidae until 255 B.C. when it became an independent kingdom (*see* EUCRATIDES; EUTHYDEMUS). Its prosperity was due to its situation on the Siberian gold route and to the fact that it lay on the main trade line from east to west. *See* W. W. Tarn, *The Greeks in Bactria and India*, 1938.

Baetica, one of the three provinces into which Augustus divided Spain (*see* HISPANIA). Called after the River Baetis (mod. Guadalquivir), it was separated from Lusitania by the River Anas (Guadiana) and from Tarraconensis by an imaginary line drawn from the Anas to the Charidemus promontory on the Mediterranean.

Bagoas, a eunuch, minister of Artaxerxes III, Ochus (q.v.), and his successor Arses (q.v.), both of whom he poisoned. He attempted to do likewise with the next king, Darius III, Codomannus, whom he had elevated to the throne; but the attempt failed and Bagoas was put to death (336 B.C.).

Baiae (mod. Baia), city of Campania, 10 miles west of Neapolis, on the Gulf of Puteoli. In Roman times it was a watering-place with warm sulphur springs (Pliny, *Hist. Nat.* xxxi. 4). It had baths, of which there are remains, and some palatial residences. Nero built a villa here, and Hadrian died in one that had belonged to Julius Caesar. Baiae was renowned for its immorality, and Cicero once apologized for defending a man who had lived there. *See also* BAULI.

Balagrae (-ai), town of Cyrenaica. Excavations begun in 1957 have revealed a Roman theatre of the 2nd century A.D. In close topographical association with the ancient temple of Asclepius, a much older edifice which appears to have been reconstructed in the reign of Claudius or Nero.

Balbinus, Decimus Caelius, elected emperor by the senate, together with M. Clodius Pupienus Maximus, in A.D. 238. *See* PUPIENUS.

Balbus, Lucius Cornelius (1st century B.C.), a native of Gades in Hispania Ulterior. He served under Pompey against Sertorius (q.v.), and received from him the Roman citizenship. Returning to Rome with Pompey, he lived on intimate terms with him and also with Caesar. In 56 B.C. he was accused of having illegally assumed Roman citizenship, but was defended by Cicero (*Pro Balbo*) and acquitted. During the civil wars he managed Caesar's personal affairs at Rome (*see* OPPIUS, GAIUS, 2), and afterwards found favour with Octavian, who raised him to the consulship in 40 B.C., the first man of foreign extraction to hold it.

Baleares (also called **Gymnesiae**) **Insulae,** eastern group of the modern Balearic islands off the east coast of Spain, chief of which were Majorca and Minorca; they supplied expert slingers to the Roman armies. The western group, including Iviza and Formentera, was called *Pityusae Insulae.*

Ballista (from Gk *ballein,* **to** throw), a piece of Roman artillery for hurling either darts or stones up to 57 lb. in weight and for distances up to 400 yards.

Barca, city of Cyrenaica (q.v.), about 11 miles from the sea. Originally the settlement of a Libyan tribe, the Barcaei, it was colonized *c.* 560 B.C. by seceders from Cyrene (*see* BATTIADAE). In 510 B.C. it was taken by the Persians, who removed most of the inhabitants to Bactria; and under the Ptolemies its ruin was completed by the erection of its port into a new city with the name of Ptolemais.

Barsinē: 1. Daughter of Artabazus (q.v.), was married to Alexander the Great and bore him a son, Heracles. She and her son were put to death by Polysperchon in 309 B.C.

2. Elder daughter of Darius III, Codomannus, by his sister and wife Stateira (q.v.). She too was married to Alexander (325 B.C.) at Susa, but was murdered by order of Roxana shortly after his death.

Basilica, a Roman hall used mainly for the administration of justice, but often also for other business. The earliest was that of M. Porcius Cato (3rd century B.C.). At first these buildings were constructed with or without pillars dividing the interior into aisles. From about 50 B.C. the plan became more elaborate: there were often double aisles, arcades opening on to the forum, and clerestory windows to give added light. This was the prototype of the Christian church, since many basilicas were used as such after Constantine. One of the largest of these halls, the plan of which shows a further advance in building technique, was the Basilica Nova of Maxentius in Rome, completed by Constantine *c.* 313; it measured 265 feet by 195 feet by 114 feet. *See also* LONDINIUM.

Bassae (-ai), town of Arcadia, on Mt Cotylium about five miles from Phigaleia (q.v.). Here is a well-preserved temple of Apollo Epicurius, built in the 5th century B.C. to commemorate deliverance from a plague and designed by the architect Ictinus. The complete interior frieze, representing the combat between the Lapithae and the Centaurs, is now in the British Museum.

Bassus, Aufidius, *see* AUFIDIUS BASSUS.

Bassus, Caesius, Roman lyric poet in the reign of Nero. He was a friend of Persius (q.v.), whose sixth satire is addressed to him and whose works he edited. Bassus was killed in the eruption of Vesuvius (A.D. 79). Quintilian praises him, and some attribute to him a work *On Metres* of which large fragments of a prose epitome are extant.

Bassus, Saleius, Roman epic poet of the 1st century A.D. None of his works has survived, but he is said to have fallen upon hard times and to have received from the emperor Vespasian a gift of half a million sesterces.

Bastarnae, a Germanic people originally inhabiting the Carpathians from Galicia southward, but first heard of *c.* 200 B.C., serving under Perseus of Macedonia on the lower Danube. Defeated by Thracians (cf. Livy, xl. 57, 58), they returned north; but they left some of their number on the island of Peuce in the Danube, who were thenceforward known as Peucini. Subdued by the Romans in 28 B.C., the Bastarnae became subject allies. They ultimately amalgamated with the Goths and were settled by the emperor Probus (q.v.) on the south bank of the Danube. According to Tacitus (*Germania,* 46) they were 'a squalid and slovenly people, and the features of their nobles got something of the Sarmatian (Mongolian) ugliness from intermarriage.'

Batavi, a German tribe inhabiting the island formed by the Rhine and the Waal, which was called after them Insula Batavorum. When Tacitus wrote the *Germania* (A.D. 98) they were allies of Rome, not liable to taxation but supplying contingents of auxiliary troops. *See* CIVILIS, JULIUS; EQUITES SINGULARES AUGUSTI; HERULI; SABINUS, JULIUS.

Bathycles (Bathuklēs), Greek sculptor, probably of the late 6th century B.C., a native of Magnesia ad Maeandrum in Lydia. He made the throne for a colossal statue of Apollo at Amyclae (q.v.).

Bathyllus (-thullos): 1. Of Samos, a beautiful youth loved by Anacreon (q.v.).

2. Of Alexandria, freedman and favourite of Maecenas (q.v.), perfected the imitative dance or ballet called *pantomimus. See* Juvenal, vi. 63.

Battering Ram, *see* ARIES.

Battiadae (-ai), a family which ruled Cyrene (q.v.) for eight generations. (1) BATTUS I, of Thera, led a colony to Africa and founded Cyrene *c.* 630 and died 590 B.C. (2) ARCESILAUS I (590–574), his son. (3) BATTUS II (574–*c.* 560), son of the last; under him a fresh band of settlers came from Greece. (4) ARCESILAUS II (*c.* 560–550), son of No. 3, in whose reign political unrest caused some of the population to secede and found the rival city of Barca (q.v.). (5) BATTUS III (550–530), son of No. 4. The recent secession, and the fact of his lameness which was thought to have disgraced his house, prompted his subjects to seek advice from Delphi. Demonax of Mantinea arrived as arbitrator; he reformed the constitution on the basis of a limited monarchy and divided the citizens into tribes. (6) ARCESILAUS III (530–519), son of No. 5. His son, (7) BATTUS IV, and the latter's son, (8) ARCESILAUS IV (died 450 B.C.), attempted to annul the new constitution. This, together with family quarrels, resulted in the extinction of the dynasty, which gave place to a republic.

Bauli, Roman villa resort near Baiae (q.v.). Pompey had a villa in the surrounding hills. Another, on the shores of the Lacus Lucrinus, belonged to the orator Hortensius; it afterwards became imperial property and was the scene of Agrippina's murder by Nero. Caligula built a bridge of boats from Bauli to Puteoli.

Bavius and **Maevius,** malevolent poetasters who attacked the work of Virgil (*Ecl.* iii. 90) and of Horace (*Epod.* x).

Bebryces (Bēbrukes): 1. Mythical people of Bithynia. *See* AMYCUS.
2. Iberian people dwelling on the Mediterranean coast north and south of the Pyrenees.

Bedriacum, *see* BETRIACUM.

Belgae, a people formed, probably in the 2nd century B.C., by the fusion of Celtic and Germanic tribes on the lower Rhine. In Caesar's time they inhabited one of the three great divisions of Gaul, that north and east of the Seine and Marne, and included among several tribes the Bellovaci, Nervii, Remi, and Eburones. In 57 B.C., after the defeat of Ariovistus, they conspired against Caesar, who defeated them on the Aisne. They also took part in the rising of Vercingetorix (q.v.) in 52 B.C. A group of the Belgae migrated to Britain *c.* 75 B.C. and spread from Kent northwards over the Thames. A second group entered Wessex *c.* 50 B.C. and spread westwards, perhaps as far as the Bristol Channel and the lower reaches of the Severn. *See* T. R. Holmes, *Caesar's Conquest of Gaul,* 2nd ed., 1911; Hawkes and Dunning, 'The Belgae of Gaul and Britain' in *Archaeological Journal,* lxxxvii, 1930. *See also* GALLIA; COMMIUS.

Bellerophōn, in Greek legend, son of the Corinthian king Glaucus by Eurymede, and grandson of Sisyphus, was originally called Hipponoüs, and received the name Bellerophon from slaying the Corinthian Belerus. To be purified from the murder he fled to Proetus, King of Argos, whose wife Antea, or Sthenoboea, fell in love with him; but as her offers were rejected, she accused him to her husband of having attempted her chastity. Proetus sent him to his father-in-law, Iobates, King of Lycia, with a letter in which Iobates was requested to put the young man to death. Iobates sent him to kill the monster Chimaera (q.v.), thinking that he was sure to perish in the contest. After obtaining possession of the winged horse Pegasus (q.v.), Bellerophon rose with him into the air, and slew the Chimaera with his arrows. Iobates, thus disappointed, sent Bellerophon against the Solymi and next against the Amazons. In these contests also he was victorious; and on his return to Lycia, being attacked by the bravest Lycians, whom Iobates had placed in ambush for the purpose,

Bellerophon slew them all. Iobates, now seeing that it was impossible to get rid of the hero, gave him one of his daughters in marriage, and made him his successor to the throne. At last Bellerophon drew upon himself the hatred of the gods, and, consumed by grief, wandered lonely through the Aleian field. This is all that Homer says respecting Bellerophon's later fate: some traditions relate that he attempted to fly to heaven upon Pegasus, but that Zeus sent a gadfly to sting the horse, which threw the rider, who fell to earth and became lame or blind in consequence. For Bellerophon's occurrence in Christian art *see* article by Joan Toynbee in *Journal of Roman Studies, LIV*, 1964.

Bellona, Roman goddess of war, corresponding to the Greek Enyo. She was generally represented as sister or wife of Mars. Her temple at Rome, dating from 296 B.C., was situated in the Campus Martius; there the senate met to debate a general's request for a triumph, and to receive foreign ambassadors. *See also* FECIALES.

Bellovaci, tribe of the Belgae (q.v.) inhabiting the territory around modern Beauvais, which perpetuates their name.

Benacus, Lacus (mod. Lago di Garda), lake in Gallia Cisalpina (Transpadana), at whose southern extremity is the beautiful promontory of Sirmio (mod. Sermione), a favourite resort of Catullus.

Beneventum (mod. Benevento), originally Maleventum, chief town of the Samnites (*see* SAMNIUM). Captured by the Romans *c.* 277 B.C., it was used by them as a base from which they defeated Pyrrhus (q.v.) in 275 B.C. The name was changed in 268 when a Roman colony was established. The importance of Beneventum was largely due to its being the junction of several high roads, including the Via Appia and the Via Traiana. There are interesting remains dating mostly from imperial times, particularly the Arch of Trajan.

Berenice (-kē), the Macedonian form of *Pherenike*, i.e. 'bringing victory'.

1. Wife of Ptolemy I, Soter, and mother of Ptolemy II, Philadelphus.

2. Daughter of Ptolemy II, Philadelphus, and wife of Antiochus II, Theos, King of Syria, who divorced Laodice in order to marry her, 252 B.C. On the death of Ptolemy, 246, Antiochus recalled Laodice, who poisoned him and murdered Berenice and her son.

3. Daughter of Magas, King of Cyrene, and wife of Ptolemy III, Euergetes. She was murdered by her son, Ptolemy IV, Philopator, on his accession to the throne, 221 B.C. A lock of her hair, which she dedicated for her husband's safe return from his Syrian expedition, was said to have become a constellation (*Coma Berenices*).

4. Otherwise called Cleopatra, daughter of Ptolemy VIII, Lathyrus, succeeded her father on the throne, 81 B.C., and married Ptolemy X (Alexander II), who murdered her nineteen days after their marriage.

5. Daughter of Ptolemy XI, Auletes, and eldest sister of the famous Cleopatra, was enthroned by the Alexandrines when they drove out her father, 58 B.C. She married Archelaus, but was put to death with her husband, when Gabinius restored Auletes, 55.

6. Niece of Herod the Great, married Aristobulus, who was put to death 7 B.C. She was the mother of Agrippa I.

7. Daughter of Agrippa I, married her uncle Herod, King of Chalcis, by whom she had two sons. After the death of Herod, A.D. 48, Berenice, then twenty years old, lived with her brother, Agrippa II, not without suspicion of incest. She gained the love of Titus, who was only withheld from making her his wife by fear of offending the Romans.

Berenice : 1. (formerly Hesperides or Euhesperides), coastal town of north Africa, north-east of modern Benghazi. Founded by the Greeks of Cyrenaica, it was named Berenice by Ptolemy III after his wife.

2. Seaport town of Egypt on the Sinus Immundus (Foul Bay). Founded in 285 B.C. by Ptolemy II, who named it after his mother, it became the chief emporium for the commerce of Egypt with Arabia and India. There were emerald mines in the neighbourhood.

Beroea (Beroia; mod. Aleppo; native Halab), ancient city of Syria, dating at least from the 2nd millennium B.C. It was enlarged by Seleucus Nicator (312–280 B.C.), who called it after a Macedonian town of the same name about 20 miles south-west of Pella.

Berossus (Bērossos), a priest of Bel at Babylon (3rd century B.C.), who translated into Greek a Babylonian treatise on astrology and astronomy. He also published (250 B.C.) a history of Babylon in three books. Fragments of the latter work have been preserved.

Berytus (mod. Beirut), ancient Phoenician seaport on the coast of Syria. It was captured by Tryphon in 140 B.C., and again in 15 B.C. by M. Vipsanius Agrippa, who made it a military colony (*see* COLONIA). Lavishly adorned by the Herod family, Berytus was in Roman times pre-eminent as a seat of learning; the school of Roman law was among the official law schools of the empire.

Bessus (-os), satrap of Bactria under Darius III, Codomannus. After the battle of Gaugamela (331 B.C.) he seized Darius, whom he murdered in the following year when pursued by the conqueror. He then fled to Bactria and assumed the royal title, but was betrayed by two of his followers to Alexander, who put him to death (329 B.C.).

Bestia, Lucius Calpurnius, tribune of the plebs at Rome in 121 B.C. As consul in 111 he was entrusted with the war against Jugurtha (q.v.), but was bribed by the latter to conclude an ignominious peace, for which he was tried and condemned after his return. He is to be distinguished from two other men likewise named, one of whom was among the Catilinarian conspirators in 63 and an adherent of Antony in 43; the other was unsuccessfully defended by Cicero for bribery while canvassing for the praetorship in 57 B.C.

Betriacum or **Bedriacum,** a small place in northern Italy between Cremona (q.v.) and Verona, where the forces first of Otho and then of Vitellius were defeated in A.D. 69.

Bias, a native of Priene in Ionia, son of Teutamus and one of the Seven Sages of Greece, *fl. c.* 570 B.C. According to Herodotus, he advised his fellow citizens at the time of the Persian invasion to migrate to Sardinia. *See* F. W. A. Mullach, *Fragmenta Philosophorum Graecorum,* 1860.

Bibaculus, Marcus Furius, Latin poet, born at Cremona in 103 B.C. His bitter satirical verses, written in iambics, are compared by

Quintilian with those of Catullus, and are said to have been directed even against the emperor Augustus. He is possibly not the person ridiculed by Horace (*Sat.* i. 10, 36; ii. 5, 50), or the author of an *Aethiopis* and a poem on the Rhine sometimes attributed to him.

Bibracte (mod. Mont-Beuvray), chief town of the Aedui (q.v.) in the time of Julius Caesar. It was situated on a hill, 2,500 feet above sea level, and excavations have revealed an advanced stage of civilization. Augustus transferred the population to his new town of Augustodunum (mod. Autun) in the plain below. Near Bibracte, in 58 B.C., Julius Caesar defeated the Helvetii (q.v.) and thus concluded his first campaign in the conquest of Gaul (*Bell. Gall.* i. 23–7). *See* J. Déchelette, *L'Oppidum de Bibracte*, 1903.

Bibulus, Marcus Calpurnius, curule aedile 65 B.C., praetor 62 and consul with Julius Caesar 59. He was unable to resist the powerful combination of Caesar, Pompey and Crassus; after an ineffectual attempt to oppose Caesar's agrarian law he retired, and it was said in joke that the consulship was that of Julius and of Caesar. In the civil war he commanded Pompey's fleet in the Adriatic and died (48 B.C.) while holding this command off Corcyra. He married Porcia, the daughter of Cato Uticensis. His younger son Lucius was appointed by Antony commander of his fleet and afterwards governor of Syria, in which capacity he died (*c.* 32 B.C.).

Bilbilis, town of Hispania Tarraconensis (*see* HISPANIA), near modern Calatayud. It was the birth-place of the poet Martial.

Biōn: 1. Greek bucolic poet, *fl. c.* 100 B.C. He was born at Phlossa, near Smyrna, but probably spent most of his life in Sicily. Though much inferior to Theocritus (q.v.), he rises considerably above his usual standard in the *Lament for Adonis*. *See* the Oxford edition by U. Wilamowitz-Moellendorff, 1905, and verse translation by A. S. Way, 1913.

2. Greek philosopher and moralist, usually called Bion of Borysthenes, i.e. of Olbia in Sarmatia; *fl. c.* 280 B.C. He was sold as a slave, when young, to a rhetorician who gave him his freedom and made him his heir. Bion then studied philosophy at Athens, and afterwards spent some time at the court of Antigonus II, Gonatas. From there he moved to Rhodes, where he taught philosophy. He died at Chalcis in Euboea. Only fragments of his *Diatribae* survive; but his influence on later satirists was considerable and his acid wit is alluded to by Horace: 'Bioneis sermonibus et sale nigro' (*Ep.* ii. 2, 60). *See* R. Dudley, *A History of Cynicism*, 1937.

Bisaltae (-ai), a Thracian people inhabiting fertile territory on the lower Strymon, where there were also silver mines. They were subject to Macedonia (q.v.), *c.* 460–168 B.C., and thereafter to the Romans, under whom their territory was included in Macedonia Prima. Groups of the Bisaltae penetrated south to the peninsulas of Acte and Pallene, and east to the River Nestos.

Bithynia, district of Asia Minor. Bounded north by the Propontis, Thracian Bosporus and Euxine; east by Paphlagonia; west and south-west by Mysia; south by Phrygia and Galatia. Occupied at an early date by Thracian tribes, it was included in the kingdom of Lydia, and subsequently (546 B.C.) in that of Persia. In the 4th century B.C. it became an independent kingdom (capital Prusa) under native princes (*see* NICOMEDES; PRUSIAS) and remained so until the death of Nicomedes IV (74 B.C.), who bequeathed it to Rome. Bithynia then became a Roman province, which was often administered together with that of Pontus (q.v.). Among the most celebrated governors of the joint provinces was Pliny the Younger (q.v.).

Bitōn and **Kleobis**, sons of Cydippe, a priestess of Hera at Argos, celebrated for the love and reverence in which they held their mother. On one occasion, during a festival of Hera, they drew her chariot a distance of about five miles, and Cydippe prayed to the goddess to grant them what was best for mortals. That night they died while sleeping in the temple. The statues of Biton and Kleobis at Delphi have been unearthed.

Bituriges, a Celtic people of Gaul, who at an early date had split up into two branches: (1) *Bituriges Cubi*, with their capital at Avaricum (mod. Bourges, which perpetuates their name), joined the rebellion of Vercingetorix (q.v.) in 52 B.C. The town was taken by assault and the population massacred (Caesar, *Bell. Gall.* vii. 24–8). Next year the Bituriges submitted; in 28 B.C. their territory was included in Aquitania. (2) *Bituriges Vivisci* inhabited a strip of land between the Atlantic and the left bank of the Garonne, with their capital at Burdigalia (mod. Bordeaux).

Boadicea, *see* BOUDICCA.

Bocchus: 1. King of Mauretania (q.v.) and father-in-law of Jugurtha (q.v.). In 108 B.C. he joined the latter in his war with Rome, but three years later handed him over to Sulla (q.v.). The Romans in consequence added western Numidia (q.v.) to his kingdom.

2. Son and successor of the preceding, reigning jointly with his younger brother Bogud. They supported Caesar against Pompey; but after Caesar's murder (44 B.C.) Bocchus sided with Octavian, Bogud with Antony. Bocchus, however, managed to oust his brother, and was confirmed as sole ruler by Octavian. He died in 33 B.C.

Boeotia (Boiōtia), district of central Greece. Bounded north by Locris; west by Phocis; south by Attica, Megaris and the Corinthian Gulf; north-east by the Strait of Euboea. For the chief natural features *see* CEPHISSUS, 2; COPAÏS; HELICON. By far the most important city was Thebae (Thebes), which, though it never stood to Boeotia as Athens did to Attica, nearly always exercised hegemony. For a summary, therefore, of Boeotia's political history *see* THEBES. Other towns were Orchomenus, Plataea, Tanagra and Thespiae (qq.v.). Boeotia was the scene of five historic battles: two at Chareonea, two at Coroneia, and one at Haliartus (qq.v.). The Boeotian League consisted of independent city-states (about eleven at the end of the Peloponnesian war) under the presidency of Thebes. Each elected a Boeotarch to handle war and foreign affairs; each sent 60 delegates to the federal assembly, but had its own council; and each supplied contingents of about 1,000 infantry and 100 cavalry to the federal army. The Boeotians, though traditionally dull-witted (probably because of the country's foggy winters and sultry summers), produced such men as Hesiod, Pindar, Epameinondas, Pelopidas and Plutarch (qq.v.). *See* W. R. Roberts, *The Ancient Boeotians*, 1895.

Boii, a Celtic people who in the 5th century B.C. inhabited Trans-alpine Gaul, though there has been some dispute as to their more remote origins. About 400 B.C. the majority of them migrated in two groups. One crossed the Pennine Alps and the Po to settle in northern Italy. Here they waged a long struggle with Rome until their final subjugation in 191 B.C. The second group crossed the Rhine and occupied territory on the Danube, which was afterwards known as Boiohemum (mod. Bohemia). They were eventually exterminated (c. 50 B.C.) by the Dacians. Meanwhile, however, in 58 B.C. about 30,000 Boii accompanied the migration of the Helvetii (q.v.) with whom they were defeated by Caesar near Bibracte (q.v.). Caesar allowed the survivors to settle in Aeduan territory (see AEDUI) between the Allier and the Loire.

Bolbitinē, modern Rosetta, town on the west bank of the western mouth of the Nile. In 1779 there was discovered on a site four miles to the north a basalt stele with a sacerdotal decree in favour of Ptolemy V, Epiphanes, inscribed in hieroglyphic, demotic and Greek. This is the so-called Rosetta Stone, which gave Champollion the key to the decipherment of hieroglyphic; it was ceded to Britain in 1801 and is now in the British Museum.

Bomilcar, a Numidian, confidential agent of Jugurtha (q.v.), who secured for him the assassination at Rome of Massiva (q.v.) in 111 B.C.

The name was also borne by two Carthaginians, a general and an admiral, of the late 4th and late 3rd century B.C. respectively.

Bona Dea ('the Good Goddess'), a Roman deity, variously described as the sister, wife or daughter of Faunus (q.v.), and herself called Fauna or Faula. She was worshipped at Rome as a chaste and prophetic deity, revealing her oracles only to females as Faunus did to males. Her festival was celebrated every year in December, in the house of a consul or praetor, since the sacrifices on this occasion were offered for the whole Roman people. The solemnities were conducted by the Vestals, and no male was allowed to be present in the house. P. Clodius Pulcher (see CLODIUS) profaned the mysteries of Bona Dea by entering the house of Caesar disguised as a female lutist in 62 B.C., when Caesar was praetor.

The mystic rites, attended only by women, may have given rise to abuses in the shape of female debauchery (see Juvenal, vi. 314–41), and even to burlesque imitation among the effeminate gentry of Rome (ibid., ii. 82–91).

Bononia (formerly Felsina; mod. Bologna), town of Gallia Cispa-dana, founded c. 500 B.C. by the Etruscans and called Felsina. By 196 B.C. it was in possession of the Boii (q.v.) and had probably by this time acquired the name Bononia. In 189 B.C. it was made a Latin colony (see COLONIA). In 187 B.C. it was connected with Ariminum and Placentia by the Via Aemilia, and some twelve years later with Aquileia. In 90 B.C. Bononia was granted Roman citizen-ship, and in 43 B.C. was Mark Antony's base of operations against Decimus Brutus. There are now no visible remains of the ancient city.

Boreas, personification of the north wind. In mythology he was son of Astraeus by Eos, and brother of Eurus, Zephyrus, Notus and

Chione. Dwelling in a cave on Mt Haemus in Thrace, he carried off Orithyia, daughter of Erechtheus, King of Athens, and begot by her Zetes, Calais and Cleopatra (*see* ZETES). Boreas was said to have helped the Athenians during the Persian war by destroying the enemy's ships; he was consequently worshipped at Athens, where a festival called Boreasmoi was celebrated in his honour.

Borysthenes (Borusthenēs), name of a river in Sarmatia, now called the Dnieper. It flowed into the Euxine not far from the mouth of the Hypanis (Bug), where stood a town sometimes known as Borysthenes (*see* BION, 2), but better known as Olbia (q.v.).

Bosporus Cimmerius (Bosporos Kimmerios; mod. Straits of Kerch), uniting the Palus Maeotis with the Euxine, formed with the River Tanais (mod. Don) part of the boundary between Europe and Asia. It derived its name from the Cimmerii (q.v.), who were supposed to have inhabited the adjacent Chersonesus Taurica (q.v.) until driven out by the Scythians.

Bosporus, Kingdom of, *see* CHERSONESUS TAURICA.

Bosporus Thracicus (Bosporos Thrakikos), strait connecting the Propontis (Sea of Marmora) with the Euxine.

Boudicca, often but wrongly called Boadicea. Her husband Prasutagus ruled the Iceni in Britain as autonomous prince under Roman suzerainty. On his death without male issue in A.D. 61 the Romans annexed his territory, but Boudicca resisted. She was scourged, her daughters raped and many of the tribal chiefs were plundered. There was widespread discontent in Britain at this time, due to heavy taxation and other acts of oppression, and the result was an insurrection involving the whole south-east of the province. The governor, Suetonius Paulinus, and most of his army were absent in north Wales. Before they could come to grips with the rebels Verulamium, Camulodunum and Londinium had been sacked, and the Ninth Legion on its way from Lindum practically annihilated. The entire province was in danger. Paulinus, however, eventually met the insurgent forces, probably between London and Chester, inflicted a crushing defeat, and destroyed all remaining pockets of resistance. Boudicca committed suicide by poison. *See* D. R. Dudley and G. Webster, *The Rebellion of Boudicca*, 1962.

Boulē, the Council at Athens, consisting of 500 members chosen annually by lot, fifty from each tribe. Each group of fifty served (in an order determined by lot) as what were called *prutaneis* (i.e. a presiding or superintending sub-committee of the whole council) for a period of 36 days in the case of the first four *prutaneis* and 35 days in that of the other six; and each of these periods was called a *prutaneia*.

The fifty *prutaneis* for the time being shared a common table in the Tholos (a circular building, the floor of which can now be seen in the Agora; *see* ATHENS), for which purpose they received a sum of money from the state. They summoned meetings of the full Boule on every day except holidays, prepared its agenda and decided where the meetings were to be held. They also summoned meetings of the Ecclesia (q.v.) four times in every *prutaneia*, and submitted its agenda.

The main duty of the Boule was to discuss and prepare measures to be laid before the Ecclesia. For a detailed account of its minor judicial and executive functions, as well as of procedure on the part of the *prutaneis* in carrying out their duties described above, *see* Aristotle, *Athenian Constitution*, 44–9.

Bovianum Undecimanorum, chief town of the Pentri, in Samnium, 18 miles south of Aesernia, on the road from Beneventum to Corfinium; taken by Sulla (q.v.) in 89 B.C. It was later called Undecimanorum after veterans of the Legio XI Claudia, whom Vespasian settled there.

Bovillae, town of Latium on the Via Appia (*see* APPIA, VIA), a colony of Alba Longa and a member of the Latin League (q.v.). After the destruction of Alba Longa, Bovillae became the centre of the cult of the *gens* Julia, and as such was important under the early empire. It was here that Clodius (q.v.) was killed (52 B.C.); here too the equites met the body of Augustus on its way from Nola to Rome. There are remains of a circus, a theatre and other buildings.

Branchidae (-khidae), *see* DIDYMA.

Brasidas, son of Tellis, a Spartan general during the Peloponnesian war. In the first year of hostilities (431) he distinguished himself by the relief of Methone, for which he received his country's thanks, 'the first officer', says Thucydides, 'who obtained this notice during the war' (ii. 25). He again behaved with great gallantry as captain of a galley at Pylos in 425 (iv. 11, 12). Next year, having saved Megara from an Athenian attack, he took command of a small force with which he gained possession of many towns in Thessaly that were subject to the Athenians, among them, and most important of all, Amphipolis. In 422 he won a brilliant victory over Cleon, who had been sent by the Athenians to recover Amphipolis, but fell in action. Buried at Amphipolis, he was afterwards worshipped there as a hero (v. 11). Thucydides has nothing but admiration for the character and conduct of Brasidas, and even allows (iv. 84) that he was 'not a bad speaker for a Lacedaemonian'.

Brauron, *see* IPHIGENEIA.

Brennus: 1. Leader of the Gauls who defeated a Roman army on the Allia and sacked Rome (390 B.C.). According to tradition he besieged the Capitol for six months and then agreed to depart on condition of receiving 1,000 lb. of gold; but Camillus (q.v.) arrived as the bullion was being weighed, and routed the Gallic host.

2. Leader of the Gauls who invaded Greece in 279 B.C. but was defeated near Delphi.

Brigantes, a tribe inhabiting north Britain between the Forth and the Humber at the time of the Roman Conquest. Subdued by Petillius Cerealis (A.D. 71–4), they revolted about 120, destroyed the Ninth Legion at Eburacum (York), and were not finally subjugated until the reign of Antoninus Pius (138–61). A branch of the tribe settled in south-east Ireland.

Briseis, daughter of a Trojan priest Brises. A captive of Achilles, she was taken from him by Agamemnon, an event which caused Achilles to withdraw from the fighting and thus marks the beginning of the *Iliad*.

Britain (Lat. Britannia; *see also* ALBION), Roman province in the island now including England, Wales and Scotland. Its most northerly limit varied between Hadrian's Wall (q.v.) and the Antonine Wall (q.v.), as will be explained below.

Pytheas (q.v.) of Massilia visited the island and left some account of it in his *Periplus*; but the Romans first became directly acquainted with Britain through the two expeditions of Julius Caesar (55 and 54 B.C.). There had long been a steady infiltration of Roman ideas and culture into the southern parts of the country by the time of the invasion under Claudius (A.D. 43). In that year four legions—II Augusta, IX Hispana, XIV Gemina Martia, and XX Valeria Victrix, together with their auxiliary troops (*see* AUXILIA), landed on the coast of Kent under the command of Aulus Plautius (q.v.). They advanced on London (*see* LONDINIUM), where Claudius spent a few days in their midst, and then, having crossed the Thames, captured Camulodunum (q.v.). By 47 the entire country south of the Humber and east of the Severn was partly annexed and partly formed into protectorates under native client-rulers. *See also* CUNOBELIN; CARATACUS.

The next thirty years were devoted to the more difficult task of subduing the tribes of Wales and Yorkshire. Ostorius Scapula (q.v.) defeated the Silures in south Wales; Suetonius Paulinus (q.v.) started out in A.D. 61 to occupy Mona (Anglesey), but was obliged to turn back and quell a serious revolt led by Boudicca (q.v.). For the next ten years Britain as a whole was quiet, though the army was mutinous. The Fourteenth Legion was withdrawn *c.* 67, its place being taken soon afterwards by Legio II Adiutrix. Under Vespasian (q.v.), Petillius Cerealis (71–4) conquered the Brigantes (q.v.); his successor, Julius Frontinus, extinguished the last resistance of the Silures and established the camp at Isca (q.v.).

Julius Agricola (q.v.) was governor of Britain from A.D. 77 to 84, and this period witnessed a decisive advance northwards. In seven campaigns he defeated the Ordovices in central and north Wales, and conquered Mona; established garrisons between Solway Firth and the Tyne (78), between the Clyde and Forth (80), and along the Moray Firth facing the coast of Ireland (81); and penetrated into Caledonia where he won the battle of Mons Graupius. Agricola was recalled in 84, and Legio II Adiutrix was withdrawn at the same time or very soon afterwards.

Little is known of the following years until *c.* 120, when the Brigantes revolted and destroyed the Ninth Legion. In 122 Hadrian visited the province, bringing with him Legio VI Victrix to replace the vanished Ninth. He ordered the building of his famous wall (*see* HADRIAN'S WALL) between Tyne and Solway, which was intended to mark for all time the northern limit not only of Roman Britain but of the empire itself. Henceforward, for about 170 years, the province was held by three legions: II Augusta, VI Victrix and XX Valeria Victrix, with their bases at Isca (Caerleon), Eburacum (York) and Deva (Chester) respectively. About 143 the frontier was moved north to Agricola's Forth-Clyde line, and the Antonine Wall (q.v.) was built. But Hadrian's Wall was not abandoned; it served as a second line of defence, and the intervening space was treated as a military zone.

Irruptions of the Caledonians had become so serious by 208 that the emperor Septimius Severus in person renewed Agricola's attempt to conquer them. Before his death at Eburacum (q.v.), in 211, he had re-established Hadrian's Wall as the northern boundary. He had also divided the province into two, *Britannia Superior* and *Inferior*; it is uncertain how long this arrangement lasted, but by the 4th century the number had been increased to five and even (for a while) to six.

The Caledonians were in arms again by 275. At the other end of the province Saxon pirates were beginning to raid the long-established and peaceful settlements close to the Kent and Sussex coasts. More-over, about 286 Carausius (q.v.) proclaimed himself emperor of Britain, and Maximian was obliged to recognize his authority in 289. Constantius Chlorus (q.v.) recovered the province, and under Constantine, although Saxon raiders continued to menace the south-east and the coastline, there was again a period of general peace and prosperity. *See* Tacitus, *Agricola*; R. G. Collingwood and J. N. L. Myres, *Roman Britain and the English Settlements*, 1937; I. A. Richmond, *Roman Britain* (Pelican History of England), 1955; I. D. Margary, *Roman Roads in Britain* (2 vols.), 1955, 1957; British Museum, *Guide to the Antiquities of Roman Britain*, 1955; *Ordnance Survey Map of Roman Britain*, 3rd ed., 1956.

Britannicus, only son of the emperor Claudius by Messalina (q.v.), was born in A.D. 41. After Messalina's death (48) Claudius married his own niece, Agrippina the younger, who persuaded him to adopt her own son by a previous marriage and to give him precedence. That son consequently ascended the throne in A.D. 54, and is known to history as the emperor Nero, who caused Britannicus to be poisoned in the following year.

Britomartis, originally a mother-goddess of eastern Crete. A later myth identified her with Dictynna, a similar goddess of western Crete. She was described as a nymph, a daughter of Zeus, whom Minos pursued for nine months, until, to escape from him, she leaped from a cliff into the sea. To account for the name Dictynna, she was said to have been saved by being caught in a fisherman's net (*diktuon*). She escaped to Aegina, and was there worshipped as Aphaea (q.v.). At least as early as Euripides, Britomartis-Dictynna was identified with Artemis (q.v.).

Bructeri, a German tribe inhabiting the basin of the Lippe and the upper basin of the Ems. They submitted to Nero Claudius Drusus (q.v.) in A.D. 12. Their power was destroyed towards the end of the first century by the Angrivarii coming from the lower basin of the Weser.

Brundisium or **Brundusium** (mod. Brindisi), seaport town of Calabria and terminus of the Via Appia (*see* APPIA, VIA). Situated on a small cape, it had an inner and outer harbour, the second of which was enclosed by a mole and a number of small islands. Brundisium was taken by the Romans from the Sallentini in 267 B.C., and a Latin colony was established there in 245 B.C. It was developed into the principal naval station on the Adriatic and became the chief point of embarkation for Greece and Asia. A journey to Brundisium is the subject of one of Horace's satires (I. v), and here Virgil died on his return from Greece in 19 B.C.

Bruttii (Gk Brettioi), tribe occupying the south-western peninsula of Italy. Their territory, to which the name Italia was first applied, was known as the *ager Bruttius* or simply Bruttii; it was separated from Lucania by a line drawn from the mouth of the Liris on the west to a point slightly south of the Crathis on the east. The Bruttii had many contacts with Greece, as is shown by their language and numerous Greek objects in their tombs; but in the 4th century B.C. they joined the Lucanians in a war against the Greek colonies. In the several campaigns of the Pyrrhic war they assisted Pyrrhus (q.v.) against Rome, and after his defeat were deprived of half their territory. Having sided with Hannibal in the second Punic war, they lost their independence. Augustus joined the district with Lucania (q.v.) to form the third region of Italy (*see* ITALIA), which was placed by Diocletian (q.v.) under a *corrector*. The country was noted for pitch as well as for its cattle, corn, olives and fruit. Before the Hannibalian campaigns it was also a noted centre of shipbuilding. *See* G. Slaughter, *Calabria, the First Italy*, 1939.

Brutus, Decimus Junius: 1. Surnamed Gallaecus on account of his victory over the Gallaeci, in Lusitania, when consul in 138 B.C. He was patron of the poet Actius (q.v.).

2. Consul in 77 B.C.

3. An officer who served under Caesar both in Gaul and during the civil wars, but took part in the conspiracy which ended in Caesar's death. Brutus then hurried to Cisalpine Gaul, which province had been promised him by Caesar, and prepared to defend it against Antony (*see* ANTONIUS, MARCUS, 3), who had obtained it by vote of the people. Antony besieged him in Mutina until his own defeat by Octavian and the consuls (April 43 B.C.), but Brutus was betrayed to him later in the same year and put to death.

Brutus, Lucius Junius, legendary figure of Roman history, son of M. Junius by Tarquinia, sister of Tarquinius Superbus. After the murder of his elder brother, Lucius escaped by pretending to be an idiot (*brutus*). The death of Lucretia (q.v.) led to the expulsion of Tarquinius, and Brutus, who had led the Roman people in this achievement, was elected first consul with L. Tarquinius Collatinus (510 B.C.). He is said to have had both his own sons put to death for attempting to restore the royal house of Tarquin, and to have fallen in battle the same year fighting against Aruns, son of Tarquinius Superbus.

Brutus, Marcus Junius: 1. Husband of Servilia, half-sister of Cato Uticensis. He supported Lepidus in 78 (*see* LEPIDUS, MARCUS AEMILIUS, 1), and was slain in Cisalpine Gaul by order of Pompey.

2. Son of the preceding, born *c.* 86 B.C. After his father's death he was brought up by his uncle Cato, and accordingly joined the senatorial party on the outbreak of civil war in 49. After the battle of Pharsalus (48), he was not only pardoned by Caesar, but received many marks of favour and confidence, being made governor of Cisalpine Gaul in 46 and praetor in 44. Nevertheless, he was one of the leading conspirators against his benefactor's life; and Caesar's last words ('You too, my child'), addressed to him, together with previous favours, strengthened a common belief that Brutus was in fact

Caesar's son by an adulterous union with Servilia. Following the dictator's death Brutus spent a short time in Italy, and then took possession of the province of Macedonia. In 42 he was joined by Cassius, governor of Syria, and their united forces were opposed to those of Octavian and Antony (*see* ANTONIUS, MARCUS, 3; AUGUSTUS). Two battles were fought in the neighbourhood of Philippi. In the first Brutus was successful, though Cassius was defeated; in the second Brutus also was overwhelmed, and put an end to his life.

Brutus married Porcia, daughter of Cato. He wrote various works, none of which has survived; but he was a friend of Cicero, who dedicated to him several of his writings and gave the name Brutus to his celebrated dialogue on illustrious orators.

Bryaxis (Bru-), Greek sculptor, born at Athens 372 B.C. He worked in both stone and bronze, and was one of the school of Scopas who adorned the Mausoleum at Halicarnassus. Bryaxis died in 312 B.C. A base with horsemen in relief, attributed to him, has been discovered at Athens.

Brygus (Brugos), Athenian potter of the 6th century B.C. He employed an artist known as the Brygus Painter, and is identified by nine red-figure pieces.

Bucephala (Boukephalē), city on the Hydaspes in North India, built by Alexander the Great in memory of his charger, Bucephalus, which died there (326 B.C.).

Bucolic War. During the reign of Marcus Aurelius a revolt of the Bucolic or native troops, recruited for home service in Egypt, was joined by the whole native population. Suppressed only after several years of fighting, it did untold harm to the country's agriculture, and marks the beginning of its decline under heavy taxation, especially as the province of Africa was now Egypt's equal as a source of Rome's corn supply.

Bulla, a heart-shaped case containing an amulet, worn round the neck of free-born Roman children. Boys laid it aside on assuming the *toga virilis*; girls on marriage.

Bulla Regia, city of Numidia and once the residence of that country's kings. Under the Roman Empire it was on the road from Carthage to Hippo Regius and received numerous benefits, particularly from Hadrian.

Burrhus, *see* NERO; SENECA, L. ANNAEUS.

Byzantium (Buzantion), city on the Thracian Bosporus, founded by Megarians and Argives under Byzas, *c.* 657 B.C., on the site of what is now the most easterly of the seven hills of Istanbul (Constantinople). Its geographical situation made it a place of great strategic and commercial importance. Destroyed by the Persians under Darius I, it was recolonized by the Spartan Pausanias in 479; a large population of Athenians and Spartans settled there, and the city became a bone of contention between those two states.

About 472 B.C. it was seized by Cimon, son of Miltiades (qq.v.), but in 440 it revolted and returned to its former allegiance. Alcibiades won the city through the treachery of the Athenian party in 408 B.C., but it was recaptured by Lysander three years later. Under the Spartans it was in danger of pillage by the Ten Thousand (*see* TEN THOUSAND,

EXPEDITION OF THE), who, however, were dissuaded by Xenophon. In 390 Thrasybulus wrested Byzantium from the Spartan oligarchy and restored democracy and Athenian influence. After resisting an attempt by Epameinondas to recover it for Sparta, the city co-operated with Rhodes, Chios and other states in securing their independence of Athenian suzerainty; but on the approach of Philip of Macedon it sought the help of Athens, and Phocion (q.v.) obliged Philip to raise the siege. The deliverance of the city through a miraculous flash of light, which revealed the advancing Macedonians, led the Byzantines to erect an altar dedicated to torch-bearing Hecate and to stamp a crescent on their coinage, an emblem subsequently adopted by the Turks.

Included for a short while in the empire of Alexander, Byzantium regained its independence and thereafter withstood the attempted invasions of Scythians and Gauls. It became an allied city of Rome, but its powers were curtailed by Claudius I and abolished altogether by Vespasian. In A.D. 196 Septimius Severus razed it to the ground, but rebuilt a large portion of it under the name Augusta Antonina. It checked a Gothic invasion under Claudius II, and its fortifications were strengthened in the early years of the 4th century A.D. Constantine chose the site as his new seat of empire, and built a new city on the site of the old (330). *See* CONSTANTINOPLE.

C

Cabeiri (Kabeiroi), fertility gods, probably of Phrygian origin. At first indefinite in number, they were afterwards four: two males, Axiokersos and his son Kadmilos; and two females less important, Axieros and Axiokersa (not referred to in the rest of this article). As early as the 5th century B.C. they were regarded as protective deities of sailors, for which reason they were sometimes identified with the Dioscuri (q.v.). At Thebes in Boeotia, as a result of Orphic influence, they were represented as an elder (? Dionysus) and a child. The Romans, among whom their cult was extremely popular, identified them with the *Penates publici* (*see* PENATES).

Little is known of the worship of the Cabeiri, which existed in Asia Minor, Macedonia, northern and central Greece, but above all in the islands of Lemnos and Samothrace. Strabo says that their rites were similar to those of the Curetes and of Bendis in Thrace.

Cacus, son of Vulcan, was a giant who lived in a cave on the Aventine at Rome. When Hercules came to Italy with the oxen taken from Geryon (*see* TWELVE LABOURS OF HERACLES, 10), Cacus stole some of them; and since he dragged the animals backwards to his cave, it was impossible to tell which way they had gone. But when the remaining oxen passed by the cave those inside began to bellow. Hercules thereupon slew Cacus, and in honour of his victory dedicated the Ara Maxima.

Cadmus (Kadmos), son of Agenor (q.v.), King of Phoenicia, by Telephassa, and brother of Europa (q.v.). When Europa was carried off by Zeus, Agenor sent Cadmus in search of her. The search proving fruitless, he settled in Thrace and sent to Delphi for advice. The oracle instructed him to follow a certain cow and build a town on the spot where she sank down with fatigue. Cadmus found the cow in Phocis, followed her into Boeotia and built the town as directed. He called it Cadmea, which afterwards became the citadel of Thebes.

Intending to sacrifice the cow to Athena, he sent some men to draw water at the neighbouring well of Ares. This well was guarded by a dragon, who killed them. Cadmus in turn slew the dragon and, on the advice of Athena, sowed its teeth, out of which there grew armed men called 'Sparti' (i.e. Sown). These warriors destroyed each other, all but five who were the ancestors of the Thebans.

Athena appointed Cadmus King of Thebes, and Zeus gave him as wife Harmonia (q.v.), daughter of Ares by Aphrodite. The marriage was attended by all the Olympian gods, and Cadmus presented his bride with a *peplos* and necklace which he had received from Hephaestus. Harmonia bore him four daughters (Semele, Agave, Ino and Autonoë) and a son, Polydorus. *See* PENTHEUS; THEBAN LEGEND. Cadmus and Harmonia were ultimately changed into serpents and transferred by Zeus to Elysium (q.v.). Cadmus was also alleged to have introduced into Europe from Phoenicia an alphabet of sixteen letters.

Caecilia, Via, highway of Italy, constructed probably by the consul L. Caecilius Metellus Diadematus in 117 B.C. It ran from a point on the Via Salaria, 35 miles from Rome, through Amiternum and Interamna Praetuttiorum, to the sea at Castrum Novum (148 miles).

Caecilius, Greek rhetorician and critic of the early 1st century A.D. A native of Calacte in Sicily, he spent his working life at Rome. Of his several critical works, which ranked him as inferior only to Dionysius of Halicarnassus (q.v.), mere fragments have survived.

Caecilius, Quintus, Roman eques who adopted his nephew Atticus (*see* POMPONIUS ATTICUS, TITUS) and left him a fortune of ten million sesterces.

Caecilius Statius, Roman comic poet, a friend of Ennius. Originally a slave, he was by birth an Insubrian Gaul and a native of Mediolanum. He was eventually given his freedom, and died *c.* 168 B.C. Though only three hundred lines of his works survive, we know the titles of some forty plays.

Caecina, Aulus, author of a libellous work against Caesar, for which he was exiled in 48 B.C. He recanted, and was pardoned chiefly through the intercession of Cicero, who had defended his father Aulus Caecina in a lawsuit (69) and who probably used the son's expert knowledge of Etruscan divination in his own treatise *De divinatione.*

Caecina Alienus, Aulus, quaestor in Spain at the time of Nero's death. He served in turn under Galba, Vitellius and Vespasian; but having conspired against the last, he was put to death by order of Titus.

Caecubus Ager, marshy district of Latium near Fundi; famous in the time of Horace for its wine (caecubum).

Caepio, Quintus Servilius, Roman consul in 106 B.C., was sent in the following year to Gallia Narbonensis to oppose the Cimbri (q.v.), by whom he and the consul Maximus were defeated at Arausio (q.v.) with the loss, it is said, of 80,000 troops and 40,000 camp-followers. Caepio survived the battle, but in 95 he was charged by the tribune C. Norbanus with misconduct of the war, condemned and imprisoned.

Caere or **Agylla** (mod. Cervetri), one of the twelve cities of Etruria, about 25 miles north-west of Rome and about 5 miles from the sea, with its port at Pyrgos. In 390 B.C., when the Gauls invaded Italy, the vestal virgins were given refuge at Caere, and a treaty with Rome was made in the same year. Having sided with Tarquinii against Rome in 353 B.C., Caere was partly incorporated in the Roman state without internal self-government or the right of voting, a status known thenceforward as *Jus Caeritum.* Magnificent finds from the Etruscan necropolis can be seen in the Vatican and the Villa Julia at Rome. *See* D. Randall-MacIver, *Villanovans and Early Etruscans,* 1924; *The Etruscans,* 1927.

Caesar, name of a patrician family, of the Julia *gens,* which traced its legendary origin to Iulus, the son of Aeneas (q.v.). The name was assumed by Augustus as the adopted son of the dictator C. Julius Caesar, and was by Augustus handed down to his adopted son Tiberius. It continued to be used by Caligula, Claudius and Nero, as members either by adoption or female descent of Caesar's family; but though the family became extinct with Nero, succeeding emperors still retained the name among their titles. When Hadrian adopted

Aelius Verus, he allowed the latter to take the title of Caesar; and from this time, though the title of Augustus continued to be confined to the reigning prince, that of Caesar was also granted to the heir presumptive to the throne.

Caesar, Gaius Julius, Roman general and statesman, one of the greatest military geniuses of all time, was born probably on 12th July 102 B.C. (100 is the traditional date). He was closely connected with the popular party by the marriage of his aunt Julia with Marius (q.v.); and *c*. 85, though only seventeen years of age, he repudiated Cossutia, to whom his parents had betrothed him while very young, and married Cornelia, daughter of L. Cornelius Cinna, leader of the party. Sulla commanded him to put away his wife, but he refused and was consequently proscribed. He concealed himself for some time in the country of the Sabines, till his friends obtained his pardon from Sulla. Seeing, however, that he was not safe at Rome, he went to Asia, where he served his first campaign under M. Minucius Thermus, and, at the capture of Mytilene (80), was rewarded with a civic crown for saving the life of a fellow soldier. On the death of Sulla, in 78, he returned to Rome, and in the following year gained renown as an orator by his prosecution of Cn. Dolabella for extortion in the province of Macedonia. To perfect himself in oratory he resolved to study at Rhodes under Apollonius Molo, but on the voyage thither was captured by pirates, and obtained his liberty only by a ransom of fifty talents. At Miletus he manned some vessels, overpowered the pirates and conducted them as prisoners to Pergamum, where he crucified them—a punishment with which he had frequently threatened them in sport when he was their prisoner.

On his return to Rome Caesar devoted all his energies to acquiring popular favour. His liberality was unbounded; and as his private fortune was not large, he soon contracted enormous debts. But he gained his object, became the favourite of the people and was raised by them in succession to the highest offices of state. He was quaestor in 69, aedile in 65, when he spent enormous sums upon the public games and buildings, and was elected pontifex maximus in 63. In the debate in the senate on the punishment of the Catilinarian conspirators he opposed their execution in a very able speech, which made such an impression that their lives would have been spared but for the arguments of Cato in reply. In 62 he was praetor, and in the following year went as propraetor into Further Spain, where he subdued the Lusitanians. On his return to Rome he was elected consul for 59 along with Bibulus (q.v.), a warm supporter of the aristocracy. After his election, but before taking office, he formed that coalition with Pompey and M. Licinius Crassus, usually known as the First Triumvirate. Pompey had become estranged from the aristocracy, since the senate had opposed the ratification of his acts in Asia, and of an assignment of lands which he had promised to his veterans. Crassus, in consequence of his immense wealth, was one of the most powerful men at Rome, but was a personal enemy of Pompey. They were reconciled by Caesar, and the three entered into an agreement to support one another, and to divide the power in the state between them.

During his consulship, since he enjoyed the support of Pompey and

Crassus, Caesar was able to carry all his proposals. He brought forward such measures as secured for him the affections of the poorest citizens, of the equites, and of the powerful Pompey; having done which he was able to obtain for himself the provinces he desired. By a vote of the people, proposed by the tribune Vatinius, Cisalpine Gaul and Illyricum, with three legions, were granted him for five years; and to these the senate, under popular threats, added Transalpine Gaul, with another legion and for the same period. Caesar foresaw that the struggle between the different parties at Rome must eventually be terminated by the sword, and he had therefore resolved to obtain an army, which he might attach to himself by victories and rewards. In the course of the same year he allied himself more closely to Pompey by giving him his daughter Julia in marriage.

During the next nine years Caesar was occupied with the subjugation of Transalpine Gaul, in the course of which he made two punitive expeditions to Britain (q.v.), 55 and 54 B.C., and twice crossed the Rhine. Also in 55 (winter) he met Pompey and Crassus at Luca, and it was agreed that his command should be prolonged for another five years, namely, from 1st January 53, to the end of December 49. But his success in Gaul had begun to excite Pompey's jealousy; and the death of Julia in childbirth, in 54, broke one of the few links that held them together. Pompey was thus led to rejoin the aristocratical party, by whose assistance he hoped to retain his dominant position at Rome. The object of this party was to deprive Caesar of his command, and to compel him to come to Rome as a private citizen to sue for the consulship. Caesar offered to resign his command if Pompey would do the same; but the senate would not listen to any compromise. Accordingly, on 1st January 49, the senate passed a resolution that Caesar should disband his army by a certain day or be regarded as an enemy of the state. Two of the tribunes, M. Antonius and Q. Cassius, put their veto upon this resolution, but their opposition was set at naught, and they fled for refuge to Caesar's camp. Under the plea of protecting the tribunes, Caesar crossed the Rubicon, which separated his province from Italy, and marched south. Pompey, who had been entrusted by the senate with the conduct of the war, soon discovered how greatly he had overrated his own popularity and influence. His troops deserted to his rival in crowds; town after town in Italy opened its gates to Caesar, whose march was like a triumphal progress. Meantime Pompey, with the magistrates and senators, had fled from Rome to Brundisium, and on 17th March embarked for Greece. Caesar, who had reached the outskirts of that city a week earlier, was unable to follow for want of ships. Shortly afterwards he set out for Spain, where Pompey's legates, Afranius, Petreius and Varro, commanded powerful armies. After defeating Afranius and Petreius, receiving the submission of Varro and terminating the siege of Massilia, Caesar returned to Rome, where he had in the meantime been appointed dictator by the praetor M. Lepidus. He resigned this office at the end of eleven days, after holding the consular comitia, in which he himself and P. Servilius Vatia Isauricus were elected consuls for the next year.

At the beginning of January 48, Caesar crossed over to Greece, where Pompey had collected a formidable army. At first the campaign was in Pompey's favour; Caesar was repulsed before Dyrrhachium with considerable loss, and was obliged to retreat towards Thessaly. Here, on the north bank of the River Enipeus, opposite Old Pharsalus, a decisive battle was fought between the two armies on 9th August 48. Pompey was completely defeated. He fled to Egypt, pursued by Caesar, but was murdered before the latter's arrival. *See* POMPEY. Soon after reaching Egypt, Caesar became involved in a war, usually called the Alexandrian war, which was not brought to a close till the latter end of March 47. He had meanwhile been fascinated by Cleopatra, who about this time bore him a son, Caesarion (q.v.). He returned to Rome through Syria and Asia Minor, and on his march through Pontus defeated Pharnaces (q.v.), son of Mithradates the Great, at Zela. He reached Rome in September (47), and before the end of the month set sail for Africa, where Scipio and Cato had collected a large army. The war was terminated by the defeat of the Pompeian army at the battle of Thapsus, 6th April 46. Caesar returned to Rome in the latter end of July and celebrated a triumph (q.v.) for his victories to date. He was now the undisputed master of the Roman world, but he used his victory with the greatest moderation. Unlike other conquerors in civil wars, he freely forgave all who had borne arms against him, and declared that he would make no difference between Pompeians and Caesarians. One of the most important of his measures this year (46) was the reformation of the calendar (*see* JULIAN CALENDAR). Meantime the two sons of Pompey, Sextus and Gnaeus, had collected a new army in Spain. Caesar set out towards the end of the year, and brought the war to a close by the battle of Munda (q.v.), on 17th March 45. Cn. Pompey was killed shortly afterwards, but Sextus made good his escape.

Caesar reached Rome in September, and entered the city in triumph. Possessing royal power, he did not prevent Antony from offering him the diadem in public on the festival of Lupercalia (15th February 44); but, seeing that the proposition was not favourably received by the people, he declined it for the present. But Caesar's power was not witnessed without envy. The Roman aristocracy resolved to remove him by assassination. The conspiracy had been set afoot by Cassius, a personal enemy, and there were more than sixty persons privy to it. Many of these persons had been raised by Caesar to wealth and honour; and some of them, such as M. Brutus, lived with him on terms of the most intimate friendship. It has been the practice of rhetoricians to speak of the murder of Caesar as a glorious deed, and to represent Brutus and Cassius as patriots; yet they cared not for the republic, which was rotten to the core, but only for themselves; and their object in murdering Caesar was to gain power for themselves and their party. Caesar had many warnings of his approaching fate, but he disregarded them all, and fell by the daggers of his assassins on the Ides or 15th of March 44. *See also* CALPURNIA; CORNELIA, 2; POMPEIA, 1.

Gaius Julius Caesar was among the greatest men of antiquity. He was gifted by nature with the most varied talents, and was distinguished by extraordinary attainments in the most diversified pursuits.

During the whole of his busy life he found time for the prosecution of literature, and was the author of many works, the majority of which have been lost. The purity of his Latin and the clearness of his style were celebrated by the ancients themselves, and are conspicuous in his *Commentarii*, which are his only works that have come down to us. Of these *De Bello Gallico* (seven books with an eighth by Hirtius, q.v.) gives an account of his campaigns in Gaul; while *De Bello Civili* narrates the history of the civil wars down to the outbreak of hostilities at Alexandria. *De Bello Alexandrino* is from an unknown hand, possibly one of Caesar's staff, who prepared it for Hirtius by whom it may have been partially revised. There is some reason to think that *De Bello Africo* and *De Bello Hispaniensi* were written respectively by a tribune of the Fifth and an officer of the Tenth Legion. For these last three works *see* the edition with translation by A. G. Way (Loeb Library), 1955. There is a good edition of *De Bello Gallico* by T. Rice Holmes (1914); *see also* his translation (1908). The best English edition of *De Bello Civili* is that of A. G. Peskett, with translation (Loeb Library), 1916. There is a modern translation of the *Commentaries* by J. Warrington in Everyman's Library (1953). *See* T. Rice Holmes, *Caesar's Conquest of Gaul*, 2nd ed., 1911, and *The Roman Republic*, 3 vols., 1923; M. Cary and F. E. Adcock, *The Cambridge Ancient History*, vol. ix, 1932; G. Walter, *Caesar* (translated by Emma Craufurd), 1953; M. Gelzer, *Caesar*, 1968.

Caesar, Lucius Julius: 1. Consul in 90 B.C., fought in the Social War (q.v.), and afterwards proposed the *Lex Julia de Civitate*, which granted citizenship to the Latins and Socii who had remained faithful to Rome. He was censor in 89; but he belonged to the aristocratical party and was put to death by Marius (q.v.) two years later, together with his brother Caesar Strabo Vopiscus (q.v.).

2. Son of C. Julius Caesar Strabo Vopiscus, and uncle by his sister Julia of Mark Antony (*see* ANTONIUS, MARCUS, 3). He was consul in 64 B.C. and, like his father, a member of the aristocratical party which he afterwards, however, seems to have deserted. In 52 he was one of Caesar's legates in Gaul, and continued to serve him in Italy during the civil war. After Caesar's death (44) Lucius took part with the senate against Antony, by whom he was proscribed (43), but was pardoned through his sister's influence.

3. Son of the preceding. He joined Pompey on the outbreak of civil war (49 B.C.), and was sent by him with abortive proposals for peace. Later that year, when in command of a fleet, he failed to intercept Curio's passage from Sicily to Africa. After the battle of Thapsus (46), though pardoned by Caesar, he was murdered by the latter's troops, probably because he had massacred some freedmen and slaves of the dictator.

Caesar Strabo Vopsicus, Gaius Julius, curule aedile in 90, candidate for the consulship in 88 and slain by Marius (q.v.), together with his brother (*see* CAESAR, LUCIUS JULIUS, 1), in 87 B.C. He was one of the principal orators and poets of his age, and is represented as one of the speakers in Cicero's *De Oratore*.

Caesaraugusta (mod. Zaragosa, Saragossa), name given to the Celtiberian town of Salduba when it was made a Roman colony by

Augustus in 25 B.C. Situated on the River Ebrus, it was the chief commercial and military station of the region, and an administrative centre first of Hispania Citerior and afterwards of Tarraconensis (*see* HISPANIA).

Caesarea Mauretaniae, formerly Iol, ancient coastal city of the Phoenicians in Mauretania; capital of Juba II (*see* MAURETANIA), who called it Caesarea in honour of Augustus.

Caesarea-Mazaca (mod. Kaisarieh). Mazaca, the capital of the kings of Cappadocia (q.v.), was named Caesarea probably by Claudius I. It was destroyed by the Persian king Sapor I in A.D. 260.

Caesarea Palestinae (mod. Kaisarieh), seaport town built (25–13 B.C.) by Herod the Great on a Phoenician site known as Straton's Tower, and named Caesarea in honour of Augustus. The town and magnificent harbour works are described in some detail by Josephus (*Jewish Antiquities*, xv. 9, 6). It was here that the Jewish revolt began (A.D. 66) and that Vespasian was proclaimed emperor (69). After A.D. 7 it was capital of Judaea (q.v.) and residence of the procurators.

Caesarea Philippi (formerly Paneas; mod. Banias), city of Palestine. Augustus made a gift of the district to Herod the Great, who erected a temple to the emperor. Herod's son, Philip the Tetrarch, enlarged the town, renamed it Caesarea in honour of Augustus, and added his own name as a title to distinguish it from Caesarea Palestinae (q.v.). It was at Caesarea Philippi that Our Lord gave the famous charge to St Peter (Mark viii. 27) and that Titus held gladiatorial games after the fall of Jerusalem (A.D. 70).

Caesarion, son of Julius Caesar by Cleopatra, born in 47 B.C. After his mother's suicide he was put to death by order of Augustus (30 B.C.).

Caestus, general name for the ancient boxing-glove, of which there were three varieties. The first, called *meilichae*, consisted of rawhide straps, used chiefly for practice; the second, *sphaerae*, had small metal leather-covered balls; while the third, *murmekes*, were studded with nails.

Caiatia (mod. Caiazzo), city of Campania on the Volturnus, 11 miles north-east of Capua. It was occupied by the Romans in or before 306 B.C.; but having rebelled in the Social War (q.v.) it was deprived of its municipal status, which was not restored until imperial times. There are remains of ancient walls, and a Roman cistern beneath the present Piazza del Mercato is still in use.

Caietae Portus, harbour of Latium, five miles south-west of Formiae (q.v.). The district was a favourite summer resort of the Roman aristocracy. On the neighbouring promontory is the tomb of Munatius Plancus who founded Lugdunum (q.v.).

Calabria (called by the Greeks Iapygia), in Roman history, the name applied to the heel or south-eastern extremity of Italy, terminating in the Promontorium Sallentinum upon which stood a village called Leuca. The peninsula is bounded west and east by the Tarentine Gulf and the Adriatic respectively. Despite the lack of rivers, its soil was fertile, and ancient writers frequently mention its pastures, olives, vines and fruit trees. Although Calabria once boasted thirteen populous cities, only Brundisium and Tarentum (qq.v.) retained their importance at the end of the 1st century B.C. Augustus joined Calabria with Apulia and the territory of the Hirpini to form the second region of Italy; Diocletian placed it together with Apulia under a *corrector*.

Calagurris (mod. Calahorra), city of north-east Spain, birth-place of Quintilian (q.v.). It is famous chiefly for its defence by Sertorius (q.v.) against Pompey (76–72 B.C.), the garrison being reduced to cannibalism before its capitulation. Under Augustus the inhabitants received Roman citizenship; later the name was altered to Calagurris Nassica to distinguish it from nearby Calagurris Fibularensis. There are remains of an aqueduct and an amphitheatre.

Calamis (**Ka-**), Athenian sculptor and embosser, *fl.* 480–450 B.C. He was famous for his figures of horses and for a colossal statue of Apollo at Apollonia Pontica (*see* APOLLONIA, 2) which was thirty cubits high.

Calatia, town of Campania on the Via Appia, six miles south-east of Capua (q.v.), of which it was a dependent. During the Samnite Wars (q.v.) it was a place of some strategic importance and was twice taken and retaken by the opposing sides. Calatia shared the doom of Capua in 211 B.C. Its walls were repaired by the censors in 174, and a colony (*see* COLONIA) was established there by Julius Caesar in 59 B.C.

Calatinus, Aulus Atilius, Roman general during the first Punic war, consul in 258 B.C. As dictator in 249 he conducted operations in Sicily, the first Roman dictator to command an army outside Italy.

Calauria (Kalaureia), small island off the coast of Argolis opposite Troezen, with a temple of Poseidon in which the orator Demosthenes (q.v.) committed suicide (322 B.C.).

Calchas (Kalkhas), son of Thestor, a soothsayer with the Greek army before Troy. An oracle had declared that he would die if he met another of his profession superior to himself. This happened at Clarus, near Colophon, where he encountered Mopsus (q.v.) and died of envy. In historical times there was an oracle of Calchas in Apulia.

Calchedon (Kalkhēdōn), town of Bithynia, on the Propontis almost opposite Byzantium. It was founded from Megara in 685 B.C. and lent its support alternately to Athens and Sparta. It was eventually (*c.* 140 B.C.) included in the kingdom of Bithynia, which was bequeathed by Nicomedes IV to Rome in 74 B.C. Partly destroyed by Mithradates the Great of Pontus, Calchedon was restored and appears to have flourished under the empire.

Caledonia, Roman name for northern Britain (q.v.), first used by Lucan (A.D. 64).

Cales (mod. Calvi), city of Campania on the Via Latina, eight miles north-west of Casilinum (q.v.). Taken by the Romans from the Aurunci in 335 B.C., Cales became the centre of Roman authority in Campania, and was an important base during the campaigns against Hannibal. Its prosperity was greatly increased by the export of black glazed pottery. There are extensive remains.

Caligula, Roman emperor, A.D. 37–41, son of Germanicus and Agrippina the elder, was born in A.D. 12, and was brought up among the legions in Germany. His real name was Gaius Caesar, and he was always called Gaius by his contemporaries; Caligula was a diminutive nickname (= bootikins) given him by the soldiers from his wearing

in his boyhood small *caligae*, or soldiers' boots. He won the favour of
Tiberius, who raised him to office and held out to him hopes of the
succession. On the death of Tiberius (37), which was either caused or
accelerated by Caligula, the latter succeeded to the throne. He was
saluted by the people with the greatest enthusiasm as the son of
Germanicus, and his first acts gave promise of a just and beneficent
reign; but at the end of eight months his conduct suddenly altered.
After a serious illness, which probably weakened his mental powers,
he appeared as a sanguinary and licentious maniac. In his madness he
built a temple to himself as Jupiter Latiaris, and appointed priests to
attend to his worship. He also caused trouble in Judea by threatening
to erect his statue for worship in the temple (*see* PHILO JUDAEUS).
His extravagance was monstrous. To replenish the treasury he exhausted Italy and Rome by his extortions, and then, in 39, marched
into Gaul, which he plundered. With his troops he advanced to the
ocean, as if intending to cross over into Britain; he drew them up in
battle array, and then gave them the signal—to collect shells, which
he called the spoils of conquered Ocean. The Roman world was
exasperated. Four months after his return to the city, on 24th
January 41, he was murdered by C. Cassius Chaerea (q.v.), tribune of
a praetorian cohort, Cornelius Sabinus and others. His wife Caesonia
and his daughter were likewise put to death. *See* J. P. V. D. Ballsdon,
The Emperor Gaius, 1934.

Calleva Atrebatum (mod. Silchester), a Romano-British town in
Hampshire, about 10 miles south of Reading. The whole site was
excavated between 1899 and 1909.

Callias (Kall-) and **Hipponicus (-kos)**, names borne alternately by
members of an Athenian family who were hereditary torch-bearers
(*dadukhoi*) at the Eleusinian Mysteries during the 5th and 4th centuries B.C.

1. Callias, fought at Marathon (490 B.C.). He was sent on a mission
to the court of Artaxerxes I (448), but on his return was accused of
treason and fined fifty talents.

2. Hipponicus, son of the preceding, joint commander, with
Eurymedon, of the Athenian force which invaded Boeotia (426), and
fell at the battle of Delium (424 B.C.).

3. Callias, son of the preceding, a notorious profligate and spendthrift, for which he was ridiculed by Aristophanes in the *Frogs* and
Birds. The scenes of Plato's *Protagoras* and Xenophon's *Symposium*
are laid at his house. He commanded the Athenian hoplites at Corinth
in 392 B.C. (*see* IPHICRATES).

Callicrates (Kallikratēs), architect with Ictinus of the Parthenon
(q.v.).

Callicratidas (Kallikratidas), Spartan admiral, commanded the fleet
which was defeated by the Athenians at Arginusae (406), where he
was killed.

Callimachus (Kallimakhos): 1. Greek grammarian and poet, was a
native of Cyrene. He lived at Alexandria in the reigns of Ptolemy
Philadelphus and Euergetes, and was cataloguer at the library there,
from about 260 until his death *c.* 250 B.C. Among his pupils were
Eratosthenes, Aristophanes of Byzantium and Apollonius Rhodius.

He wrote numerous works on an infinite variety of subjects, but of these we possess only some of his poems, which are characterized by labour and learning. Among fragments which have more recently come to light on Egyptian papyri, the chief is part of a poem in four books on the origins of various local rituals. All that survives has been edited with translation by A. W. Mair (Loeb Library), 1921. *See also* translation by G. M. Young, 1934.

2. Athenian sculptor of the late 5th century B.C., said to have invented the Corinthian column. According to the elder Pliny his work was marred by an excess of detail.

Callinus (Kallinos), earliest of the Greek elegiac poets, a native of Ephesus. He is supposed to have lived in the late 7th and early 6th centuries B.C. A few fragments of his work are extant.

Calliope (Kalliopē), the muse of epic poetry, *see* MUSES.

Callipus (Kallipos), Greek astronomer, born at Cyzicus, *c.* 370 B.C. He developed Eudoxus's system of concentric spheres and died in 300 B.C.

Callirrhoë (Kallirrhoē), 'fair flow', in Greek legend, daughter of the river-god Acheloüs and wife of Alcmaeon (q.v.). The name was also given to a spring in the south-east quarter of Athens. This was afterwards called Enneakrounos, 'Nine Springs', because its waters were distributed by as many conduits.

Callisthenes (Kallisthenēs), Greek historian and nephew of Aristotle, born at Olynthus *c.* 360 B.C. He accompanied Alexander the Great to Asia. Having rebuked the conqueror for his adoption of oriental manners, he was charged with complicity in the conspiracy of Hermolaus (q.v.) and was thrown into prison (328), where he died. None of his works survives.

Callisto (Kallistō), an Arcadian nymph and companion of Artemis (q.v.) in the chase. She was beloved by Zeus, who changed her into a she-bear. But Hera caused Artemis to slay Callisto during the chase, and Zeus placed her among the stars with the name Arctos (q.v.).

Callistratus (Kallistratos): 1. Athenian poet of uncertain date, author of an extant poem on Harmodius and Aristogeiton.

2. Athenian general and orator (4th century B.C.). In 361 he was condemned to death for having advised a temporary occupation of Oropus by the Thebans, which they subsequently refused to evacuate. He escaped to Methone in Macedonia; but returning to Athens, in 355, he was executed. It was his defence while on trial that persuaded Demosthenes (q.v.) to study oratory.

3. Alexandrian grammarian of the early 2nd century B.C. Some fragments of his commentaries on Greek poets survive.

4. A pupil of Isocrates (q.v.), who wrote a history of Heraclea Pontica.

5. Greek sophist and rhetorician of the 3rd century B.C. His extant *Ekphraseis*, a description of fourteen statues by famous artists, has been edited with translation by A. Fairbanks (Loeb Library, with Philostratus' *Eikones*), 1931.

Calpe, the modern Rock of Gibraltar, opposite Abyla (q.v.), with which it formed the *Herculis Columnae* (Pillars of Hercules).

Calpurnia, daughter of L. Calpurnius Piso and third wife of Caesar, whom she married in 59 B.C. She tried to prevent him attending the senate on 15th March 44 B.C., and after his murder transferred his money and private papers to Mark Antony.

Calpurnius Siculus, Titus (1st century A.D.), Roman poet, author of seven eclogues imitated from Theocritus. *See* the edition with prose translation by J. W. and A. M. Duff in *Minor Latin Poets* (Loeb Library), 1934.

Calvinus, Gnaeus Domitius, Roman general. He was tribune of the plebs in 59, when he supported Bibulus (q.v.) against Caesar; praetor in 56 and consul in 53 B.C. He took part with Caesar during the civil war, and was sent by him to intercept Scipio's approach from the East (48). Later he was joined by Caesar, commanded the centre at Pharsalus and was then dispatched with three legions to the province of Asia. Towards the end of 48 he was defeated by Pharnaces (q.v.) at Nicopolis, and is last heard of in Africa (46 B.C.).

Calvus, Gaius Licinius Macer, Roman poet and orator, whose father was prosecuted by Cicero for extortion and committed suicide. He died *c.* 47 B.C. His contemporary reputation was very high, but practically nothing of his work is extant.

Calydon, town of Aetolia (q.v.). According to Pliny it stood about seven miles from the sea on the River Euenus, and was supposed to have been founded by Calydon, son of Aetolus (q.v.). It was connected in legend with the hunting of the Calydonian boar (*see* MELEAGER). The inhabitants of Calydon were removed by Augustus to Nicopolis (q.v.). There are remains of a two-mile circuit of walls, also of a temple dedicated to Artemis Laphria, which housed a chryselephantine statue of the goddess.

Calypso (Kalupsō), nymph and queen of Ogygia, an island in the Ionian Sea. Here Odysseus was shipwrecked, and was detained by Calypso for seven years. *See* E. Bradford, *Ulysses Found,* 1964.

Camarina, city on the south coast of Sicily, 17 miles south-east of Gela. Founded from Syracuse in 598 B.C., it made an unsuccessful attempt to assert its independence forty-five years later (553). In 491 the city and its territory was transferred by Syracuse to Hippocrates of Gela; but in 484 it was destroyed by Gelon, and its inhabitants removed to Syracuse. It was refounded, however, by Gela in 461; abandoned by order of Dionysius I of Syracuse in 405; restored by Timoleon in 339; destroyed by the Romans in 258. The architectural remains are not impressive, but important finds have been made in the cemeteries. *See* B. Pace, *Camarina* (in Italian), 1927.

Cambyses (Kambusēs), Greek form of the Persian name Kambujia, which was borne by the father and son of Cyrus the Great (q.v.). The son was associated with his father in the kingdom from 530 until 528 B.C., when Cyrus died and Cambyses became sole monarch. In 525 he conquered Egypt with the help of Polycrates of Samos and some Greek mercenary troops. Before setting out on this expedition, he had murdered his brother Smerdis. In 522 the Magian Gaumata pretended to be Smerdis; Cambyses started from Egypt against him, but was not successful and committed suicide early in the next year. Herodotus had received a less probable tradition that he died in Syria of an accidental wound.

Camenae, nymphs having a grove and spring outside the Porta Capena at Rome. They were sometimes identified with the Muses (cf. Juvenal, iii. 16). *See* EGERIA.

Camerinum, more anciently **Camers** (mod. Camerino), town of Umbria, on the borders of Picenum. It became an ally of Rome in 310 B.C. and subsequently a Latin colony (*see* COLONIA).

Camers, *see* CAMERINUM.

Camillus, Marcus Furius, one of the great heroes of the Roman republic, censor in 403 B.C.; he was six times consular tribune and five times dictator. In his first dictatorship (396) he captured Veii, but in 391 was accused of an unfair distribution of its spoils and went into exile at Ardea. Recalled as dictator in the following year, he routed the Gauls under Brennus (q.v.) and was hailed as the second Romulus. In his last dictatorship (367), though eighty years of age, he again defeated the Gauls, and died two years later of the pestilence.

Campania, district of Italy, bounded east by the Apennines, south and west by the sea, north by the River Liris. Capua (q.v.) was the principal city. The soil of Campania was extremely fertile, yielding three or four grain crops annually; fruit and vegetables were plentiful; roses supplied the perfume factories of Capua; and the region was famous for its wines. The climate and scenery, especially on the coast, earned for Campania the title *felix,* and the vicinity of Neapolis was a favourite summer resort of wealthy Romans (*see* BAIAE; PUTEOLI; STABIAE). Augustus made Latium (q.v.) and Campania the first administrative region of Italy (*see* ITALIA); but from the time of Diocletian Campania was included in Latium.

Campi Raudii, plain, near Vercellae in northern Italy, where Marius defeated the Cimbri, 101 B.C.

Campus Martius, 'field of Mars', an open space to the north-west of Rome (q.v.), outside the city walls until included within the Aurelian circuit (3rd century A.D.). Belonging originally to the Tarquins, it was dedicated to Mars (q.v.), after their expulsion, as a place for athletic and military exercises. In course of time it was adorned with numerous public buildings, including the Circus Flaminius (*see* CIRCUS), and was used as a general recreational centre, the meeting-place of the *comitia curiata* (*see* COMITIA), and a place where foreign ambassadors were received.

Camulodunum (mod. Colchester), named after Camulos, the Celtic god of war, was capital of the British chieftain Cunobelin (q.v.), ruler of the Trinobantes. After his death and the Roman conquest of south Britain (q.v.), Claudius established a *colonia* of discharged legionaries (*c.* A.D. 48), which was known officially as *Colonia Victricensis Camulodunum.* The place was stormed and burnt in the rising of Boudicca (A.D. 61), but it soon recovered and became one of the most important towns of Roman Britain.

Candace, title of several queens of Aethiopia. One of them, Ameniremas, invaded Egypt in 24 B.C., but was repulsed by the imperial prefect C. Petronius. *See* AETHIOPIA.

Candaules (Kandaulēs), Greek name for the last king of the second (Heraclid) dynasty of Lydia. He exposed his wife to Gyges, one of his generals, who was driven by her to slay Candaules.

Canephorae (Kanēphorai), maidens who carried the sacred baskets in the Panathenaic procession at Athens (*see* PANATHENAEA).

Cannae, village of Apulia near which Hannibal overwhelmingly defeated the Romans under Aemilius Paulus and Terentius Varro on 2nd August 216 B.C. The battle was fought on the right bank of the River Aufidus, somewhat below the village of Cannae. A large military cemetery has been found near by. The battle of Cannae has been described as 'one of the supreme tactical masterpieces in the military history of the ancient world'.

Canopus, coastal town of Lower Egypt, 15 miles east of Alexandria, before the foundation of which it was the principal port for Greek trade. It was here, in 239 B.C., that Ptolemy III received the title 'Euergetes' by decree of an assembly of priests. Osiris was worshipped at Canopus under the form of a human-headed jar; he was identified with Menelaus's pilot Canopus, who was said to have been buried there.

Cantabria, district on the north coast of Spain (*see* HISPANIA), including the territory around modern Santander and Bilbao and the mountains behind. The inhabitants, known as Cantabri, were savage mountaineers who long resisted Roman arms; and Horace speaks of the 'Cantabrum indoctum iuga ferre nostra' (*Odes*, ii. 6, 2). Though attacked at intervals from 150 B.C. onwards, they were not finally subdued until about 19 B.C. Under the empire Cantabria was part of Hispania Tarraconensis.

Canusium (mod. Canosa), city of Apulia on the right bank of the Aufidus, and 85 miles east-north-east of Beneventum on the Via Traiana. Traditionally founded by Diomedes (q.v.), its culture even in classical times was partly Greek: the coinage bore Greek legends, and Horace tells us (*Sat.* i. 10, 30) that in his time both Greek and Latin were spoken there. Polychrome vases were manufactured in the 3rd century B.C., and the city was noted for its export of Apulian wool. Canusium placed itself under the sovereignty of Rome in 318 B.C. and remained faithful to her until it revolted in the Social War (q.v.). A *municipium* (q.v.) under the early empire, it was made a *colonia* (q.v.) by Herodes Atticus (q.v.), who gave it its first adequate water supply.

Capaneus (Ka-), son of Hipponoüs and father, by his wife Evadne, of Sthenelus. One of the Seven against Thebes (*see* THEBAN LEGEND, 3), he was struck by Zeus with lightning while scaling the wall. As his body burned, Evadne leaped into the flames. (*See* Aeschylus, *Seven against Thebes*.) His son Sthenelus was one of the Epigoni (*see* THEBAN LEGEND, 5), after which he served with Diomedes in the Trojan War.

Capena, city of southern Etruria; a dependant of Veii (q.v.), after the fall of which it became subject to Rome. There are tombs of the 8th and 7th centuries B.C. in the neighbourhood.

Capernaum (mod. Tell Hūm), on the northern shore of the Sea of Galilee, was in the time of Christ a Roman garrison town, administrative centre and customs station. St Luke (vii. 5) speaks of a centurion who loved the Jewish nation and had built them a synagogue. This synagogue was destroyed by an earthquake, but its complete ruins have been excavated and identified. *See* G. Orfali, *Capharnaum et ses ruines*, 1922.

Capito, Gaius Ateius, Roman jurist in the reigns of Augustus and Tiberius. He and his contemporary Antistius Labeo were reckoned the highest authorities of their day, and founded two legal schools afterwards known as Sabinian and Proculian respectively. *See* PROCULUS; SABINUS, 2.

Capitolium, the temple of Jupiter Optimus Maximus at Rome, situated on the south-western summit of the Mons Capitolinus, which was named after the temple. The site of the temple is now covered in part by the *Palazzo Caffarelli*, while the northern summit, which was formerly the Arx, is occupied by the church of *Ara Coeli*. The building was said to have been begun by the Tarquins, but not to have been dedicated till the first year of the republic, 509 B.C., by the consul Tarquinius Collatinus. It was burnt down in the civil wars, 83, and twice afterwards in the time of the emperors. After its third destruction in the reign of Titus it was again rebuilt by Domitian with greater splendour than before. The Capitol contained three cells under the same roof: the middle cell was the temple of Jupiter, hence described as *media qui sedet aede Deus*, and on either side were the cells of his attendant deities, Juno and Minerva. The Capitol was one of the most imposing buildings at Rome, and was adorned as befitted the majesty of the king of the gods. It was in the form of a square, namely 200 feet on each side, and was approached by a flight of 100 steps. The gates were of bronze, and the ceilings and tiles gilt. In the Capitol were kept the Sibylline books. Here the consuls upon entering on their office offered sacrifices and took their vows; and hither the victorious general, who entered the city in triumph, was carried in his triumphal car to return thanks to the father of the gods. The Capitoline hill (which, like the other hills of Rome, had its contour much altered by cutting away and levelling) consisted of a central part, flanked by two nearly equal heights. Between the Arx and the Capitolium lay the *Asylum* traditionally founded by Romulus. The Capitoline hill was in early times known also as *Mons Tarpeius*; but in later times the name *Rupes Tarpeia* was applied only to one portion of the cliff. Here are rock-hewn chambers which extended under the great temple of Jupiter and were used as secret treasuries. *See* T. Ashby and S. Platner, *Topographical Dictionary of Ancient Rome*, 1920; L. R. Muirhead, *Rome and Central Italy*, 1956.

Cappadocia, district of Asia Minor, to which different boundaries were assigned at different times. Under the Persian Empire it included the whole territory inhabited by a people called Leucosyri (q.v.) by the Greeks and 'Cappadocians' by the Persians, i.e. the whole north-eastern part of Asia Minor east of the River Halys and north of the Taurus range. At some date before the time of Xenophon this territory was divided to form Pontus (q.v.) and Cappadocia. It is with the latter only that this article is concerned.

Cappadocia became independent of Persia in the time of Alexander the Great, and continued to be governed by a line of native princes (*see* ARIARATHES; ARIOBARZANES), with some interference from Pontus, until 41 or 34 B.C., when Antony gave the kingdom to Archelaus (see ARCHELAUS, 5). He was deposed in A.D. 17, and Tiberius made Cappadocia a Roman province to which Vespasian added Armenia Minor (q.v.) in A.D. 70.

The principal towns were the capital, Mazaca (see CAESAREA-MAZACA), Tyana and Archelais (founded by Archelaus). There was a famous temple of Artemis Taurica at Comana (q.v.). Cappadocia was an important centre of the slave trade; it was also noted for its horses (the Roman emperors kept studs of race-horses there), its great flocks of sheep and its mines of quartz, salt and silver. See Th. Mommsen, *Provinces of the Roman Empire* (trans.), 1886; E. Chantre, *Mission en Cappadoce*, 1898.

Capreae (mod. Capri), a small island off Campania (q.v.), opposite the Promontorium Minervae. Famous principally as the residence of Tiberius (q.v.) during the last ten years of his life, it was later the place of banishment of the wife and sister of Commodus (q.v.). Remains include those of twelve villas built by Tiberius and numerous cisterns. See H. E. Trower, *The Book of Capri*, 1924.

Capua, chief city of Campania (q.v.) and one of the most important in the whole of Italy, on the Via Appia (q.v.) which connected it with Rome in 312 B.C. It soon became notorious for its luxury, and this blight undermined the morale of the Samnites who conquered it late in the 5th century B.C. and of Hannibal's troops who wintered there in 216–215 B.C. Capua allied itself with Rome in 338 B.C. and remained faithful to her until after the defeat of Cannae (216). It was taken by the Romans after a long siege in 211, and, together with its dependent towns, Casilinum, Calatia and Atella (qq.v.), was deprived of all privileges and became part of the *ager publicus* (q.v.). Capua was celebrated for bronze-work, perfumes, unguents and wine. Remains include rich tombs, baths, a theatre, an amphitheatre and a wonderful Mithraeum.

Caracalla, Roman emperor, A.D. 211–17, was son of Septimius Severus, and was born at Lugdunum, A.D. 188. His proper name was Marcus Aurelius Antoninus, Caracalla being a nickname derived from a long tunic worn by the Gauls, which he adopted as his favourite dress after he became emperor. He accompanied his father to Britain in 208; and on the death of Severus, at Eburacum (211), Caracalla and his brother Geta succeeded to the throne, according to their father's will. He assassinated Geta, and, with him, many of the most distinguished men in the state. He added extravagance to cruelty, and visited the eastern and western provinces of the empire, for the purposes of extortion and plunder. He was about to set out on further expeditions across the Tigris, but was murdered at Edessa by Macrinus, the praetorian prefect. Caracalla gave to all free inhabitants of the empire the name and privileges of Roman citizens.

Carales (mod. Cagliari), principal town of Sardinia (q.v.), situated on the south coast; founded probably by Carthaginians. It became a Roman *municipium* (q.v.) under Julius Caesar. In imperial times its importance was due mainly to its fine harbour, where a detachment of the *classis Misenensis* (see MISENUM) was stationed. There are extensive remains of Punic and Roman tombs, an amphitheatre, reservoirs and baths.

Caratacus or **Caractacus**, Latin form of the Celtic name Caradoc borne by a chieftain of the Catuvellauni in Britain (q.v.), son of Cunobelin (q.v.). Having led the resistance against Aulus Plautius and Ostorius Scapula, he was taken prisoner by the latter in A.D. 50 and sent with his family in chains to Rome, where Claudius spared their lives.

Carausius, Marcus Aurelius, a Gallic officer in the service of Maximian, who placed him in command of the garrison at Gessoriacum (Boulogne). Accused of being in league with the Frankish and Saxon pirates whom it was his business to destroy, he was condemned to death by the emperor, but fled to Britain and proclaimed himself independent sovereign (A.D. 286). A Roman fleet was dispatched to recover the island, but was wrecked in a storm, and Maximian recognized Carausius as ruler of Britain. Carausius maintained his position undisturbed until 293, when he was murdered by Allectus, commander of his guards, just as Constantius Chlorus was preparing an invasion. *See* P. H. Webb, *The Reign and Coinage of Carausius*, 1908.

Carbo, Gaius Papirius: 1. Tribune of the plebs in 131 B.C., and in the following year one of the commissioners appointed to give effect to the agrarian law of Tiberius Gracchus. He deserted the popular party, went over to the optimates, and in his consulship (120) successfully defended Opimius, the murderer of Gaius Gracchus. In 119, however, he was accused by L. Licinius Crassus of putting citizens to death without trial, and committed suicide.

2. Son of the preceding. As tribunes in 90 or 89 B.C. he and his colleague M. Plautius Silvanus carried the *Lex Plautia Papiria*, which offered the Roman franchise to every Italian ally domiciled in Italy at that date, provided he made personal application to the praetor at Rome within sixty days.

Carbo, Gnaeus Papirius, nephew of C. Papirius Carbo (tribune of the plebs 131 B.C.). He was one of the leaders of the Marian or popular party, and thrice consul (85, 84 and 82). Defeated by Sulla's general Metellus Pius near Faventia (q.v.), he fled, but was overtaken by Pompey at Cossyra and put to death.

Cardea, a Roman divinity, presiding over the hinges of doors, that is, over family life.

Caria, mountainous district of Asia Minor, bounded north by Lydia and Ionia, east by Lycia and Phrygia, west and south by the Aegean. The coastline is a succession of long promontories forming deep inlets, and is fringed with numerous islands. The native inhabitants consisted of (*a*) Carians, who were akin to the Lydians and Mysians, and (*b*) Caunians, a wilder people, who dwelt in the eastern part of the country and who, though speaking the same language as the Carians, were considered by them a different race. There were Greek colonies along the coast, of which the most famous were Cnidus and Halicarnassus (qq.v.).

Caria was at an early date absorbed into the kingdom of Lydia (q.v.). When the latter was destroyed by Cyrus (q.v.) in 546 B.C. Caria too passed under the sovereignty of Persia. But a line of native princes managed to establish themselves, and their authority extended in course of time even to the Greek cities. After the death of

Alexander, Caria was included in the empire of the Seleucids, then in the kingdom of Pergamum (q.v.), and finally in the Roman province of Asia (q.v.).

Carinus, Marcus Aurelius, Roman emperor A.D. 283–4, elder son of Carus (q.v.) who appointed him to govern the western provinces of the empire. Having won some successes against German tribes, he handed over command to his legates and went off to enjoy himself in Rome. On the death of Carus he succeeded to the throne jointly with his brother Numerianus (q.v.), but in the following year he was assassinated by some of his own officers during a battle against Diocletian on the River Margus, in Moesia.

Carna, Roman divinity, regarded as the protector of the physical well-being of man. Her festival was celebrated 1st June, and was believed to have been instituted by Brutus in the first year of the republic. Ovid confounds this goddess with Cardea (q.v.).

Carnea (Karneia), from *karnos*, 'ram', a festival held at Sparta in the month Carneus (Aug.–Sept.), in honour of the ram-god, Apollo Carneios. The old ram-god was probably worshipped in Laconia before the Dorian invasion, and the Dorians, taking over his worship from the conquered people, identified him with Apollo under the title of Carneios. *See* L. R. Farnell, *Cults of the Greek States*, vol. iv, 1907.

Carneades (Karneadēs), Greek philosopher, born at Cyrene in 214 B.C.; studied under Diogenes the Stoic and Hegesinus. The most important of Greek sceptics, he founded the third or New Academy (*see* ACADEMY), and was a strenuous opponent of Stoic epistemology. In 155 the Athenians sent him to Rome with Diogenes and Critolaus (q.v.), to protest against a fine imposed upon Athens by the Roman authorities for some trespass on the territory of Oropus. There he delivered two speeches, for and against justice, which so impressed his audience that Cato had him ordered out of the city. Carneades died in 129 B.C.

Carnuntum, Roman fortress town on the Danube, belonging first to Noricum, but after A.D. 16 to Pannonia. In A.D. 6 it was used by Tiberius in his campaign against Maroboduus; later it became the centre of the Roman defences between Vindobona and Brigetio, then (under Trajan or Hadrian) the permanent quarters of the Fourteenth Legion. Hadrian created it a *municipium* (q.v.) with the name Aelium Carnuntum. Marcus Aurelius had his headquarters there during the war against the Marcomanni (172–5). Septimius Severus (q.v.) was proclaimed emperor at Carnuntum (A.D. 193). Carnuntum was originally a Celtic town and a market for amber on its way to Italy from the north. There are considerable Roman remains.

Carnutes, a Celtic people of central Gaul between the Sequana (Seine) and Liger (Loire). Their principal towns were Autricum (Chartres) and Cenabum (Orleans). At the time of Caesar's conquest of Gaul the Carnutes were dependants of the Remi (q.v.); but they joined the rebellion of Vercingetorix (q.v.) in 52 B.C., during which Cenabum was burned. They sent 12,000 men to relieve Alesia, but were involved in the Gallic disaster. In the following year they attacked the Bituriges (q.v.); the latter appealed to Caesar, and the

Carnutes were forced to submit. Augustus created them a *civitas foederata*, which meant that they retained their own political institutions and were obliged only to render military service to the empire. In A.D. 275 Aurelian raised Cenabum to the rank of a *civitas* with the name Aurelianum, and it took the place of Autricum as the national capital.

Carpi, a Dacian tribe (*see* DACIA) established on the lower Danube from the 1st century B.C. During the third century A.D. they made an unsuccessful attempt to invade the Roman Empire. Then they made common cause with the Goths (*see* GOTHI) and shared their fortunes until both were defeated by the emperor Claudius II (269). Repulsed time and again under Diocletian and Galerius, most of them were eventually settled in Pannonia and Moesia.

Carrhae, town in Mesopotamia, near which a Roman army of about 39,000 men under M. Licinius Crassus (*see* CRASSUS, MARCUS LICINIUS) was virtually annihilated by the Parthian mounted archers under Surenas (53 B.C.). The battle of Carrhae has been described as 'the first great failure of the flexible infantry legion evolved from the Hannibalic wars and the reforms of Marius'. It was one of the turning points in military history.

Carseoli (mod. Carsoli), Italian city on the Via Valeria, founded in the country of the Aequi (q.v.) between 302 and 298 B.C., soon after the establishment of Alba Fucens (q.v.), the road to which it was doubtless intended to protect. It was sacked during the Social War (q.v.).

Carteia, *see* TARTESSUS.

Carthage (Gk Karchēdōn; Lat. Carthago), city on the north coast of Africa, situated on a peninsula in the Sinus Uticensis about 12 miles east of modern Tunis. Founded *c.* 700 B.C. from Tyre (*see* DIDO), it was by the middle of the 6th century B.C. mistress of a great Phoenician commercial empire whose numerous colonies were scattered throughout the Mediterranean area. For an account of the political institutions of Carthage *see* Aristotle, *Politics*, ii.

Carthage enters the recorded history of the classical world in 550 B.C. when she conquered most of eastern Sicily. Fourteen years later the Carthaginians defeated the Phocaeans and Massaliotes on the coast of Corsica. In about 500 B.C. they conquered Sardinia and the Baleares (qq.v.). In 480 B.C. a Carthaginian army intended for the final subjugation of all Sicily was defeated before Himera by the combined forces of Syracuse and Acragas (qq.v.; *see also* GELON; THERON). The war, however, continued on and off for more than a hundred years (*see* AGATHOCLES; DIONYSIUS THE ELDER; DIONYSIUS THE YOUNGER).

Meanwhile, in 509 B.C., Carthage had entered into a commercial treaty with Rome; but during the 220 years since that date the power of Rome had greatly increased, and conflict with the Carthaginian Empire was inevitable. It proved to be one of the most remarkable and most decisive struggles of history (*see* PUNIC WARS) and ended with the defeat and destruction of Carthage in 146 B.C. when all her territories became subject to Rome. The city remained virtually in ruins until it was rebuilt and made a *colonia* (q.v.) by Augustus with the name Colonia Julia Carthago. During the first two centuries of the imperial age Carthage was described by Pomponius Mela, Strabo and Herodian as one of the greatest and most wealthy cities of the empire.

In the heyday of her glory Carthage had a flourishing industry in woven goods, while Sicily, Italy and Greece alike welcomed her exports of Negro slaves, ivory, metals, precious stones and all the products of central Africa. *See* R. B. Smith, *Carthage*, 1911; H. P. Hurd, *The Topography of Punic Carthage*, 1934; B. H. Warmington, *Carthage*, 1960.

by P. Cornelius Scipio Africanus after one of the greatest sieges in history (*see* SCIPIO, AFRICANUS MAJOR). The city stood at the head of a fine natural harbour; its territory included important gold and silver mines which were a source of great wealth to both the Carthaginians and the Romans. *See* B. H. Liddell Hart, *A Greater than Napoleon: Scipio Africanus*, 1926.

Carus, Marcus Aurelius, Roman emperor, A.D. 282-3, born at Narona in Illyricum. A senator and prefect of the praetorian guards, he was proclaimed emperor by the troops after the murder of Probus (q.v.). Leaving his elder son Carinus (q.v.) to govern the western provinces, he started out with the younger, Numerianus (q.v.), on an expedition against the Persians. After successful campaigns against the Quadi and Sarmatians on the Danube, he conquered Mesopotamia and eventually crossed the Tigris. Here he was assassinated, probably at the instigation of Arrius Aper (q.v.), the praetorian prefect.

Caryae (Karuai), town of Laconia near the Arcadian border. It had a temple of Artemis, at which a ritual dance was performed by Lacedaemonian virgins in honour of the goddess. Hence, probably, the sculptured figures known as caryatids.

Casilinum, city of Campania, three miles north-west of Capua, where the Via Appia and Via Latina (qq.v.) joined and crossed the River Volturnus. It offered an heroic resistance to Hannibal, but was taken by him in 215 B.C. Retaken by the Romans in the following year, it was subsequently their base of operations against Capua (q.v.).

Casinum, town of Campania on the Via Latina (q.v.), 40 miles north-west of Capua. The amphitheatre survives. On the adjoining mountain (1,715 ft), now occupied by the abbey of Monte Cassino, are remains of an older Volscian town of the same name.

Cassander (Gk Kassandros), King of Macedonia, was born *c.* 350 B.C., son of Antipater. His father, on his death-bed (319), appointed Polysperchon regent and conferred on Cassander the secondary dignity of chiliarch. Dissatisfied with this arrangement, Cassander made an alliance with Ptolemy I, Soter, and Antigonus I, and declared war on Polysperchon. He then turned his arms against Olympias (q.v.), who had murdered Philip Arrhidaeus and Eurydice (brother and sister-in-law of Alexander), and put her to death (316). He

Carthago Nova ('New Carthage'; mod. Cartagena), town on the south-east coast of Spain (*see* HISPANIA), founded by the Carthaginian Hasdrubal (*see* HASDRUBAL, 1) *c.* 227 B.C. In 209 B.C. it was captured

was now without a rival in Macedonia, and therefore formed a coalition with Lysimachus, Ptolemy and Seleucus I, Nicator, against Antigonus; and a treaty made in 311 recognized him as general in Europe during the minority of Alexander IV. But in 310 he murdered Alexander and his mother. In 303, in face of the threat from Demetrius Poliorcetes (q.v.), Cassander revived the coalition, and after the defeat and death of Antigonus at Ipsus (301), was acknowledged as King of Macedonia. He died in 297 B.C.

Cassandra (Kass-), in Greek legend, daughter of Priam and Hecuba, and twin sister of Helenus. When she grew up her beauty persuaded Apollo to confer upon her the gift of prophecy, upon her promising to comply with his desires; but when she had become possessed of the prophetic art, she refused to fulfil her promise. Thereupon the god ordained that no one should believe her prophecies. On the capture of Troy she fled into the sanctuary of Athena, but was torn away from the statue of the goddess by Ajax, son of Oïleus. On the division of the booty, Cassandra fell to the lot of Agamemnon, who took her with him to Mycenae. Here she was killed by Clytaemnestra, and was subsequently deified.

Cassia, Via, Roman road built probably in 187 B.C. between Rome and Florence. It connected with the Via Clodia and the Via Ciminia (q.v.).

Cassiopeia, in Greek legend, wife of Cepheus (q.v.) and mother of Andromeda. After her death she was placed among the stars.

Cassiterides, the 'Tin Islands', name given by ancient geographers and other writers to islands somewhere near the west coasts of Europe. They cannot be certainly identified, but T. Rice Holmes (*Ancient Britain,* 1907) has advanced powerful arguments in favour of the British Isles.

Cassius Longinus, Gaius : 1. Roman general and the leading spirit in the conspiracy against Caesar's life. As quaestor of Crassus in 53 B.C. he distinguished himself by withdrawing the remnants of their scattered army after the disaster at Carrhae (q.v.), and managed to inflict two defeats upon the Parthians (52 and 51). On the outbreak of civil war in 49 he was tribune of the plebs, joined the senatorial party and accompanied Pompey to Greece. After Pharsalus (48) he was pardoned by Caesar, who made him praetor in 44 and promised him the province of Syria for the next year. Cassius, however, maintained his secret hostility to Caesar, and organized the conspiracy which bore its fruit on the Ides of March, 44 B.C. Later he went to Syria, although the senate had conferred it upon Dolabella and given Cassius Cyrenaica instead. He defeated Dolabella, who committed suicide, and then, having plundered Syria and Asia, joined M. Junius Brutus (q.v.) in Macedonia, where, after his defeat at Philippi, Cassius ordered one of his freedmen to kill him (42 B.C.).

2. Roman jurist of the Sabinian school (*see* CAPITO, GAIUS ATEIUS); consul in A.D. 30, governor of Asia 40–1 and of Syria 45–50. Banished to Sardinia by Nero (65) for possessing among his ancestral images a bust of the preceding (Caesar's murderer), he was recalled by Vespasian. He was the author of a work on the civil law in ten books.

Cassius Longinus, Lucius, tribune of the plebs in 137 B.C. and author of the celebrated legal maxim *cui bono?* The meaning of this often misused phrase is 'Who profits by [this crime?]'

Cassius Parmensis, Gaius, so called from Parma, his birth-place, Roman poet whose work was esteemed by Horace. He was one of Caesar's murderers and afterwards took an active part on the side first of Sextus Pompeius and then of Antony. He was put to death by order of Octavian (30 B.C.).

Cassivellaunus, British chieftain who ruled over territory immediately north of the Thames, and who was chosen to command the native forces on the occasion of Caesar's second invasion (54 B.C.). His stronghold, however, was captured and he came to terms. See *Bell. Gall.* v. 8, 11; 18–22.

Castalia or **Fons Castalius,** fountain rising in a cave on Mt Parnassus near Delphi. Sacred to Apollo and the Muses, it was treated by late Greek writers and Latin poets as a source of inspiration. Its water was used in the purification of pilgrims to Delphi.

Castor (Kastōr), one of the Dioscuri (q.v.).

Castrum Minervae, town of the Sallentini in Calabria, 10 miles south of Hydruntum, with an ancient temple of Minerva. It was said to have been founded by Idomeneus and to have been the first place at which Aeneas landed in Italy.

Castulo (mod. Cazlona), town of Hispania Tarraconensis (*see* HISPANIA) with silver and lead mines in the neighbourhood.

Catana (Katanē), *see* CATINA.

Catilina, Lucius Sergius, called in English **Catiline,** was born into an impoverished patrician family at Rome *c.* 109 B.C. He appears first as a zealous partisan of Sulla (q.v.), taking an active part in the proscription and committing at least one murder with his own hand. Quaestor in 77, praetor in 68 and governor of Africa 67–66 B.C., he sued for the consulship in this last year. But he had already been charged with extortion in his province, and was therefore disqualified. He then formed a conspiracy to murder the new consuls on the day of their installation, but the date was postponed and nothing was achieved.

Catiline now planned a much more formidable scheme, and circumstances favoured him; for the younger nobility and Sulla's veterans looked for some change to relieve their wants, and the masses were thoroughly discontented. Catiline had used bribery to secure his acquittal on the charge of extortion, so that he was free to act. His purpose was to secure the consulship for 63 B.C. with C. Antonius as his colleague (*see* ANTONIUS, GAIUS, 1). Then Rome would be set on fire, opponents of the revolution would be put to death, debts would be cancelled and the rich would be proscribed. But as it happened, Catiline was not elected: the voters chose Cicero (q.v.) and Antonius, and Catiline determined to follow the course of open war. For this he was not unprepared: the conspirators, many of them men of rank and influence, had already enlisted troops, collected money and arms, and even secured the backing of slaves. It was decided to murder Cicero on the morning of 7th November; but the plan failed, and on the 8th Cicero launched his attack with the first Catilinarian oration— 'Quousque tandem, Catilina, abutere patientia nostra?' Catiline fled the city to his army in Etruria, where the standard of revolt had already been raised by one of Sulla's veterans, C. Manlius. On the 9th Cicero delivered the second oration before the people in the Forum; Catiline and Manlius were declared public enemies, and Antonius was sent against them with an army. In the meantime correspondence had been intercepted from those conspirators who had remained in the city to some ambassadors of the Allobroges (who happened to be at Rome) inviting their assistance. With this evidence of treason in hand, Cicero at once ordered the arrest of Lentulus, Cethegus and others, who were put to death (5th December).

In the first days of January 62 Catiline was defeated near Pistoriae by the forces of Antonius, and died fighting valiantly. *See* Sallust, *Bellum Catilinarium*; E. H. Hardy, *The Catilinarian Conspiracy*, 1924.

Catina (Gk *Katanē*) or **Catana**, city on the east coast of Sicily, founded from Naxos in 729 B.C. The principal events in its history are as follows: Hiero I of Syracuse removed the population to Leontini, replacing them with 10,000 Syracusans and Peloponnesians and changing the name Katane to Aitna, 467 B.C. In 461 B.C. the former inhabitants regained possession of the city and revived the old name. Katane was an ally of Athens during the Syracusan expedition, 415–413 B.C. Dionysius I plundered it in 403 B.C., sold the population into slavery and replaced them with Campanian mercenaries. During the first Punic war (263 B.C.) the city became subject to Rome; it was devastated by an eruption of Aetna in 123 B.C. and became a Roman colony under Augustus.

Among numerous Roman remains, which include a theatre and several baths, the most important are those of an amphitheatre. This is surpassed in size by the one at Verona and by the Colosseum (q.v.) alone. *See also* CHARONDAS.

Cato, Marcus Porcius (232–147 B.C.), Roman statesman surnamed 'the Elder' or 'the Censor' to distinguish him from his great-grandson (*see* next article), was born at Tusculum. Between 217 and 191 B.C. he served in the second Punic war and in the campaigns against Antiochus III. With the Roman victory over Antiochus at Thermopylae (191) his military career ended. But he took a more than active part in civilian affairs during the remainder of his life, being particularly opposed to the increasing luxury of Roman society. Elected censor with L. Valerius Flaccus in 184, he applied himself with the utmost vigour to the duties of his office, regardless of hostility and opposition; but all his efforts failed to revive simpler habits.

Sent to Africa as one of the Roman commissioners to arbitrate between Masinissa (q.v.) and the Carthaginians, he was persuaded that Rome could never be safe while Carthage continued to exist. From this time, whenever he was called upon to address the senate, and even though the subject of debate bore no relation to Carthage, he invariably ended with the words 'Delenda est Carthago' ('Carthage must be destroyed').

Cato was a gifted orator. His work on the *Origins* of Rome is lost; but we possess his *De Re Rustica*, a treatise on agriculture. *See* text and translation by H. D. Ash (Loeb Library). *See also* C. W. Oman, *Seven Roman Statesmen*, 1902.

Cato, Marcus Porcius (Uticensis) (95–46 B.C.), called Cato the
Younger to distinguish him from his great-grandfather (*see* preceding
article), posthumously surnamed Uticensis from the place of his death.
In early childhood he lost both parents, and was brought up in the
household of his maternal uncle M. Livius Drusus. As a young man he
devoted himself to the study of oratory, and became an adherent of
the Stoic school, in which capacity he was soon conspicuous for
unbending rectitude. Tribune of the plebs in 63, he supported Cicero
in proposing death for the fellow conspirators of Catiline, and from
this time he was one of the most active leaders of the senatorial party.
He sided with Pompey on the outbreak of civil war (49), and after
Pharsalus went first to Corcyra and thence to Africa, where he joined
Metellus Scipio (*see* METELLUS, 5). Following Caesar's victory at
Thapsus (46), when it became clear that all was lost, Cato was shut
up in Utica, of which he had been appointed governor. He would
almost certainly have been pardoned by the victor had he chosen to
ask for clemency; but he cared no more for life. Having withdrawn to
his bedroom, he read Plato's *Phaedo* and committed suicide.

Cato, Publius Valerius, Roman poet and grammarian, born in Cisal-
pine Gaul *c.* 100 B.C. During the civil strife in the days of Marius and
Sulla he lost his property, and according to Suetonius (*De Gram-
maticis*) the later years of his long life also were beset with poverty.
Cato was the leader of a school, called by Cicero *novi poetae*, who
modelled their work upon the mythological epics and elegies of the
Alexandrians. He may be the author of an extant poem entitled
Dirae (edited by F. Näke, 1847).

Catullus, Gaius Valerius (84–*c.* 54 B.C.), Latin poet, born at Verona.
Having squandered his property he went in the train of the pro-
praetor Memmius to Bithynia (57), where he visited his brother's
tomb near Troy and wrote the wonderful lament *Multas per gentes*.
His love poetry is addressed to 'Lesbia', who is identified with
Clodius Pulcher's sister Clodia. His political verses include a disgusting attack on Caesar, who nevertheless treated him with the
utmost courtesy. As a poet Catullus is notable for his mastery of the
Latin language, which he endows with the flexibility and melody of
Greek, and for his expression of every phase of emotion. A paraphrase
of Callimachus's *Lock of Berenice* and the wild pulsating *Attis* are
masterpieces. *See* edition by R. A. B. Mynors, 1964; verse translation
by F. O. Copley, 1964; *also* A. L. Wheeler, *Catullus and the Traditions
of Ancient Poetry*, 1934; E. A. Havelock, *The Lyric Genius of Catullus*,
1939.

Catulus, Gaius Lutatius, Roman admiral, consul in 242 B.C. when he
occupied Lilybaeum and Drepanum with 200 ships. As proconsul in
the following year his fleet defeated the Carthaginians off the Aegates
(q.v.), although he himself was prevented by a wound from taking
part in the action. This victory ended the first Punic war.

Catulus, Quintus Lutatius: 1. Consul in 102 B.C. with C. Marius
(q.v.). As proconsul in the following year he shared the victory of
Marius over the Cimbri (q.v.). Subsequently, however, he supported Sulla (q.v.), and during the massacres of 87 B.C. put an
end to his life by means of the vapour from a charcoal fire. Catulus

was also distinguished as an orator and poet; two of his epigrams have survived (*see* W. W. Merry, *Fragments of Roman Poetry*, 1898).

2. Son of the preceding. As consul in 78 B.C. he opposed the attempt of his colleague, M. Aemilius Lepidus, to overthrow the Sullan constitution, and defeated him with the help of Pompey. He died in 61 B.C. at the age of about fifty-nine.

Caucasus, a range of mountains, 900 miles long and stretching from the eastern shores of the Pontus Euxinus (Black Sea) to the Caspian. That the Greeks had knowledge of this region from very early times is shown by the legends of Prometheus and the Argonauts (qq.v.), and also by the presence of maritime colonies established by Miletus on the Euxine during the 7th century B.C.

Caudium, town of Samnium on the road from Capua to Beneventum. In the neighbourhood were the *furculae Caudinae* (Caudine Forks), narrow passes where the Roman army surrendered to the Samnite general Herennius and was made to pass under the yoke, 321 B.C.

Caulonia (Kaulōnia), town on the east coast of Bruttii, an Achaean colony founded either as an outpost of Croton or from Greece itself. It was an ally of Croton and Sybaris in the 7th century, and of Athens during the Peloponnesian war. It was twice sacked: by Dionysius I of Syracuse in 389 and by Campanian troops under Pyrrhus (q.v.). Excavations have revealed considerable remains of fortifications belonging to the 7th–6th century B.C., together with houses and a temple of later date.

Cecrops (Ke-), in Greek legend, first king of Attica as distinct from the city of Athens (*see* ERECHTHEUS; XUTHUS). He was said to have divided the country into twelve communities, to have introduced bloodless sacrifices and burial of the dead, to have taught his subjects the worship of the Olympian gods and to have invented the art of writing. He was umpire in the dispute between Athena and Poseidon for possession of Attica.

Celaenae (Kelainai), city of Phrygia, situated on an important east–west trade route at the sources of the Maeander and Marsyas. It possessed a cave which was the traditional scene of the punishment of Marsyas (q.v.). Celaenae was the starting-point of the younger Cyrus's march against Artaxerxes II in 401 B.C. It resisted Alexander and obtained terms from him in 333. Capital of Antigonus I, it was later refounded on another site by Antiochus I, Soter, and called Apamea (q.v.).

Celaeno (Kelainō), one of the Harpies (q.v.).

Celeus (Kēleos), legendary king of Eleusis, and father of Demophon and Triptolemus. He received Demeter (q.v.) with hospitality at Eleusis, when she was wandering in search of her daughter. The goddess, in return, wished to make his son Demophon immortal, and placed him in the fire in order to destroy his mortal parts; but the child's mother Metaneira screamed aloud at the sight, and Demophon was destroyed by the flames. Demeter then bestowed great favours upon Triptolemus (q.v.). Celeus is described as the first priest and his daughters as the first priestesses of Demeter at Eleusis.

Celsus, Aulus Aurelius Cornelius (25 B.C.–A.D. 50), Latin medical writer. His *De Medicina* has been printed in more than 100 editions since 1478. He preferred if possible to let nature take its course; but the eighth and final book, on surgery, points to the fact that many of the most delicate and serious operations were performed in his time. *See* text, with translation by W. H. Spencer (Loeb Library).

Celtae, the Celts, a name applied by ancient writers to two loosely divided groups of peoples living north of the Alps and called by the Greeks *Keltoi*. The first of these groups, inhabiting north-western Europe, was tall, fair-haired and blue- or grey-eyed. The second is found along the great mountain chain from south-western France, in Savoy, in Switzerland, the Po valley and Tyrol, as also in Auvergne, Brittany, Normandy, Burgundy, the Ardennes and the Vosges; they were of medium height, chestnut-haired and hazel-eyed.

The expansion of the Celts from their original habitat in central Europe took place between about 500 B.C. and the beginning of the Christian era. The first of these great migratory movements was towards the Mediterranean coast of Gaul (*see* GALLIA), into Spain (*see* CELTIBERIA) and into northern Italy (*see* Livy, v. 34). A second invasion of Italy in 391 B.C. (*see* SENONES) destroyed the Etruscan power and ended in the occupation of Rome, 390 B.C. (*see* ALLIA; BOII; CENOMANI). The Celts were paid to abandon the city and its territory, but they continued to occupy large tracts of northern Italy as far south as Sena Gallica in Picenum and formed a standing threat for about two hundred years.

About 280 a huge army of Celts defeated the Macedonians, overran Thessaly and penetrated into Phocis with a view to capturing Delphi; but the shrine and treasury were saved, thanks largely to the Aetolian League, 279 B.C. A part of this great host had waited in Thrace. It was now joined by the survivors from Greece; together they marched to the Hellespont and some settled near Byzantium until they were annihilated by the Thracians some time after 220 B.C. Others crossed into Asia Minor and dominated the whole area west of Taurus until their defeat by Attalus I (q.v.) of Pergamum, after which they were confined to a narrow strip of territory afterwards known as Galatia (q.v.). *See* H. Hubert, *Rise of the Celts*, 1934.

Celtiberia, name given by ancient writers to the north-east portion of the central plateau of Spain. The Celtiberi were the descendants of Celts (*see* CELTAE) who had crossed the Pyrenees and mingled with the native Iberians. Their troops served as mercenaries in the armies of both Carthage and Rome. Subdued in 179 B.C. by Tib. Sempronius Gracchus, they revolted in 153 B.C. and were not finally overcome until twenty years later, after the fall of Numantia. They took up arms once again under Sertorius (q.v.); but after his death, in 72 B.C., they were gradually romanized.

Cenchreae (Kenkhreai), the eastern harbour of Corinth, on the Saronic Gulf. *See* CORINTH.

Cenomani, a people of north-western Gaul; their territory corresponded roughly with the old province of Maine, and the name of their chief town, Civitas Cenomanorum (formerly Vindinum), survives in modern Le Mans. Some of the Cenomani took part in the Celtic invasion of northern Italy *c.* 400 B.C. (*see* CELTAE) and occupied territory between the Addua, the Adige and the Po, from which they had driven the Etruscans and where their principal towns were Brixia and Verona. Having sided with Rome in the Gallic war of 225 B.C. and during the campaigns against Hannibal, they joined the Gallic revolt under Hamilcar (q.v.) in 200. Defeated by Gaius Cornelius three years later, they finally submitted and received Roman citizenship with the rest of Gallia Transpadana in 49 B.C. That branch of the tribe which had remained in Transalpine Gaul contributed a force of 5,000 men to the army of Vercingetorix (q.v.) in 52 B.C. Augustus established them as a tributary community within the province of Gallia Lugdunensis (*see* GALLIA).

Censorinus (3rd century A.D.), Italian grammarian and chronologist, author of an extant Latin treatise *De die natali* (A.D. 238), on the influence of the stars and various methods employed in the division and calculation of time. The best edition with commentary continues to be that of H. Lindenbrog (1614).

Censors, Roman magistrates whose duties were to superintend the quinquennial census, and to regulate public morals. In the execution of this latter function they could remove the names of offenders from the equestrian and senatorial lists. The censorship was instituted in 443 and was last filled as an independent office in 22 B.C. The censors, two in number, were originally elected for a whole *lustrum* (five years), but in 433 the period was reduced to eighteen months. *See* W. E. Heitland, *Roman Republic*, 1923.

Centaurs (Gk Kentauroi) are represented in mythology and legend as inhabiting Mt Pelion in Thessaly. Homer speaks of them as wild beasts, but in later accounts they appear as half horses and half men, and are said to have been the offspring of Ixion and a cloud. Another account makes them the offspring of Centaurus (son of Ixion and Nephele) who mated with mares. The Centaurs are famed in Greek legend for their fight with the Lapithae, which ended by the Centaurs being expelled from their country and taking refuge on Mt Pindus, on the frontiers of Epirus. Chiron (q.v.) is the most celebrated of them all. We know that hunting the bull on horseback was a national custom in Thessaly, and that the Thessalians were skilled riders, whence probably the tradition as to the Centaurs' form. *See* P. Baur, *Centaurs in Ancient Art*, 1912.

Centorbi, *see* CENTURIPAE.

Centum Cellae (mod. Civitavecchia), seaport town 35 miles northwest of Rome. It was founded by Trajan, who built an excellent harbour. Near this was a naval cemetery. Remains include a Roman house under the 16th-century castle, and baths of Trajan's time at a place once called Aquae Tauri, where there were warm springs, three miles to the north-east.

Centumviri, ancient civil court at Rome, with jurisdiction in matters of debt and of real property. The Centumviri were originally appointed by the urban praetor; but in Cicero's time, when they numbered 105, they were elected by the Comitia Tributa (*see* COMITIA). The number was increased by Augustus, and had reached 180 towards the end of the 1st century.

Centurion (Lat. *centurio*), *see* LEGION.

Centuripae, formerly **Centorbi** (Gk Kentoripa), town of the Siculi, in Sicily, on the River Symaethus, 28 miles north-west of Catina. An ally of Athens against Syracuse, it remained independent, except for a brief period of subjection to Agathocles (q.v.), until the second Punic war, when it was included in the Roman province of Sicily. Though a flourishing place in Cicero's day, it suffered during the war against Sextus Pompeius (q.v.) and never regained its prosperity.

Ceos (Keōs), an island of the Cyclades (q.v.), 14 miles from the coast of Attica. The principal town, Iulis, was the birth-place of the lyric poets Simonides and Bacchylides, of the philosopher Ariston, and of the physician Erasistratus (qq.v.). Ceos fought with the Greeks at Artemisium and Salamis, joined the Delian League (q.v.) and (377 B.C.) the Athenian alliance; but it revolted in 363, and after its subjugation in the following year Athens assumed a monopoly of trade in the island's red earth, its most valuable product. The code of laws by which Ceos was governed was greatly admired; one remarkable clause forbade citizens to protract their lives beyond the age of sixty.

Cephallenia (Kephallēnia), largest island of the Ionian Sea, separated from Ithaca by a narrow channel. There are Greek and Roman remains. In the Peloponnesian war Cephallenia was an ally of Athens, to whom it was presented more than five hundred years later by the emperor Hadrian; but there is record of its being subsequently free and autonomous.

Two of the principal towns were Palē and Samē. The former supported the Aetolians in 218 B.C. and was vainly besieged by Philip V of Macedon. In 189 B.C. the whole island surrendered to Rome, but Samē afterwards revolted and a siege of four months was necessary before it was reduced.

Cephalus (Kephalos), in Greek legend, husband of Procris, a daughter of Erechtheus, King of Athens. His love for his wife caused him to reject the advances of Eos (q.v.), who thereupon advised him to test the fidelity of Procris, metamorphosed him into a stranger and sent him with rich presents to his home. Procris was tempted by these splendid gifts to yield to the stranger, who immediately revealed his identity, and she fled in shame to Crete. Artemis gave her a dog and a spear, which would never miss their object, and sent her back to Cephalus disguised as a youth. In order to obtain the dog and spear, Cephalus offered himself as the youth's lover, and Procris in turn revealed her identity. This led to a reconciliation. Procris, however, still feared Eos and used to watch Cephalus when he went out hunting, until one day he accidentally slew her with the unerring spear.

Cepheus (Kē-), King of Aethiopia and father of Andromeda by Cassiopeia. After their deaths both he and his wife were placed among the stars.

Cephisodotus (Kēphisodotos), name of two Greek sculptors of the 4th century B.C., one a cousin and the other a son of Praxiteles. The former, besides executing a number of statues for Megalopolis (founded 370 B.C.), produced a celebrated figure of Peace carrying the infant Wealth. The son made portraits of Menander, Lycurgus and others.

Cephissus (Kēphissos): 1. The largest river of Attica (q.v.). Rising in the western slopes of Parnes, it flows past Athens and enters the Saronic Gulf near Phalerum.

2. River flowing through Phocis and Boeotia into Lake Copais.

Ceramicus (Kerameikos), district of Athens (q.v.) which derived its name from the numerous pottery factories established there. It was the chief burial ground of the city and has been largely excavated.

Cerasus (Kerasos), a colony of Sinope on the coast of Pontus, at the mouth of a river of the same name. It is chiefly celebrated as the place whence Europe obtained the cherry, which, according to Pliny, was brought back to Rome by Lucullus (q.v.) on his return from the East in 68 B.C.; but this probably refers to one or more particular strains, for there is evidence that the Romans possessed the tree much earlier.

Cerberus (Kerberos), a dog which guarded the entrance to Hades. Some poets represent him with 50 or 100 heads; but later writers describe him as a monster with only 3 heads, with the tail of a serpent and with serpents round his neck. His den is usually placed on the farther side of the Styx, at the spot where Charon landed the shades of the departed. Heracles dragged him to the upper world (*see* TWELVE LABOURS OF HERACLES, 12).

Cercopes (Kerkōpes), mischievous spirits who were changed into monkeys, and in that shape robbed Heracles when he was asleep. The hero seized them and carried them off slung upside-down from a pole laid across his shoulder. Their jests on the subject of his hairiness, viewed from that position, so amused him that he let them go.

Cerealis or **Cerialis, Petillius,** Roman general, related to the emperor Vespasian. He was legate of the Ninth Legion in Britain when it was almost annihilated in the rising of Boudicca (q.v.), A.D. 61. Consul in 69, he put down the revolt of Civilis (q.v.) in the following year, and was appointed governor of Britain in A.D. 71. *See* BRITAIN.

Ceres, Italian goddess of whose early history little is certain. She represented the fertility of earth as producer of corn. It is clear from the details of her cult at Rome, dating from 496 B.C., that she was very early identified with Demeter (q.v.). Her temple, built on the Aventine in 493, was later a plebeian centre, since the corn trade, of which Ceres came to be regarded as patron, was largely in plebeian hands. The chief festival of Ceres, called *Cerealia* or *Ludi Ceriales*, was held annually from 12th to 19th April; it was instituted before 202 B.C.

Cerialis, *see* CEREALIS.

Cerretani, an Iberian people inhabiting modern Cerdagne (Catalonia and Pyrénées-Orientales). They were famous for the curing of some really excellent hams.

Cethegus, Gaius Cornelius, one of the Catilinarian conspirators (*see* CATILINA). He remained in Rome when Catiline left the city, and was executed with Lentulus and others (5th December 63 B.C.).

Cethegus, Marcus Cornelius, Roman general and orator, pontifex maximus and curule aedile 213 B.C., praetor 211, censor 209, consul 204. In the following year he and the praetor P. Quintilius Varus defeated Hannibal's brother Mago (q.v.) in Cisalpine Gaul and drove him from the peninsula. Cethegus died in 196 B.C. As an orator he is praised by both Ennius and Horace

Ceyx (Kēux), King of Trachis in Thessaly and husband of Alcyone (q.v.).

Chabrias (Kha-), Athenian general and mercenary. In 378 B.C. he was one of the commanders of the forces sent to the aid of Thebes against Agesilaus II, when he adopted that manœuvre for which he became celebrated—ordering his men to await the attack on the left knee with their spears pointed against the enemy and their shields resting on the ground. A statue was afterwards erected at Athens to Chabrias in this posture. He was killed at the siege of Chios, 357 B.C. *See* H. W. Parke, *Greek Mercenary Soldiers*, 1933.

Chaerea, Gaius Cassius, a tribune of a praetorian cohort in A.D. 41, when he led the conspirators who slew Caligula (q.v.). For this service to mankind he was rewarded with death by the new emperor, Claudius.

Chaeronea (Khairōneia), town of Boeotia, about seven miles from Orchomenus (q.v.), of which it was a dependency until the 4th century B.C. Chaeronea was the last obstacle to an invading army coming from the north into central Greece. It was here that Philip II of Macedon defeated the Athenians and Thebans in 338 B.C., thus establishing the Macedonian supremacy in Greece; here too Mithradates the Great of Pontus was defeated by L. Cornelius Sulla in 86 B.C.

The most famous of Chaeronea's sons was Plutarch (q.v.). Remains include the ancient citadel, known as the Petrarchos, and a seated lion which marks the grave of those Boeotians who died in battle against Philip. Pausanias (ix. 40) relates that at Chaeronea divine honours were paid to the sceptre of Agamemnon.

Chalcidice (Khalkidikē), peninsula of Macedonia between the Thermaic and Strymonic Gulfs. It terminates in three smaller peninsulas which, from west to east, were named Pallene, Sithonia and Athos (q.v.).

Chalcis (Khalkis), chief town of Euboea (q.v.) on the strait of Euripus. Originally an Ionian settlement, it became a great centre of industry and colonization. In the 8th and 7th centuries B.C. it founded no fewer than thirty small towns on the peninsula of Chalcidice and several important cities in Sicily. Among the exports of Chalcis, which were carried not only in its own ships but also in those of its allies Corinth and Samos (qq.v.), were metal-work, purple and pottery. Its prosperity, however, was reduced by wars with Athens. Later it was used as a military base by Antiochus III of Syria (192 B.C.) and Mithradates the Great of Pontus (88 B.C.).

Chares (Kharēs): 1. Athenian general, born *c.* 400 B.C. He contrived for many years to maintain his influence with the people in spite of his disreputable character, and in 357 obtained sole command by denouncing his colleagues, Iphicrates (q.v.) and Timotheus, to the assembly. Next he entered the service of Artabazus, a revolted Persian satrap, but was recalled by the Athenians on the complaint of Artaxerxes III, Ochus. Chares was subsequently one of the Athenian commanders at Chaeronea (338 B.C.).

2. A sculptor of the 5th century B.C., a native of Lindus in Rhodes and a favourite pupil of Lysippus (q.v.). His principal work was the statue of Helios known as the Colossus of Rhodes (q.v.).

Charites (Khariteis), in Latin **Gratiae**, the personification of all that is meant by the English word 'grace', and called by us the Graces. This personification by a plurality of persons is at least as old as Homer, who speaks of the Charites. In mythology they are represented as three in number, daughters of Zeus, named Euphrosyne, Aglaia and Thalia. They are usually found in the service of other deities, lending their qualities to all that delights the hearts of gods and men. Poetry, however, is their special favourite, whence they are friends and companions of the Muses.

Chariton (Kharitōn), Greek novelist, a native of Aphrodisias in Caria. His date, which is much disputed, has been placed anywhere between the 2nd and the 4th century A.D. His *Chaereas and Callirrhoë* has been edited with a translation by E. W. Blake, 1938-9.

Charon (Kharōn), legendary son of Erebus and Nyx, ferried the shades of the dead across the Styx (or Acheron). For this service he was paid with an obol, a small coin, which was placed in the corpse's mouth before burial. Charon is represented in art as an aged man with dirty beard and ragged dress.

Charondas (Kha-), law-giver of Catina in Sicily, who legislated (c. 500 B.C.) for his own and other cities of Chalcidian origin in Italy and Sicily. According to Aristotle (*Pol.* ii. 1274b) he was the first to introduce prosecution for perjury.

Charybdis (Kharubdis), *see* SCYLLA AND CHARYBDIS.

Chatti, Latin form of the name borne by one of the most powerful German tribes, living between the Rhine and the Weser.

Chauci, Latin form of the name borne by a German tribe inhabiting territory between the mouths of the Ems and Elbe. Tacitus describes them as the noblest of their race, but they disappear as a distinct people after their devastation of Gaul in the 3rd century A.D.

Chersonesus (Khersonēsos), name derived from Greek *khersos*, dry, *nēsos*, island, and applied by ancient geographers to four peninsulas: C. Thracica, modern Gallipoli; C. Taurica (q.v.), modern Crimea; C. Cimbrica, modern Jutland; C. Aurea, probably the modern Malay peninsula.

Chersonesus Taurica or **Tauris** (mod. Crimea), commonly known as the **Kingdom of Bosporus.** During the 7th century B.C. Chersonesus Taurica received numerous Greek colonies. Among them was Panticapaeum (q.v.), which came to be called Bosporus because of its situation on the Bosporus Cimmerius (q.v.). About 438 B.C. the tyrant of Panticapaeum, Spartocus, declared himself King of Bosporus and founded a dynasty which gradually extended its authority over the whole region. This kingdom endured until about 110 B.C., when it became subject to Mithradates the Great of Pontus. After his death (63 B.C.) it was conferred by Pompey on Pharnaces (q.v.), son of Mithradates. In 47 B.C. Pharnaces was murdered by his regent Asander, who ruled until his death in 16 B.C., when the kingdom was granted by Augustus to Polemon (q.v.) of Pontus. The kingdom of Bosporus was the first state consisting of a mixed population to adopt the Greek language and culture. Its great prosperity, reflected in the magnificent archaeological discoveries at Panticapaeum, was due mainly to its exports of wheat. *See* E. H. Minns, *Scythians and Greeks*, 1913; M. Rostovzeff, *Iranians and Greeks in South Russia*, 1922.

Cherusci, a Germanic tribe inhabiting both sides of the Visurgis (Weser). Their most famous chieftain was Arminius (q.v.). Owing to internal dissension, they lost their pre-eminence to the Chatti (q.v.). *See* Tacitus, *Germania,* 36.

Chilon (Kheilōn), a Spartan, son of Damagetus and one of the Seven Sages of Greece (q.v.), *fl. c.* 556 B.C. He is said to have died of joy while embracing his son who had just been victorious in boxing at the Olympic games.

Chimaera (Khimaira), a fire-breathing monster, the fore part of whose body was that of a lion, the hind part that of a dragon, and the middle that of a goat. In art, however, she is often represented as a lion with a goat's head in the middle of the back. She made great havoc in Lycia and the surrounding countries, and was at length killed by Bellerophon (q.v.). The origin of this creature must probably be sought in a volcano of the same name near Phaselis, in Lycia.

Chione (Khionē): 1. Daughter of Daedalion, mother of Autolycus by Hermes and of Philammon by Apollo.

2. Daughter of Boreas by Orithyia, and mother of Eumolpus.

Chios (Khios), one of the largest islands of the Aegean, opposite the peninsula of Clazomenae on the coast of Ionia. It was an independent and powerful maritime state having close ties with Miletus. Together with Miletus, Chios submitted to the Persians in 546 and, when Miletus revolted, sent 100 ships to her aid (494 B.C.). The revolt was a failure; Chios was once again subject to Persia and some of her vessels were in the Persian fleet at Salamis. Freed by the Greek victory at Mycale (479 B.C.), she joined the Delian League (q.v.) and was long one of the most favoured allies of Athens, having political independence and a navy of her own. In 413 B.C., however, she revolted; renewed her alliance with Athens after the Peloponnesian war, but severed it once again in 357 B.C.

Chios was generally considered to be one of the best governed of Greek states, but became the prey of factions in the second half of the 4th century B.C. She managed, however, to retain her independence and was recognized by Rome as a free and allied state.

Chios was noted for its wine, trade in which was helped by the presence of Maroneia, a Chian colony, on the coast of Thrace. The island was equally famous for its school of epic poets known as the Homeridae, and for a number of celebrated sculptors. There are no outstanding remains.

Chirisophus (Khirisophos), Spartan general sent to aid Cyrus the younger against his brother Artaxerxes. After the battle of Cunaxa (401 B.C.) he was one of those who assisted Xenophon in conducting the retreat of the Ten Thousand (q.v.).

Chiron (Kheirōn), wisest of the Centaurs (q.v.). He was the son of Cronus by Philyra, and lived on Mt Pelion. Instructed by Apollo and Artemis, he was renowned for his skill in hunting, medicine, music, gymnastics and prophecy. Jason, Achilles and many other Greek heroes are described as pupils of Chiron in these arts. Heracles was his friend, but when fighting the other centaurs (*see* PHOLUS) he accidentally struck Chiron with one of his poisoned arrows. Though immortal, Chiron desired to live no longer. He therefore gave his immortality to Prometheus (q.v.) and was placed by Zeus among the stars as Sagittarius.

Chiton (Khitōn), the Greek undershirt. Over it was worn the *himation* and *chlamys*.

Choerilus (Khoirilos): 1. Athenian tragic poet, *fl.* 524 B.C. He is said to have competed with Aeschylus and Pratinas, to have written 150 plays and won the prize thirteen times, and to have improved the masks and dresses. Only fragments of his work survive. *See* A. Nauck, *Tragicorum Graecorum Fragmenta*, 1889.

2. Samian epic poet of the late 5th century B.C., resided for some time after 404 B.C. at the Macedonian court. Fragments of his poem on the Persian war are extant.

3. Carian epic poet of the 4th century B.C. He accompanied the expedition of Alexander (334) as court poet, and is ridiculed by Horace (*Ep.* ii. 1, 232; *Ars Poet.* 357). Fragments are preserved.

Chronology. The Greeks reckoned their day from sunset to sunset, marking off the day period, as well as the night period, into three divisions. Years were distinguished in various ways—at Athens by the name of the chief archon, at Sparta by that of the chief ephor. For a fixed date by which all reckonings might be adjusted, they chose the year when the record of Olympic victors began (776 B.C.), but this was never used for ordinary reckoning. The normal Athenian year was divided into twelve months consisting alternately of thirty and twenty-nine days. The first of these months was Hecatombaion which usually began with the first new moon after the summer solstice, but occasionally a new moon earlier or two later. The order of the succeeding months was: Metageitnion, Boedromion, Pyanopsion, Maimacterion, Poseideon, Gamelion, Anthesterion, Elaphebolion, Munychion, Thargelion and Scirophorion.

The Romans reckoned their day from midnight to midnight, marking off the day period, as well as the night period, into twelve hour divisions (the hours varying according to the season). A particular year was usually designated by the names of the year's consuls (cf. Horace's Address to a Wine-jar, 'O nate mecum consule Manlio' = 65 B.C.). Later Roman writers reckoned from the Foundation of the City (viz. 753 B.C.). For the Roman year *see* JULIAN CALENDAR.

Chryse (Khrusē), city on the coast of the Troad. Here was a temple of Apollo Smintheus. *See* next article.

Chryseïs (Khruseïs), in the Trojan epic, daughter of Chryses, priest of Apollo Smintheus at Chryse (q.v.), was taken prisoner by Achilles. In the distribution of the booty she was given to Agamemnon. Chryses came to the Greek camp to solicit her ransom, but was repulsed by Agamemnon. Thereupon Apollo sent a plague among the Greeks, and Agamemnon was obliged to restore her to her father to appease the anger of the god. See *Iliad*, i.

Chrysippus (Khrusippos), Greek Stoic philosopher, born at Soli in Cilicia 280 B.C.; studied at Athens, first at the Academy under Arcesilaus, then under Cleanthes, whom he succeeded as head of the Stoa (232). He died in 207 B.C. Only fragments of his alleged 750 treatises survive.

Cicero, Marcus Tullius: 1. Roman statesman, orator, philosopher and man of letters, born near Arpinum, 3rd January 106 B.C. He and his brother Quintus displayed such aptitude for learning that their father removed with them to Rome, where they received instruction from the best teachers in the capital, among them Archias (q.v.) of Antioch. After receiving the *toga virilis* (91), the young Marcus studied under Q. Mucius Scaevola, and in later years, during the civil war, under Phaedrus the Epicurean, Philo of Larissa, chief of the fourth Academy (q.v.), Diodotus the Stoic and Apollonius Molon. Having carefully cultivated his powers, Cicero came forward as a pleader in the Forum, as soon as tranquillity was restored by the final overthrow of the Marian party. His first extant speech was delivered in 81, when he was 26 years of age, on behalf of P. Quintius. Next year, 80, he defended Sex. Roscius of Ameria, charged with parricide by Chrysogonus. In 79 he went to Greece, partly that he might avoid Sulla, whom he had offended, but partly also that he might improve his health and complete his course of study. At Athens he formed that friendship with Pomponius Atticus which lasted until his death, and at Rhodes he once more placed himself under the care of Molon. After an absence of two years, Cicero returned to Rome (77). He again came forward as an orator in the Forum and was again successful. In 75 he was quaestor in Sicily, returned to Rome in 74, and for the next four years was engaged in pleading causes. In 70 he distinguished himself by the impeachment of Verres (q.v.), and in 69 he was curule aedile. In 66 he was praetor, and while holding this office he defended Cluentius in the speech still extant, and delivered his celebrated oration in favour of the Manilian law, which appointed Pompey to the command of the Mithradatic war. Two years afterwards he gained the great object of his ambition, and, although a *novus homo*, was elected consul, with C. Antonius as colleague. He took office on 1st January 63. Not having any real sympathy with the popular party, Cicero now deserted his former friends, and connected himself closely with the aristocracy. His consulship was made memorable by the conspiracy of Catiline, which was suppressed by Cicero's prudence and energy. *See* CATILINA. For this service he received the highest honours. But as soon as he had laid down the consulship, he had to contend with the popular party, and especially with the friends of the conspirators. He had also mortally offended Clodius (q.v.), who, in order to have his revenge, brought forward a bill banishing anyone who should be found to have put a Roman citizen to death untried. The triumvirs, Caesar, Pompey and Crassus, left Cicero to his fate; his courage failed him, he voluntarily retired from Rome before the measure of Clodius was put to the vote and crossed over to Greece (58 B.C.). Meanwhile his friends at Rome were exerting themselves on his behalf, and obtained his recall from banishment in the course of next year (57). Taught by experience, Cicero would no longer join the senate in opposition to the triumvirs, and retired to a great extent from public life. In 51 he was compelled to go to the East as governor of Cilicia. He returned to Italy towards the end of 50, and arrived in the neighbourhood of Rome on 4th January 49, just as the civil war between Caesar and Pompey broke out. After long hesitating which side to join, he finally determined to throw in his lot with Pompey, and crossed over to Greece in June. After the battle of Pharsalus (48), Cicero was not only pardoned by Caesar, but, when the latter landed at Brundisium in September 47, he greeted Cicero with the greatest kindness and respect, and allowed him to return to Rome. Cicero now retired into privacy, and during the next three or four years composed the greater part of his philosophical and rhetorical works.

The murder of Caesar on 15th March 44, brought him once again into public life. He put himself at the head of the republican party and in his Philippic orations attacked M. Antony with unmeasured vehemence. But this proved his ruin. On the formation of the triumvirate between Octavian, Antony and Lepidus (27th November 43), Cicero's name was in the list of the proscribed. He endeavoured to escape, but was overtaken by the soldiers near Formiae. His slaves were ready to defend their master with their lives, but Cicero commanded them to desist, and offered his neck to the executioners. They instantly cut off his head and hands, which were conveyed to Rome, and, by the orders of Antony, nailed to the rostra.

Cicero perished on 7th December 43, when he had nearly completed his 64th year. By his first wife, Terentia, he had two children, a daughter Tullia (q.v.), whose death in 45 caused him the greatest sorrow, and a son Marcus (see below). His wife Terentia, to whom he had been united for thirty years, he divorced in 47, and soon afterwards married a young and wealthy maiden, Publilia, his own ward, but this new alliance was speedily dissolved.

As a statesman and a citizen, Cicero was weak, changeful and excessively vain; his only great work was the suppression of Catiline's conspiracy. It is as an author that he deserves the highest praise. In his works the Latin language appears in its greatest perfection. They may be divided as follows. I. Rhetorical Works. Of these there were seven, which have come down to us more or less complete. The best known is the De Oratore, written at the request of his brother Quintus. II. Philosophical Works. (1) Political Philosophy. Under this head we have De Republica and De Legibus, both of which are written in the form of dialogues. A large portion of both works is preserved. (2) Philosophy of Morals. In his work De Officiis, which was written for the use of his son Marcus, at that time residing at Athens, the tone of his teaching is pure and elevated. He also wrote De Senectute and De Amicitia, which are preserved. (3) Speculative Philosophy. Under this head the most noted of his works are De Finibus, or inquiry into 'the chief good', and the Tusculan Disputations. (4) Theology. In De Natura Deorum he gives an account of the speculations of the ancients concerning a Divine Being, which is continued in De Divinatione. III. Orations. Of these fifty-six have come down to us. IV. Epistles. Cicero during the most important period of his life maintained a close correspondence with Atticus, and with a wide circle of literary and political friends and connections. We now have upwards of 800 letters, undoubtedly genuine, extending over a space of twenty-six years, and commonly arranged under Epistolae ad Familiares, ad Diversos, ad Atticum and ad Quintum Fratrem. There are critical editions of the complete works by C. F. Müller (1880–96) and in the Oxford Classical Texts. Texts with translations of most works are in the Loeb Library, and there are innumerable editions of separate treatises, orations, etc. The best edition of the Letters is that of R. Y. Tyrrell and L. C. Purser (1904–18). *See* T. Rice Holmes, *The Roman Republic*, 1923; F. R. Cowell, *Cicero and the Roman Republic*, 1948.

2. Only son of the preceding, born in 65 B.C. After serving with Pompey in Greece (48), he was sent to study rhetoric at Athens, where he preferred a gay life, much to the chagrin of his father, who dedicated to him at this period the *De Officiis*. After the murder of Caesar he served as military tribune under Brutus in Macedonia. The defeat at Philippi drove him for refuge to Pompeius in Sicily; but in 39 he took advantage of a general amnesty to return to Rome and riotous living. None the less he found favour in the sight of Octavian, who made him his colleague in the consulship, 30 B.C., and by a singular coincidence it was Cicero to whom was addressed the dispatch announcing Antony's suicide, and who was entrusted with the execution of a decree ordering that all statues of Antony were to be destroyed. He was afterwards governor of Asia or Syria, but nothing more is known of him.

Cicero, Quintus Tullius, brother of the orator, was born c. 102 B.C.; aedile in 67, praetor in 62 and governor of Asia 61–58. In 54 he went to Gaul as one of Caesar's legates, and distinguished himself by his courage and ability. In 51 he accompanied his brother, who had been appointed governor of Cilicia, and joined Pompey on the outbreak of civil war (49). After the battle of Pharsalus (48) he was pardoned by Caesar, but perished in the proscriptions of 43 B.C. shortly before his brother. Cicero made an unhappy marriage with Pomponia, daughter of T. Pomponius Atticus. Their son Quintus, born c. 67 B.C., sided with Antony after Caesar's death (44), but deserted to Brutus and Cassius, and was put to death, together with his father.

Cilicia, a district on the south coast of Asia Minor between Pamphylia and Syria, bounded on the north by the Taurus range. The principal river was the Cydnus, upon which stood Tarsus (q.v.). The western part of Cilicia is intersected by offshoots of the Taurus, while the eastern part includes much larger tracts of level country. The former was known as Cilicia Trachea, which was once a source of timber for the Egyptian fleets; Cilicia Pedias was a large producer of flax and grapes. Though forming a satrapy of the Persian Empire from the time of Darius, it continued to be governed by native princes until it was included in the dominions of Alexander. After his death it fell to the Seleucidae (q.v.). Its plains were settled by Greeks, and the old inhabitants were driven back into the mountains of Cilicia Trachea, where they remained virtually independent, practising brigandage by land and piracy by sea, until subdued by Pompey (67 B.C.). Cilicia Pedias had meanwhile (103 B.C.) become Roman territory, and in 64 B.C. Pompey organized it and Trachea as a single province. Reorganized by Caesar in 47, it became, about twenty years later, part of the province Syria-Cilicia-Phoenice. Under Diocletian (c. A.D. 297) it formed, together with Egypt and Syria, the Diocese of the East (Oriens). Among the most important products of Cilicia in

Roman times was a cloth made of goat's hair and used in the manufacture of tents. The preparation of this cloth, rather than the actual making of tents, was probably the trade practised by St Paul.

Cimber, Lucius Tillius (*not* Tullius), one of Caesar's murderers (44 B.C.), although he had previously received from him the province of Bithynia.

Cimbri, a Teutonic tribe, probably from the Cimbric peninsula (Jutland), who, after warring for several years with the Celts on the Danube, defeated a Roman army under Cn. Papirius Carbo near Noreia in 113 B.C. Four years later they defeated M. Julius Silanus in southern Gaul, and in 105 annihilated the combined armies of Maximus and Q. Servilius Caepio (q.v.) at Arausio. But instead of crossing the Alps, the victorious Cimbri, fortunately for Rome, moved into Spain; but they were repulsed by the Celtiberi (*see* CELTIBERIA). Turning back (103 B.C.) they overran Gaul as far as the Seine and were joined near Rouen by the Teutones and Ambrones. This great host now marched southwards by different routes: the Teutones and Ambrones intended entering Italy from the west; the Cimbri (who had recently been joined by the Helvetii, q.v.), via the eastern passes of the Alps. The former were routed by Marius (q.v.) at Aquae Sextiae in 102; the latter, having forced their way to the Po, were annihilated by Marius and Q. Lutatius Catulus in 101 on the Raudine Plain (*Campi Raudii*) near Vercellae.

Ciminia, Via, Roman road which parted from the Via Cassia (*see* CASSIA, VIA) at Sutrium, passed along the east side of the Lacus Ciminius, and rejoined it at Aquae Passeris, north of Viterbo.

Cimmerii (Kimmerioi), an ancient people of the far north or west of Europe. Homer (*Od.* xi. 12–19) refers to them as living in a land of perpetual darkness, while Herodotus considers them as the early inhabitants of southern Russia (*see* BOSPORUS CIMMERIUS). Passing from legend to historical fact, we know that in the 7th century B.C. northern nomads, whom Herodotus (iv. 12) calls Cimmerians, entered Asia Minor and captured Sardis in 657 during the reign of Ardys, by whose grandson Alyattes they were eventually expelled.

Cimolus (Kimolos), island in the Aegean, about one mile north-east of Melos (q.v.), an important source of fuller's earth.

Cimon (Kimōn), Athenian admiral and statesman of the 5th century B.C. On the death of his father Miltiades (q.v.), in 489, he was imprisoned because of his inability to pay the latter's fine of fifty talents. This was eventually paid by Callias on his marriage with Cimon's sister Elpinice; but according to Aristotle (*Ath. Con.* 27) Cimon was afterwards possessed of great wealth. He commanded the Athenian fleet during the Persian Wars (q.v.), winning the battle of the Eurymedon in 468 or 467. The death of Aristides and the ostracism of Themistocles (qq.v.) left Cimon without a rival at Athens for some years, and to him was due the extension of Athenian authority throughout the islands of the Aegean. But his influence gradually waned as that of Pericles (q.v.) increased. In 461 he was ostracized through the machinations of the popular party; but he was subsequently recalled (451), and it was through his activity that a five-year truce was signed between Athens and Sparta in 450. In 450 hostilities with Persia were renewed, and Cimon was given the naval command. He sailed to Cyprus with 200 ships, but died while besieging Citium in the following year.

Cimon (Kimon) **of Cleonae,** Greek painter, *fl. c.* 460 B.C., is said to have been the first to use perspective.

Cincinnatus, Lucius Quintius, legendary or semi-legendary hero of the early Roman republic, a model of the old Roman frugality and integrity. After serving as consul in 460 B.C., he returned to his farm which he cultivated with his own hands. In 458 he was called from the plough to the dictatorship, in order to deliver the consul Minucius and his army from a perilous situation during hostilities against the Aequi. His task fulfilled, and having held office for only sixteen days, he returned once again to his farm. For the events of his second dictatorship (440 B.C.) *see* MAELIUS, SPURIUS.

Cineas (Kin-), a Thessalian, friend and minister of Pyrrhus (q.v.), King of Epirus. He was believed to be one of the most eloquent men of his day, and after the battle of Heraclea (280 B.C.) he was sent to Rome by Pyrrhus with proposals for peace. Though he spared no arts of persuasion, his offers were rejected by the senate at the instigation of Appius Claudius Caecus (q.v.).

Cinna, Gaius Helvius, Roman poet and friend of Catullus. As tribune of the plebs in 44 B.C., he was murdered by the mob, who mistook him for his namesake L. Cornelius Cinna after the assassination of Julius Caesar. Some remains of his *Smyrna* and *Propempticon Pollionis* are extant.

Cinna, Lucius Cornelius: 1. Roman magistrate and politician, leader of the popular party at Rome during Sulla's absence in the East (87–84 B.C.), Before setting out for Greece, Sulla had allowed the election of Cinna as consul for 87 with Cn. Octavius upon condition of his taking an oath not to alter the constitution as then existing. But as soon as Sulla had left Italy, Cinna began his attempt to overpower the senate and bring about the return of Marius (q.v.). Defeated by his colleague, Octavius, in the Forum, he was forced to flee the city and was deposed; but he soon returned, together with Marius, took possesion of Rome, massacred Sulla's adherents and was consul again in 86, 85 and 84. Learning, however, of Sulla's impending return, his own troops put him to death in this last year.

2. Son of the preceding, joined M. Lepidus in his attempt to overthrow the Sullan constitution in 78 B.C. In 44 B.C. he was privy to the assassination of Caesar.

Cippus, a low pedestal used by the Romans as milestones, boundary posts, funeral memorials, etc.

Circe (Kirkē), mythical sorceress, daughter of Helios and Perse. She dwelt in the island of Aeaea (q.v.), upon which Odysseus was cast. His companions drank a magic potion which Circe offered them, and were changed into swine, all except Eurylochus who brought the news to his leader. Odysseus, having received from Hermes a root called 'molu', which fortified him against enchantment, drank the cup without injury and then compelled Circe to restore his companions to their former shape. After this he remained for a whole year with her, and she became by him the mother of Telegonus (q.v.).

Circeii, an ancient town of Latium on an isolated promontory (Circeius Mons) about 80 miles south-east of Rome; founded as a Roman colony (*see* COLONIA). Because this promontory has the appearance of an island when viewed from a distance, some Latin poets believed it to have been the island of Circe (q.v.), though the true origin of the name is quite uncertain. Extensive remains include prehistoric fortifications as well as villas of the republican and imperial periods. Noteworthy among the latter is a residence of Domitian, which included an area of about 300,000 square yards.

Circumvallation, Lines of, a continuous line of entrenchments round a besieged place, facing outwards to resist a relieving force. Lines of contravallation, of less circumference, faced inwards as a precaution against an attempt at sortie by the besieged.

Circus. The Roman circus was used mainly for chariot racing, was oval or oblong in shape, and the tiers of seats formed a crescent round one end; the opposite end was straight. Down the centre ran a fence (*spina*), to separate the outward from the return course, and at each end of it were three conical pillars (*metae*) marking the turning-points. The races began and finished at the straight end, where also were the main entrance and stalls (*carceres*) to accommodate horses and chariots. *See* ROME: *Circuses*.

Cirta (afterwards Constantina; mod. Constantine), city of Numidia, 50 Roman miles from the sea; capital of Syphax and of Masinissa (qq.v.) and his successors. Its position on a height, almost completely surrounded by the River Ampsaga (mod. Rummel), rendered it virtually impregnable. During the 3rd century A.D. Cirta derived great wealth from its marble quarries and copper mines. It was restored by Constantine the Great, after whom it was renamed. There survive six arches (each about 60 feet high) of an aqueduct over the Ampsaga valley. *See also* JUGURTHA.

Cisseus (Kis-), a Thracian king whose daughters, Hecuba and Theano, were married respectively to Priam and Antenor (qq.v.).

Cithaeron (Kithairōn), mountain range separating Boeotia from Megaris and Attica. It is associated in mythology with Actaeon, Pentheus and Oedipus (qq.v.). On Cithaeron there took place the mystic rites of Dionysus (q.v.) and also the Daedala (q.v.) in honour of Hera.

Citium (Kition), town on the north-east coast of Cyprus (q.v.). The earliest remains date from the latter part of the second millennium B.C.; but in historical times Citium, an important seaport and market, was the centre of Phoenician influence in the island, belonging possibly to Tyre. It appears to have been the administrative headquarters during the Assyrian protectorate, 709–668 B.C., and is listed as an ally of Assyria in this latter year. During the Greek revolts in the 5th and 4th centuries B.C. Citium remained loyal to Persia. For an account of ancient remains *see* J. L. Myres in *Journal of Hellenic Studies*, xvii.

Civilis, Julius, a Batavian officer in the Roman army, who, after Nero's death (A.D. 69), induced his people to revolt and was supported by the neighbouring German tribes. The Roman garrisons were driven out; two legions were blockaded in Castra Vetera (near modern Xanten) and the survivors eventually massacred. Civilis was next joined by some cohorts of Batavian auxiliaries as well as by the troops sent against him by Vespasian, and the rebellion spread to Gaul, where the Roman troops, urged by Julius Classicus and Julius Tutor, two commanders of auxiliaries, were also defeated, A.D. 70. In the same year, however, the Gauls submitted, and Civilis was defeated by Petillius Cerealis at Augusta Treverorum and at Vetera. He surrendered upon honourable terms; the Batavians returned to their allegiance, and nothing more is heard of Civilis. *See* B. Henderson, *Civil War and Rebellion in the Roman Empire*, 1908.

Claros (Kl-), town on the coast of Ionia, near Colophon, with a celebrated temple and oracle of Apollo.

Claudia, Quinta, a Roman matron. When a vessel conveying the image of Cybele to Rome had stuck fast in a shallow at the mouth of the Tiber, the soothsayers announced that only a chaste woman could move it. Claudia, who had been accused of incontinency, seized the rope, and the vessel forthwith followed her, 204 B.C.

Claudia Nova, Via, Roman road built by the emperor Claudius in A.D. 47 and intended to connect the road systems of northern and southern Italy. It links the Via (Claudia) Valeria with the Via Caecilia and Via Salaria at Foruli near Amiternum.

Claudius I, Roman emperor A.D. 41–54. He was Tiberius Claudius Drusus Nero Germanicus, younger son of Nero Claudius Drusus (died 9 B.C.) and nephew of the emperor Tiberius. Claudius was born at Lugdunum on 1st August 10 B.C. When he grew up he devoted himself to literary pursuits, but was not allowed to take part in public affairs. He had reached the age of fifty when he was raised by the soldiers to the imperial throne, after the murder of Caligula (q.v.). Claudius was not cruel, but the weakness of his character made him the slave of his wives and freedmen, and thus led him to consent to acts of tyranny. He was married four times. At the time of his accession his third wife, the notorious Valeria Messalina (q.v.), had governed him for some years, together with the freedmen Narcissus, Pallas and others. After the execution of Messalina, A.D. 48, a fate which she richly merited, Claudius was still more unfortunate in choosing for his wife his niece Agrippina. She prevailed upon him to set aside his own son, Britannicus, and to adopt her son, Nero, that she might secure the succession for the latter. Claudius soon regretted this and was poisoned by Agrippina, 54. In his reign the southern part of Britain (q.v.) was made a Roman province. *See* V. M. Saramuzza, *The Emperor Claudius*, 1940.

Claudius II, surnamed Gothicus, Roman emperor A.D. 268–70. Member of an obscure Illyrian family, Marcus Aurelius Claudius rose by sheer ability to high command in the armies of Decius, Valerian and Gallienus. On the death of Gallienus he was raised to the throne, and soon afterwards (269) won a great victory over the Goths at Naïssus in Moesia, whence his surname. He died of the plague at Sirmium.

Claudius, Appius, one of the Decemviri (q.v.) at Rome in 451 and 450 B.C. His attempt upon Virginia (q.v.) led to the abolition of the decemvirate, and Claudius, impeached by Virginius, either committed suicide in prison or was executed (446 B.C.).

Claudius Caecus, Appius, surnamed Caecus ('Blind'), because he had lost his sight in early or middle life. As censor in 312 B.C., to which office he was appointed without having previously been consul, he built the first aqueduct, and also the Via Appia (q.v.) from Rome to Capua. He retained the censorship for four years, despite the law which limited its tenure to eighteen months. Claudius was twice consul (307 and 296 B.C.), and in his old age he induced the senate to reject the terms of peace offered by Pyrrhus (*see* CINEAS).

Claudius Pulcher, Appius, brother of P. Clodius Pulcher (q.v.), whom he joined in opposing Cicero's recall from exile (57 B.C.). Claudius was governor of Cilicia in 63. He sided with Pompey during the civil war, crossed over with him to Greece in 49, but died before the battle of Pharsalus.

Claudius (more usually spelt Clodius) **Pulcher, Publius,** *see* CLODIUS PULCHER, PUBLIUS.

Claudius Sabinus Regillensis, Appius, legendary figure of early Roman history. He is said to have been a Sabine by birth and a native of Regillum or Regilli, where he bore the name Attus Clausus. He came to Rome in 504 B.C. and was received into the ranks of the patricians, while lands beyond the River Anio were assigned to his followers, who were formed into a new patrician *gens*. Claudius is represented as entertaining bitter hatred towards the plebeians, whose secession to the Sacred Mount (q.v.) in 494 was due in large measure to his conduct.

Clazomenae (Klazomenai), one of the twelve federated cities of Ionia (q.v.), on the Gulf of Smyrna. Its original site was an isthmus connecting the mainland with the peninsula of Erythrae; but when the Persians began to encroach upon Ionian territory the inhabitants moved their city to an island in the bay. Alexander the Great connected this island to the mainland by means of a pier, remains of which can still be seen. During the 5th century B.C. Clazomenae was subject for a while to Athens; under the Romans it came within the province of Asia but was exempt from taxation. It is famous as the birth-place of Anaxagoras (q.v.), and also for its painted terra-cotta sarcophagi (6th century B.C.).

Cleanthes (Kleanthēs), Stoic philosopher, born at Assos in the Troad, some time around 301 B.C. He studied first under the Cynic Crates (q.v.), and afterwards under Zeno, whom he succeeded as head of the Stoa in 263 B.C. Much of his *Hymn to Zeus* is extant (*see* text and translation with notes by E. H. Blakeney, 1921; verse translation by A. S. Way, 1934). Cleanthes died by voluntary starvation in 232 B.C.

Clearchus (Klearkhos), Spartan general. He served in the Peloponnesian war, and at its close persuaded his countrymen to send him with an army into Thrace, the peoples of which were then astir. Recalled by the ephors, he refused to obey their orders, was condemned to death and took refuge with Cyrus, who was planning to overthrow his brother, the Persian king Artaxerxes Mnemon. Clearchus collected for him a large force of Greek mercenaries (*see* CYRUS, 2; TEN THOUSAND; XENOPHON) and marched with him in 401 B.C. After the defeat and death of Cyrus at Cunaxa, Clearchus and the other Greek generals were made prisoner and put to death through the treachery of Tissaphernes.

Cleisthenes (Kleisthenēs), Athenian statesman, son of Megacles and Agariste, who was daughter of the Sicyonian tyrant Cleisthenes. Upon the expulsion of the Peisistratids (510 B.C.), he was head of the Alcmaeonidae (q.v.). Finding he could make no headway against his political rivals, he won over the people by offering to place the constitution on a more democratic basis than that of Solon's regime, which had fallen into desuetude during the tyranny. Isagoras, however, called in the assistance of Cleomenes I of Sparta, and two years of strife followed. In 508 Cleisthenes and his party emerged victorious, and he set about his work of reform, the principal elements of which were as follows: (1) The four ancient tribes were abolished and ten new ones created in their stead. (2) The numbers of the Boule (q.v.) were raised from 400 to 500. (3) The country was divided into thirty *trittyes* (three to a tribe), each containing a certain number of demes. Every man registered in the *deme* was enfranchised and voted in the Ecclesia. (4) The introduction of ostracism (q.v.).

Cleitomachus (Kleitomakhos), Greek philosopher of the 2nd century B.C., a Carthaginian by birth. He studied under Carneades (q.v.) at Athens, and succeeded him as head of the Academy (q.v.) in 129 B.C.

Cleitor (Kleitōr) or Clitor, town of Arcadia, with a spring which was supposed to deprive anyone who drank from it of his taste for wine.

Cleobulus (Kleoboulos), of Lindus in Rhodes, one of the Seven Sages of Greece, *fl. c.* 580 B.C. Both he and his daughter Cleobule were famous for their skill in propounding riddles.

Cleombrotus (Kleombrotos): 1. Son of the Spartan king Anaxandrides. His elder brother Leonidas (*see* LEONIDAS, 1) was killed at Thermopylae, 480 B.C., leaving an infant son Pleistarchus. For this child Cleombrotus was appointed regent, but died soon afterwards.

2. King of Sparta, son of Pausanias (*see* PAUSANIAS, 1), grandson of the preceding and great-nephew of Leonidas. He succeeded his brother Agesipolis I in 380 and reigned until 371, when he fell at the battle of Leuctra.

3. King of Sparta, son-in-law of Leonidas II (*see* LEONIDAS, 2), in whose place he was made king by the party of Agis IV in 242 B.C. About two years later Leonidas returned, and Cleombrotus was banished to Tegea.

4. An Academic philosopher of Ambracia, said to have killed himself after reading Plato's dialogue on the immortality of the soul (*Phaedo*). *See* Milton, *Paradise Lost*, iii. 473.

Cleomenes (Kleomenēs): (A) Name of three kings of Sparta.

1. Son of Anaxandrides, reigned 520–487 B.C., a man of enterprising but violent character. In 510 he commanded the force with whose aid Hippias was driven from Athens, and later assisted Isagoras and the oligarchs against Cleisthenes. In 491 he bribed the priestess of Delphi in order to bring about the deposition of his colleague Damaratus (*see* DAMARATUS), but soon afterwards went mad and committed suicide.

2. Son of Cleombrotus I (*see* CLEOMBROTUS, 2), reigned from 371 to 309 B.C.

3. Son of Leonidas II (*see* LEONIDAS, 2), reigned 235–222 B.C. He

married the widow of Agis IV, whose example he followed in attempting to restore the old Spartan constitution. He succeeded, and put the ephors to death. His struggle with the Achaean League (q.v.) and Antigonus Doson ended in his defeat at Sellasia (222); after which he fled to Egypt and committed suicide two years later.

(B) Athenian sculptor of the 1st century B.C. He executed the Medicean Venus now at Florence.

Cleon (Klēon) was originally a tanner, and entered public life as an opponent of Pericles. On the latter's death, 429 B.C., Cleon became the favourite of the people, and for about six years of the Peloponnesian war (428–422) was head of the war party. In 427 he advocated in the assembly that the Mytilenaeans should be put to death. In 425 he won his greatest success by taking prisoner the Spartans in the island of Sphacteria, and bringing them in safety to Athens. Puffed up by this achievement, he obtained command of an Athenian army to oppose Brasidas (q.v.) in Thrace; but he was defeated by Brasidas, under the walls of Amphipolis, and fell in the battle, 422. Aristophanes and Thucydides both speak of him as a vile, unprincipled demagogue. The most remarkable attack by Aristophanes occurs in the *Knights* (424). Here Cleon figured as one of the *dramatis personae*; and, in default of an artificer bold enough to make the mask, he was represented by the poet himself with his face smeared with wine lees.

Cleopatra (Kl-): 1. Daughter of Philip II of Macedon by his wife Olympias. In 336 B.C. she was married to Alexander I, King of Epirus, and it was at their wedding feast that Philip was assassinated (*see* PAUSANIAS, 2).

2. Eldest daughter of Ptolemy XI, Auletes, born 69 B.C. On the death of her father (51) she became joint sovereign of Egypt with her brother Ptolemy XII (q.v.), whom the dead ruler's will directed her to marry. She was expelled by the young king's guardians, Pothinus and Achillas; but having won the support of Caesar (*see* CAESAR, GAIUS JULIUS), he replaced her on the throne in conjunction with Ptolemy XIII. She had a son by Caesar, called Caesarion, and she afterwards followed him to Rome, where she appears to have been at the time of his death (44). She then returned to Egypt, and met Antony (*see* ANTONIUS, MARCUS, 3) in Cilicia (41). Being then in her twenty-eighth year, and in the perfection of matured beauty, she completely won the heart of Antony. In the war between the latter and Octavian, Cleopatra accompanied her lover, and was present at the battle of Actium (31), during which she retreated with her fleet, and thus hastened the loss of the day. She fled to Alexandria, where she committed suicide in the following year (30 B.C.). Cleopatra died in the thirty-ninth year of her age, and with her ended the dynasty of the Ptolemies in Egypt, which was now made a Roman province. *See* E. R. Bevan, *History of Egypt under the Ptolemaic Dynasty*, 1927.

Cleruchy (Klēroukhia), name given to colonies planted by Athens in conquered territory. The settlers retained Athenian citizenship and the land assigned to them was Attic soil. The cleruchs were liable to military service and taxation like their fellow citizens at home.

Clio (Kleiō), the Muse of history, *see* MUSES.

Clitomachus, *see* CLEITOMACHUS.

Clitumnus, river of Umbria, rising eight miles from Spoletium and falling into the Tinia, a tributary of the Tiber. Virgil mentions the white sacrificial cattle that grazed on its banks. The Clitumnus was personified as a minor deity, in whose honour there was a temple, close to the source.

Clitus (Kleitos), a Macedonian general and friend of Alexander the Great, whose life he saved during the passage of the Granicus (334 B.C.). In 328 he was slain by Alexander at a banquet, when both parties were heated with wine and Clitus had provoked the king with insolent language.

Cloaca Maxima, the largest drain of ancient Rome. It ran from the southern extremity of the Forum to the Tiber. *See* ROME.

Clodius (or **Claudius**) **Pulcher, Publius,** notorious Roman profligate and politician. In 62 B.C. he profaned the mysteries of Bona Dea (q.v.); in the following year, when quaestor, he was brought to trial, but secured his acquittal by bribery. He had attempted to prove an alibi; but Cicero's evidence showed that Clodius was with him in Rome only three hours before the time when he claimed to have been at Interamna. In order to revenge himself upon Cicero (q.v.), he had himself adopted into a plebeian family that he might obtain the formidable tribunician power. As tribune in 58, and supported by the triumvirs, Caesar, Pompey and Crassus, he drove Cicero into exile; but he was unsuccessful in opposing the orator's recall in the following year. For the subsequent events of his life, and his death, *see* MILO, TITUS ANNIUS.

Cloelia, in Roman legend, a virgin who was one of the hostages given to Lars Porsena of Clusium (*see* PORSENA). She escaped from the Etruscan camp and swam across the Tiber to Rome. She was sent back by the Romans, and Porsena, impressed by her courage, not only set her free, but even allowed her to take some of her fellow hostages along with her. In addition, he was said to have presented her with a richly caparisoned horse and to have sent the Roman people a statue of a woman on horseback. The story may have been invented, like that of Cocles (q.v.), to explain a primitive statue.

Clotho (Klōthōn), one of the Fates, *see* MOIRAE.

Clubs, known in Greek as *hetaireiai* and in Latin as *sodalitates*, were more in the nature of medieval guilds than of what we now call a club. Their main purposes were religious observance, trade organization, and even privateering; but they were sometimes formed with political aims or became involved in political activities. Some clubs, moreover, were founded for or included meals in common and mutual conversation. Cicero (*De Senectute*) mentions one such club at Rome, which provided him with an opportunity to air his views, and some have seen in him the first club bore.

Cluentius Habitus, Aulus, a native of Larinum in Samnium. In 74 B.C. he accused his own stepfather, Statius Albius Oppianicus, of attempting to procure his death by poison. Oppianicus was condemned, but it was believed that Cluentius had bribed the judges. In 66, therefore, Oppianicus's son charged Cluentius with triple murder by poison. The accused was defended by Cicero (*Pro Cluentio*) and acquitted.

Clusium (mod. Chiusi), one of the most powerful cities of the Etruscan federation (*see* ETRURIA), situated on a hill at the south end of the valley of the Clanis on the Via Cassia. As a member of the federation it took up arms in the 7th century B.C. against Tarquinius Priscus; headed the attempt to restore Tarquinius Superbus at the end of the 6th century B.C.; and was besieged by the Celts (*see* CELTAE) in 391 B.C. It was subject to Rome before 125 B.C. In imperial times the grain and grapes of Clusium were famous. Today the place is more celebrated for remains from numerous Etruscan cemeteries in the neighbourhood; these are of great archaeological importance and can be seen in the museums at Chiusi, Florence and Palermo (*see* D. Randall-MacIver, *Villanovans and Early Etruscans*, 1924). Another item of archaeological interest is the elaborate system of rock-hewn passages under the town; they were probably drains.

Clymene (Klumenē): 1. Daughter of Oceanus and Tethys, mother of Prometheus, Epimetheus and Atlas.

2. Mother of Phaëthon by Helios.

3. A relative of Menelaus and companion of Helen, with whom she was carried off by Paris.

Clytaemnestra (Klutaimnēstra), daughter of Tyndareus (q.v.), King of Sparta, and wife of Agamemnon, *see* ATREIDS, LEGEND OF THE.

Cnidus (Knidos), city of Caria (q.v.) in Asia Minor, built partly on the mainland and partly on the island of Triopion; these were connected by a bridge and also by a causeway which formed two harbours. Cnidus was one of the six cities of the Dorian Hexapolis (q.v.). It had considerable commerce, exported a famous wine and was the birth-place of the astronomer Eudoxus. The temple of Aphrodite contained a celebrated statue of the goddess by Praxiteles (q.v.). In 1857–8 C. T. Newton excavated the entire circuit of the walls (much of them in an excellent state of preservation), the agora and theatre, an odeum, several temples, numerous lesser buildings, and the seated statue of Demeter now in the British Museum.

The city was subject at one time to Persia, at another to Athens; and it was off Cnidus in 394 B.C. that Conon (q.v.) defeated the Spartan navy. This victory may have been commemorated by the colossal marble lion discovered by Newton about three miles southeast of the walls and now in the British Museum. Under Rome Cnidus enjoyed the status of a free city in return for help against Antiochus III.

Cocalus, mythical king of Sicily. He received Daedalus (q.v.) on his flight from Crete and, with the assistance of his daughters, slew Minos (q.v.).

Cocles, Horatius, legendary Roman hero, said to have defended the Pons Sublicius, together with Sp. Lartius and T. Herminius, against the army of Porsena while the Romans broke down the bridge behind them. When the work was nearly finished, Horatius sent back his two companions. As soon as the bridge had been completely destroyed he plunged into the Tiber and swam across to the city. The story was invented probably to explain a primitive statue of Vulcan opposite the Pons Sublicius.

Cocytus (Kōkutos), 'wailing', river in Epirus, a tributary of the Acheron (q.v.) and, like the latter, supposed to be connected with the underworld.

Codrus (Kodros), in Greek legend, last king of Athens. When the Dorians invaded Attica from Peloponnesus, an oracle declared that they would conquer if the Attic king's life was spared. Codrus therefore determined to sacrifice his life for his country. He entered the Dorian camp in disguise, picked a quarrel with some soldiers and was killed. When the Dorians understood what had happened they returned. No one was considered worthy to succeed so glorious a king; the royal dignity was abolished at Athens, and Medon, son of Codrus, was said to have been appointed first archon (q.v.). Aristotle, however (*Ath. Con.* 3), says that the archonship 'is believed by most authorities to have been created *in the reign of* Medon. Others date it from that of Acastus [Medon's successor], arguing from the oath still taken by the archons to carry out their duties "as in the days of Acastus"'.

Coele-Syria, 'Hollow Syria', name originally given to the great valley between the ranges of Lebanon and Anti-Lebanon. During the 3rd century, however, in the wars of the Ptolemies and Seleucids, it was applied to the whole of southern Syria.

Coeus (Kō-), one of the Titans (q.v.), father of Asteria and Leto (qq.v.) by Phoebe (q.v.).

Cohort, *see* LEGION.

Coinage: 1. *Greek.* In the classical period there were two main systems of coinage: the Euboic and Aeginetan. The former was used at Athens, and in both the standard was silver. The following table shows the weights in each system:

Euboic		*Aeginetan*
36·86 kgs.	TALENT	37·80 kgs.
431 gms.	MINA	630 gms.
4·31 gms.	DRACHMA	6·30 gms.
0·72 gms.	OBOL	1·05 gms.

The talent and mina were in the form of bullion. There were also minted didrachms, tridrachms and tetradrachms, with the value of 2, 3 and 4 drachmas respectively. A gold stater had the value of 20 drachmas, and there was a copper $\frac{1}{8}$ obol. Athenian coins usually bore on the obverse the head of Athena, the reverse an owl, crescent or olive branch and the inscription AΘE. The art of coining reached its highest perfection in the 5th and 4th centuries B.C.

2. *Roman.* The fundamental unit was the As, a bar of bronze originally weighing 1 Roman pound, i.e. 327·45 gms. By 187 B.C. the weight of the as had been reduced to 1 uncia (ounce) = $\frac{1}{12}$ Roman pound. Bronze coins date from *c.* 290 B.C., and about thirty years later silver coinage began. The Sestercius was equal to $2\frac{1}{2}$ (later 4) asses; the Denarius was of 20 (later 16) unciae. There were also gold Aurei and Solidi of various weights. Republican coins bore on the obverse the head of a god, on the reverse a ship's prow. Those of the empire

had the reigning emperor's head and a symbol of Rome. From Augustus to Aurelian the minting of gold and silver was controlled by the emperor, of bronze by the senate. Thereafter all coinage was under imperial control. It is impossible to fix a satisfactory value for ancient coins in terms of modern currency; but if some comparison is required it is probably safe to regard the Greek drachma and the Roman sestercius as equivalent to about 8*d*. of our money (1951). *See* H. Mattingly, *Roman Coins*, 1928; J. G. Milne, *Greek Coinage*, 1931.

Colchis (Kolkhis), district of Asia Minor at the eastern extremity of the Euxine. Chief town Dioscurias; principal river, Phasis. Colchis was famous for its linen, on account of which, and of certain physical peculiarities, Herodotus believed the inhabitants to be of Egyptian origin. They probably had some commercial intercourse with the Mediterranean, which is no doubt reflected in the statement of Apollonius Rhodius (*Argon.* iv. 279) that they possessed ancient tablets showing road and sea routes.

Though included in the Persian dominions, Colchis enjoyed a large measure of independence. Nothing is known of its history between the destruction of the Persian Empire by Alexander and the Mithradatic wars, when it seems to have owed allegiance of some sort to the kingdom of Pontus. After the defeat of Mithradates by Pompey (63 B.C.) it became Roman territory and was ultimately incorporated with Pontus (q.v.).

Colchis was renowned as the home of Medea (*see* ARGONAUTS; JASON AND MEDEA) and as the land *par excellence* of sorcery.

Collatia, town of Latium, 10 miles east of Rome on the Via Collatina. It was the legendary scene of the rape of Lucretia (q.v.). *See also* COLLATINUS, LUCIUS TARQUINIUS.

Collatinus, Lucius Tarquinius, in the legendary history of Rome, son of Aruns and nephew of Tarquinius Priscus; surnamed Collatinus from the Sabine town of Collatia (q.v.), of which his father had been made governor. The rape of his wife Lucretia by Sextus Tarquinius, son of Tarquinius Superbus (q.v.), led to the latter's expulsion. Collatinus and L. Junius Brutus (q.v.) then became the first consuls; but since the people could not endure the rule of any of the hated race of Tarquin, Collatinus resigned from office and went into retirement at Lavinium.

Collytus (Kollutos), a deme of Attica, within the walls of Athens. It was the deme of Plato and the residence of Timon the misanthrope.

Colonia, a Roman settlement in conquered territory. When its purpose was to relieve population at home and to serve as a centre of romanization among the new subjects, it generally consisted of civilians. But when it was intended chiefly as a precaution against rebellion the colonists were retired veterans of the army. The *Colonia Romana* was made up exclusively of Romans, who retained their citizenship; the *Colonia Latina* included Romans who, on becoming colonists, lost their citizenship, and also Latins, i.e. persons who possessed only limited (Latin) rights.

Colonia Agrippina or **Agrippinensis** (mod. Köln, Cologne), Roman colony planted (A.D. 50) by Claudius on a site known previously as

Oppidum Ubiorum, capital of the Ubii, and so called in honour of the emperor's wife, Agrippina the Younger (q.v.), who was born there. It became the chief town of Germania Secunda and enjoyed Latin rights (see COLONIA).

Colonus (Kolonos), deme of Attica, little more than a mile to the north-west of Athens: celebrated for a temple of Poseidon, a grove of the Eumenides (q.v.) and the tomb of Oedipus. It was the birth-place of Sophocles, who describes it in his *Oedipus Coloneus*.

Colophon (Kolophōn), city of Ionia (q.v.) about two miles from the sea between Lebedus and Ephesus, on the River Halesus. The port was called Notium. Colophon was the mother city of Smyrna (q.v.); it was famous for its luxury, and was the birth-place of Xenophanes and Mimnermus (qq.v.). Sacked by Gyges of Lydia in 665 B.C., it gradually declined in favour of Notium, until part of the population was transferred by Lysimachus (q.v.) to Ephesus (287 B.C.).

Colossae (Kolossai), city of Phrygia, on the River Lycus. Its pros-perity was ruined by the foundation near by of Laodicea (q.v.). It was the seat of an early Christian church, to which St Paul addressed his Epistle to the Colossians.

Colosseum or **Amphitheatrum Flavianum,** one of the most famous of Roman buildings, was begun by Vespasian on a site previously occupied by part of Nero's Golden House, and completed by Titus in A.D. 80. At this date it consisted of three arcaded stone storeys and an upper gallery of wood. The latter was rebuilt in stone during the 3rd century. The plan of the Colosseum is elliptical, the longer axis measuring 615 feet, and the shorter 510 feet. The total height is about 160 feet. It held about 45,000 spectators, and was restored no fewer than seven times between its first completion and A.D. 523. *See* J. H. Middleton, *The Remains of Ancient Rome,* vol. ii, 1892.

Colossus of Rhodes, The, one of the Seven Wonders of the World, a bronze statue of the sun-god Helios, with whom Apollo was later identified. It was made by Chares (q.v.) of Lindus from the spoils left behind by Demetrius Poliorcetes (q.v.) in 304 B.C. The Colossus, which took twelve years to make, was seventy cubits high and stood near (but *did not* bestride) the harbour. It was thrown down by an earthquake *c.* 224 B.C., and the pieces lay where they fell for nearly one thousand years; then they were purchased as scrap from the Saracens by a Jewish merchant.

Columbarium, Roman architectural term, originally denoting a pigeon house, but afterwards applied to a sepulchral building with niches for funerary urns. Columbaria were erected by *sodalitates* (see CLUBS), the slaves and freedmen of distinguished families, and other groups. They were generally in the form of an open courtyard, the inner side of whose wall contained the niches. Among the most remarkable of these buildings was that built early in the 1st century A.D. by the freedmen of Livia on the Via Appia.

Columella, Lucius Junius Moderatus (1st century A.D.), born at Gades in Spain. His extant *De re rustica,* a work on agriculture which influenced many subsequent writers in this field, and *De arboribus* (on trees) are edited with translation by H. B. Ash and others (Loeb Library).

Columna Rostrata, a column set up in the Forum at Rome to commemorate the victory of Duilius (q.v.) over the Carthaginian fleet off Mylae (260 B.C.). It was so called because it was decorated with the beaks (*rostra*) of the captured ships.

Comana: 1. (Mod. Shahr) city of Cappadocia (q.v.), sometimes called Comana Chryse or Aurea to distinguish it from Comana in Pontus (*see* below). There was a famous temple of Mā-Enyo, a nature-goddess whom the Greeks identified with Artemis Taurica (*see* ARTEMIS). The city was no more than an appanage of the temple; it was governed by the chief priest, who was always a member of the royal family (*see* ARCHELAUS, 4, 5). Comana was made a Roman colony under Caracalla and received many favours from subsequent emperors until the reign of Constantine. It was a place of some strategic importance: it lay at the eastern end of a pass through which ran the road from Caesarea-Mazaca to Melitene (qq.v.), a road which Septimius Severus made the principal military highway to the eastern frontier of the empire.

2. City of Pontus on the River Iris; said to have been founded from Comana Chryse. The moon-goddess, also identified with Artemis, was worshipped here with a magnificence equal to that used in the service of her Cappadocian sister.

Comitia, an assembly of the Roman people convened by a magistrate in order to put a question to them and obtain their binding response. The earliest political organization of the Roman people was based upon its division into thirty patrician *curiae* (ten to each of three tribes) made up of *gentes*. The legislative assembly of these *curiae*, which voted as a body, came to be called the *comitia curiata*. It conferred the *imperium* and *potestas* upon magistrates after their election; it inaugurated certain priests, e.g. the *flamines* and *rex sacrorum*; and it regulated the internal affairs of the *curiae* and their *gentes*. But it had become a mere formality by the time of the Punic wars.

Meanwhile, however, the plebeians had won the right to become freeholders of land and its appurtenances. This made them liable for military service, and they were enrolled accordingly in the military units called *centuriae*. The resultant body was the *comitia centuriata*, which from 508 until 287 B.C. was the principal Roman assembly. It elected the higher magistrates, passed laws submitted to it by the senate, declared war and tried capital cases.

All the same, the *comitia centuriata* was found inadequate for the expression of plebeian claims, and the creation of the tribunate (493) led to the establishment of an exclusively plebeian assembly, known as *concilium plebis* (471 B.C.). It was organized on the basis of another division of the people into thirty territorial tribes; and its functions were to elect the plebeian magistrates, to try cases of injury to the latter, and to present petitions through the consuls to the *comitia centuriata*. Finally, by the *Lex Hortensia* in 287 B.C., its decisions (*plebiscita*), obtained the force of law binding the entire community.

The tribal organization was next extended to the whole people, giving rise to the *comitia tributa*, which first appears as a legislative assembly in 357 B.C. and whose rights gradually increased. It elected the inferior magistrates; tried and punished by fine various civil offences, as also cases of neglect of duty on the part of a magistrate, embezzlement of public funds and mismanagement of a war. As regards legislative functions, the *comitia tributa* had at first only the right to frame resolutions for submission to the senate; but in the later republic it was the usual source of laws passed by the whole people.

See A. H. J. Greenidge, *Roman Public Life*, 1901; G. W. Botsford, *The Roman Assemblies*, 1909.

Commagene (Kommagēnē), the north-easternmost district of Syria, lying between the Taurus and the Euphrates. It formed part of Alexander's empire, after which it enjoyed independence under a succession of native princes until the death of Antiochus III of Commagene, in A.D. 17, when it became Roman territory. Another Antiochus, surnamed Epiphanes, received back the kingdom from Caligula in 38 but was dethroned in 72 by Vespasian, who included Commagene in the province of Syria. *See* ANTIOCHUS (B).

Commentarii, a term used originally to denote memoranda, aids to memory. Hence it came to be applied to such various compilations as notes of speeches, to assist orators; family records; personal diaries; and memoirs of public events (e.g. the *Commentarii* of Caesar). Under the empire, the *commentarii principis* formed a register of the emperor's official acts, while the *commentarii diurni* was a daily court journal. *See also* ACTA.

Commius, King of the Atrebates, in Gaul, to which dignity he had been advanced by Caesar. In 55 B.C. he was sent by Caesar to Britain with instructions to visit as many tribes as possible and exhort them to acknowledge Roman supremacy. As soon as he arrived, however, the Britons clapped him in irons, and he was not released until they sued for peace after Caesar's landing later in the year. In 53 he was left with a force of cavalry to keep an eye on the Menapii when Caesar set out to deal with Ambiorix. Next year he joined the great revolt under Vercingetorix, and was one of the leaders who attempted to relieve Alesia. In 51 he was joint commander, with Correus, of the Bellovaci, but submitted during the winter of that year. See *Bell. Gall.* viii. 23; Dio xlviii. 1–9. Commius led the second Belgic migration to Britain *c.* 50 B.C., and founded a kingdom with Calleva Atrebatum (Silchester) as capital.

Commodianus (*fl. c.* A.D. 250), Christian Latin poet, born in Africa and converted late in life. His *Instructiones* and *Carmen apologeticum* (edited by B. Dombast, 1887) are of interest as providing an early example of metrical quantity yielding to accent, and as foreshadowing by their grammatical irregularities the evolution of Romance languages.

Commodus, Lucius Aelius Aurelius, Roman emperor A.D. 180–92, son of Marcus Aurelius and Faustina, born at Lanuvium in A.D. 161, and associated with his father in the empire at the age of fifteen. On the death of Marcus (whom he had accompanied in the war against the Quadi and Marcomanni), Commodus made peace and hurried back to Rome. In 183 an attempt was made upon his life, and having indulged himself in a pitiless blood-bath, he emptied the treasury by unheard-of expenditure on gladiatorial and wild-beast shows. In these latter the emperor himself took part and claimed divine honours as Hercules. Several more plots were betrayed or abandoned. In 192, however, one of his concubines, Marcia, and the praetorian prefect Laetus, discovered that their names were on a list of those doomed to die. Marcia administered poison; but it worked too slowly, and Narcissus, a celebrated athlete, undertook to strangle him.

Compsa, ancient city of the Hirpini (q.v.) near the sources of the Aufidus.

Comum (mod. Como), town of Gallia Cisalpina (Transpadana) on the Lacus Larius (Lake Como). Having suffered damage from the Rhaetians, it was restored in 89 B.C. by Cn. Pompeius Strabo and granted Latin rights (*see* COLONIA). In 59 B.C. it received 5,000 colonists sent by Julius Caesar and was called Novum Comum. The place was the centre of an important iron industry and was the birthplace of the two Plinys. The younger Pliny founded a school at Comum; it was supported by subscriptions of the local magnates, who formed a board of governors.

Concordia, Roman goddess of civic concord. She had several temples at Rome, of which the oldest (dedicated by Camillus in 367 B.C.) stood on the Capitoline. It was restored by Livia, wife of Augustus, and consecrated by Tiberius in A.D. 10. Concordia is represented in art as a matron, holding in her left hand a *cornucopia* or sceptre, and in her right an olive branch or a *patera.*

Concordia, town of Gallia Cisalpina (Transpadana), 31 miles west of Aquileia; an important road centre. Originally a village, it was made a colony (*see* COLONIA) by Augustus. Later it became an important place, having a strong garrison and a large arms factory. Many valuable inscriptions have been found in the garrison cemetery; and there are remains of walls, forum and theatre.

Confarreatio, in Roman law, the ancient patrician form of marriage, so called because bride and bridegroom shared a cake of spelt (*panis farreus*) in presence of the pontifex maximus, flamen dialis and ten witnesses. The marriage thus contracted could be dissolved only by a ceremony of equal solemnity called *diffareatio*. In later republican times *confarreatio* became generally obsolete.

Conon (Konōn): 1. Athenian admiral during the Peloponnesian war. After the Athenian defeat at Aegospotami (q.v.) in 405 B.C., Conon escaped with eight ships and took refuge with Evagoras (q.v.) in Cyprus, where he remained for some years. In 394, as joint commander of a Persian fleet, he gained a decisive victory over the Spartans off Cnidus. Then he returned to Athens, where he restored the long walls and the fortifications of Peiraeus. Later, while on an embassy from Athens to the Persian court, he discovered his life to be in danger, but managed to escape to Cyprus, where he died *c.* 390 B.C.

2. Greek grammarian and mythographer, lived at Rome in the time of Caesar and Augustus. He published a collection of myths and legends relating to the founding of colonies, of which an epitome survives.

Conovium, a Roman fort, four and a half miles from modern Conway in north Wales. It was built *c.* A.D. 112 and excavated in 1926–7 (see *Arch. Camb.*, 1926–7 seq.).

Consentes Dii, twelve Roman gods, six male and six female, who formed the council of Jupiter. The full list is unknown, but it included Summanus, Vulcan, Saturnus, Mars, Juno and Minerva (qq.v.).

Consentia (mod. Cosenza), town of the Bruttii, on the Via Popilia. Alexander I of Epirus (*see* ALEXANDER: *Kings of Epirus*) was buried here, *c*. 330 B.C. It became subject to Rome in 204 B.C., but remained essentially Greek in culture. According to Varro (q.v.) its apple-trees bore fruit twice yearly, and Pliny speaks highly of its wine.

Constantine the Great, Flavius Constantinus, illegitimate son of Constantius I, Chlorus (q.v.), by Flavia Helena, born at Naissus (mod. Nish) in Upper Moesia, 27th February A.D. 274. Sent to the court of Diocletian (q.v.) in 302, practically as a hostage, he later served under Galerius on the Danube. After the abdication of Diocletian and Maximian in 305, he escaped and joined his father, who was about to leave on an expedition to Britain. Constantius died on 25th July 306 at Eburacum (York), where the troops acclaimed his son as Augustus. Constantine, however, wrote to Galerius acknowledging that dignity to be vested in Flavius Valerius Severus (q.v.), but asking for recognition as Caesar. His request was granted. The revolt of Maxentius (q.v.) later in that year led to his recognition as Augustus by Maximian (q.v.), whose daughter Fausta he married. In 308 Diocletian and Galerius declared these arrangements null and void. Galerius retained his position in the East, Licinius (q.v.) was appointed Augustus of the West, and the title 'Son of the Augusti' was conferred upon Constantine and Maximin Daia (q.v.).

Constantine, however, did not cease to call himself Augustus, and in 310 he put to death Maximian, who had attempted to resume the purple. The death of Galerius in 311 led to a coalition of Maxentius and Maximin, which caused Licinius to ally himself with Constantine. Constantine crossed the Alps in 312 and won a great victory at Saxa Rubra (q.v.) over Maxentius, who was drowned in attempting to cross the river at the Milvian bridge. It was before this battle that Constantine adopted the Christian monogram ☧ and placed it on the *labarum* (q.v.), owing, so his biographers related, to a vision (or a dream) in which he saw a cross in the sky with the Greek words '*En toutō nika*' ('By this conquer'). He then disbanded the Praetorian Guard (q.v.), which was never revived. In 313 Constantine gave his half-sister Constantia in marriage to Licinius, and by the Edict of Milan granted toleration to Christianity throughout the empire. Licinius had been Augustus of the East since 311; Constantine held the West. There was a short period of war between them in 314, but the inevitable conflict was postponed. Then, in 323, Licinius began hostilities which ended in his defeat and internment. Constantine was now sole master of the empire.

The principal events in the last thirteen years of his reign were the convocation of the Council of Nicaea, at which Constantine himself presided; the foundation (326) and dedication (330) of Constantinople (q.v.); the settlement of 300,000 Sarmatians on Roman territory in 334; and finally the outbreak of war with Sapor II of Persia in 337. Constantine was about to take the field when he fell sick, and died soon afterwards at Nicomedia, receiving baptism shortly before the end from Eusebius, Bishop of Caesarea. For a full account of Constantine's conversion to Christianity and its consequences, and of his dealings with the Church, *see* H. Daniel-Rops, *The Church of Apostles and Martyrs* (translated by Audrey Butler), 1960. For his important social and administrative reforms see *Cambridge Medieval History*, vol. i, 1911.

Constantinople (Konstantinopolis; mod. Istanbul), city founded by Constantine the Great through the enlargement of Byzantium (q.v.) in A.D. 326. It was completed in 330 and solemnly dedicated on 11th May in that year. The walls of old Byzantium included the land nearest the head of the promontory, together with the following sites and buildings: the acropolis and its temples, the Tetrastoon (chief market-place), the Hippodrome begun but left unfinished by Septimius Severus, two theatres on the southern slopes of the acropolis, and the Strategion, a military training ground. All these were incorporated in the new city with the addition of the imperial palace, the first church of Hagia Sophia and the Forum of Constantine. Constantine's walls, however, took in a much larger area: they were drawn at a distance of about two miles to the west, taking in the third and fourth, together with parts of the fifth and seventh hills. The suburb of Blachernae on the sixth hill, and that of Galata across the Golden Horn, stood within their own fortifications, but were considered parts of the city. Very little remains of the original buildings, except the five-mile line of walls, some traces of Constantine's palace, an aqueduct and a system of large water-tanks. The remainder of Constantinople's glorious history and the antiquities lie outside the scope of this volume. *See* C. Diehl, *Constantinople*, 1924.

Constantius, Flavius Valerius, surnamed Chlorus ('pale'), Roman emperor and father of Constantine the Great (q.v.), born of Illyrian parentage *c.* A.D. 250. In 293 he was adopted and appointed Caesar by Maximian (q.v.), and received the provinces of Britain, Gaul and Spain; recovered Britain from Allectus (*see* CARAUSIUS) in 297; defeated the Alamanni in 298, and strengthened the Rhine frontier; and he did his best to minimize the sufferings of his Christian subjects in the persecution of 303 (*see* DIOCLETIAN). On the abdication of Diocletian and Maximian in 305 he was raised to the dignity of Augustus, but died at Eburacum in the following year while on an expedition against the Picts and Scots.

Consul, the highest ordinary magistrate in republican Rome. There were two consuls elected annually by the *comitia centuriata* (*see* COMITIA), taking office on 15th March until 153 B.C. and thereafter on 1st January. They were the highest civil authority and also the supreme commanders of the army. They convened the senate and presided over it. They were the medium through which foreign affairs were brought to the senate, and they carried the decrees of the senate into effect. They also convened the assembly of the people and presided. They conducted the elections, put legislative measures to the vote, and carried the decrees of the people into effect. The two consuls could act only if in unanimous agreement. Under the empire the consuls held office for only two to four months, and only those taking office on 1st January gave their names to the year; their successors were known as *consules suffecti*, a title formerly given to those who took the place of consuls who had died while in office. *See* J. E. Greenidge, *Roman Public Life*, 1901.

Consus, an ancient Roman divinity, originally, it seems, of the corn store bins. In course of time the meaning of his cult was forgotten, and he was regarded as the god either of good counsel (*consilium*) or of secret deliberations (*condita*). But it also happened that his festival on 21st August and 15th December (i.e. after harvest and seed-sowing) was celebrated with horse and chariot races in the Circus Maximus, where his altar was always covered with earth except on these occasions. Hence he also became Neptunus Equester (*see* NEPTUNUS; POSEIDON).

Copais, lake (now dry) in Boeotia. Formed chiefly by the River Cephissus (*see* CEPHISSUS, 2) and called Cephesis in the *Iliad*, it was famous for its eels. Remains of drainage works are visible (*see* AQUEDUCTS).

Cora (mod. Cori), an ancient town of the Volsci (q.v.), about 35 miles south-east of Rome. There are remains of cyclopean walls. On the site of the acropolis is a small Doric temple of the 1st century B.C.

Corbulo, Gnaeus Domitius, Roman general in the reigns of Tiberius, Claudius and Nero. While governor of Germania Inferior in A.D. 47, he made a successful punitive expedition against the Frisii, and was about to undertake another against the Chauci when he received orders from Rome to withdraw behind the Rhine. Following the occupation of Armenia (q.v.) by the Parthians under Vologaeses I, early in Nero's reign (*see* TIRIDATES), Corbulo was sent out to deal with the situation. Having reorganized the legions of Syria, he launched his offensive in 58; captured Artaxata and Tigranocerta in 59; and in the following year established a Roman nominee, Tigranes, on the Armenian throne. But the new king was driven out (61) by the Parthians, whose territory he had invaded. Corbulo therefore concluded an armistice whereby both sides should evacuate Armenia pending arbitration by the imperial government. Nero, having resolved to annex the country, sent Paetus to take the necessary steps, while Corbulo protected Syria. The overwhelming defeat of Paetus at Rhandeia in 62 led to Corbulo's reinstatement as commander-in-chief. He crossed the Euphrates (63), and at his approach Tiridates submitted. In 67 Nero, who was then in Greece, summoned Corbulo, and on his arrival at Cenchreae ordered him to commit suicide. Corbulo, acknowledging the justice of this sentence, obeyed, though it is not certain whether he was in fact guilty of conspiracy.

Corcyra (Kerkura or Korkura; mod. Corfu), island in the Ionian Sea, identified by some with Homer's Scheria. Colonized from Corinth (q.v.) *c.* 700 B.C., it quickly prospered; but unlike most Corinthian colonies it maintained an independent and indeed hostile attitude towards the mother city, and *c.* 664 B.C. their fleets fought the first recorded naval action in Greek history. In 435 B.C., during one of its recurrent disputes with Corinth, Corcyra invoked the assistance of Athens, and this was one of the principal immediate causes of the Peloponnesian War (q.v.). During that war it was an important Athenian naval base until 410, when it ceased to take any part in hostilities owing to internal unrest; but a renewal of its Athenian alliance in 375 brought it once again into conflict with Sparta. In the hellenistic period Corcyra was besieged by Cassander (q.v.), and occupied in turn by Agathocles, Pyrrhus (qq.v.) and Illyrian pirates. From these last it was delivered (229 B.C.) by the Romans, who made it a free state but used it as a naval station. It was one of Octavian's bases against Antony in 31 B.C., but was finally eclipsed by the foundation of Nicopolis (q.v.). *See* Herodotus, viii. 168; Thucydides, i–iii; Xenophon, *Hellenica*, vi. 2; Polybius, ii. 9–11.

Corduba (mod. Cordova), city which, under the Roman Empire, was capital of the province of Hispania Baetica (*see* BAETICA). Founded probably by the Carthaginians, it was occupied by the Romans under Marcus Marcellus in 152 B.C. and soon afterwards became the first Latin *colonia* (q.v.) in Spain. After the battle of Munda (q.v.) in 45 B.C. it was severely punished by Caesar for having supported the sons of Pompey, and 20,000 of its inhabitants were massacred. Under Augustus it became a *municipium* (q.v.). Corduba's prosperity in imperial times was due (*a*) to its situation on the River Baetis (then navigable to the city) and on the Via Augusta (a great commercial high road built by Augustus from northern Spain), and (*b*) to the neighbouring mines, cornlands and pastures. It was the birth-place of the two Senecas and of Lucan (qq.v.).

Cordus, Aulus Cremutius (1st century B.C.), Roman historian, author of a history of the civil wars and the reign of Augustus from 43 B.C. to 18 B.C. In consequence of a gibe against Sejanus (q.v.), he was charged with treason as having praised Brutus and Cassius, and starved himself to death (A.D. 25). Only a few fragments of the work survive.

Corfinium, ancient city of the Paeligni in the valley of the Aternus, seven miles north of Sulmo. During the Social War (q.v.) in 90 B.C. it was chosen by the allies as the capital and seat of government of their newly founded state under the name Italica. In the imperial period it was an important road centre on the Via Valeria.

Corinium (mod. Cirencester), a Romano-British town. Founded probably as a military station in the 1st century A.D., it afterwards became a civilian city, of which the ruins include a huge forum and basilica, some traces of the walls, an amphitheatre, a monumental gate and the foundations of a bridge.

Corinna (Ko-), Greek lyric poetess, *fl. c.* 500 B.C., a native of Tanagra in Boeotia. She is said to have instructed Pindar and to have won five victories over him in poetic contests. Almost nothing was known of her work until the discovery in modern times, at Hermopolis in Egypt, of a papyrus containing parts of three poems. These are narrative verses, written in Boeotian dialect (the only specimens thereof at present known). They are believed to follow a primitive pattern, and on that account to provide a fair idea of pre-Homeric poetry of this kind. *See* text with commentary edited by Sir Maurice Bowra in J. U. Powell and E. A. Barber's *New Chapters in the History of Greek Literature*, vol. iii, 1933.

Corinth (Gk Korinthos; Lat. Corinthus), Greek city one and a half miles south of the isthmus which connects Peloponnesus with central Greece. Its territory was small and unfertile; but its geographical situation early made it an important industrial and commercial centre, and it was famed for its wealth and luxury. Corinth was built upon two terraces on the lower slopes of its citadel, which towered over the surrounding plain to a height of 1,886 feet and was known as Acro-Corinthus. It was connected by long walls with the port of Lechaeum on the Corinthian Gulf and by a line of forts with that of Cenchreae on the Saronic Gulf. Its greatness in the 8th and 7th centuries B.C. is attested by numerous colonies, among the most famous of which were Syracuse and Corcyra (qq.v.).

The main stream of Corinthian history begins with the tyranny (c. 657–581 B.C.) established by Cypselus (q.v.) and continued by his son Periander (q.v.). Under these two men Corinth extended her influence along the whole coastline of the Saronic Gulf, and controlled the Italian and Adriatic trade routes. The tyranny was succeeded by an oligarchy. The prosperity of Corinth was now enormous. Her shipyards had long been famous. Her manufactures included textiles, bronze work, perfumes, and pottery made from a famous yellow clay. Her trade was mainly towards the West, which she inundated with her ceramics in exchange for corn, of which she became the principal *entrepôt* in the East. But an economic crisis set in c. 550 B.C., when exports began to fall because of Athenian competition. Towards the end of the 6th century B.C. Corinth joined the Peloponnesian League under Sparta; but her great wealth and strategic position assured her a large measure of independence. She took part in the Persian war of 480 B.C. and was friendly towards Athens until the emergence of Athenian sea-power. The succeeding enmity between the two states culminated in the active part played by Corinth in the Peloponnesian war, for the outbreak of which she was largely responsible. From 395 B.C. her alliances varied according to expediency. The attempt of Timophanes to establish a new tyranny (344 B.C.) was foiled by his brother Timoleon (q.v.). In 338 B.C., after the battle of Chaeronea (q.v.), Philip placed a Macedonian garrison in the citadel. This garrison was expelled by Aratus in 243 B.C., and Corinth became for a time a member of the Achaean League (q.v.). After another period of Macedonian rule she was restored to the league in 196 B.C. by T. Quinctius Flamininus (q.v.); but the revival of her political and commercial prosperity made her the mainstay of resistance to Rome. Consequently the city was sacked and destroyed by L. Mummius after the defeat of the league in 146 B.C. For a century Corinth lay in ruins; but in 46 B.C. it was rebuilt and colonized by Julius Caesar. Augustus made it capital of the province of Achaea, and Hadrian enriched it with public works.

Extensive excavations have been carried out since 1896 by the American School of Classical Studies at Athens. Remains include the Agora (see *American Journal of Archaeology*, 1896, sqq.), the temple of Apollo, the Fountain of Priene and the theatre.

Corinthiacus Isthmus (Isthmus of Corinth), often called simply 'The Isthmus', lay between the Corinthian and the Saronic Gulfs. *See*

CORINTH. Four unsuccessful attempts were made to dig a canal through the isthmus.

Coriolanus, hero of an early Roman legend. His original name was C. or Cn. Marcius, and he received the surname Coriolanus on account of his bravery at the storming of the Volscian capital Corioli. His haughty bearing towards the commons excited their fear and dislike; and he was impeached and condemned to exile, 491 B.C. He took refuge with the Volsci, and promised to assist them in war against the Romans. Attius Tullius, King of the Volsci, appointed him general of the Volscian army, and Coriolanus advanced unresisted till he came to the Cluilian dike close to Rome, 489. Here he encamped, and the Romans in alarm sent to him embassy after embassy. But he would listen to none of them. At length the noblest matrons of Rome, headed by Veturia, his mother, and Volumnia, his wife, with his two little children, came to his tent. His mother's reproaches, and the tears of his wife, bent his purpose. He led back his army, and lived in exile among the Volsci till his death; though other traditions relate that he was killed on his return.

Cornelia: 1. Daughter of Scipio Africanus, mother of the tribunes Tiberius and Gaius Gracchus, and of Sempronia, wife of Scipio Africanus the younger. After the murder of Gaius (121 B.C.) she retired to Misenum and devoted the remainder of her life to Greek and Latin literature.

2. Daughter of L. Cornelius Cinna and first wife of Julius Caesar, to whom she was married *c.* 85 B.C. and to whom she bore his only child Julia. She died before 69 B.C.

3. Daughter of Q. Cornelius Metellus Pius Scipio. She was married first to P. Licinius Crassus, younger son of the triumvir, and secondly (as his third wife) to Pompey the Great. She accompanied Pompey to Egypt after Pharsalus, witnessed his murder at Alexandria, and then returned to Rome, where she later received from Caesar the ashes of her husband.

Cornificius, Latin author of a lost work on rhetoric, mentioned by Quintilian. His date is uncertain, but there is some reason to believe that he may be the man generally called 'Auctor ad Herennium', whose *Rhetorica* in four books (*c.* 85 B.C.) is extant, ed. F. Marx, 1894.

Cornucopia or **Cornu Copiae,** the 'horn of plenty', a goat's horn generally depicted as filled with flowers and fruit. *See* ACHELOÜS; AMALTHEIA.

Cornus, town on the west coat of Sardinia (q.v.). Its capture by the Romans in 215 B.C. marked the end of the rebellion of that year. There are Phoenician and Roman tombs.

Cornutus, Lucius Annaeus, Roman Stoic philosopher of the 1st century A.D. Among his pupils were Lucan and Persius, the latter of whom pays a moving tribute to him in the fifth Satire (30–51). He revised the *Satires* with a view to publication, but after the author's premature death he left the task of editing them to Caesius Bassus (q.v.). Cornutus was banished by Nero *c.* 66 for having slighted the emperor's projected history of the Romans, and no more is heard of him. None of his own works (on rhetoric) has survived.

Coroneia (**Ko-**), town of Boeotia near which the Thebans defeated the Athenians in 447 B.C. Here also Agesilaus II of Sparta (*see* AGESILAUS) defeated the combined forces of Thebes, Athens, Argos and Corinth in 394 B.C.

Corsica (Gk Kurnos), island of the Mediterranean, north of Sardinia. Honey, wax, timber and granite were its chief products. It was colonized by the Phocaeans (*see* ALALIA) *c.* 560, who were soon driven out by the Etruscans, and these in turn by the Carthaginians. The Romans gained a footing in the island during the first Punic war, but did not establish themselves there until the middle of the 2nd century B.C. Made to form a single province with Sardinia (q.v.) in 227 B.C., it was separated therefrom under Nero in A.D. 67.

Cortona, 18 miles south-east of Arretium, was one of the twelve cities of the Etruscan confederation. There are well-preserved remains of Etruscan walls and a Roman reservoir.

Coruncanius, Tiberius, consul with P. Valerius Laevinus in 280 B.C. He was the first plebeian to be pontifex maximus, and the first person at Rome to give public instruction in law.

Corvus, Marcus Valerius, semi-legendary figure of early Roman history. When serving as military tribune in 349 B.C. he accepted the challenge of a gigantic Gaul to single combat and was assisted by a raven (Lat. *corvus*) which flew in the face of the barbarian. He is said to have been six times consul and twice dictator, during which time he won a memorable victory over the Samnites at Mt Gaurus (q.v.) in 343 B.C.

Corybantes (Koru-), in Greek mythology, demi-gods who stand in the same relation to the Great Mother of the Gods (q.v.) as do the Curetes (q.v.) to Zeus. They were, in fact, often identified with the Curetes. The ritual of their cult included an orgiastic dance which was supposed to be a cure for mental derangement.

Corycian Cave, vast cave in the side of Mt Parnassus (q.v.), about seven miles north of Delphi (q.v.), in which the inhabitants of Delphi took refuge during the Persian invasion, 480 B.C. It is said to be capable of holding 3,000 people.

Cos (Kōs), island of the Sporades (q.v.) off the coast of Caria, noted for its wine, ointments and the famous transparent garments called in Latin *Coae vestes*. Settled by Dorians from Epidaurus, Cos was a member of the Delian League (q.v.) in the 5th century B.C. Having resisted Athenian aggression (357–355), it became subject for a few years to Halicarnassus (q.v.). It was used as a naval base and largely benefited by the Ptolemies. The Romans made it a free city. Among its most famous men were Hippocrates, Apelles, Philetas and Theocritus (qq.v.). Near the town of Cos there was a precinct of Asclepius (q.v.), the home of a celebrated medical school (*see* A. J. Brock, *Greek Medicine*, 1929). This has been excavated.

Cosa, ancient Etruscan city on the south-west of Italy, near the Via Aurelia (q.v.). It stands on a promontory, through the east end of which there is an Etruscan cutting, made to drain a lagoon. Cosa became a Roman colony (*see* COLONIA) in 273 B.C. T. Annius Milo (q.v.) was put to death here in 48 B.C.

Cotta, Gaius Aurelius, Roman statesman and orator, born *c.* 124 B.C. As consul in 75 he carried a law abolishing the rule which, since the time of Sulla, had disqualified tribunes of the plebs from holding higher offices. He was governor of Gaul in the following year, and died suddenly on his return to Rome in 73 B.C. He is one of the speakers in Cicero's *De Oratore* and *De natura deorum*.

Cotta, Lucius Aurelius, brother of Gaius (*see* preceding article). When praetor in 70 B.C. he carried the *Lex Aurelia Judiciaria*, which abolished the provision of Sulla's constitution whereby jurors were chosen exclusively from the senate. Henceforward senators, equites and *tribuni aerarii* were to be equally qualified. In 66 Cotta and L. Manlius Torquatus accused the consuls-elect for the following year of bribery, and were chosen in their stead. It was Cotta who proposed an act of public thanksgiving for Cicero's suppression of Catiline's conspiracy. Later he became a partisan of Caesar, after whose death he withdrew from public life.

Cottii Regnum, 'Kingdom of Cottius', a district of Liguria (q.v.) which included a considerable length of the highway over the pass of the Alpes Cottiae into Gaul (*see* ALPES). The chief town was Segusio. Under Nero the kingdom became the province of Alpes Cottiae. *See* COTTIUS.

Cottius, ruler of several Ligurian tribes (Cottii) in the Cottian Alps (*see* previous article). Son of King Donnus, he submitted to Augustus and was confirmed by him in authority, with title of imperial prefect, over the fourteen tribes which his father had governed as king. Besides the triumphal arch at Segusio (q.v.), Cottius built roads over the Alps. Claudius restored the royal title to his family, which became extinct in the reign of Nero.

Cotytto (Kotuttō), a Thracian goddess, whose orgiastic festival, Cotyttia, resembled that of Phrygian Cybele. Her worshippers were called Baptae. The cult was introduced at Athens and Corinth.

Crannon, *see* LAMIAN WAR.

Crantor (Krantōr): 1. In Greek legend, armour-bearer of Peleus, slain by the centaur Demoleon.

2. Academic philosopher (*fl. c.* 300 B.C.), a native of Soli in Cilicia. He studied at Athens under Xenocrates and Polemon, and was the author of several works, none of which has survived. Cicero commends him, and made much use of his treatise *On Grief* both in the third book of his *Tusculan Disputations* and in the *Consolatio* which he composed on the death of his daughter Tullia.

Crassus, Lucius Licinius, Roman orator, born 140 B.C. He was consul in 95 B.C. with Q. Mucius Scaevola, and their measures against the unlawful assumption of Roman citizenship were among the chief causes of the Social war. Crassus is one of the principal speakers in Cicero's *De Oratore*, where he is believed to represent the author's own views.

Crassus, Marcus Licinius, Roman politician and financier, born *c.* 115 B.C. He fought with Sulla against the Marian party (83–82), and on the latter's defeat was allowed to buy at nominal prices the confiscated estates of the proscribed. These formed the basis of his enormous wealth, which he increased by usury, slave-trading and other means. He worked silver mines, cultivated farms and built houses which he let at high rents. All this made him the richest, and of course the greediest, man in Rome. As praetor in 71 he managed, rather surprisingly, to crush the revolt of Spartacus (q.v.). In 70 he was consul with Pompey (q.v.), and entertained the populace at a banquet of 10,000 tables. Jealousy, however, sprang up between the two men; and after Pompey's departure from Rome (67), Crassus enabled Caesar (q.v.) to pay his debts in return for political support. But in 60 Pompey's hostility to the senate, which had refused to ratify his Eastern settlement, and Crassus's greed for power as a gateway to still greater riches, enabled Caesar to reconcile them and to form with himself what is known as the First Triumvirate. Crassus was again consul with Pompey in 55, when a law was passed assigning them the provinces of Syria and Spain respectively for five years. In November of that year he started out to make war on the Parthians, who had given Rome no provocation. In 54 he devastated Mesopotamia; and in 53, after plundering the Temple of Jerusalem, he began his second invasion of Parthian territory. But he sustained an overwhelming defeat at Carrhae (q.v.), was taken prisoner and subsequently murdered at an interview with the victorious general Surenas. His younger son, Publius, who had served under Caesar in Gaul, fell in the battle.

Crassus, Publius Licinius: 1. Roman orator, statesman and jurist. He was consul with L. Valerius Flaccus in 131 B.C., and was given command against Aristonicus (q.v.), a claimant to the throne of Pergamum. In the following year, when on his way home after a successful campaign, he was taken prisoner by a small Thracian force near Leucae and put to death.

2. Father of M. Licinius Crassus (*see* preceding article); consul in 97 B.C., and afterwards governor of Further Spain. He was an adherent of Sulla, and committed suicide when Marius and Cinna entered Rome in 87 B.C.

Craterus (Krateros), one of the generals of Alexander the Great, upon whose death (323 B.C.) he became joint regent of Macedonia and Greece with Antipater (*see* ANTIPATER, 1). In 322 he assisted the latter in suppressing the Greek revolt (*see* LAMIAN WAR), but fell in battle against Eumenes of Cardia (q.v.), 321 B.C.

Crates (Kratēs): 1. Athenian poet of the Old Comedy, *fl. c.* 470 B.C. According to Aristotle he was the first to substitute more general subjects and a well-developed plot for mere political lampoons on individuals (*Poetics*, 5); while Aristophanes tells us that he was the first to represent a drunkard on the stage (*Knights*, 37 ff.).

2. Athenian philosopher who succeeded Polemon (q.v.) as head of the Old Academy; succeeded in turn by Arcesilaus (q.v.).

3. Cynic philosopher of the late 4th century B.C., a native of Thebes in Boeotia. Among his pupils was Zeno of Citium, so that he forms a link between the Cynic and the Stoic schools. The extant letters attributed to him are spurious.

4. Greek grammarian and Stoic philosopher of the 2nd century B.C., a native of Mallus in Cilicia. While head of the library at Pergamum he wrote a commentary on Homer, in which he maintained that the Homeric poems were allegorical, meant to expound philosophical and scientific truths. About 170 B.C. he was sent by Attalus

II on an embassy to Rome, where his lectures aroused interest in grammatical and critical subjects for the first time among the Romans.

Crathis (Kra-), river of Italy between Lucania and Bruttii, flowing into the sea near Sybaris (q.v.). Its waters were supposed to dye the hair blond. It is to be distinguished from another river of the same name, in Achaea, which fell into the sea near Aegae.

Cratinus (Kratinos), Greek poet of the Old Comedy, born at Athens *c.* 520 and died in 423 B.C. Little is known of his life, and only a few fragments of his work have survived. Aristophanes speaks of him as a drunkard, but compares his style to a rushing torrent. He is said to have written twenty-one comedies and to have won the prize nine times; his *Bottle*, of which the plot is known and which constitutes an admission of his own weakness, defeated the *Clouds* of Aristophanes in 423. Persius (i. 123) writes of Cratinus's 'bold breath', referring to his attacks on Pericles, then at the height of his power. These attacks were represented by at least three comedies: *Nemesis, Archilochi* and *Dionysalexandros*. The argument of the last has been preserved (*see* B. P. Grenfell and A. S. Hunt, *Oxyrhynchus Papyri*, iv. 1904).

Cratippus (Kratippos): 1. Greek historian, *fl. c.* 375 B.C. He was probably a native of Athens, and his work appears to have been a continuation of Thucydides down to the year 394 B.C. A portion of this work is believed to have been discovered at Oxyrhynchus in 1896 (*see* B. P. Grenfell and A. S. Hunt, *Oxyrhynchus Papyri*, v. 1905).

2. Greek philosopher of the Peripatetic school, a native of Mitylene and a contemporary of Cicero, who held him in the highest esteem and whose son was among his pupils at Athens (*see* CICERO, MARCUS TULLIUS, 2). In 44 B.C. he succeeded Andronicus of Rhodes as head of the Lyceum.

Cremera (mod. Fosso della Valchetta), small stream in Etruria falling into the Tiber about six miles north of Rome and famous for the defeat of the three hundred Fabii. *See* FABIUS VIBULANUS, QUINTUS.

Cremona, town of Gallia Cisalpina on the north bank of the Padus (mod. Po). It was founded as a Roman colony (*see* COLONIA), together with Placentia (q.v.), in 218 B.C. as a defence against Gallic tribes. Having espoused the cause of Vitellius, it was captured and destroyed by Antonius after the second battle of Betriacum in 69 B.C. Rebuilt almost at once, it never recovered its prosperity, but continued to be an important road centre. Virgil began his education at Cremona.

Creon (Krēon): 1. King of Corinth, whose daughter Glauce was married to Jason. *See* JASON AND MEDEA.

2. Brother of Jocasta and father of Menoeceus and Haemon. *See* THEBAN LEGEND, 1 and 4.

Creophylus (Kreophulos), one of the earliest Greek epic poets, a native of Samos. He was said to have been a friend of Homer and to have written a poem on the *Capture of Oechalia*. Others attributed this work to Homer himself, and said that the latter gave it as a present to Creophylus.

Cresilas (Krē-), Cretan sculptor, born at Cydonia and *fl. c.* 450 B.C.

Copies of his 'Wounded Amazon' and portrait of Pericles survive. *See* E. A. Gardner, *Handbook of Greek Sculpture*, 1915.

Crete (Krētē), island in the Mediterranean. Its fertile soil produced corn in abundance, copper was mined, and purple dye was extracted from the murex. The high civilization which has been brought to light by modern archaeology, and which is called Minoan, lasted through its several stages from the late 4th to the late 2nd millennium B.C. It belonged therefore to the distant past at the opening of the period covered by this volume (*see* the articles AEGEAN CIVILIZATION and CRETE in Everyman's Encyclopaedia. *See also* Sir Arthur Evans, *The Palace of Minos*, 5 vols., 1921–36; J. O. S. Pendlebury, *The Archaeology of Crete*, 1939, and *A Handbook of the Palace of Minos*, 1954). It was indeed, as the recent decipherment of the Linear B Script shows, a true ancestor of the classical Greek language and culture; but its date and the fact that it has left no written historical records, places it outside the scope of the present article.

Homer speaks of Crete as an island of 100 cities, and there are remains of the classical Greek and Roman periods. It never became united, and the 'Cretan Constitution' discussed in the second book of Aristotle's *Politics* was no doubt generally prevalent among the various city-states. This assumption is borne out by the fact that Aristotle says that it bore a close resemblance to the constitution of Sparta, and that the population of Crete in classical times was Dorian.

Crete preserved its independence until the 1st century B.C., supplying skilled archers to the armies of Rome and other nations. But it incurred the hostility of Rome, first by its alliance with Mithradates the Great (q.v.) of Pontus, and afterwards by its active support of the Cilician pirates (*see* CILICIA). It was conquered by Q. Caecilius Metellus (*see* METELLUS, 6), 69–67 B.C., and became a Roman province. It was subsequently united with the province of Cyrenaica (q.v.) by Augustus, and was incorporated by Constantine in the prefecture of Illyria. *See* CURETES; GORTYNA; MINOS; MINOTAUR; TITANS; ZEUS.

Creusa (Kreousa): 1. Daughter of Priam and Hecuba (qq.v.), wife of Aeneas and mother of Ascanius (qq.v.); she perished on the night of the fall of Troy (Virgil, *Aen.* ii).

2. Otherwise Glauce (*see* GLAUCE, 3).

3. Daughter of Erechtheus (q.v.) and wife of Xuthus (q.v.).

Criobolium (Kriobolion), sacrifice of a ram in the cult of Attis (q.v.). It was often performed jointly with that of a bull (*taurobolium*), which was in honour of the Great Mother of the Gods (q.v.); and on such occasions the altar was dedicated to both divinities.

Crissa and **Cirrha**, towns of Phocis, regarded by some writers as identical; but it seems more probable that Crissa lay inland, southwest of Delphi, while Cirrha was its port on the Crissaean Gulf. The inhabitants of these towns taxed pilgrims frequenting the Delphic oracle, in consequence of which the Amphictyons declared war (*c.* 595 B.C.) and eventually destroyed them. The rich Crissaean plain was declared sacred to Apollo, and its cultivation forbidden. *See* SACRED WARS.

Critias (Kri-), Athenian orator and politician of the late 5th century

B.C. In his youth he was a pupil of Gorgias and Socrates. Imprisoned for having taken part in the mutilation of the Hermae (q.v.), 415 B.C., he afterwards helped to put down the Four Hundred (q.v.), but in 404 was one of the Thirty Tyrants (q.v.) set up at Athens by the Spartans. He was killed in battle against Thrasybulus (q.v.) in the same year.

Critius (Kritios) and **Nēsiotēs**, Athenian sculptors (5th century B.C.) who replaced the statues of Harmodius and Aristogeiton which had been removed from the Acropolis by the Persians in 480.

Critolaus (Kritolaos), Greek philosopher of the Peripatetic school. In 155 B.C. he accompanied Carneades (q.v.) and Diogenes the Babylonian (*see* DIOGENES, 3) on an Athenian embassy to Rome.

Croesus (Kroisos), last king of Lydia, of the Mermnad dynasty, reigned 560–546 B.C. He completed the conquest of Ionia, begun by his father Alyattes (q.v.), and extended the Lydian Empire as far east as the River Halys. His enormous wealth, attributed in legend to the gold-bearing sands of the Pactolus, was based upon commercial enterprise.

A famous story, the truth of which is open to dispute, tells how Solon (q.v.) visited the court of Croesus and, in reply to the monarch's question as to who was the happiest man he had ever known, assured him that none should be deemed happy until he had died a happy death.

After the conquest of the Median Empire by Cyrus the Great (549 B.C.), Croesus attempted to arm himself against the Persian menace by means of alliances with Babylon, Egypt and Sparta. Then, on advice from the Delphic oracle, he took the offensive by invading Cappadocia. An indecisive battle was fought, and Croesus returned to Sardis, his capital, to obtain reinforcements. There he was surprised by Cyrus, who captured the city and took Croesus prisoner (546 B.C.).

The subsequent history of Croesus, though familiar to readers of Herodotus, is in fact uncertain. According to the latter, he was condemned by Cyrus to be burned alive. As he stood on the burning pyre, Apollo, grateful for the victim's generosity to Delphi (where he had dedicated magnificent gifts), sent a shower of rain which put out the flames. Simultaneously, Croesus, remembering his interview with Solon, had invoked the latter's name; and Cyrus, wondering at the miracle and associating it with the cry of 'Solon!' asked who it was that he had called upon. Having learned the facts, he not only spared the life of Croesus, but made him his friend.

According to Bacchylides (q.v.), Croesus tried unsuccessfully to avoid being taken prisoner by burning himself on a funeral pyre; and it has been maintained by G. B. Grundy (*The Great Persian War*, 1901) that he actually died on his own pyre.

According to Ctesias (q.v.), who makes no mention of any attempt to burn the conquered king, Croesus lost his throne but was appointed by Cyrus governor of a Median province.

Crommyon (Krommuōn), town in the territory of Megara, on the Saronic Gulf, celebrated in Greek legend for the killing of the wild sow by Theseus.

Cronus (Kronos), in Greek mythology, son of Uranus and Gē, youngest of the Titans (q.v.). He sometimes appears as King of the Golden Age, and was identified by the Romans with Saturnus (q.v.). It is probable that Cronus originated as an agricultural deity of some pre-hellenic people.

Croton (Krotōn), Greek town on the east coast of Bruttii (q.v.); founded by Achaeans, 710 B.C., seven miles north-west of the Lacinian promontory. It soon became wealthy and powerful; for its harbour, though not good, was the only one between Tarentum and Rhegium. Croton was also the seat of a medical school (*see* ALCMAEON, 2). Celebrated for its successes at the Olympic Games (q.v.) from 588 onwards, Milon (q.v.) was its best-known athlete. Between 540 and 530 B.C. Pythagoras (q.v.) established himself here with three hundred disciples. In 510 B.C. Croton captured and destroyed Sybaris; but soon afterwards the Pythagoreans were expelled. A Crotonian ship was present at Salamis in 480 B.C. In the same year, however, Croton was defeated by the Epizephyrian Locrians and the Phlegeans, from which time it gradually declined. Having suffered from the depradations of Dionysius I, the Bruttii, Agathocles and Pyrrhus (qq.v.), it became subject to Rome in 277 B.C. It revolted after Cannae (q.v.), and was Hannibal's winter quarters for three years. The site has disappeared, but on the neighbouring promontory there are traces of the famous temple of Hera Lacinia, which was approached from Croton by a processional way.

Crucifixion, a form of capital punishment inflicted by the Romans only on slaves, prisoners of war and criminals of the lowest class, but never on a Roman citizen. It seems to have been borrowed from Carthage, where it was in common use. Under the Romans scourging was an invariable preliminary to crucifixion, and after that terrible ordeal the victim carried his cross to the place of execution, where he was stripped naked. The cross might take any one of four forms. If it was a *crux simplex*, i.e. an upright stake, the condemned was either impaled thereon or simply tied. If a *crux commissa* (T), a *crux immissa* (†) or a *crux decussata* (X) was employed, he was fastened to it with cords or by nails driven through his hands (or wrists) and feet. In all cases he was then left to die of exhaustion, thirst and wounds.

Crypteia (Kru-), from Greek *kruptein*, 'to hide', the Spartan secret police. The constant danger of a helot revolt (*see* HELOTS) led to a rule whereby the ephors (q.v.), on taking office, proclaimed war against the helots, which meant that any Spartan who slew a helot was free from the guilt of homicide. The ephors then dispatched a body of young Spartans, who formed the *crypteia*, to spy upon the helots and assassinate any whom they thought dangerous. The following account of the *crypteia* at work during the Peloponnesian war is given by Thucydides (v. 80). In 425 B.C. 'the helots were invited by a proclamation to pick out those of their number who claimed to have most distinguished themselves against the enemy, in order that they might receive their freedom; the object being to test them, as it was thought that the first to claim their freedom would be the most high-spirited and the most apt to rebel. As many as 2,000 were selected accordingly, who crowned themselves and went round the temples, rejoicing in their new freedom. The Spartans, however, soon afterwards did away

with them, and no one ever knew how each of them perished.' *See*
A. H. J. Greenidge, *Handbook of Greek Constitutional History*, 1896.

Ctesias (Ktēsias), Greek historian of the late 5th and early 4th
century B.C. A native of Cnidus, in Caria, he studied medicine and
became private physician to the Persian king Artaxerxes II, Mnemon,
whom he accompanied in the war against Cyrus the Younger (401).
The most important of his works was *Persica* in twenty-three books, a
history of Assyria, Babylon and the Persian Empire down to 398 B.C.
It was written in opposition to Herodotus, whose very high standing
at Athens, coupled with the fact that it claimed to be based on the
Persian royal archives, caused the work to be considered by the
Greeks as totally unreliable. None of Ctesias's works has survived;
but there are abridgments of the *Persica* and the *Indica* (an account
of India) in Photius, and other writers have preserved fragments of
both works.

Ctesiphon (Ktēsiphōn), ancient city on the left bank of the Tigris,
about three Roman miles east of Seleucia (*see* SELEUCIA, I). First
mentioned by Polybius in 220 B.C., it became headquarters of the
Parthians in 129 B.C., and in the 2nd century A.D. metropolis of the
Persian (Sassanid) Empire. There are remains of a huge vaulted hall,
once part of the Sassanid palace.

Cui bono, *see* CASSIUS LONGINUS, LUCIUS.

Cumae (Gk Kumē), Greek city on the west coast of Campania,
founded from Chalcis *c.* 750 B.C. It extended its power around the
Gulf of Puteoli, founding in turn Parthenope and Dichearchia
and dominating the harbours in that area. It was off Cumae that
Hieron I (q.v.) of Syracuse defeated the Etruscan fleet in 474 B.C.
Occupied by the Samnites before the end of the 5th century, it
became subject to Rome *c.* 340 B.C. Under the empire Cumae still
possessed a good deal of territory, but was a quiet country town
yielding pride of place to the fashionable resorts of Baiae and Puteoli.
The site is now deserted; but there are some remains, and in the acropolis hill are caves famous in legend as the seat of the Cumaean Sibyl
(*see* ORACLES; SIBYL).

Cunaxa, a small town on the Euphrates, famous for the battle
between Cyrus the Younger (q.v.) and his brother Artaxerxes II (q.v.)
in 401 B.C. *See also* TEN THOUSAND, EXPEDITION OF THE.

Cunobelin, British king at Camulodunum *c.* A.D. 10–40. Before his
death he had extended his rule over south-east Britain and done much
to familiarize his subjects with Roman fashions.

Cupido (English Cupid), Latin name (meaning Desire) for the god of
love, Eros (q.v.), identical with Amor (q.v.). His representation in art
and literature as an irresponsible 'cherub' with bow and arrow is due
to Alexandrian influence. *See also* PSYCHE.

Curator, in Roman law, the legally appointed guardian of a
prodigus (spendthrift) or of a *furiosus* (person of unsound mind).
The term was also used of one who had charge of the estate of an
adolescens, that is, of a person less than twenty-five years old, but
more than fourteen in the case of a boy and more than twelve in the
case of a girl.

Cures, a Sabine town near the left bank of the Tiber, about 26 miles from Rome. According to legend, it was from here that Titus Tatius led the Sabine settlers to the Quirinal (*see* QUIRITES). Cures was also the traditional birth-place of Numa Pompilius (q.v.).

Curetes (Kourētes), probably meaning ' young men ', were in Greek mythology demi-gods attendant on the infant Zeus (q.v.) in Crete (*see* TITANS), though they are sometimes confused with the Corybantes (q.v.). According to the legend they danced and clashed their weapons so that Cronus would not hear his cries, a story invented no doubt to explain the war-dances which were a feature of their cult in historical times. The discovery of a hymn in their honour has suggested to some scholars that the real origin of the Curetes is to be sought in the worship (dating perhaps from the 2nd or 3rd millennium B.C. in Crete) of a fertility-god who came to be called *Zeus Kouros*; in other words, that adolescent lads (*kouroi*) worshipped a god who was imagined to be of their own age. *See* J. E. Harrison, *Themis*, 2nd ed., 1927; M. P. Nilsson, *Minoan-Mycenaean Religion*, 1927.

Curia, *see* COMITIA.

Curio, Gaius Scribonius : 1. Roman consul in 76 B.C., a personal enemy of Caesar. He supported Clodius (q.v.) when the latter was accused (61 B.C.) of profaning the mysteries of Bona Dea (q.v.). Appointed pontifex maximus in 57, he died in 53 B.C. He had some reputation as an orator, and was a friend of Cicero.

2. Son of the preceding, husband of Fulvia, the future wife of Mark Antony. Curio belonged at first to the senatorial party and was tribune of the plebs in 50 B.C.; but he was bought over by Caesar and used his power as tribune against his former friends. Soon after the outbreak of civil war (49 B.C.) he was sent by Caesar to Sicily as propraetor. Having driven the senatorial governor, Cato, from the island, he crossed with his army to Africa, where he was defeated and slain by Juba (*see* Caesar, *Bell. Civ.* ii).

Cursor, Lucius Papirius, Roman general, five times consul (between 326 and 313 B.C.) and twice dictator (325 and 309 B.C.). He gained a number of successes over the Samnites; but his greatest victory was won in the year of his second dictatorship, in honour of which he celebrated a magnificent triumph. Livy (vii, ix) ranks him, as a general, next to Alexander the Great.

Cursus honorum, the order in which a Roman succeeded to the several degrees of office: quaestor, aedile, praetor, consul (qq.v.). An interval of at least two years was required between each. Sulla fixed the minimum age for the consulship at forty-three.

Curtius, Manlius, the hero of one of three legends created to explain the *Lacus Curtius*, a pond in the Forum Romanum. The legend goes that in 362 B.C. the earth in the Forum gave way, and a great chasm appeared, which the soothsayers declared could be filled up only by throwing into it Rome's greatest treasure; that thereupon Curtius, a noble youth, mounted his steed in full armour, and declaring that Rome possessed no greater treasure than a brave and gallant citizen, leaped into the abyss, upon which the earth closed over him. The second legend states that one Mettius Curtius, a Sabine general, when pursued by Romulus, jumped into a swamp in the valley afterwards occupied by the Forum. According to the third legend, the place was struck by lightning in 445 B.C., and enclosed as sacred by the consul Gaius Curtius.

Curtius Rufus, Quintus, Roman rhetorician, *fl.* A.D. 41–54. He wrote a worthless history of Alexander the Great in ten books; but the first two are lost, and of the remaining eight only parts have survived.

Cybele (Kubelē), *see* GREAT MOTHER OF THE GODS.

Cyclades, group of islands in the Aegean Sea, so called because they encircled (Gk *kuklos*, circle) Delos (q.v.). The central island is Syros (q.v.); others are Melos, Thera, Naxos, Ceos, Cimolus, Paros, Andros and Seriphos.

Cyclopes (Kuklōpes), 'round-faced'. Homer speaks of these creatures as a race of gigantic shepherds dwelling in a land that was afterwards identified with Sicily. Later they were said to have only one eye, in the centre of the forehead (*see* ACIS; POLYPHEMUS). According to Hesiod they were sons of Uranus and Gē, and were three in number: Arges, Steropes and Brontes (*see* TITANS). Later authors say they were killed by Apollo for having supplied Zeus with the thunderbolt that slew Asclepius, and represent them as the workmen of Hephaestus (q.v.).

The epithet 'cyclopean' is applied in architecture to walls built of unhewn stone, such as are found in many parts of Greece and Italy.

Cydippe (Kudippē): 1. Mother of Biton and Kleobis (*see* BITON). 2. *See* ACONTIUS.

Cydnus (Kudnos), river of Cilicia. Rising in the Taurus mountains and flowing by Tarsus (q.v.), it was celebrated for the coldness of its waters, in which Alexander the Great nearly lost his life while bathing.

Cyllene (Kullēnē): 1. Mountain of Arcadia. It was sacred to Hermes, who was said to have been born in a cave there and had a temple on the summit.

2. Seaport town of Elis.

Cylon (Kulōn), an Athenian of noble family, who won an Olympic victory in 640 B.C. In 632 he led an armed insurrection and seized the Acropolis, hoping to make himself tyrant of Athens. Under stress of famine (for they were closely besieged), Cylon and his adherents were driven to take sanctuary at the altar of Athena. The archon Megacles, an Alcmaeonid (*see* ALCMAEONIDAE), induced them to leave their refuge by promising to spare their lives. In the event, however, they were all put to death, excepting Cylon, who escaped. Years later, in consequence of misfortunes which were believed to have resulted from this sacrilegious act, the Alcmaeonidae were condemned to perpetual banishment from Athens. *See* EPIMENIDES.

Cynesii (Kunēsioi), a people whom Herodotus describes as dwelling in the west of Europe 'beyond the Celts'. They were most probably inhabitants of what is now southern Portugal, between the Guadiana and the Atlantic.

Cynosarges (Kunosargēs), a gymnasium outside Athens, dedicated to Heracles and originally intended for the use of those who were not of pure Athenian blood. Here taught Antisthenes (q.v.), whence his followers are believed to have been called Cynics, though others hold the name to have been derived from their dog-like (Gk *kuōn*, dog) contempt of this world's goods.

Cynoscephalae (Kunoskephalai), mountains of Thessaly between Pharsalus and Larissa, the summits of which were thought to resemble dogs' heads (Gk *kunos*, of a dog; *kephalē*, head). They are celebrated for the victory of Pelopidas over Alexander, tyrant of Pherae (365 B.C.), and for that of T. Quinctius Flamininus over Philip V of Macedon (197 B.C.).

Cynossema (Kunossēma), promontory of the Thracian Chersonnesus. The name means 'dog's tomb'. *See* HECUBA.

Cyprus (Kupros), an island of the Mediterranean, first appears in history *c.* 1500 B.C., and excavations have revealed a Neolithic culture of the 4th millennium B.C. Before the mid 7th century B.C. there were both Greek and Phoenician cities in the island. During the 6th century B.C. the whole of Cyprus had voluntarily surrendered to Darius I of Persia. The Greek cities joined the Ionian revolt (499 B.C.); but the Phoenician states remained loyal to Persia, and the rising was soon put down. In 480 B.C. Cyprus furnished 150 ships to the fleet of Xerxes, and the island was subject to Persia throughout the 5th century. The Greek cities revolted again under Evagoras (q.v.) in 391 B.C.; backed by Athens till 387, they were rent by internal feuds, and the attempts failed after an effort of fifteen years. All the Cypriot states, Greek and Persian alike, welcomed Alexander after his victory at Issus (333 B.C.). After his death the island passed to the Ptolemies and remained subject to them for most of the following period until 58 B.C. In the latter year it was annexed by Rome and attached to the province of Cilicia. Augustus made it a separate province, and among its subsequent governors was Sergius Paulus, who was converted by St Paul (A.D. 46). During the Ptolemaic period a number of Jewish settlements were made in Cyprus. A Jewish revolt in A.D. 116–17 was suppressed by Hadrian, who expelled all Jews from the island. Cyprus was one of the chief sources of copper, and one of the main centres of the cult of Aphrodite (q.v.).

Cypselus (Kupselos), tyrant of Corinth *c.* 657–627 B.C. Aristotle (*Pol.* 1310*b*) says that he began as a demagogue, and he obtained power by driving out the ruling clan of the Bacchidae. According to Herodotus the government of Cypselus was harsh; but other and less prejudiced accounts represent him as popular. His commercial and colonial enterprise certainly brought great wealth to Corinth, and he made magnificent gifts to Delphi and Olympia. His name provided a legend which no doubt lent an air of divine approval to his seizure of power. It was said that while he was still a babe an oracle or soothsayer warned the Bacchidae that he would be their undoing; that the Bacchidae sent men to kill him; but that his mother saved him by hiding him in a chest (*kupselē*), which was afterwards shown in the Heraeum at Olympia (*see* Pausanias, v. 17–19).

Cyrenaica, a district on the north coast of Africa, between the Syrtis Major and Marmarica. Its northern half was called Pentapolis (Gk *pente*, five; *poleis*, cities) from the five cities of Cyrene, Barca, Apollonia (qq.v.), Hesperis and Teucheira. Cyrenaica was subjugated by Ptolemy I. Under his successors Hesperis was known as Berenice, Teucheira as Arsinoë; Barca was eclipsed by its port, which was given the rank of a city and named Ptolemais (q.v.). In this period also

Cyrenaica suffered from the commercial rivalry of Egypt and of Carthage. Ptolemy VIII bequeathed the kingdom to his illegitimate son Ptolemy Apion, who, on his death in 96 B.C., bequeathed it in turn to Rome. Later it became a Roman province (*see also* CRETE), which was divided into two by Diocletian.

Cyrene (Kurēnē), chief city of Cyrenaica (q.v.), situated about eight miles from the coast on a plateau 1,800 ft above sea level. It was founded *c.* 630 B.C. by colonists from Thera, led by one Battus (*see* BATTIADAE). The dynasty established by him ended *c.* 450 B.C., and the subsequent republic was interrupted by periods of tyranny. Having submitted to Alexander the Great in 331, Cyrene, with the rest of Cyrenaica, became subject to the Ptolemies, passed to Rome under the will of Ptolemy Apion in 96 B.C., and was included in the province of Cyrenaica. It continued to be a great city until the Jewish revolt of A.D. 115–16; but reprisals taken by the imperial government dealt it an irreparable blow, and in the 4th century it is described as deserted. Extensive ruins have been excavated. These include the temple of Apollo founded by Battus I and reconstructed by Augustus, with a huge open-air altar (25 yards long) in front of it; the temple of Artemis (early 6th century B.C.); Roman baths; and much fine sculpture. The most remarkable features of the place, however, are the cemeteries, especially those along the rock-hewn road leading to Apollonia, where the sepulchres rise tier upon tier in the northern buttresses of the plateau.

Cyrene was the birth-place of Callimachus the poet, Carneades and Aristippus (qq.v.), the last of whom founded the Cyrenaic school of philosophy. In its heyday it was also the seat of a famous medical school. *See* C. G. B. Hyslop, *Guide to Cyrene*, 1943; F. Chamoux, *Cyrène sous la monarchie des Battalids*, 1953.

Cyrus (Kuros), Greek form of the Persian name Kurush, borne by two members of the Achaemenid dynasty.

1. Surnamed the Great, founder of the dynasty and of the Persian Empire. In 558 B.C., as head of the Persian clan of Pasargadae, he became king of Anshan, a vassal state of the Median Empire. In 553 he revolted, overthrew the empire of the Medes (549) and that of Croesus (q.v.), after which his general Harpagus subdued the whole western seaboard of Asia Minor. Babylon fell to the arms of Cyrus in 538, and in the following year he permitted the Jews to return to Palestine. At his death (528), on an expedition against the Massagetae, his empire extended from the Aegean and the confines of Egypt to the rivers Indus and Jaxartes. The conquests of Cyrus are important in Greek history as bringing the Greeks of Ionia into closer touch with the scientific achievements of Babylonia.

2. Called the Younger, second son of Darius II, Ochus, and Parysatis. In 408 B.C. he was sent by his father as satrap of Lydia, Phrygia and Cappadocia, with command of the Persian troops. He assisted Lysander and the Spartans in the Peloponnesian war, and already had his eye upon the throne when his elder brother Artaxerxes II, Mnemon, became king in 404. Accordingly he found a pretext for assembling a large army, including 13,000 Greek mercenaries, and set out from Sardis in the spring of 401. Having crossed the Euphrates at

Thapsacus, he marched downstream to Cunaxa (q.v.), 500 stadia from Babylon, where he met the army of Artaxerxes. The Greek troops were victorious, but Cyrus himself was slain. *See* TEN THOUSAND, EXPEDITION OF THE.

Cythera (Kuthēra), island about eight miles off the most southerly point of Laconia (q.v.), celebrated for its murex beds and its honey. There was a famous temple of Aphrodite, who was supposed to have emerged here from the sea.

Cyzicus (Kuzikos), town of Mysia (q.v.), founded from Miletus in 756 B.C. During the Peloponnesian War (q.v.) it was held alternately by Athens and Sparta, but became, together with the other Greek cities of Asia, subject to Persia by the Peace of Antalcidas (q.v.) in 387 B.C. Included in the kingdom of Pergamum (q.v.) *c.* 190 B.C., it accordingly passed to Rome in 133 B.C. and became part of the province of Asia. Cyzicus was held for the Romans against Mithradates in 74 B.C., and in return was granted an extension of its territory and other privileges. There are traces of the great temple of Venus, begun by Hadrian and completed by Marcus Aurelius (A.D. 167), which was sometimes reckoned among the seven wonders of the world. It was destroyed by earthquake in the 6th century A.D. *See* F. W. Hazluck, *Cyzicus*, 1910.

D

Dacia, district of central Europe. It was roughly equivalent to modern Roumania with Transylvania; the capital was Sarmizegethusa. When not engaged in war the population was occupied chiefly with agriculture and the mining of gold and silver. In the time of Augustus they made formal recognition of Roman supremacy, but continued to cross the Danube and ravage the province of Moesia (q.v.). After several reverses Rome emerged successful from two wars (A.D. 85–9) against the Dacians under their king Decebalus (q.v.). Trajan conducted two Dacian campaigns, A.D. 101–2 and 105–7, which ended in the conquest of all Dacia and its establishment as a Roman province. This, however, was abandoned by Aurelian (*see* GOTONES), who fixed the Danube as the frontier.

Daedala (Dai-), a Boeotian festival celebrated at Plataea in honour of Hera. The rites included a 'sacred marriage' and a curious fire ceremony described by Pausanias (ix. 3, 3).

Daedalus (Daidalos), 'cunning craftsman', a legendary Athenian. Excelling in the arts of sculpture and architecture, he gave instruction to his nephew Perdix, who soon surpassed him in skill and ingenuity. This aroused jealousy in Daedalus, who slew the young man and was condemned to death by the Council of Areopagus. But he escaped to Crete, where his accomplishments earned him the friendship of King Minos (q.v.) and his queen Pasiphaë; and when the latter gave birth to the Minotaur, Daedalus built the labyrinth in which the monster was to be kept (*see* THESEUS). Having at length offended Minos, he was imprisoned. Pasiphaë released him; but as Minos had set a watch on every port, Daedalus made wings for himself and his son Icarus, which he fastened on with wax. Daedalus flew safely over the Aegean (*see* COCALUS). Icarus, however, soared too near the sun: the wax melted, the wings fell away and he tumbled into the sea and was drowned.

Dalmatia, part of Illyria (q.v.). After the Roman subjugation and total annexation of Illyria in 168 B.C., Dalmatia continued rebellious. It was finally subdued by Tiberius in A.D. 9, when it became part of the Roman province of Illyricum (q.v.). Late in the 1st century A.D. it was made a separate province, which was later divided by Diocletian (q.v.) into Dalmatia and Praevalitana. These were included respectively in the dioceses of Pannonia and Moesia.

Damaratus (-os) or **Dēmaratus (-os),** Eurypontid king of Sparta *c.* 510–491 B.C. Deposed through the intrigues of his colleague Cleomenes I in favour of Leotychidas, he took refuge at the court of Darius. The latter gave him Pergamum and other cities, where his descendants still ruled at the beginning of the 4th century B.C. Damaratus accompanied Xerxes on his invasion of Greece (480).

Damascus, city of Syria and one of the most ancient in the world.

Its prosperity from early times was due to its situation on caravan routes from Egypt, Mesopotamia, Persia and the Far East. Subject in turn to the Pharaohs of the XVIIIth dynasty, to a line of native kings, to Assyria and to the Persians, it first emerges into classical history in 333 B.C. when it was betrayed to Parmenion (q.v.) after Alexander's victory at Issus. Thereafter it shared the fate of Syria in the wars of the Diadochi (q.v.) and under the Seleucidae (q.v.), Aretas (q.v.), Tigranes (q.v.) of Armenia, and finally the Romans. See DECAPOLIS; SYRIA. Damascus was celebrated in classical times for its Chalyborian wine, dried fruits, linen, cloths and cushions, as well as for its sword blades.

Damocles (-klēs), a Syracusan courtier of Dionysius I. Having praised the happiness of Dionysius in extravagant terms, he was invited by the tyrant to a banquet at which he found himself seated under a naked sword suspended by a single hair. See Cicero, *Tusc.* v. 21; Horace, *Odes*, iii. 1. 17.

Damōn and Phintias (*not* Pythias), two Pythagoreans of Syracuse renowned for their friendship. Phintias was condemned to death by Dionysius I, but in order to settle his affairs he obtained a short respite upon condition that Damon would suffer in his place if he failed to return. He presented himself for execution before the expiry of his time, and Dionysius freed them both, asking admission to their friendship. See Cicero, *De Officiis*, iii. 45.

Damophōn, Messenian sculptor of uncertain date, but commonly believed to have lived in the 2nd century B.C. He is mentioned by Pausanias, and fragments of an original group attributed to him have been excavated at Lycosura (q.v.) in Arcadia.

Danaë (Gk Danaa), daughter of Acrisius, see PERSEUS.

Danaids, The, the fifty daughters of Danaüs (q.v.).

Danaüs (-os), son of Belus and twin brother of Aegyptus. Aegyptus, King of Egypt, had fifty sons and Danaüs fifty daughters. Danaüs, for some obscure reason, feared those fifty lads and fled with his brood to Argos, where he was chosen king. Thither the sons of Aegyptus followed, demanding their cousins in marriage (*see* Aeschylus, *Suppliants*). Danaüs dared not refuse, but he gave each lady a dagger with which to slay her husband on the wedding night. All the sons of Aegyptus were thus murdered, excepting Lynceus, who was spared by Hypermestra and afterwards avenged his brothers by killing Danaüs, whom he succeeded as King of Argos. According to some poets the Danaids (daughters of Danaüs) were punished in Hades by being everlastingly compelled to fill a sieve with water. For the descendants of Lynceus and Hypermestra see PERSEUS.

Danubius or **Danuvius**, Latin name for the River Danube from its source to the Iron Gates. From this point to its mouth it was called the Ister.

Daphnai, Greek name for Tahpanhes (mod. Defenneh), a fortress near the Syrian frontier of Egypt, on the Pelusian arm of the Nile. A garrison of Carian and Ionian Greek mercenaries was established there by Psammetichus I (666–611 B.C.). Daphnai gave asylum to Jewish refugees, among whom was the prophet Jeremiah, after the destruction of Jerusalem by the Babylonians in 588 B.C. The prosperity of the place was terminated abruptly when Amasis II gave Naucratis (q.v.) a monopoly of Greek trade, *c.* 550 B.C.

Daphnē, 'laurel', daughter of the river-god Ladon, in Arcadia, by Gē; but some legends make her father one of two other river-gods, Peneus in Thessaly or Amyclas in Laconia. Ovid says that, when pursued by Apollo, she called upon her mother and was changed into a laurel, which was thenceforward Apollo's favourite tree. According to others, she was loved by Leucippus, son of Oenomaus, King of Pisa in Elis. He disguised himself as a girl and joined Daphne's companions; but his sex was revealed while bathing, and he was slain by the nymphs.

Daphnē, a beauty spot four miles west of Antioch (q.v.) in Syria. It was celebrated for a grove and temple of Apollo, and a pleasure-ground, theatres, etc.

Daphnis, in Greek legend, a Sicilian shepherd and the inventor of bucolic poetry. Son of Hermes by a nymph, he was discovered by shepherds in a laurel grove and reared by them. A naiad to whom he proved faithless blinded him, and Hermes translated him to heaven. In the first Idyll of Theocritus, however, his death is caused by unrequited love, because he had offended Aphrodite and Eros.

Dardanus (-os), legendary son of Zeus and the Pleiad Electra, founder of Dardanus on the Hellespont, eponymous ancestor of the Dardanians in Troas and progenitor (through Aeneas) of the Romans. His original home was Arcadia, whence he emigrated to Samothrace and subsequently to Troas. Here he married Batea, daughter of Teucer and became ancestor of the Trojan royal house. *See also* DEUCALION.

Dareios, generally written in English **Darius**, Greek form of the Persian name Daryavaush, which was borne by three kings of the Achaemenid dynasty.

1. Son of Hystaspes, one of the seven Persian chiefs who overthrew the usurper Smerdis. They agreed among themselves that the one whose horse neighed first at a given time and place should be king, and the lot fell upon Darius (522 B.C.). He divided the empire into twenty satrapies, quelled a Babylonian insurrection (*c.* 516) and invaded Scythia (513), which expedition took him into the interior of modern Russia, but was obliged to retreat. He then sent part of his forces to subdue Thrace and Macedonia. The revolt of the Ionian Greeks in 499 was ultimately suppressed (*see* ARISTAGORAS), but the intervention of Athens, which had led to the burning of Sardis, caused Darius to invade the Greek mainland. His army was defeated at Marathon (q.v.) in 490 B.C., and he determined upon a new and more powerful offensive. But after three years of preparation he had to postpone his scheme in order to deal with rebellion in Egypt. He died in 485 B.C., leaving the fulfilment of his plans to Xerxes (q.v.).

2. Surnamed Ochus, son and successor (425 or 424 B.C.) of Artaxerxes I, Macrocheir (*see* ARTAXERXES). He obtained the crown by putting to death his brother Sogdianus, and married Parysatis by whom he had two sons, Artaxerxes II, Mnemon, and Cyrus the Younger (qq.v.). Darius was governed by eunuchs, and the weakness of his rule

was manifest in repeated insurrections among his satraps. He died in 404 B.C.

3. Surnamed Codomannus, was raised to the throne by Bagoas in 336 B.C., after the murder of Arses (qq.v.). He was defeated by Alexander the Great (q.v.) at the Granicus (334), at Issus (333) and at Gaugamela (331). After the last battle he was seized and put to death (330) by Bessus (q.v.), satrap of Bactria.

Darēs Phrygius (Phrugios), legendary priest of Hephaestus at Troy, mentioned by Homer (*Iliad*, v. 9). To him was attributed an account of the destruction of Troy earlier than the Homeric poems. This work—if indeed it ever existed—is lost; but there is an extant Latin prose work, *Daretis Phrygii de excidio Troiae historia*, purporting to be a translation by Cornelius Nepos of the Greek original. The Latin work, however, is of much later date (? 5th century A.D.). Together with Dictys Cretensis (q.v.) it was the chief source of medieval versions of the Trojan story.

Darius, *see* DAREIOS.

Datamēs, a Carian general in the service of the Persian king Artaxerxes II, Mnemon. He revolted and defeated the generals sent against him, but was assassinated in 362 B.C. Cornelius Nepos (q.v.), who wrote his life, calls him the bravest of all barbarian generals, excepting Hamilcar and Hannibal.

Datum (Daton), Thracian town on the Strymonic Gulf, subject to Macedonia. Near by were the gold mines of Mt Pangaeus; hence the phrase 'a Datum of good things'.

Daulis, town of Phocis, the legendary capital of Tereus (q.v.).

Dea Dia, *see* ARVAL BROTHERS.

Dead Sea, lake of southern Palestine in which the River Jordan terminates. The name was first used by late Greek writers such as Pausanias, Galen, Justin and Eusebius. To Josephus it was 'the asphalt sea' or 'the Sodomitish sea', and it is from him that there dates the tradition that its waters cover Sodom and Gomorrah. Modern archaeologists are inclined to accept this view, and in 1960 divers located ruins in the south-east corner of the lake.

Decapolis (Dek-), a league of ten cities (Gk *deka,* ten; *poleis,* cities) on the eastern side of the upper Jordan and the lake of Tiberias. It was formed soon after 63 B.C. as a means of defence against the neighbouring Bedouin. The ten cities were Damascus, Philadelphia (qq.v.), Raphana, Scythopolis, Gadara (q.v.), Hippos, Dion, Pella (q.v.), Gerasa (q.v.) and Kanatha. They were linked by good roads and maintained uninterrupted communication with Greece and the Mediterranean ports. They were subject to the Roman governor of Syria. *See* G. A. Smith, *Historical Geography of the Holy Land,* 1895.

Decebalus, King of the Dacians (*see* DACIA), to whom Domitian agreed in A.D. 90 to pay an annual subsidy. He was defeated by Trajan (q.v.) and committed suicide (A.D. 106).

Decelea (Dekeleia), an Attic deme on the pass leading over Mt Parnes to Oropus and Chalcis. Its traditional friendship with Sparta (*see* DECELUS), together with the fact that it commanded the Athenian plain, led the Spartans to fortify Decelea as a permanent military base in the last ten years of the Peloponnesian war (413–404 B.C.).

Decelus (Dekelos), eponymous hero of Decelea (q.v.). He was said to have told the Dioscuri (q.v.) where Theseus had hidden their sister Helen (q.v.) at Aphidnae (q.v.). Hence the traditional friendship of Decelea with Sparta (Herodotus ix. 73).

Decemviri, 'ten men', name given at Rome to various temporary or permanent commissions appointed to carry out legal or religious functions.

1. *Decemviri legibus scribundis* took office in 451 B.C. They were all patricians; their terms of reference were to draw up a code of laws that would secure the plebeians against magisterial caprice, and during their tenure of office all other magistracies were in abeyance. At the end of that year they presented to the *comitia centuriata* a code in ten sections. A new commission was appointed for 450-449; some of its members were plebeians, and only Appius Claudius (q.v.) had sat on the previous board. They added two more sections to the code, thus completing the *Lex duodecim tabularum* (*see* TWELVE TABLES, LAW OF THE); but their tyrannical behaviour, and in particular the affair of Virginia (q.v.), led to their enforced abdication before their term was ended.

2. *Decemviri agris dandis adsignandis* were appointed as circumstances required to administer the distribution of public land (*see* AGRARIAN LAWS).

3. *Decemviri stlitibus judicandis*, an occasional body of jurors with the praetor as their president and concerned mainly with the status of individuals. Later they became a permanent and independent committee elected by the *comitia tributa*.

4. *Decemviri sacris faciundis* were a permanent board of five patricians and five plebeians, created in 367 B.C. to look after the Sibylline Books and to celebrate the Apolline and Secular games. *See also* DUUMVIRI.

Decius, Gaius Messius Quintus Trajanus, Roman emperor A.D. 249-51, born near Sirmium in 201. While campaigning on the Danube, he was proclaimed emperor by his troops, who obliged him to return to Italy and oppose the reigning emperor Philip the Arabian (q.v.). Philip was defeated and slain near Verona, and Decius ascended the throne. Meanwhile the Goths had invaded Moesia and Pannonia, and Decius at once took the field against them. Surprised by the emperor while besieging Nicopolis in Moesia, they abandoned operations and attacked the Thracian city of Philippopolis. Decius followed; but he was defeated near Beroë, and Philippopolis surrendered. The Goths, whom Decius had surrounded, offered to give up their booty and prisoners in return for a safe conduct. Decius refused; the enemy was obliged to fight, and both the emperor and his son fell in the battle. The reign of Decius was marked by one of the most severe persecutions of the Christians. *See* H. Daniel-Rops, *The Church of Apostles and Martyrs* (translated by Audrey Butler), 1960.

Decurio, a member of the town council (*senatus*) in a Roman *municipium* (q.v.). The number of *decuriones* was normally one hundred, and the qualification for office (held for life) was fixed in each town by a *lex municipalis*; the method of appointment varied. They were convened by the chief magistrate, who presided at their sessions and was obliged to carry out their decisions. Under the empire, owing to the heavy taxation to which they were collectively subjected, it became necessary to compel the qualified members of *municipia* to take office.

The term *decurio* was also applied to a cavalry officer in command of ten men.

Dēianeira, daughter of Oeneus (q.v.). The river-god Acheloüs and Heracles both loved her; the latter was victorious, and she became his wife. She unwittingly caused the death of Heracles, and killed herself in despair. *See* HERACLES.

Dēidameia, mother of Neoptolemus by Achilles. *See* LYCOMEDES.

Deinarchus (-khos), last of the ten Attic Orators (q.v.), born at Corinth *c.* 361 B.C. and settled at Athens before 336, when he was already in demand as a writer of speeches for litigants. In the affair of Harpalus (q.v.) he composed the prosecution speeches, *Against Demosthenes, Against Aristogeiton* and *Against Philocles,* all extant. Pro-Macedonian in sympathy, he was condemned to death after the restoration of the democracy by Demetrius Poliorcetes (q.v.) in 307 B.C., but escaped execution by going into exile at Calchis in Euboea. He was able to return in 292, and died probably in the next year.

Deinocrates (-kratēs), Greek architect of the 4th century B.C. He designed for Alexander the regular ground plan of Alexandria (q.v.), and constructed the funeral pyre of Hephaestion (q.v.).

Deïotarus, tetrarch of Galatia and an ally of Rome. In return for assistance during the third Mithradatic war, Pompey gave him the title of king and enlarged his territory by the addition of Lesser Armenia. Deïotarus sided with Pompey in the civil war, joining him at its outset with 600 cavalry and sharing his flight after Pharsalus. He was pardoned by Caesar in 47 B.C., and, though deprived of some territory, was left with the royal title. But he was subsequently accused by his own grandson of having attempted to murder Caesar while the latter was his guest. He was defended by Cicero (*Pro rege Deïotaro*), but before the case was ended Caesar was murdered, and no verdict was reached. Antony restored his confiscated territory in return for a large sum of money, and on the renewal of civil war Deïotarus joined Brutus and Cassius; but he supported the triumvirs after Philippi (42 B.C.) and lived out the remainder of his long reign in peace.

Deiphobus (-os), in Greek legend, son of Priam and Hecuba. He married Helen after the death of Paris, and was slain by Menelaus at the fall of Troy.

Delator, a common informer. The term was first used in imperial times of those who gave notice of moneys owing to the *fiscus* (q.v.), and then by extension to those who gave information of any criminal act (especially treason) or brought a public accusation. The practice was open to every kind of abuse in the interest of greed or spite, and the plague of *delatores* reached its greatest dimensions under Tiberius. Those who had served Nero in this way were ordered by Titus to be publicly flogged and exiled. Trajan banished those who had abetted the cruelty of Domitian; while Constantine made the profession of *delator* a capital offence.

Dēlia, quinquennial festival of the Ionians, celebrated in the island of Delos in honour of Apollo.

Delian League, a confederation of Ionian Greek city-states, under the hegemony of Athens and with its headquarters at Delos, founded in 478 B.C. Dissolved at the end of the Peloponnesian war (404 B.C.), it was revived in 377 and lasted until the victory of Philip at Chaeronea, 338 B.C.

The original purpose of the first league was to destroy the few remaining Persian strongholds and to protect the member-states against any revival of the Persian menace. Its organization, and the assessment of tribute in money or ships payable by each member, were the work of Aristeides. The affairs of the league were managed by a synod which met under the presidency of the Athenian delegates, in the temple of Apollo and Artemis at Delos. Athens also appointed a board of 'Hellenotamiai' to administer the league's treasury and receive the contributions of those allies who paid in money.

After the victory of Cimon (q.v.) on the Eurymedon (467 B.C.) the great majority of members grew tired of personal service with the fleet, and exchanged their contribution of ships for money payments. This arrangement added enormously to the strength of Athens, whose original hegemony of a free association of autonomous states quickly developed into a veritable empire. Any attempt to secede from the league was now regarded as treason, and put down as such. Of several measures which were taken in succeeding years, and which marked the inferior status of the allies, the most significant was the removal of the treasury from Delos to Athens in 454.

The resentment engendered by Athenian imperialism, as well as by the forcible establishment of democracies to suit Athenian interests in states where other forms of government had prevailed, led to numerous secessions; and the ultimate defeat of Athens in the Peloponnesian war marked the end of an empire which was already in an advanced state of dissolution.

The second league was formed in order to resist Spartan aggression; but after 371 B.C. it too gradually fell to pieces. No attempt was made to re-create the former empire of Athens, and by the time of Philip's victory at Chaeronea (338 B.C.) the Delian League had little more than nominal existence.

Delium (Dēlion), town on the coast of Boeotia. Here the Athenians were routed by the Boeotians under Pagandas in 424 B.C.

Dēlos (*see also* ASTERIA; ORTYGIA, 1), smallest island of the Cyclades (q.v.) and headquarters of the Delian League (q.v.). The most popular of many legends states that Delos was a drifting island until Zeus anchored it on behalf of Leto (q.v.), as a birth-place for Apollo and Artemis. Before 426 B.C. an annual festival in honour of Apollo was attended by delegations from the various Ionic states, including Athens; after that date it was celebrated in the third year of each Olympiad (*see* CHRONOLOGY, *Greek*). The precinct and temple of Apollo, which were among the most hallowed sites of the Greek world, have been excavated by the French School at Athens since 1877, together with other public and private buildings. All these are of great archaeological importance (see *Fouilles de Délos,* 1878 ff.).

From the close of the Persian to that of the Peloponnesian war Delos was under Athenian hegemony. It was independent for a short time after 404 until 338 B.C., and again from 332 until 166. In this latter year the Romans restored control of its worship to Athens; but they granted it certain privileges which resulted in great commercial prosperity, especially after the destruction of Corinth in 146 B.C., when it became an important centre of trade between southern Europe and the Asiatic coast. During the Mithradatic wars it remained loyal to Rome and was sacked by Menophanes in 87 B.C. From this blow it never recovered, and Pausanias's *Itinerary of Greece* (2nd century A.D.) describes it as deserted. *See* W. A. Laidlaw, *History of Delos*, 1933.

Delphi (oi-), called Pytho by Homer and Herodotus (*see* PYTHON), a place in Phocis (q.v.) celebrated for its temple and oracle of Apollo. It lay in a glen about six miles from the Corinthian Gulf, bounded on the north by the Phaedriades (the undercliffs of Parnassus) and on the south by Mt Cirphis. Through this glen the River Pleistus flows in a westerly direction and receives the waters of a brook which rises as the Castalian fountain (*see* PARNASSUS) in a gorge of the Phaedriades. Delphi was supposed to be the centre of the earth, and the exact spot was marked by a stone called the Omphalos (navel). The temple of Apollo, the treasuries (that of Thebes has been rebuilt with the original blocks), theatre, stadium (*see* PYTHIAN GAMES), monuments, offerings, etc., were situated at various levels on the north side. What is left of all these has been excavated by French archaeologists (see *Fouilles de Delphe*, the official account, and summary in J. G. Frazer's *Pausanias*, vol. v). Delphi is said to have escaped plunder by the Persians through the intervention of Apollo himself, but it was looted by the Phocians in 448 (*see* AMPHICTYONIC LEAGUE; SACRED WARS). Some of its treasures were requisitioned by Sulla in 86 B.C.; others were removed by Nero. Constantine transferred the sacred tripod and its support of intertwined serpents to the Hippodrome at Constantinople.

The Oracle. Delphi appears to have been a sacred place at least from the second millennium B.C., the sanctuary of a pre-hellenic chthonian deity whose shrine and oracle were taken over by Apollo (q.v.). Questions were submitted in writing; they were put to the Pythia (priestess) by male 'prophets', and her answers were edited, generally in hexameter verses, by the same officials. Before taking her seat on the tripod in the inner shrine she chewed the sacred bay and drank from a spring called Cassotis; but how the ensuing trance or 'frenzy' was actually induced we do not know. The oracle of Delphi foretold to an emissary of Julian the Apostate its approaching doom. It was abolished by the emperor Theodosius in A.D. 390. *See* ORACLES.

Delphinia, an annual festival celebrated at Athens in honour of Apollo on 6th or 7th Munychion. Instituted traditionally by Theseus (q.v.) to commemorate his voyage to Crete, its occurrence in early spring, when navigation began, suggests that it was originally intended to propitiate a sea-god who was afterwards confused with Apollo.

Demadēs, Athenian orator, born *c.* 380 B.C. Pro-Macedonian in sympathies, he was not above accepting bribes from the patriots, and he was eventually put to death by Antipater for having intrigued with Perdiccas (319 B.C.). None of his speeches has survived.

Dēmaratus (-os), *see* DAMARATUS.

Dēmētēr, with whom the Romans identified Ceres (q.v.), was one of the great divinities of the Greeks, goddess of earth's fruits, especially of the corn. In mythology she was the daughter of Cronus and Rhea, and sister of Zeus, by whom she became the mother of Persephone. Zeus, without the knowledge of Demeter, had promised Persephone to Aïdoneus; and while the unsuspecting maiden was gathering flowers in the Nysian plain in Asia, the earth suddenly opened and she was carried off by Aïdoneus. *See* HADES. After wandering in search of her daughter, Demeter learnt from the Sun that it was Aïdoneus who had carried her off. Thereupon she quitted Olympus in anger and dwelt upon earth among men, conferring blessings wherever she was kindly received, and severely punishing those who repulsed her (*see* CELEUS). As the goddess still continued angry, and would not allow the earth to produce its fruits, Zeus sent Hermes into the lower world to fetch back Persephone. Aïdoneus consented, but gave Persephone part of a pomegranate to eat. Demeter returned to Olympus with her daughter, but as the latter had eaten in the lower world, she was obliged to spend one-third of the year with Aïdoneus, residing with her mother for the remainder of the year. The earth now brought forth fruit again. This is the ancient legend as preserved in the Homeric hymn. In the Latin poets the scene of the rape is near Enna, in Sicily; and Ascalaphus, who had alone seen Persephone eat anything in the lower world, revealed the fact, and was in consequence turned into an owl by Demeter. The meaning of the legend is obvious: Persephone, who is carried off to the lower world, is the seed-corn, which remains concealed in the ground part of the year; Persephone, who returns to her mother, is the corn which rises from the ground, and nourishes men and animals. In Attica Demeter was worshipped with great splendour. The Athenians pretended that agriculture was first practised in their country, and that Triptolemus (q.v.) of Eleusis was the first who invented the plough and sowed corn. Every year at Athens the festival of the Eleusinia was celebrated in honour of Demeter and Persephone (*see* MYSTERIES). In works of art Demeter is represented in full attire. Around her head she wears a garland of corn-ears, of a simple riband, and in her hand she holds a sceptre corn-ears or a poppy, sometimes also a torch and the mystic basket. For the religious significance of the Demeter cult *see* T. W. Allen, W. R. Halliday and E. E. Sikes, Introduction to the Hymn to Demeter, in their second edition of the *Homeric Hymns* (1936), and the references there given. Cf. also L. R. Farnell, *The Cults of the Greek States* (1896–1909), vol. iii, pp. 29 ff.

Dēmētria, an Athenian festival of Demeter (q.v.), in which her votaries employed the common fertility rite of flogging one another with whips of twisted bark.

Demetrius (Dēmētrios), King of Bactria. Before succeeding his father Euthydemus (q.v.), he had negotiated the treaty whereby Antiochus recognized the independence of the Bactrian throne. and had conquered large parts of northern India and Afghanistan. Demetrius was eventually defeated by Eucratides (q.v.) *c.* 175 B.C.

Demetrius (Dēmētrios): (A) Name of two Antigonid kings of Macedonia.

1. Surnamed Poliorcetes (Poliorkētēs), son of Antigonus I, Cyclops (q.v.), and Stratonice, born in 337 B.C. During his father's lifetime he was engaged in constant warfare: first against Ptolemy I, Soter, and Cassander, during which he restored the Athenian democracy (307) and destroyed the naval power of Egypt (306); secondly, against the Rhodians. In this latter campaign he conducted the famous siege of Rhodes (305), and constructed those formidable engines which earned him the surname Poliorcetes (Besieger). But he failed to capture the city, and concluded a treaty (304). *See* COLOSSUS OF RHODES. In 301 Demetrius and his father were confronted with the triple alliance of Seleucus I, Nicator, Ptolemy I and Lysimachus (qq.v.), who defeated them at the battle of Ipsus (301). Antigonus was slain, and Demetrius fled to Ephesus. He was subsequently reconciled with Seleucus, and in 294 obtained the throne of Macedonia. In 288, however, he was driven out by a coalition of Pyrrhus (q.v.), Ptolemy and Lysimachus. He crossed to Asia, but was there deserted by his own troops and surrendered to Seleucus (285). The latter kept him in strict but honourable confinement, and he died in 283 B.C.

2. Grandson of the preceding and son of Antigonus II, Gonatas, whom he succeeded in 239 B.C. Soon afterwards the Achaean and Aetolian leagues combined against him, but he more than held his own. A war with invaders from the north was less successful: Demetrius II was overwhelmingly defeated by the Dardanians, and died in 229 B.C.

(B) Name of three Seleucid kings of Syria (*see also* ANTIOCHUS).

1. Surnamed Soter, son of Seleucus IV, Philopator, during whose lifetime he was sent to Rome as a hostage. After his father's death (175 B.C.) he escaped, and obtained the throne by murdering his cousin Antiochus V, Eupator. The outstanding event of his reign was a conflict with the Maccabees. Demetrius was killed in battle against the usurper Alexander Balas (*see* ALEXANDER, (C) 1) in 150 B.C.

2. Surnamed Nicator, took refuge in Crete on his father's death, but regained the throne *c.* 147 B.C., with the assistance of Ptolemy VII, Philometor. Hated for his cruelty, he was driven out by Tryphon (q.v.), who set up Antiochus, the infant son of Balas. Demetrius went to Babylon, and from there marched against the Parthians (140), who defeated and took him prisoner. He remained in captivity for ten years, at the end of which (*c.* 129) he regained his throne on the death of his brother who had ousted the son of Balas. He next undertook an expedition against Egypt; but during his absence Ptolemy VII, Physcon, installed another pretender, Alexander Zebina, who later defeated him near Damascus. Demetrius escaped to Tyre, where he was assassinated in 126 B.C.

3. Surnamed Euergetes Philometor, son of Antiochus VIII, Grypus. Ptolemy X, Lathyrus, helped him to regain part of his paternal dominions in Syria from his cousin Antiochus X, Eusebes, and he kept his court at Damascus. He next attempted to dethrone his

brother Antiochus XI, Epiphanes, but was taken prisoner by the Parthians and held until his death in 88 B.C.

Demetrius (Dēmētrios), Greek Cynic philosopher of the 1st century A.D., born at Sunium. After living for some time at Corinth he settled in Rome, where he formed a close friendship with Thrasea Paetus and Seneca, but was banished by Vespasian.

Dēmētrius (-os) Phalēreus, Greek orator, statesman and Peripatetic philosopher, born at Phalerum, near Athens, c. 345 B.C., and a pupil of Theophrastus. In 317 he was appointed governor of Athens by Cassander (q.v.); but on the restoration of the democracy by Demetrius Poliorcetes in 307 (see DEMETRIUS, (A) 1) he was condemned to death and escaped to Egypt, where he died as the result of snake-bite in 283 B.C. Demetrius is said to have suggested to Ptolemy I, Soter, the foundation of the Alexandrian library. He was a prolific author in many fields, but none of his works has survived.

Democedes (Dēmokēdēs), Greek physician. After practising at Aegina, Athens and Samos, he was taken prisoner along with Polycrates (q.v.) in 522 B.C. and sent to Darius at Susa. There he acquired fame by curing the king's foot and the breast of Atossa, his queen. In order to regain his freedom he used the good offices of Atossa to have himself sent with some Persian nobles to explore the coast of Greece with a view to the projected invasion. He escaped at Tarentum and settled at Croton, where he married the daughter of Milo the athlete.

Demochares (Dēmokharēs), Athenian orator and statesman, born c. 355 B.C. In 322 he made public protest against the surrender of the anti-Macedonian orators to Antipater, and then went into exile. He returned to Athens after the restoration of democracy by Demetrius Poliorcetes (307), but was banished in 303 because he had ridiculed a decree which overpraised Demetrius. Recalled in 298, he did good work in putting the city in a proper state of defence; but, having made an unpopular alliance with the Boeotians, he was again banished (c. 296). He finally returned c. 287, and died in 275 B.C.

Democritus (Dēmokritos), Greek philosopher who developed the atomic theory of Leucippus (q.v.). He was born c. 470 or 460 B.C. at Abdera in Thrace. He spent his large inheritance travelling in Egypt and the East, and died in extreme old age. Many legends gathered round his name, but none is supported by reliable evidence.

According to Diogenes Laertius (q.v.) he was the author of seventy-two works. These ranged over several fields, but only fragments have survived. The purity of their style is said to have been comparable with that of Plato. See C. Bailey, *The Greek Atomists*, 1928.

Dēmophōn, name of two characters in Greek legend.

1. Son of Theseus (q.v.). Having served with the Greeks against Troy, he was on his way home when he fell in love with Phyllis, daughter of the Thracian king Sithon. Pending the marriage, he went on a visit to Attica, but was absent longer than expected. Phyllis thought he had abandoned her; she committed suicide, and was changed into a tree.

2. *See* CELEUS.

Dēmosthenēs: 1. Athenian general in the Peloponnesian war. In

426 B.C., after an initial setback, he defeated a joint Spartan and Ambraciot force at Olpae and annihilated the Ambraciot survivors at Aedomenes. These two victories destroyed the enemy's influence in north-western Greece. In 425 it was largely due to Demosthenes that the Spartans in Sphacteria were defeated and taken prisoner. Next year, however, he failed to take Megara, and his unsuccessful invasion of Boeotia was followed by the Athenian defeat at Delium. In 413 he was sent to reinforce Nicias (q.v.) at Syracuse, and during the disastrous retreat of their forces Demosthenes and his troops were surrounded in an orchard, where he surrendered and was put to death.

2. The greatest of the ten Attic Orators, born in 384 or 383 B.C. His father, also named Demosthenes, who belonged to the deme of Paeania, was a master-cutler, swordsmith and upholsterer; his mother's name was Cleobule. The elder Demosthenes died when his son was seven years old, leaving him and his sister, together with a comfortable fortune, to the care of guardians who proved dishonest. When he came of age, therefore, Demosthenes found himself with only a small fraction of what was due to him. With the help of Isaeus (q.v.), he embarked upon a series of lawsuits against the defaulters; but though he obtained judgment he failed to recover his inheritance. He then became a professional writer of speeches for litigants, and sometimes spoke himself. It is to this period that his biographers attributed those doubtless apocryphal stories of his efforts to overcome an impediment of speech, from which he probably did in fact suffer and which seems to have gone hand in hand with a far from athletic physique. It is said, for instance, that he used to fill his mouth with pebbles and declaim on the seashore to make himself audible above the thunder of the waves; that he recited poetry while running uphill to acquire perfection in breathing; that he copied out the *History* of Thucydides eight times in order to improve his style, and so forth.

About 355 B.C. Demosthenes entered the sphere of practical politics. His initial efforts were directed to those reforms in public life which he saw to be necessary if Athens was to play her part in the impending struggle against foreign aggression. The principal speeches in this cause are *Against Androtion* (355), *Against Leptines* (354) and *On the Navy Boards* (354). His first direct approach to foreign policy (352) is represented chiefly by the two speeches *For the Megalopolitans* and *Against Aristocrates*.

In the next period Demosthenes was concerned almost exclusively with the immediate problem of Macedonian expansion. His outstanding performances at this time, while he tried to rouse his fellow citizens to a sense of the peril, are the three *Philippics* (351, 344 and 341) and the three *Olynthiacs* (349 and 348). Thus for fourteen years he continued the struggle against Philip, and neither bribes nor threats could turn him from his purpose. His impassioned oratory did bestir the Athenians, and did create some degree of unity among the city-states; but the Macedonian phalanx was irresistible, and swept away the glory that was Greece at Chaeronea, 338 B.C.

Notwithstanding this misfortune, Demosthenes continued to serve Athens; and in 336 it was proposed by Ctesiphon that he should receive a golden crown from the state, and that his splendid services should be publicly acknowledged in the theatre at the Great Dionysia. But Aeschines (q.v.) at once gave notice of his intention to prosecute Ctesiphon for having proposed an unconstitutional measure. The trial was delayed, for reasons unknown to us, until 330, when Aeschines delivered his speech *Against Ctesiphon*. This was in effect an attack upon the whole public life of Demosthenes, who replied with his tremendous oration *On the Crown*. His victory was complete.

In 324 Demosthenes was accused with eight others of having received money from Harpalus (q.v.). The charge, in retrospect, was manifestly absurd, at least in the case of Demosthenes; but he was found guilty and imprisoned. He soon managed to escape, and fled first to Aegina, then to Troezen. On the death of Alexander (323) the Greek states revolted, and Demosthenes returned in triumph; but in the following year the confederates were overwhelmed at Crannon, and Antipater threatened to lay siege to Athens unless the leading patriots were surrendered to him. Demosthenes and others were condemned to death by the Ecclesia, and fled to Aegina, whence Demosthenes removed alone to the island of Calauria (q.v.). Hither he was followed by some emissaries of Antipater, who tried to lure him from the sanctuary of Poseidon in which he had sought refuge. But rather than surrender he took poison (322 B.C.).

Sixty orations of Demosthenes have come down to us. *See* the edition by S. H. Butcher, *Demosthenis Orationes*, 1903. There are numerous editions of separate speeches. The public orations have been translated by A. W. Pickard-Cambridge, 1912 (published in Everyman's Library, 1961). *See also* S. H. Butcher, *Demosthenes*, 1881; A. W. Pickard-Cambridge, *Demosthenes and the Last Days of Greek Freedom*, 1914; C. D. Adams, *Demosthenes and his Influence*, 1927.

Dentatus, Manius Curius, Roman general, probably a Sabine by birth, was considered in later times a model of old Roman simplicity and frugality. His decisive victory over the Samnites during his first consulship (290 B.C.) terminated an intermittent war of fifty years (*see* SAMNIUM). As consul for the second time (275) he defeated Pyrrhus (q.v.) near Beneventum, and in his third consulship (274) he finally subdued the Samnites and Lucanians. Dentatus was censor in 272, when he began to build an aqueduct, but died (270 B.C.) before its completion.

Deucalion (-kaliōn), the Greek 'Noah', was son of Prometheus and King of Phthia. When Zeus caused a flood by pouring water on the earth, he and his wife Pyrrha escaped in a chest which he had previously made on the advice of his father. After floating for nine days the chest grounded on Mt Parnassus. Deucalion stepped from the chest and offered sacrifice to Zeus, who granted him a single boon. He chose men, and the god told him to throw stones over his head; these became men, while those thrown likewise by Pyrrha became women. This story occurs in the *Bibliotheke* attributed to Apollodorus (q.v.). It is somewhat elaborated by Ovid (*Metam.* i. 243–415). There is a Boeotian version in which Deucalion becomes Ogyges, founder of Thebes, and an Arcadian version, where he is replaced by King

Dardanus. Other accounts substitute Mt Gerania or Mt Othrys in Thessaly for Parnassus.

Deva, a Roman fortress in Britain (q.v.), on the site of modern Chester; built *c.* A.D. 78. From A.D. 122 it was occupied by Legio XX, Valeria Victrix. Unlike many legionary fortresses it never became a town. Excavation of an amphitheatre within the fortress area was begun in 1960.

Dexippus (-os), Greek general and historian of the 3rd century A.D., who bore the Roman *praenomen* and *nomen* Publius Herennius. He defeated the Heruli when they invaded Greece in 269, and a statue was erected in his honour. The inscribed base of this figure is extant: it informs us that Dexippus was an hereditary priest of the Eleusinian family of the Ceryces, and that he had been king-archon and archon eponymous at Athens. Dexippus wrote three works, of which fragments survive: an epitome of Arrian's *Ta met' Alexandron*; a history of the wars between Rome and the Goths in the 3rd century; and a chronological history from the earliest times to A.D. 270.

Diadochi (-dokhoi), 'Successors', name given to the Macedonian generals who fought for the empire of Alexander the Great (q.v.). They were Antigonus and his son Demetrius Poliorcetes, Seleucus, Ptolemy, Eumenes and Lysimachus (qq.v.). The kingdoms which **they** formed are known as hellenistic.

Diadochi, Wars of the, a series of conflicts (321–281 B.C.) in which the Diadochi (*see* preceding article) fought for possession of Alexander's empire. In the first of these (321) Perdiccas was murdered by his own troops while invading Egypt, and Craterus was defeated and killed in Asia by Eumenes. The second was fought between Antigonus and Eumenes (316); it ended with the capture of Eumenes, who was put to death.

The next stage is represented by an ineffectual attempt on the part of Antigonus to dispose of Cassander; it ended in stalemate. Meanwhile, however, the struggle between Antigonus and Ptolemy had begun. Demetrius was beaten at Gaza (312), but made good his defeat at Myus, occupied Athens and restored the democracy (307), and in 305 began the famous siege of Rhodes (*see* DEMETRIUS, (A) 1). In 301, while on his way to confront Cassander in Thessaly, he was recalled to Asia by his father in order to meet a new threat in the shape of a coalition between Ptolemy, Seleucus and Lysimachus. The ensuing defeat and death of Antigonus at Ipsus (301) led to the partition of Antigonus's kingdom, mostly to the advantage of Seleucus.

The final stage in the wars of the Diadochi begins with the death of Cassander in 297 B.C. Three years later Demetrius Poliorcetes secured the throne of Macedonia, but surrendered to Seleucus in 285. Ptolemy died in 283, and two years later Lysimachus was defeated and slain by Seleucus at the battle of Coron. In the following year Seleucus himself, the last of the Diadochi, was murdered by Ptolemy Ceraunos.

Diagoras (5th century B.C.), Greek poet and sophist, a native of Melos, surnamed 'the Atheist'. In consequence of his attacks upon popular religion, he was condemned to death at Athens (411) and fled first to Pallene and then to Corinth, where he died. None of his works is extant.

Diana, ancient Italian divinity; probably in origin a woodland deity who became associated with the peasant family and thus became a fertility goddess. Perhaps as a result of Etruscan influence, she was early identified with Artemis (q.v.), many of whose attributes she consequently assumed. The most famous shrine of Diana was at Aricia (q.v.) in the Alban Hills: here she was worshipped with curious rites in conjunction with a woodland god, Virbius. Her cult was believed to have been introduced upon the Aventine at Rome by Servius Tullius.

Diaulos, 'double course': 1. Greek foot race over a distance of about a quarter of a mile. 2. The colonnade surrounding the main court of a Greek palaestra.

Dicast (Gk Dikastēs), a member of the judiciary at Athens. All male citizens over thirty years of age were qualified to serve in this capacity, provided they had not been deprived of civic rights and were not indebted to the state. Six thousand were chosen annually by lot, and they served in panels called *dikasteria*. Payment was introduced by Pericles, and in the time of Aristotle was at the rate of three obols a day. For a detailed account of the complicated procedure of assigning dicasts to the various courts *see* Aristotle, *Athenian Constitution*, 63 ff.

Dichaearchus (Dikhaiarkhos), Greek Peripatetic philosopher, historian and geographer, *fl. c.* 320 B.C. A native of Messana in Sicily, he was a pupil of Aristotle and a friend of Theophrastus. Only fragments of his works survive.

Dictator, an extraordinary magistrate of the Roman republic, whose office was created (501 B.C.) to deal with situations which could not be safely entrusted to the consuls with their divided authority (*see* CONSUL). He was supposed to be nominated at discretion by one of the consuls, but in fact the senate intimated both the necessity and the nominee. Once nominated, his *imperium* was confirmed by the *comitia curiata* (*see* COMITIA), and all other magistrates became his subordinates. He was attended by twenty-four lictors (q.v.), who, at least in the early period, bore the axes with the *fasces* (q.v.) even within the city walls. The latter privilege emphasized the dictator's power of life and death; but that power was circumscribed in 300 B.C. by the *Lex Valeria* which made it subject to the right of appeal (*provocatio*) within the city boundaries.

The main purposes of the dictatorship were as follows: (*a*) To handle a military crisis, during which, however, the dictator's authority was limited to Italy. (*b*) To put down civil strife. (*c*) To exercise criminal jurisdiction. In any of these cases he was termed 'administrative' and held office for six months. After 216 B.C., during the second Punic war, we find several innovations, e.g. the election of a dictator by the people, his command of an army outside Italy, etc.

A dictator might also be appointed to perform such minor functions as holding elections, celebrating games or exercising religious rites. In these cases he retired as soon as the particular duty was fulfilled.

The dictatorship in its true character, as described above, must be distinguished from the so-called dictatorships of the late republic. That of Sulla (q.v.) was a provisional government, that of Caesar (q.v.) a temporary monarchy; and it was in order to prevent its further use for such purposes that it was abolished by law in 44 B.C.

Dictynna (Diktunna), *see* BRITOMARTIS.

Dictys Cretensis, the reputed author of an extant work in Latin (translated from a Greek original) on the Trojan war, divided into six books, and entitled *Ephemeris Belli Trojani*. In the preface we are told that it was composed by Dictys of Cnossus, who accompanied Idomeneus to the Trojan war; but it probably belongs to the time of the later Roman Empire. *See* the edition by F. Meister, 1873; N. E. Griffin, *Dares and Dictys*, 1907. *See also* DARES PHRYGIUS.

Didius Salvius Julianus, Marcus, Roman emperor 28th March–2nd June A.D. 193, grandson of Salvius Julianus, a jurist in the reign of Hadrian, and son of a distinguished general. On the death of Pertinax the praetorian guards put up the throne for auction, and it was eventually knocked down to Didius. The senate grovelled, true to form; but the disgusting farce was too much for the people and for the troops stationed in the provinces. The legions of Britain, Illyricum and Syria revolted and proclaimed Septimius Severus (q.v.), who commanded in Pannonia. When Severus marched on Italy the praetorians were cowed; the senate somersaulted and condemned Didius to death, and he was executed. *See* the account by Dio Cassius (lxxiii. 11–17).

Dido or **Elissa**, the reputed founder of Carthage (q.v.). She was daughter of the Tyrian king Belus, and sister of Pygmalion, who succeeded to the crown after the death of his father. Dido was married to her wealthy uncle, Acerbas, who was murdered by Pygmalion. Upon this she sailed from Tyre with his treasures, accompanied by some noble Tyrians, and passed over to Africa. Here she purchased as much land as might be enclosed with the hide of a bull, but she ordered the hide to be cut up into the thinnest possible strips, and with them she surrounded a spot on which she built the citadel called Byrsa. Around this fort the city of Carthage arose. The neighbouring king, Iarbas, jealous of the prosperity of the new city, demanded the hand of Dido in marriage, threatening Carthage with war in case of refusal. Dido had vowed eternal fidelity to her dead husband; but as the Carthaginians expected her to comply with the demands of Iarbas, she pretended to yield, and under pretence of soothing the *manes* of Acerbas by expiatory sacrifices, she erected a funeral pile, on which she stabbed herself in presence of her people. After her death she was identified with Tanit, the tutelary goddess of Carthage. Virgil introduces the story of Dido into the *Aeneid*, but with various modifications. According to the traditional chronology, there was an interval of more than 300 years between the capture of Troy (1184 B.C.) and the foundation of Carthage (853 B.C.); but Virgil makes Dido a contemporary of Aeneas, with whom she falls in love on his arrival in Africa. When Aeneas hastened to seek the new home which the gods had promised him, Dido, in despair, destroyed herself on a funeral pyre.

Didymus (Didumos), Greek scholar and grammarian, nicknamed

Chalcenterus, i.e. 'brazen-bowelled', because of his enormous industry. He was born 63 B.C., and worked at Alexandria and Rome. There are extant fragments of his treatise on Aristarchus's recension of Homer; and the surviving scholia on Pindar, Sophocles and Aristophanes are derived from his commentaries. Didymus is said to have written more than 3,500 books. He died in A.D. 10.

Dio Cassius, whose correct name was Cassius Dio Cocceianus, Roman historian, born *c.* A.D. 150 at Nicaea in Bithynia. His father was Cassius Apronianus, governor first of Dalmatia and then of Cilicia under Marcus Aurelius; his maternal grandfather was Dio Chrysostom (*see* next article). He went to Rome in 180, and held many responsible offices, both there and in the provinces, under Commodus, Caracalla, Septimius and Alexander Severus. He returned to Nicaea soon after 229, and died there in 235.

The principal work of Dio Cassius, who wrote in Greek, was a History of Rome in eighty books, from the landing of Aeneas in Italy to A.D. 229. Books xxxvii–liv have survived intact, together with large parts of xxxvi and lv–lx. These cover the period 68 B.C.–A.D. 47. The contents of the missing portions are known from an 11th-century epitome of Xiphilinus and from the 12th-century *Manual of Universal History* by Zonaras, who followed Dio closely. *See* edition and translation of the extant books by E. Cary, 9 vols. (Loeb Library).

Dio Chrysostom (Gk *Khrusostomos*, golden mouthed), Greek sophist and rhetorician, born at Prusa in Bithynia *c.* A.D. 40. He afterwards settled at Rome, was banished by Domitian, but returned on the accession of Nerva (96). His subsequent movements are unknown, but he is believed to have died *c.* 115. Eighty speeches attributed to Dio Chrysostom have survived; they are really essays on political, moral and philosophical subjects. *See* text and translation by J. W. Cohoon and H. Lamar Crosby, 5 vols. (Loeb Library).

Diocese (Gk *dioikēsis*, administration). The political reforms begun by Diocletian and completed by Constantine divided the civil administration of the empire among thirteen 'dioceses', subdivided into 120 'provinces'. These dioceses (of which Oriens was the largest, Britain the smallest) were governed by praetorian prefects, proconsuls or vicars, the provinces by rectors or exarchs.

Diocletian, Gaius Aurelius Valerius Diocletianus, Roman emperor A.D. 284–305, born of obscure parentage at Dioclea, near Salona in Dalmatia, 245. After a distinguished career in the army under the emperors Aurelian and Probus, he accompanied the Persian expedition of Carus (q.v.), upon whose death and that of Numerianus (q.v.) he was proclaimed emperor by the troops at Calchedon. The assassination of Carinus (q.v.) quickly followed, and Diocletian was acknowledged everywhere. In order to deal with the barbarian menace on the northern frontiers he appointed Maximian (q.v.) joint Augustus in 286. In 293 the work of government was further divided by the creation of two Caesars, Constantius Chlorus and Galerius (qq.v.). Diocletian made important administrative divisions of the provinces, and was responsible for far-reaching military and financial reforms which were completed by Constantine. First, the provinces were grouped in twelve *dioceses*, the largest of which (Oriens) contained four. Under Constantine these dioceses were themselves included in the four praefectures of Italy, the Gauls, the Orient and Illyria. Second, there was created a vast bureaucracy directly subject to the emperor, which would gradually oust local autonomy. Third, a new system of taxation was introduced, which in rural districts amounted to forced contributions of labour and produce, and so led to the ultimate serfdom of the country populations; while the municipal councils were made responsible for city taxes. The attempt to stabilize prices in 301 was a complete failure as also was an attempt to revive the old religion by a severe persecution of the Christians in 303. For military reforms *see* ROMAN ARMY. Diocletian has sometimes been compared with Augustus and described as second founder of the empire. It is true that both faced roughly the same problems, but their circumstances were different. As Rostovtzeff has shown, Augustus succeeded in restoring not only the State but also the prosperity of the people. Diocletian and Constantine sacrificed the interests of the people to the preservation of the State.

Diocletian and Maximian abdicated in 305, and Diocletian retired to his great palace at Salona (q.v.), where he lived until his death in 313. *See* M. Rostovtzeff, *Social and Economic History of the Roman Empire*, 1926.

Diodorus Cronus (Diodōros Kronos), Greek philosopher of the Megarian school, *fl.* 4th century B.C. His great dialectical skill, which won him the nickname of 'Dialectician', is illustrated by a famous sophism. The impossible, argued Diodorus, cannot proceed from the possible; nor can a past event become other than it is. But if an event, at a given moment, had been possible, it would have given rise to an impossibility. Therefore the original event also was impossible.

Diodorus (-ōros) **Siculus**, Greek historian, a native of Agyrium in Sicily, was a contemporary of Julius Caesar and Augustus. His *Bibliotheca historica*, 'Historical Library', in forty books was an unreliable annalistic work covering a period from the remotest ages to the beginning of Caesar's Gallic war (58 B.C.). We possess Books i–v and xi–xx, namely, the mythical history of Egypt, Assyria, Aethiopia and Greece, and the years 480–302 B.C. Of the rest only fragments survive. *See* the text and translation by C. H. Oldfather (Loeb Library).

Diodotus (-os), a Seleucid satrap of Bactria (q.v.), who rebelled against Antiochus II *c.* 255 B.C. and founded an independent kingdom. As his power spread over neighbouring provinces, Arsaces (q.v.), chieftain of the Parni, fled before him into Parthia (q.v.) and became founder of the Parthian Empire. Diodotus died *c.* 238 and was succeeded by his son Diodotus II; but the latter was overthrown by Euthydemus (q.v.).

Diogĕnĕs: 1. Greek natural philosopher, *fl. c.* 460 B.C., a native of Apollonia in Phrygia. In his poem *On Nature*, of which large fragments survive, he attempted to reconcile the theories of Anaximenes and Anaxagoras (qq.v.) by accepting air as the primary element but endowing it with intelligence. Aristophanes ridicules his views as those of Socrates (*Clouds*, 264 ff.).

2. Called 'the Cynic', Greek philosopher, born at Sinope in Pontus

c. 412 B.C. Settling later in Athens he was attracted by the teaching of Antisthenes (q.v.) and became his pupil. The stories told of his acid tongue and the austerity of his life are held by some to be probably true; but others maintain that they cannot be relied upon except as caricature. On a voyage to Aegina he was captured by pirates and sold as a slave to Xeniades of Corinth. At Corinth he spent the remainder of his life as tutor to the two sons of Xeniades and preaching self-control. He died in 323 B.C. Diogenes believed that virtue consisted in the avoidance of all physical pleasure, that pain and inconvenience in their several forms were conducive to goodness. *See* F. Sayre, *Diogenes of Sinope*, 1938.

3. Surnamed the Babylonian, Greek Stoic philosopher of the 2nd century B.C., a pupil of Chrysippus. He succeeded Zeno of Tarsus as head of the Stoa at Athens, and later, in 155 B.C., was sent with Carneades and Critolaus (qq.v.) on the Athenian embassy to Rome.

Diogenes Laërtius (Diogēnēs Laërtios), Greek biographer of whose life nothing whatever is known. He lived probably during the reign of Alexander Severus (A.D. 222–35), and may have been an adherent of the Epicurean school. Some believe that he was born at Laërte in Cilicia, while others derive his surname from the family of the Laërtii, whom they assume to have been his patrons. Diogenes was the author of an extant book, *Lives of the Philosophers*, an uncritical work of no philosophical value, but affording much precious information on the private lives of those with whom it deals. Among the treasures it has preserved is the will of Aristotle. *See* the edition with translation by R. D. Hicks (Loeb Library). *See also* R. Hope, *The Book of Diogenes Laërtius*, 1930.

Diomedeae Insulae, five small islands in the Adriatic, north of the promontory of Garganum in Apulia. They were named after Diomedes, son of Tydeus, who was buried in one of them (*see* DIOMEDES, 2). In the largest of them, called Trimerus (mod. San Domenico), died Julia, grand-daughter of Augustus (*see* JULIA, 6).

Diomēdēs: 1. Legendary king of the Bistones in Thrace, whose man-eating mares were carried off by Heracles. *See* TWELVE LABOURS OF HERACLES, 8.

2. Son of Tydeus (q.v.) by Deipyle, and successor of Adrastus (q.v.) as King of Argos. According to the *Iliad*, his father was killed before Thebes while Diomedes was still a boy, but he was afterwards represented as one of the Epigoni. Diomedes sailed against Troy with eighty ships; was, next to Achilles, the bravest of the Greeks; and enjoyed the special favour of Athena. *See also* GLAUCUS, 2.

Later stories represent him as helping Odysseus (q.v.) to carry off the palladium from Troy, after the fall of which he returned to Argos and found his wife Aegiale living in adultery with Hippolytus (or Cometes, or Cyllabarus). He therefore quitted Argos and went to Aetolia. He subsequently set sail for home, but was driven by a storm on to the coast of Daunia (Apulia) in Italy, where he married Euippe, daughter of the king, and lived there until his death at an advanced age. He was buried in one of the islands named after him (*see* DIOMEDEAE INSULAE); and his companions, inconsolable at their loss, were changed into birds.

Dion, tyrant of Syracuse, where he was born in 408 B.C., son of Hipparinus and son-in-law of Dionysius the Elder (q.v.). A close friend of Plato (q.v.), who had visited the court of Dionysius, he took advantage of the latter's death (367) to invite Plato to Syracuse with a view to withdrawing the new tyrant, Dionysius the Younger, from his vicious courses and to training him up as a philosopher-king. But the historian Philistus (q.v.) stirred up trouble between Dion and Dionysius, and the former was banished. Dion resided at Athens until 357, when he landed at Syracuse with a small force and was welcomed as the new ruler. Dionysius meanwhile was absent in Italy. He hurried back, but was defeated and driven into exile. In the following year (356) Heracleides (q.v.) secured Dion's expulsion; but his own incompetence led to the speedy recall of Dion, who remained in power until his assassination in 353 B.C.

Diōnē, cult-partner of Zeus at Dodona (q.v.). In Olympian mythology, however, Hera is the wife and partner of Zeus, and classical writers from Homer onwards give various accounts of Dione. According to the *Iliad* she was mother of Aphrodite by Zeus. Hesiod represents her as a daughter of Oceanus; later poets make her nurse or mother by Dionysius or Tantalus of Pelops and Niobe, or even a daughter of Uranus and Gē.

Dionysia (-nusia), festivals of Dionysus (q.v.), particularly the five celebrated annually in Attica. These were the *Little* or *Rustic Dionysia*, a country festival in the month Poseidon (December); the *Lenaea* at Athens in the next month, Gamelion; the *Anthesteria* in the following month, Anthesterion; the *Great* or *City Dionysia*, in Elaphebolion (late March); and the *Oschophoria*, in Pyanepsion (end of October).

Dionysius (-nusios): 1. 'The Elder', tyrant of Syracuse, was born *c.* 432 B.C. He started his career in a government office, but was soon recognized as an able demagogue. Owing to the mismanagement of a war against Carthage by the Syracusan commander, Dionysius succeeded in having himself appointed sole general with full powers (405), and this date marks the beginning of his tyranny. His measures to secure his position at home included the fortification of Epipolae, the crushing of his political opponents, and the depopulation of Naxos, Catina and Leontini (qq.v.), which he turned over to foreign mercenaries and Sicels. Next he turned his arms against the Carthaginians, who were at that time the strongest power in Sicily. Two wars (397–396 and 392) went in his favour, and the authority of Carthage was limited to the north-west corner of the island. In 391 he crossed with an army to the mainland, and the capture of Rhegium in 386 made him the leading power in Magna Graecia. In 383 war was resumed with Carthage; it ended in 378 with the overwhelming defeat of Dionysius, and Carthage recovered the whole of Sicily west of the River Halykas.

The character of Dionysius has been painted in the darkest colours by some ancient writers, who saw in him the prototype of autocracy at its worst. But whilst he deprived Syracuse of her freedom, he made her the most prosperous city and the most formidable power in Europe. He enjoyed friendly relations with both Sparta and Athens, sent magnificent delegations to the Olympic games and entertained such men as Plato (q.v.) at his court. He even fancied himself as a dramatist, in which capacity he often competed at Athens, and at length won the prize at the Lenaean festival in the year of his death, 367 B.C.

2. 'The Younger', son and successor of the preceding. He was driven out by Dion (q.v.) in 357, and fled to Locri. After the murder of Dion (353), Dionysius regained possession of Syracuse, but was again expelled by Timoleon (q.v.) in 343 B.C. He then retired to Corinth, where he spent the remainder of his life, and according to some authorities was reduced to support himself by keeping a school.

Dionysius (-nusios) of Halicarnassus, Greek historian and rhetorician, who settled in Rome early in the reign of Augustus. His *Roman Antiquities* in twenty books covered the history of Rome from mythical times to 264 B.C. Books i–ix have survived intact, together with most of x and xi. Of the remainder we possess fragments and an epitome. More important are his critical works. These include *The Arrangement of Words*; *Commentaries on the Attic Orators* (Lysias, Isaeus, Isocrates, Deinarchus); *On the Admirable Style of Demosthenes*; *On Thucydides*; two *Letters to Ammaeus* on Demosthenes and Thucydides, and a *Letter to Cn. Pompeius* on Plato.

The *Roman Antiquities* are edited by E. Cary with his revision of Spelman's translation (Loeb Library). The *Arrangement of Words* was edited with translation in 1910 by W. Rhys Roberts, whose translation of the three *Letters* was published in 1901.

Dionysius (-nusios) Periēgētes, Greek author of an hexameter poem entitled *Periēgēsis tēs oikoumenēs*, a description of the world. He probably lived *c.* A.D. 300, perhaps at Alexandria. His work was long used as a school text-book; it was translated into Latin by Avienus and by Priscian in the 4th and early 6th century A.D. *See* E. H. Warmington, *Greek geography*, 1934.

Dionysius (-nusios) Thrax, author of the first Greek grammar, *fl. c.* 100 B.C. He was born at Alexandria, son of a Thracian father (whence his surname), studied under Aristarchus of Samothrace and later taught rhetoric at Rhodes. The grammar was edited by G. Uhlig (1884), and there is an English translation by J. Davidson (1874). Only fragments of other works by Dionysius have survived.

Dionysus (Dionusos), called also by the Lydian name **Bacchus** (Bakkhos), is believed to have been originally a Thracian fertility god worshipped in the form of a bull with orgiastic rites. He represents the irrational element in man in contrast to Apollo (q.v.), who means all that we understand by self-discipline. The date of his entry into Greece is uncertain, but his cult spread rapidly (being specially popular with women), in face of official opposition which is perhaps reflected in the numerous cult-myths which grew around his name (*see* PENTHEUS). Under the influence of Apollo the orgies were gradually toned down, and Dionysus is found associated with Apollo at Delphi.

In classical mythology he was the son of Zeus and Semele, the daughter of Cadmus of Thebes. Before his birth, Semele was persuaded by Hera, who came to her in disguise, to request the father of the gods to appear to her in the same glory in which he approached his own wife Hera. Zeus unwillingly complied, and appeared to her in thunder and lightning. Semele, being seized by the flames, gave premature birth to a child; but Zeus saved the boy, sewed him up in his thigh and thus preserved him till he came to maturity.

After his birth Dionysus was brought up by the nymphs of Mt Nysa (Nysiads). When he had grown up, Hera drove him mad. He went to Egypt, thence proceeded through Syria, then traversed all Asia, teaching the inhabitants of the different countries of Asia the cultivation of the vine and introducing among them the elements of civilization. After he had thus gradually established his divine nature throughout the world, he took his mother out of Hades, called her Thyone and rose with her into Olympus.

Various mythological beings are described as the offspring of Dionysus; but among the women who won his love none is more famous than Ariadne (q.v.). In Homer Dionysus does not appear as one of the great divinities; he is simply described as the god who teaches man the preparation of wine. As the cultivation of the vine spread in Greece, the worship of Dionysus likewise spread; and after the time of Alexander's expedition to India, the celebration of the Bacchic festivals assumed more and more their wild and dissolute character. On account of the close connection between the cultivation of the soil and the earlier stages of civilization, he is regarded as a law-giver and a lover of peace. As the Greek drama had grown out of the dithyrambic choruses at the festival of Dionysus, he was also regarded as the god of tragic art. In the earliest times the Graces or Charites were the companions of Dionysus; but afterwards we find him accompanied in his expeditions and travels by Bacchantic women, called Lenae, Maenades, Thyiades, Mimallones, Clodones, Bassareae or Bassarides, all of whom are represented in works of art as raging with madness or enthusiasm, their heads thrown backwards, with dishevelled hair, and carrying in their hands thyrsus staffs (entwined with ivy, and headed with pine-cones), cymbals, swords or serpents. Sileni, pans, satyrs, centaurs and other beings of a like kind are also the constant companions of the god. The animal most commonly sacrificed to him was the ram. Among the things sacred to him, we may notice the vine, ivy, laurel and asphodel; the dolphin, serpent, tiger, lynx, panther and ass. Dionysus himself is generally depicted as a youthful god. The form of his body is that of a man, but approaches the female by its softness and roundness. For his position in later mystical religion see ORPHISM. See especially W. K. C. Guthrie, *The Greeks and their Gods*, ch. vi, for a discussion of Dionysus and his worship.

Diophantus (-os), Greek mathematician of Alexandria, *fl.* 3rd century A.D. He is said to have been the discoverer of algebra, and his writings were the starting-point of Fermat's work. The six surviving books of Diophantus's *Arithmetica*, and a work on polygonal numbers, have been edited by Sir T. L. Heath (1910).

Dioscoridēs, Pedianos, Greek doctor who served in the Roman Army during the reign of Nero, a native of Anazarba in Cilicia. His *Materia Medica*, an account of 600 or so medicinal herbs, together with a description of many animal products useful in medicine, has been translated by R. T. Gunter (1934). The text was edited by K. Sprengel in 1829.

Dioscuri (Dioskouroi), 'lads of Zeus', in Greek and Roman mythology, the joint name of Castor and Polydeuces (Latin, Pollux), twin sons of Leda, and brothers of Helen and Clytaemnestra. According to Homer they are the sons of Tyndareus (q.v.) and Leda, while Helen is daughter of Leda by Zeus. Later tradition made the Dioscuri sons of Zeus (hence 'Dioscuri') and Leda. The god visited her in the form of a swan, and she brought forth two eggs, one containing the Dioscuri, the other Helen. Yet another version makes Zeus the father of Polydeuces, and Tyndareus of Castor and Clytaemnestra.

According to this last version Polydeuces, as son of Zeus, was immortal, whereas Castor was subject to old age and death. In a battle with Idas and Lynceus (qq.v.), Castor fell by the hand of Idas (whom Zeus promptly killed with a flash of lightning), and Polydeuces slew Lynceus. At the request of Polydeuces, Zeus allowed him to share his brother's fate and to live on alternate days in the underworld and with the gods; or he rewarded their attachment by placing them among the stars as Gemini.

They were also said to have taken part in the expedition of the Argonauts (q.v.), during which they founded the city of Dioscurias in Colchis, and Polydeuces killed the Bebrycian king Amycus in a boxing match. For their rescue of Helen from Aphidnae *see* THESEUS.

The Dioscuri received divine honours at Sparta, whence their cult spread throughout the Dorian world. Poseidon had given them power over the winds and waves, and they were worshipped particularly as the friends of sailors, to whom they appeared during storms in the shape of what is now known as St Elmo's fire. Hence too, perhaps, it was that they came later to be identified with the Cabeiri (q.v.).

The Dioscuri are usually represented in works of art as youthful horsemen, with egg-shaped helmets, crowned with stars, and with spears in their hands. At Rome, their worship was introduced at an early date. They were believed to have assisted the Romans against the Latins in the battle of Lake Regillus; and the dictator A. Postumius Albinus during the battle vowed a temple to them. This temple was erected in the Forum, opposite the temple of Vesta. The equites (q.v.) regarded the Dioscuri as their patrons. *See* J. Rendel Harris, *The Cult of the Heavenly Twins*, 1906.

Diphylus (-phulos), Greek poet and actor of the new Attic comedy, a contemporary of Menander (q.v.), born at Sinope and died at Smyrna. The *Casina*, *Asinaria*, *Rudens* and *Commorientes* of Plautus are adaptations from Diphylus.

Dirce (-kē), wife of Lycus, *see* ANTIOPE, 2.

Dōdōna, in Epirus (q.v.), the seat of the most ancient of hellenic sanctuaries, with an oracle of Zeus (*see* DIONE; ORACLES). Responses were obtained by interpretation of the rustling of wind in an old oak-tree. In order to render the sounds more distinct brazen vessels were sometimes hung in the tree. Sometimes, too, recourse was had to the cooing of doves in the branches or to the murmur of a fountain. The *Iliad* describes Dodona as the abode of Selli, who may have been the original priests. The later priestesses were called *peleiai* (doves). During the 19th century excavations revealed what were thought to be remains of a temple. But it has been suggested more recently (1929) that there was no actual temple, only an altar surrounded by tripods. Among those who are recorded as having consulted the oracle at Dodona are Croesus and Lysander. Athens sought its advice on several occasions; but its principal clients were the Acarnanians, Aetolians and Boeotians. *See* P. Gardner, *New Chapters in Greek History*, ch. xiv, 1892; J. Friedrich, *Dodonorica*, 1935.

Dolabella, Publius Cornelius (*c.* 80–43 B.C.), Roman general and husband of Cicero's daughter Tullia. Soon after the outbreak of civil war (49) he transferred his allegiance from Pompey to Caesar, with whom he fought at Pharsalus (48), and later in Africa and Spain. On Caesar's death he seized the consulship and sided with Brutus and his fellow conspirators. Bribed by Antony he again changed sides and accepted the province of Syria. Having plundered Greece and Asia on his way there, he murdered Trebonius, proconsul of Asia, who had denied him admission to Smyrna. Cassius was sent to take his place, and besieged him in Laodicea. To avoid capture Dolabella ordered one of his soldiers to kill him.

Domitianus, Titus Flavius, called in English **Domitian,** Roman emperor A.D. 81–96, born at Rome, A.D. 51, the younger son of Vespasian. Although he held the rank of Caesar, he took little or no part in public affairs during the reign of his father (69–79) and that of his brother Titus (79–81). On his accession there was every sign that he meant to govern well, nor were these hopes disappointed during the first years of his rule. Abroad, however, things did not go well. His defeat of the Chatti in 83 and his extension of the north-east frontier (*see* LIMES GERMANICUS) were later offset by his failures against the Quadi, Sarmatae and Marcommanni; and war against the Dacians, though the outcome of its several campaigns was not always in their favour, ended with Domitian having to buy peace and undertake payment of an annual subsidy to their king Decebalus (A.D. 90).

Meanwhile the recall of Agricola (q.v.), whose achievements in Britain (q.v.) had roused the emperor's jealousy, foreshadowed a change; and the revolt of Antonius Saturninus in Upper Germany (88 or 89) marked the turning point in the career of Domitian, who behaved thenceforward as a madman. The rebellion was suppressed without much difficulty, but anyone to whom he took dislike, no matter for what reason, was charged with conspiracy and put to death. These victims included his cousin Flavius Clemens, husband of his niece Domitilla, who was banished on suspicion of favouring Christianity. The monstrous tyranny could no longer be endured, and Domitian was murdered in his bedroom by Stephanus, a freedman of Clemens, on 18th September A.D. 96. *See* the Life by Suetonius; Dio Cassius, lxvi and lxvii; Tacitus, *Agricola* 18–22; *Histories*, iii and iv; Juvenal, *passim*.

Dorian Hexapolis, The, a league formed by six Dorian settlements on the coast of Caria and neighbouring islands. They were Lindus, Ialysus and Camirus in Rhodes, the island of Cos, and Cnidus and Halicarnassus on the mainland.

Dorians, The. According to Greek traditions Aegimius, King of Doris (q.v), was driven from his dominions by the Lapithae (q.v.) but was reinstated by Heracles. When, therefore, the sons of Heracles were expelled from Peloponnesus they took refuge in Doris; and it was in order to restore their descendants (*see* HERACLIDAE) that the Dorians invaded that territory, whence the invasion is often called the Return of the Heraclidae.

The true facts about this prehistoric migration, which took place in successive waves between *c.* 1250 and *c.* 1100 B.C., are inevitably uncertain; but the following summary account represents the theory most widely accepted today. The migration began from the Danube valley by way of the Morava and the Vardar. Somewhere in modern Servia it split up into 2 groups. Group I crossed the Pindus into Epirus, and then moved southward occupying Acarnania, Aetolia, Locris and Phocis. The more adventurous crossed the Gulf of Corinth to establish themselves in Elis and Achaea. During the early years of this movement, branches of the group (known later as Boeotians and Thessalians), recrossed Pindus and occupied the territories known in classical times as Boeotia and Thessaly. Meanwhile Group II remained east of Pindus and came down through Thessaly to the River Spercheus and the Maliac gulf. Here it too split up. *Section* 1 forced its way by land into Central Greece, and occupied what was later called Doris. Then it, like Group I, crossed the Gulf of Corinth; but taking a more easterly course than the latter, it moved via Achaea and Arcadia into Laconia and Messenia. *Section* 2 embarked on the Maliac gulf, sailed through the Euboean strait, rounded Attica and landed near Nauplia. It then conquered Argolis and spread outwards to Epidaurus and Aegina, Corinth and Megara. Some scholars, however, maintain, on the strength of certain myths, that section 2, after passing the Euboean strait, continued south-east to conquer south Asia Minor and several Aegean islands, including Crete; only then did it turn back and conquer Argolis. The Dorians destroyed the ancient Mycenean civilization, with which perished the art of writing (Linear B script). In classical times they predominated in Peloponnesus and had also settled in the Sporades and Crete, in Caria (*see* DORIAN HEXAPOLIS), as well as in several colonies on the east and south coasts of Sicily. Their rivalry with the Ionians (q.v.) lay behind the internal conflicts of Hellas down to the 4th century B.C. and is exemplified most typically in the Peloponnesian war (q.v.).

Dōris, district of central Greece, between Mts Oeta and Parnassus, containing the source of the Cephissus (q.v.). Though quite small, and possessing only four townships, it commanded the road from Heraclea to Amphissa. It was the traditional home of the Dorians (q.v.), on which account they were assisted by a Spartan army in 457 B.C. and again in the second Sacred war (*see* SACRED WARS). *See* Herodotus, i. 56, viii. 31; Thucydides, i. 107, iii. 92.

Drachma (Drakhmē), *see* COINAGE, 1.

Dracon (-kōn), author of the first written code of laws at Athens, said to have been framed during his year as Archon Eponymous (621 B.C.). The laws of Draco carried the penalty of death for almost every transgression, and became proverbial for their severity. They were all abolished by Solon (q.v.) except those dealing with homicide.

Drepanum (-on), meaning 'sickle': 1. (mod. Trapani), town on the north-west coast of Sicily, founded by the Carthaginians, and the place where Anchises (q.v.) was said to have died.

2. Town of Bithynia, the birth-place of Helena, mother of Constantine the Great, and called after her Helenopolis.

Drusilla: 1. Daughter of Germanicus and Agrippina, believed to have had incestuous relations with her brother, the emperor Caligula, who deified her after her death in A.D. 38.

2. Daughter of Herod Agrippa I, king of the Jews. *See* FELIX, ANTONIUS.

3. Mother of the emperor Tiberius. *See* LIVIA DRUSILLA.

Drusus, Marcus Livius, name of two Roman politicians.

1. Tribune of the plebs with C. Gracchus (q.v.), 122 B.C. In that year Gracchus proposed certain measures of reform which Drusus threatened to veto. The senate, anxious to discredit and be rid of Gracchus, persuaded Drusus to propose similar measures that went even further than those which he had challenged. The bill passed, contrary to the expectations of Drusus who would have nothing to do with carrying out its provisions. In return for his services he received the consulship (112) with the title *patronus senatus*. In the following year, as governor of Macedonia, he was the first Roman commander to reach the Danube. The year of his death is uncertain.

2. Son of the preceding, tribune of the plebs in 91 B.C. His measures for judicial reform were unpopular alike with the senate and with the *equites*; but he managed to force them through the *Comitia* by including them in a single bill with some subsidiary proposals which appealed to the mob. Drusus then made known his determination to secure for the Italians the long-desired franchise. Senatorial opposition increased: the laws of Drusus were declared null and void as having been carried against the auspices, and Drusus himself was murdered by an unknown assassin. His death was the signal for the Social War (q.v.).

Drusus, Nero Claudius, Roman general, son of Tiberius Claudius Nero (*see* NERO, TIBERIUS CLAUDIUS) by Livia Drusilla (q.v.), and younger brother of the emperor Tiberius. He was born in the house of Augustus (38 B.C.) three months after the latter's marriage with Livia. In 13 B.C. he helped his brother to subdue the Rhaeti and Vindelici; then, as governor of the three Gauls, he pacified those provinces, which were on the brink of revolt. He then turned to deal with the Germans beyond the Rhine, and in the course of three triumphant campaigns (12–9 B.C.) advanced as far as the Albis (Elbe). On his return he was thrown from his horse, and died thirty days later. Drusus was among the most distinguished men of his age. His military genius went hand in hand with beauty of person and grace of manner; so that he was popular with the army and the people. He married Antonia, daughter of Mark Antony, who bore him three children: Germanicus, Claudius (qq.v.), and Livilla (*see* LIVIA, 2).

Drusus Caesar, sometimes called Drusus junior to distinguish him from his uncle Nero Claudius Drusus (*see* preceding article), was born *c.* 15 B.C., son of the emperor Tiberius. In A.D. 14, on the accession of Tiberius, he quelled a mutiny of troops in Pannonia, was governor of Illyricum in A.D. 17, and in A.D. 21 received the *tribunicia potestas* which marked him out as heir to the throne. Sejanus (q.v.), who aspired to imperial honours, seduced his wife Livilla and obtained her co-operation in poisoning her husband (A.D. 23).

Dryads, *see* NYMPHS.

Dryope (Druopē): 1. Husband of Andraemon (*see* ANDRAEMON, 2), mother of Amphissus by Apollo. She was afterwards carried off by the Hamadryads and became a nymph.

2. Wife of Anius (q.v.).

Duilius, Gaius, Roman general during the first Punic war. As consul in 260 B.C. he defeated the Carthaginian fleet off Mylae. This was the first victory ever won by the Romans at sea; it was due entirely to the foresight of Duilius, who, appreciating the inexperience of his troops, transformed the battle into something closely resembling an action on land by the use of grappling irons and boarding bridges. *See* COLUMNA ROSTRATA.

Duoviri, *see* DUUMVIRI.

Duris (Douris), Greek historian whose parents were natives of Samos (q.v.). He was born *c.* 340 B.C. and studied under Theophrastus. As a lad he won a prize at the Olympic games. Later in life he seems to have returned to Samos, of which he was for some time ruler. His works included a History (371–281 B.C.); a Life of Agathocles; *Annals of Samos*; and various critical treatises. Only fragments survive, but the ancient authorities do not appear to have held his writings in much esteem.

Durnovaria (mod. Dorchester), Romano-British town and an important road centre. Many remains have been unearthed. Near by, at Maumbry Rings, there are remains of a Roman amphitheatre.

Durovernum (mod. Canterbury), town of the Cantii in Britain (q.v.). Extensive Roman remains have been brought to light since 1950.

Duumviri or **Duoviri,** 'two men', joint officials under the Roman republic and early empire, appointed to carry out a variety of functions whether at Rome or in the colonies and municipalities.

Duumviri aediles, colonial magistrates for finance and building.

Duumviri iure dicundo, municipal magistrates concerned with the administration of justice.

Duumviri quinquennales, municipal officers elected every fifth year, for one year, to perform the duties of censorship.

Duumviri sacrorum, officials who originally had charge of the Sibylline books (*see* DECEMVIRI).

Duumviri aedi bocandae, whose duty under the early republic was to supervise the building of a temple.

Duumviri navales, officials to equip a fleet. Originally appointed by the consuls, they were chosen by the people after 311 B.C.

Duumviri perduellionis, earliest court for trying cases of treason.

Duumviri viis extra urbem purgandis, assistants of the aediles (q.v.), to whom they were responsible for keeping clean the streets outside the walls of Rome. Their duties were taken over by the *curatores viarum* before 12 B.C.

Dyrrachium (mod. Durres, formerly Durazzo), name given by the Romans late in the 4th century B.C. to the ancient Greek city of Epidamnus in Illyria, which had been founded jointly from Corcyra and Corinth towards the end of the 7th century. Enmity developed between Epidamnus and Corcyra, and the resulting hostilities helped to precipitate the Peloponnesian War (q.v.). In 312 B.C. Epidamnus was seized by Glaucias, King of Illyria; but soon afterwards it passed to the Romans, who changed its name to Dyrrachium. Its importance was mainly due to its being the western terminus of the Via Egnatia (q.v.) on the Adriatic. Here Pompey worsted Caesar in 48 B.C. Augustus settled a colony of veterans (*c.* 30 B.C.), which later became a *civitas libera*.

E

Ebora (mod. Evora), town of Hispania Ulterior and afterwards in Lusitania (*see* HISPANIA). From 80 to 72 B.C. it was the headquarters of Sertorius (q.v.). Later it received privileges from Julius Caesar and was known as Liberalitas Julia.

Eburacum or **Eboracum** (mod. York), Roman town of Britain (q.v.). It was founded *c.* A.D. 78 as fortress of the Ninth Legion, after the annihilation of which (*c.* A.D. 120) it was occupied by the Sixth Legion. The site was that now occupied by York Minster, and the walls can be partly traced. A civilian town grew up on the other side of the river, near the present railway station; it attained municipal status. The emperors Septimius Sever·· and Constantius Chlorus (qq.v.) both died at Eburacum. *Colonia* (q.v.) *c.*160

Ecbatana (Ek-), Greek name of the capital of Media (q.v.), which in Old Persian was called Hangmatána (mod. Hamadan). Though surrounded by seven walls and possessing a citadel, Ecbatana was captured by Cyrus in 550, and later by Alexander the Great in 330 B.C.

Ecclesia (Ekklēsia), the general assembly of freemen at Athens, including all men who had completed their eighteenth year and who had not been deprived of civic rights. It was convened by the *prutaneis* (*see* BOULE); discussion was limited to an agenda prepared by the Boule, but the Ecclesia might instruct the latter to include any matter on the next agenda.

There were four ordinary meetings in each *prutaneia*. One of these (probably the first) was called the 'sovereign', at which (*a*) magistrates who were considered to be performing their duties satisfactorily were confirmed in office; (*b*) impeachments were introduced; (*c*) inventories were read of property confiscated by the state; (*d*) claims to inheritances and wards of state were heard; (*e*) the Boule reported on general security and the corn supply. At the 'sovereign' meeting in the sixth *prutaneia*, besides the foregoing items of business, (*a*) a vote was taken as to whether or not the power of ostracism should be exercised in that year; (*b*) complaints against professional accusers were heard, and also cases involving non-performance of promises made by individuals to the state.

The second ordinary meeting in each *prutaneia* was devoted to the hearing of formal petitions, and anyone might then address his fellow citizens on any matter, public or private. The third and fourth ordinary meetings were assigned for other purposes, but were bound to discuss three religious subjects, three secular and three arising from the introduction of foreign ambassadors.

Emergency meetings, and those which the country people were required to attend, were summoned respectively by the herald of the Boule with a trumpet and by special messengers. *See* NOMOTHETAI.

Pay for attending the Ecclesia was introduced at the beginning of the 4th century B.C. The rate rose from one to two and then to three obols, until the time of Aristotle, when it was one and a half drachmas for the 'sovereign' meeting and one drachma for the other three.

Voting was by show of hands and a simple majority. When, however, the issue affected an individual's rights (e.g. in the case of ostracism) the ballot was secret and a vote of at least 6,000 was required in favour of the motion.

The regular meeting-place of the Ecclesia was the Pnyx. From the 5th century B.C. onwards it met sometimes in the Theatre of Dionysus, and this was its regular place in the 3rd century B.C. The business of the Ecclesia was preceded by certain formalities, which included a report on the weather omens; and the assembly was promptly dismissed if the signs foretold thunder, rain or an eclipse.

See Aristotle, *Athenian Constitution*, ed. J. E. Sandys, 1912; A. H. J. Greenidge, *Handbook of Greek Constitutional History*, 1896.

Echidna (Ekh-), in Greek legend a monster, half woman and half serpent, became by Typhon (q.v.) mother of the Chimaera, of the many-headed dog Orthus, of the dragon who guarded the apples of the Hesperides, of the Colchian dragon, of the Sphinx, of Cerberus, of Scylla, of the Lernaean Hydra, of the eagle which consumed the liver of Prometheus, and of the Nemean lion. She was killed in her sleep by hundred-eyed Argus (*see* ARGUS, 1).

Echo (Ēkhō), in later Greek mythology, an Oread or mountain nymph personifying disembodied sound or echo. According to Ovid (*Metam.* iii. 356 ff.) she kept Hera talking and thus prevented her spying on Zeus during one of his amours. The goddess punished her by depriving her of speech, except the power to repeat the last words uttered by someone else. In this condition she fell in love with Narcissus (q.v.); but as her affection was not returned she faded away until there was nothing but her voice. Longus (q.v.) says that she refused the advances of Pan, who caused her to be torn to bits by frenzied shepherds. Earth concealed her remains, which continue to sing and imitate other sounds.

Ecnomus (Eknomos), a promontory in Sicily, 24 miles south-east of Agrigentum. Off this promontory a Roman fleet defeated the Carthaginians in 256 B.C. In the plain a little to the north Agathocles (q.v.) was defeated by Hamilcar in 310 B.C.

Edessa: 1. Greek name for the ancient Mesopotamian city of Urhāi (mod. Urfa). According to Pliny it was also called Antioch, perhaps because it was rebuilt by Antiochus IV Epiphanes. After the death of Alexander (323 B.C.) Edessa was included in the Seleucid kingdom until about 132 B.C., then it became the capital of an independent state (Osroëne) ruled by a native dynasty and remained more or less autonomous until Hadrian made it a dependency of Rome. Caracalla made Edessa a Roman colony in 216 and was murdered near by in the following year. Gordian restored the native state in 242, but in 244 it again became directly subject to Rome. *See* R. Duval, *Histoire d'Édesse*, 1892.

2. (formerly Aegae). The original capital of Macedonia, about 46 miles west of Thessalonica. After the seat of government was removed

by Philip II to Pella (q.v.) it remained the royal burial-place, but the royal tombs were plundered by the Gallic mercenaries of Pyrrhus (q.v.). Philip himself was murdered at Edessa in 336 B.C. In Roman times the place remained important as commanding the Via Egnatia (q.v.).

Eetiön, *see* AEETION.

Egeria, spirit of a stream (from which the Vestals drew water for their rites) in the grove of the Camenae, just outside the Porta Capena at Rome; also of a stream in the grove of Diana at Aricia (q.v.). She was imagined to have been the lover of Numa (q.v.) and to have advised him in the matter of his religious forms. It was said that on Numa's death she retired weeping to Aricia, where Diana changed her into a stream. Egeria was worshipped by pregnant women, and also as a prophetic deity, in association with Diana and the Camenae.

Egesta or Aegesta (Aig-), Greek name for Segesta (q.v.).

Egnatia, Via, name given to the stretch of the Via Appia between Gnatia (q.v.) and Brundisium. The continuation of this road from Dyrrachium (q.v.) to Byzantium, the Via Egnatia properly so called, was the great military highway between Italy and the East.

Egypt (Gk Aiguptos; Lat. Aegyptus) was bounded, in ancient times, north by the Mediterranean, east by Palestine (*see also* ARABIA, I) and the Red Sea, west by the Libyan desert. The southern boundary was Aethiopia (q.v.), the division being at the First Cataract, near Syene. From Syene the Nile flowed due north for some 500 miles through a valley whose average width is about seven miles to a point just below Memphis. Here the river divided into seven branches (now only two), which flowed through a low alluvial plain, called from its shape the Delta, into the Mediterranean. The whole district thus described is periodically laid under water by the overflowing of the Nile from April to October. The subsiding waters leave behind a rich deposit of mud, which forms the fertile soil of Egypt. Westward, but forming part of Egyptian territory, were five oases in the Libyan desert (*see* AMMON).

The history of Egypt is divisible into four periods: from the earliest times to 525 B.C.; from 525 to 332 B.C.; from 332 to 30 B.C.; and 30 B.C. onwards. During the first of these periods Egypt was governed by a long succession of native and other dynasties, and there was considerable trade with Minoan Crete and Mycenean Greece. The Homeric poems show some slight acquaintance with Egypt and its river, and refer to the wealth and splendour of Thebes with its 'hundred gates'. The Pharaohs from Psammetichus (Psamêtk) I to Psammetichus III, i.e. from 664 to 525 B.C., all appear to have employed Greek mercenaries (*see* DAPHNAI).

The second period begins with the Persian conquest under Cambyses (q.v.) in 525 B.C. Egypt now became a satrapy of Persia. It remained so until 332 B.C., with the exception of about sixty years (*c*. 405–341 B.C.), during which Greek mercenaries (*see* H. W. Parke, *Greek Mercenary Soldiers*, 1933) again helped to secure Egyptian independence (*see* AGESILAUS II; CHABRIAS; IPHICRATES). Herodotus visited the country *c*. 440 B.C.

The third period opens in 332 B.C., after the battle of Issus, when Alexander was welcomed by the Egyptians as their liberator. During his year's sojourn he founded Alexandria (q.v.), went on pilgrimage to the oracle of Ammon, reorganized the government, and entrusted taxation and control of the armed forces to Greek officials. After his death in 323 B.C., Egypt fell to the Ptolemies and remained subject to them until 30 B.C., when it became a Roman province.

This year marks the commencement of the fourth period. Augustus treated Egypt as part of his personal domain. Upon its fertile soil depended the Roman corn supply, and a rebellious governor, by holding back the grain ships, might reduce the capital to starvation. Augustus therefore placed the province under an imperial prefect of equestrian rank; and no senator was allowed to hold office, or even to enter the country, without the emperor's leave. Except that Romans replaced Greeks in most of the higher positions, the old order of government was largely retained; the prefect took the place of the Ptolemaic king, his power being limited by right of appeal to Caesar. The first prefect was C. Cornelius Gallus (q.v.). His successor, Aelius Gallus, attempted unsuccessfully to conquer Arabia Felix (q.v.) with a view to obtaining the spice trade; but the valuable Indian trade was secured for Egypt by Claudius. The third prefect, C. Petronius, repelled an Ethiopian invasion (see AETHIOPIA). Other events in the history of Egypt under Rome were the great Jewish revolt in the reign of Trajan, the Bucolic War (q.v.) in that of Marcus Aurelius, the brief conquest by Zenobia (q.v.), and the persecutions of Christians under Septimius Severus, Decius, Diocletian and Galerius (qq.v.). *See* J. G. Milne, *A History of Egypt under Roman Rule*, 3rd ed., 1924; E. Bevan, *A History of Egypt under the Ptolemaic Dynasty*, 1927.

Eilithyia (-thuia), Greek deity who assisted women in childbirth. In the *Iliad* the Eilithyiae (plural) are called daughters of Hera; but in the *Odyssey* and later poets there is only one goddess of this name. She was often identified with Artemis or Hera, and accordingly by the Romans with Juno Lucina (see JUNO).

Eirene, *see* IRENE.

Elagabalus or **Heliogabalus**, Roman emperor A.D. 218–22, born at Emesa *c*. 205. His real name was Varius Avitus; his mother, Soaemias, was a daughter of Julia Maesa, aunt of Caracalla. On the death of Caracalla (217), Varius and his cousin Alexander Severus were taken by their grandmother from Rome to Emesa, where Varius was appointed high priest of the Syro-Phoenician sun-god Elagabalus (Gk Heliogabalus). He enjoyed great popularity among the Syrian legions, because of his personal beauty and the gorgeous ceremonies over which he presided; and this popularity was enhanced by a rumour, originating from Maesa herself, that he was an illegitimate son of Caracalla. An insurrection ended in the defeat and death of Macrinus (q.v.) and the proclamation of Varius as emperor under the name Marcus Aurelius Antoninus (218). He chose, however, to reign as Elagabalus, in honour of his heavenly patron. But the abominable vices and extravagance of their master shocked even the Roman rabble: the second of two attempts by the emperor's partisans to murder Alexander resulted in a mutiny of the praetorian guards, in which Elagabalus and his mother were slain. *See* Gibbon, *Decline* *and Fall*, ch. vi; G. Duviquet, *Héligabale*, 1903; J. S. Hay, *The Amazing Emperor Heliogabalus*, 1911.

Electra (Elektra), name of three figures in Greek legend.

1. Daughter of Oceanus, wife of Thaumas, and by him mother of Iris and the Harpies (qq.v.).

2. One of the Pleiades (q.v.); mother by Zeus of Dardanus (q.v.) and Iasion. According to Hyginus (q.v.) she is represented in the constellation Pleiades by the dim star which faded when Troy fell.

3. Daughter of Agamemnon. She does not occur in the Homeric list of his daughters, but was identified by later writers with Laodice. *See* ORESTES.

Eleia, *see* ELIS.

Eleusis, city and deme of Attica, about 14 miles north-west of Athens. It was situated on a ridge near the Bay of Eleusis, opposite the island of Salamis. Its fame is due to the Eleusinian Mysteries (*see* MYSTERIES). To the west of the town lay the Rharian, where Demeter (q.v.) was said to have sown the first seeds of corn. The entire sacred precinct, including the great Hall of Initiation, has been excavated; many of the buildings were erected or restored in Roman times. *See* K. Kourouniotes, *Eleusis* (Eng. trans.), 1936.

Eleutheropolis (mod. Beit Jibrin), city of Palestine, 25 miles from Jerusalem on the road to Gaza. The original site, known in Old Testament times as Mareshah, was about one mile south-west of Beit Jibrin. Having been sacked by Judas Maccabaeus (163 B.C.) and taken by John Hyrcanus (110 B.C.), it was restored to independence by Pompey (63 B.C.); but twenty-three years later it was destroyed by the Parthians. Rebuilt by the Romans as a fortress on the present site with the name Baitogabra, it was favoured by Septimius Severus, who called it Eleutheropolis ('free city') in A.D. 200. In the neighbourhood are caves and the site of a second-century Roman villa. The former contain paintings of the Roman period; in the latter was found (1922) a wonderful mosaic. *See* H. Thiersch and J. P. Peters, *Painted Tombs in the Necropolis of Marissa*, 1905; F. M. Abel, 'Découvertes recentes à Beit-Djebrīn' in *Revue Biblique*, 1924.

Elis or **Eleia,** country of Peloponnesus; bounded north by Achaea, east by Arcadia, south by Messenia and west by the Ionian Sea. It was divided into three districts: Hollow (or Lowland) Elis, Pisatis and Triphylia. *Hollow Elis*, famous for its horses, cattle and byssus, was the most northerly of the three; it was watered by the rivers Peneus and Ladon, and its principal towns were Elis, Cyllene and Pylos. *Pisatis* stretched south from Hollow Elis to the right bank of the River Alpheus (q.v.), where was the scene of the Olympic games (*see* OLYMPIA). *Triphylia* extended south from the Alpheus (q.v.) to the northern boundary of Messenia.

The original inhabitants of the country, under the name of Epeians, were said to have taken part in the Trojan war. At the time of the Dorian invasion (*c.* 1000 B.C.), according to tradition, Elis fell to the share of Oxylus and the Aetolians. They intermingled with the Epeians and formed a powerful kingdom in the north, which before the end of the 8th century B.C. had established supremacy over the whole country, and acquired the right of celebrating the Olympic games which had hitherto belonged to Pisatis. A long struggle ensued for the possession of this privilege. The Pisatans regained it in 668 and again in 664; but in 572 B.C. the contest ended with their subjugation and the destruction of their city by the Eleans. After the Peloponnesian war, during which the Eleans had defected from the Spartan alliance, the Spartans deprived them of Triphylia and the mountainous parts of Hollow Elis, together with the presidency of the games. After the Spartan defeat at Leuctra, in 371 B.C., the Eleans attempted to recover this territory, but were prevented by the Arcadian League (see ARCADIA). In 366 B.C. war broke out between the Eleans and the league. The former appealed to their old enemy, Sparta, who obliged the Arcadian troops to withdraw, and the whole country became once more subject to the Eleans, who also resumed their rights at Olympia. After Chaeronea (q.v.), in 338 B.C., Elis allied herself with the Macedonian conquerors until the death of Alexander, when she joined the Aetolian League (q.v.). Coming eventually within the Roman province of Achaea, she was allowed certain privileges owing to the sanctity of Olympia. For legends connected with Elis see PELOPS.

Elissa, see DIDO.

Elpēnŏr, one of the companions of Odysseus (q.v.) who were changed by Circe (q.v.) into swine. One day, after being restored to human shape, he drank too much wine and fell asleep on Circe's flat roof, but tumbled off and broke his neck. Elpenor's was the first shade encountered by Odysseus in the underworld.

Elymi (Elumoi), a people who, with the Sicani (q.v.), were the earliest inhabitants of Sicily. They appear to have originated in Asia Minor, where they had already come under Greek influence. Their chief towns were Segesta and Eryx (qq.v.).

Elysium (Elusion), the pre-hellenic paradise, which the Greeks identified with their Islands of the Blessed (q.v.). In Homer it forms no part of the realms of the dead, but lies in the far west, on the banks of Oceanus; it is a land of perfect happiness, governed by Rhadamanthus (q.v.). Pindar makes Rhadamanthus and Cronus (qq.v.) joint rulers. To Elysium, according to Homer, only favoured heroes were transported, being carried there alive and endowed with immortality (see CADMUS). In Hesiod, however, it is already a place for the blessed dead, and from the time of Pindar it was believed that admission was the reward only of a good life. In the Latin poets it is a part of Hades (q.v.).

Emerita Augusta (mod. Mérida), capital of Lusitania (see HISPANIA), on the River Anas (Guadiana). Founded by the Romans in 25 B.C., it soon became one of the finest cities in the peninsula. The river was spanned during the reign of Trajan by a granite bridge consisting of eighty-one arches and measuring 2,575 feet in length. Other Roman remains include parts of the city wall, a triumphal arch, an aqueduct, a theatre and a bridge over the River Alba Regia.

Emesa, city of Syria on the Orontes, with a famous temple of the Sun; birth-place of Elagabalus (q.v.), who rebuilt the temple; made a Roman colony by Caracalla (see COLONIA). It was at Emesa that Aurelian subdued the rebellion of Zenobia (q.v.).

Empedocles (c. 490–430 B.C.), Greek philosopher and statesman, born at Acragas in Sicily of a distinguished democratic family. Having helped to overthrow an oligarchy at Acragas he refused the proffered crown and retired later to Peloponnesus, where he died. Empedocles enjoyed the highest renown among the ancients for his learning, his eloquence and his medical knowledge. Of his poem on nature and his purificatory hymns only fragments have survived. First among the pluralists, who opposed the teaching of Parmenides and the Eleatic school, Empedocles held as his central thesis that there are four ultimate elements (fire, air, water, earth) eternally united and eternally parted by two active corporeal forces which he called love and strife. See J. Burnet, *Early Greek Philosophy*, 4th ed., 1930.

Among the legends that grew up around Empedocles's name, the most famous is one which tells how he threw himself into the crater of Mt Aetna in order that his sudden disappearance might cause him to be thought a god; but the volcano threw up one of his sandals and thus revealed the manner of his death.

Endymion (Endumiōn), in Greek legend, a beautiful young shepherd or hunter whom Selene (the moon) visited each night as he slept an eternal sleep in a cave on Mt Latmos, in Caria. Various reasons were alleged to account for his sleep; but the most common explanation was that it had been imposed by the goddess herself in order that she might enjoy Endymion's company undisturbed.

Enna, see HENNA.

Ennius, Quintus (239–169 B.C.), Latin poet, born at Rudiae in Calabria. While serving as a centurion in the Roman army in Sardinia during the second Punic war he attracted the notice of Cato the elder (*see* CATO, I), who brought him in his train to Rome (204 B.C.). Here he made a living by teaching Greek and adapting Greek plays for the Roman stage until 189 B.C. when he accompanied M. Fulvius Nobilior (q.v.) on his Aetolian campaign. Through the influence of Nobilior's son he afterwards obtained Roman citizenship, and spent the remainder of his life in Rome.

Horace and Cicero bear witness to his intelligence and pleasing character as revealed in writings that covered a wide range. These included many tragedies (mostly adaptations from or translations of Euripides) and miscellanies on a great variety of subjects, but his fame rests chiefly upon the *Annales*, an epic poem in dactylic hexameters on the history of Rome, of which about 600 lines have survived. This work, which marks him as the father of Latin poetry, inspired Virgil's *Aeneid*. It lacks the polish of Virgil and Lucretius, but its merit and the conception that lay behind it are summed up in a celebrated phrase of Ovid: 'Ingenio maximus, arte rudis'. The fragments have been edited by E. M. Steuart (1925). *See also* E. Norden, *Ennius und Vergilius*, 1915.

Ēōs, 'Dawn', daughter of Hyperion (q.v.), sister of Helios (the sun) and Selene (the moon). By her husband Astraeus she was mother of Boreas, Eurus, Zephyrus and Notus, and by Tithonus of Memnon (qq.v.). *See also* CEPHALUS; ORION.

Epameinōndas (c. 418–362 B.C.), Theban general. In 385 he fought on the Spartan side at Mantineia, where he saved the life of Pelopidas (q.v.). He broke the power of Sparta and established the hegemony of Thebes (q.v.), first by his victory at Leuctra (q.v.) in 371, and then in the following year by his liberation of Messenia (q.v.). In 369 he led the Boeotian forces into the isthmus of Corinth, secured Sicyon for Thebes and founded Megalopolis (q.v.). Twice again, in 366 and 362, he successfully invaded Peloponnesus. In the second of these campaigns he defeated the newly formed Spartan League at Mantineia (q.v.), but was killed in the hour of victory. He is said to have fallen by the hand of Gryllus (q.v.), son of Xenophon. Epameinondas was one of the most outstanding of the ancient Greeks, both as a military leader and as a man of the highest ability and integrity; but his achievements died with him.

Ephebeum (Ephēbeion), a hall set apart in Greek palaestra (q.v.) for the exercises of youths between sixteen and eighteen years of age.

Ephebi (Ephēboi), name given at Athens to a class of young men from eighteen to twenty years of age. A detailed account of their admission to its ranks, of their organization and of their duties is given by Aristotle in the forty-second chapter of the *Constitution of Athens* (Everyman's Library, No. 710, with *Politics*). After about 300 B.C. the character of the institution underwent a radical change, becoming social rather than military in purpose; but it survived until the end of the 3rd century A.D. *See also* G. Gilbert, *The Constitutional Antiquities of Athens*, 1895.

Ephesus (-os), one of the twelve Ionian cities of Asia Minor, situated on the lower slopes of Coressus and Prion, near the mouth of the River Caÿster. In the adjacent plain, about a mile east-north-east of the city, stood the famous temple of Artemis (*see* below), for which Ephesus was chiefly celebrated. The commercial prosperity of the place was due partly to the fertility of the neighbourhood, but more to the fact that it commanded the Caÿster basin and had ready access to those of the Hermus and Meander.

Traditionally founded from Athens by Androclus, son of Codrus, it was later subject in turn to Lydia and Persia. After 466 B.C. (*see* EURYMEDON) it paid tribute for a time to Athens, and was the headquarters successively of Lysander and Agesilaus (qq.v.). In 334 B.C. it was visited by Alexander the Great, after whose death it belonged first to Lysimachus (q.v.) and then to the Seleucids. Following the defeat of Antiochus III by the Romans (190 B.C.), the latter gave Ephesus to Eumenes II of Pergamum (q.v.), whose son, Attalus III, bequeathed his kingdom to the Roman people. Ephesus now became one of the chief cities and ports of the province of Asia.

The Artemision (Temple of Artemis). Before the Ionian settlement, the city supplanted by Ephesus was situated farther south, at Ortygia in the foothills of Mt Solmissus. Here was a sanctuary dedicated to the primitive Asiatic nature-goddess, whom the Greeks identified with Artemis (q.v.). About 750 B.C. a small shrine was established in the plain near Ephesus; it was soon enriched by the Greeks with numerous works of art. Sacked by the Cimmerii (q.v.) c. 650 B.C., it was rebuilt on a slightly larger scale. About fifty years later this shrine was replaced by a temple of regular Hellenic form, designed, according to tradition, by the Cretan Chersiphron and his son

Metagenes, and said to have been the first building in which the Ionic order was used. This temple was greatly enlarged with the help of Croesus (q.v.). It took 120 years to complete and was dedicated *c.* 425 B.C. In 356 B.C. (traditionally on the night of Alexander's birth, but the date is suspect) it was set on fire by an exhibitionist named Herostratus and destroyed. The fifth and last temple, designed by Deinocrates (q.v.), was ranked among the seven wonders of the world, though it was greatly inferior in most respects other than size to its predecessors. It was finished by 300 B.C. With the Artemision of Ephesus there is generally associated the hideous many-breasted figure of the goddess wrapped below the waist in a shroud. This, however, is probably of foreign origin, dating from the hellenistic or Roman period. Nothing is known about the statue (if any) in the first shrine; but it seems that in the early Ionian period at any rate she was depicted as a natural mother, sometimes with a child. *See* RHOECUS.

The city of Ephesus (which has been partly excavated, yielding like the temple much fine sculpture) was destroyed, together with the Artemision, by the Goths in A.D. 262. Both were to some extent restored, but neither regained its former magnificence and prosperity. Ephesus was the birth-place of Heraclitus and Callinus (qq.v.). *See* J. T. Wood, *Discoveries at Ephesus*, 1877; D. G. Hogarth (ed.), *Excavations at Ephesus*, 2 vols., 1908.

Ephialtēs : 1. The Malian traitor who, while Leonidas was defending the Pass of Thermopylae, guided the Persians through the defile of Anopaea and thus enabled them to fall upon his rear (480 B.C.).

2. Athenian statesman, supported Pericles against Cimon (qq.v.). His democratic reforms (462–461 B.C.) limited the power of the Areopagus (q.v.).

Ephor, 'overseer', title of the highest magistrates at Sparta. Five in number, they were elected annually and the senior, like the eponymous archon at Athens, gave his name to the year. Except in the sphere of military command in the field, the board of ephors had almost unlimited powers in both home and foreign affairs. They presided over meetings of the Gerousia and Apella (qq.v.), saw that the kings ruled according to law, decided civil actions at law, regulated taxation, negotiated with foreign ambassadors and sent out military expeditions. *See* A. H. J. Greenidge, *Greek Constitutional History*, 1896; L. Whibley, *Companion to Greek Studies*, 1916.

Ephorus (-os), Greek historian of the mid 4th century B.C., born at Cyme in Asia Minor. He was the author of a universal history from about 1100 to 340 B.C. Despite hostile criticism, it was used by many later historians, among them Polybius. Only fragments have survived. *See* G. L. Barber, *The Historian Ephorus*, 1935.

Epicaste (Epikastē), name given in Homer to Jocasta (q.v.).

Epicharmus (-kharmos), Greek comic poet, born in the island of Cos *c.* 530 B.C. Early in life he went to Megara in Sicily, but after its destruction by Gelon (484) removed to Syracuse and lived at the court of Hieron I until his death *c.* 440 B.C. Thirty-five titles and a few fragments have survived. *See* G. Norwood, *Greek Comedy*, 1931.

Epictetus (Epiktētos): 1. Greek Stoic philosopher, born at Hierapolis in Phrygia *c.* A.D. 55. In boyhood he was a slave of Epaphroditus, one of Nero's officials, but attended the lectures of Musonius Rufus and was subsequently manumitted. He taught first at Rome, but was expelled with other philosophers by Domitian and settled at Nicopolis in Epirus, where he passed the remainder of his life and died *c.* 135. Epictetus wrote nothing, and what we know of his teaching is derived from the *Discourses,* preserved and published by Arrian, who has also left us the *Encheiridion,* a resumé in aphoristic form of the main doctrines of the other work. *See* text and translation by W. A. Oldfather (Loeb Library), 1926.

2. Athenian potter and vase painter of the late 6th century B.C.

Epicurus (Epikouros), Greek philosopher, founder of the Epicurean school, was born at Samos in 341 B.C. He began the study of philosophy at an early age, and in 310 began to teach, first at Mitylene and afterwards at Lampsacus. In 306 he settled at Athens and purchased a garden, the famous *Kēpoi Epikourou* (*see* 'GARDEN, THE'), where he established his school. Here, surrounded by his friends and pupils, he spent the remainder of his life. He taught that man's duty was to attain personal happiness and peace of heart by overcoming irrational desires and fears. Although he appears to have been a prolific writer and, according to Diogenes Laertius, was the author of 300 volumes, there remain only some fragments of his great work *On Nature,* three letters, his will and a compendium of his doctrine in forty-four short propositions, written for his pupils to learn by heart. The extant remains have been edited with translation by Cyril Bailey (1926). *See* E. Zeller, *Stoics, Epicureans and Sceptics,* 1880; W. Wallace, *Epicureanism,* 1902; C. Bailey, *The Greek Atomists and Epicurus,* 1928.

Epidamnus (-os), *see* DYRRACHIUM.

Epidaurus (-os), city on the east coast of Argolis. Situated on a peninsula, with a natural harbour on the northern side, and backed by a fertile plain enclosed by mountains, it was a place of some commercial importance. Conquered from Ionian colonists by Dorians from Argos under Deiphontes, Epidaurus in turn made settlements in the neighbouring islands and in Asia Minor, as well as founding Aegina (q.v.). The government passed from monarchy, through oligarchy, to tyranny, then (5th century B.C.) back to oligarchy.

The fame of Epidaurus rested principally upon the sacred precinct (*hieron*) of Asclepius (q.v.), which lay about eight miles inland. The temple of Asclepius dates from about 460 B.C., and an inscription referring to building contracts has survived. Much of the sculpture was by Timotheus (q.v.); Thrasymedes of Paros was responsible for the chryselephantine statue of the god. South of this temple was the altar and a small temple of Artemis. South-west stood a circular building of extraordinary beauty, now known as the Tholos, but called in the building contracts Thymele; it was designed by Polycleitus the younger. North of this was the Abaton, a long portico on two levels, where the patients slept, saw certain visions and went away cured. In later times this faith-healing declined, and the priests substituted what may be compared with modern spa treatment. Other buildings were the stadium, baths, gymnasia, hospitals and above all the magnificent theatre (4th century B.C.) of which the orchestra and almost every seat are intact. All these, together with the *hieron*, have been excavated. *See* Proceedings of the Greek Archaeological Society, 1881–4 and 1889; Sir J. G. Frazer, *Pausanias*, vols. iii and iv.

Epigoni (oi), *see* THEBAN LEGEND, 5.

Epimenidēs, Cretan poet and prophet of the early 6th century B.C., whose story is in great part mythical. According to one legend he was sent by his father to look for a lost ewe, but while sheltering from the noonday sun in the Dictaean cave he fell into a sleep which lasted fifty-seven years.

His visit to Athens, however, appears to be an historical fact. It is mentioned by Plato, who says that it took place *c.* 500 B.C. Aristotle tells us that after the expulsion of the Alcmaeonidae (q.v.) Epimenides came and purified the city; so that the date of his visit was in fact about a century earlier (*c.* 596 B.C.).

Many works were attributed by the ancients to Epimenides, and St Paul (Titus, i. 12) has preserved one of his verses: 'The Cretans are always liars, evil beasts, slothful bellies.'

Epimētheus ('afterthought'), brother of Prometheus (q.v.). Zeus, to punish mankind, gave him Pandora (q.v.).

Epiphanēs, 'Illustrious', title given to the Seleucid kings Antiochus IV and Antiochus XI, and also to Ptolemy V of Egypt.

Epirus (Ēpeiros), i.e. 'the mainland' in relation to Corcyra (q.v.) and neighbouring islands, district of north-western Greece; bounded north by Illyria and Macedonia, east by Thessaly, south by Acarnania and the Ambracian Gulf, west by the Ionian Sea. Among the principal towns were Ambracia, Palaeste and Phoenice. The country was celebrated for its cattle and horses. Dodona (q.v.) was the seat of a famous oracle.

According to tradition the Epirots consisted of fourteen independent tribes. Of these the most important were the Chaones, the Molossians and the Thesprotians. The Molossian rulers, who claimed descent from Neoptolemus, son of Achilles, gradually extended their sway over the whole of Epirus. One of them, Arymbas II, was a man of great culture. His niece, Olympias (q.v.), was married to Philip II of Macedon, who placed her brother Alexander on the throne with the title of king (*see* ALEXANDER: *Kings of Epirus*). Alexander was succeeded by his first cousin Aeacides, whose son and successor, Pyrrhus (q.v.), is famous in Roman history. After three more reigns the dynasty ended, and Epirus was governed by an annually elected magistrate. Having sided with Perseus, King of Macedon, in 168 B.C., it was devastated by the Romans and never recovered. In 146 B.C. it was included in the Roman province of Macedonia. *See* G. N. Cross, *Epirus*, 1930.

Epithalamium (-on), song in praise of a bride and bridegroom, performed in Greece by a small choir of boys and girls at the door of the nuptial chamber, but at Rome by girls only. As a literary form it was brought to perfection by such poets as Sappho, Anacreon, Stesichorus, Pindar, Theocritus and (in Latin) by Catullus.

Epona, a goddess, patroness primarily of horses, but also of asses and mules. Her cult was popular especially in Gaul, Germany and the Danubian territories. It was not introduced into Rome until imperial times, when she was sometimes styled Augusta and invoked on behalf of the emperor and his family. It is noteworthy that such images of and inscriptions relating to Epona as have been found at Rome were unearthed on the site of barracks once occupied by the *Equites Singulares Augusti* (q.v.).

Eponina, wife of Julius Sabinus (q.v.).

Epōpeus, son of Poseidon and King of Sicyon, *see* ANTIOPE, 2.

Eporedia (mod. Ivrea), town of Gallia Cisalpina (Transpadana), about 30 miles north-east of Augusta Taurinorum (Turin), just where the road from Vercellae to Augusta Praetoria Salassorum (q.v.) entered the valley of the Durius. Belonging originally to the Salassi, it was occupied in 143 B.C. by the Romans, who coveted the neighbouring gold mines. Eporedia was made a Roman *colonia* (q.v.) in 100 B.C.

Equites, originally the cavalry corps of the Roman army, but subsequently a political order. They consisted at first of three patrician *centuriae* which were later increased to six. The addition of twelve plebeian *centuriae* was attributed to Servius Tullius, and eighteen remained the number throughout the republican period.

The equites were chosen from the wealthiest citizens, but service was so costly that state aid was given towards the keep of mounts, and its recipients were called *equites equo publico*. Early in the 4th century B.C. their ranks were swelled by volunteers who kept horses of their own, *equites equo privato*; and as vacancies came to be filled in this way, service in the cavalry, with either a public or a private horse, was made obligatory for all Roman citizens possessed of a certain income.

The equites were selected originally by the *curiae* (*see* COMITIA), then successively by the kings, the consuls and (after 443 B.C.) by the censors (*see* CENSORS), by whom they were reviewed every five years in the Forum. Those whose physique and character, horses and equipment were approved, passed muster; those who failed were dismissed. This quinquennial inspection (*recognitio*) must be distinguished from the *transvectio*, an annual procession on 15th July from the temple of Mars to the Aedes Castoris, in commemoration of the help given by the Dioscuri (q.v.) at the battle of Lake Regillus (496 B.C.). Both events, abandoned before the end of the republic, were revived and combined by Augustus.

As Rome extended her territory and was supplied with far more efficient cavalry by allied and subject peoples, the equites lost their military character. They became first and foremost a class of wealthy men who obtained huge fortunes by speculation, handled state contracts and farmed the public revenues (*see* PUBLICANI). Gaius Gracchus (q.v.) used them as a foil to the aristocracy, giving them control of the jury-courts as well as of the revenues of Asia, and the right to wear a gold ring. *See also* OTHO, LUCIUS ROSCIUS. Sulla restored the courts to the senate (82 B.C.), but at the same time raised 300 of the equites to senatorial rank; but the *Lex Aurelia* (70 B.C.) provided that juries were to be drawn in equal numbers from senators, equites and *tribuni aerarii*, and Caesar replaced the last with equites. Under Augustus many civil posts were filled by equites, but they now became once more primarily soldiers and civil servants rather than financiers.

Equites Singulares Augusti. The bodyguard of the emperor Augustus, recruited mainly from Germans and Batavians (*see* BATAVI), was abolished by Galba but revived with the above title by Trajan or Hadrian. It consisted mainly of the best provincial cavalry with a sprinkling of Roman citizens. Stationed in Rome, except when the emperor left the city, the force was divided in the reign of Septimius Severus into two corps, each of which was commanded by a tribune under the orders of the prefect of the Praetorian Guard (q.v.) and occupied separate quarters (*see* EPONA). They were subsequently replaced by the Protectores Augusti.

Erasistratus (-os), Greek physician and physiologist, *fl. c.* 300 B.C., born at Iulis in the island of Ceos. About 294 he was physician at the court of Seleucus Nicator, but later settled at Samos and founded a school of medicine. He discovered the difference between sensory and motor nerves, and believed the heart to be the origin of veins and arteries. Only fragments of his works survive.

Eratō, muse of erotic poetry and music. *See* MUSES.

Eratosthenēs, Greek mathematician and scientific writer, born at Cyrene *c.* 276 B.C. A pupil of Callimachus (q.v.) at Alexandria, he later studied philosophy under Ariston and Arcesilaus (qq.v.) at Athens. About 235 he returned to Alexandria, where he became tutor to the future Ptolemy IV, Philopator, and succeeded Apollonius Rhodius as head of the Library. Eratosthenes's most famous work was a systematic treatise on geography, of which Strabo (q.v.) made extensive use; but he wrote also on astronomy, geometry, philosophy, history and grammar. Only fragments survive. His most remarkable achievement was the measurement of the earth. He found the circumference to be 252,000 stadia, which gives for the diameter about 7,850 miles, only 50 miles less than the true polar diameter. *See* Sir T. L. Heath, *Greek Astronomy*, 1932.

Erebus (-os), in Greek mythology, son of Chaos, and father by his sister Nyx (Night) of Aether (the clear air) and Hemera (Day). The name means 'darkness', and was used of the dark space through which the shades passed to Hades.

Erechtheum (Erekhtheion), a temple on the site of an older shrine on the Acropolis at Athens, called after Erechtheus (q.v.) to whom part of it was dedicated. According to Pausanias it contained a shrine of Athena Polias, an altar of Poseidon and Erechtheus, one of Zeus Hypatos, one of Butes and one of Hephaestus. Building started between 431 and 421 B.C., but the temple was not completed until 409. Seriously damaged by fire soon afterwards, it was repaired in the early years of the 4th century, and the west end reconstructed during the Roman period (late 1st century A.D.). The most notable feature of the Erechtheum is the caryatid porch.

Erechtheus (-khtheus) or **Erichthonius (-kthonios),** legendary king of Athens, sometimes identified with Erichthonius but more often distinguished from him. According to Homer, Erechtheus was the son of Gē (Earth), brought up by Athena. In the later story Erichthonius, son of Hephaestus and Gē, was entrusted by Athena to the three daughters of Cecrops (Aglauros, Herse and Pandrosos) in a chest which they were forbidden to open. Herse and Pandrosos disobeyed, and when they saw the infant with the form of (or entwined by) a serpent, they went mad and hurled themselves from the Acropolis. Athena then made herself responsible for Erichthonius, who eventually drove out Amphictyon and seized his throne. He established the worship of Athena at Athens, instituted the festival of Panathenaea and built an Erechtheum (q.v.) in honour of Athena Polias.

Erechtheus (-khtheus), legendary king of Athens, grandson of the preceding, son and successor of Pandion. When Eumolpus (q.v.) attacked Athens in support of the Eleusinians, Erechtheus was promised victory if he would sacrifice one of his four daughters; and when one was chosen by lot the others resolved to die with her. Eumolpus was slain and Erechtheus won the day, but he himself was killed by Zeus with a thunderbolt at the request of Poseidon.

Eretria, coastal town of Euboea (q.v.), on the Euripus about 15 miles south of Chalcis (q.v.). In early times it had an extensive commerce, and founded colonies in western and northern Greece, besides acquiring dependencies among the Cyclades. Destroyed by the Persians before Marathon (q.v.) because it had, together with Athens, assisted the Ionian revolt, it was rebuilt and afterwards enjoyed membership of the Delian League (q.v.). Eretria declined to insignificance under Macedonian and Roman rule. Excavations by the American School at Athens include remains of walls, temples of Dionysus and Apollo, and an interesting theatre. It was to Eretria that Menedemus (q.v.) transferred the Elean school of philosophy.

Eridanus (-os), legendary river, at the mouth of which were the Electrides (Amber Islands). Originally placed beyond the limits of the Greek world, it was later, by both Greek and Roman authors, identified with the Padus (mod. Po). The earlier belief may echo an ancient river trade in amber between Jutland and the Mediterranean. *See also* PHAËTHON.

Erinna, Greek poetess who died at the age of nineteen. The opinion, deriving from Suidas, that she was contemporary with Sappho has been abandoned. She lived probably on the island of Telos during the first half of the 3rd century B.C. Three of her epigrams are preserved in the *Greek Anthology*; but her fame rests chiefly on the *Distaff*, a poem in memory of Baucis. *See* C. M. Bowra, *Greek Poetry and Life*, 1936, pp. 325–42.

Erinyes (Erinuēs), less correctly **Erinnyes,** in Greek mythology, were hideous avenging deities, probably personified curses or ghosts of murdered people (*see* FURIAE). Their function was to torment those who had violated the laws of society (especially those who had murdered a near relative) on a basis of strict justice and with no regard to mitigating circumstances. As dwellers in the underworld they were often identified at Athens with the Eumenides (q.v.). Hesiod makes them spring, with the Gigantes, from the blood of Uranus (*see* TITANS); Aeschylus represents them as daughters of Night, Sophocles of Darkness. Their number likewise varied. Euripides was the first to speak of them as three, to whom Alexandrian writers gave the names Alecto, Tisiphone and Megaera.

Eriphyle (-phulē), daughter of Talaus, wife of Amphiaraus and mother of Alcmaeon (qq.v.).

Eris (Lat. Discordia), 'Strife,' in Greek mythology, a sister of Ares according to Homer, and in Hesiod a daughter of Nyx (Night). Later legends represent her as ultimately responsible for the Trojan war, in that it was she who, angry because she had not been invited, flung the golden 'apple of discord' among the guests at the wedding of Peleus and Thetis. *See* PARIS.

Eristics or **Megarians**, a group of sophists led by Eucleides of Megara (q.v.). Their dialectic had as its purpose to 'floor' their opponents rather than to discover truth; and it was through such men as these that the name 'sophist' acquired a disreputable connotation.

Erōs, in Greek mythology, the god of love. He does not occur in Homer, but Hesiod represents him as a son of Chaos, and he seems originally to have been the god not merely of passion but of love's fertility. In later mythology he is the son of Aphrodite by Zeus, Ares or Hermes (*see also* IRIS). His brother Anteros, the god of mutual love, who punishes those who spurn the love of others, is sometimes described as his opponent. From hellenistic times onward Eros becomes a mischievous child (*see* CUPID).

Erymanthus (Erumanthos), mountain in Arcadia, legendary haunt of the Erymanthian boar (*see* TWELVE LABOURS OF HERACLES, 4). In the same mountain is the source of the Erymanthus, a tributary of the Alpheus.

Erysichthon (Erusikhthōn), son of Triops and brother of Iphimede (q.v.). Having cut down trees in a grove sacred to Demeter, he was punished with a hunger so fearful that he devoured his own flesh.

Erythrae (Eruthrai), Ionian city of Asia Minor (*see* IONIA), situated on a peninsula in the Bay of Erythrae, opposite the island of Chios, and alleged to have been founded by Knopos, son of Codrus. Good wine was produced in the neighbourhood. Towards the end of the Peloponnesian war Erythrae withdrew its long-standing allegiance to Athens; but an extant inscription shows that it welcomed Conon (q.v.) after the battle of Cnidus (394 B.C.). There are considerable remains of walls and towers dating from the hellenistic period, also of a theatre on the northern slope of the Acropolis.

Eryx (-ux), a mountain near Drepanum in the north-west of Sicily, on the summit of which was a temple of Aphrodite. It was built, according to Virgil, by Aeneas, but most probably in fact by the Phoenicians. The latter introduced the worship of their goddess Astarte, whom the Greeks identified with Aphrodite (q.v.). Aphrodite herself was identified by the Romans with Venus (q.v.), and the worship of Venus Erycina was introduced at Rome from Sicily at the beginning of the second Punic war. Anchises (q.v.) was said to have been buried on Mt Eryx. At the foot of the mountain was a town of the same name (mod. Erice), founded by the Elymi (q.v.).

Eteoclēs, son of Oedipus by Jocasta, *see* THEBAN LEGEND.

Etruria (called by the Greeks Turrhenia, whence Latin **Tyrrhenia**), a district of Italy which in early times appears to have included the whole or most of the territory between the Tiber and the Alps. By the end of the 5th century B.C., however, this had been greatly reduced, and by about 100 B.C. was confined within the Arno, the Apennines and the Tiber. Augustus made it the seventh region of Italy (see ITALIA).

The Etruscans, a highly civilized people from whom the Romans appear to have derived many of their religious and political institutions (see TARQUINIUS), are considered to have originated in Asia Minor and to have reached the west coast of Italy some time before the end of the 9th century B.C. They came, probably, in small isolated bands, whose superior arms and organization enabled them to subdue the native peoples whom they encountered. Numerous small city-states were formed, joined in a loose confederation (chiefly for religious purposes) with headquarters at the shrine of Voltumna (see VERTUMNUS) above the Lacus Volsiniensis.

The Etruscans themselves constituted a small ruling hierarchy, the backbone of whose power was the native Italian races subject to them. Nevertheless they held their own against Greeks and Carthaginians until 474 B.C., when their defeat by Hieron I of Syracuse near Cumae marked the beginning of a decline. The later history of the Etruscans is one of a long struggle with Rome, to which they became subject after their defeat by Cornelius Dolabella in 283 B.C. In 91 B.C. they received the Roman franchise; and the military colonies established in Etruria, first by Sulla and then by Augustus, destroyed the national character of the people, and the country became romanized.

Many Etruscan sites have been excavated, yielding numerous and splendid works of art. See ARRETIUM; CAERE; CLUSIUM; PERUSIA; POPULONIA; RUSELLAE; TARQUINII; VETULONIA; VOLATERRAE; VOLSINII. See also D. Randall-MacIver, *The Etruscans*, 1927; M. Johnstone, *Etruria Past and Present*, 1930; R. Bloch, *The Etruscans*, 1958.

Euboea (Euboia), largest island of the Aegean, about 90 miles long and from 30 to 40 miles wide, lying along the coasts of southern Thessaly (see ARTEMISIUM), Boeotia and Attica. It is divided from the mainland by a strait which at its narrowest point was called Euripus. The population consisted of various tribes: Histiaei and Ellopes in the north; Curetes and Abantes (the latter prominent in Homer) in the centre; Dryopes from Thessaly in the south. The chief products were corn, cattle, iron, copper, medicinal herbs and (in Roman imperial times) marble. The two most important cities were Chalcis and Eretria (qq.v.). Long subject to Athens, Euboea revolted in 411 B.C. and retained its independence until 338, when it fell to Macedon and afterwards to Rome.

Eubulides (-boulidēs), Greek philosopher, contemporary of Aristotle and successor of Eucleides (q.v.) as head of the Megarian school.

Eucleides (-kleidēs) of Megara, Greek philosopher and founder of the Megarian school, born c. 450 B.C. A disciple of Socrates, he was also acquainted with Plato, and the eristic tendencies of his school (see ERISTICS) prepared the way for the scepticism of the New Academy. He was succeeded by Eubulides (q.v.).

Euclid (Gk Eukleidēs), Greek mathematician, born at Alexandria c. 330 B.C. His life is practically a blank, but many of his treatises, including the famous elements (*Stoikheia*), have come down to us. This work, which includes five books on plane geometry, one on proportion, three on the properties of numbers, one on incommensurable magnitudes and three on solid geometry, was for centuries the textbook on geometry in all schools, and has only in comparatively recent years been superseded on the Continent and in the U.S.A. His *Data* (*Dedomena*) contains ninety-five theorems in which it is shown that, given certain hypotheses, other things are deducible. The *Phainomena* deals with the appearances produced by celestial motions. The musical treatises entitled *Introduction to Harmony* and *Section of the Scale*, and the *Optics* and *Katoptrics*, etc., are of doubtful authenticity. *See* T. L. Heath, *The Thirteen Books of Euclid's Elements* (trans.), 2nd ed., 3 vols., 1926.

Eucratides (-kratidēs), King of Bactria (q.v.), obtained the throne by defeating Demetrius, son of Euthydemus (q.v.), *c.* 175 B.C. He was murdered *c.* 150 B.C. by his son, and from this time the Bactrian kingdom gradually fell to pieces.

Eudemus (-dēmos), a native of Rhodes and pupil of Aristotle, whose *Metaphysics* and *Physics* he revised. The *Eudemian Ethics* is probably no more than an edition of a course on ethics by Aristotle. Many fragments of his work on the history of astronomy and mathematics have been preserved; *see* the editions by Spengel (1866) and Mullach (1881).

Eudoxus (-os): 1. Greek astronomer and geometer (*c.* 408–355 B.C.), born at Cnidus. In early life he attended lectures by Plato, and later devised the hypothesis of concentric spheres to explain the stationary points and retrogradations in the motion of the planets. The theory is a remarkable piece of pure spherical geometry, representing the first attempt to furnish a mathematical basis for astronomy. *See* Sir T. L. Heath, *Greek Astronomy*, 1932.

2. Greek navigator (*fl. c.* 130 B.C.) who was sent by Ptolemy VII, Euergetes, to explore the Arabian Sea. After two successful voyages he left the service of Ptolemy and made several independent voyages along the west coast of Africa.

Eugubine (or **Iguvine**) **Tables.** These tablets, seven in number, were discovered during the 15th century at Iguvium (mod. Gubbio), in Umbria. They contain large texts, engraved on both faces of the tablets, and have been recognized as parts of the liturgy of a sacred brotherhood at Iguvium. Tables I–IV and part of V are in Umbrian script, which is not only an offshoot of the Etruscan, but is so close to its classical form that some Etruscologists consider it as Etruscan. These tables are attributed by some scholars to the 5th or 4th, by others to the 3rd or 2nd century B.C. The rest of Table V and Tables VI and VII are written in Roman characters and are assigned to the 1st century B.C.

Euhemerus (-hēmeros), a native of Messana in Sicily, founder of the historical theory known as euhemerism, *fl.* late 4th century B.C. at the court of Cassander. While voyaging to the Indian Ocean he discovered (so he claimed) an island called Panchaea, and on it a number of inscriptions representing the gods of Hellas as mere humans, deified after death because of their superior strength and abilities. His

Hiera Anagraphē (Sacred History) led to his being accused of atheism and his name became a byword for mendacity. Later, however, many adopted the theory, which was simplified in order to eliminate extravagances and leave a number of commonplace and credible stories. Aeolus became an ancient mariner; the Cyclopes, a race of savages inhabiting Sicily; Atlas, an astronomer; Scylla and Pegasus, fast-sailing pirates.

Eumenēs: (A) Of Cardia, secretary to Philip II of Macedon and Alexander the Great, and one of the latter's generals. On the death of Alexander he obtained the government of Cappadocia and Paphlagonia, defeated Craterus (q.v.) in 321, but was himself defeated and slain by Antigonus I (q.v.) in 316 B.C.

(B) Name of two kings of Pergamum.

1. *Eumenes I*, 263–241 B.C., nephew and successor of Philetaerus.

2. *Eumenes II*, 197–159 B.C., son and successor of Attalus I (q.v.). Having maintained his father's alliance with Rome, especially in the wars against Antiochus III and Perseus, he received large accessions of territory (*see* PERGAMUM). To commemorate a victory over the Gauls in 180 he built the great sculptured altar of Zeus at Pergamum, which is probably the 'throne of Satan' mentioned in the Apocalypse (ii. 13), and which was excavated in 1878. It was Eumenes II also who founded the great library at Pergamum, at which time he is said to have invented parchment. The library was given by Antony to Cleopatra and transferred to Alexandria.

Eumenidēs ('kindly ones') or **Semnai** ('revered ones'), goddesses worshipped at the foot of the Areopagus at Athens, at Colonus and even outside Attica. Their cult was similar to that of Gē (earth), and they were probably pre-hellenic chthonian spirits concerned mostly with fertility; but the fact that they came to have certain moral and social functions caused them to be wrongly identified, at least from the time of Aeschylus (*see* his *Eumenides*), with the Erinyes (q.v.), of whom their name must be considered as a euphemism.

Eumenius, Latin panegyrist of Greek descent, born at Augustodunum (mod. Autun) in Gallia Lugdunensis *c.* A.D. 260, and died not earlier than 311. He was private secretary to Constantius Chlorus, who in 296 appointed him head of the restored *Scholae Maenianae*, a famous college at Augustodunum. Eumenius was by far the best orator of his time. Five of his addresses have survived. The first is on the restoration of schools and was delivered at Augustodunum in 297. The remainder were delivered at Augusta Treverorum (Trier) as follows: congratulations to Constantius Chlorus (297) on victories in Britain; panegyric on Constantine (310); thanksgiving to Constantine (310) for favours done to the city; festal speech on the marriage of Constantine and Fausta (307). *See* E. Bährens (ed.), *Panegyrici Latini*, 1874.

Eumolpus (-os), 'good singer', eponymous ancestor of the Eumolpidae (*see* MYSTERIES), but an otherwise shadowy figure of Greek legend. According to one version he is son of Poseidon by Chione, daughter of Boreas; after various adventures he becomes king in Thrace, is invited to help the Eleusinians in their war with Erechtheus (q.v.), and is killed in battle.

Another version represents him as son of Earth and a native of Eleusis where he helped to found the mysteries and became father of the Ceryces.

Finally, he is son, father or pupil of Musaeus (q.v.).

Eunus (-os), a Syrian slave at Enna in Sicily, leader of the slaves in the first Servile war, 136–132 B.C. *See* SERVILE WARS.

Eupalinus (-os), Greek architect of the 6th century B.C., a native of Megara. He constructed the wonderful subterranean aqueduct at Samos in the time of the tyrant Polycrates (q.v.). *See* AQUEDUCTS.

Eupatridae (-ai), the ancient nobility of Attica. Towards the end of the 8th century B.C. they had entire control of the administration and were the only dispensers of justice in the state. Their power was greatly curtailed by publication of Draco's criminal code and by the reforms of Solon; by the middle of the 6th century it had vanished altogether, though the clan continued to exist. *See* L. Whibley, *Companion to Greek Studies*, 1923.

Euphorbus (-bos): 1. A Trojan warrior, son of Panthous (q.v.). He was killed by Menelaus.

2. Physician to King Juba II (q.v.) at Rome, and brother of Antonius Musa (q.v.).

Euphorion, Greek poet and grammarian, born at Chalcis in Euboea *c.* 275 B.C. After making a fortune at Athens, he was invited (221) by Antiochus III of Syria to help with the foundation of the royal library at Antioch, and held the post of librarian until his death. Fragments of his work survive.

Euphranor, Greek sculptor and painter of the mid 4th century B.C., a native of Corinth. Pliny gives lists of his work.

Euphronius (-os), Athenian potter and vase painter of the late 6th and early 5th century B.C. The artist whom he employed to decorate those vases of which he himself was only the potter is known as the 'Panaitios painter'.

Eupolis, Athenian poet of the Old Comedy, born *c.* 446 B.C. He is ranked by Horace as one of the greatest writers of that school. In the elegance and purity of his style he was reputed the equal of Aristophanes, and the rival of Cratinus in his command of irony and sarcasm. The plays of Eupolis numbered seventeen, with which he won the prize seven times; among the best known were *Kolakes, Marikas, Baptai, Demoi* and *Poleis*. Eupolis died in 411 B.C., but it is not true that he was drowned by Alcibiades for having attacked him in the *Baptai. See* T. Kock, *Comicorum Atticorum Fragmenta*, vol. i, 1880; J. U. Powell, *New Chapters in the History of Greek Literature*, 3rd series, 1933; G. Norwood, *Greek Comedy*, 1931.

Eupompus (-os), Greek artist, founder of the great school of painting at Sicyon, which flourished in the 4th century B.C. He is best remembered for the advice he gave Lysippus (q.v.): 'Follow nature rather than any master.'

Euripides (*c.* 484–407 B.C.), last of the great Attic tragedians, born at Phlya, son of Mnesarchus and Cleito; his wife's name was Melite. There are no good grounds for accepting the calumnies of ancient writers, especially Aristophanes, that Euripides was a misogynist and that his mother was of low birth. Nor need we hesitate to reject the story that he was twice married and embittered by the infidelity of both wives. In his youth Euripides was an outstanding athlete, winning prizes both at Athens and Eleusis. He was also a skilled painter, and his plays contain several references to this art. He received a good education and early came under the influence of such thinkers as Protagoras, Anaxagoras and Socrates (qq.v.). In later life his outspoken antagonism to the war party at Athens drove him further and further into isolation until, in about 408, he went into voluntary exile, dying next year at the court of Archelaus, King of Macedon.

Euripides began his career as a dramatist in 455, winning third place with *Pleiades*. Not till 442 did he secure the first prize, and only four times in all. The scientific and philosophic thought revealed in his work, often approaching religious scepticism, did not find favour with his contemporaries. He represented the new moral and social influ- ences that were affecting Athens; in the next century his popularity increased tenfold, and many considered his dramas superior to those of Aeschylus and Sophocles (qq.v.). He is noted pre-eminently as a master of pathos and for his delineation of female character. He is interested in the experiences of the ordinary individual rather than in that of mythological or legendary beings, drawing his characters with a fine realistic touch. Euripides has been called the most modern of the three great Athenian dramatists and the 'forerunner of Rationalism'. The criticism of Aristophanes (*Frogs* and *Thesmophoriazusae*) and others is hostile in the extreme, but he was much admired by Cicero and Quintilian.

Euripides was essentially a realist whose art reflected the humours and passions of daily life, and the vehicle he used as his medium was a drama of archaic plots and simple style, not unmixed with sheer incongruity; but, seen through his rationalism, the plays became a formidable weapon of propaganda for the 5th-century Illumination. For Euripides plot is almost immaterial; several of his plays seem, in point of plot, to be much the same as those of Phrynicus (q.v.). But he made such innovations as (*a*) the prologue, which takes the form of a versified programme; and (*b*) the *deus ex machina* or god who appears at the end to wind up the plot.

Eighteen certainly authentic plays by Euripides have survived: *Cyclops* (sole surviving complete specimen of a satyr play); *Alcestis*, 438; *Medea*, 431; *Hippolytus*, 428; *Andromache*, *c.* 430; *Hecuba*, *c.* 425; *Heraclidae*; *Suppliant Women*; *Heracles*; *Ion*; *Trojan Women*, 415; *Iphigeneia in Tauris* and *Helen*, 414–412; *Electra*; *Phoenissae*, *c.* 410; *Iphigeneia at Aulis*; *Bacchae* (posthumously produced), 406. The *Rhesus* which has come down to us is of doubtful authenticity, but Euripides is known to have written an early play with that title.

See the complete critical edition by Gilbert Murray (Oxford Classical Texts), 2 vols., 1901–9 (vol. ii revised and brought up to date, 1913). There are numerous editions and translations of separate plays; the best complete verse translation is that of A. S. Way (3 vols., 1894–8 (Everyman's Library, 2 vols., 1951). *See also* A. W. Verrall, *Euripides the Rationalist*, 1895; G. Murray, *Euripides and his Age*,

1914; F. L. Lucas, *Euripides and his Influence*, 1924; W. N. Bates, *Euripides: A Student of Human Nature*, 1964.

Europa, in Greek legend, daughter of the Phoenician king Agenor, but of Phoenix according to the *Iliad* (xvi. 321). Her beauty charmed Zeus, who took the form of a bull and emerged from the waves as Europa and her attendants were playing on the seashore. Encouraged by his tameness, Europa climbed on his back, whereupon the god rushed back into the water and swam with her to Crete. Here she became by Zeus the mother of Minos, Rhadamanthus and Sarpedon (qq.v.). *See also* CADMUS.

Eurus, personification of the south-east wind; son of Astraeus by Eos and brother of Boreas (q.v.).

Eurybatus (Eurubatos), an Ephesian, said to have been entrusted by Croesus (q.v.) with the raising of mercenaries in Peloponnesus in preparation for his war with Cyrus. But Eurybatus deserted to the Persians, and his name was afterwards used as a byword of treachery.

Euryclea (Eurukleia), in the *Odyssey*, nurse of Odysseus, whom she recognized on his return from Troy, thanks to a scar he revealed while taking a bath.

Eurydice (Eurudikē): 1. In Greek legend the wife of Orpheus (q.v.). *See also* ARISTAEUS.

2. Wife of Philip Arrhidaeus (q.v.), half-brother of Alexander the Great (q.v.). She and her husband were put to death by Olympias, 317 B.C.

Eurymedon (Eurumēdon), river in Pamphylia, near the mouth of which Cimon (q.v.) won a decisive naval victory over the Persians in 468 or 467 B.C.

Eurystheus (Eurus-), *see* HERACLES.

Euterpē, the muse of lyric poetry. *See* MUSES.

Euthydemus (Euthudēmos), a native of Lydian Magnesia, who overthrew the dynasty of Diodotus (q.v.) and made himself King of Bactria, *c.* 230 B.C. He was acknowledged by Antiochus III, the Great, in 206 after three years of hostilities. The date of his death is unknown; he was succeeded by his son Demetrius (q.v.).

Eutrēsis, town of Boeotia, with a temple and oracle of Apollo, between Thespiae and Plataea. It is mentioned by Homer and was said to have been the residence of Amphion (q.v.) and Zethus before their return to Thebes. The site was identified and remains of a Bronze Age palace unearthed in 1924–5. *See* Goldman, *Excavations at Eutresis in Boeotia*, 1931.

Eutychides (-tukhidēs), of Sicyon, Greek sculptor of the late 4th century B.C. and a pupil of Lysippus (q.v.). His statue of Fortune, made for the city of Antioch *c.* 300 B.C., is represented by copies and on coins in various museums.

Euxinus (-os), now called in English the Black Sea, was known to the Greeks at a very early date, as is clear from the legend of the Argonauts. Many Greek cities and commercial emporia were founded on its southern shores.

Evagoras (Eu-), King of Salamis in Cyprus, 410–374 B.C. He claimed descent from Teucer, half-brother of Telamonian Ajax. Evagoras was friendly towards Athens, and gave refuge to Conon (q.v.) after his defeat at Aegospotami in 405; he also obtained Persian help for Athens against Sparta, and was present at the Athenian victory of Cnidus (394). From 391, however, Evagoras and the Persians were virtually at war. Until 387 he was supported by Athens, but her assistance was withdrawn when he refused to recognize the Peace of Antalcidas. He carried on successful hostilities alone until 376, when he was defeated at Citium and soon afterwards concluded peace. He remained King of Salamis under the suzerainty of Persia until 374, when he was assassinated by a eunuch from motives of private revenge. A panegyric by Isocrates (q.v.) is extant. *See also* Xenophon, *Hellenica,* iv. 8; Diodorus Siculus, xiv. 115, xv. 2–9.

Evander (Euandros), in late Roman legend, son of Hermes by the goddess Carmenta. About sixty years before the Trojan war he led a colony from Pallantion in Arcadia to Italy, and there built a town, Pallanteum, at the foot of the Palatine hill, which town was subsequently incorporated into Rome. Evander was supposed to have instituted the festival of Lupercalia, and to have taught the natives various arts of peace and social life. He is represented by Virgil as welcoming Aeneas and helping him against the Rutuli.

Exēkias, Athenian potter and vase painter of the 6th century B.C. *See* W. Technau, *Exekias,* 1936.

F

Fabius, name of one of the most ancient and most distinguished patrician *gentes* at Rome, claiming descent from Hercules and a daughter of Evander (q.v.); one of the two *gentes* entrusted with management of the Lupercalia (q.v.). The next five articles deal with the principal members of its most outstanding families.

Fabius Ambustus, Marcus, father of three sons who were sent as ambassadors to the Gauls while the latter were besieging Clusium (391 B.C.), but subsequently took part in the fighting. The Gauls claimed that this was a violation of the law of nations, and demanded their surrender. Instead the young men were appointed consular tribunes for 390, when their father was pontifex maximus; whereupon the Gauls marched on Rome, defeated a Roman army on the Allia (q.v.) and captured the city.

Fabius Maximus, Quintus, name of two Roman generals.

1. Surnamed Rullianus, master of the horse to L. Papirius Cursor (q.v.) during the second Samnite war. Though degraded by Cursor for having fought a (successful) action contrary to orders, Fabius was appointed dictator in 315. He was defeated by the Samnites at Lautulae in that year, but this was offset in 310 by his victory over the Etruscans at Lacus Vadimonis. In his fifth consulship (295) he won the battle of Sentinum (q.v.) against a combined force of Etruscans, Umbrians, Samnites and Gauls.

2. Grandson of the preceding; surnamed Cunctator, 'delayer', because of his cautious tactics in the war against Hannibal (q.v.). He was five times consul (233, 228, 215, 214, 209 B.C.). In 217, following the disasters of the Trebia and Lake Trasimene, he was chosen dictator (q.v.) by the people. During the sixth month of his tenure he avoided direct encounter with the enemy, moved his camp from highland to highland, where the Numidian horse and Spanish infantry could not follow, watched Hannibal's movements and cut off his stragglers and foragers. At Rome, however, and in his own camp the caution of Fabius was misinterpreted, and the people divided the command between him and his master of horse, M. Minucius Rufus, who was soon afterwards entrapped and would have been destroyed but for the speed and energy of Fabius. His resignation of the dictatorship was quickly followed by the rout of Cannae (q.v.). During his third and fourth consulship Fabius and his colleague M. Claudius Marcellus besieged Capua, and in his fifth he took Tarentum, which Hannibal had occupied since 212. In the closing years of the second Punic war Fabius appears to less advantage. A new generation of commanders had gone over to the offensive, and he dreaded the influence of Scipio whose plan for the invasion of Africa he resolutely opposed. He died in 203 B.C.

Fabius Pictor, Gaius, Roman artist, was surnamed Pictor from his having adorned the temple of Salus (q.v.), which the dictator C.

Junius Bubulcus dedicated in 302 B.C. and which was burnt down in the reign of Claudius. These were the earliest Roman paintings on record.

Fabius Pictor, Quintus, grandson of the preceding, the earliest known Roman historian (he wrote in Greek), was born c. 254 B.C. His work, which covered the period from the landing of Aeneas in Italy to the second Punic war (in which he served), was among the chief sources used by Polybius (q.v.). Fragments have survived. *See* H. Peter, *Historicorum Romanorum Fragmenta,* 1883.

Fabius Vibulanus, Quintus, consul in 484, 481 and 479 B.C. In the last year his brother and colleague Caeso espoused the cause of the plebeians, a move which roused hostility to the entire family. Thereupon another brother, Marcus, led an emigration of the *gens* (300 souls according to tradition), which settled on the banks of the Cremera (q.v.) and built a fortress. Here for two years they defended themselves against attack by the forces of Veii (q.v.), but were cut off and destroyed on 18th June 477. The whole *gens* perished, excepting Marcus's son Quintus, from whom all subsequent Fabii were descended.

Fabricius, Gaius, surnamed Luscinus ('one-eyed'), consul in 282 B.C. when he defeated the Bruttians and Lucanians, who were besieging Thurii. In 280 he was one of the ambassadors sent to Pyrrhus (q.v.) at Tarentum in order to negotiate a ransom of prisoners. Later propagandists told how Pyrrhus, impressed by the integrity of Fabricius, who would not be lured by the offer of bribes, released the prisoners without ransom. During his second consulship (278 B.C.) he negotiated the peace which was followed by Pyrrhus's withdrawal from Italy. Before returning to Rome he won several victories over the Samnites, Lucanians and Bruttians, for which he was granted a triumph. As censor in 275 he distinguished himself by the severity wherewith he endeavoured to suppress the growing taste for luxury. But those frugal habits for which he was admired by ancient writers are suspect: he died so poor that provision had to be made for his daughter out of public funds.

Fabricius, Lucius, was superintendent of highways in 62 B.C., when he built a new bridge of stone connecting the city with the island in the Tiber and called after him Pons Fabricius.

Faesulae (mod. Fiesole), city of Etruria, three miles north-east of Florentia. There are considerable remains of early walls, of an Etruscan temple and of a Roman theatre.

Falerii, one of the twelve Etruscan cities, originally situated on a height some 32 miles north of Rome and 2 miles west of the Via Flaminia (q.v.). The majority of the inhabitants were of a tribe known as Falisci, who, since they were considered of the same stock as the Aequi (q.v.), were often called Aequi Falisci; but the dominant element was Etruscan. Subjugated by Rome in 394, Falerii revolted in 241 B.C., when it was destroyed and deprived of half its territory. A new (Roman) town was built 3 miles to the north-west, in the plain. Remains of the old city include four wooden temples and many rock tombs. The walls of the second city are well preserved and offer a splendid example of Roman military architecture: over a mile in circumference, they are at some points 56 feet high and have a mean width of roughly 8 feet. There were eighty towers, of which about fifty are preserved.

Falernus Ager, district in the north of Campania (q.v.). It produced some of the finest wines in Italy.

Falisci, *see* FALERII.

Fama, *see* OSSA.

Fanum Fortunae (mod. Fano), town in Umbria, where the Via Flaminia (q.v.) reached the Adriatic coast. Augustus established a colony (*see* COLONIA) here in A.D. 9 and walled the town. A triumphal arch in his honour is still standing. There were also a temple of Augustus, another of Jupiter and a basilica designed by Vitruvius (q.v.).

Fasces, Roman emblems of authority over life and limb, carried by lictors (q.v.), in the left hand and on the left shoulder, before the higher magistrates (excluding censors) and behind the bier at their funerals. The *fasces* consisted of bundles of elm or birch rods bound with a red strap. Outside the city these bundles enclosed an axe, the head of which protruded about one-third of the way from the top; and, at least under the earlier republic, a dictator was entitled to the axe even within the city boundaries. The reason for this removal of the axe from the *fasces* was the right of appeal to the people (*provocatio*) from a capital sentence *at Rome*, but not elsewhere. The custom of lowering the *fasces* in presence of the *comitia* (q.v.) was attributed to P. Valerius Publicola. A victorious general who had been hailed 'imperator' by his troops had his *fasces* crowned with laurel, which always adorned those borne before the emperors.

Fasti. This word, meaning 'lawful', was originally an adjective qualifying the noun *dies*, 'days', so that *fasti dies* denoted those days on which legal business could be transacted without impiety. Later *fasti* was used as a noun and was applied to various sorts of lists or registers. Of these the two main classes were as follows:

1. *Fasti Diurni,* an official year-book, with dates and directions for religious ceremonies, market-days, etc. It was first published on tables posted in the Forum by Gnaeus Flavius in 304 B.C. After the introduction of the Julian Calendar (q.v.), Caesar published new *Fasti,* to illustrate the first six months of which Ovid (q.v.) wrote his work of the same name.

2. *Fasti Magistrales,* also called *Fasti Annales* or *Historici.* These included (*a*) chronicles of events issued by the various offices of state (e.g. *fasti consulares*); (*b*) lists of those who had been granted a triumph (*fasti triumphales*); (*c*) lists of the year's memorable events, with particular reference to prodigies, published by the pontiff and called *Annales Pontificum.*

Faunus, in Latin mythology, one of the oldest Italian gods. He was worshipped as the protector of agriculturists and shepherds, and also as an oracular divinity. He was subsequently identified with the Greek Pan (q.v.) and represented with the horns and legs of a goat. Later again we find mention of Fauni (plural), who were identified with the Satyrs (q.v.). What Faunus was to men, his wife Fauna or Faula was to women. *See also* BONO DEA.

Faustina, Anna Galeria, younger daughter of Antoninus Pius and wife of Marcus Aurelius (q.v.). According to Dio Cassius and others she was a woman of gross profligacy, and was said to have instigated the revolt of Avidius Cassius. Whatever the truth of these allegations, it is certain that to the end of her life she retained the emperor's devotion and esteem, and that she founded charitable schools for orphan girls. Faustina died in A.D. 175 or 176 at Halala in Cappadocia, whither she had accompanied her husband.

Faventia (mod. Faenza), town on the Via Aemilia (q.v.), about 35 miles, south-west of Ravenna. Noted for its linen and vines, it was also the scene of a battle in which Q. Caecilius Metellus Pius (*see* METELLUS, 4) defeated Papirius Carbo and C. Norbanus in 82 B.C.

Favonius, the Latin name for Zephyrus (q.v.).

Favorinus, Greek sophist and sceptical philosopher of the 2nd century A.D., born at Arelate (mod. Arles) in Gaul, but spent most of his time travelling in Italy, Greece and the East. A great scholar and a powerful orator, he was on intimate terms with some of the leading thinkers and writers of his day, while his familiarity with Hadrian is commemorated in a well-known story. Once, when silenced by the emperor during an argument, Favorinus dryly acknowledged that it was futile to criticize the logic of the master of thirty legions. Only a few fragments of his many works have survived. *See* Philostratus, *Vitae sophistarum*, i. 8; L. Legré, *Favorin d'Arles*, 1900.

Feciales or **Fetiales,** a Roman college of twenty priests holding office for life. Their duty was to ' maintain the laws of international relationship '. When a state was considered to have acted in a manner hostile to Rome, two members of the college were sent to make a formal demand for redress. If this was not forthcoming within thirty days, the *Feciales* reported back to Rome; and if war was declared they crossed the enemy border and cast a twin-pointed javelin of cornel wood. Somewhat later, in order to avoid long journeys for the performance of this rite, a column (*columna bellica*) was erected at Rome to represent hostile territory, and into it the javelin was flung. The *Feciales* also performed certain rites at the conclusion of peace treaties.

Felix, Antonius, a Greek freedman who, after serving as prefect of Samaria, was appointed by Claudius procurator of Judaea in A.D. 51 or 52 and held that position until A.D. 60. Soon after taking office he married Drusilla, daughter of Agrippa I and wife of King Azizus of Emesa, whom he persuaded to leave her husband. Though not devoid of intelligence, the character of Felix is assessed by Tacitus in a memorable phrase: 'He revelled in cruelty and lust, wielding the power of a king with the mind of a slave.' For St Paul's appearance before Felix (A.D. 58) *see* Acts xxiii, xxiv.

Felsina, *see* BONONIA.

Fenestella, Roman historian and encyclopaedist, lived in the reign of Tiberius (A.D. 14–37). His *Annales* not only took account of historical events, but also discussed such varied subjects as strange occurrences, the origin of political institutions and social customs, literary history, agriculture, etc. *See* H. Peter, *Historicorum Romanorum Fragmenta*, 1883.

Ferentum or **Ferentis**, city of Etruria, about six miles north of Viterbo near the Via Cassia (q.v.); birth-place of the emperor Otho. There are Roman remains, including walls, baths and a theatre.

Feronia, ancient Italian divinity whose principal sanctuary was at Anxur (q.v.). At her festival a great fair was held, during which offerings were made of first fruits of the fields.

Fescennia, city of Etruria, six miles north-west of old Falerii (q.v.), whence most authorities believe the Romans to have derived the so-called *Fescennini Versus* (q.v.).

Fescennini Versus, early form of Italian poetry, consisting of obscene and abusive verse-dialogues sung by masked dancers at vintage, harvest, weddings and other rustic festivals. It is generally agreed that they were named after Fescennia (q.v.), where the Romans first became acquainted with them. Originally intended as fertility or luck charms, the Fescennine verses were also believed to avert the evil eye. Horace's statement that they became so abusive that a law was made to check them, probably means that the provision of the Twelve Tables (q.v.) against *malum carmen* was extended to cover libel.

Festus, Porcius, succeeded Felix (q.v.) as procurator of Judaea in A.D. 60. For his dealings with St Paul in the same year *see* Acts xxiv, xxv.

Festus, Sextus Pompeius, Roman grammarian of the 2nd century A.D. Much of the second half of his epitome of the *De Verborum significatu* by Verrius Flaccus (q.v.) has survived, and sheds a good deal of light on Roman antiquities. *See* the edition of W. M. Lindsay, 1913.

Fetiales, *see* FECIALES.

Fidenae, town of Latium, about six miles north of Rome on the Via Salaria (q.v.). Commanding the high road and a ferry over the Tiber, it was long a bone of contention between Rome and Veii. In early imperial times the ferry connected an estate belonging to Livia (*see* LIVIA, 2) with her villa near Saxa Rubra (q.v.) across the river.

Fides Publica, Roman goddess personifying the honour of the people. Each year, on 1st October, the three *flamines majores* (*see* FLAMEN) drove to the Capitol, where they offered sacrifice in her honour.

Fidius occurs in the expression *Medius Fidius*, 'So help me the god of truth'. This *Dius Fidius* was identified with Sancus (q.v.) and was later regarded as synonymous with the Greek *Zeus Pistios*. The *me-* is a demonstrative particle as in *mehercule, mecastor*.

Figulus, Publius Nigidius (*c.* 98–45 B.C.), Roman scholar and, with the exception of M. Terentius Varro (q.v.), the most learned man of his time. He was praetor in 58, sided with Pompey in the civil war, was banished by Caesar after Pharsalus (48) and died in exile. Figulus was a Pythagorean, and his endeavour in numerous works to revive Pythagorean teaching and the occult sciences led to his being credited with preternatural powers. Other subjects dealt with in his writings were cults and ceremonies, grammar, orthography and antiquities. The surviving fragments have been edited by A. Swoboda (1889).

Fimbria, Gaius Flavius, son of C. Flavius Fimbria who was consul in

104 B.C. One of the most violent partisans of Marius and Cinna (87 B.C.), he was sent to Asia in 86 as legate to Valerius Flaccus (*see* FLACCUS, LUCIUS VALERIUS, 1), who dismissed him for insubordination. Soon afterwards Fimbria procured the assassination of Flaccus by his own troops at Nicomedia and took command of the army. He carried on war with Mithradates with some success, but in 84 B.C. was attacked by Sulla and committed suicide.

Firmum Picenum (mod. Fermo), town of Picenum, founded as a Latin colony in 264 B.C. as the centre of Roman authority after the subjugation of the Picentes. Originally governed by five quaestors, it became a Roman *colonia* (q.v.) with full rights in 42 B.C. and was the headquarters of the Fourth Legion.

Fiscus, the treasury or privy purse of the Roman emperors, established by Augustus. It was filled largely with the profits of imperial domains in Egypt and elsewhere, and is to be distinguished from the *Aerarium* (q.v.).

Flaccus, Lucius Valerius : 1. Consul with Marius (q.v.) in 100 B.C., when he helped to subdue the insurrection of Saturninus (q.v.). On the death of Marius in 86, Flaccus was elected consul in his place and was sent to Asia against Mithradates. There he was murdered by his troops at Nicomedia (*see* FIMBRIA).

2. Latin poet, wrote in the reign of Vespasian (A.D. 69–79). We possess his *Argonautica*, an heroic poem in eight books on the Argonauts (q.v.). *See* text and translation by J. H. Mozely (Loeb Library).

Flaccus, Marcus Valerius, a supporter of the Gracchi, and one of the commissioners for carrying out Tiberius's agrarian law after the latter's death in 133 B.C. As consul in 125 he unsuccessfully proposed to grant Roman citizenship to all the allies in Italy, and in the following year was sent to deal with the Salyes (q.v.). This campaign, though successful, did not end the war. In 122 he was sent with Gaius Gracchus (q.v.) to found a colony at Carthage, and was killed together with him in 121 B.C.

Flaccus, Marcus Verrius, Roman grammarian, lived in the reign of Augustus, to whose grandsons, Gaius and Lucius Caesar, he was tutor. He was author of the first recorded dictionary of the Latin language. *See* FESTUS, SEXTUS POMPEIUS.

Flaccus, Quintus Fulvius, Roman general, son of M. Fulvius Flaccus who was consul in 264 B.C. Quintus was four times consul: 237 and 224, when he carried on successful operations in Liguria and Gallia Cisalpina; during the second Punic war, 212–211 when, with his colleague Appius Claudius Pulcher, he defeated Hanno near Beneventum and ended the siege of Capua (*see* FABIUS MAXIMUS, QUINTUS, 2); 209, when he crushed the last embers of revolt in Lucania and Bruttii.

Flaccus, Quintus Horatius, *see* HORACE.

Flamen, the title of certain members of the priestly college at Rome, consecrated to offer daily sacrifice to particular gods in the state pantheon. There were originally three *flamines*: *flamen Dialis*, *flamen martialis* and *flamen quirinalis*, that is, of Jupiter, Mars and Quirinus (qq.v.). There were always patricians. Later the number was increased to fifteen, and those mentioned above were called *majores* *(see* FIDES PUBLICA); the other twelve, called *minores*, were plebeian, but they became fewer towards the end of the republican period.

The *flamines* were chosen for life, but could be made to resign *(a)* if they neglected their duties, or *(b)* if an evil omen occurred while they were performing their rites. With the exception of the *flamen Dialis*, who will be discussed below, the *flamines* had as their official dress a white conical cap *(apex)*, a mantle *(laena)* and a laurel wreath.

By far the most honourable of these priests was the *flamen Dialis*. He had a seat in the senate and was entitled to a curule chair. His insignia were a white cap *(pileus* or *albogalerus)* topped with an olive branch and a woollen thread; a thick woollen *toga praetexta* woven by his wife; a sacrificial knife; and a rod to keep the people at a distance when on his way to sacrifice. His marriage took the form of *confarreatio* (q.v.). His wife, called *flaminica Dialis*, assisted him in his religious duties, and on her death (which alone could dissolve the marriage) he was obliged to resign. He was not allowed to absent himself from Rome for a single night, and he was protected from ritual defilement by an elaborate code of regulations. Thus he was not permitted *(a)* to see fetters, an army or people working; *(b)* to touch a horse or anything unclean; *(c)* to swear an oath. *See* the article by C. Jullian in Daremberg and Saglio's *Dictionnaire des Antiquités*, 1877–1919.

Flaminia, Via, the chief northward highway from Rome, named after the censor C. Flaminius (q.v.), who in 220 B.C. continued an earlier road from Spoletium to Ariminum. Crossing the Tiber on the Pons Mulvius (built by M. Aemilius Scaurus in 109 B.C.), two miles north of the city, it crossed the River Nar at Narnia and continued thence via Carsulae and Mevania to Forum Flaminii (in imperial times by way of Interamna and Fulginiae, where a branch diverged to Perusia); thence to Nuceria and over the main ridge of the Apennines to Cales, Forum Sempronii, Forum Fortunae, Pisaurum and Ariminum *(see* AEMILIA, VIA). The total distance was 209 miles, until the Interamna-Fulginiae diversion increased it by six miles.

The Via Flaminia was restored by Augustus, who rebuilt all the bridges except the Pons Mulvius. Vespasian drove a new tunnel through the pass of Intercisa between Cales and Forum Sempronii (A.D. 77).

Flamininus, Titus Quinctius, Roman general and statesman, born *c.* 228 B.C. He was consul in 198 and received command of the war against Philip V of Macedon, whom he defeated at Cynoscephalae in the following year.   He later, (195) attended the Isthmian games and proclaimed the Greek states free, and before returning home (194) secured the release of 1,200 Italian captives who had been sold as slaves during the Hannibalic war.

In 192, on the outbreak of hostilities with Antiochus III of Syria, Flamininus returned to Greece as civil representative of Rome, rallied the Greek states, strengthened an alliance with Philip, and thus did much to bring about the Roman victory at Thermopylae (191). In 183 he went as ambassador to King Prusias of Bithynia, to demand the surrender of Hannibal (q.v.), and died about ten years later. *See* the life by Plutarch.

Flaminius, Gaius, Roman general and statesman. As tribune of the plebs in 232 B.C. he carried an agrarian law for distributing some newly acquired public land in Picenum. During his first consulship (223), after a dangerous setback, he won a victory over the Insubrian Gauls on the Addua. While censor in 220 he built the Circus Flaminius in the Campus Martius at Rome, and continued the Via Flaminia (q.v.) from Spoletium to Ariminum. He was consul for a second time in 217, when he was defeated and slain by Hannibal (q.v.) at the battle of Lake Trasimene.

Flora, Italian goddess of flowers. Her festival, the Floralia, was instituted in 238, was at first celebrated at irregular intervals, but became annual after 173 B.C. It lasted from 28th April to 3rd May and included licentious exhibitions on the stage.

Florentia (mod. Firenze; Eng. Florence), city of Etruria, founded at an unknown date, probably as a Roman *colonia* (q.v.), and described by Florus (q.v.) as a *municipium* (q.v.).

Florianus, Marcus Annius, uterine brother of the emperor Tacitus (q.v.), upon whose death (March A.D. 276) he was proclaimed emperor at Rome. In June of the same year he was murdered by his troops at Tarsus, while marching against Probus (q.v.).

Florus, Roman historian, lived under Trajan and Hadrian. His brief sketch of Roman history, from the foundation of Rome to 25 B.C., is extant, and is professedly derived from Livy. *See* the edition with translation by E. Forster (Loeb Library), 1929. *See also* FLORUS, PUBLIUS ANNIUS.

Florus, Publius Annius, Latin poet and rhetorician, sometimes identified with the historian Florus (*see* preceding article). He was born in Africa, but was in Rome during the reign of Domitian, before whose death (A.D. 96) he left Italy and established a school of rhetoric at Tarraco in Spain. He was certainly in Rome again during the reign of Hadrian. Florus is generally considered to be the author of twenty-six trochaic tetrameters, *De qualitate vitae*, of five hexameters, *De rosis*, and of three trochaic dimeters addressed to Hadrian (*see* J. W. and A. M. Duff, *Minor Latin Poets*, Loeb Library). The introduction to his dialogue *Virgilius orator an poeta* is also extant (*see* C. Halm's edition of the historian Florus, 1854). He was most probably not, as has been suggested, the author of *Pervigilium Veneris* (q.v.).

Formiae (mod. Formia), town of Latium on the Via Appia (*see* FUNDI) at the north-west extremity of the Bay of Caieta. The neighbourhood was popular as a resort of Roman nobles, many ruins of whose villas have been excavated. The most famous of these was one belonging to Cicero, near which he was murdered in 43 B.C.; but its exact site cannot now be determined.

Fortuna, an Italian goddess; originally a bringer of fertility, she was afterwards identified with the Greek Tyche, the personification of chance. At Praeneste (q.v.) was a famous sanctuary of Fortuna, with an oracle called the 'Praenestine lots'. This sanctuary, the nucleus of which was a small cave, was enlarged by Sulla to occupy five enormous terraces, which, resting on huge substructures of solid masonry and connected by stairways, towered above one another on the hill in the form of the side of a pyramid, crowned on the highest terrace with the small round temple of Fortuna. This mighty structure was the largest sanctuary in Italy; it was visible from many parts of Latium, from Rome, and even from the sea.

Forum, Latin name for an open space where the people of a city met for the transaction of public business, and for the sale and purchase of provisions. It was level, generally rectangular in shape, and surrounded by porticoes and public buildings. *See* ROME.

Forum Appii, post station on the Via Appia (q.v.), 43 miles southeast of Rome, and according to Horace the usual terminus of the first day's journey from the capital. In his day the stretch of road through the Pomptine marches (*see* POMPTINAE PALUDES) enjoyed less favour than a canal which started at Forum Appii. It was at Forum Appii that the Christians of Rome met St Paul (Acts xxviii. 15).

Forum Julii (mod. Fréjus), a Roman colony (*see* COLONIA), founded, according to some, by Julius Caesar (45 B.C.) with veterans of the Eighth Legion, but more probably by Augustus, as a port independent of Massilia. It became an important naval station and arsenal. There are ruins of a large amphitheatre, an aqueduct and various buildings. Forum Julii was the birth-place of Agricola (q.v.).

Forum Traiani, town of Sardinia on the road from Carales to Olbia and on the River Thyrsus. There are noteworthy remains of Roman baths built over hot springs.

Fosse Way, The, English name of a series of Roman roads in Britain, running from Lindum (Lincoln) to Isca Dumnoniorum (Exeter) via Ratae (Leicester), Venonae (High Cross), Corinium (Cirencester) and Aquae Sulis (Bath).

Four Hundred, The, an oligarchical government at Athens which came to power in 411 B.C. Its work was a catalogue of failures; it was ousted later in the same year. *See* Aristotle, *Athenian Constitution*, xxviii, 5–xxxiv, 1; W. S. Ferguson, 'The Oligarchical Movement in Athens', ch. xi in *Cambridge Ancient History*, vol. v.

Frentani, a Samnite tribe dwelling on the Adriatic coast of Italy, between the Sagrus on the north and the Frento on the south. They submitted to Rome in 305 or 304 B.C.

Fretum Gaditanum, Latin name for the Straits of Gibraltar. *See* ABYLA; CALPE.

Frisii, a Germanic people who, in the 1st century A.D., dwelt between the mouths of the Scaldis (Scheldt) and Amisia (Ems). They were made tributary to Rome by Drusus, and remained *socii* until the withdrawal of the legions to the left bank of the Rhine by Claudius in 47. In 70 they took part in the rebellion of Civilis (q.v.).

Frontinus, Sextus Julius (*c.* A.D. 40–103), Roman soldier and author. As governor of Britain (q.v.) from 74 until he was superseded by Agricola (q.v.) in 78, he distinguished himself by subduing the Silures. In 97 he was appointed superintendent of aqueducts (q.v.) at Rome. Two of his works have survived. The first, *De aquis urbis Romae*, is a history and description of the city's water supply, together with an account of its use and upkeep (*see* the great edition, with English translation by C. Herschel, 1899; 1913). The second, *Strategemata*, is a collection of examples of military stratagems drawn from Greek and Roman history. There is a text and translation by C. E. Bennett of both works in the Loeb Library, 1925.

Fronto, Marcus Cornelius (*c.* A.D. 100–70), Italian grammarian, rhetorician and advocate, born at Cirta in Numidia, but spent most of his life at Rome. He was tutor to M. Aurelius and L. Verus, and some of his correspondence with the future emperors and their adoptive father, Antoninus Pius, was discovered in palimpsest by Cardinal Mai at Milan and Rome early in the 19th century. These letters reveal a pedantic mind, but are evidence of the most sincere friendship. *See* the edition with translation by C. R. Haines (Loeb Library), 1919.

Fucinus, Lacus (mod. Lago di Fucino), a lake (drained since 1875) in central Italy, in the country of the Marsi (q.v.), 37 miles in circumference and 65 feet deep. To avoid the frequent flooding of this lake, the emperor Claudius ordered the construction of an emissarium, or artificial channel to carry its waters into the River Liris (*see also* NAUMACHIA). The emissarium, which employed the labour of 30,000 men for eleven years (A.D. 52–63), was three and a half miles long and had no fewer than forty shafts. It is in an almost perfect state of preservation, having been repaired in the reign of Trajan.

Fulvia, a Roman matron, notorious for her profligacy and ambition. Married first to Clodius (q.v.), and secondly to C. Scribonius Curio (q.v.), she later (*c.* 44 B.C.) became the wife of Mark Antony (q.v.). She exercised considerable influence in Rome during the civil war that followed Caesar's murder, and showed a bitterly vindictive spirit in the proscriptions. She instigated an unsuccessful revolt against Octavian (*see* AUGUSTUS) during Antony's absence in the East. Besieged in Perusia, she managed to escape to Athens, but was coldly received by her husband and died (40 B.C.) at Sicyon.

Fundi (mod. Fondi), in Latium, a former town of the Volsci (q.v.), after whose conquest by Rome in 338 B.C. it was granted, together with Formiae (q.v.), limited citizenship and later (188 B.C.) full citizenship. These favours were due to the fact that Fundi had always granted the Roman armies free passage through their territories. Their goodwill in this matter was all the more valuable to Rome after 312 B.C. in that the Via Appia (q.v.) ran through a narrow pass between the two towns. There are remains of walls.

Furiae, a mere Latin translation of the Greek name Erinyes (q.v.), corresponding to no Latin deities.

G

Gabii, city of Latium, 12 miles east of Rome on the Via Praenestina; traditionally a colony from Alba Longa (q.v.) and captured by Tarquinius Superbus. Though clearly an important place, its early history is uncertain. It had declined to insignificance in the reign of Augustus, but flourished again under Hadrian. The 'Cinctus Gabinus', a mode of wearing the toga (q.v.), seems to have originated here. In the neighbourhood are stone quarries used in the building of Rome. Remains include a temple dedicated probably to Juno and dating from the sacred half of the 3rd century B.C.

Gabinius, Aulus, Roman soldier and politician. While tribune of the plebs in 67 B.C., he proposed the *Lex Gabinia*, which gave Pompey supreme command in the war against the pirates, and carried other measures to check abuses in the senate. As consul in 58 he helped Clodius to drive Cicero into exile, and took office in the following year as proconsul of Syria. The principal events of his governorship (57–54) were the reinstatement of Hyrcanus II in the Jewish high priesthood, and the restoration of Ptolemy XI, Auletes (q.v.), to the throne of Egypt. But while he was engaged in the latter undertaking, his province was the scene of new disorders in the shape of rebellion against Hyrcanus and widespread brigandage. These were put down; but the damage they had caused to tax-farming interests led to the prosecution of Gabinius on his return to Rome. He went into voluntary exile, was recalled by Caesar in 49, and died on active service against M. Octavius in Illyricum, 48 B.C.

Gadara, city of Coele-Syria and a member of the Decapolis; birth-place of Philodemus, Meleager the anthologist, Menippus and Theodorus the rhetorician. The city was probably of Greek origin. It was taken by Antiochus III (q.v.) and by Alexander Jannaeus. Restored by Pompey in 63 B.C., it was given by Augustus to Herod the Great. Gadara was occupied by Vespasian during the Jewish wars, and the citizens dismantled its walls; but under the Antonines it recovered its prosperity, as may be seen from the ruins of three theatres and other once imposing structures. Three miles north of the city were the hot springs and baths of Amatha, much favoured by Roman residents in the time of Strabo. Note that Gadara is unconnected with the episode of the Gadarene swine, which probably took place near Kersa on the shores of the Lake of Galilee.

Gaetulia, name given by Latin writers to a district of north Africa, which extended roughly from the southern slopes of the Atlas to the Atlantic and included the northern oases of the Sahara. The inhabitants, who were Berbers, were noted as horse breeders and were said to produce purple dye.

Gaia or Gē, *see* TITANS.

Gaius, Roman jurist who lived in the reigns of Antoninus Pius and Marcus Aurelius. He wrote an elementary treatise on Roman law,

entitled *Institutionum Commentarii*, in four books. This was rediscovered in palimpsest by Niebuhr at Verona (1816). Its authenticity
was at first disputed, but has been confirmed by the discovery in
1933 of fragments on Egyptian papyri. *See* the edition by G. Stude-
mund and P. Krüger, 1923; there is a text with English translation
by E. Poste, 1875.

Gaius Caesar, son of M. Vipsanius Agrippa (q.v.) by Julia, daughter
of Augustus. On the death (12 B.C.) of Agrippa, whom Augustus had
considered his most suitable heir, he adopted Agrippa's two sons,
Gaius and Lucius, conferring upon them the title Caesar. This
question of the imperial succession had long been a source of anxiety
to the emperor, and he was once again disappointed: Lucius died in
A.D. 2, Gaius two years later; and Augustus turned at length to
Tiberius (q.v.).

Galatia: 1. District of Asia Minor occupied (278–277 B.C.) by Gauls
who had withdrawn from the army of Brennus (*see* BRENNUS, 2) and
crossed into Asia Minor at the request of Nicomedes I of Bithynia
(*see* NICOMEDES). It was bounded north by Bithynia and Paphlagonia,
east by Pontus, south by Lycaonia and Cappadocia, west by Phrygia.
During the next forty years the Gauls overran the entire peninsula
west of Taurus, but were defeated several times by Attalus I of
Pergamum, who obliged them (230 B.C.) to settle within the limits
indicated above. In 64 B.C. the kingdom of Galatia became a client
state of Rome; but in 52 B.C. Rome recognized Deiotarus (q.v.) as
king. The dominant Gallic element soon intermingled with the far
more numerous native population and gradually became hellenized,
though they long retained their own language and social customs.

2. The Roman province constituted by Augustus in 25 B.C. after
the death of Amyntus, third king of Galatia. It included the territory
described above, Pisidia and Isauria, together with parts of Phrygia
and of Lycaonia. These boundaries varied from time to time. *See*
A. H. M. Jones, *The Cities of the Eastern Roman Provinces*, 1937.

Galba, Servius Sulpicius, Roman emperor, June A.D. 68–January 69,
born near Terracina 24th December 5 B.C. As praetor in 20 and consul
in 33 he proved his ability as a soldier in Gaul, Germany, Africa and
Spain. In 41, after the assassination of Caligula, he was urged by his
friends to seize the throne; but he declined and remained loyal to
Claudius. In 61 he was living in retirement when Nero appointed him
governor of Hispania Tarraconensis. On Nero's death he was chosen
emperor by the praetorian guards, and marched on Rome. But the
troops and the people soon came to detest him for his austerity and
meanness: a conspiracy was formed by M. Salvius Otho (q.v.), and
Galba was murdered. His character is summed up in the immortal
phrase of Tacitus: 'Capax imperii nisi imperasset ('Worthy of empire if
he had never been emperor'). *See* the Lives by Plutarch and Suetonius;
see also B. W. Henderson, *Civil War and Rebellion in the Roman
Empire*, A.D. 69–70, 1908.

Galen (Galēnos), Greek physician, born A.D. 130 at Pergamum, son
of Nicon, an architect. Nicon personally superintended his son's
elementary education, and then sent him, at the age of fourteen, to
study mathematics, logic and philosophy with the best teachers in the

town. The boy learned the doctrines of Plato and Aristotle, of Epicureanism and Stoicism; but when he was seventeen Nicon had vivid dreams, as a result of which he caused his son to take up medicine also. Galen was therefore put to study at the Asclepieum, and later, after Nicon's death, he continued his medical studies at Smyrna, Corinth and Alexandria. Returning to Pergamum in 157, he was appointed physician to the gladiators, but found the work distasteful and settled in Rome (161), where he soon made a name for himself and was welcomed in the highest society. At that time, however, medical practice was corrupt, and Galen's outspoken criticisms roused such violent hostility that he was obliged to leave Rome. He had scarcely reached Pergamum when he was recalled by the emperors Marcus Aurelius and Lucius Verus, who meant him to accompany them on their expedition against the Marcomanni (157). Galen managed to excuse himself and was left in Rome to look after the health of the young heir-apparent Commodus. Little is known of his subsequent career. He died, probably in Sicily, in A.D. 200.

Practically nothing remains of his philosophical treatises. The corpus of his medical writings includes 162 works and some fragments. Only 98 are considered genuine; 19 are held to be doubtful and 45 spurious. See the standard edition by C. G. Kühn, 20 vols., 1821–33. The only work yet available in English is that on *The Natural Faculties*, edited with translation by A. J. Brock (Loeb Library), 1916. *See also* A. J. Brock, *Greek Medicine*, 1929.

Galerius, whose full name was Galerius Valerius Maximianus, was born near Sardica in Thrace. After a distinguished military career under Aurelian and Probus, he was given the title Caesar, along with Constantius Chlorus (q.v.), by Diocletian and Maximian (A.D. 293). He assumed the title of Augustus on the abdication of the two latter in 305, and, intending to make himself master of the whole empire on the death of Constantius, he secured the promotion to the rank of Caesar of Flavius Valerius Severus, a loyal servant, and Maximinus Daia (q.v.), his nephew. His plans, however, were upset by the proclamation of Constantine (q.v.) at Eburacum and the action of Maximian and Maxentius in Italy. Galerius devoted most of his remaining years to pleasure. But it was at his instigation that the first edict of persecution against the Christians was published (24th February 303), and he continued this policy until the general edict of toleration was issued in his name and those of Licinius (q.v.) and Constantine, A.D. 311, in which year also he died.

Galeus, 'lizard', in Greek mythology, son of Apollo and Themisto, from whom the Galeotae, a family of soothsayers at Megara Hyblaea in Sicily, claimed to be descended.

Gallaecia (mod. Galicia), district of Lusitania. Its inhabitants were defeated with great slaughter in 138 B.C. by the consul D. Junius Brutus (q.v.).

Gallia, name given by the Romans to the two chief districts inhabited by Celtic-speaking peoples.

1. GALLIA CISALPINA, between the Alps and the Apennines; it was divided by the Padus (Po) into *Cispadana* and *Transpadana*, south and north respectively of the river (but *see also* ITALIA). It had been

practically conquered by Rome and formed into a province by 222 B.C., but it was not until 191 B.C. that the Boii (q.v.) were finally subjugated. After it had become romanized it was sometimes known as *Gallia Togata*, and about 42 B.C. it was made part of Italy. Among the most famous sons of Gallia Cisalpina were Virgil, Livy, Catullus, Cornelius Nepos and the two Plinys (qq.v.).

2. GALLIA TRANSALPINA, bounded by the Alps, the Mediterranean, the Pyrenees, the Atlantic and the Rhine. Greeks from Phocaea (q.v.) in Asia Minor founded the colony of Massilia (q.v.) *c.* 600 B.C. The Romans began the conquest of Gallia Transalpina in 125 B.C.; four years later they formed the south-eastern part of the country into the province of *Gallia Narbonensis* (called by Caesar The Province), and constituted its port, Narbo (q.v.), a *municipium* (q.v.). This province was gradually extended northwards up the Rhône, and as a result of Caesar's Gallic campaigns (58–51) the whole of Gaul to the Rhine and the Atlantic became Roman territory.

Augustus divided this large area into four provinces: (*a*) *Gallia Narbonensis*, between the Alps, Mediterranean and Cevennes and up the Rhône to Vienne (q.v.). By A.D. 70 it had become completely romanized. (*b*) *Aquitania*, from the Pyrenees to the Liger (Loire). (*c*) *Lugdunensis*, named after its capital Lugdunum (q.v.), between the Liger and Sequana (Seine), stretching south-eastward from modern Brittany to Lugdunum. (*d*) *Belgica*. In these last three provinces the Roman language and culture made slower progress, especially in country places. Narbonensis was governed by a proconsul; each of the other three by a pro-praetorian legate. No garrison was stationed in any of the four.

Shortly afterwards, that part of Belgica which bordered on the Rhine was organized into two military districts called *exercitus*. Between A.D. 80 and 90 these became the twin provinces of *Germania Superior* (or *Prima*) and *Germania Inferior* (or *Secunda*), the former including territory east of the Rhine that was bounded by the Limes Germanicus (q.v.). The foregoing arrangements were modified by Diocletian (q.v.). *See* O. Brogan, *Roman Gaul*, 1953.

Gallienus, Publius Licinius Egnatius, Roman emperor A.D. 260–268, son of Valerianus (q.v.), born *c.* 218. He was associated with his father in the empire in 253, and when Valerian was taken prisoner by Sapor I of Persia (260), Gallienus took no steps to obtain his release. His miserable reign witnessed incursions by invaders from all sides, the sack of many Greek cities by the Goths, widespread rebellion (*see* THIRTY TYRANTS, 2) and the ravages of pestilence. Gallienus was killed by his own troops while besieging Mediolanum.

Gallio, Junius Annaeus, born at Corduba, elder son of M. Annaeus Seneca (q.v.) the rhetorician, and brother of L. Annaeus Seneca (q.v.) the philosopher. His original name was L. Annaeus Novatus, but he was adopted at Rome by L. Junius Gallio, a rhetorician. He was banished (A.D. 41) and recalled (49) together with his brother. As governor of Achaea, in 53, he dismissed the charge of heresy brought by the Jews of Corinth against St Paul (Acts xviii, 12–17). Gallio survived his brother Seneca, but in 65 he committed suicide or was put to death by order of Nero.

Gallus, Cornelius, Roman poet. Born at Forum Julii in Gaul, he went to Rome at an early age and rose to distinction under Julius Caesar and Augustus. He was appointed by the latter first prefect of Egypt (q.v.), in which capacity he subdued the natives of Upper Egypt and received ambassadors from Aethiopia (q.v.) at Philae, and established a nominal protectorate over the frontier district which had been abandoned by the later Ptolemies. Eventually, however, he incurred the emperor's displeasure, was sent into exile and committed suicide (26 B.C.). Ovid ranked him first among Roman elegiac poets. All his works have perished, though some believe him to have been the author of the *Ciris* attributed by Suetonius to Virgil.

Gallus, Gaius Sulpicius, Roman general, statesman and orator. Under L. Aemilius Paulus he commanded the Second Legion in the war against Perseus of Macedon, and (being a student of astronomy) predicted a lunar eclipse on the night before the battle of Pydna (168 B.C.). He was consul in 166, and devoted the remainder of his life to study.

Gallus, Gaius Vibius Trebonianus, Roman emperor A.D. 251–3, successor of Decius (q.v.). He concluded peace with the Goths on terms dishonourable to Rome. When the barbarians renewed their attack in the following year they were routed by Aemilianus (q.v.), who was proclaimed emperor by his troops. Gallus marched against him, but was defeated and killed.

Gallus Saloninus, Gaius Asinius, son of C. Asinius Pollio (q.v.), married Vipsania (q.v.), divorced wife of the emperor Tiberius, who hated him on that account. A pretext was found for having him thrown into prison, where he languished four years and died in A.D. 33. Gallus was the author of a work unfavourable to Cicero, to which the emperor Claudius replied.

Games, Greek, *see* ISTHMIAN GAMES; NEMEAN GAMES; OLYMPIC GAMES; PYTHIAN GAMES.

Games, Roman, *see* LUDI APOLLINARES; LUDI MAGNI; LUDI MEGALENSES; LUDI SAECULARES; GLADIATORS; NAUMACHIA.

Ganymedes (Ganumēdēs), according to Homer, son of Tros, King of Troy. Because of his exceeding beauty he was carried off by Zeus to serve as his cup-bearer, in which capacity he was responsible for the annual flooding of the Nile, and was later identified with the constellation Aquarius. Zeus compensated the father with a stud of immortal horses.

The many variants of this myth are of some interest. Thus he is often (*see* HERACLES) called son of Laomedon; the carrying off is done not by Zeus, but by his eagle or by the god in shape of an eagle; and the horses become a golden vine. The popular Latin form of his name, moreover, was Catamitus. This appears to derive from an ancient (? Dorian) tradition (6th century B.C.) that the ravisher (who according to a Cretan version was Minos) entertained an unnatural passion for the boy.

'Garden, The', name given to the Epicurean school of philosophy (*see* EPICURUS), in the same way that the 'Academy' and the 'Porch' are used respectively to denote the Platonic and Stoic schools. The name arose from the fact that Epicurus taught in the gardens at

Athens, and it has sound authority in the statement of Diogenes Laertius (*Lives of the Philosophers*, x. 10) that the disciples of Epicurus were known as 'those from the gardens' ('hoi apo tōn kēpōn').

Gargettus (-os), an Attic deme, birth-place of Neocles, father of Epicurus (q.v.).

Gaugamela, town in the Persian province of Adiabene, near which Alexander the Great (q.v.) with 47,000 troops defeated a great host under Darius III, Codomannus (q.v.), in 331 B.C. This famous action is often called the battle of Arbela, because it was at Arbela, 32 miles east of Gaugamela, that Darius placed his magazines and harems before moving westward to meet the enemy. The battle of Gaugamela has been described as 'one of the supreme tactical masterpieces in the military history of the ancient world'. See *Cambridge Ancient History*, vol. vi; E. W. Marsden, *The Campaign of Gaugamela*, 1964.

Gaurus, Mons, volcanic range in Campania (q.v.), between Cumae and Neapolis. It produced good wine and was the scene of a Samnite defeat by M. Valerius Corvus in 343 B.C.

Gaza, ancient city of Palestine, taken and sacked by Alexander the Great after an obstinate resistance (332 B.C.). The Romans made it an important place (named Minoa) and gave it to Herod the Great.

Gē or **Gaia**, *see* TITANS.

Gela, city on the south coast of Sicily, founded by colonists from Crete and Rhodes in 690 B.C. In 582 B.C. Gela itself founded Acragas (*see* AGRIGENTUM). It obtained power and wealth, particularly under its tyrant Hippocrates, who died in 491 B.C. He was succeeded by Gelon (q.v.), who transported half the population to Syracuse, leaving his brother Hieron (q.v.) to govern those who remained. Between 466 and 405 it regained some of its former prosperity; but in the latter year it was abandoned by order of Dionysius I (q.v.), and although the inhabitants returned, 4,000 of them were put to death by Agathocles in 311 B.C. Gela was destroyed by the Mamertines (q.v.) *c.* 281 B.C., after which the survivors were removed by Phintias, tyrant of Agrigentum. Aeschylus (q.v.) died at Gela in 456 B.C. There are unimportant remains of Greek temples.

Gellius, Aulus (*c.* A.D. 123–65), Latin author and grammarian, born in Rome. There he spent most of his life, except for a period of residence at Athens while studying philosophy. He was the author of a work entitled *Noctes Atticae* in ten books, nine of which have survived. It is composed of notes upon a very wide variety of subjects, and is particularly valuable on account of its numerous quotations from lost authors, and also because of the light it throws upon the period. *See* text and translation by J. C. Rolfe (Loeb Library), 1927–8.

Gelōn, tyrant of Gela and Syracuse (qq.v.). On the death of Hippocrates in 491 B.C., his cavalry commander, Gelon, succeeded him. In 485 his help was sought by the oligarchical party at Syracuse. He thus became master of that state, a mastery which extended to the whole of Sicily after his great victory over the Carthaginians at Himera (q.v.) in 480.

Gemoniae (*scalae*) or **Gemonii** (*gradus*), a flight of steps cut out of the Aventine hill at Rome, down which the bodies of criminals strangled in the prison were dragged before being thrown into the Tiber.

Genava (mod. Geneva), in Caesar's time a town in the extreme north of Gallia Narbonensis, in what had formerly been the territory of the Allobroges (q.v.). It lay at the point when the Rhône emerged from the Lacus Lemannus (mod. Lake of Geneva) and was crossed by a bridge. *See* Caesar, *Bell. Gall.* i. 7.

Genius, meaning the 'begetter', was an early Roman private cult, a divinity personifying the male capacity of a family or *gens* to reproduce itself, and residing exclusively in the *paterfamilias* (*see* PATRIA POTESTAS) or head of the clan. For the corresponding female capacity *see* JUNO. At all weddings a bed called *lectus genialis* was prepared for the *genius* and *iuno* of the married couple.

In course of time, with the growth of individualism and owing largely to contact with the Greek idea of guardian spirits (*daimones*), the genius came to personify the individual's appetites and natural desires; so that *genio indulgere* and *genium defraudare* meant respectively to lead a life of pleasure and of austerity. This new conception was carried to a point at which the genius was transformed into a man's higher self, even into his personal character or temperament, and as such was worshipped by him, especially on his birthday.

It had always been a mark of respect to honour or swear by another's genius; and since every genius was essentially divine, a popular cult of the emperor's genius developed as early as the reign of Augustus. Other developments were the genii of places, of buildings and of corporations great or small.

Genua (mod. Genoa), seaport town of Liguria, occupied by Greeks in the 4th century B.C. Destroyed by the Carthaginians in 204 B.C., it was restored by the Romans and became at some unknown date a *municipium* (q.v.). According to Pliny it produced the best wine in Liguria; its chief exports were timber, honey and skins.

Gerasa, city of Palestine, 20 miles east of the Jordan, and a member of the Decapolis (q.v.). Said to have been originally colonized by veterans of Alexander the Great, it was captured by Alexander Jannaeus *c.* 83 B.C. and several times thereafter destroyed and rebuilt by the Jews and Romans. Under the Antonines it rose to great prosperity, and there are many splendid architectural remains. From the reign of Trajan, Gerasa belonged to the province of Syria until *c.* 160, when it was included in that of Arabia Petraea.

Gergovia, chief town of the Arverni (q.v.), about eight miles from the Puy de Dôme. Caesar attacked it unsuccessfully in 52 B.C. (*Bell. Gall.* vii. 36–8). Under Augustus the place was dismantled and the inhabitants resettled in a new Roman town named Augustonemetum (mod. Clermont-Ferrand) four miles away in the plain.

Germania, a country bounded west by the Rhine, east by the Vistula and Carpathians, south by the Danube, north by the North Sea and the Baltic. For the principal tribes whose names occur in Roman history *see* AESTII; ALAMANNI; ANGLI; BATAVI; BRUCTERI; CHATTI; CHAUCI; CHERUSCI; FRISII; GOTONES; LANGOBARDI; MARCOMANNI; QUADI; SEMNONES; SUEBI; SUGAMBRI; TENCTERI; TEUTONES; UBII. For Roman attempts to extend the imperial frontier beyond the Rhine *see* (in this order) DRUSUS, NERO CLAUDIUS;

TIBERIUS; VARUS; GERMANICUS; VESPASIAN; DOMITIAN. For the establishment of the two Roman provinces, *Germania Superior* and *Inferior*, on the west bank of the Rhine, *see* GALLIA; *see also* AGRI DECUMATES; COLONIA AGRIPPINA; LIMES GERMANICUS; MOGUNTIACUM. *See* Caesar, *De Bell. Gall.*, i. 31 ff., iv. 1–19, vi. 21 ff.; Velleius Paterculus, ii. 105 ff.; Tacitus, *Annales*, i. 38 ff., ii. 5 ff., 44 ff., 62 ff., 68; and *Germania, Histories* iv.; T. R. Holmes, *Caesar's Conquest of Gaul*, 1911; T. Mommsen, *The Provinces of the Roman Empire* (trans.), 1909.

Germanicus Caesar, Nero Claudius, Roman general. He was born in 15 B.C., son of Nero Claudius Drusus by Antonia, daughter of Mark Antony, and was adopted by his uncle, the future emperor Tiberius, during the lifetime of Augustus. He assisted Tiberius in his campaigns against the Pannonians and Dalmatians (A.D. 7–10), and against the Germans (A.D. 11 and 12). Germanicus was commanding in Germany when the legions there and in Pannonia mutinied on the death of Augustus (A.D. 14). After restoring order among the troops he undertook the conquest of Germany, with such success that he might soon have reduced the entire country between the Rhine and the Elbe. In A.D. 17, however, Germanicus was recalled by Tiberius, who appointed him commander-in-chief in the East, but secretly ordered the governor of Syria, Gnaeus Calpurnius Piso (*see* PISO, GNAEUS CALPURNIUS), to thwart him at every turn. In A.D. 19 Germanicus died in Syria, and it was commonly believed that he had been poisoned by Piso. His wife Agrippina the elder bore him nine children, among whom were the emperor Caligula and Agrippina the younger, mother of Nero. *See* Tacitus, *Annales*, ii. iii.

Gerousia, the council of elders at Sparta. It consisted of twenty-four members, all over sixty years of age, elected by the Apella (q.v.) and holding office for life, plus, *ex officio*, the two kings and five ephors (*see* EPHOR). The Gerousia prepared all business which was to be submitted to the Apella and had power to nullify perverse decisions of the latter. Besides possessing a large measure of political and criminal jurisdiction, it formed the highest executive committee of the state. *See* Aristotle, *Politics* ii; A. H. J. Greenidge, *Handbook of Greek Constitutional History*, 1896.

Geryon (Gēruon), *see* TWELVE LABOURS OF HERACLES, 11.

Geta, Publius Septimius, younger son of the emperor Septimius Severus, born A.D. 189 at Mediolanum. On the death of Severus (211) Caracalla (q.v.) and his brother Geta were proclaimed joint emperors. A scheme for dividing the empire between them was proposed, but rejected; whereupon Caracalla arranged that they should meet in their mother's apartments and be reconciled. There Geta was assassinated in his mother's arms by centurions who had been sent by Caracalla (A.D. 212).

Getae, a Thracian people who believed the human soul to be immortal. They inhabited the right bank of the Danube near its mouth, but moved north of the river in the reign of Philip II of Macedon. Alexander the Great, before his expedition to Asia, invaded their new territory unopposed; but they worsted two other Macedonian armies, in 326 and 292, before their own defeat by the Gauls *c.* 278 B.C. From this time they were generally called Daci, to whom they were in fact closely akin.

Gigantes, the giants, sprang from the blood of Uranus (*see* TITANS). They attacked Olympus, armed with rocks and tree-trunks; but the gods, assisted by Heracles (q.v.), defeated them and buried them under Mt Aetna. It is probable that the story of their war with the gods arose from the spectacle of volcanic eruptions. *See also* ALOIDAE.

Glabrio, Manius Acilius : 1. Roman general. When consul, in 191 B.C., he defeated Antiochus the Great at Thermopylae.

2. Son of the jurist P. Mucius Scaevola (q.v.). As praetor urbanus in 70 B.C. he presided at the impeachment of Verres (q.v.). In 67 he was consul with C. Calpurnius Piso, and introduced the *Lex Acilia Calpurnia* against illegal canvassing at elections. In that year also he superseded Lucullus in the government of Cilicia and the command of the third Mithradatic war, but he proved ineffective and was succeeded in turn by Pompey.

Gladiators, professional combatants who fought to provide public entertainment. The custom of gladiatorial fights is supposed to have come from the East, and to have been borrowed by Rome from the Etruscans. Its origin is probably to be found in the practice of honouring heroes who had died in battle by sacrificing the lives of captives. The practice spread to the funerals of all important men, the sacrifice being rendered more interesting to the spectators by the captives dying in conflict with one another, and later still it became an independent form of public amusement. The first gladiatorial fight in Rome of which we have knowledge took place in 264 B.C., being arranged by Marcus and Decimus Brutus for their father's funeral. In 217 B.C. Scipio Africanus arranged an exhibition at New Carthage; in 207 B.C. twenty-four pairs of gladiators fought in the Forum at Rome; while Julius Caesar, Titus and Trajan all gave huge gladiatorial shows. Augustus made some attempt to limit the number of such exhibitions, but they had become so popular that this was impossible. They were unsuccessfully prohibited by Constantine (A.D. 325) and finally abolished by Theodoric (A.D. 500).

The gladiators were slaves, prisoners or criminals, who were bought and trained for the business, or freemen of the lowest class, who fought for hire. They were sworn to fight to the death, and any show of cowardice was punished with death by torture. The defeat of one of the combatants was marked by a cry of 'Habet!' from the spectators, who then decided his fate, turning their thumbs upwards if they wished him to be killed by the victor. The winner was rewarded with a branch of palm, and sometimes received his freedom.

There were several types of gladiators, such as the *andabatae*, who fought blindfolded; the *mirmillones*, who fought with sword and shield; the *retiarii*, who had as weapons a net and a three-pronged lance; and the *Thraces*, who used a short sword and round buckler. They were occasionally mounted. Discharged gladiators were known as *rudiarii*, from the *rudis*, a wooden sword, with which they were presented. The practice of gladiatorial fights never found much favour in Greece.

Glauce (-kē): 1. One of the nereids, the name Glauce being only a personification of the colour of the sea.

2. Daughter of Cychreus, King of Salamis, and first wife of Telamon (q.v.).

3. Otherwise Creusa, daughter of Creon, King of Corinth (*see* CREON, 1), and wife of Jason (*see* JASON AND MEDEA).

Glaucus (-kos), name of four persons in Greek legend.

1. Son of Sisyphus and father of Bellerophon, was torn to pieces by his own mares for having despised the power of Aphrodite.

2. Son of Hippolochus and grandson of Bellerophon, succeeded Sarpedon (q.v.) as commander of the Lycians in the Trojan war. There were ties of hospitality between Glaucus and Diomedes (*see* DIOMEDES, 2), and when the two men recognized each other in battle, they abstained from fighting and exchanged arms. Glaucus was eventually slain by Telamonian Ajax.

3. Son of Minos, King of Crete, and Pasiphaë. When a boy he fell into a cask of honey and was drowned. A soothsayer, appointed by Apollo for this purpose, discovered the body, and was ordered by Minos to restore the boy to life. Having failed to do so, he was condemned to a similar death, but a serpent revealed a herb which brought both bodies to life.

4. A fisherman of Anthedon in Boeotia, who became a marine deity by eating part of a herb sown by Cronus. He was believed to pay annual visits to the coasts and islands of Greece, where fishermen and sailors eagerly awaited his prophecies.

Glevum (mod. Gloucester), headquarters of the Second Legion *c.* 50–*c.* 75. *Colonia* (q.v.) *c.* 97.

Glycon (Glukōn), Athenian sculptor of the 1st century B.C. He made the 'Farnese Hercules' (now at Naples), a copy of an earlier work by Lysippus.

Golden Fleece, The, *see* ARGONAUTS; JASON AND MEDEA; PHRIXUS.

Gordianus, Marcus Antonius, name of three Roman emperors, father, son and grandson. The father, a man of high intellectual gifts and moral integrity, was governor of Africa when he was proclaimed emperor on the death of Maximinus I in A.D. 238. Being then eighty years old he associated his son with him in the empire. Two months later the younger Gordian fell in battle, and his father committed suicide. The grandson was chosen emperor by the soldiers in Rome, later in the year 238, after the murder of Balbinus and Pupienus (qq.v.). He was only twelve years old at the time. Gordian reigned until A.D. 244, when he was assassinated by the troops at Zaitha with the connivance of the praetorian prefect, who seized the throne and is known as the emperor Philip the Arabian (*see* PHILIPPUS).

Gordium (-on), Phrygian city on the River Sangarius, residence of Gordius (q.v.) and his successors.

Gordius (-os), legendary king of Phrygia and father of Midas (q.v.). During civil strife in that country the inhabitants were told by an oracle that a wagon would bring them a king. Shortly afterwards appeared Gordius, a peasant, riding in his wagon, and the people at once acknowledged him as king. Gordius dedicated the cart to Zeus, which was laid up on the acropolis at Gordium. The pole was fastened to the yoke by a knot of cornel bark so cunningly tied that the two ends were invisible; but another oracle declared that whoever managed to undo the strangely tied knot would reign over Asia. Alexander the Great, after several fruitless attempts, cut it with his sword, thus circumventing an oracle which he nevertheless claimed to have fulfilled. *See* ADRASTUS, 2.

Gorgias, Greek sophist and rhetorician, born at Leontini in Sicily *c.* 483 B.C. In 427 he was head of an embassy sent to ask Athenian help against Syracuse. He afterwards settled at Athens, where he introduced the art of rhetoric, and did much to establish the Attic dialect as the language of literary prose. He is the principal speaker in Plato's *Gorgias.* Fragments of his work *On Nature or the Non-existent* survive; the genuineness of two rhetorical exercises (edited with the speeches of Antiphon (q.v.) by F. Blass in 1881) is extremely doubtful.

Gorgōn, according to Homer (*Od.* xi. 633), a monster of the underworld, whose head (*Il.* v. 741) is fixed in the centre of Zeus's aegis (q.v.). In Hesiod there are three Gorgones: Stheno, Euryale and Medusa, the daughters of Phorcys and Ceto, who dwell in the far west (*see also* GRAEAE). Later tradition places them in Libya. Euripides (*Ion.* 1002) takes up the old Athenian legend of a single Gorgon and represents it as a monster produced by Gē (Earth) and slain by Athena.

The Gorgons were depicted as winged females, their heads covered with serpents in place of hair, and having enormous teeth. Medusa alone of the three was mortal; hence Perseus (q.v.) was able to kill her by cutting off her head. From her blood sprang Pegasus (q.v.). The head turned anyone who beheld it into stone. Some authorities believe that the figure of Medusa derives from a ritual mask; others connect her with the staring or pursuing faces which occur in nightmares.

Gortyna (-tuna), city of Crete, once next in importance to Knossos. Here, in 1884, was discovered an inscription known as the Code of Gortyna, a body of laws in two parts, the second and later of which dates from about 450 B.C. *See* J. Kohler and E. Ziebarth, *Das Stadtrecht von Gortyn,* 1912.

Gotones (Goths), a German tribe inhabiting the middle basin of the Vistula, with settlements also in the island of Gottland in the Baltic. At the beginning of the 3rd century A.D. they extended their frontiers southward, ravaging the whole country as far as the lower Danube. The emperor Decius (q.v.) was defeated and slain by them in Moesia, A.D. 251. His successor, Gallus, paid them tribute, and during the next twenty years they made frequent attacks on the maritime districts of Greece and Asia Minor. It was in face of Gothic pressure that the emperor Aurelian abandoned Dacia (q.v.). Constantine made peace with their king Ariaric.

Gracchus, Gaius Sempronius, Roman statesman, younger son of Tib. Sempronius Gracchus, by Cornelia, daughter of Scipio Africanus the elder, and brother of Tib. Sempronius Gracchus (*see* No. 3 in next article). As tribune of the plebs in 123 B.C., he proposed reforms more extensive than his brother's, and such was his influence with the people that all his measures passed into law. The first of these was renewal of his brother's legislation. He also transferred judicial functions from the senate to the equites (q.v.), and provided that in future, *before* the consular elections, the senate should determine the two provinces which would be assigned to the new consuls. Gracchus was elected tribune a second time, for 122 B.C. The senate, however, resolved to destroy his influence with the people. They sent him with M. Valerius Flaccus (q.v.) to found a colony at Carthage, and persuaded one of his colleagues, M. Livius Drusus (*see* DRUSUS, MARCUS LIVIUS, 1), to propose measures even more popular than those of Gracchus. The people were duped, and the popularity of Gracchus waned. He failed to obtain the tribunate for the following year (121), and when his term of office had expired his enemies moved to repeal some of his enactments. He appeared in the Forum to oppose these proceedings, and a riot ensued. His supporters fought furiously in his defence; but they were worsted, and Gracchus flew to the grove of the Furiae, where he ordered one of his slaves to kill him. About 3,000 of his friends were slain, while many were thrown into prison and there strangled. *See* T. Rice Holmes, *The Roman Republic*, vol. i, 1923, pp. 17–30.

Gracchus, Tiberius Sempronius: 1. Roman general in the second Punic war; consul 215 and 213 B.C. In 212 he died in battle against Hannibal's brother Mago at Campi Veteres in Lucania. His body was sent to Hannibal, who honoured it with a splendid funeral.

2. Father of the tribunes (*see* 3 below and GRACCHUS, GAIUS SEMPRONIUS). While tribune of the plebs in 185 B.C. he rendered services to Scipio Africanus Major (q.v.), and was rewarded with the hand of his daughter Cornelia (*see* CORNELIA, 1), who bore him twelve children; but all died young except the two tribunes and a daughter Cornelia, who was married to Scipio Africanus the younger. Gracchus was twice consul and once censor. He subdued the Celtiberi in 179, and died in 151 B.C.

3. Roman statesman, elder surviving son of the preceding, born *c.* 168 B.C. As he grew up his sympathy was roused by the distressed condition of Italy, large tracts of which were completely deserted, while the huge estates of a few wealthy men were cultivated only by slave labour; and he resolved to remedy this state of affairs by creating an industrious middle class of agriculturists. With this end in view, when tribune of the plebs in 133 B.C., he proposed a Bill for the renewal and enforcement of the Licinian Rogations (*see* LICINIUS, 1), and to the section under which no one might hold more than 500 *jugera* of public land he added a clause permitting a father of two sons to hold an additional 250 *jugera* in respect of each. The measure was opposed by the aristocracy; but it eventually passed into law, and commissioners were appointed to execute its provisions. In the same year (133) Attalus III (q.v.) of Pergamum bequeathed his kingdom and his personal fortune to the Roman people, and on the proposal of Gracchus part of this legacy was divided among the poor, to enable them to buy farming implements, etc. When the time came for the election of tribunes for the following year Tiberius was again a candidate, but was assassinated by P. Cornelius Scipio Nasica Serapio. *See* T. Rice Holmes, *The Roman Republic*, vol. i, 1912, pp. 1–19.

Graeae (Graiai), 'old women' or 'hags', sisters of the Gorgones (*see* GORGON). They were three in number: Pemphredo, Dino and Enys; their hair was grey from birth, and they had only one eye and one tooth between them. *See also* PERSEUS.

Granicus (-kos), small river of Mysia, the scene of Alexander's first great victory over Darius III, Codomannus, in 334 B.C.

Grattius, Latin poet of the Augustan age, author of *Cynegetica*, an hexameter poem on hunting, of which 541 lines are extant. *See* edition and translation by J. W. and A. M. Duff in *Minor Latin Poets* (Loeb Library).

Great Mother of the Gods, a divinity whose worship originated in Asia Minor, and who was called by the Greeks and Romans Cybele or other names (e.g. Dindymene) derived from the chief centres of her cult. The Great Mother was known in Boeotia in the 6th century B.C., but did not reach Attica until about two hundred years later. She was soon identified by the Greeks with Rhea (*see also* ATTIS); but she was sometimes accepted without Attis, and identified with Gē or Demeter. In 204 B.C. her cult was introduced at Rome from Pessinùs in Galatia, in consequence of a Sibylline prophecy. Here she was variously identified with Maia, Ops, Rhea, Tellus and Ceres. A temple was erected on the Palatine, and in it was laid up the sacred symbol of the goddess, a meteoric stone supposed to have fallen from heaven and formerly kept at Pessinus. The worship of the Great Mother was in the hands of a high priest and priestess, together with a whole train of minor officials. (It was forbidden to Roman citizens until imperial times.) Her annual festival was originally on 4th April, but from the reign of Claudius it lasted from 15th to 27th March. *See* LUDI MEGALENSES.

Greece (Gk Hellas; Lat. Graecia). The Greeks of classical times called themselves Hellenes (*see* HELLEN) and their country Hellas. But the name Hellenes, as used to designate the inhabitants of the peninsula as opposed to the barbarians (i.e. non-Greek speaking peoples), was of comparatively late origin. In Homer the Hellenes are a people of Phthiotis in southern Thessaly. The names Graeci and Graecia, as general names for the people and country of Greece, were used only by the Romans, who extended to the whole region the name of the first tribe they encountered on the Greek mainland (at Dodona, in Epirus). In its widest and loosest application 'Hellas' signified the abode of the Hellenes, mainland and colonies alike (*see* MAGNA GRAECIA). More specifically, Hellas was the land which, prior to the Macedonian conquests, lay south of the Cambunian and Araunian mountains, and included the following districts: Acarnania, Achaea, Aetolia, Arcadia, Argolis, Attica, Boetia, Corinth, Doris, Elis, Epirus, Laconia, Locris, Megaris, Messenia, Phocis, Sicyon, Thessalia. *See* ACHAEANS; DORIANS; IONIANS. *See also* S. Casson, *Ancient Greece*, 1922; J. L. Myres, *Who were the Greeks?*, 1930.

Greek Drama, *see* THEATRE.

Griffin (Gk *Grups*; Lat. *Gryphus*), a fabulous animal, belief in which came apparently from the East. It had the body of a lion and the head and wings of an eagle. Griffins were supposed to dwell in the Rhiphaean mountains and to fight with the Arimaspi (q.v.) for the gold of that region.

Gryllus (Grullos), elder son of the historian Xenophon, slain at the battle of Mantineia (362 B.C.), in which he is said to have killed Epameinondas (q.v.).

Gyarus (Guaros), a small island of the Cyclades lying south-west of Andros. In Roman imperial times it was used as a place of banishment.

Gylippus (Gulippos), the Spartan commander at Syracuse 414–413 B.C. His arrival found the Syracusans on the point of negotiating surrender; yet within a year he annihilated the Athenian armament and destroyed all reasonable hope of final victory for Athens in the Peloponnesian war (*see* Thucydides, vii). In 404 he was commissioned by Lysander to convey a sum of money from Athens to Sparta; but on the way he embezzled a large part of it, was discovered and went into exile.

Gymnasium (Gumnasion), originally a public school for the training of competitors in Greek games, who exercised naked (*gumnos*). It is to be distinguished from the palaestra, a private school in which boys were trained in physical exercises; but the word 'palaestra' was often applied to that part of the gymnasium set aside for boxing and wrestling.

The gymnasium formed a large complexus of buildings, with separate places for the various kinds of exercise, a stadium, baths and a covered portico for use in bad weather. It also possessed an outer portico, where philosophers and other teachers expounded their views. The trainees were under a regular hierarchy of officials responsible for their maintenance, their morals, their exercises and their health.

The Romans in republican times viewed the gymnasium with profound suspicion, holding it useless for military training and conducive to immorality. The first public gymnasium at Rome was built by Nero and another by Commodus.

Gymnesiae Insulae, *see* BALEARES.

Gythium (Guthion), the harbour and arsenal of Sparta, from which it was about 30 miles distant, on the Laconian Gulf.

H

Hadēs, originally **Aidēs** (the 'Unseen'), Greek god of the under-world, often called euphemistically Pluto (q.v.). The Romans knew him as Dis, Orcus or Tartarus. Hades was son of Cronus and Rhea (*see* TITANS); his wife was Persephone, daughter of Demeter (q.v.). Sacrifices offered to him consisted of black sheep, and the offerer while thus engaged turned away his face from the altar. The name Hades was also given to his kingdom, a kind of shadowy world akin to Hebrew *Sheol*.

Hadrian's Wall in Britain (q.v.), the great northern frontier system constructed by the Romans as a continuous and permanent barrier between Tyne and Solway. It was intended as an operational base against direct attack by the Caledonians and also as a defence against barbarian infiltration from the north. The wall was designed by Hadrian (*see* HADRIANUS) as part of his plan for the consolidation of the empire during his visit to Britain in A.D. 122, but the work was largely executed by the governor Aulus Platorius Nepos (122–6). The wall runs for a distance of a little over 73 miles, from Wallsend-on-Tyne to Bowness-on-Solway. Hadrian's Wall is the most powerful and most impressive of all Roman frontier works. It consists of (1) a stone and turf wall with sixteen associated forts for troops of a fighting garrison; (2) a line of fortlets at intervals of one Roman mile with signal turrets at intermediate points, both for the use of a patrolling garrison; (3) a deep flat-bottomed ditch south of the wall proper, known as the *vallum*, which served as a civil boundary; and (4) a road system for military communications and supplies. *See* D. Harrison, *Along Hadrian's Wall*, 1950; J. Collingwood Bruce, *Handbook to the Roman Wall* (ed. I. A. Richmond), 1957.

Hadrianus, Publius Aelius (A.D. 76–138), called in English **Hadrian,** Roman emperor, born 24th January at Italica in Hispania Baetica, where his family, originally from Atria in Picenum, had resided for nearly 200 years. On his father's death, in 85 or 86, he was placed under the guardianship of M. Ulpius Traianus (afterwards the emperor Trajan) and Caelius Attianus (a future praetorian prefect). He spent the next six years at Rome, but at the age of fifteen returned to Italica and joined the army. Summoned by Trajan to Rome in 93, he held various minor civil posts; then he went as tribune to the Second Legion at Aquincum (q.v.), and remained there until 99, when he returned to Rome with Trajan, and in the following year the empress Plotina arranged a marriage between him and Trajan's great-niece Vibia Sabina.

Hadrian's public career from this date until his accession may be summarized briefly as follows: quaestor, 101; tribune of the people, 105; praetor, 106; distinguished himself in both Dacian campaigns, 101–2 and 105–7; *legatus praetorius* of Lower Pannonia, 107; *legatus* in the Parthian campaign, 113–17. In this last year Trajan fell sick and set out for home, leaving Hadrian as commander of the army and governor of Syria. Hadrian was at Antioch when he learned of his adoption by Trajan, and two days later of the emperor's death. It is not certain that the formalities of adoption had been completed, but Hadrian's succession was confirmed by the army and the senate.

The empire at this moment was threatened on all sides, and Hadrian took immediate steps to remove the danger. He abandoned Assyria, Mesopotamia and Armenia, which had been conquered and annexed by his predecessor. Next he pacified the lower Danube, and then (118) hurried to Rome to remove the unfavourable impression created by the execution of four consulars who were alleged to have conspired against him.

The first of his two great journeys round the empire (121–6) included Gaul, Germany, Britain, Spain, Mauretania, Asia Minor, the Aegean islands, Athens, central and southern Greece, and Sicily. Among the most outstanding events of this journey are the building of Hadrian's Wall (q.v.) in 122, and his initiation into the Eleusinian Mysteries at Athens (125). The second journey (128–34) took in Athens (where he completed and dedicated the buildings begun during his first visit, notably the Olympieum), Asia Minor, Syria, Palestine (where he ordered the rebuilding of Jerusalem (q.v.)). Arabia, and Egypt (see ANTINOÜS). On his way back to Europe he was recalled (133) to deal with the Jewish revolt, which had broken out in the previous year; but in 134 he entrusted the command to Julius Severus, returned to Rome and passed the remainder of his life between the capital and his beautiful villa at Tibur. He died at Baiae on 10th July A.D. 138, and was succeeded by Antoninus Pius (q.v.).

Hadrian was probably the most capable ruler who ever sat upon a throne. He introduced various administrative, financial and legal reforms, and his magnificent buildings, especially at Athens and Rome, were among the glories of the empire. See B. W. Henderson, *Life and Principate of the Emperor Hadrian*, 1923; M. I. Rostovtzev, *Social and Economic History of the Roman Empire*, 1926; W. Weber, 'Hadrian', *Cambridge Ancient History*, vol. viii, 1936; Marguerite Yourcenar, *Memoirs of Hadrian* (trans. G. Frick), 1955. This last work is fictional, but of the greatest value. See also S. Perowne, *Hadrian*, 1960.

Hadrumetum or **Adrumetum** (Gk Adeumēs or Adeumetōs; mod. Susa), town on the north coast of Africa, founded from Tyre (q.v.) long before Carthage, to which it afterwards became subject. It was captured by Agathocles (q.v.) in 310 B.C., and gave refuge to Hannibal and the remnants of his army after Zama (202 B.C.). Caesar landed there at the beginning of the African war in 46 B.C. Under the Roman Empire Hadrumetum belonged to the province of Africa; it was made a Latin colony by Trajan, and was the birth-place of Decimus Clodius Albinus (q.v.).

Haedui, *see* AEDUI.

Haemon (Haimōn), son of Creon and nephew of Jocasta, *see* THEBAN LEGEND, 4.

Hagelaidas, *see* AGELADAS.

Halaesa, town on the north coast of Sicily, founded in 403 by Archonides, tyrant of Herbita. In the first Punic war it was the first town to surrender to the Romans and became a prosperous port.

Halcyone (-kuonē), *see* ALCYONE.

Haliartus (-os), town of Boeotia, south of Lake Copaïs. Destroyed by the Persians in 480 B.C., it was afterwards rebuilt, and it was here that Lysander (q.v.) was killed in 395 B.C.

Halicarnassus (mod. Budrum), city of Asia Minor on the southwest coast of Caria, opposite the island of Cos; founded by Dorians from Troezen and Argos. With the rest of the coast of Asia Minor, Halicarnassus became subject to Persia. The satrap Lygdamis obtained power as tyrant, and was succeeded by his daughter, Artemisia I, who was present with Xerxes at the battle of Salamis (480 B.C.). After the Persian wars it enjoyed a period of relative autonomy under the hegemony of Athens (*see* DELIAN LEAGUE); but the Peace of Antalcidas (387 B.C.) restored it to the suzerainty of Persia. Another satrap, Mausolus (q.v.), made himself independent ruler of Halicarnassus, and raised it to the height of its prosperity. His wife and successor, Artemisia II, immortalized herself and her husband by the celebrated mausoleum which she erected to his memory (*c.* 352 B.C.). Among the sculptors who worked on this great building were Scopas, Bryaxis, Leochares and Timotheus (qq.v.). Fragments, including the statue of Mausolus, are preserved in the British Museum. Halicarnassus was the birth-place of the historians Herodotus and Dionysius (qq.v.).

Halirrhothius (-os), in Greek legend, son of Poseidon and Euryte. He attempted the rape of Alcippe, daughter of Ares, but was slain by her father. Ares was brought to trial by Poseidon on the hill at Athens which was called thenceforth Areopagus. According to another story Halirrhothius was ordered by Poseidon to cut down the olive-trees sacred to Athena, but missed his aim at one of them and inflicted on himself a mortal wound.

Hamilcar, surnamed Barca ('lightning'), a Carthaginian general and father of Hannibal (q.v.). He was appointed to command his country's forces in Sicily during the first Punic war (247 B.C.), at a time when Rome was mistress of the island; but he maintained himself for years, notwithstanding all the efforts of the Romans to dislodge him, first in the neighbourhood of Panormus and subsequently in a stronger position on Mt Eryx. After the naval victory of Catulus in 241, which ended the first Punic war, Hamilcar had to carry on war in Africa against the rebellious mercenaries (*see* MERCENARIES, WAR OF THE), whom he subdued after a struggle lasting three years (240–238). In 238 he went to Spain in order to win new territory for Carthage and thus make good her loss of Sicily. In the course of nearly nine years he obtained possession of large areas of the peninsula, partly by force of arms and partly by negotiation. He was drowned while campaigning against the Vettones in 229 B.C. and left three sons: Hannibal, Hasdrubal and Mago.

Hannibal, a common name among the Carthaginians signifying the grace or favour of Baal. The most celebrated was the son of Hamilcar Barca (*see* preceding article), born in 247 B.C. He was only nine years

old when his father took him to Spain and made him swear lifelong
hostility to Rome. Child though he then was, Hannibal never forgot
his vow, and devoted his subsequent career to its fulfilment. At the
time of his father's death (229) he had already shown such courage and
skill in warfare that he was appointed to carry out most of the operations planned by Hamilcar's son-in-law and successor, Hasdrubal
(see HASDRUBAL, 1). On the assassination of Hasdrubal (221), Hannibal was elected commander-in-chief by the army, and their choice was
approved by the government at Carthage. In two campaigns he
subdued the whole country south of the Iberus, with the exception of
Saguntum (q.v.). In the spring of 219, therefore, Hannibal laid siege
to Saguntum, which he captured after a desperate resistance of nearly
eight months. Now Saguntum, lying south of the Iberus, did not come
within the treaty concluded (226 B.C.) between Rome and Carthage,
defining their respective spheres of influence. But it had formed an
alliance with Rome, who treated the attack as a violation of the
treaty and demanded the surrender of Hannibal. Carthage refused,
and the second Punic war began.

In the spring of 218 Hannibal left his winter quarters at Carthago
Nova and marched into Italy via the Pyrenees, southern Gaul and
the Alps. On reaching Gallia Cisalpina he defeated the consul P.
Cornelius Scipio (q.v.) first on the Ticinus and then more decisively
on the Trebia. Having wintered in this area, he marched early in 217
into Etruria, through the marshes on the banks of the Arnus, where
his troops suffered severely and he himself lost the sight of one eye as
a result of an attack of ophthalmia. The consul Gaius Flaminius
hurried north to oppose him, but was overwhelmingly defeated and
slain on the shores of Trasimenus (q.v.). A new Roman army was
assembled and placed under the command of a dictator, Q. Fabius
Maximus (q.v.), who avoided a general action and attempted only to
harass the Carthaginian forces. In the following year (216) the consuls L. Aemilius Paulus and C. Terentius Varro marched into Apulia
with an army of 90,000 men, but Hannibal routed them on the right
bank of the Aufidus, just below Cannae (q.v.). This annihilating defeat
was followed by the revolt against Rome of most of the peoples in
southern Italy. Hannibal established his winter quarters at Capua
(q.v.), which had espoused his cause; but Capua was noted for its
luxury and enervating climate, and the havoc wrought by these
among his troops was a favourite theme of rhetorical exaggeration in
later times.

Notwithstanding his many great victories, the efforts of Hannibal
had so far been in vain. Rome remained unsubdued, and the 'delay-
ing' strategy of Fabius was resumed. Hannibal was often successful
in subsequent campaigns, but his forces gradually weakened. His sole
object now was to hold what he had won in the south until his brother
Hasdrubal should reinforce him (see HASDRUBAL, 2). But Hasdrubal's
coming was delayed, and his crossing of the Alps in 207 was followed
at once by his defeat on the Metaurus by the consuls C. Claudius
Nero and M. Livius Salinator. Hasdrubal was killed in action, and his
fate decided the outcome of the war, especially as Hannibal was fast
losing the support of his government at home (see HANNO, 2). He

withdrew his forces to the peninsula of Bruttii, where he stood his ground for nearly four years (207–203). Towards the end of 203 he crossed to Africa, in order to oppose Scipio, but was decisively beaten at Zama, 202 B.C. (*see* SCIPIO AFRICANUS MAJOR). In the following year a treaty was concluded which ended the second Punic war, but in which Hannibal saw the frustration of his whole life's work. In 193 he was obliged by the jealousy of Rome and the hostility of a powerful group at Carthage to flee his country. He took refuge with Antiochus III of Syria, who was then on the eve of war with Rome; but after the defeat of Antiochus in 190, the victors demanded Hannibal's surrender as a condition of peace. Hannibal had foreseen the danger and fled to the court of Prusias, King of Bithynia. Rome, however, could not rest while he lived, and T. Quinctius Flamininus (q.v.) was sent to overawe the helpless monarch. Hannibal, realizing that escape was impossible, took poison which he had long carried in a ring (133 B.C.).

When comparing Hannibal with other great captains of antiquity it is necessary to bear in mind the circumstances in which he was placed. Feebly and grudgingly supported by his government (*see* HANNO, 2), he stood alone at the head of an army composed of mercenaries from many lands. Yet not only did he retain the devotion of these men, unshaken by any change of fortune, for a period of more than fifteen years, but he trained up one army after another; and long after the veterans who had followed him across the Alps had dwindled to an inconsiderable remnant, his new levies were as invincible as their predecessors. *See* W. Morris, *Hannibal*, 1897; A. R. Bonus, *Where Hannibal Passed*, 1925; H. Lamb, *Hannibal*, 1959.

Hanno: 1. Carthaginian navigator of the late 6th century B.C. The extant *Periplus* attributed to him is believed by some to be a Greek translation of the Punic original which Hanno is known to have written. It describes a voyage along the west coast of Africa for the purpose of exploration and colonization. *See* translation in M. Cary and E. Warmington, *Ancient Explorers*, 1929.

2. Carthaginian general and statesman, surnamed 'the Great', apparently for military achievements in Africa of which nothing is known. In 240 B.C. he caused a revolt of the mercenaries by withholding their pay (*see* MERCENARIES, WAR OF THE), and failed miserably in the command against them. As a statesman he was leader of the aristocratic party and the principal adversary of Hamilcar Barca (q.v.) and his family. For thirty-five years, from the landing of Barca in Spain until the return of Hannibal (q.v.) from Italy, he appears continually to have thwarted the efforts of that family and to have advocated peace with Rome.

Harmodius (-os) and Aristogeitōn, two Athenians celebrated for their attempt to destroy the Peisistratid tyranny (*see* PEISISTRATUS) in 514 B.C., an attempt concerning the details of which there was some doubt even in the time of Thucydides. Harmodius, says the latter, 'was then in the flower of youthful beauty, and Aristogeiton, a citizen in the middle rank of life, was his lover and possessed him'. The beauty of Harmodius excited the lust of Hipparchus, brother of the tyrant Hippias; but Harmodius would have none of him; he told Aristogeiton, who became obsessed with fear that Hipparchus might deprive him of the lad by force. A second attempt by Hipparchus met with no better result, and by way of revenge he insulted the sister of Harmodius by inviting her to carry one of the sacred baskets in a religious procession and then declaring that she had never been invited because of her unworthiness.

Harmodius and Aristogeiton now determined to end the tyranny by murdering Hippias and Hipparchus at the Great Panathenaea, having communicated their intention to a few friends. When the time arrived the conspirators noticed one of their accomplices talking with Hippias, and jumped to the conclusion that they had been betrayed. Hippias was not at hand, but they rushed upon Hipparchus and slew him. Harmodius was immediately cut down by the guards. Aristogeiton escaped, but was afterwards caught, put to the torture and finally stabbed to death by Hippias.

The foregoing version of the story is that of Thucydides (vi. 54–9), omitting, however, one episode which is expressly and on good grounds denied by Aristotle, whose account (*Ath. Con.* 18) differs from that of Thucydides in that he attributes the improper designs upon Harmodius not to Hipparchus, but to Thessalus, his youngest brother.

Four years later (510 B.C.) Hippias was expelled and the tyranny ended. Harmodius and Aristogeiton were looked upon by succeeding generations at Athens as patriots, deliverers and martyrs. To be born of their blood was among the highest of honours and carried exception from *leitourgiai* (q.v.).

Harmōnia, in Greek legend, daughter of Ares and Aphrodite (or of Zeus and the Pleiad Electra), and wife of Cadmus (q.v.). At the wedding, at which all the gods were present, Cadmus (or one of the heavenly guests) gave Harmonia a necklace, which had been made by Hephaestus and which brought disaster upon all who possessed it. *See* ALCMAEON; AMPHIARAUS; PHAYLLUS.

Harpalus (-os), a Macedonian, appointed by Alexander the Great receiver-general for Asia and satrap of Babylon. Having embezzled large sums he fled, and in 325 B.C. arrived off Sunium with an army of mercenaries and an immense treasure. His admission to Athens was opposed by the orator Demosthenes (q.v.); but Harpalus obtained an entry without his troops, and scattered gold among the politicians, in the hope of raising Athens against Alexander. Demosthenes now joined Phocion in advocating submission to Alexander, whose power he understood; and he accordingly proposed the detention of Harpalus and sequestration of his treasures until Alexander's officers should come to claim them. But Harpalus escaped, and half the money, though formally lodged in the Acropolis under the direction of Demosthenes and others, was found to have disappeared. Demosthenes was forthwith charged with having been bribed to connive at the flight of Harpalus. After an inquiry by the Areopagus, he and others were sent for trial. Demosthenes was sentenced to a fine of fifty talents and, on the assumption that he would not be able to find the money, was denied the legal respite and imprisoned. Harpalus meanwhile had taken refuge in Crete, where he was murdered (323 B.C.).

Harpies (Gk Harpuai, 'snatchers'), mythical beings, probably wind-spirits (cf. Homer, *Odyssey*, i. 241; xx. 66), who were considered as having abducted persons who had disappeared without trace. They were sometimes connected with the powers of the underworld, in which capacity they carried off the daughters of Pandareos (q.v.)— a scene represented on the 'Harpy Tomb' from Xanthus in Lycia, now in the British Museum. The number of the Harpies is nowhere stated. One of them, Podarge, became, according to Homer (*Il*. xvi. 150), mother of the horses of Achilles; while in Hesiod, Aello and Ocypete were daughters of Thaumas.

In neither of these early poets are the Harpies in any way repellent. Later (e.g. in the story of the Argonauts) they are disgusting monsters: birds with women's faces pale with hunger. Virgil calls one of them Celaeno, and places them in the Strophades.

Harpocrates (-kratēs), Greek form of the name of an Egyptian deity Harpa-khruti, i.e. 'the child Horus'. He was adopted by the Greeks and worshipped both by them and by the Romans, probably because he bore some resemblance to Apollo as enemy of the powers of darkness (*see* Herodotus, ii. 144). Statues of Harpa-Khruti showed him in the conventional attitude of childhood, i.e. with finger on lips; but the Greeks and Romans, mistaking the significance of this attitude, made him the god of silence, in which capacity he became patron of the later mystical schools of philosophy.

Harpocration (-kration), **Valerius**, Greek grammarian, a native of Alexandria. Some believe him to have lived in the 2nd century A.D., but others place him much later. His partly extant *Lexicon* is a collection of notes on events and persons mentioned by the ten most famous orators, together with explanations of legal and commercial terms. *See* the edition by W. Dindorf, 1853.

Haruspices, Etruscan diviners (*see* TAGES) who practised at Rome and were especially popular in early republican times. By the 1st century B.C. they had fallen into disrepute, though there was a college of sixty haruspices at Rome under the empire. The haruspices must be carefully distinguished from the augurs (q.v.), not only because of their different methods of divination, but also by virtue of the fact that they never formed part of the state religion. The principal branch of their pseudo-science was the interpretation of the divine will from the appearance of a victim's entrails; but they also interpreted unusual phenomena of nature and prescribed expiatory sacrifices.

Hasdrubal, name of three Carthaginian generals.

1. Son-in-law of Hamilcar (q.v.), on whose death (229 B.C.) he succeeded to the command in Spain (*see also* HANNIBAL). He founded Carthago Nova, and concluded with Rome a famous treaty (226 B.C.) which established the River Iberus as the boundary between Roman and Carthaginian spheres of influence. Hasdrubal was murdered by a slave whose master he had put to death, and was succeeded in the command by Hannibal (221 B.C.).

2. Son of Hamilcar and brother of Hannibal (qq.v.). When the latter set out for Italy (218), Hasdrubal was left to command in Spain, and there fought for some years against the two Scipios (*see*

SCIPIO, PUBLIUS CORNELIUS). In 207 he crossed the Alps and descended into Italy, but was defeated and slain on the Metaurus. His head was cut off and thrown into Hannibal's camp.

3. Son of Gisco, served in Spain during the second Punic war and must be carefully distinguished from 2 above.

Hēbē, Greek goddess of youth, daughter of Zeus and Hera, and was cup-bearer to the gods before the rape of Ganymedes (q.v.). After the deification of Heracles she became his wife. Later she was represented as the goddess of youth, with powers of rejuvenation. At Rome she was called Juventas.

Hecataeus (Hekataios), name of two Greek historians.

1. A native of Miletus, *fl.* 6th–5th century B.C. In 500 he endeavoured to dissuade his countrymen from revolting against Persia, and in 494, when they were obliged to submit, it was he who persuaded the conqueror to restore the autonomy of the Ionian city-states. Fragments of his *Histories* survive. This was the first serious prose history, giving a systematic account of Greek mythology and traditions, though its critical principles left much to be desired. Fragments are also extant of a geographical work, *Travels round the Earth*, of which some hold Hecataeus to have been the author; but the attribution seems to rest upon inconclusive evidence.

2. A native of Abdera in Thrace, or of Teos, *fl.* late 4th century B.C. He accompanied Ptolemy I, Soter, on an expedition to Syria and on a voyage up the Nile. Fragments remain of his *Aiguptiaka* and *Peri Huperboreōn*, which were used by Diodorus Siculus.

Hecate (Hekatē), 'worker from afar', Greek goddess, probably originating in a pre-hellenic chthonian deity but possibly an hellenic adaptation of Thracian Bendis. She is first mentioned by Hesiod, who represents her as daughter of the Titan Perses (*see* TITANS), whose universal power enables her to confer wealth and all the blessings of daily life. In later tradition Hecate is the chief goddess of magic arts. Accompanied by ghosts and hell-hounds she visited crossroads, where, on the last day of the month, eggs and fish were left as offerings to her. Creatures sacrificed to Hecate were black puppies and black female lambs; while pillars, called Hecataea and resembling Hermae (q.v.), were erected at crossroads and doorways, particularly in Attica. Her only occurrence in mythological legend is connected with Demeter (q.v.): she witnessed the rape of Persephone, and, with lighted torch, helped Demeter in her search. Her association with night led to her frequent identification with the moon (*see* SELENE) and hence with Artemis (q.v.). Earlier artists depicted Hecate clad in a long flowing robe and carrying flaming torches. Later she is given three bodies set back to back, enabling her to look all ways at once from the crossroad.

Hecatoncheires (Hekatonkheires), 'hundred handed', three monsters begotten by Uranus and Gē. *See* TITANS.

Hector (Hektōr), son of Priam and Hecuba, husband of Andromache and father of Astyanax (Scamandrius). He was the principal hero of Troy, slew Patroclus and was himself slain by Achilles (q.v.). Apollo and Aphrodite preserved his body from corruption and mutilation. Priam, protected by Hermes, sued for and obtained the corpse, which was given a magnificent funeral. In historical times Hector was worshipped in the Troad and at Tanagra in Boeotia.

Hecuba (Gk Hekabē), in Greek legend, daughter of the Phrygian king Dymas (or of Cisseus, a Thracian monarch, or of the river-god Sangarius) and wife of Priam, to whom she bore Hector, Paris and many other children. After the fall of Troy she was carried off as a slave by the Greeks. On the coast of Thrace she avenged the murder of her son Polydorus (q.v.), was changed into a dog and leapt into the sea from the promontory Cynossema ('dogs tomb'). *See* EURIPIDES, *Hecuba*.

Hēgemōn of Thasos, Greek poet of the Old Comedy, *fl.* 420 B.C. He invented a kind of parody, whereby through slight alterations in the wording of famous poems he reduced them from the sublime to the ridiculous. *See* Aristotle, *Poetics*, ii. 5.

Hēgēsias: 1. Greek rhetorician and historian of the late 4th century B.C., born at Magnesia in Lydia. He is said by Strabo to have founded the florid 'Asiatic' style of prose, for which he is ridiculed by Cicero and others. Fragments of a work on Alexander the Great survive. *See* F. Jacoby, *Fragmente der griechischen Historiker*, vol. i, 1927.

2. Greek philosopher of the Cyrenaic school, *fl.* 250 B.C. In broad outline he followed the doctrines of Aristippus (q.v.); but the emphasis which he placed upon indifference to life and contempt of death, together with his insistence upon the folly of seeking happiness where the soul is for ever imprisoned in a suffering frame, drove many of his pupils to suicide. It is said that this gloomy strain in his teaching became so alarming that Ptolemy II, Philadelphus, forbade him to lecture. Hegesias also maintained the wisdom of complete egoism, and the instability and unreality of such 'figments of the brain' as kindness and friendship.

Hegesippus (Hēgēsippos), Athenian orator and statesman, a contemporary and supporter of Demosthenes (q.v.). In 343 B.C. he was one of the ambassadors sent to Philip of Macedon to discuss the restoration of the island of Hallonesus; and in reply to Philip's subsequent offer to resign the island, or submit the question of ownership to arbitration, Hegesippus delivered the oration *De Halonneso* which was formerly attributed to Demosthenes and is still included in some editions of his works.

Helena or **Helenē**, in Greek mythology, daughter of Zeus by Leda, and sister of the Dioscuri (q.v.). For her abduction in early youth *see* THESEUS. After her return from this adventure she was married to Menelaus (q.v.), King of Sparta, to whom she bore a daughter Hermione (q.v.). Later she was seduced by Paris (*see* PARIS, 1) and carried off to Troy, and this event was the *casus belli* of the Trojan war. After the death of Paris Helen was married to his brother Deiphobus (q.v.; *see also* HELENUS). On the fall of Troy she was reconciled to Menelaus, with whom she returned to Sparta and spent the remainder of her life in peace.

According to another version (*see* Euripides, *Helen*), Paris, on his voyage to Troy with Helen, was driven ashore on the coast of Egypt, where the king, Proteus, detained the real Helen; a phantom substitute was carried off to Troy, and Helen herself recovered by Menelaus on his way home from the Trojan war.

There are varying accounts of Helen's end. According to the *Odyssey*, Menelaus and Helen were fated not to die, but to be transported to Elysium (q.v.). Others relate that she and Menelaus were buried at Therapnae in Laconia, and it is known that Helen was worshipped there in historical times as the goddess of beauty. A third legend states that after the death of Menelaus she was driven out by her stepsons, that she fled to Rhodes, and that there she was hanged from a tree by her former friend Polyxo (*see* TLEPOLEMUS) who thus avenged her husband's death at Troy. She was in fact worshipped at Rhodes in a temple dedicated to Helena Dendritis ('tree-goddess'). Finally, some said that after death she was married to Achilles in the island of Leuce, and bore him a son named Euphorion. With her brothers, the Dioscuri, she was a patroness of sailors.

This curious admixture of the human and divine is almost certainly due to the fact that Helen was originally a pre-hellenic fertility-goddess, probably of Laconia. Thus even in the *Odyssey*, where she has a purely human status, marriage with her is stated to be Menelaus's title to a place in Elysium. *See* J. Pollard, *Helen of Troy*, 1965.

Helena, wife of Constantius Chlorus and mother of Constantine the Great. She appears to have been of humble origin, perhaps the daughter of an innkeeper. She died at the age of about eighty (*c.* A.D. 327). It is certain that, at an advanced age, she made a pilgrimage to Palestine, where she visited the holy places and founded several churches. But the tradition of her having discovered the True Cross is not well supported: it seems to have been unknown to the Pilgrim of Bordeaux (333), Eusebius and Cyril of Jerusalem, appearing only in the West towards the end of the 4th century.

Helenus, in Greek legend, son of Priam and Hecuba, and twin brother of Cassandra. In the *Iliad* he is a seer and a fighting man. Later poets tell various stories. It is said, for instance, that after the death of Paris (q.v.) Helenus contended with Deiphobus for possession of Helen, and that, being worsted, he withdrew to Mt Ida, where he was captured by the Greeks (or deserted to them of his own free will, or was ensnared by a stratagem of Odysseus), and revealed to them their dependence on the arrows of Philoctetes, as well as that of Troy on the Palladium. He also advised the Greeks to build the wooden horse. After the fall of Troy, Helenus and Andromache were assigned to Neoptolemus (q.v.), whom he persuaded to settle in Epirus. When Neoptolemus died Helenus married Andromache and became King of Epirus, where he welcomed Aeneas (Virgil, *Aen.* iii. 294 ff.). According to another story, he was buried at Argos, where his tomb was shown.

Helicon (-kon), mountain range between Lake Copaïs in Boeotia and the Corinthian Gulf. Owing, probably, to its great fertility, to the absence of snakes and poisonous plants and to the neighbourhood of Ascra, home of the poet Hesiod, Helicon was sacred to the Muses. They had a temple on the eastern slopes, which has been excavated; the sculptures adorning it and the surrounding grove were removed by

Constantine to embellish his new capital. Near by were two celebrated fountains, Aganippe and Hippocrene (qq.v.).

Heliodorus (Hēliodōros), Greek sophist of the 3rd century A.D., a native of Emesa in Syria, author of *Aethiopica*, the oldest and best of surviving Greek romances. *See* the translation by Sir Walter Lamb (Everyman's Library), 1961.

Heliogabalus, *see* ELAGABALUS.

Hēliopolis, 'city of the sun' (mod. Baalbek), in Syria, seat of the worship of Baal, whose symbol was the sun. The place was of commercial importance, being on the direct route from Egypt, the Red Sea and Tyre to Asia Minor and Europe. The imposing remains date from the Roman period (1st and 2nd century A.D.).

Hēlios (Lat. Sol), in Gk mythology god of the sun. He was the son of Hyperion and Thea, and a brother of Selene (the Moon) and Eos (Dawn). Homer describes Helios as rising in the east from Oceanus, traversing the heavens, and descending in the evening into the darkness of the west and Oceanus. Later poets embellished this simple notion. They tell of a magnificent palace of Helios in the east, from which he starts in the morning in a chariot drawn by four horses. They also assign him a second palace in the west, and describe his horses as feeding upon herbs growing in the Islands of the Blessed. Helios is described as the god who sees and hears everything. The island of Thrinacia (Sicily) was sacred to him, and there he had flocks of sheep and oxen, which were tended by his daughters, Phaetusa and Lampetia. He was worshipped in many parts of Greece, and especially in the island of Rhodes, where the famous colossus was a representation of the god. The sacrifices offered to him consisted of white rams, bears, bulls, goats, lambs, and especially white horses, and honey. Among the animals sacred to him, the cock is especially mentioned.

Hellas and **Hellenes**, *see* GREECE.

Hellē, daughter of Athamas and Nephele, and sister of Phrixus (q.v.).

Hellēn, in Greek legend, son of Deucalion (q.v.) and Pyrrha; father of Aeolus, Dorus and Xuthus, and through them ancestor of all the Hellenes.

Hellespont, The (Gk Hellēspontos; Lat. Fretum Hellesponticum; mod. Dardanelles), strait connecting the Propontis with the Aegean. East and west of its narrowest point (about one mile in width) stood the cities of Abydos and Sestos. *See* HERO AND LEANDER; PHRIXUS.

Helots (Gk Heilōtes or Heilōtai), Spartan serfs, probably the original inhabitants of Laconia who were enslaved by the Achaeans before the Dorian conquest. Later, following the second Messenian war (*see* MESSENIA), the Messenians were reduced to the status of helots; that is to say, they were State slaves bound to the land, but assigned to individual Spartiates (*see* SPARTA) to cultivate their holdings upon the following conditions: (1) their masters could not emancipate or sell them off the land, or (2) increase their annual rent, which was payable in kind.

The helots were employed in war as peltasts (q.v.) or as rowers in the fleet, and from the Peloponnesian war onwards they served on occasion as hoplites (q.v.); those who distinguished themselves by bravery in action might be emancipated by the State. The wretched status of so large a group, which some say amounted to about half the Spartan population, produced more than one revolt, which led in turn to constant mistrust and frequent cruelty on the part of the government (*see* CRYPTEIA). *See also* MOTHONES; NEODAMODES.

Helvetii, a Celtic people who in Caesar's time occupied territory bounded west by the Jura, south by the Rhône and the Lake of Geneva, north and east by the Rhine to Lake Constance, and thus corresponding to the western part of modern Switzerland. In 107 B.C. two of their tribes, the Tigurini and Tungri, had defeated a Roman army under L. Cassius Longinus on the shores of the Lake of Geneva. Subsequently, in 102 B.C., the Helvetii accompanied the Cimbri (q.v.) in their invasion of Italy, but managed to reach home safely. In 58 B.C., upon the advice of Orgetorix, one of their chiefs, they resolved to migrate and seek a new home in the more fertile plains of Gaul, but were defeated by Caesar near Bibracte and driven back into their own territories. These territories, known as *ager Helvetiorum*, were included by Augustus in the province of Gallia Belgica (*see* GALLIA), by Tiberius in Germania Superior. The Helvetii enjoyed their greatest prosperity under Vespasian, and gradually adopted Roman language and customs. *See* T. R. Holmes, *Caesar's Conquest of Gaul,* 1899.

Helvidius Priscus, Roman senator and Stoic philosopher of the 1st century A.D., son-in-law of Thrasea Paetus (q.v.). His strong republican sympathies found expression even in the senate, and led to his banishment by Nero (66). Recalled by Galba, he continued his opposition to the imperial regime, and as praetor in 70 he actually flouted the dignity and authority of Vespasian. This resulted in a second banishment, and he was put to death soon afterwards by order of the emperor. *See* Tacitus, *Hist.* iv. 5; Dio Cassius, lxvi. 12, lxvii. 13; Suetonius, *Vespasian.*

Henna or **Enna,** town of the Siculi (q.v.) situated almost in the centre of Sicily at an altitude of 2,600 feet. It surrendered to Dionysius I of Syracuse in 397 and was the headquarters of the slave revolt 136–132 B.C. In each case its strong natural position would have rendered it impregnable but for treachery. Henna possessed a temple of Demeter, from which Verres (q.v.) carried off the bronze statue of the goddess. Four miles distant from Henna is the lake of Pergusa, traditional scene of the rape of Persephone (q.v.).

Hephaestion (Hēphaistiōn): 1. Macedonian general and friend of Alexander the Great (q.v.), who called him 'my Patroclus'. His services in Bactria and India, where he superintended the foundation of cities and colonies, were rewarded (324 B.C.) with a golden crown and the hand of Alexander's sister-in-law Drypetis. Hephaestion died suddenly in the same year at Ecbatana; his body was cremated at Babylon on a vast funeral pyre designed by the architect Deinocrates (q.v.), and temples were built in his honour.

2. Greek grammarian of the late 2nd century A.D., a native of Alexandria. His *Manual of Metres,* the only complete surviving work on that subject, has come down to us. *See* the edition by T. Gaisford, 1855.

Hephaestus (Hēphaistos), Greek god of fire, with whom the Romans subsequently identified Vulcanus (q.v.). The original home of his worship was probably Mt Olympus in Lycia, where natural gases still escape from the soil. Thence the cult spread to other places in Asia Minor and to some of the islands, notably Lemnos. It reached Athens *c.* 600 B.C., but seems never to have penetrated the rest of mainland Greece. Hephaestus having been recognized as the god of fire in general, his worship was also adopted in volcanic regions, e.g. the Aeoliae Insulae (q.v.), whence it spread to Sicily and parts of Campania. Since fire is indispensable for the working of metals, Hephaestus came to be regarded as the divine smith and patron of craftsmen, and his cult was especially popular at Athens, which had a large industrial population.

According to Homer, Hephaestus was a son of Zeus and Hera. He was born lame, and was thrown down from heaven by his mother immediately after birth; but he was rescued by the sea-goddesses Eurynome and Thetis, dwelt with them for nine years and then returned to Olympus. There, however, he took his mother's part in a quarrel with Zeus, and was again hurled from heaven, this time by Zeus himself. He was a whole day falling, landed at evening in the island of Lemnos, but again returned. His palace in Olympus contained his workshop with anvil and twenty pairs of bellows that worked spontaneously at his bidding. He made the armour of Achilles, the fatal necklace of Harmonia and other things famed in legend. Later accounts place that workshop beneath various volcanoes.

Charis is the wife of Hephaestus in the *Iliad*, Aphrodite in the *Odyssey*, Aglaia (youngest of the Charites) in Hesiod. During the best period of Greek art he was usually represented as a middle-aged man with beard and unkempt hair; he wears a round, close-fitting cap and sleeveless tunic, and carries a hammer or other instrument. *See* L. R. Farnell, *Cults of the Greek States*, v. 1909.

Hēra. In classical times the predominant feature of this great goddess was her patronage of marriage and female life. She was the chief pre-hellenic deity of Argos, and W. K. G. Guthrie suggests that she may originally have been worshipped as the embodiment of the fruitful earth (*The Greeks and their Gods*, pp. 66 ff.). In mythology she is the daughter of Cronus and Rhea, and sister and wife of Zeus, to whom she bore Ares, Hephaestus and Hebe. It was natural, as H. J. Rose points out, that the Greeks should eventually yield to so powerful a goddess the honour of being wife to their own chief god. The character of Hera is described by Homer as jealous and quarrelsome; the many stories which illustrate this unlovable quality may reflect an early conflict between her ancient worship and that of the newcomer, Zeus. She was worshipped especially at Argos where stood her temple, the Heraeum, which has been excavated. But in addition to this famous sanctuary her cult was followed in Samos, and elsewhere throughout the Greek world. In art the ideal type of the goddess was found in the statue by Polycleitus (q.v.) in the Heraeum at Argos.

Heraclea (Hēracleia), name of several cities founded by Greek settlers:
1. In Lucania (q.v.), between the rivers Aciris and Siris; founded

from Tarentum *c.* 433 B.C. Here Pyrrhus (q.v.) defeated a Roman army under Valerius Laevinus, 280 B.C. Two years later Rome made a treaty with Heraclea, and in 89 B.C. granted the inhabitants Roman citizenship by the *Lex Plautia Papiria*. The *Lex Iulia Municipalis* (46 B.C.), of which a part has been found, created Heraclea a *municipium* (q.v.).

2. Heraclea Lyncestis, in Macedonia, on the Via Egnatia (q.v.). It was capital of Pelagonia, one of the four districts into which the Romans divided that province.

3. Heraclea Minoa, on the south coast of Sicily, 20 miles north-west of Agrigentum; founded from Selinus. Taken by Lacedaemonian colonists under Euryleon *c.* 502 B.C., it afterwards became subject to the Carthaginians, who used it as a base during the first Punic war.

4. Heraclea Pontica, on the coast of Bithynia, founded from Megara *c.* 560 B.C.

5. Heraclea ad Latmum, on the border of Caria and Ionia, at the foot of Mt Latmus. Near by was the burial cave of Endymion (q.v.). There are magnificent remains of the city walls dating from about 300 B.C.

See also PERINTHUS; TRACHIS.

Heracles, called by the Romans Hercules, a Greek hero, later worshipped as a god. It is now commonly supposed that he was originally an historical figure, perhaps a lord of Tiryns, whose military prowess led to the Homeric legend of his having met and conquered Death; and that in consequence there grew around him the stories of the 'Twelve Labours' and other legends arising from the claims of various city-states.

In classical mythology Heracles was the son of Zeus by Alcmene (q.v.), the wife of Amphitryon, of Thebes in Boeotia. On the day on which Heracles was to be born, Zeus boasted of becoming the father of a hero destined to rule over the race of Perseus, who was the grandfather both of Amphitryon and of Alcmene. Hera prevailed upon him to swear that the descendant of Perseus, born that day, should be the ruler. Thereupon she hastened to Argos, and there caused the wife of Sthenelus, the son of Perseus, to give birth to Eurystheus; whereas she delayed the birth of Heracles, and thus robbed him of the empire which Zeus had destined for him. Zeus was enraged, but could not violate his oath. Alcmene brought into the world two boys, Heracles, the son of Zeus, and Iphicles, the son of Amphitryon, who was one night younger than Heracles. As the latter lay in his cradle, Hera sent two serpents to destroy him, but the infant hero strangled them with his own hands. As he grew up he was instructed by Amphitryon in driving the chariot, by Autolycus in wrestling, by Eurytus in archery, by Castor in fighting in heavy armour, and by Linus in singing and playing the lyre. Linus was killed by his pupil with the lyre, because he had censured him; and Amphitryon, to prevent similar occurrences, sent him to feed his cattle. In this manner he spent his life till his eighteenth year.

His first great adventure happened while he was watching the oxen of Amphitryon. A lion, which haunted Mt Cithaeron, made havoc among the herds of Amphitryon and Thespius, King of Thespiae.

Heracles promised to deliver the country of the monster; and Thespius, who had fifty daughters, rewarded Heracles by making him his guest, so long as the chase lasted, and by giving up his daughters to him. Heracles slew the lion, and henceforth wore its skin as his ordinary garment, and its mouth and head as his helmet. (Others related that the lion's skin of Heracles was taken from the Nemean lion.) He next defeated and killed Erginus, King of Orchomenus, to whom the Thebans used to pay tribute. In this battle Amphitryon lost his life; but Creon rewarded Heracles with the hand of his daughter, Megara, by whom he became the father of several children. The gods made him presents of arms, and he carried a huge club which he had cut for himself in the neighbourhood of Nemea. Soon afterwards Heracles was driven mad by Hera, and in this state he killed his own children by Megara and two of Iphicles. In his grief he sentenced himself to exile, and went to Thespius, who purified him. He then consulted the oracle of Delphi as to where he should settle. The Pythia ordered him to live at Tiryns, and to serve Eurystheus for the space of twelve years (*see* TWELVE LABOURS OF HERACLES), after which he should become immortal.

After performing the twelve labours, Heracles returned to Thebes, gave Megara in marriage to Iolaus and sought the hand of Iole, daughter of the Oechalian king Eurytus. The latter had promised his daughter to the man who should conquer him and his sons in shooting with the bow. Heracles defeated them, but Eurytus and his sons, with the exception of Iphitus, refused to surrender Iole, because he had murdered his own children. Shortly afterwards he killed his friend Iphitus in a fit of madness. Though purified from this murder, he was, nevertheless, attacked by a severe illness. The oracle at Delphi declared that he would be restored to health if he would serve three years for wages, and surrender his earnings to Eurytus as an atonement. Accordingly he became a servant to Omphale, Queen of Lydia and widow of Tmolus. Later writers describe Heracles as living effeminately during his residence with Omphale: he spun wool, it is said, and sometimes dressed as a woman. But according to other accounts he performed great feats during this time, undertaking an expedition to Colchis, which brought him into connection with the Argonauts (q.v.), taking part in the Calydonian hunt, and meeting Theseus on his landing from Troezen on the expedition against the Amazons. When the time of his servitude had expired, he sailed against Troy, took the city and killed Laomedon (q.v.). Next he marched against Augeas (*see* TWELVE LABOURS, 5). He then proceeded against Pylos, which he took, and killed the whole family of Neleus (q.v.), with the exception of Nestor. Finally he went to Calydon, where he obtained Deianeira (q.v.), the daughter of Oeneus, for his wife, after fighting with Acheloüs (q.v.).

After Heracles had been married to Deianeira nearly three years, he accidentally killed a boy, Eunomus, at a banquet in the house of Oeneus. In accordance with the law, he went into exile, taking Deianeira with him. On their road they came to the River Evenus, across which the centaur Nessus carried travellers for a small sum of money. Heracles himself forded the river, but asked Nessus to carry

Deianeira across. Nessus attempted to outrage her: Heracles heard her screams, and shot an arrow into the heart of Nessus. The dying centaur called out to Deianeira to take his blood with her, as it was a sure means of preserving the love of Heracles.

After this he took up his abode at Trachis, whence he marched against Eurytus of Oechalia. He took the city, killed Eurytus and his sons and carried off Iole. On his way home he landed at Cenaeum, a promontory of Euboea, erected an altar to Zeus, and sent his companion, Lichas, to Trachis, in order to fetch him a garment, which he intended to use during the sacrifice. Deianeira, afraid lest Iole should supplant her in the affections of her husband, steeped it in the blood of Nessus. But the blood had been poisoned by the arrow of Heracles (*see* PHILOCTETES; TWELVE LABOURS, 2), and the poison penetrated into all his limbs. He wrenched off the garment, but it stuck to his flesh, and with it he tore away whole pieces from his body. In this state he was conveyed to Trachis. Deianeira, on seeing what she had done, hanged herself. Heracles commanded Hyllus, his eldest son by Deianeira, to marry Iole as soon as he should arrive at the age of manhood. He then ascended Mt Oeta, raised a pile of wood, on which he placed himself, and ordered it to be set on fire. When the pile was burning a cloud came down from heaven, and amid peals of thunder carried him to Olympus, where he was honoured with immortality, became reconciled to Hera and married her daughter Hebe.

In course of time the cult of Heracles spread throughout Hellas, particularly among the Dorians. In Italy it was connected by Roman writers with the hero's expedition to fetch the oxen of Geryon (*see* TWELVE LABOURS, 10). They stated that Hercules, on his return, visited Italy, where he abolished human sacrifices among the Sabines, established the worship of fire, and slew Cacus, a robber, who had stolen his oxen. The aborigines, and especially Evander, honoured Hercules with divine worship; and Hercules entrusted the care of his worship to two distinguished families, the Potitii and Pinarii. *See* introductions to the *Hercules Furens* of Euripides, edited by E. H. Blakeney, 1904, and L. R. Farnell, *Greek Hero Cults*, 1921.

Heraclidae (Hērakleidai), descendants of Heracles. The name was applied more particularly to Hyllus and his descendants, who led the Dorian invasion of Peloponnesus (*see* DORIANS).

Heraclides (Hērakleides): 1. A Syracusan who commanded the mercenary troops of Dionysius II, and who shared the exile of Dion (q.v.). He helped to establish the latter in power (357 B.C.), but in the following year secured his expulsion. On his restoration Dion spared Heraclides, whose loyalty, however, remained suspect, and he was put to death by order of Dion (354 B.C.).

2. Greek astronomer, born at Heraclea in Pontus *c.* 388 B.C. He went far towards anticipating the Copernican system by two capital discoveries: (1) the rotation of the earth about its own axis, and (2) the revolution of Venus and Mercury about the sun. He died in 315 B.C. *See* Sir T. L. Heath, *Greek Astronomy*, 1932.

Heraclitus (Hērakleitos), Greek philosopher, born at Ephesus *c.* 540; died *c.* 475 B.C. He attempted to reconcile the multiplicity and unity, change and stability of the universe by positing an eternal state of flux, a conflict of opposites, controlled by Logos which may best be described as Active Order; and he held true wisdom to be the soul's perception of this order. Heraclitus was one of the earliest writers of Greek prose. The surviving fragments of his work have been edited (with some spurious letters) by Ingram Bywater (1877) and translated in J. Burnet's *Early Greek Philosophy* (4th ed., 1930). For a very clear account of the Heraclitean system, which won for its author the title 'dark' or 'obscure', *see* B. Fuller, *History of Greek Philosophy*, 1923, pp. 118 ff.

Herculaneum, city of Campania, on the coast between Neapolis and Pompeii. It joined the Italian allies in the Social War (q.v.), but submitted in 88 B.C. In late republican and early imperial times it enjoyed great prosperity and included many luxurious villas. In A.D. 63 it was partially destroyed by an earthquake, and had scarcely completed restoration work when it was overwhelmed, together with Pompeii and Stabiae (qq.v.) by the eruption of Vesuvius in August 79. Whereas Pompeii was buried by the shower of small stones and the rain of ashes, Herculaneum lay beneath a coat of lava, 70 to 100 feet below the present level of the ground, and was therefore more difficult than its neighbour to excavate. The site was discovered accidentally in 1720, between which date and 1780 many fine sculptures and paintings were found. In 1753 the so-called Villa Suburbana yielded a library once owned by an Epicurean. It consisted of 1,803 papyri and included works by Epicurus, Polystratus, Chrysippus and Philodemus (qq.v.). Unfortunately the most primitive methods were used to unroll these badly damaged papyri; but many have been published (*Herculanensium voluminum quae supersunt*, Naples, 1793–1809; *Collectio altera*, 1862–76). *See* C. Waldstein and L. Shoobridge, *Herculaneum, Past, Present and Future*, 1908; A. W. van Buren, *A Companion to the Study of Pompeii and Herculaneum*, 1933.

Hercules, *see* HERACLES.

Herculis Columnae, *see* ABYLA; CALPE.

Herennius, Gaius Pontius, Samnite general who defeated the Roman army near Caudium (q.v.) in 321 B.C. In 292 he himself was defeated by the consul Fabius Rullianus, after whose triumph, according to some accounts, he was put to death.

Hermae. From early times posts, or mere heaps of stones, were set up by the Greeks to mark boundaries (cf. Lat. *Terminus*) or distances along roads. These were related to the cult of Hermes (q.v.). With the growth of artistic taste and the development of anthropomorphism these crude objects were supplanted (*c.* 5th century B.C.) by regularly shaped pillars tapering downwards, crowned with a head (generally of Hermes) and having a phallus half way up. These were called Hermae. In cities they were erected at street corners and at the doors of houses. They were held in great respect, if not actually worshipped, as appears from the alarm and indignation caused at Athens by their mutilation in 415 B.C., on the eve of the Sicilian expedition (*see* ALCIBIADES; ANDOCIDES). *See* J. G. Frazer, *The Golden Bough* (3rd ed.), ix, ch,. i; Thucydides, vi. 27.

Hermaphroditus (-deitos), in Greek legend of the hellenistic age, son of Hermes and Aphrodite. He had inherited the beauty of both his parents, and thus excited the passions of the nymph of a fountain at Salmacis in Caria. As he was one day bathing in the fountain, she prayed to the gods that she might be for ever united with him. Her request was granted, but the resulting form retained the characteristics of each sex. The idea is of oriental origin, but is a common theme of later Greek art.

Hermeias or **Hermias**, a eunuch who had been perhaps a banker's clerk and had thriven sufficiently to purchase mining property in the neighbourhood of Mt Ida. He eventually succeeded Eubulus as tyrant of Atarneus and Assos, and, like his predecessor, maintained himself as an independent prince in defiance of Persian claims. In 346 B.C. he became a pupil of Aristotle (q.v.), who had established a school at Assos and who married Pythias, niece and adoptive daughter of Hermeias. In 342, very soon after Aristotle had settled at Pella, Hermeias was seized by the Persians, tortured and crucified.

Hermēs, in Greek mythology, son of Zeus and Maia, daughter of Atlas. He was identified by the Romans with Mercurius (q.v.). The earliest centre of his cult was Arcadia, where Mt Cyllene was reputed to be his birth-place and where he was worshipped as a god of fertility with phallic images (*see* HERMAE). His position as a protector of sheep and cattle is recognized in the *Iliad*; but the *Odyssey* speaks of him mainly as messenger or herald of the gods, and also as conductor of the dead to Hades, whence he is associated with the underworld and dreams. It was doubtless owing to his character as herald that he came to be looked upon as the god of roads and doorways, and as patron of travellers; while his position as deity of good luck, and of commerce and gain in general, probably derived from his character as a god of fertility. Cunning and dishonesty being often bound up with gain, Hermes is shown from Homer onwards as endowed with these qualities; thus within a few hours of his birth he stole some of the oxen of Apollo.

Cleverness may be regarded as the source of those less dignified and more practical inventions and institutions of civilization, whose loftier and more fundamental counterparts were attributed to Apollo. Hermes, therefore, is closely associated with the latter: he invented the cithara, presided at public games and watched over some forms of popular divination. Among things sacred to him were the palm-tree, the tortoise, the number 4 and several kinds of fish. Sacrifices offered to him included incense, honey, cakes, pigs and especially lambs and kids. In archaic art he was represented (apart from the Hermae) as a bearded man wearing a long chiton, and often a cap or broad-brimmed hat and winged sandals. Sometimes he appears in his pastoral character, bearing a sheep on his shoulders; or again as a messenger of the gods, with herald's staff. From the late 5th century B.C., however, he is depicted as a nude and beardless youth, typical of the perfect athlete, and this type was probably fixed a century later by the famous statue by Praxiteles at Olympia.

Hermes Trismegistus, *see* HERMETICA.

Hermēsianax, Greek elegiac poet of the Alexandrian school; born at Colophon, he lived *c.* 330 B.C. A single fragment (about 100 lines) has been preserved by Athenaeus (xiii. 597). It was part of a poem in three books dedicated to Leontion, and gives examples of the power of love. *See* the edition of Athenaeus (with translation) by C. B. Gulick (7 vols., Loeb Library).

Hermetica, ancient Greek and Latin writings that contain religious or philosophical teachings ascribed to 'Hermes Trismegistus', i.e. the Egyptian Thoth, with whom Hermes was identified. These writings, instead of being (as was once imagined) the remains of ancient wisdom, dating perhaps from the time of Moses—or even earlier—belong to the period when Christianity was first beginning to expand over the Roman Empire. They are Neoplatonist documents, of importance as evidence of religious thought and speculation in the early 3rd century A.D. The doctrine of these writings appears to be that of 'salvation without a saviour': there can be no salvation apart from the true *gnosis* (= knowledge), which comes partly by instruction, partly by initiation. They presuppose, as a basis of speculation, the *Timaeus* of Plato, and frequently appeal to the theory of the domination of this lower (sensible) world by astrological influences. There are few, if any, traces of Jewish or Christian teaching in the *Hermetica*; and their value, from a philosophical standpoint, is small. The best things in the collection are the four thanksgiving 'Hymns', which strike a high note of mystical devotion (*see* S. Angus, *The Mystery Religions and Christianity*, 1925). The *Hermetica* have been edited with translation and notes by W. Scott and A. S. Ferguson (4 vols.), 1924–36.

Hermias, *see* HERMEIAS.

Hermionē, in Greek legend, daughter of Menelaus and Helen. She had been promised to Orestes, son of Agamemnon, before the Trojan war; but Menelaus, after his return, married her to Neoptolemus (q.v.). After the latter's death, however, she was married to Orestes and bore him a son Tisamenus.

Hermippus (-os), Athenian poet of the Old Comedy, lived during the Peloponnesian war. Of his forty plays fragments of nine are extant (*see* T. Kock, *Comicorum Atticorum Fragmenta*, i., 1880). He was a bitter opponent of Pericles, and according to Plutarch (*Pericles*, 32) he prosecuted Aspasia (q.v.) for impiety and immorality.

Hermogenēs, Greek rhetorician, a native of Tarsus, *fl.* A.D. 170. He was so precocious that he was appointed to teach while still a boy, and it is not surprising that he lost his wits at the age of twenty-five. Of his *Art of Speaking* we possess the sections 'On Legal Issues', 'On the Invention of Arguments', 'On the Various Kinds of Style', 'On the Method of Effective Speaking' and 'Rhetorical Exercises'. *See* the edition by H. Rabe, 1913.

Hermolaus (-os), a Macedonian youth and page of Alexander the Great (q.v.), against whose life he formed a conspiracy in 328 B.C. The plot was discovered, and Hermolaus was stoned to death.

Hermopolis (mod. Ashmounein), Greek name of an ancient Egyptian city which stood on the Nile a little below the confines of Upper Egypt. Papyri discovered here (*see also* OXYRHYNCHUS) have resulted in important additions to Greek literature. Excavations have also revealed Graeco-Egyptian murals.

Hermunduri, a German tribe inhabiting the basin of the Saale. In the time of Augustus they were in alliance with Rome and were permitted to occupy northern Bavaria. They were probably the only Suebic tribe (*see* SUEBI) not subject to the empire of Maroboduus (q.v.).

Hernici, ancient people of Latium, between the Volsci (q.v.) on the south and the Aequi and Marsi on the north. They were not finally subdued by Rome until 306, and they appear to have received full Roman citizenship by 225 B.C. Their chief town was Aletrium (q.v.).

Hērō and Leander (-dros), in Greek legend of the hellenistic age, the characters of a love-story handled in modern times by Marlowe and Byron. Hero, virgin priestess of Aphrodite at Sestos, was seen at a festival by Leander of Abydos. They fell in love, and he used to swim across the Hellespont at night to visit her, guided by a light in her tower. One wild night the lamp was blown out and Leander was drowned; next day Hero saw his body, threw herself into the sea and perished likewise.

Herodas or **Herondas** (Gk Hēroidas or Herōndas), Greek writer of mimes (short verse dialogues describing scenes from everyday life). Until 1891 he was little more than a name, but in that year Sir Frederick Kenyon published the *editio princeps* of seven mimes and fragments of an eighth, discovered (1890) in an Egyptian papyrus. *See also* the edition (with translation) by W. Headlam and A. D. Knox, 1922.

Hērodēs: 1. Commonly called Herod the Great, was born *c.* 73 B.C., son of the Idumaean Antipater (*see* ANTIPATER, 3) who served under Caesar in the Alexandrine war and was appointed by him procurator of Judaea. At the age of twenty-five Herod was appointed by his father ruler of Galilee. The anarchical state of Palestine in 40 B.C. caused Herod to go to Rome, where the senate, persuaded by Mark Antony, declared him King of Judaea. Returning to Palestine in the following year, he laid siege to Jerusalem with Roman troops in 37, and captured the city. Meanwhile he had married as his second wife the Hasamonaean princess Mariamne.

The next years were a period of violence and intrigue, during which his enemies more than once seemed to have prevailed, and of which the most tragic episode was the death of Mariamne. Despite his love for her, he gave ear to malevolent whispers of adultery, and had her put to death (28 B.C.). But none was better fitted than Herod to dispose of his enemies in time, whether by fair means or foul; and by 25 B.C. he was undisputed master of his kingdom, dependent only on the goodwill of imperial Rome. He put down brigandage with a heavy hand, restored the temple at Jerusalem, built fortresses and founded splendid cities; all of which earned the favour and support of Augustus.

But Herod, for all his energy and undeniable ability, was at heart a craven coward, as is plain from the bloody deeds of his last years. The great popularity of his two sons by Mariamne, Alexander and Aristobulus, alarmed him so that he had them strangled. Then, when already on his death-bed, he learned that his eldest son, Antipater, had been plotting against him. He accused him before the Roman governor and obtained leave from the imperial authorities to put him to death. Five days after the execution Herod himself died (4 B.C.). The birth of Jesus Christ took place in this year; it is known to have occurred in the year of Herod's death, but it is equally certain that the latter must be placed four years before the date generally accepted as the first of the Christian era. Consequently Herod must have ordered the massacre of the Innocents (Matt. ii. 16) while on his death-bed.

2. Surnamed Antipas, son of the preceding by the Samaritan Malthace. On his father's death he obtained the provinces of Galilee and Peraea with the title of tetrarch, while the kingdom of Judaea devolved upon his elder brother Archelaus. Herod married Herodias, wife of his brother Philip (not 3 below), she having, in defiance of Jewish law, divorced her husband, and he being already married to a daughter of the Arabian king Aretas. John the Baptist denounced these proceedings and was put to death (Matt. xiv. 3–12). It was also to this Herod that Christ was sent by Pilate (Luke xxiii. 6–12). In A.D. 39 Antipas went to Rome to solicit a kingly crown from the emperor; but his brother-in-law, Agrippa I (q.v.), influenced Caligula against him, and he was deprived of his dominions and banished to Lugdunum in Gaul, where Herodias voluntarily shared his exile. The year of his death is uncertain.

3. Surnamed Philippos and commonly known as Herod Philip, son of Herod the Great and Cleopatra of Jerusalem. On his father's death he was appointed tetrarch of Ituraea and other districts east and north-east of the Sea of Galilee. His reign was peaceful and happy to the end. He died in A.D. 34.

4. Name of two kings of Judaea commonly called Herod Agrippa. See AGRIPPA.

See A. Jones, *The Herods*, 1938; F. O. Busch, *The Five Herods*, 1958.

Herodes Atticus, Tiberius Claudius, Greek rhetorician, born *c.* A.D. 101 at Marathon in Attica. He taught rhetoric at Athens and also at Rome, where the future emperors Marcus Aurelius and Lucius Verus were among his pupils. Antoninus raised him to the consulship in 143. Herodes spent much of his enormous wealth upon the adornment of Athens, where the imposing remains of his great Odeum can still be seen. He died in A.D. 177.

Herodianus (-os), Greek historian of the 3rd century A.D., author of an extant history of the Roman Empire from the death of Marcus Aurelius to the accession of Gordian III (A.D. 180–238). His work, though defective in many ways, gives most interesting accounts of the death both of Commodus and of Pertinax. *See* the edition by K. Stavenhagen (Teubner), 1922 ; trans, E. C. Echols, 1962.

Herodianus, Aelius, Greek grammarian of Alexandria, who settled at Rome under Marcus Aurelius (A.D. 161–80). We possess several epitomes of his work *On Universal Prosody*, together with a complete treatise *On Anomalous Words* (*see* the edition by A. Lentz, 1867–70). Another work, on difficult words and peculiar forms in Homer, is lost.

Herodotus (Hērodotos), Greek historian, born at Halicarnassus (q.v.) *c.* 484 B.C., son of Lyxes and Dryo (or Rhaeo). He left home at an early age to escape the persecution of Lygdamis, tyrant of Halicarnassus, who had put to death his uncle Panyasis (q.v.) for alleged treasonable activities. By this time Herodotus was far advanced on that long road of reading which seems to have taken in most of the literature then available in verse and prose. He had also embarked upon the great series of intermittent journeys which in a period of seventeen years carried him through twenty-four degrees of latitude and thirty-one of longitude: mainland Greece and the Aegean isles; Asia Minor and Mesopotamia; the uttermost shores of the Euxine, Scythia and Thrace; Syria and Palestine; Magna Graecia and Egypt.

During his seven or eight years of exile he resided, when not travelling, in Samos. He returned to Halicarnassus after the expulsion of Lygdamis, but left again c. 447 B.C. and settled at Athens, where the draft (or perhaps the first part) of his *History* won such approval that the Ecclesia voted him an award of ten talents. Herodotus was dissatisfied, however, with his alien status, and Athenian citizenship was not to be had without great cost and trouble. Consequently, in 444 B.C., he sailed from Peiraeus with the colonists who were going to found Thurii; and there, except for an occasional journey (e.g. to Athens c. 430), he lived until his death c. 424 B.C., completing or retouching and elaborating his great work.

The purpose of Herodotus was to give an account of the struggle between Persia and the Greeks (490–470 B.C.); but he devotes the first two-thirds of the composition to a magnificent introduction which enables him not only to trace back the enmity between East and West to legendary origins, but also to expatiate upon the geography, antiquities and manners of nearly all the nations of the known world. In order to form a right judgment of his historical value, it is well to distinguish those parts in which he speaks from personal observation from those in which he merely repeats what he was told by priests and others. In the latter case he was often deceived; but when he relies upon what he himself had seen he is a model of accuracy. *See* the editions by H. Stein, 1869–71, and A. D. Godley (Loeb Library, with translation). *See also* the translation by G. Rawlinson (1860), revised by A. W. Lawrence, 1935; W. W. How and J. Wells, *Commentary on Herodotus*, 1928; J. E. Powell, *The History of Herodotus*, 1930.

Hērōn, of Alexandria, Greek scientist and geometer. His date is uncertain; it may fall anywhere between 150 B.C. and A.D. 250. He was the author of four surviving mechanical works: *Pneumatica, Automatopoietice, Belopoeica* and *Cheiroballistra*; his *Mechanics* is extant only in an Arabic adaptation. Of his geometrical writings only the *Metrica* has come down to us in its original form. Except for the *Belopoeica* (ed. C. Wescher in *Poliorcétique des Grecs*, 1867), all the works by or attributed to Heron are published in *Heronis Alexandrini opera quae supersunt omnia*, edited by W. Schmidt, L. Nix, H. Schöne and J. L. Heiberg, 5 vols. (1899–1914). *See also* Sir Thomas Heath, *History of Greek Mathematics*, 1921.

Herostratus (Hērostratos), an Ephesian who, in order to immortalize his name, set fire to the temple of Artemis at Ephesus. This event was said to have taken place on the night that Alexander the Great was born—a coincidence of dates which renders the whole story suspicious.

Heruli, a Teutonic tribe from the Jutland peninsula. During the reign of Gallienus (A.D. 260–8) they joined the Goths (*see* GOTONES) in ravaging the Black Sea and Aegean coasts; but in 289 they were active around the Rhine estuary, and in the following century they and the Batavi (q.v.) supplied troops to the Roman army.

Hesiod (Gk Hēsiodos), earliest of the Greek didactic poets, lived probably at the very end of the 8th century B.C. He and his brother Perses were born at the village of Ascra in Boeotia, whither their father had emigrated from Aeolic Cyme in Asia Minor. Hesiod began life as herdsman of his father's flocks, and seems never to have risen above the status of a small peasant farmer. After the father's death Hesiod became involved in a dispute with his brother Perses over their inheritance. Judgment went for Perses; Hesiod retired to Naupactus, and is said to have been murdered by the sons of his host in the sacred precinct of Nemean Zeus at Oeneon in Locris. Subsequently Ascra was destroyed by the Thespians, its inhabitants settled at Boeotian Orchomenus, and the Delphic oracle ordered the translation of Hesiod's remains to that place.

Three extant works are attributed to Hesiod. There is no reason to doubt the genuineness of the first, *Works and Days,* which contains ethical precepts, advice on husbandry and a calendar of the months with observations on the days most propitious or otherwise for rural and nautical undertakings. It was generally believed by the ancients that Hesiod wrote a *Theogony,* an attempt to systematize the many legends of gods and heroes with particular reference to their descent. But the form in which this work has come down to us consists of various recensions with many later additions and interpolations. Finally we have the *Shield of Heracles,* which is now recognized as spurious, and some fragments of other works. The best editions of Hesiod are those by F. A. Paley (1883), V. von Wilamowitz-Moellendorff (1928) and T. A. Sinclair (1932). *See* the translations by A. W. Mair (Oxford Translations Library), 1908; H. G. Evelyn White, with text and the *Homeric Hymns* (Loeb Library); A. S. Way, 1934.

Hesione (Hēsionē), daughter of Laomedon (q.v.), King of Troy, who was obliged to chain her to a rock, in order to be devoured by a sea-monster and thereby appease the wrath of Apollo and Poseidon. Heracles (q.v.) undertook to save her if Laomedon would give him the stud of immortal horses which his grandfather Tros (q.v.) had received from Zeus in compensation for the rape of Ganymedes (q.v.). Heracles killed the monster; but Laomedon, faithless as ever, broke his promise. Heracles took Troy, slew Laomedon and gave Hesione to Telamon (q.v.). Hesione's brother Priam, Laomedon's successor, sent Antenor (q.v.) to demand her return, and the refusal of the Greeks was one cause of the ill feeling that led to the Trojan war.

Hesperidēs, 'Daughters of Evening', in Greek mythology, the guardians of the golden apples which Gē gave Hera on her marriage to Zeus. According to Hesiod they were daughters of Erebus and Night; in later accounts of Atlas and Hesperis, or of Phorcys and Ceto. The Hesperides were usually represented as three in number, Aegle,

Erytheia and Hesperethusa (or Hesperis); but sometimes they appear as four or seven. In the earliest legends they are said to dwell in the extreme west, on the River Oceanus; others place them among the Hyperboreans (q.v.) or near Mt Atlas. The apples grew on a tree continually watched by a dragon called Ladon; and the fact that this name belonged also to a river in Arcadia has led some to suggest that the garden of the Hesperides was originally located in that country. *See also* ATALANTA; ERIS; HIPPOMENES, 1; TWELVE LABOURS OF HERACLES, 11.

Hestia, in Greek mythology, goddess of the hearth (*see* VESTA), daughter of Cronus and Rhea, was one of the twelve great divinities of the Greeks. When Apollo and Poseidon sought her hand in marriage she vowed to remain a virgin and was appointed by Zeus to preside over sacrifices. Hestia was worshipped principally as goddess of the family hearth; but as a city is only an extension of the family, she had also, at least in many states, a public cult at the city hearth in the *prutaneion* or town hall, where the fire round which the magistrates assembled continually burned and was regarded as a place of refuge for suppliants. When a colony was about to leave, the emigrants took from this hearth the fire which would burn on the civic hearth of their new home. Later philosophies thought of Hestia as personifying the earth as centre of the universe, and identified her with Cybele and Demeter.

Hibernia or **Ivernia,** the island of Ireland, which was called by the Greeks Ierne. Ireland was never occupied by the Romans; but from the middle of the 3rd century A.D. its inhabitants (more usually called Scotti) availed themselves of the prevailing disorder in the empire to make raids upon Britain, where they learned something of Roman military defence works and military organization.

Hiempsal, name of two kings of Numidia.

1. Son of Micipsa and cousin of Jugurtha (q.v.), who assassinated him in 118 B.C.

2. Son of Mastanabal and half-brother of Jugurtha. Expelled from his kingdom by a Numidian faction supported by Cn. Domitius Ahenobarbus, leader of the Marian party in Africa (81 B.C.), he was restored by Pompey in the same year. The date of his death is unknown, but he was alive in 62 B.C. He wrote a number of works in Punic, which are quoted by Sallust.

Hierapolis: 1. City of Syria, with a sanctuary of Atagartis. For an account of the orgiastic rites performed there *see* the tract *De Dea Syria* attributed to Lucian.

2. City of Phrygia, birth-place of Epictetus (q.v.) and seat of an early church (Col. iv. 13), which supplanted the pagan cult of Cybele under the name Leto. Remains include an avenue of tombs and a well-preserved theatre.

Hierōn, name of two tyrants of Syracuse.

1. Brother and successor of Gelon (q.v.), reigned 478–467 B.C. He removed the populations of Naxos and Catina (which was renamed Aetna) to Leontini (q.v.), and won an important victory over the Etruscans at Cumae (474). To celebrate this latter achievement he dedicated at Olympia a bronze helmet which is now in the British

Museum. Hieron was a generous patron of literature, and entertained Aeschylus and Simonides at his court.

2. Illegitimate son of Hierocles, a Syracusan noble, reigned 270–216 B.C. Appointed commander-in-chief by the soldiers and citizens in 275, he defeated the Mamertines (q.v.) in 270 and was chosen ruler with the kingly title. His renewed attack on Messana (q.v.), which was still held by the Mamertines, in 264 B.C. precipitated the first Punic war. Hieron took the side of Carthage, but he was defeated by the consul Appius Claudius, besieged in Syracuse, and obliged to sign a treaty with Rome; the terms provided that he should govern south-eastern Sicily and the east coast as far as Tauromenium. Hiero remained a loyal and useful ally of Rome until his death in 216 B.C. He was an admirer of Theocritus, whose sixteenth idyll depicts the prosperity of Syracuse under his government.

Hieronymus (-numos), Greek general and historian, a native of Cardia. He accompanied Alexander the Great to Asia, and after Alexander's death (323 B.C.) joined Eumenes against Antigonus. Taken prisoner by the latter, he was pardoned and appointed superintendent of asphalt beds in the Dead Sea. Antigonus's son, Demetrius Poliorcetes, made him polemarch of Thespiae in Boeotia, and he died at the court of Antigonus II, Gonatas, at the age of 104. Hieronymus wrote a history of the Diadochi covering the period 323–272 B.C., some fragments of which remain.

Himera, city on the north coast of Sicily, near the mouth of a river of the same name; birth-place of Stesichorus (q.v.). It was founded in 648 B.C. by Chalcidian inhabitants of Zancle and exiles from Syracuse. Here the Carthaginians were defeated by Gelon (q.v.) in 480 B.C. (*see* THERON). In 408, however, it was taken by the Carthaginians, who razed it to the ground and built a new town on the opposite side of the river. This, from a hot spring in the vicinity, was called Thermae Himeraeae; it soon became a Greek city, and was the birth-place of Agathocles (q.v.).

Hippalus (-os), Greek merchant-navigator, *fl.* 150 B.C. His discovery of the south-east monsoons opened up the Arabia–India sea route. *See* E. H. Warmington, *Commerce between the Roman Empire and India*, 1928.

Hipparchus (-khos): 1. Son of Peisistratus (q.v.).

2. Greek astronomer (*fl.* 161–126 B.C.), born at Nicaea in Bithynia. He did not follow the heliocentric theory of his predecessor Aristarchus of Samos (q.v.), but other aspects of his achievement have caused him to be considered the greatest astronomer of antiquity. He is the first person known to have used trigonometry in his work; he made great improvements in astronomical instruments; and he compiled a catalogue of fixed stars to the number of 850 or more. Hipparchus also (1) discovered the Precession of the Equinoxes; (2) calculated (with the aid of Babylonian records) the length of the mean tropic year to within about 6½ minutes, and that of the mean lunar month to within less than a second of the figures now accepted; (3) improved on Aristarchus's estimates of the sizes and distances of the sun and moon, and observed the changes in their apparent diameters. The astronomy of Hipparchus takes its definitive form in the *Syntaxis*

(commonly called *Almagest*) of Ptolemy (*c.* A.D. 150), which held the field until the time of Copernicus. *See* Sir Thomas Heath, *Greek Astronomy*, 1932.

Hippasus (-os), a native of Metapontum and one of the earliest disciples of Pythagoras. Though always reckoned among the Pythagoreans, he followed Heraclitus in holding fire to be the primary element.

Hippias: 1. Son of Peisistratus (q.v.).

2. Greek sophist, born at Elis in Peloponnesus about the middle of the 5th century B.C. He settled at Athens, where he met Socrates and lectured on politics, mathematics, music and astronomy. He aimed not to give his pupils knowledge, but to supply them with those weapons of argument which would enable them to discuss any and every subject. His methods are expounded in the *Hippias major* and *minor* of Plato, whence it appears that he laid great emphasis on the meaning of words, the value of rhythm and literary style.

Hippocrates (-krates), Greek physician, born in the island of Cos *c.* 460 B.C. He wrote, taught and practised at home, travelled extensively in mainland Greece, and died at Larisa in Thessaly *c.* 377 B.C. As to the extant works bearing his name, there is no agreement as to which are genuine; *see* edition (with translation) of the most important by W. H. S. Jones and E. T. Withington, 4 vols. (Loeb Library). The best known is the *Aphorism*, which opens with the famous words: 'Life is short, and the art [of medicine] is long; the occasion fleeting, experience deceitful and judgment difficult.' *See* A. J. Brock, *Greek Medicine*, 1929.

Hippocrene (Hippokrēnē), i.e. fountain of the horse, a spring on Mt Helicon (q.v.) sacred to the Muses and Apollo, and hence a reputed source of poetic inspiration. According to legend it was produced, like its namesake at Troezen and Peirene at Corinth, by the stamping of Pegasus's hoof. *See also* AGANIPPE.

Hippodameia: 1. Daughter of Oenomaus, King of Pisa in Elis.

2. Wife of Pirithoüs (q.v.).

Hippodrome (Gk Hippodromos), Greek building for horse and chariot races, corresponding to the Roman circus (q.v.). It was usually constructed on the slope of a hill so that the material excavated from one side could be used to form an embankment for the other. The length was generally between 600 and 700 feet, the width of the arena about 400 feet. One end was semicircular, the other square; tiers of seats ran round the circular ends and two long sides, and down the centre was a division. At Constantinople, where there are many remains of the great hippodrome begun by Septimius Severus in A.D. 203 and finished by Constantine in 330, much of the area was supported not on the usual embankment, but on tiers of enormous vaults.

Hippolyte (-lutē), in Greek legend, queen of the Amazons (q.v.). She wore a girdle given to her by her father Ares, and was slain by Heracles (*see* TWELVE LABOURS OF HERACLES, 8). According to another story she was ravished by Theseus (q.v.) and became the mother of Hippolytus; while others again say that it was her sister Antiope whom Theseus carried off, that to avenge her Hippolyte invaded Attica, but was defeated by Theseus and fled to Megara where she died of grief.

Hippolytus (-lutos), in Greek legend, son of Theseus (q.v.) by Hippolyte (q.v.), queen of the Amazons, or by her sister Antiope. He was a famous charioteer and hunter, and a favourite of Artemis. His stepmother Phaedra fell in love with him, but when he rejected her advances she denounced him to Theseus as having attempted to dishonour her. Theseus, to whom Poseidon had granted three wishes, banished Hippolytus and prayed for his destruction. As Hippolytus was driving his chariot along the shore at Troezen, a sea-monster came from the waves and frightened the horses. Hippolytus was thrown, became entangled in the reins and was dragged along until he died. According to a version which seems to have originated at Epidaurus, Asclepius (q.v.) was persuaded by Artemis to restore Hippolytus to life; according to Italian traditions he was renamed Virbius by Diana (q.v.) and transported to Aricia. He was also worshipped at Troezen. Hippolytus was originally the male consort of Artemis (q.v.) as Mediterranean mother-goddess; cf. **Adonis** and **Aphrodite** (qq.v.).

Hippomenēs: 1. In Boeotian legend, son of Megareus and suitor of Atalanta (q.v.), who was defeated by him in a foot-race with the help of three golden apples of the Hesperides (q.v.).

2. Fourth and last of the decennial archons at Athens, deposed by the Attic nobles (*see* EUPATRIDAE) because of a barbarous punishment inflicted by him upon his daughter. This event must be placed somewhere between 752 and 682 B.C., which latter date marks the beginning of annual archonship; but the details of the story are doubtless apocryphal.

Hippōn, Greek eclectic philosopher, a native of Samos. He lived chiefly at Athens, taught that water is the primary element, and denied all existence save that of things known through the five senses. Aristotle considered that the meanness of his intellect hardly entitled him to the name philosopher.

Hippōnax, Greek iambic poet, a native of Ephesus. Driven out by the tyrant Athenagoras (*c.* 540 B.C.), he settled at Clazomenae and spent the rest of his life in poverty. Only a few fragments of his satires are extant. According to some he was the inventor of parody (*see also* HEGEMON). *See* B. J. Peltzer, *De parodica Graecorum poesi,* 1855.

Hipponicus (-kos), son of Callias 1 (q.v.) and father of Callias 2, was killed at the battle of Delium in 424 B.C. His daughter Hipparete was married to Alcibiades.

Hirpini, Samnite tribe of southern Italy, inhabiting territory that was bounded south by the Lucani, south-west by the Campani, east and north-east by the Apuli and Frentani. On the north they were politically identical with the Caraceni and Pentri, with whom they formed the Samnite alliance in the wars of the 4th century B.C. After the defeat of the Samnites (q.v.) by Sulla, in 82 B.C., they were given the Roman franchise.

Hirtius, Aulus, Roman historian and statesman, born *c.* 90 B.C. He was one of Caesar's legates in Gaul, but during the civil war remained at home as Caesar's agent and general man of business. As consul with C. Vibius Pansa in 43 B.C., he was killed in battle against Mark Antony at Mutina. Hirtius is recognized as author of the eighth book of Caesar's *Gallic War*. *De Bello Alexandrino* may also be his work, based upon conversations with Caesar himself and upon written material supplied by a member of Caesar's staff. It was also probably at the request of Hirtius that *De Bello Africo* and *De Bello Hispaniensi* were prepared by two soldiers (*see* CAESAR, GAIUS JULIUS) as a basis for literary revision by Hirtius, had he lived.

Hispalis (mod. Seville), town of Hispania Ulterior, and, from the time of Augustus, of Baetica (*see* HISPANIA). It was an important Roman town in the 2nd century B.C., and in 45 B.C. was captured by Caesar, who called it Colonia Julia Romula. The chief Roman remains are those of an aqueduct which consisted of 410 arches. *See* W. Gallichan, *The Story of Seville*, 1903.

Hispania (mod. Spain and Portugal). The Greeks and Romans had no accurate knowledge of the peninsula before the second Punic war (218–201 B.C.). It is first mentioned by Hecataeus (q.v.) as Iberia. But this name indicated only the east coast; the west coast beyond the Pillars of Hercules was called Tartessis.

The native inhabitants, called by classical writers Iberi, dwelt on both sides of the Pyrenees and were found in southern Gaul as far east as the Rhône. Celts later crossed the Pyrenees and intermarried with the Iberi, whence the mixed race of Celtiberi (*see* CELTIBERIA). But there were several tribes, both of Iberians and Celts, which never mingled. The pure Iberians, from whom the modern Basques claim descent, included the Cantabri, Astures, Vascones and other groups in the Pyrenees and on the north coast. The pure Celts lived chiefly on the River Anas (mod. Guadiana) and in Gallaecia, the extreme north-west. There were also Phoenician and Carthaginian settlements on the coasts, the most important of which were Gades, Carthago Nova and Tartessus (qq.v.); among Greek colonies were Saguntum (q.v.) and Emporiae. Lastly, the Roman conquest introduced a strong Roman element.

Spanish history begins with the Carthaginian invasion under Hamilcar (q.v.) in 238 B.C. (*see also* HANNIBAL; HASDRUBAL). During the second Punic war the Carthaginians were driven out of the country by Scipio Africanus Major (q.v.) in the four years 210–207 B.C. Rome now possessed the former Carthaginian dominions south of the Iberus; but many tribes in the centre retained their independence, while those in the north and north-west were scarcely known. Nearly two centuries would elapse before Rome had managed to subdue the whole peninsula. Celtiberia was subdued by the elder Cato in 195, and again by Tib. Sempronius Gracchus (father of the tribunes) in 179 B.C. The Lusitani, who long resisted under the leadership of Viriathus (q.v.), were obliged to submit (in 138 B.C.) to D. Junius Brutus, who penetrated as far as Gallaecia (*see* BRUTUS, DECIMUS JUNIUS, 1). But they were not yet finally conquered. By the capture of Numantia (q.v.) by Scipio Aemilianus Africanus (q.v.) in 133 B.C. Rome obtained sovereignty over the centre and over Lusitania south of the Tagus; northern Lusitania was won by Julius Caesar (60 B.C.). The Astures,

Cantabri and other tribes in the extreme north were subjugated by Augustus.

At the end of the second Punic war the Romans divided Hispania into two provinces: (1) *Hispania Citerior*, north-east of the Iberus; (2) *Hispania Ulterior*, south-west of that river. Augustus made a new division and formed three provinces: (1) *Hispania Tarraconensis*, by far the largest, including the whole north-west, centre and south-east; (2) *Hispania Baetica*, separated from Lusitania on the north and west by the River Anas, and from Tarraconensis by an irregular line drawn from the Anas to a point about longitude 3° E. on the Mediterranean; (3) *Lusitania*, corresponding very nearly to modern Portugal. The respective capitals of these three provinces were Tarraco, Hispalis and Augusta Emerita. *See* C. H. V. Sutherland, *The Romans in Spain, 217 B.C.–A.D. 117*, 1939.

Histiaeus (-aios), tyrant of Miletus under the Persian king Dareios I. When Dareios invaded Scythia, in 513 B.C., Histiaeus was left with other Greek tyrants to guard the bridge of boats over the Danube. He successfully resisted a proposal to break the bridge (*see* MILTIADES) and leave the Persians to their fate, for which he was rewarded with some territory in Thrace. Dareios, however, became suspicious of his ultimate intentions, invited him to Susa, and prevented him from returning. Aristagoras (q.v.), his kinsman, ruled Miletus in his place; and when the Ionian revolt broke out Histiaeus persuaded Dareios that only he could quell it. He was accordingly allowed to depart (496 B.C.). But on reaching the coast he found himself suspected by the local satrap, and was driven to establish himself as a pirate at Byzantium. He was eventually taken prisoner by the Persian general Harpagus and sent to Artaphernes, brother of Dareios and satrap of Sardis, who had him crucified (494 B.C.).

Homer (Gk Homēros), name given to the author(s) of the two great Greek epics, *Iliad* and *Odyssey*, which appear to date from some time between *c.* 810 and 730 B.C. Except for the fact that these poems derive from the west coast of Asia, nothing whatever is known about the author(s). Homer was supposed in antiquity to have been blind, and seven cities, listed in the following hexameter, claimed to be his birth-place: 'Smyrna, Rhodos, Colophon, Salamis, Chios, Argos, Athenae.' Such was the universal traditional belief until 1795, when there appeared F. A. Wolf's *Prolegomena*, which endeavoured to show that *Iliad* and *Odyssey* were not two complete poems, but small, separate epic songs, celebrating single exploits of the heroes, and that these lays were for the first time collected and written down by Peisistratus (q.v.) or under his supervision. These views started a controversy which is not yet settled and probably never will be. The following, however, may be regarded as the most probable conclusions: (1) An abundance of heroic lays preserved the memory of the Trojan war. (2) These unconnected songs were, for the first time, united by a great genius called Homer, who is responsible for the poetical unity which we must acknowledge within each poem. There are facts which have led some scholars to declare that even if *Iliad* and *Odyssey* were each produced by an individual, those individuals were not identical. But the prevalent opinion today does not view the evidence as cogent against the more than superficial unity apparent between the two poems. (3) As writing was little practised in the centuries immediately succeeding, many interpolations crept in, the poems became dismembered, returned to their original state as separate songs and were preserved by rhapsodes who sang at private banquets and public festivals. (4) Solon directed the attention of his countrymen to the Homeric poems, but their re-collection and committal to writing belongs to Peisistratus, from whose time the *Iliad* and *Odyssey* were recited in their entirety at the quadrennial festival of Panathenaea (q.v.) at Athens.

The ancients attributed other poems to Homer, but the claims of none of them can stand investigation. The hymns which still bear Homer's name, the *Batrachomyomachia* ('Battle of Frogs and Mice') and the lost *Margites* are clearly of later origin.

The bibliography of Homer is legion; for English-speaking students the best editions of the text with commentary are (1) of the *Iliad* by W. Leaf, 1900–2, and by T. W. Allen, 1931; (2) of the *Odyssey* by Merry, Riddell and Monro (1886–1901). *See* the verse translations of both *Iliad* and *Odyssey* by S. O. Andrew and M. Oakley in Everyman's Library. *See also* J. A. Scott, *The Unity of Homer*, 1921; M. P. Nilsson, *Homer and Mycenae*, 1932; Gilbert Murray, *The Rise of the Greek Epic*, 4th ed., 1934; S. E. Basset, *The Poetry of Homer*, 1938; G. S. Kirk, *The Homeric Poems as History*, 1964.

Honos, Roman divinity, the personification of honour. A temple dedicated to her was built at Rome in 234, converted into a double shrine of Honour and Virtue by M. Claudius in 208 B.C. and restored by the emperor Vespasian. Another temple of Honour and Virtue was built by Marius.

Hoplites (Gk Hoplitai), Greek heavy-armed infantry as distinct from the peltasts (q.v.). Organized on a basis of tribes (ten regiments at Athens) and property qualification, they wore a bronze helmet, breastplate and greaves, and carried a round shield, while their offensive weapons consisted of an iron sword and 9-foot spear.

Horace, Quintus Horatius Flaccus, Latin poet, born 8th December 65 B.C. at Venusia on the borders of Apulia and Lucania. His father, a freedman, was either a collector of taxes or of payments at auctions. He would not send his son to the local school, but took him to Rome and seems thereafter to have devoted his time and modest fortune to his son's education. In the capital Horace attended the best schools, one of which was kept by Orbilius Pupillus (q.v.), and then, at the age of about eighteen, proceeded to Athens where he studied Greek poetry and philosophy. When Brutus came to Greece after the death of Caesar, Horace joined his army. He was present at Philippi (42 B.C.) and shared the republican rout.

Having obtained his pardon Horace returned to Rome, where his small paternal estate had been confiscated; but he managed to raise sufficient money to buy a clerkship in the quaestor's office. Meanwhile some of his poems had attracted the notice of Varius and Virgil, who introduced him to Maecenas (39). Horace soon became a close friend of the latter, and found favour with the emperor Augustus. About the year 34 B.C. Maecenas gave him a small property among the

Sabine hills, about 15 miles north-east of Tibur, the site of which has been discovered in recent times. The peace and beauty of this place, to which he loved to retire, filled his heart with joy (*satis beatus unicis Sabinis*). In the summer of 8 B.C. the dying Maecenas said to Augustus: 'Be mindful of Horatius Flaccus as of me.' But on 27th November in the same year Horace also died, at the age of fifty-seven. He was a man of short stature, with dark eyes, but prematurely grey and inclined to stoutness. His health was not robust, a fact which must have both helped and encouraged him in the more frugal habits which he cultivated in later life. He never married.

The surviving works of Horace consist of two books of *Satires*, dealing rather with the folly than with the wickedness of vice; the *Epodes* (completed soon after 31 B.C.), in which there is much bitterness, provoked, it would seem, by some personal hatred or sense of injury; four books of *Odes*, which, if they lack the highest inspiration of lyric poetry, are unrivalled as works of refined art, as examples of the most skilful felicities of language and metre; two books of *Epistles*, the most polished of his writings; the *Carmen Saeculare*, an ode written by command of the emperor to be sung by a chorus of boys and girls in the Secular games exhibited by Augustus in 17 B.C.; finally, the unfinished letter to the Pisos *On the Art of Poetry*. See complete text by F. Klinger, 2nd ed., 1950; also with translation by C. E. Bennett and H. R. Fairclough (Loeb Library). There is an English version of the complete works by Lord Dunsany and Michael Oakley (Everyman's Library), 1961. *See also* W. Y. Sellar, *Horace and the Elegiac Poets*, 1899; J. F. D'Alton, *Horace and his Age*, 1917; A. Y. Campbell, *Horace, a new Interpretation*, 1924; T. R. Glover, *Horace*, 1932; L. P. Wilkinson, *Horace and his Lyric Poetry*, 1945; A. Noyes, *Portrait of Horace*, 1947; E. Fraenkel, *Horace*, 1957.

Horae (Hōrai), in Greek and Latin mythology, the Seasons. The *Iliad* represents them as guardians of the gates of Olympus, the *Odyssey* as bringing round the seasons. In Hesiod, who calls them daughters of Zeus and Themis, they are three in number (Eunomia, Dikē and Eirēnē) and watch over the processes of agriculture. In classical Athens there were two Horae, Thallo and Carpo, goddesses respectively of flowers and spring and of the fruits of summer; a festival, Horaea, was celebrated in their honour. In hellenistic mythology the Horae were again the four seasons, but daughters of Helios and Selene. Later, when the day was divided into twelve equal parts, each was called a *hora*, whence English 'hour'.

Horatii, in Roman legend, three brothers who fought with three Curiatii from Alba, to determine whether Rome or Alba should rule in Latium. The contest was long undecided: two of the Horatii fell, but the three Curiatii were severely wounded. Seeing this, the surviving Horatius, who was still unhurt, pretended to flee, and vanquished his opponents by encountering them severally. He shouldered the spoils and started back towards Rome. As he approached the Porta Capena, his sister Horatia met him, and recognized the mantle of one of the Curiatii, her betrothed. Her immoderate grief stirred the wrath of Horatius, who stabbed her, exclaiming: 'So perish every Roman woman who bewails a foe!' For this murder he was condemned by the magistrates to be scourged and hanged from a tree. The people, however, commuted the sentence and prescribed a new form of punishment, and Horatius, with veiled head and escorted by his father, was made to pass under a yoke or gibbet (*tigillum sororium*). The story was no doubt invented to explain some religious rite whose meaning had long since been forgotten.

Hortensius, Quintus: 1. Roman dictator (287 B.C.). When the plebeians, oppressed by their patrician creditors, seceded to the Janiculum he was commissioned to end the strife, and passed the *Lex Hortensia* which made *plebiscita* (resolutions of the plebeian assembly) binding on the whole people without senatorial confirmation.

2. Surnamed Hortalus, Roman forensic orator, born 114 B.C. He made his reputation at the age of nineteen with a speech in defence of Nicomedes III (q.v.) of Bithynia, which gave him undisputed leadership of the bar. This position he retained until 70 B.C. (the year before his consulship), when he lost it to Cicero upon the trial of Verres; but after 63 B.C. Cicero joined the aristocratic party, so that, despite their traditional rivalry, the two men were often on the same side in political cases. Hortensius died in 50 B.C. None of his speeches has survived. His eloquence was of the florid 'Asiatic' style, better heard than read, and his manner was somewhat affected; but he had a wonderful memory and a magnificent voice. He was rich, and lived in princely style. His only son, named like himself, was put to death by Mark Antony after Philippi (42 B.C.).

Hostius, Roman epic poet of the 2nd century B.C., whose lost *Bellum Histricum* commemorated the victory of C. Sempronius Tuditanus over the Illyrian Iapydes in 129 B.C. *See* E. Bährens, *Fragmenta poetarum Romanorum*, 1884.

Hyacinthus (Huakinthos), originally a pre-hellenic god. In mythology he was a beautiful youth, beloved by Apollo and Zephyrus. He returned the love of Apollo; but as he was playing at quoits with the god, Zephyrus, out of jealousy, caused the quoit of Apollo to strike the head of the youth and kill him on the spot. From the blood of Hyacinthus there sprang the flower, hyacinth, on the leaves of which appeared the exclamation of woe, AI, AI, or the letter *upsilon*, being the initial of his name. Hyacinthus was worshipped at Amyclae as a hero, and a festival, Hyacinthia, was celebrated in his honour.

Hybla, name of three Sicilian towns founded by the Siculi (q.v.): 1. *Hybla Major*, on the River Symaethus; probably the Hybla famous for its honey, but others identify this with 2. *Hybla Minor* on the east coast north of Syracuse, which was later the site of a Dorian colony known as Megara Hyblaea. 3. *Hybla Heraea* in the south of the island, on the road from Syracuse to Agrigentum.

Hyccara (Hukkarē), town on the north coast of Sicily, founded by the Sicani (q.v.). It was taken by the Athenians in 415 B.C. and its inhabitants sold into slavery. Among these was Timandra, mistress of Alcibiades and mother of Laïs (*see* LAÏS, 2).

Hydaspes (mod. Jhelum), northernmost of the five great tributaries of the River Indus, on whose banks Alexander the Great defeated Porus (q.v.) in 326 B.C.

Hygieia (Hu-), Greek goddess of health, whose cult first appears at

Titane near Sicyon. Here she was worshipped simply as a female aspect of Asclepius (q.v.), not as an independent or associate deity; her cult indeed did not reach Epidaurus until late, long after the worship of Asclepius reached Athens in 420 B.C. It is at Athens that she first emerges as a distinct personality, exercising the functions already attributed to Athena Hygieia. At this stage she was not considered as related to Asclepius, whose wife was called Epione. Gradually, however, she came to be regarded as his daughter, and in the Orphic hymns as his wife. In 293 B.C. the cult of Asclepius and that of Hygieia were introduced at Rome from Epidaurus, and Hygieia was soon identified with Salus (q.v.).

Hyginus: 1. Surnamed Gromaticus, 'the Surveyor', Latin writer on land-surveying, flourished in the time of Trajan (A.D. 98–117). The treatise *De Munitionibus Castrorum*, usually attributed to him, is almost certainly of a much later date.

2. Gaius Julius Hyginus, a scholar of great learning and versatility. Probably a native of Spain, he was a freedman of Augustus, who placed him in charge of the Palatine library. His numerous works are lost; the *Fabularum Liber* and *De Astronomia*, which have come down to us under his name, are probably later abridgments.

Hylas (Hulas), in Greek legend, son of Theiodamas, King of the Dryopes. He was a favourite of Heracles and accompanied him on the Argonautic expedition (*see* ARGONAUTS); but having landed at Kios, on the coast of Mysia, he was carried off by the nymphs of a spring where he had gone to draw water. Heracles, seeking him in vain, threatened to devastate the land, and it was to commemorate this traditional event that the inhabitants of Kios wandered once a year crying 'Hylas!' The story was of course invented to explain the custom, whose meaning had been long since forgotten. It dates from Theocritus, but there are references in Aeschylus and Aristophanes.

Hyllus (Hullos), son of Heracles by Deianeira, and husband of Iole (q.v.). With other sons of Heracles he was driven from Peloponnesus by Eurystheus (q.v.), and was later slain in battle by the Arcadian king Echemus when he attempted to return (*see* HERACLIDAE).

Hymen or **Hymenaeus** (Humēn *or* Humenaios), personification of the refrain of a song sung at Greek weddings. He was represented variously as the son either of Apollo by a Muse or of Dionysus by Aphrodite. In this last capacity he was a fertility-god. In Attica, on the other hand, he was described simply as a dashing youth with nothing divine about him. He fell in love with a girl, disguised himself as a woman in order to accompany her in a procession to Eleusis, and saved the whole party from a gang of pirates who attacked them on the way. Of course he married the girl and lived so happily ever afterwards that his name became a by-word of matrimonial bliss and was invoked in wedding hymns.

Hymettus (Humettos), mountain of Attica, bounding the Athenian plain on the south-east. It was famous (as it still is) for its honey, and also produced a bluish marble which, though used for both building and sculpture, was less highly valued than the pure white marble of Pentelicon (q.v.).

Hyperbolus (Huperbolos), Athenian demagogue of servile origin.

During the Peloponnesian war (417 B.C.) he attempted to get rid of Nicias or Alcibiades (qq.v.) by calling for a vote of ostracism (q.v.). But the parties endangered combined to defeat him, and Hyperbolus himself was ostracized: an application of that dignified punishment (*see* Aristotle, *Pol.* 1284*a–b*) by which it was thought to have been so debased that it was never again employed. Hyperbolus was murdered by the oligarchs at Samos in 411 B.C.

Hyperboreans (Gk Huperboreoi), probably meaning 'carriers over', not 'beyond the North Wind', a legendary people closely connected with the cult of Apollo. According to Herodotus, two maidens, escorted by five men, were sent by the Hyperboreans with certain offerings to Delos. Finding that their messengers did not return, the Hyperboreans adopted the method of wrapping their offerings in wheat straw and requesting their immediate neighbours to hand them to the next people, and so on until they reached Delos. That such articles were brought to Delos in historical times is clear, and they must have come from somewhere; but unfortunately we have no record of the early stages of their journey.

Hypereides (Hupereidēs), one of the ten Attic Orators; born at Athens *c.* 390 B.C. and studied under Isocrates (q.v.). From 346 he supported the anti-Macedonian policy of Demosthenes (q.v.), but was one of the ten public prosecutors on the latter's impeachment in 324 (*see* HARPALUS). He then assumed leadership of the patriotic party, and was chiefly responsible for the Lamian War (q.v.). After Crannon, in 322, he took refuge in Aegina, where he was seized by the emissaries of Antipater and put to death. Hypereides has been called by Jebb 'the Sheridan of Athens'. Most of the surviving fragments of his speeches were discovered in Egyptian papyri in 1847 and 1892. *See* the Oxford text, edited by Sir F. G. Kenyon, 1907. *See also* R. C. Jebb, *Attic Orators*, ii. 381, 1888.

Hyperion (Huperiōn), one of the Titans (q.v.), father of Helios (q.v.), who is himself called Hyperion in Homer.

Hypermestra (Hupermestra), daughter of Danaüs and wife of Lynceus, son of Aegyptus, *see* DANAÜS.

Hypnos (Hup-), in Greek mythology, the personification of sleep, called in Latin *Somnus*; son of Nyx (q.v.) and brother of Thanatos (q.v.).

Hypsipyle (Hupsipulē), in Greek legend, daughter of Thoas, King of Lemnos. When the Lemnian women murdered all the men in the island, Hypsipyle saved her father. Soon after this the Argonauts (q.v.) called at Lemnos and she conceived by Jason a son, Euneus, who was king during the Trojan war. Subsequently the Lemnian women discovered that Thoas was alive, and obliged Hypsipyle to leave the island. During her voyage she was captured by pirates and sold to the Nemean king Lycurgus, who entrusted her with the care of his son Archemorus (q.v.) or Opheltes.

Hyrcanus (Hurkanos), name of two Jewish high priests of the Hasamonean family.

1. *John* (*Johanan*) *Hyrcanus I* (*c.* 175–104 B.C.), son of Simon Maccabaeus, early won fame as a general against the Syrians. He became high priest and governor of Judaea (135), and founded the

Jewish monarchy, which continued in his family until Herod seized Judaea. There was much warfare during his reign.

2. *John* (*Johanan*) *Hyrcanus II*, grandson of the preceding, born *c.* 79 B.C. His brother Aristobulus disputed the throne with him until his death (49 B.C.). Antipater and later Pompey (63) supported Hyrcanus as a less formidable foe, and Judaea lost her independence. In 40 Hyrcanus was captured by the Parthians, and lived in Babylonia till invited back by Herod (36), who in 30 B.C. had him executed on a charge of treason.

I

Iacchus (Iakkhos), personification of the Eleusinian invocation 'iakkh' ō iakkhe'. In the Mysteries he was regarded as son of Zeus by Demeter, but was later identified with Bacchus (see Dionysus.)

Iamblichus (-khos), Neoplatonist philosopher of the time of Constantine. Born at Chalcis in Coele-Syria, he studied at Rome under Porphyry, and later taught in Syria. His extant writings are parts of a larger work on Pythagorean philosophy. They are: On the Pythagorean Life; Exhortation to Philosophy (embodying much of Aristotle's lost Protrepticus); On the General Science of Mathematics; On the Arithmetic of Nicomachus; The Theological Principles of Arithmetic. Another two, On the Egyptian Mysteries and the Book of Mysteries, are now considered to have been written by members of his school. See T. Whittaker, The Neoplatonists, 2nd ed., 1918.

Iapetus (-os), one of the Titans (q.v.), father of Atlas, Prometheus and Epimetheus (qq.v.).

Iapydia, territory in the north of Illyria (q.v.). The Iapydes were a mixed race of Celts and Illyrians dwelling between the rivers Ansia and Tedanius. They were finally subdued by the Romans in 34 B.C.

Iapygia (Iapugia), Greek name for Calabria (q.v.).

Iazyges, a Sarmatian tribe dwelling on the shores of the Maeotis (Sea of Azov), where they were allies of Mithradates the Great of Pontus. During the first century A.D. they moved to the plains east of the Theiss.

Iberia: 1. Name given by early Greek navigators to the east coast of Spain and the south coast of France as far east as the Rhône. Towards the end of the 1st century B.C. it had come to be used of the whole Spanish peninsula.

2. A country corresponding to part of modern Georgia between the Black and Caspian seas.

Ibycus (Ibukos), Greek lyric poet of the 6th century B.C., born at Rhegium and lived at the court of Polycrates (q.v.) at Samos. The extant verses attributed to him are believed to have been supplemented in modern times by the discovery of a papyrus at Oxyrhynchus containing some fifty lines of a poem in honour of Polycrates (see J. U. Powell, New Chapters in the History of Greek Literature, 1933). Some scholars, however, reject the attribution.

A well-known story is related of Ibycus. While travelling through a wood near Corinth he was murdered by robbers, but before he died he called upon a passing flock of cranes to bear witness of the crime. Some time later one of the murderers was present at the Isthmian games when some cranes appeared. He foolishly cried out 'Look! the witnesses of Ibycus!' and the guilty men were thus discovered.

Icarius (Ikarios), in Greek legend, an Athenian who welcomed Dionysus to Attica and was taught by him the cultivation of the vine.

He gave some of his wine to a party of shepherds, who became intoxicated, and whose companions, believing Icarius to have poisoned them, murdered and buried him. His daughter Erigone, helped by his dog Maera, found his grave after a long search, and hanged herself from a nearby tree. The story was invented probably to explain the curious rite of hanging small objects from trees at a religious festival.

Icarus (Ikaros), *see* DAEDALUS.

Icĕnī, an ancient British tribe inhabiting what are now the counties of Norfolk and Suffolk. Their chief town was Venta Icenorum (Caister), about three miles from Yarmouth. *See also* BOUDICCA.

Ichthyophagi (Ikhthuophagoi), 'fish eaters', name given by ancient writers to various coast-dwelling peoples (of whom they knew little or nothing) in such localities as the Red Sea, Aethiopia and the Persian Gulf.

Iconium (Ikonion), city of Phrygia. The Romans treated it as belonging to Lycaonia (q.v.). From 25 B.C. until about A.D. 295 it was included in the province of Galatia (q.v.) and then in Pisidia (q.v.). There were numerous Roman settlers, chiefly merchants, at Iconium, and Hadrian created the town a Roman *colonia* (q.v.) *c.* A.D. 130. St Paul paid three visits here, in A.D. 47, 50 and 53.

Ictinus (Iktinos), Athenian architect of the 5th century B.C. With Callicrates (q.v.) he designed the Parthenon (q.v.). He was also responsible for the temple of Apollo at Bassae (q.v.), and for the second Telesterion at Eleusis.

Ida: 1. Mountain range of Mysia, celebrated in legend as the scene of the rape of Ganymedes (q.v.) and of the judgment of Paris (q.v.). In Homer it is from the summit of Ida that the gods watch the battles in the plain of Troy.

2. Mountain in the centre of Crete, associated in mythology with the legend of Zeus (q.v.).

Idas, in Greek legend, son of Aphareus by Arone, and brother of Lynceus with whom he took part in the Calydonian hunt (*see* MELEAGER) and the expedition of the Argonauts (q.v.). Idas and Apollo (q.v.) were both in love with Marpessa, daughter of Evenus. Idas carried her off in a winged chariot given him by Poseidon, and a fight with Apollo ensued. Zeus, however, intervened and left the decision to Marpessa. She chose Idas, fearing that Apollo would desert her when she grew old. *See also* DIOSCURI.

Idomeneus, In Greek legend king of Crete; son of the Cretan Deucalion. According to Homer he led her subjects against Troy and returned home safely with the survivors. A much later story tells that on the return journey he was overtaken by a violent storm, and vowed to sacrifice to Poseidon the first living thing he should meet on landing. This happened to be his own son, whom he promptly sacrificed; but the island was visited by a plague, and Idomeneus was driven into exile. He settled first in Calabria, then at Colophon, where he died and was buried (Virgil, *Aem.* iii. 121, 400, 531). The Cretans, however, showed his grave at Knossos, where he was worshipped as a hero. *See* H. J. Rose, *Handbook of Greek Mythology*, 1928.

Iduiē, wife of Aeëtes, King of Colchis, and mother of Medea. *See* JASON AND MEDEA.

Idumaea. In the Old Testament Edom is the mountainous district between the Dead Sea and the eastern head of the Red Sea. The decline of the kingdom of Judea enabled the Edomites to extend their sway over the southern parts thereof as far as Hebron, while their original territory was occupied by the Nabataeai (q.v.). Thus in later Jewish and in Roman history Idumaea includes the southern portion of Judea and a small area in the north of Arabia Petraea (*see* ARABIA). *See also* PETRA.

Idus, the Ides, name given in the Roman calendar to the 13th day of the month, except in March, May, July and October, when it falls on the 15th.

Iernē, Greek name for Hibernia (q.v.).

Iguvium (medieval Eugubium; mod. Gubbio), town of Umbria on the southern slopes of the Apennines. In the ruins of a nearby temple of Jupiter were discovered the seven bronze tablets bearing Umbrian inscriptions (*c.* 400–90 B.C.) and known as the *Tabulae Iguvinae* or Eugubine Tables (q.v.), now in the Palazzo dei Consoli at Gubbio. *See* C. D. Buck, *Grammar of Oscan and Umbrian*, 1928.

Ilerda (mod. Lerida), town of Hispania Citerior on the Sicoris (mod. Segu), afterwards in Hispania Tarraconensis (*see* HISPANIA), in the neighbourhood of which Caesar defeated the Pompeian generals Afranius and Petreius (49 B.C.). The manœuvres of Caesar in this campaign have been declared by military historians to have been 'seldom rivalled and never surpassed'. See *Bell. Civ.* i. 39–81; T. Rice Holmes, *The Roman Republic*, vol. iii, 1923.

Ilia or **Rhea Silvia,** mother of Romulus and Remus (*see* ROMULUS).

Ilipa, town of Carthaginian Spain (*see* HISPANIA), not far from Hispalis (mod. Seville). In the neighbourhood P. Cornelius Scipio (*see* SCIPIO AEMILIANUS AFRICANUS) defeated Hasdrubal Gisco (q.v.), thus finally destroying the Carthaginian power in Spain. Scipio's generalship on this occasion made the battle 'one of the supreme tactical masterpieces in the military history of the ancient world'. *See* B. H. Liddell Hart, *A Greater than Napoleon: Scipio Africanus.*

Illyria, a country stretching along the eastern shore of the Adriatic between modern Fiume and Durazzo, and inland to Macedonia. Its three main districts were Dalmatia, Iapydia and Liburnia. Greek colonies were established on the coast in the late 7th or early 6th century B.C. (*see* EPIDAMNUS; SALONA). An Illyrian kingdom came into being *c.* 383 B.C., and continued, despite unsuccessful conflicts with Macedon and Rome, as well as internal dissensions, until 168 B.C. In that year Rome conquered and annexed the country after it had sided with Perseus of Macedon. Following the final subjugation of Dalmatia in A.D. 9, the latter, with Iapydia and Liburnia, were formed into the Roman province of Illyricum (*see* ILLYRICUM, I).

Illyricum: 1. Roman province formed in A.D. 9 from the three Illyrian districts of Dalmatia, Iapydia and Liburnia. *See* ILLYRIA. The spread of Roman civilization in this province was rapid. Illyricum produced excellent soldiers, some of whom rose from the ranks of the legions to the imperial throne. Its importance was increased by the presence of gold-mines in the interior and of commercial cities on the coast, as well as by the passage of the Via Egnatia (q.v.). *See* Th. Mommsen, *Provinces of the Roman Empire*, edited by F. Haverfield, 1909.

2. One of the four prefectures established by Diocletian. It included Pannonia, Noricum, Crete and the whole Balkan peninsula except Thrace.

Illyricus Limes, name given in the 2nd century A.D. to a large area which included Noricum, Pannonia, Moesia, Dacia and Thrace.

Ilus (-os), in Greek legend, son of Tros by Callirrhoë, and founder of Ilium, which was also called Troas (Troy) after his father.

Ilva (Gk Aithalia; mod. Elba), island off the west coast of Italy, famous for its iron mines and smelting furnaces (*see* POPULONIA); whence its Greek name, which means 'soot island'.

Imagines, Roman name for the wax portrait-masks of deceased ancestors. They were highly valued possessions of those whose forbears included curule magistrates. When a member of such a family died, the *imagines* were worn by actors in the funeral procession.

Imbros, island of the Aegean off the southern extremity of the Chersonesus Thracicus. It was a seat of the worship of the Cabeiri (q.v.; *see also* SAMOTHRACE).

Imperator, 'commander-in-chief', a title which, from the 2nd century B.C., was conferred on a Roman general by acclamation of his troops after a victory. Under Augustus a principle was established according to which all honours of war, no matter by whom earned, belonged to the emperor. From the reign of Vespasian onwards the title 'Imperator' became the emperor's official *praenomen*, though it was also added after the *cognomen*, with a number to indicate how many times he had been so hailed following a victory of the imperial armies.

Inarime, poetic name for the island of Aenaria (q.v.).

India. Although there appears to have been some trade between India and Asia Minor in the time of Homer, and although the country is mentioned by Hecataeus of Miletus, Herodotus and Ctesias (qq.v.), the first direct contact between India and the Greek world dates from the expedition of Alexander the Great (q.v.), 327–326 B.C. Alexander got no farther than the Hyphasis (mod. Beas); but he established military settlements of Greeks and allies in the Punjab, in Sind and in Bactria (q.v.), and their cultural influence can be detected at many points. Seleucus Nicator took Bactria and India after Alexander's death. He crossed the Hyphasis and made war upon the Prasii, who dwelt along the upper Ganges. In Roman times there was much direct trade with India until the 3rd century A.D. when communication was interrupted by the Arabs and Persians. *See* H. Rawlinson, *Intercourse between India and the Western World*, 1926; W. W. Tarn, *The Greeks in Bactria and India*. 1938.

Infamia, a term of Roman law, denoting the effects of condemnation for certain specified offences, e.g. theft, fraud, bankruptcy and some kinds of immoral behaviour. The consequences of *infamia* included loss of personal status, of the right to vote or stand for public office, certain disabilities regarding marriage and the making of wills, and disqualification from acting for another at law.

Ino̅, daughter of Cadmus (q.v.), sister of Agave and Autonoë (*see* PENTHEUS), and wife of Athamas (q.v.).

Insubres, a Celtic people of Gallia Cisalpina (Transpadana). They had crossed the Alps and occupied the territory of a previous tribe, whose name they had assumed and where they built the city of Mediolanum (q.v.). The Insubres were frequently engaged in hostilities with Rome from 225 until 194 B.C., when they were subdued by L. Valerius Flaccus. *See also* MARCELLUS, MARCUS CLAUDIUS, I.

Interamna, 'between streams', name of two towns in Italy.

1. Interamna Nahartium (mod. Terni), in Umbria, situated upon and almost surrounded by the River Nar; birth-place of the historian Tacitus.

2. Interamna Lirenas, in Latium, about five miles south-east of Aquinum on the northern bank of the Liris between two of its tributaries. Founded by the Romans as a Latin colony in 312 B.C., it was intended as a military base in the Samnite wars.

Internum Mare, Roman name for the Mediterranean Sea, which was called by most Greek writers *hē esō thalatta, hē entos thalatta* or, more fully, *hē entos Herakleiōn stēlōn thalatta*, but by Herodotus *hēde hē thalatta*. From its washing the coasts both of Greece and of Italy, it was also called sometimes by both Greeks and Romans 'our sea'. The term Mare Mediterraneum occurs first in Solinus (q.v.), *c.* A.D. 200.

Iō, in Greek mythology, daughter of Inachus, first king of Argos. She was loved by Zeus, who changed her into a heifer, thinking thereby to conceal her from Hera. The goddess, aware of this metamorphosis, placed her in charge of hundred-eyed Argus, who was, however, slain by Hermes at the command of Zeus. Hera then tormented Io with a gadfly, which drove her in a state of frenzy from land to land, until at length she found rest on the banks of the Nile. Here she recovered her human form and bore a son by Zeus, named Epaphus, who became King of Egypt and built Memphis. The wanderings of Io were a favourite theme with the ancients, and the Bosporus (*Ox-ford*) was said to have derived its name from her swimming across it. Io was sometimes identified with Isis (q.v.).

Iobatēs, King of Lycia, *see* BELLEROPHON.

Iolaus (-os), in Greek legend, son of Iphicles and Automedusa. Iphicles was half-brother of Heracles; Iolaus the hero's companion and charioteer, and first to offer him sacrifices as a demi-god. After death Iolaus obtained permission from the gods of the underworld to help the sons of Heracles. He slew Eurystheus, and then returned to the shades.

Iolcus (-kos), town of Magnesia in Thessaly. It was celebrated in Greek legend as the home of Pelias and Jason, and as the starting-point of the expedition of the Argonauts (q.v.).

Iolē, in Greek legend, daughter of Eurytus, King of Oechalia. She was loved by Heracles (q.v.), after whose death she married his son Hyllus (q.v.).

Iōn, son of Apollo by Creusa, daughter of Erechteus and wife of Xuthus. He was legendary ancestor of the Ionians (q.v.). *See* Euripides, *Ion.*

Iōnia, a narrow strip of land with adjacent islands on the west coast of Asia Minor, bounded north by the Hermus, south by the Maeander and east by Lydia. It was colonized in prehistoric times by Ionian Greeks (*see* IONIANS). In historical times there were twelve Ionian cities, each independent but forming a league which was mainly social and religious in character, and had its sanctuary in the temple of Poseidon on Mount Mycale (q.v.), where an annual festival, the Panionia, was celebrated.

These cities were (south to north) Miletus, Myus, Priene, Ephesus, Colophon, Lebedus, Teos, Erythrae, Clazomenae and Phocaea, together with the island cities of Samos and Chios (qq.v.). Smyrna (q.v.), originally Aeolic, was occupied by Ionians and subsequently admitted to the league.

Ionia became subject first to Croesus (q.v.) of Lydia, then (545 B.C.) to Persia. The revolt of 499 B.C. (*see* ARISTAGORAS; HISTIAEUS) was followed by the defeat of the Ionian fleet off Lade, the destruction of Miletus, and the reconquest of all the Ionian city-states. They regained their freedom under the hegemony of Athens (*see* DELIAN LEAGUE) after the Persian wars, but were restored to Persia by the peace of Antalcidas (q.v.). Thereafter they were subject to Alexander the Great and his successors, and finally to Rome, when they were included in the province of Asia (q.v.). *See* D. H. Hogarth, *Ionia and the East*, 1909.

Ionian Sea, that part of the Mediterranean which extends roughly from the Tarentine Gulf to Crete, and between Italy and Epirus south of a line drawn from Hydruntum to Oricum.

Ionians, name given to the earliest hellenic invaders of Greece, *c.* 1980 B.C. Coming originally from the steppes north of the Black Sea they certainly first crossed the Balkan range, from which point the classic theory represents them as gradually occupying Greece in a direct north–south movement. On the basis, however, of archaeological evidence some recent authorities have maintained that after traversing the Balkans the Ionians turned south-east, crossed the Hellespont and occupied north-west Asia Minor. Later, according to this new theory, they turned back, perhaps under pressure of other invaders (?the 'Cuneiform' Hittites) and travelled via Thrace, northern Chalcidice, Macedonia, and so down to occupy the whole of continental Greece and Peloponnesus. Later (*c.* 1580–*c.* 1450) they were driven from large areas of their territory by Achaeans (q.v.) and Aeolians, being confined thereafter chiefly to Attica, Euboea, many of the Aegean islands and Ionia (q.v.). For legends *see* CODRUS; HELLEN.

Ionopolis, *see* ABONOUTEIKHOS.

Iophōn, son of the poet Sophocles. He was believed to owe much of his success to the help of his father. *See* SOPHOCLES.

Iphicles (-klēs): 1. Son of Amphitryon by Alcmene (qq.v) and half-brother of Heracles (q.v.). By his wife Automedusa, daughter of Alcathoüs (q.v.), he was the father of Iolaus (q.v.).

2. One of the Argonauts (q.v.), celebrated as a runner.

Iphicrates (-kratēs), Athenian general, son of a shoemaker, born at Rhamnon *c.* 415 B.C. He remodelled the Athenian light infantry (*see* PELTASTS), with which he annihilated a battalion of Spartan hoplites in 392. Iphicrates married a daughter of the Thracian king Cotys and died in 353 B.C.

Iphigeneia, in Greek legend, daughter of Agamemnon and Clytaemnestra. According to the most usual story Agamemnon had incurred the wrath of Artemis, who produced a calm which prevented the Greek fleet sailing from Aulis against Troy. The seer Calchas announced that only the sacrifice of Iphigeneia would appease the goddess. Iphigeneia was sent for on pretence of marrying her to Achilles; but at the last moment Artemis relented, substituted a hind, bear or bull for the intended victim and carried her off to Tauris (q.v.). There Iphigeneia became priestess in the temple of Artemis, and had to sacrifice all strangers. When Orestes (q.v.) and Pylades arrived, she managed to flee with them, taking the image of the goddess, which Orestes had been sent to fetch. Among the places which claimed in historical times to possess the true statue and some vestiges of the old rite of human sacrifice were Brauron in Attica, where a pretence was made of cutting a man's throat in the presence of the goddess, and Sparta, where boys were flogged till the blood ran, in the ritual of Artemis Orthia. Iphigeneia, who may have been originally a by-form of Artemis herself, was said to have died either at Brauron or at Megara, and to have been transported to Leuce where she was married to Achilles. *See* Euripides, *Iphigeneia at Aulis* and *Iphigeneia in Tauris*; H. J. Rose, *Handbook of Greek Mythology*, 1928.

Iphimedē, daughter of Triops, wife of Aloeus and mother by Poseidon of the Aloidae (q.v.).

Iphis: 1. A youth of Cyprus (*see* ANAXARETE).

2. A Cretan girl changed by Isis into a boy (Ovid, *Met.* ix. 666 ff.).

Ipsus (-os), in Phrygia, the scene of a battle (301 B.C.) in which Antigonus and his son Demetrius were defeated by Lysimachus and Seleucus.

Ira, mountain fortress in Messenia (q.v.), where Aristomenes (q.v.) resisted the Spartans for eleven years. Its capture by the Spartans in 666 B.C. ended the second Messenian war.

Irene (Eirēnē), Greek goddess of peace, called in Latin Pax. According to Hesiod she was a daughter of Zeus and Themis, and one of the Horae (q.v.). On the Acropolis at Athens there was a statue of Irene holding the infant Ploutos (wealth). At Rome a temple of Pax was built by Vespasian, and a festival celebrated in honour of Pax and others on 30th April (*see* SALUS).

Iris, daughter of Thaumas by the oceanid Electra; personification of the rainbow; and messenger of the gods, particularly of Zeus and Hera. Her name occurs frequently in the *Iliad*, but never in the *Odyssey*, where Hermes (q.v.) exercises her functions. In the earlier poets Iris is a virgin goddess, but Alcaeus makes her the wife of Zephyrus and mother of Eros (qq.v.).

Isaeus (Isaios), one of the ten Attic Orators; born, probably at Chalcis in Euboea, *c.* 420 B.C. Having studied under Lysias (q.v.), he started on his career as a *logographos*, i.e. a writer of forensic speeches for others, in which he limited himself to private causes. In 366 he assisted Demosthenes (q.v.) in the latter's prosecution of his guardians, and died *c.* 350 B.C. Eleven speeches of Isaeus have survived intact, all of them dealing with questions of inheritance. There are editions by W. Wyse (1904) and by E. S. Forster (Loeb Library, with translation).

Isauria, district of Asia Minor on the north side of the Taurus, between Pisidia and Cilicia (qq.v.). The piratical excursions of the Isauri brought about the intervention of Rome. After their conquest in 78 B.C. by the consul L. Servilius, who received the surname 'Isauricus', they were made subject to the kingdom of Galatia (q.v.); but this step put an end neither to their predatory habits nor to their *de facto* independence.

Isca (mod. Caerleon-on-Usk), in Britain (q.v.), fortress of the Second Legion from about A.D. 75 until late in the 3rd century. Established by the Roman governor, Sextus Julius Frontinus (q.v.), it was the base and focal point of a network of roads spreading west and north into Wales. The fortress and its amphitheatre had already been excavated when, in 1954, digging began on the site of a disused racecourse between the fortress and the river. Here was situated the civilian town inhabited by the wives and families of the legionaries.

Isis, an Egyptian goddess, wife of Osiris and mother of Horus. She was identified by Herodotus with Demeter (q.v.), and it is as a corn-goddess that she is represented by Frazer in *Adonis, Attis, Osiris* (1907). Later, when the Egyptians depicted her wearing the horns of a cow, she was sometimes identified by the Greeks with Io (q.v.). Her cult and that of Serapis (q.v.) were brought to Greece early in the 3rd century B.C.

Sulla introduced the worship of Isis at Rome *c.* 80 B.C., but it was fiercely resisted by the government until the reign of Caligula. The most important temple of Isis at Rome stood in the Campus Martius; that at Pompeii is the best preserved. Her priests and servants wore linen garments, whence her title 'linigera'. *See* S. Dill, *Roman Society*, ch. v, 1906.

Islands of the Blessed (Gk *Hai tōn makariōn nēsoi*; Latin *Fortunatae* or *Fortunatorum insulae*), the hellenic paradise (*see* ELYSIUM). They are mentioned first by Hesiod.

Ismarus (-os), town of Thrace, near Maronea, famous for its wine.

Ismēnē, daughter of Oedipus by Jocasta, *see* THEBAN LEGEND, 2.

Isocrates (-kratēs), Greek rhetorician and one of the ten Attic Orators, born at Athens in 436 B.C., son of a wealthy flute manu-facturer. He received a first-class schooling, and when the Pelopon-nesian war ruined his family's fortunes, he turned his gifts to good account by setting up as an educator. In this capacity he held a middle course between the pure philosophy of Socrates and the pseudo-science of the sophists. He quickly rose to fame, having at one time no fewer than one hundred pupils who stayed with him three or four years at a charge of ten *minae* (*see* COINAGE), and made a fortune that ranked him in the wealthiest class of citizens. He remained active till the end, dying soon after the battle of Chaeronea (338 B.C.), two years short of his centenary.

Owing to a weak voice and extreme shyness, Isocrates never spoke in the courts or addressed a public gathering. As with Plato and Demosthenes, it seems probable that everything he published has survived. This includes (1) two rhetorical exercises and a manifesto *Against the Sophists*; (2) some court speeches, nearly all of them written probably as specimens for his pupils, though the one *Against Pasion* seems to have been intended for delivery in a case heard at Byzantium; (3) nine letters; (4) a number of political pamphlets in the form of harangues or open letters. Upon one of these last, the *Panegyric* (c. 380 B.C.), the fame of Isocrates principally rests. Its theme is one that had obsessed him for years—the union of all Greek states, but with the sole aim of enriching themselves by conquest of the crumbling Persian Empire. As to matter, the *Panegyric* is an example of that political thinking and advice which was not unnaturally treated by his countrymen with steady indifference, if not with actual contempt; but as literature it is a masterpiece, illustrating to perfection a prose style which influenced the greatest of his contemporaries. *See* the complete edition by Benseler and Blass (Teubner), 1880; also text with translation by G. Norlin and L. Van Hook (Loeb Library).

Issa, island in the Adriatic off the coast of Dalmatia. Said to have been colonized originally from Lesbos, it received Parian settlers under the auspices of Dionysius I of Syracuse during the 4th century B.C. The inhabitants were fine sailors, and their fleet assisted the Roman admiral Duilius (q.v.) at the battle of Mylae in 260 B.C. They were again of service to Rome in the first Macedonian war (215 B.C.).

Issedones, people of central Asia inhabiting the Tarim basin, terminus of a trade route from Scythia (*see* Herodotus, iv. 26). Probably of Tibetan race, they had wives in common and murdered their old folk, whose flesh they devoured and made the skulls into drinking-cups.

Issus, city of Asia Minor, in Cilicia (q.v.), in the neighbourhood of which Alexander the Great (q.v.) defeated Darius III, Codomannus, in 333 B.C. Here also, in A.D. 194, Septimius Severus defeated Pescennius Niger (qq.v.).

Ister, *see* DANUBIUS.

Isthmian Games, one of the four great pan-hellenic festivals (*see* GREEK GAMES), dating from 581 B.C. and held on the Isthmus near Corinth (q.v.) in spring of the second and fourth years of each Olympiad. They were celebrated in honour of Poseidon, and were the most popular of such gatherings, owing to the attractions of neighbouring Corinth. The chief prize was a crown of wild celery, and some of the victors are commemorated in the fourth book of Pindar's *Epinikeia*. *See* E. N. Gardiner, *Greek Athletic Sports and Festivals*, 1910.

Istria, peninsula at the head of the Adriatic. Inhabited by fierce Illyrian pirates (*see* ILLYRIA), it was subdued in 177 B.C. by the Romans under C. Claudius Pulcher. In the reign of Augustus it was added to Italy (*see* ITALIA). Oil was its chief product; the principal towns were Tergeste and Pola.

Italia (mod. Italy), name originally given by the Greeks to the territory of the Oenotri in the southern part of the Bruttian peninsula (*see* BRUTTII). It appears to be a Graecized form of Italic 'Vitelia', probably meaning calf-land or grazing land. In the time of Thucydides the synonymous names Italia and Oenotria were used of the two districts afterwards known as Lucania (q.v.) and Bruttii; Campania and Latium (qq.v.) were known as Ausonia, Calabria as Iapygia. After the Roman conquest of Tarentum, in 272 B.C., 'Italia' signified all the country then subject to Rome, namely, the entire peninsula from the Bruttii and Calabria in the south to a line drawn between the rivers Arnus and Rubicon in the north. Beyond this line, to the foot of the Alps, lay Gallia Cisalpina (*see* GALLIA), which remained officially a province until the end of the republic, though from the time at least of Polybius (q.v.) it was unofficially spoken of as part of Italy.

Augustus, however, formally included Gallia Cisalpina in Italy, which he divided for purposes of administration into eleven *regiones* as follows: (1) Latium and Campania, including the Volsci, Hernici, Aurunci and Picentini; (2) Apulia and Calabria, together with the Hirpini; (3) Lucania and Bruttii, bounded north by a line between the rivers Silarus and Bradanus; (4) the Samnites (excepting the Hirpani) and Sabines, bounded north by Picenum and south by Apulia; (5) Picenum, on the Adriatic between the Matrinus and the Aesis; (6) Umbria, including the Ager Gallicus (q.v.), bounded north by the Ariminus and south by the Aternus; (7) Etruria, between the Tiber, the Tyrrhenian Sea and the Macra; (8) Gallia Cispadana, bounded north by the Padus from just above Placentia to its mouth, south by the Apennines from the Trebia to the Ariminus; (9) Liguria, extending along the coast from the Varus to the Macra, and inland to the Padus from its source to just above Placentia; (10) Venetia, from the Padus to the Alps and Adriatic, together with Istria (q.v.), and westward to the Addua. (11) Gallia Transpadana, the remainder of Gallia Cisalpina from the Padus and the Addua to the foot of the Alps. *See also* MAGNA GRAECIA. *See* J. Whatmough, *Foundations of Roman Italy*, 1937; *Everyman's Classical Atlas*, edited by Professor J. O. Thompson, 1961.

Italica: 1. (mod. Santiponce), town of Hispania Ulterior, afterwards in Hispania Baetica (*see* HISPANIA), on the west bank of the River Baetis (mod. Guadalquivir); founded during the second Punic war by P. Scipio Africanus who settled some of his veterans there. It was the birth-place of the emperors Trajan and Hadrian.

2. *See* CORFINIUM.

Italiotes (-ōtai), collective name for the inhabitants of Magna Graecia (q.v.).

Ithaca (-ke), small island in the Ionian Sea, off the coast of Epirus, traditionally the home of Odysseus (q.v.). Against this identification, however, certain geographical and topographical difficulties have been advanced, based chiefly on accounts in the *Odyssey*. According to Dörpfeld, who is not entirely supported by the results of excavation, Ithaca is to be identified not with this island but with Leucadia (q.v.). *See* W. Dörpfeld, *Alt-Ithaka*, 1927; Sir R. Rodd, *Homer's Ithaca*, 1927.

Ithōmē, fortress town of Messenia (q.v.) and afterwards (369 B.C.) the acropolis of Messene (q.v.). Its capture from Aristodemus (q.v.) by the Spartans ended the first Messenian war.

Itinerarium Antoninum, *see* ANTONINE ITINERARY.

Itius Portus (probably mod. Wissant), harbour at which Julius Caesar embarked for his second expedition to Britain (54 B.C.). See *De Bello Gallico*, v. 2, iv. 21–3; T. Rice Holmes, *Ancient Britain*, pp. 552–94, 1907, and *Classical Review*, May 1909. For the view that Itius Portus is to be identified with Boulogne *see* H. Stuart Jones, *English Historical Review*, xxiv. 115, 1909.

Ituraea, district on the north-eastern borders of Palestine. It had been ruled by native princes until the reign of Augustus, who gave it to the Herods. In the time of Christ it was subject to the tetrarch Philip, brother of Herod Antipas.

Itylus (Itulos), son of Zethus and Aedon, *see* AEDON.

Itys (Itus), son of Tereus (q.v.).

Iulus : 1. An alternative name for Ascanius (q.v.).

2. Elder son of Ascanius; King of Latium and founder of the *gens* Iulia. His brother Silvius drove him from the kingdom.

Ivernia, *see* HIBERNIA.

Ixiōn, in Greek legend, King of Thessaly, son of Phlegyas and husband of Dia. He murdered his father-in-law, in order to avoid paying the bridal gifts which he had promised, and was consequently shunned by all men. Zeus carried him to heaven and purified him from blood guilt; but Ixion abused the god's hospitality, and strove to seduce his wife. Embracing a cloud, which he believed to be Hera, he became father of the Centaurs (q.v.). Zeus punished him in Tartarus by binding him to a fiery wheel in perpetual motion. There are variations of the legend. *See* H. J. Rose, *Handbook of Greek Mythology*, 1928.

Iyrcae (Iurkai), a people dwelling in the upper basins of the rivers now called Tobol and Irtysh (*see* Herodotus, iv. 22). They are commonly held to have been the ancestors of the Magyars.

J

Janus, one of the oldest Latin gods. His name may be derived from the same root as *janua*, 'gate', or be the masculine form of Diana (Jana). He was 'the spirit of opening', and is represented with two (sometimes four) faces looking as many ways. He was invoked at the beginning of any enterprise before the other gods, and as the patron of all 'openings', whether concrete (e.g. the gates of public or private buildings) or abstract (e.g. the beginning of the day, month or year). His only official priest was the *Rex Sacrorum*, but every head of a household was regarded as responsible for his worship. The cult of Janus was of immemorial antiquity; and at Rome there was a covered passage (erroneously called a temple) near the Forum, supposed to have been built by Numa, which was always open in times of war and shut in times of peace. The chief festival of Janus was New Year's Day, on which people exchanged gifts in the form of sweetmeats, and copper coins showing on one side the double head of Janus and on the other a ship. The fifth month of each year was also sacred to him. *See* W. Warde Fowler, *Roman Festivals*, 1908, and *Religious Experience of the Roman People*, 1911.

Jason (Iasōn) and Medea (Mēdeia), the principal characters of one of the most famous of Greek legends. Tyro, daughter of Salmoneus (q.v.), bore three sons: Aeson to Cretheus, King of Iolcus; Pelias and Neleus (twins) to Poseidon. Aeson was excluded from the throne by his half-brothers. They also attempted the life of his son, Jason, but he was saved by his friends and entrusted to the centaur Chiron (q.v.). Neleus (q.v.) in turn was driven out by Pelias, who thus became sole ruler of Iolcus.

After many years Jason came to Iolcus demanding the kingdom, which Pelias promised to surrender to him if he would obtain and bring back the Golden Fleece (*see* PHRIXUS). Jason undertook the task (*see* ARGONAUTS). Arrived at Colchis (q.v.), and assisted by Medea, daughter of King Aeëtes and his wife Iduie, he obtained the Fleece and carried off Medea as his wife, together with her young brother Apsyrtus. Aeëtes followed in pursuit. In order to delay him, Medea killed Apsyrtus, cut his body in pieces, and strewed them along the road. Thus, while Aeëtes gathered the remains of his child, Jason and Medea made good their escape to Iolcus.

Meanwhile Pelias had murdered Aeson; and in order to avenge the death of his father, Jason persuaded Medea to use her powers as a sorceress. Instigated by her, the daughters of Pelias slew their father and boiled his dismembered body, assured that they would thus rejuvenate him. Acastus (q.v.), son of Pelias, having succeeded to the throne, expelled Jason and Medea from Iolcus. They went to Corinth, where they lived for several years until Jason deserted Medea in order to marry Glauce (or Creusa), daughter of the Corinthian king Creon. Medea, in revenge, sent Glauce a poisoned robe, which burned her to death. Creon also perished in the flames. Medea then slew the two children she had borne to Jason, after which she fled to Athens in a chariot drawn by winged dragons (*see* Euripides, *Medea*). Jason was said to have committed suicide; another tradition stated that he was crushed by the ship *Argo* as he lay beneath its poop.

Jerusalem (Gk Hierosoluma). The earliest historical notice of this fortified city occurs in the Amarna Letters, *c.* 1400 B.C., when it was garrisoned by Egyptian troops. Taken by David from the Jebusites in 1050 B.C., it was made capital of the kingdom of Israel, and of Judah after the dismemberment of Israel under Rehoboam. It was destroyed by the Babylonians in 586 B.C. and its inhabitants were carried into captivity. In 538 B.C. the Jewish exiles, having been allowed by Cyrus of Persia to return, began rebuilding the city and temple, and the work was completed in about twenty-four years. Alexander the Great made a peaceful entry into Jerusalem in 332 B.C. After his death it was subject to the Ptolemies, then to the Seleucids; but because of the attempts made by Antiochus IV, Epiphanes, to root out the national religion, the Jews rose in rebellion under the Maccabees and eventually established their independence. The city was taken by Pompey (q.v.) in 63. From this time it was virtually subject to Rome (*see* JUDAEA), except for the period 37 B.C.–A.D. 7 when it belonged to the Herods. In consequence of the great Jewish rebellion (66–70), Jerusalem was taken by Titus (q.v.; *see also* VESPASIAN) and partially destroyed. This devastation was completed in 135 when another rising was quelled. The site was ploughed, and a Roman *colonia* (q.v.), called Aelia Capitolina in honour of Hadrian (q.v.), was established. Where the Holy of Holies had stood there now rose a temple of Jupiter Capitolinus. *See* G. A. Smith, *Jerusalem*, 1907; S. Merrill, *Ancient Jerusalem*, 1908; F. M. Abel, *Jerusalem*, 1922–6.

Jocasta (Iokastē), called Epicaste in Homer, sister of Creon, mother and wife of Oedipus, *see* THEBAN LEGEND, 1 and 2.

Joppa, coastal city of Palestine, legendary scene of the rescue of Andromeda (q.v.) from the sea-monster, whose petrified form was 'discovered' by Pompey's general M. Aemilius Scaurus and transported to Rome! For St Peter's residence at Joppa *see* Acts ix. 36– x. 47. The city was destroyed by Vespasian during the Jewish war, A.D. 68.

Josephus, Flavius (A.D. 37–*c.* 101), Jewish historian and general. Having tried the Pharisees, Sadducees and Essenes before he was nineteen, he spent three years in the desert with an Essene hermit named Banos, and finally became a Pharisee (A.D. 56). In 64 he visited Rome, in order to obtain the release of some Jewish priests who had been sent there by the procurator Felix (q.v.) to stand trial for some slight offence. Thanks to the good offices of Nero's wife Poppaea he succeeded. On his return he opposed the revolutionary spirit of his countrymen, but became governor of Galilee on the outbreak of war (66). In 67 he defended Jotapata against Vespasian; the place was taken, and Josephus made prisoner. He prophesied that his captor would soon wear the imperial purple. On the fulfilment of this prophecy he was released, and was present with the Roman army at the destruction of Jerusalem (70), when his influence saved the lives of many of his friends. Having received a grant of land in Judaea, he accompanied Titus to Rome, where Vespasian gave him the freedom of the city and assigned him a handsome residence. Josephus assumed the name Flavius as a compliment to his benefactor, and spent the remainder of his years in the sunshine of imperial favour, writing (in Greek) his four celebrated works: *The Jewish War*, covering the period 170 B.C. to A.D. 70, written towards the end of Vespasian's reign; *Jewish Antiquities*, a history of the Jews from the Creation to A.D. 66, finished in A.D. 93; *Autobiography*, defending himself against an accusation of having caused the rebellion; *Against Apion*, two books in defence of the Jews. *See* complete text with translation by H. St John Thackeray and R. Marcus, 9 vols. (Loeb Library). *See also* H. St John Thackeray, *Josephus*, 1929; F. Jackson, *Josephus and the Jews*, 1930.

Juba, name of two kings of Numidia (q.v.):

1. Son and successor of Hiempsal II (q.v.). He joined Pompey on the outbreak of civil war, and inflicted an overwhelming defeat on Caesar's legate Curio in the desert (49 B.C.). He shared the defeat of Thapsus and was afterwards killed in mutual combat with M. Petreius (q.v.).

2. Son of the preceding, was a child at the time of his father's death, and was carried by Caesar to Rome. In 30 B.C. Octavian restored him to his father's throne, and gave him in marriage Cleopatra Selene, daughter of Mark Antony by Cleopatra. In 25, however, Augustus gave him Mauretania in exchange for Numidia, which then became a Roman province. Juba died between A.D. 19 and 24. Unlike his father, a thorough savage, he was one of the most learned men of his age; but only fragments survive of the twelve valuable works on historical and geographical subjects which he is known to have written.

Judaea, the southern part of Palestine. After the deposition of Archelaus, son of Herod the Great (*see* HERODES), in A.D. 7 it became merged in the Roman province of Syria under the immediate government of a procurator whose headquarters were at Caesarea Palestinae (q.v.).

Jugurtha, King of Numidia, illegitimate son of Mastanabal and grandson of Masinissa (q.v.). He lost his father at an early age, and was brought up by his uncle Micipsa, together with the latter's own sons Hiempsal and Adherbal. While in command of a Numidian force under Scipio before Numantia, in 134 B.C., he was a great favourite with the Roman officers, some of whom suggested to him the plan of making himself master of Numidia. Micipsa, on his death in 118, bequeathed his kingdom to his two sons and Jugurtha jointly; but Jugurtha contrived the assassination of Hiempsal (118), drove Adherbal from the country, seized the entire kingdom and sent envoys to Rome to defend his conduct. The senate divided Numidia, giving the western, richer and more populous half to Jugurtha, and leaving the sandy deserts of the eastern half to Adherbal. Jugurtha, however, provoked his cousin to a war of self-defence, and eventually slew him with the entire population of Cirta (112 B.C.). Some of the victims of this massacre were Roman citizens, and this, together with Jugurtha's defiance of the senate's arbitration, resulted in war. The consul L. Calpurnius Bestia (q.v.) was sent to Africa with an army (III), but Jugurtha managed to purchase from him a favourable peace. The Numidian king, however, was summoned to Rome to give an account of the negotiations. While there he procured the assassination of his cousin Massiva, who happened to be in the city at that time and who had been encouraged by Spurius Albinus, one of the consuls for 110, to claim the throne of Numidia for himself. This murder resulted in Jugurtha's dismissal and the renewal of war. Albinus was put in charge of the campaign; but it ended in a heavy Roman defeat, the expulsion of every Roman from Numidia and the conclusion of a peace ignominious to Rome (110). Next year (109) the consul Q. Caecilius Metellus was sent to Africa at the head of a new army, and by the end of 108 he had deprived Jugurtha of eastern and central Numidia. In 107 he was superseded by C. Marius (q.v.), against whom Jugurtha was supported by his father-in-law, the Mauretanian king Bocchus (q.v.). But Marius defeated their united forces near Cirta (106), and some time in the following year Sulla (q.v.) forced Bocchus to entrap Jugurtha. The latter was carried prisoner of war to Rome, where he adorned the triumph of Marius (1st January 104) and was soon afterwards strangled or starved to death in the subterranean prison of the Capitol. *See* Sallust, *Bellum Jugurthinum*; H. Last in *Cambridge Ancient History*, vol. ix, ch. iii, iv–viii.

Julia, name of many women of the Julian *gens*, of whom the most famous are:

1. Wife of the great general Gaius Marius and aunt of Gaius Julius Caesar the dictator. *See* TABLE 1.

2. Sister of Lucius Julius Caesar (consul 64 B.C.) and mother of Mark Antony.

3. Sister of Gaius Julius Caesar, and wife of M. Atius Balbus, to whom she bore a daughter Atia, afterwards mother of the emperor Augustus. *See* TABLE 1.

4. Daughter of Gaius Julius Caesar (*see* TABLE 1) by Cornelia, married to Pompey in 59 and died in childbirth 54 B.C.

5. Daughter of Augustus (his only child) and Scribonia, born 39 B.C. She was married first in 25 B.C. to her cousin Marcellus (*see* MARCELLUS, MARCUS CLAUDIUS, 3); secondly, in 21 B.C., to M. Vipsanius Agrippa (q.v.), by whom she had three sons (Gaius Caesar, Lucius Caesar and Agrippa Postumus) and two daughters (Julia and Agrippina); thirdly to Tiberius Claudius Nero, the future emperor Tiberius (q.v.). Because of her profligacy she was banished by her father to the island of Pandataria, off the coast of Campania, in 2 B.C. She was afterwards transferred to Rhegium, and died in A.D. 14. *See* TABLE 1.

6. Daughter of the preceding by M. Vipsanius Agrippa, and wife of L. Aemilius Paulus, born 18 B.C. She had the morals of her mother, and was likewise banished to the little island of Tremerus, off the coast of Apulia, in A.D. 9. She died in A.D. 28. *See also* OVID.

7. Youngest child of Germanicus (q.v.) and Agrippina, put to death by Claudius at the instigation of Messalina. *See* TABLE 2.

8. Daughter of Drusus (*d.* A.D. 43) and Livilla, sister of Germanicus. She too was killed by order of Claudius at the bidding of Messalina (A.D. 43). *See* TABLE 2.

Julia Domna, wife of the emperor Septimius Severus and mother of Caracalla (qq.v.). It was at her request that Philostratus (q.v.) wrote the Life of Apollonius of Tyana.

Julia Maesa, sister of Julia Domna, wife of Julius Avitus, and grandmother of the emperors Elagabalus and Alexander Severus.

Julia Mammaea, daughter of Julius Avitus by Julia Maesa. She was married to Gessius Marcianus and became mother of the emperor Alexander Severus (q.v.).

Julia Soemias, sister of Julia Mammaea (q.v.), wife of Sextus Varius Marcellus and mother of the emperor Elagabalus (q.v.).

Julian Calendar. The Romans developed a calendar of alternate 29- and 30-day months with an arbitrary intercalated period to keep the civil and solar years in step; but abuse by the pontiffs responsible for the correct operation of this system led to an accumulated discrepancy of about two months by the time Julius Caesar became dictator and determined to reform. Sosigenes (of whom nothing else is known) gave technical advice, and the year 46 B.C. was extended to 445 days in order to restore the vernal equinox to 25th March. The first Julian year began on 1st January 45 B.C. (709 A.U.C.). Originally this system provided leap years with alternate 31- and 30-day months, February being reduced to 29 days in the intervening years; but the emperor Augustus transferred one of these to his own month (August) in order to make it equal to Caesar's July. Then the last four months had their days re-allocated in order to avoid three 31-day months in succession.

Juno, one of the great goddesses of the Roman state religion, wife of Jupiter (q.v.) and commonly identified with the Greek Hera (q.v.). From early times Juno was worshipped as queen of heaven along with Jupiter and Minerva (*see* CAPITOLIUM). She was considered the patroness of womanhood under several forms: as *Pronuba* she watched over marriage, and the month of June was considered the most suitable time for marriage; as *Lucina*, over childbirth and newly born babes, whence she was often identified with Eilithyia (q.v.). As one of the chief guardians of the State she was the guardian of finances, and under the title *Moneta* she had a temple on the Capitoline hill which contained the mint. The most important festival of Juno was the *Matronalia*, celebrated on 1st March. The *Nonae Caprotinae* fell on 7th July, when the rites included a sham fight of maid-servants. Women also offered sacrifices to Juno (*Natalis*) on their birthdays.

Jupiter, later identified by the Romans with Zeus, was originally an elemental deity. His name signifies father (or lord) of heaven, being a contraction of *Diovis pater*. He was first worshipped as the god of rain, thunder and lightning; whence he had appropriate titles (*Pluvialis, Fulgurator,* etc.). To these, in course of time, were added others corresponding to various aspects of his power and patronage. As the special protector of Rome, he was worshipped by the consuls when they took office; and the triumph of a victorious general was a

solemn procession to the temple of Jupiter Capitolinus (*see* CAPITO-
LIUM). Jupiter was supposed to determine the course of human affairs.
He foresaw the future; and the events happening therein proceeded
from his will. He revealed the future to man through signs and the
flight of birds (*see* AUGURES; HARUSPICES). For the same reason he was
invoked at the beginning of every undertaking, together with Janus
(q.v.). Jupiter was also considered as the guardian of law, and as the
protector of justice and virtue. As he was the lord of heaven, and
consequently of light, white was sacred to him. White victims were
sacrificed in his honour; his chariot was described as drawn by four
white horses; his *flamen* wore a white cap (*see* FLAMEN); and the
consuls were attired in white when they sacrificed in the Capitol on
the day of their inauguration.

Justinus, Latin historian (2nd century A.D.), author of an extant
work, *Historiarum Philippicarum Libri XLIV*, a selection from
Pompeius Trogus's lost *Historiae Philippicae* (early 1st century A.D.).
The title *Philippicae* derives from the original purpose of the work,
which was to give an account of the Macedonian monarchy. But
Trogus permitted himself so many digressions that it formed a kind of
universal history from the rise of Assyria to the Roman conquest of
the East.

Juturna, in late Roman legend, nymph of a fountain in Latium,
famous for its healing power. Its water was used in nearly all sacrifices, and a shrine was dedicated to the nymph at Rome in the
Campus Martius. Sacrifices were offered to her on 11th January both
by the state and by private persons. Juturna was loved by Jupiter
(*see* LARUNDA). Virgil represents her as sister of Turnus.

Juvenal, Decimus Junius Juvenalis, Roman satirist, of whose life
we have few authentic particulars. His native place (if not his actual
birth-place) was Aquinum (q.v.); the approximate dates of his birth
and death are A.D. 50 and 130 respectively. He may be the Juvenalis
twice mentioned by Martial (*Epigrammata*, vii. 24, 91; xii. 18), and he
may be the author of a well-known inscription, a dedication (probably
to Ceres) by one Juvenalis who held a military rank and also some
civil offices in Aquinum (*C.I.L.*, vol. x, No. 5382). This reference to
military service agrees more or less with a story told by Apollinaris
Sidonius (5th century A.D.) that Juvenal quarrelled with Paris, a
famous *pantomimus* (ballet dancer) in the days of Domitian, and was
sent to the Egyptian frontier as an officer of a local garrison.

The works of Juvenal consist of sixteen *Satires*, the last of which is
incomplete. Internal evidence suggests that none of them is earlier
than the death of Domitian (A.D. 96), and this agrees with the tradition that he practised rhetoric until he was middle-aged, rather for his
own amusement than with any further end in view. When he turned
to satire, he did so under pressure of furious indignation at the vices
of his time.

It is a brutal, vivid and often disgusting picture that the poet draws
of the vicious Roman society of his day. The third satire, which is an
Hogarthian painting of the metropolis, appals the reader with the
glare and variety of its colours; while the sixth, which may well be
called the 'Legend of Bad Women', displays to the full the grimness

of the writer's humour, the remorselessness of his crude realism, and the sincerity of his spiritual revolt against the immoralities of the age. Like Swift, Juvenal often descends to filth and indecency, and, it must be confessed, he was far too prone to verbal luxuriance and gaudy rhetoric. Yet at his best he writes with a style as vigorous and trenchant as Tacitus, and his verses are replete no less with the learning of a patient scholar than with the worldly knowledge and wisdom of an ancient Machiavelli. The first nine satires are at the same time the finest and most virulent. The others reveal greater forbearance, loftier sentiment, but also a falling off in power. *See* editions by F. Leo, 1910; L. Friedländer, 1895; A. E. Housman, 1931. *See also* Gifford's verse translation, 1802 (revised by J. Warrington, Everyman's Library, 1954); P. de Labriolle, *Les Satires de Juvenal,* 1932; J. Wright Duff, *Roman Satire,* 1937; G. Highet, *Juvenal the Satirist,* 1962.

Juventas, *see* HEBE.

K

Kēr, in Greek mythology a goddess of death, but also a bringer of every sort of evil. The term Keres was sometimes used for the souls of the dead. In late times the Keres were likened in form to the Harpies (q.v.).

Kings of Rome. According to tradition there were seven kings of Rome: Romulus, Numa Pompilius, Tullus Hostilius, Ancus Marcius, L. Tarquinius 'Priscius', Servius Tullius and L. Tarquinius 'Superbus'. *See* separate articles.

L

Labarum, military standard of the Christian Roman emperors, an adaptation of the older cavalry standard. It was first used (A.D. 312) by Constantine the Great (q.v.) to commemorate his vision. There was an early and a later form of the *labarum*. The early form consisted of a long gilded spear or staff, with a horizontal bar towards the top, forming a cross. From this bar was suspended a square of purple cloth richly embroidered or jewelled, while the upright was surmounted by a wreath enclosing the sacred monogram ☧. In the later form, the monogram, surrounded by a golden border was placed upon the cloth.

Labdacus (-kos), father of Laius. *See* THEBAN LEGEND, I.

Labeo, Marcus Antistius, Roman jurist, whose father took part in the conspiracy against Julius Caesar and committed suicide after the battle of Philippi (42 B.C.). His was probably the most authoritative name in Roman law before the time of Hadrian, and he is considered as the founder of the so-called Proculian school (*see* CAPITO, MARCUS FONTEIUS). His republican views lost him the favour of Augustus, and Horace's *Labeone insanior* (madder than Labeo) was probably a gibe intended to please the emperor. None of his works survives, but he is quoted several times in Justinian's *Digest*.

Laberius, Decimus, a Roman knight and writer of mimes, whose pungent pen and bitter tongue attracted the notice of Caesar. In 46 B.C., at the celebrations following Caesar's triumphs, Laberius received from the dictator a quasi-royal command to act in a mime of his own composition; and his fee, equivalent to more than £5,000 of our money, increased rather than compensated for his humiliation. But when he declaimed a line in his prologue, 'He whom many fear must needs fear many', all eyes turned towards Caesar. Only a few fragments of his work survive.

Labienus, Quintus, son of Titus Labienus (*see* next article). In 40 B.C. he invaded Syria at the head of a Parthian army (*see* PACORUS). In the following year they were defeated by Antony's legate P. Ventidius (q.v.); Labienus fled to Cilicia, but was taken prisoner and put to death.

Labienus, Titus, Roman general. As tribune of the plebs in 63 B.C. he carried a law restoring to the people their right to elect the pontifex maximus, and also prosecuted C. Rabirius (q.v.). He was Caesar's principal and most trusted lieutenant throughout the Gallic campaigns, but he joined Pompey on the outbreak of civil war. His subsequent career was sometimes marred by violence and cruelty, and in the long run his military genius could not avail to save the fortunes of his friends. It is true, on the other hand, that his talents never really had free play; and it is worth noting that during the African war Labienus was in command on the two occasions when Caesar was reduced to the extremity of peril. Labienus fell in the battle of Munda (45 B.C.). *See* T. Rice Holmes, *The Roman Republic*, 3 vols., 1923.

Lacedaemon (Lakedaimōn), another name for Laconia (q.v.).

Lachesis (-khesis), in Greek mythology, one of the Moirae (q.v.).

Lacinium (mod. Capo delle Colonne), promontory on the coast of Bruttii (q.v.), about seven miles south-east of Croton, and forming the western boundary of the Tarentine Gulf. Here stood a temple of Juno Lacinia (480–440 B.C.).

Laconia (Gk Lakōnikē), south-eastern district of Peloponnesus; capital Sparta (q.v.). *See also* AMYCLAE; CARYAE; THERAPNAE. It was bounded on the west by the range of Taygetus (q.v.), on the east by a broken range extending from Mt Parnon to Cape Malea. Between lies the valley of the Eurotas. Off the south coast, around the island of Cythera (q.v.), were murex beds that yielded purple dye inferior only to the Tyrian. The history of Laconia is the history of Sparta, until 195 B.C., when T. Quinctius Flamininus (q.v.) liberated the coastal towns from Spartan dominion. These then became members of the Achaean League (q.v.), upon the dissolution of which (146 B.C.) they remained independent within the Roman province of Achaea, forming a confederation which was reorganized by Augustus.

Lacydes (Lakudēs), Greek philosopher, a native of Cyrene, succeeded Arcesilaus as head of the Academy (q.v.) *c.* 241 B.C. He lectured in a garden presented to him by Attalus I of Pergamum and known as the Lacydeum. He died *c.* 215 B.C.

Ladas, Greek athlete of the 5th century B.C., a native of Laconia. Having won the *dolichos* (20 stades) at Olympia, he collapsed and died. A monument was erected to his memory on the banks of the Eurotas, and there was a famous statue of him by Myron (q.v.) in the temple of Apollo Lyceus at Argos.

Ladōn, a dragon. *See* HESPERIDES.

Laelius, Gaius: 1. Roman general and statesman, friend of Scipio Africanus the elder. He accompanied the latter on his Spanish campaign (210–206 B.C.), went with him to Sicily in 205, and commanded the cavalry at Zama in 202 B.C. He was plebeian aedile in 197, praetor in Sicily 196, and consul in 190, when he was sent to organize the recently conquered territory in Cisalpine Gaul. The date of his death is unknown.

2. Son of the preceding, surnamed Sapiens (the Wise) because of his scholarly pursuits, or perhaps on account of his political sagacity. Born *c.* 186 B.C., he was tribune of the plebs in 151; fought under Scipio Aemilianus Africanus in the third Punic war (149–146); conducted operations against Viriathus (q.v.) in Spain (145), and was consul in 140. During the disturbed period of the Gracchi (*see* GRACCHUS, GAIUS; GRACCHUS, TIBERIUS, 2) he was a staunch supporter of the aristocrats. Laelius was a student of philosophy, a poet and one of those chiefly responsible for the introduction of Greek culture to Rome. He is one of the speakers in Cicero's *De senectute*, *De amicitia* (or *Laelius*) and *De republica*.

Laenas, name of a Roman family notorious for its arrogance and cruelty. The two best known are:

1. *Gaius Popilius Laenas*, consul in 172 B.C. He next took part in

the war against Perseus (q.v.), King of Macedonia. When the Seleucid monarch Antiochus IV, Epiphanes, invaded Egypt and was advancing upon Alexandria, he was met by three Roman ambassadors. One of them, Laenas, handed him a letter from the senate requiring him to desist from hostilities. Antiochus promised to consider the demand; but Laenas drew a circle round him with his staff and forbade him to stir out of it until he had given a decisive answer. Such arrogance alarmed the king, who at once submitted and withdrew from Egypt.

2. *Publius Popilius Laenas*, son of the preceding. As consul in 132 B.C., the year after the murder of Tiberius Gracchus (*see* GRAC-CHUS, TIBERIUS SEMPRONIUS, 2), he headed a commission appointed to proceed against the dead tribune's associates. In 123, fearing the vengeance of Gaius Gracchus, brother of Tiberius, he went into voluntary exile until the triumph of the aristocratical party in 121 B.C.

Laërtes, King of Ithaca, husband of Anticlea and father of Odysseus. He was one of the Calydonian hunters (*see* MELEAGER) and took part in the expedition of the Argonauts (q.v.). He was still alive when his son returned from Troy.

Laestrygones (Laistrugones), legendary race of cannibalistic giants in Libya. Odysseus landed on their coasts and escaped with only one ship (*Odyssey*, x). Later traditions placed the Laestrygones in Sicily or southern Latium. *See also* LAMIA.

Lagidae, the Lagids, name of a dynasty more commonly known as the Ptolemaic; founded by Ptolemy I, Soter, son of Lagus, after the death of Alexander the Great. It reigned from 323 until 30 B.C. *See* PTOLEMY.

Lagus (-os), father of Ptolemy I, Soter, *see* PTOLEMY I.

Lais, name of three Greek courtesans:

1. A Corinthian of the 5th century B.C., who counted among her lovers the Cyrenaic philosopher Aristippus.

2. Mistress of Alcibiades. Born at Hyccara in Sicily *c.* 420 B.C., she went to Corinth at the age of seven.

3. A contemporary of Alexander the Great, mistress of the painter Apelles.

Laius (-os), father of Oedipus, *see* THEBAN LEGEND, 2.

Lamachus (-khos), Athenian general and, with Nicias and Alci-biades (qq.v.), one of the commanders of the Sicilian expedition (415 B.C.). He displayed courage and ability during the first year of the campaign, but was killed before the walls of Syracuse in 414 B.C. *See* Thucydides, vii; Aristophanes, *Acharnians;* Plutarch, *Nicias.*

Lambaesis (mod. Lambessa), Roman military town in Numidia, 17 miles west of Timgad (q.v.). Its remains, together with those of the camp about 1,100 yards from the town centre, are among the most important in north Africa. The camp of Legio III, Augusta (covering more than $\frac{3}{4}$ square mile), was established here *c.* A.D. 125, and an address delivered by Hadrian to the troops was found inscribed on a pillar. The arsenal, when excavated, contained thousands of missiles. The adjoining town was already flourishing in 166, and on becoming capital of the province of Numidia (q.v.) was made a *municipium* (q.v.). *See* S. Gsell, *Les Monuments antiques de l'Algérie*, 1901, and *L'Algérie dans l'antiquité*, 1903.

Lamia, in Greek legend, a queen of the Laestrygones (q.v.) in Libya; loved by Zeus, whose jealous wife Hera robbed Lamia of her children. In revenge, Lamia seized and killed every child she could find. In later traditions she was a female bogy, and passed into Roman legend. Here the Lamiae were vampires, in the form of beautiful women who enticed young men to their arms and fed on their blood. Lamia is thus represented by Goethe in *Die Braut von Korinth* and by Keats in *Lamia*. *See* Plutarch, *De Curiosis*; G. F. Abbott, *Macedonian Folklore*, 1903; J. C. Lawson, *Modern Greek Folklore and Ancient Greek Religion*, 1910.

Lamian War. On the death of Alexander the Great, in 323 B.C., many of the Greek city-states combined in an attempt to recover their independence, but were defeated in the following year at Crannon in Thessaly by Antipater (*see* ANTIPATER, 1) and Craterus (q.v.). The war is named after Lamia, a town of Phthiotis, where Antipater was besieged.

Lampsacus (-kos), a Greek city in Mysia, on the Hellespont; founded from Miletus and Phocaea. Famous for its wine, it was also the chief seat of the worship of Priapus (q.v.).

Langobardi, ancestors of the Lombards, a German tribe. They dwelt between the territory of the Semnones (q.v.) and the mouth of the Elbe. They made formal submission to Tiberius in A.D. 5, and in 17 joined the Semnones in their revolt against Maroboduus.

Lanuvium, city of Latium, 19 miles south-east of Rome, with a temple of Juno Sospes. It became subject to Rome in 338 B.C.; but its chief magistrate and council continued to be called *dictator* and *senatus* respectively, even in imperial times. The emperor Antoninus Pius was born here.

Laocoön (-koōn), in Greek legend, Trojan priest of Apollo, whose anger he incurred by his marriage and by solemnly warning his fellow citizens against admitting the wooden horse within their walls. The vindictive god sent two huge serpents out of the sea to the altar of Poseidon, at which Laocoön, with his two sons, was officiating. They died in agony as the monsters coiled themselves about their limbs. (*See* Virgil, *Aen.* ii. 199 ff.).

The famous Laocoön group in the Vatican museum was discovered in 1506 near the Baths of Titus in Rome. Identified by Michelangelo, it was for long accepted as the original work said by Pliny (*Hist. Nat.* 36) to have been made by three Rhodian sculptors, Agesander, Polydorus and Athenodorus, and it is ascribed to the 2nd or 1st century B.C. In September 1957, however, there were found in a cave at Sperlonga, Italy, several hundred fragments of an exactly similar group. The latter was then claimed by Prof. Giulio Iacopi, the Roman archaeologist, to be the true original; all three names mentioned by Pliny occur among the fragments. Another opinion considers the new discovery *and* the Vatican group as two copies (both perhaps by the aforesaid Rhodians) of a lost original which, according to Sir Kenneth Clarke, may have been in bronze.

Laodameia, daughter of Acastus and wife of Protesilaus (q.v.).

Laodicea (-keia), name of eight cities founded by the Seleucids (q.v.) at places as far apart as the coasts of Asia Minor and Syria and the Tigris. Five of these were said to be due to Seleucus I, Nicator, after whose mother Laodice they were named. By far the most important, however, was Laodicea ad Lycum, in Phrygia, founded by Antiochus II and named after his wife. It was situated about two miles south of the Lycus and about nine miles east of its confluence with the Maeander. Here the great trade route from the Euphrates and beyond divided into two branches, one going to Ephesus via Magnesia, the other to Pergamum via Philadelphia, Sardis and Thyatira. This fact, together with the fertility of the district, which was famous for the fine white wool of its sheep, ensured the prosperity of Laodicea. Here too was a Christian church, one of the 'seven churches which are in Asia' (Apoc. i. 11; iii. 14–18).

Laomedōn, King of Troy, son of Tros and father of Priam, Hesione and other children. Apollo and Poseidon, having displeased Zeus, were sentenced to serve Laomedon for wages. Poseidon built the walls of Troy, while Apollo tended the king's flocks on Mt Ida. When the two gods had completed their sentences, Laomedon refused to pay them. Poseidon therefore sent a sea-monster to ravage the country, to which the Trojans were obliged from time to time to sacrifice a maiden. On one occasion Laomedon's daughter was chosen by lot to be the victim. For the remainder of the story *see* HESIONE.

Lapithae (-ai), a mythical people inhabiting the mountains of Thessaly. Pirithoüs (q.v.), half-brother of the Centaurs (q.v.), was their ruler. Upon his marriage with Hippodameia, the Centaurs tried to carry off his bride and the other women. A fierce battle ensued, in which the Lapithae were victorious. This fight was the subject of some of the metopes of the Parthenon (q.v.), where it symbolized the conflict between the Greeks and Persians.

Lar, or **Lars,** an Etruscan word meaning lord, king or hero. It was used as a *praenomen* and borne by Porsenna of Clusium, Tolumnius of Veii and others. *See* C. O. Müller and W. Deecke, *Die Etrusker,* 1877.

Larentalia, *see* ACCA LARENTIA.

Larentia, *see* ACCA LARENTIA.

Lares, Roman tutelary gods. Their origin is disputed; but according to the most probable opinion they were spirits of the farmland, and hence guardians of crossroads where the boundaries of farms met. From the land they were introduced by servants into the house, where they were worshipped as spirits of deceased ancestors (*see also* LEMURES) and joined the *penates* (q.v.) to form in each home a single group of household guardians. Each family honoured its *lares* and *penates*: on the hearth were placed small statues representing them. From early times also there were public *lares* and *penates*. These formed part of the state religion and were commemorated at an annual festival with games.

Larisa: 1. (mod. Larissa), city of Thessaly, on the River Peneus, and seat of the Aleuadae (q.v.). Though its geographical situation was of some strategical importance, the state as such was notoriously unstable. It sided with Athens in the Peloponnesian war.

2. Larisa Cremaste, another Thessalian town, perched high up (*cremaste* = suspended) on Mt Othrys.

Larunda, probably in origin a Sabine earth-deity. In late Roman legend she was identified with the nymph Lara, daughter of Alcmon, who told Juno of Jupiter's love for Juturna (q.v.). The god deprived her of her tongue and ordered Mercury to conduct her to the underworld. But on the way Mercury cohabited with her and became the father of two *lares* (q.v.).

Larvae, *see* LEMURES.

Lasus (-os), Greek poet, of Hermione in Argolis, *fl. c.* 510 B.C. He instructed Pindar (q.v.) in music and poetry, and was the rival of Semonides. Lasus worked at the court of the Peisistratids (q.v.) at Athens; he greatly developed the dithyramb and wrote what was probably the first book on music. Only one short fragment survives. *See* E. Diehle, *Anthologia lyrica Graeca,* 1949.

Latifundia, large agricultural estates in Italy, and elsewhere in the Roman dominions, resulting from the distribution of public land (*see* AGRARIAN LAWS). They were worked by slaves who often lived and laboured in the most barbarous conditions. When slave labour became dear, these estates employed tenants, who were soon reduced to a condition little better than serfdom.

Latin League, a confederation of the cities of Latium (q.v.), under Roman hegemony which had been established (496 B.C.) by the victory of Lake Regillus (q.v.). After Rome had subjugated much of central Italy (*see* AEQUI; ETRURIA; VOLSCI), the league was reorganized on terms somewhat less favourable to the Latins. These attempted to regain their independence (340–338), but were crushed. The league was finally dissolved: some of its members were obliged to accept the Roman franchise, others to make treaties directly with Rome.

Latina, Via, highway of Italy running south-east from Rome via Anagnia, Fregellae, Aquinum, Casinum, Venafrum, Teanum and Cales to Casilinum, where it joined the Via Appia (q.v.). The date of its construction is not known, but was probably in the early 4th century B.C. The distance from Rome to Casilinum was 135 miles; but six miles were later deducted from this total by a loop which avoided Venafrum and ran via Rufrae to rejoin the original road at modern Caianello.

Latini, some of the most ancient inhabitants of Italy, forming a league or confederation of thirty states with headquarters at Alba Longa (*see also* MAMILIUS; REGILLUS, LACUS; TARQUINIUS, LUCIUS, 2). These Latini are sometimes called 'Prisci Latini', to distinguish them from the later subjects of Rome. *See* J. Whatmough, *Foundations of Roman Italy,* 1937; A. N. Sherwin-White, *The Roman Citizenship,* 1939; R. Bloch, *The Origins of Rome,* 1960.

Latinus, in Roman legend, King of Latium and father of Lavinia, whom he gave in marriage to Aeneas. *See* Virgil, *Aen.* vii–xii.

Latium, country of the Latini (q.v.), a division of ancient Italy, which extended along the coast of the Tyrrhenian Sea, south-eastward from the mouth of the Tiber. *See* ITALIA.

Latmos, a mountain in Caria, the legendary scene of Endymion's sleep (*see* ENDYMION).

Latona, *see* LETO.

Laurium (-on), town in Attica, famous for its silver mines which were owned by the Athenian state and formed one of the chief sources of its revenue. These mines, employing slave labour, were leased for a fixed sum plus a percentage on the yield. The ancient shafts and galleries can still be seen.

Laverna, ancient Italian divinity, perhaps a spirit of the nether world. By an easy transition she came to be regarded as the patroness of thieves, whose operations were associated with darkness. At Rome was an altar of Laverna on the Aventine, near the Porta Lavernalis, and a grove on the Via Salaria.

Lavinia, daughter of Latinus (q.v.) and Amata. She was betrothed to Turnus, but given in marriage to Aeneas (qq.v.). *See* Virgil, *Aen.* vii–xii.

Lavinium (mod. Pratica), town of Latium, on the Via Appia about 20 miles south of Rome; traditionally the city of Latinus, refounded by Aeneas who named it after his wife Lavinia, daughter of Latinus. In historical times consuls and praetors sacrificed here to Vesta before taking office or leaving for their provinces. Under the empire elephants were kept in the surrounding forest-land. There are remains of several villas in the neighbourhood. One of these has been identified with that belonging to the younger Pliny and described by him in great detail (*Ep.* ii. 1); in another a copy of Myron's 'Discobolus' was found. The inhabitants of Lavinium were called Laurentes; but in spite of what was formerly believed, there was never a town called Laurentum.

Lebadeia, a Boeotian town situated at the foot of a cliff, in a cave of which was the oracle of Trophonius (*see* AGAMEDES).

Lectisternium (Lat. *lectus*, couch; *sternere*, to spread), a Roman rite of Greek origin, in which a meal was offered to gods and goddesses, represented by busts or statues. These were laid in the reclining position on a couch placed in the street, and in front of the couch a meal was set out on a table. The rite was propitiatory, and from the beginning was performed only after consulting the Sibylline Books (*see* SIBYL). According to Livy (v. 136) the first occasion was in 399 B.C., when the divinities entertained were Apollo and Latona, Hercules and Diana, Mercury and Neptune. The festival lasted for seven or eight days, and was celebrated also by private individuals: open house was kept, enemies reconciled, debts cancelled and prisoners released.

Another kind of *lectisternium* was held annually or more often in the temples of gods (e.g. Ceres) who were originally Greek. These largely replaced the older Roman *epulum* or *daps*, at which a table was laid for gods who were not visibly represented.

Lecythus (Lēkuthos), a tall vase or urn with handle, made for placing in tombs. It was often painted.

Leda, wife of Tyndareus (q.v.), mother of the Dioscuri, Helen and Clytaemnestra (qq.v.).

Legatus, a Roman military officer. *See* LEGION.

Legion (Lat. *Legio*). The Roman army consisted originally and normally of four conscript legions each made up of 3,000 infantry, 1,200 light armed troops (*velites*) and 300 cavalry. From the 1st century B.C. cavalry was always recruited outside Italy (*see* AUXILIA; EQUITES). The heavy infantry was grouped in centuries (100 men), each under an officer known as a centurion (*centurio*); two centuries formed a maniple (*manipulus*) commanded by the senior of its two centurions. There were thus thirty maniples in the legion. The sixty centurions, risen from the ranks, were responsible for discipline; and upon them really depended the conduct of battle, for the six military tribunes (*tribuni militum*) who nominally exercised joint command were chiefly concerned with administration.

The epoch-making reforms of C. Marius (q.v.) produced a volunteer, professional army, more closely bound than ever before to its commander-in-chief, looking to him for its pay and imbued for the first time with an *esprit de corps*. These Marian reforms did away with conscription; abolished the *velites* and cavalry as units of the legion proper, whose nominal strength was raised to 6,000 heavy infantry; and created a new tactical unit—the cohort (*cohors*) of three maniples (600 men). There were thus ten cohorts to a legion, each having six centurions, who were graded in fixed order of seniority thus: *primus pilus* and *posterior, princeps prior* and *posterior, hastatus prior* and *posterior*. The legion was now commanded in rotation by the six tribunes; but by the time of Caesar these had lost something of their importance to the legate (*legatus*), and appear henceforward in command of smaller units. The *legati* formed a senatorial staff (varying in number) to assist (and sometimes to impede) the general; it was Caesar himself who first placed individual legions under the command of a legate, though not every legate was at all times so employed. As to the centurions, they lost none of their importance, since the tribunes and legates were not usually professional soldiers.

Augustus formed a new military establishment, which, until the reign of Septimius Severus (A.D. 193–211), who created three new legions, included not more than thirty legions, each described by a number and sometimes by an additional title. The imperial legion numbered 5,000 heavy infantry with a small mounted guard of 120. The commander was a senatorial legate, who was superseded in the 3rd century by an equestrian prefect (*praefectus*). Constantine greatly reduced the status of the legion, which now included a mere 1,000 infantry. *See* H. M. D. Parker, *The Roman Legions*, 1928.

Leitourgiai, duties imposed by the State upon Athenian citizens of the most wealthy class. Examples of these burdensome obligations are (1) the office of choregus, who provided a chorus at the annual dramatic festivals; (2) the office of gymnasiarch, who was responsible for the upkeep of a gymnasium (q.v.) and the maintenance of athletes in training there for public games; (3) the supplying of a chorus for the sacred festival at Delos; (4) equipping a deputation to the Delphic oracle; (5) the office of trierarch who had to maintain a trireme (q.v.), found, rigged and manned by the State. The first, second and fifth were annual; the third periodic; the fourth occasional. *See* LEPTINES.

Leleges (-eis), name given by classical authors to an Asianic people occupying the Aegean islands and parts of mainland Greece before the historical period. Said to have been akin to the Carians, they were one of those people whom the Greeks classed together as 'Pelasgians' (q.v.). Homer represents them as allies of Troy.

Lēmnos, island of the northern Aegean, sacred to Hephaestus (q.v.). For other legends connected with it *see* HYPSIPYLE; ORION; PHILOC-TETES.

Lemnos became subject to Persia after the death of Polycrates (q.v.), and passed successively to Athens and Macedon. In 197 the Romans declared it free, but restored it to Athens in 166 B.C.

The island was celebrated for its medicinal earth, which was supposed to cure gangrenous wounds and snake-bites. A wagon load was dug out on one day each year under the direction of a priestess, and before being sold each block was stamped with the head of Artemis. Hence the earth itself was called in Greek *Lēmnia sphragis* (Lemnian seal) and in Latin *terra sigillata*.

Lemures, in Roman religion, ghosts of the dead. Some writers apply the name to all such, without distinction, and divide them into two classes: *lares* (q.v.) or souls of the good, and *larvae*, those of the wicked. But the common view was that *lemures* and *larvae* were identical, without reference to merit; they were propitiated at the annual festival of *lemuria* in May. *See also* MANES.

Lenaea (Lēnaia), *see* DIONYSIA.

Lentulus Crus, Lucius Cornelius, praetor in 58 and consul in 49 B.C. He accompanied Pompey to Greece, shared his flight to Larisa after the battle of Pharsalus, and reached Egypt. Here he was seized and put to death by the ministers of Ptolemy XII.

Lentulus Spinther, Publius Cornelius, Roman politician, curule aedile in 63, praetor in 60 and consul in 57 B.C. During his consulship he moved for the immediate recall of Cicero, and afterwards received Cilicia as his province. On the outbreak of civil war (49 B.C.) he joined Pompey and was given command of the garrison at Asculum, the chief town and fortress of Picenum. On hearing of Caesar's advance he fled, and was deserted by the bulk of his troops on the road. He then took refuge in Corfinium, upon the surrender of which he was pardoned by Caesar. Nevertheless, he followed Pompey to Greece, and fled to Larisa after Pharsalus, but was subsequently captured and put to death.

Lentulus Sura, Publius Cornelius, the chief of Catiline's fellow conspirators. He was quaestor to Sulla in 81, praetor in 75 and consul in 71 B.C. In the following year he and sixty-three others were expelled from the senate on account of their infamous lives, and it was this indignity that drove Lentulus to join Catiline and his crew. He counted on becoming leader of the conspiracy, and a prophecy of the Sibylline Books (*see* SIBYL) was applied to him by a gang of subservient *haruspices* (q.v.). With a view to strengthening his position, and recovering his seat in the senate, he had himself elected praetor for the fateful year 63. When Catiline left Rome Lentulus remained at the head of the conspirators, and his bungling probably saved the city from being fired; it was he who prompted negotiations with the Allobrogan ambassadors, as a result of which the secret was revealed. He was arrested, dismissed from office and strangled with others in the Capitoline prison on 5th December 63 B.C. *See* CATILINA.

Leochares (-kharēs), Greek sculptor of the 4th century B.C. One of his most famous works was a bronze group (now in the Vatican) of Ganymedes (q.v.) carried off by the eagle. He also worked on the mausoleum at Halicarnassus (q.v.).

Leōnidas, name of two Eurypontid kings of Sparta:

1. Younger son of Anaxandrides, succeeded his brother Cleomenes I in 487 B.C. When the Persians invaded Greece in 480 Leonidas was sent to hold the pass of Thermopylae (q.v.) with about 5,000 troops, of whom only 300 were Spartans. The defence was successful until Ephialtes, a Malian, betrayed a mountain path to the enemy. As soon as Leonidas understood the hopeless odds to which he was exposed, he dismissed all but 700 Spartan, Theban and Thespian troops, and made his heroic stand. He and all his men died in action (*see* Herodotus, vii).

2. Son of Cleonymus, became king in 256 B.C. Opposed to the projected constitutional reforms of his colleague Agis IV, he was deposed by the latter and succeeded by his son-in-law Cleombrotus II (242 B.C.). About two years later he was recalled, caused Agis to be put to death (241) and died *c.* 235 B.C.

Leonidas of Tarentum, Greek poet of the early or mid 3rd century B.C., author of some 100 epigrams in the Doric dialect, which form part of Meleager's *Garland* (*see* MELEAGER OF GADARA). Other fragments have been discovered in a papyrus from Oxyrhynchus (q.v.). *See* translation by E. Bevan, 1931.

Leontini (-noi), town of Sicily, the birth-place of Gorgias (q.v.). Situated about 20 miles north-west of Syracuse, it was founded in 729 B.C. by Chalcidians from Naxos (*see* NAXOS, 2). In 498 it became subject to Gela, in 476 to Syracuse and in 214 B.C. to Rome (*see* MARCELLUS, 1). *See also* HIERON, 1.

Leotychidas (Leōtukhidas): 1. Eurypontid king of Sparta 491–476 B.C. In 479 he commanded the Greek fleet which defeated the Persians off Mycale.

2. Reputed son of Agis II (q.v.). He was excluded from the throne, in favour of his uncle Agesilaus II, because of a suspicion that he was the son of an adulterous union between Agis's wife Timaea and Alcibiades (q.v.).

Lepidus, Marcus Aemilius, Roman statesman, son of M. Aemilius Lepidus (consul 78 B.C.) who attempted to overthrow the Sullan constitution. The younger Lepidus was praetor in 49 B.C., and on the outbreak of civil war he supported Caesar, who appointed him prefect of the city before setting out for Spain. Later in the same year, at Caesar's request, Lepidus took the unconstitutional step of nominating Caesar dictator, though he secured himself by carrying a law which empowered him to act. In 48 he was appointed governor of Hither Spain. In 46 he became Caesar's Master of Horse and remained in Rome when Caesar started for the campaign of Munda (November 46). On the night of 14th March 44 B.C. Caesar dined with Lepidus, and as the guests sat over their wine someone asked: 'What is the best death?' Caesar, who was busy signing letters, replied: 'A sudden one.'

Lepidus, as Master of Horse, commanded a legion which was stationed outside Rome. He was eager to avenge Caesar's murder, but was restrained by Antony and Hirtius. He was chosen to succeed Julius as pontifex maximus; Transalpine Gaul had already been assigned to him as his province for the following year; and thither towards the end of 44 he proceeded, taking office on 1st January 43.

For the events leading to the formation of the triumvirate (October 43) *see* ANTONIUS, MARCUS, 3; AUGUSTUS. Lepidus, however, was from the very start a mere puppet. In the division of provinces which followed the battle of Philippi (42) he was given Africa alone; and there he remained until 36, when Octavian summoned him to Sicily to help in the war against Sextus Pompeius. He obeyed the call, but, tired of being treated as a subordinate, attempted to secure the island for himself. Octavian quickly subdued him, stripped him of his army and provinces, though not of his office as pontifex maximus, and sent him to live under close guard at Circeii, where he died in 13 B.C.

Leptinēs, an Athenian citizen who in 354 B.C. proposed that the list of exempted persons should be abolished, and that all should be liable to the same state burdens (*see* LEITOURGIAI), except the representatives of Harmodius and Aristogeiton (q.v.). He was opposed by Demosthenes (*see* DEMOSTHENES, 2) in the speech *Against Leptines*; but despite the express statement of Dio Chrysostom (i. 388) that Leptines was defeated, there is reason to believe that the proposal became law.

Leptis Magna (mod. Lebda), an ancient Phoenician commercial settlement in what was afterwards called Tripolitania, on the north coast of Africa (q.v.). Founded from Sidon and Tyre, it was tributary to Carthage, but refused to support her during the second Punic war. In 146 B.C. the Romans declared Leptis a free city, and it was made a *colonia* (q.v.) by Trajan. It was much favoured by Septimius Severus, who was born there; and the splendid city whose ruins are among the finest in north Africa was virtually his creation. These include the harbour with its quays, the colonnaded forum, baths, theatres, circus and well-laid-out streets.

Leptis Parva (mod. Lamta), town of north Africa, 24 miles southwest of Hadrumetum. Like its greater namesake (*see* previous article), it was declared a free city after the third Punic war. Caesar made it his base before the battle of Thapsus.

Lernē, district of Argolis with a marsh where Heracles was said to have killed the Hydra. *See* TWELVE LABOURS OF HERACLES, 2.

Lesbos, island of the northern Aegean, off the coast of Mysia, early colonized by Aeolian Greeks. Its principal cities were Mytilene and Methymna (qq.v.). Early a busy centre of trade, and home of a famous school of lyric poetry (hence the legend of Orpheus's head; *see also* ALCAEUS; ARION; SAPPHO; TERPANDER), Lesbos reached the zenith of its prosperity under Pittacus (q.v.) at the end of the 7th century B.C. It was subject to Persia from 545 until 479 B.C., and afterwards joined the Delian League (q.v.). As Athens, at the head of this league, passed from hegemony to empire, only Chios and Lesbos were left independent, i.e. were allowed to retain their fleets and contribute ships instead of money. For the revolt of Lesbos in 428 B.C. *see* MYTILENE. The outcome of the Peloponnesian War (q.v.) ended Athenian domination, but most of the island was recovered by Thrasybulus (q.v.).

Lēthē, 'oblivion', Greek name for a mythical river of the underworld. The dead were supposed to drink its waters and thus become oblivious of the past.

Lētō, called in Latin **Latona,** in Greek mythology, daughter of Coeus and Phoebe (q.v.), and mother by Zeus of Apollo and Artemis. Persecuted in consequence by Hera, she wandered from place to place, and eventually reached the floating island of Delos (q.v.). Zeus anchored the island, and there Leto gave birth to the twin deities, with whom she was subsequently worshipped.

Leucadia or **Leucas** (mod. Santa Maura), island of the Ionian Sea, identified by Dörpfeld with the Homeric Ithaca (q.v.). At the southern extremity of the island was the promontory of Leucaste, on which stood a temple of Apollo. At the annual festival of the god it was once the custom to throw down suspected criminals from this point into the sea. Birds were attached to them, supposedly to break their fall; and if they reached the water uninjured, boats were ready to pick them up. This curious form of trial by ordeal gave rise to a story that the place was used as a 'lovers' leap' (*see* SAPPHO).

Leucippus (-kippos), Greek philosopher of the mid 5th century B.C., a native of Miletus. He was founder of the atomic theory of the universe, developed by his much greater contemporary Democritus (q.v.). Only one fragment of his work survives, but his teaching is summarized by Diogenes Laertius (q.v.). *See* C. Bailey, *The Greek Atomists*, 1928.

Leucosyri (Leukosuroi), i.e. 'white Syrians', Greek name for those inhabitants of Cappadocia (q.v.) who, though of Syrian race, were of lighter colour than their kinsmen beyond Taurus.

Leucothea (Leuko-), in Greek legend, a marine deity, formerly Ino. *See* ATHAMAS; MATUTA.

Leuctra (-ktrē), village in Boeotia, on the road from Plataea to Thespiae. Near here the Spartans and their allies were defeated by Epameinondas (371 B.C.).

Lex Duodecim Tabularum, *see* TWELVE TABLES, LAW OF THE.

Libanos, Greek name for the western part of that mountain range called in Scripture Lebanon. The eastern part was known as Antilibanos. Libanos was famous for its pines and cedars as early as 3000 B.C.

Liber or **Liber Pater,** ancient Italian divinity, who, with his female counterpart *Libera,* was patron of agricultural fertility and especially of viticulture. He was often identified with Bacchus (Dionysus, q.v.).

Libertas, Roman goddess of liberty. She originally personified personal freedom, but in imperial times stood for constitutional government. In works of art she was represented as a matron, wearing either a brimless felt cap (*pileus*) or a wreath of laurel.

Libitina, ancient Italian earth-goddess connected with luxuriant nature and hence with voluptuous delights. Her association with the underworld led inevitably to her transformation into the goddess of death and therefore to her later identification with Persephone (q.v.). At her sanctuary on the Esquiline at Rome deaths were registered and everything necessary for funerals was on sale or for hire. Here too were the offices of the *libitinarii* (undertakers) who carried out all funerals by contract. Some Latin poets use the name 'Libitina' in the sense of death itself.

Liburnia, a district of Illyria (q.v.), famous for its light-built warships. These became a standard pattern in the Roman fleets, and to them Augustus largely owed his victory at Actium (q.v.).

Libya (Libuē), Greek name for north Africa, excluding Egypt and Aethiopia.

Licinian Rogations, see LICINIUS, I.

Licinius : I. C. Licinius Calvus, surnamed 'Stolo', Roman magistrate. As tribune of the plebs (see TRIBUNE) from 376 to 367 B.C. he, with his colleague L. Sextius Lateranus, terminated the struggle between the patricians and plebeians. The laws which he proposed, and which were eventually (367) enacted, are known as the Licinian Rogations. They were as follows: (*a*) No more consular tribunes to be appointed; the consuls to be elected, and one of them always to be a plebeian. (*b*) Regulation of affairs between debtor and creditor. (*c*) No citizen to hold more than 500 *iugera* of public land (see AGRARIAN LAWS). (*d*) The Sibylline Books to be entrusted to a board of ten (*decemviri*), half of whom should be plebeians. Licinius himself was consul in 364 and again in 361 B.C.

2. C. Licinius Macer, Roman annalist and orator. Impeached by Cicero for extortion, he committed suicide, 66 B.C.

3. C. Licinius Macer Calvus (83–47 B.C.), Roman poet and orator, son of the preceding. His poetic style was modelled upon that of Catullus; in oratory he was leader of the anti-'Asiatic' school, denouncing even Cicero as florid and verbose. Catullus (Ode 53) makes reference to his smallness of stature.

Licinius Licinianus, Roman emperor A.D. 307–24. A Dacian peasant by birth, he was elevated to the rank of Augustus by Galerius (q.v.). On the death of Galerius (311), Licinius and Maximinus Daia (q.v.) became joint sovereigns of the East. In 313 the former married Constantia, daughter of Constantine the Great (q.v.), and later in the same year inflicted an overwhelming defeat upon his colleague Maximinus; but he himself was defeated by Constantine in 315. The conflict between Licinius and Constantine was renewed in 323: Licinius was overwhelmed, dethroned and later (324) murdered by order of his conqueror. See Gibbon, *Decline and Fall*, ch. xiv.

Lictors (Lat. *Lictores*) were officials who bore the *fasces* before Roman magistrates (see FASCES). They were generally persons of humble origin. Their town dress was the toga (q.v.), in triumphal processions a red coat, at funerals black. They walked in single file and cleared the way. Under the republic twelve lictors attended a consul, and proportionately fewer the magistrates of lower rank (see *also* DICTATOR). The emperors had twelve lictors until the number was doubled by Domitian.

Liguria, the ninth region of Italy (see ITALIA) as established by Augustus. The original inhabitants, who are believed to have come from north Africa in Neolithic times, were called by the Greeks *Ligueis* and by the Romans *Ligures*. In early times they occupied a much larger area than that contained in the Augustan region, extending along the coasts of Gaul and Italy from the mouth of the Rhône to Pisae in Etruria. They were subdued by the Romans only after a long struggle, *c.* 121 B.C.

Lilybaeum (Lilubaion) (mod. Marsala), town on the west coast of

Sicily with an excellent harbour. Founded in 398 B.C. by the Carthaginians, it was their chief fortress in the island until the latter was
made a Roman province at the end of the first Punic war (241 B.C.).

Limes Germanicus, a line of fortifications covering the Roman
provinces of Germania Superior and Rhaetia. Constructed to protect
the advances made beyond the Rhine by Vespasian and Domitian
(A.D. 74 and 83), it consisted of a chain of forts, and in the reign of
Trajan extended from Rheinbrohl on the Rhine to Falmingen on the
Danube. Hadrian strengthened the chain with a continuous palisade
of wood. Afterwards he or his successor, Antoninus Pius, planned an
advance of the frontier to take in a much larger area south of Worth
and to meet the Danube near Eining. This new *limes* consisted of
(1) an earthwork and ditch from Rheinbrohl to a point about half way
between Stuttgart and Aalen, and (2) a stone wall from there to the
Danube. We do not know exactly when this advance was carried out;
but the whole territory between the Rhine, the Danube and the Limes
Germanicus was lost under barbarian pressure *c.* A.D. 250. *See* H. F.
Pelham, *Essays on Roman History,* 1911.

Lindum (mod. Lincoln), town of Britain, a *municipium* and *colonia*
(qq.v.) on the Fosse Way (q.v.) and Ermine Street. Many Roman
remains attest the prosperity of Lindum; the most important is the
northern gate, now called Newport Arch, one of the finest surviving
examples of Roman architecture in England. Lindum was the base
of the Ninth Legion from about 47 to 71. At some date between the
latter year and 96 Lindum was made a *colonia* (q.v.).

Lindus, city of Rhodes (q.v.) on the east coast of the island. The
temple of Athena on the acropolis, and the propylaea, evidently
modelled on that of Athens, have been excavated.

Linos, an ancient pre-hellenic nature-god, but in Greek mythology
the personification of a dirge (*linos*) or lament for the departing
summer. He was son of Apollo by an Argive or Theban princess.
According to Argive tradition, Linos was exposed by his mother,
Psamathe, at birth, found and brought up by shepherds, and subsequently torn to pieces by dogs. Psamathe's grief betrayed her guilt,
and she was condemned to death by her father. Apollo, angered by
this cruelty, visited Argos with a plague, and the Argives endeavoured
to propitiate Linos and Psamathe with sacrifices and dirges.

The Theban version represented Linos as slain by Apollo himself
for having challenged the god to a musical contest. It also distinguished him from a later individual of the same name, who taught
music to and was slain by Heracles. *See* Sir J. G. Frazer, *The Golden
Bough,* 2nd ed., vol. ii, p. 252.

Liternum, town of Campania, between Cumae and the mouth of the
Volturnus. It was the place of retirement of Scipio Africanus Major
(q.v.) who died there.

Livia: 1. Sister of M. Livius Drusus (tribune of the plebs 91 B.C.).
She was married first to M. Porcius Cato, to whom she bore Cato
Uticensis (q.v.), and secondly to Q. Servilius Caepio. Servilia, her
daughter by this second marriage, was mother of M. Junius Brutus,
the murderer of Caesar.

2. Otherwise called Livilla, daughter of Nero Claudius Drusus and

sister of Germanicus. Married to Julius Caesar Drusus, son of Tiberius, she was induced by Sejanus (q.v.) to poison her husband (A.D. 23), for which crime she was put to death in A.D. 31. She must be distinguished from her niece, Julia Livilla, daughter of Germanicus and Agrippina.

Livia Drusilla, daughter of Livius Drusus Claudianus, a member of the *gens* Claudia who had been adopted by M. Livius Drusus (tribune of the plebs 91 B.C.) and committed suicide when proscribed by the triumvirs (42 B.C.). Livia was married to Tiberius Claudius Nero, to whom she bore, among other children, the future emperor Tiberius. In 38 B.C. Octavian (afterwards the emperor Augustus) compelled her husband to divorce her, and married her himself. At this time she was pregnant with a son, Nero Claudius Drusus, father of Germanicus (*see* TABLE 2). Livia had no children by Augustus, but she managed to retain his love until her death (*see* AUGUSTUS). On the accession of her son Tiberius she tried to obtain an equal share in the government. This Tiberius would not allow; but she continued to wield immense influence, both at court and in society, until her death at the age of eighty-six, in A.D. 29.

Livius, Titus, called in English **Livy** (59 B.C.–A.D. 17), Latin historian, was born and died at Patavium in Cisalpine Gaul, but spent most of his life at Rome. His great history of Rome in 142 books covered the period 742–9 B.C. The following books have survived intact: i–x (foundation of the city to 294); xxi–xxx (219–201); xxxi–xlv (201–167). Of the remainder we possess nothing but fragments, together with epitomes of all but two of the missing books. The whole work was entitled *Decades*, because it was divided into groups of ten books; hence no doubt the survival of three groups of ten and half of another. The style of Livy is clear and eloquent; but he was totally devoid of critical sense, and took no pains to distinguish fact from legend. An enthusiastic admirer of the past, an ardent patriot and a first-class story-teller, his aim was to provide a narrative which would gratify the pride of his readers while containing no manifest improbabilities or gross perversion of truth. *See* the edition by R. S. Conway, C. F. Walters and S. K. Johnson (Oxford Classical Texts), 1914–35. There is a translation by W. M. Roberts in Everyman's Library.

Livius Andronicus, *see* ANDRONICUS, LIVIUS.

Livius 'Salinator', Marcus, consul with L. Aemilius Paulus (*see* PAULUS, 1) in 219 B.C., when they campaigned against the Illyrians. On their return to Rome they were brought to trial on a charge of having made an unfair distribution of the loot among their soldiers. Livius was found guilty and retired into private life. In 207, however, he was consul a second time, with C. Claudius Nero, and together they defeated Hasdrubal on the Metaurus. As proconsul in 206 Livius was stationed with an army in Etruria, and his *imperium* was prolonged for two successive years. Censor in 204 with his former colleague, Nero, he imposed a tax on salt and thereby earned the nickname 'Salinator'.

Locri (-kroi), a people occupying two separate districts of Greece. One of these districts, sometimes referred to as Eastern Locris, was bounded north by Malis, east by the upper part of the Euboean strait, south by Boeotia, west by Doris and Phocis. The northern part was inhabited by Epicnemidian Locrians, called after their situation on the spurs of Mt Cnemis; the southern part by the Opuntian Locrians, whose chief town was Opus. The national hero of Eastern Locris was Ajax Oileus (*see* AJAX, 2). *See also* LOCRI EPIZEPHYRII.

The other district, Western Locris, was bounded north by Doris, east by Phocis, south by the Corinthian Gulf, west by Aetolia. Here the inhabitants, who were much less civilized than their namesakes, were called Ozolian Locrians; they do not appear in history before the Peloponnesian war. They resembled their Aetolian neighbours both in their predatory habits and in their methods of warfare. Their principal town was Amphissa (q.v.).

Locri Epizephyrii (Lokroi Epizephurioi), the inhabitants of Locri, a town of Magna Graecia (q.v.), founded *c.* 683 B.C. by Locrians from Eastern Locris (*see* previous article) on Zephyrium, a promontory in Bruttii. A few years later they transferred their settlement to a point on the Bruttian coast about 12 miles north, but retained their name.

Locri was the first Greek settlement to receive a written code of laws, given by Zaleucus *c.* 664 B.C. Early in the 4th century it became subject to Syracuse, and at the end of the first Punic war to Rome. Its wavering allegiance, however, led to its capture by Scipio in 205 B.C. Excavations have revealed an Ionic and a Doric temple (the former dedicated, probably, to the Dioscuri), and a sanctuary of Persephone.

Latin poets sometimes apply the epithet 'Narycian' to the place, to its inhabitants, and even to the pitch for which the Bruttian peninsula was famous. This was because Ajax Oileus, the national hero of Eastern Locris in Greece, was said to have lived at Naryx.

Locusta or **Lucusta**, a female poisoner employed by Agrippina in the murder of Claudius (A.D. 54) and by Nero for dispatching Britannicus (A.D. 55). She was put to death by Galba (A.D. 68).

Londinium (mod. London). The original site of Roman London, established very soon after A.D. 43 (*see* BRITAIN), appears to have been on the eastern side of the Walbrook stream. A pontoon bridge gave access to the southern bank of the Thames. This first settlement was destroyed by Boudicca (q.v.) in 61, and Tacitus, recording the event, speaks of London as an important centre of trade. The city was rebuilt, spreading this time up to Ludgate Hill. Its wall was constructed *c.* 140, extending from a fort near the present site of the Tower, and continuing along the Minories to Cripplegate, Newgate, Ludgate, Fleet Street and so down to the river. The area thus enclosed was 330 acres, making London the fifth largest town in the West. A more permanent bridge was also built. After this it soon became the financial and communications centre of the province. A great Basilica (q.v.), dating from about the year 80, once stood on the site of Leadenhall Market; it was the largest building of its kind outside Rome. The museums of London already contained thousands of relics of the Roman occupation when the clearance of bombed sites after the Second World War brought to light many architectural remains, among the most interesting of which was a Mithraeum (*see* MITHRAISM) now preserved under the vast pile of Bucklersbury House. See *Royal Commission on Historical Monuments, London (Roman)*, 1928;

G. Home, *Roman London*, 1948; A. Merrifield, *The Roman City of London*, 1965.

Longinus (-os), Greek rhetorician, born at Emesa *c.* A.D. 213; lectured at Athens, where Porphyrius (q.v.) was among his pupils. Later he travelled in the East, where he met Zenobia (q.v.) and was invited to teach her Greek. He obtained great influence over the queen, and soon became her chief minister. It was largely at his instigation that she threw off her allegiance to Rome, and after her defeat by the emperor Aurelian, Longinus was put to death (A.D. 273). *See also* PSEUDO-LONGINUS.

Longus (-os), Greek romance writer of the 3rd or 4th century A.D., author of an erotic work *Daphnis and Chloë. See* text and Thornley's translation revised by J. M. Edmonds (with Parthenius) in the Loeb Library.

Luca (mod. Lucca), city of Liguria (q.v.). Here Ti. Sempronius Longus withdrew after the Roman defeat on the Trebia in 218 B.C. Here too Caesar, Pompey and Crassus (qq.v.) held their celebrated conference in 53 B.C. Augustus included Luca in Etruria, which he made the seventh region of Italy (*see* ITALIA).

Lucania, district of southern Italy, bounded north by Campania and Samnium, east by Apulia and the Gulf of Tarentum, south by Bruttii, west by the Tyrrhenian Sea; separated from Campania by the River Marus and from Bruttii by the Laus. Previously called by the Greeks Oenotria, the whole territory, excepting a few Greek city-states, was conquered by the Lucani (a Sabelline tribe) from the Oenotrians *c.* 450 B.C. The Lucani were engaged in a war with Tarentum (q.v.) during the latter half of the 4th century. They subsequently (298) allied themselves with Rome, but sided with Pyrrhus (q.v.) in 281 B.C. After his withdrawal they were subdued by the Romans in 272; later they suffered the consequences of having taken the part of Hannibal against Rome in 216 B.C., and were finally ruined by their participation in the Social War (q.v.). Augustus formed Lucania and Bruttii into the third region of Italy (*see* ITALIA). The principal towns were Heraclea, Metapontum, Paestum, Sybaris and Thurii (qq.v.).

Lucanus, Marcus Annaeus, called in English **Lucan**, Roman epic poet, born at Corduba in Spain, A.D. 39. His father, L. Annaeus Mela, was a brother of Seneca the philosopher (q.v.). He was brought up at Rome, and was early introduced to the court of Nero. Here he incurred the jealous hatred of the emperor, who considered himself a poet without a peer; and having joined in the conspiracy of Piso (*see* PISO, GAIUS CALPURNIUS), his guilt was discovered, and he was obliged to commit suicide (A.D. 65).

Lucan is the author of an extant poem, *Bellum Civile*, afterwards known as *Pharsalia*. Its ten books (the last incomplete) deal with the civil war between Caesar and Pompey. The best text is that of A. E. Housman (1926). *See* translation by E. Ridley, 2nd ed., 1919.

Lucceius, Lucius, Roman orator and historian, friend and correspondent of Cicero. Having failed to obtain the consulship in 60 B.C., he withdrew altogether from public life and wrote a history (now lost) of the Social and Civil wars. Cicero requested him (*Ad. Fam.* v. 12) to write a history of his (Cicero's) consulship; but there is no evidence that he undertook the work.

Luceria, town of Apulia, on the road from Beneventum to Sipontum; famous for its wool. The temple of Minerva was said to have been founded by Diomedes (*see* DIOMEDES, 2) and to contain the Trojan Palladium (*see* PALLADIUM).

Lucian (Gk Loukianos), Greek sophist and satirist, born at Samosata in Commagene *c.* A.D. 125. After practising for some time as an advocate at Antioch, he set up as a sophistic rhetorician and travelled as such in Asia Minor, Macedonia, Greece, Italy and Gaul. About A.D. 165 he settled at Athens, where he remained for about twenty years, until he accepted an official post in Egypt. He died probably *c.* A.D. 190. The sixty-five genuine works of Lucian include rhetorical declamations, literary criticism, biography, romance and satirical dialogues. Among the most interesting or entertaining (for Lucian was one of the world's greatest wits) are *Dialogues of the Gods*; *Dialogues of the Dead*; *Zeus Confounded*; *Zeus Tragedian*; *Sale of Lives*; *The Incredulous*; *Symposium*; *Charon*; *Menippus*; *Demonax*; *Twice Accused*; *The Fisherman*; *Timon*. His *True History* inspired Rabelais's *Voyage of Pantagruel*, Swift's *Gulliver's Travels* and Cyrano de Bergerac's *Journey to the Moon*. The best complete edition of Lucian's works is that by C. Jacobitz, 1905. There is a good English translation by H. W. and F. G. Fowler, 1905. *See also* text and translation by A. M. Harmon, 8 vols. (Loeb Library); M. Caster, *Lucien et la pensée religieuse dans son temps*, 1938.

Lucifer, *see* PHOSPHOROS.

Lucilius, Gaius, Roman satirist, born at Suessa Aurunca in Campania, *c.* 180, and died at Neapolis (mod. Naples) *c.* 102 B.C. He was the first to mould Roman satire into that form which was afterwards developed by Horace, Juvenal and Persius. Surviving fragments are printed with translation by E. H. Warmington in *Remains of Old Latin* (Loeb Library), 1938. *See also* J. Wight Duff, *Roman Satire*, 1937.

Lucilius Junior, friend of the younger Seneca, author of *Aetna*, a poem on the origin of volcanic activity. It appears to have been written some time between A.D. 65 and 79.

Lucina, title of Juno (q.v.) as patroness of child-bearing and new-born infants.

Lucretia, in Roman legend, wife of L. Tarquinius Collatinus (q.v.). Her rape by Sextus Tarquinius (q.v.) led to her own suicide, the expulsion of the kings, and the founding of the Roman republic (*see* TARQUINIUS, LUCIUS, 2).

Lucretius Carus, Titus (*c.* 99–55 B.C.), Roman poet about whose life authentic information is entirely lacking. His *De Rerum Natura* is a didactic poem in six books on Epicurean philosophy, and is addressed to C. Memmius Gemellus, who was praetor in 58 B.C. The chief aim of the poem is to free men from superstition, to accustom them to the idea of complete annihilation at death, and to rid them of the idea of divine interference in human affairs. Gods there are, beings a little higher than mortals, but to them also death and corruption come, bringing total eclipse; of mortal concerns they live in supreme contempt. Throughout the universe the atom alone is eternal and incorruptible. These theories are expounded by Lucretius with a passionate eloquence, fervour and power that are quite unparalleled in Latin literature. The definitive edition, with commentary, *apparatus criticus* and *prolegomena*, is that of C. Bailey, 3 vols., 1947. *See* G. D. Hadzeits, *Lucretius and his Influence*, 1934; E. E. Sikes, *Lucretius*, 1936.

Lucrinus, Lacus, lake in Campania, half a mile north of the Lake of Avernus (q.v.), separated from the Sinus Puteolanus by an embankment. Its waters remained salt; they were renowned for their state-owned fisheries, which were leased to contractors, and also for their oyster beds, which were said to have been laid down by Sergius Orata *c.* 100 B.C. Cicero, among many wealthy Romans, had a villa, known as Academia, on the shores of Lucrinus. Its remains disappeared in 1538, when the lake was partly filled up by a volcanic eruption which produced the crater of Montenuovo.

Lucullus, Lucius Licinius, Roman general. As consul in 74 B.C. he was given command of the third Mithradatic war (*see* MITHRADATES). On his return to Rome he devoted himself to a life of luxury, and his name is still a byword for good living. A story is told that one evening, when no guests were present, his butler failed to serve the usual sumptuous repast. 'Do you not know', exclaimed the master, 'that tonight Lucullus is dining with Lucullus?' He was also a patron of letters, and himself wrote a (lost) history of the Social War (q.v.) in Greek. *See* J. B. Cobban, *Senate and Provinces*, 1935.

Lucusta, *see* LOCUSTA.

Ludi Apollinares, a Roman festival established in 212 and annual after 211 B.C. It consisted chiefly of theatrical performances.

Ludi Magni or Maximi, games held annually in the Circus (q.v.) at Rome; instituted, according to tradition, by Tarquinius Priscus in honour of Jupiter Capitolinus. They consisted of a chariot race, a sham fight on horseback (*ludus Troiae*), a military review and gymnastic contests.

Ludi Megalenses, Roman games in honour of the Great Mother of the Gods (q.v.), instituted 204 B.C. From 191 B.C. they were celebrated annually on 5th April; but from the reign of Claudius (A.D. 41–54) they lasted from 4th to 10th April.

Ludi Saeculares, Roman games celebrated at the beginning or end of each *saeculum*, a period which the Romans took to be 100 or 110 years, according to circumstances. Horace (q.v.) composed his *Carmen Saeculare* for the celebration of 17 B.C., and the games were also held in A.D. 248 to commemorate the city's millennium.

Lugdunum or Lugudunum (mod. Lyons), town of Transalpine Gaul in the territory of the Segusiavi, at the confluence of the rivers Rhodanus (Rhône) and Arar (Saône); birth-place of the emperors Claudius and Caracalla. A Roman colony was founded here by L. Munatius Plancus in 43 B.C. and the place quickly developed into the most important town of western Europe. Early in the reign of Augustus it was made the hub of four great Roman roads, the common capital of the three newly established provinces (Narbonensis, Aquitanica and Lugdunensis, in which last it was situated), the seat of an annual assembly of deputies from the Gallic cantons, and the centre of the Gallic worship of Rome and Augustus. The same emperor adorned it with temples, aqueducts and a theatre. Destroyed by fire in A.D. 59 it was rebuilt at the expense of Nero; and after the great fire of Rome (A.D. 64) it repaid this generosity with a lavish contribution to the relief fund. The great prosperity of Lugdunum was due mainly to its control of the immense commercial traffic up and down its two rivers. For the rhetorical contest instituted here by Caligula and referred to by Juvenal (i. 44) *see* Suetonius, *Caligula*, 20.

Lugii, a German tribe. In the time of Augustus they inhabited the upper basin of the Oder. Together with all the Suebic tribes (*see* Suebi) and the Sarmatian Iazyges (q.v.) they took part in the Marcomannic war of 161–80 (*see* Marcomanni). It appears that the Lugii were identical with or a subdivision of the later Vandals (q.v.).

Lugudunum, *see* Lugdunum.

Luna (mod. Luni), harbour town on the River Macra; originally in Liguria (q.v.), but from the time of Augustus a frontier town of Etruria (q.v.). The harbour itself, called Lunae Portus, was in use before 205 B.C., when Ennius sailed thence for Sardinia; but the town dates only from the foundation of a Roman *colonia* (q.v.) in 177 B.C. Luna was famous for its marble (Carrara), and produced good wine.

Lupercalia, yearly Roman festival of purification, celebrated on 15th February in honour of Lycaean Pan (or Faunus), whose cult was said to have been introduced by Evander (q.v.). Others believe that it was in honour of the wolf that suckled Romulus and Remus. The festival took place at the foot of the Palatine hill, near the cave of Lupercus, in which was a bronze statue of a wolf. The officiating priests (*luperci*) sacrificed goats and dogs, with whose blood they touched the foreheads of two youths, and the blood was wiped off with wool dipped in milk, the youths being obliged to smile throughout. The skins of the victims were then cut into long lashes called *februa* (Lat. *februare*, to purify); with these the *luperci* ran along the city walls, slashing anyone they met as a purificatory rite. Women were eager to receive a cut, to remove barrenness. *See* W. Warde Fowler, *Roman Festivals*, 1899.

Lupus, Publius Rutilius (*fl.* A.D. 30), Roman rhetorician, author of *Skhēmata Lexeōs*, a treatise on the figures of speech, itself an abridgment of a similar work by the rhetorician Gorgias of Athens (1st century B.C.). *See* edition by C. Halen in *Rhetores latini minores*, 1863.

Lusitania, *see* Hispania.

Lutetia (mod. Paris), town of the Parisii; situated on what is now called the Île de la Cité, in the River Sequana (Seine), and connected with both banks by two wooden bridges on sites now occupied by the Pont Notre-Dame and the Petit-Pont. These bridges were broken and the town burned by the Gauls when threatened by Labienus in 52 B.C. (*see* Caesar, *Bell. Gall.* vii. 58).

By the 1st century A.D. Lutetia was a Roman town, which had spread to the left bank and occupied much of what is now known as the Montagne Sainte-Geneviève. It was destroyed by barbarian invaders in the 3rd century.

Lycaeon (Lukaion), mountain in Arcadia, sacred to Zeus (q.v.), where human sacrifice was offered until the 1st cent. A.D.

Lycaon (Lukaōn), in Greek legend, a king of Arcadia who, when visited by Zeus, served the god with a dish of human flesh. He and all his sons, excepting Nyctimus, were thereupon slain with a flash of lightning or, according to others, changed into wolves. *See* R. P. Eckels, *Greek Wolf-lore*, 1937.

Lycaonia (Lukaōnia), inland territory of Asia Minor. Its boundaries varied greatly at different times, but at its greatest extent it was bordered north by Galatia, east by Cappadocia, south by the Taurus range, west by Pisidia and Phrygia. The principal towns in the time of St Paul were Iconium, Derbe and Lystra (Acts xiv; xvi). Lycaonia remained virtually independent of Persia, but was included in the dominions of Alexander the Great. After his death it passed to the Seleucids (q.v.), until the defeat of Antiochus III, when the Romans gave it to Eumenes II of Pergamum. Part of it was added to Galatia, *c.* 160 B.C., and the eastern half to Cappadocia in 129 B.C. *See* W. M. Ramsay, *Historical Geography of Asia Minor*, 1890, and *Cities of St Paul*, 1907.

Lyceum (Lukeion), a gymnasium and garden with covered walks at Athens (q.v.), near the temple of Apollo Lyceus. Aristotle (q.v.) taught here, whence the name was afterwards applied to his school of philosophy.

Lycia, coastal district in the south-west of Asia Minor between Caria and Pamphylia. Homer, who gives the Lycians a prominent place in the *Iliad*, represents them, under their leaders Sarpedon (q.v.) and Glaucus (*see* GLAUCUS, 2), as allies of Troy. Lycia received Greek colonies at an early date; various sites have yielded fine examples of both Greek and native art, many of which are now in the British Museum.

The country was never subdued by Lydia (q.v.); and though conquered by the Persians in 546, it was freed by Cimon (q.v.) *c.* 468 B.C. The Peace of Antalcidas (q.v.) subjected it once again to Persia; but it continued to enjoy a very large measure of independence. This independence was scarcely affected by its incorporation in the dominions of Alexander and the Seleucids, or even by its submission to Rome. In the reign of Claudius, however, it was definitely annexed to the Roman Empire and united with Pamphylia (q.v.). The principal towns were Xanthus, Myra and Patara.

Lycomedes (Lukomēdēs), King of Scyros, to whose court Achilles (q.v.) was sent, disguised as a girl, by his mother, in order to prevent his going to the Trojan war. This plan was frustrated by Odysseus (q.v.). Meanwhile, however, Achilles had become by Deidameia, daughter of Lycomedes, the father of Neoptolemus (q.v.). Theseus (q.v.) was killed by Lycomedes.

Lycon (Lukōn), Greek philosopher, a native of Troas, and disciple of Straton (q.v.), whom he succeeded as head of the Peripatetic school in 269 B.C.

Lycophron (Lukophrōn), Greek poet and grammarian, born at Chalcis in Euboea, but lived at Alexandria under Ptolemy II, Philadelphus (283–246 B.C.). His extant poem *Cassandra*, on the fall of Troy, is a work of proverbial obscurity. *See* text with translation by A. W. Mair in *Callimachus, Lycophron and Aratus* (Loeb Library).

1921. More valuable than the poem itself are the *scholia* of Tzetzes, published by E. Scheer, 1908.

Lycosura (Lukosoura), city of Arcadia, traditionally founded by Lycaon (q.v.). The temple of Despoina (i.e. Persephone) housed a colossal group by Damophon (q.v.) of Messene, showing Despoina and Demeter seated, with Artemis and the Titan Anytus standing by. Remains of both temple and sculptures were discovered in 1889.

Lycurgus (Lukourgos): 1. Traditional founder of the Spartan constitution. Many scholars find no evidence for the real existence of Lycurgus; they suppose him to have been a pre-hellenic Arcadian deity whose cult was adopted at Sparta, where indeed sacrifices were offered to him in historical times. According to the legend, Lycurgus was son of the Spartan king Euonomus and brother of Polydectes. The latter succeeded his father, and died leaving his queen with child. This ambitious woman offered to destroy the infant at birth if Lycurgus would share the throne with her. He pretended to agree; but when she gave birth to a son (Charilaus), he proclaimed the child king and acted as his guardian. Later, in order to avoid suspicion of designs upon the throne, he left Sparta and travelled in Crete, Ionia, Egypt and India. On his return Lycurgus found the state a prey to anarchy and licentiousness. He therefore made a new division of property, and remodelled the whole constitution, military and civil. Then, having obtained approval of his work from the Delphic oracle, he again left Sparta, having exacted an oath from the people that they would make no alteration in his laws until he returned. In order to ensure the permanence of his establishment, he never did come back, and none knew how or where he died.

2. Legendary king of the Edones in Thrace, driven mad and killed for having persecuted Dionysus and his votaries.

3. Legendary king of Nemea, and father of Archemorus (q.v.).

Lycurgus (Lukourgos), one of the ten Attic Orators, born at Athens *c.* 390 B.C., and died in 324 B.C., before the affair of Harpalus (q.v.). From 338 to 326 B.C. he was in charge of the state finances, and distinguished himself by his ability and probity. As a statesman he was a warm supporter of Demosthenes, but most of his speeches were for the prosecution in criminal cases; only one is extant, *Against Leocrates* (330 B.C.). *See* R. C. Jebb, *Ten Attic Orators*, 1888.

But the chief glory of Lycurgus is the use he made of public funds to beautify the city of Athens (q.v.) and to enhance the splendour of religious celebrations. Among other works he built the Stadium, and completed the theatre of Dionysus, which latter he adorned with statues of the great tragic poets. Moreover he established state texts of the tragic drama, to which actors were obliged to adhere.

Lycus (Lukos), brother of Nycteus and uncle of Antiope, *see* ANTIOPE, 2.

Lydia, district of varying boundaries in Asia Minor. The original territory seems to have consisted of the upper Hermus region and the plain of Sardis; but two of its monarchs, Alyattes and Croesus (qq.v.), gradually extended their dominions to form a commercial empire which included the whole of Asia Minor west of the River Halys (excepting Lycia, q.v.), with Sardis as its capital. In 546 this empire became subject to Persia, from whom it passed to Alexander the Great, and subsequently to the Seleucids. Following their defeat of Antiochus III, in 190 B.C., the Romans gave Lydia to Eumenes II of Pergamum (q.v.), whose son Attalus III bequeathed his kingdom to Rome. Lydia was thus included in the province of Asia, bounded north by Mysia, east by Phrygia, south by Caria and west by the Aegean Sea.

The Lydians are said to have been the first people to coin money (c. 700 B.C.). They were celebrated likewise for their music and their system of physical training. Highly civilized at an early date, they undoubtedly exercised a profound influence on the culture of the Ionian city-states which lay between them and the sea.

Lynceus (Lunkeus): 1. Son of Aegyptus and husband of Hypermestra, see DANAÜS.

2. Son of Apharaeus and brother of Idas (q.v.).

Lysander (Gk Lusandros), Spartan general and statesman during the latter part of the Peloponnesian war. Appointed to command the Spartan fleet on the west coast of Asia Minor, he enlisted the aid of Cyrus the Younger (q.v.), who supplied him with large sums of money. This flood of Persian gold, at a time when the Athenian treasury was almost exhausted, enabled Lysander to win the crowning victory at Aegospotami (q.v.) in 405 B.C. and thus bring the war to an end. In the following year he entered Athens, and compelled the Ecclesia (q.v.) to vote for an oligarchy (see THIRTY TYRANTS, 1). It was through the influence of Lysander that the Spartan king Agesilaus II succeeded his half-brother Agis II, excluding the latter's son Leotychides (see LEOTYCHIDAS, 2) in 401 B.C. Lysander accompanied Agesilaus to Asia Minor (396 B.C.); but the king purposely thwarted all his designs, and on his return Lysander planned to alter the constitution by abolishing hereditary kingship and making the throne elective. But before he could achieve this purpose he was killed in action beneath the walls of Haliartus in Boeotia (395 B.C.). *See* the Life by Plutarch.

Lysias (Lusias), one of the ten Attic Orators, born at Athens 458 B.C., son of Cephalus, a native of Syracuse. In 443 he sailed with the colonists (among whom was Herodotus) who went to found Thurii; but he returned to Athens in 412. During the rule of the Thirty Tyrants (q.v.) in 404 he was imprisoned, but escaped and joined Thrasybulus (q.v.), to whom he rendered useful service. Lysias died in 380 B.C. He wrote speeches for others in a style remarkable for its unadorned simplicity. About thirty of these are extant. *See* the edition with translation by W. R. M. Lamb (Loeb Library). *See also* R. C. Jebb, *Attic Orators*, 1888; K. Freeman, *The Murder of Herodes and other Trials*.

Lysimachus (Lusimakhos), one of the generals of Alexander the Great, upon whose death (323 B.C.) he obtained the province of Thrace, and assumed the title of king in 306. He joined the coalition against Antigonus I, and, together with Seleucus I, defeated and slew him at Ipsus (301). In 288 Lysimachus and Pyrrhus (q.v.) expelled Demetrius I from Macedonia. Pyrrhus held the Macedonian throne until the following year, when he was driven out by Lysimachus.

Towards the end of his life Lysimachus put to death his son Aga-thocles. This terrible crime alienated his subjects, and eventually Seleucus invaded his Asian territories. The two monarchs fought at Corupedion, where Lysimachus was killed (281 B.C.).

Lysippus (Lusippos), Greek sculptor, a native of Sicyon; born *c.* 336 B.C. and died *c.* 270 B.C. He has been described as the 'greatest figure in the sculpture of the second half of the fourth century'. He was originally a workman in bronze, and most of his statues were executed in that medium. He was the first to introduce portrait sculpture, and made many representations of Alexander the Great. Several existing statues seem to be copies of his, notably the 'Apoxyomenus' in the Vatican.

Lysis (Lusis), Greek philosopher, a native of Tarentum (*d. c.* 390 B.C.). He was a member of the Pythagorean school, and has been credited with many of the works usually attributed to Pythagoras himself.

Lysistratus (Lusistratos), Greek sculptor of the 4th century B.C., brother of Lysippus (q.v.). According to Pliny (*Nat. Hist.* 35, 153) he was the first sculptor to take impressions of human faces in plaster.

M

Macedonia (Mak-), country of Europe to the north of Greece, originally called Emathia. The kingdom of Macedon is said to have been founded by Perdiccas I (q.v.) *c.* 700 B.C. Little is known of it until the reign of Amyntas I (q.v.). Philip II (q.v.) enlarged its boundaries and eventually conquered the whole of Greece; his son Alexander the Great (q.v.) established a vast empire. After Alexander's death (323 B.C.) this empire dissolved (*see* DIADOCHI); but the kingdom remained and continued powerful until conquered by the Romans in 168 B.C. (*see* PERSEUS). Macedonia became a Roman province in 148 B.C. (*see* METELLUS, 2). *See* S. Casson, *Macedonia, Thrace and Illyria*, 1926.

Macer, Aemilius (died 16 B.C.), Latin didactic poet, born at Verona, a friend of Ovid (q.v.). Imitating Nicander (q.v.), he wrote a poem, entitled *Theriaca*, on antidotes against snake-bite; another (*Ornithogonia*) was about birds. He must be distinguished from a poet of the same name (*fl.* A.D. 12) who wrote on the Trojan war.

Machanidas (Makh-), tyrant of Sparta, defeated and slain by Philopoemen (q.v.) in 207 B.C. *See also* NABIS.

Machaon (Makhaōn), in Greek legend, son of Asclepius (q.v.). According to the *Iliad* he and his brother Podalirius were surgeons in the Greek army before Troy. Together they led the Thessalian forces and were killed during the siege.

Macrinus, Marcus Opilius Severus, Roman emperor April A.D. 217–June 218, born of humble parentage at Caesarea in Mauretania, A.D. 164. At the instigation of his patron, Plantianus, he was admitted to the service of the emperor Septimius Severus, and after holding several responsible offices, became prefect of the praetorians under Caracalla (q.v.). On the latter's death he was proclaimed emperor by the troops, but was murdered in the following year by the generals of Elagabalus, who succeeded him.

Madauros, city of Numidia (q.v.) and birth-place of Apuleius (q.v.); became a Roman colony (*see* COLONIA) towards the end of the 1st century A.D. It was famous for its schools.

Maecenas, Gaius, Roman statesman and patron of literature, born of an equestrian family between 74 and 64 B.C., probably at Arretium. He was descended both on the paternal and on the maternal side from Etruscan ancestors, a fact of which he was extremely proud; his father's house was descended also from the Cilnii, a distinguished family of Arretium, while his mother came from the Maecenates, another leading family of that town. Maecenas was for long a close friend and the chief minister of Augustus. In later years a coolness sprang up between them, and Maecenas withdrew from public life; but this did not prevent his bequeathing his great fortune to the emperor, from whose liberality it had been largely derived. Maecenas died in 8 B.C. His chief title to immortality is his patronage of Horace, Virgil and Propertius (qq.v.).

Maecianus, Lucius Volusius, Roman jurist, author of several legal works as well as of *Distributio*, a partly extant treatise on numerical divisions, weights and measures. He held many official posts under Antoninus Pius, and also under Marcus Aurelius whose law tutor he had been. A complete list of these officers was found at Ostia in 1930. The last of them was governor of Alexandria, in which capacity he took part in the rebellion of Avidius Cassius (q.v.) and was murdered by the troops. *See* the edition of his *Distributio* by F. Hultsch in *Metrologicorum scriptorum reliquiae*, ii. 1866.

Maelius, Spurius (died 440 B.C.), a wealthy plebeian who bought up corn in Etruria during a famine at Rome and sold it at a nominal price to the people. The patricians accused him of aspiring to king-ship, and appointed Cincinnatus (q.v.) dictator. C. Servilius Ahala (q.v.), master of the horse, summoned Maelius to appear before the dictator; but he refused to go, and Ahala slew him in the Forum. His property was confiscated, his house pulled down and its vacant site (henceforth known as Aequimaelium) left as a memorial of his fate (Livy, iv. 13). The tale is no doubt in part, if not altogether, legendary.

Maenius, Gaius, consul in 338 B.C. with L. Furius Camillus. He captured the Antiate fleet, and the beaks (*rostra*) of the ships were fixed and gave their name to a platform used by public speakers in the Forum at Rome. One of his descendants erected the famous balcony (*Maenianum*) of the Basilica Porcia, supported by the *columna Maenia*.

Maevius, *see* BAVIUS.

Magna Graecia (Gk *Hē megalē Hellas*), collective name first given in the 6th century B.C. to the Greek city-states on the east coast of what the Romans later called Bruttii, i.e. the 'toe' of Italy. It was gradually extended to include those on the west coast and even Sicily. The inhabitants were known collectively as Italiotes.

Magnēsia: 1. Name of two cities in Asia Minor: (*a*) *Magnesia ad Maeandrum*, in Ionia, on a small tributary of the Maeander. The fact that it was not a member of the Ionian League supports the tradition that it was founded by colonists from Thessaly (*see* 2 below) and Crete. Its political history follows that of Ionia (q.v.); commercially it enjoyed great prosperity until Roman imperial times, when it disappears from history. Themistocles (q.v.) died here in 457 B.C. (*b*) *Magnesia ad Sipylum*, 40 miles north-east of Smyrna, famous for the battle in which Antiochus III (q.v.) was defeated by a Roman army under L. Cornelius Scipio in 190 B.C. In the neighbourhood was the rock-hewn figure of 'Niobe' (q.v.), probably intended to represent the goddess Cybele (q.v.).

2. District of eastern Thessaly (q.v.), between the Vale of Tempe and the Pagasaean Gulf.

Mago: 1. Carthaginian general, youngest son of Hamilcar Barca and brother of Hannibal. He took part in the latter's Italian cam-paigns (218–216 B.C.), and joined his elder brother Hasdrubal in Spain. Here he was defeated by M. Junius Silanus (207), and again (this time together with Hasdrubal) by Scipio Africanus at Silpia

(206). Soon afterwards he was ordered by his government to invade
Liguria (205). In 203, however, he was defeated in Gallia Cisalpina and
recalled to Carthage, dying of wounds on the voyage.

2. Reputed author of a Punic work on agriculture which was
brought to Rome and translated by order of the senate after the
destruction of Carthage. The book was regarded as a standard
authority, and is often referred to by later writers.

Maia, in Greek mythology, daughter of Atlas and Pleione. She was
the eldest and most beautiful of the Pleiades. In a grotto on Mt
Cyllene (Arcadia) Maia bore Hermes (q.v.). She was identified by the
Romans with an ancient Italian divinity of spring, also called Maia,
or Maiesta, the cult-partner of Volcanus.

Mamertines, *see* MESSANA.

Mamilius, Octavius, in Roman legend, a distinguished citizen of
Tusculum, son-in-law of Tarquinius Superbus (*see* TARQUINIUS,
LUCIUS, 2), on whose behalf he roused the Latins and was killed at the
battle of Lake Regillus (496 B.C.).

Mamurra, Roman of the equestrian order. Born at Formiae, he was
Caesar's *praefectus fabrum* in Gaul, and we learn from three odious
references in Catullus (xxix, lvii, xlii. 4) that they were believed to
enjoy unnatural relations. The accusation is probably groundless.
Certain it is, however, that Mamurra made a great fortune thanks to
Caesar's liberality. He was the first person at Rome to cover all the
walls of his house with slabs of marble, and to have all the columns
thereof made of solid marble.

Mandubii, a Gallic tribe, probably dependants of the Aedui (q.v.),
inhabiting part of what is now the Côte d'Or. Their stronghold was
Alesia (q.v.), to which they admitted Vercingetorix (q.v.) and his
forces in 52 B.C. During the siege that followed, the Mandubii,
together with their wives and children, were driven from the place, in
order to reduce the stress of famine, and were left to die of starvation
between the foot of the hill and the Roman lines of circumvallation,
which they were not allowed to pass. *See* Caesar, *Bell. Gall.* vii. 78.

Manes, in Roman religion, spirits of the dead considered as
divinities, to be distinguished from the *lemures* (q.v.) who were
simply ghosts. The name was derived from old Latin *manus*, 'good'.
In course of time the *di manes* were identified with the deceased
ancestors of a family, and even with the gods of the underworld (cf.
the inscription D.M.S.—*dis manibus sacrum*—on many Roman
tombs).

Manilius, Roman poet, author of a poem in five books called
Astronomica and written in the reign of Augustus or Tiberius. Incomplete, and probably never published, the *Astronomica* is a work of
great learning and considerable literary merit. *See* the edition by
A. E. Housman, 1932; *see also* text and translation by H. W. Garrod,
1911.

Manilius, Gaius, tribune of the plebs in 66 B.C., when he proposed a
law conferring upon Pompey supreme command of the war against
Mithradates. It was supported by Cicero (*Pro Lege Manilia*) and
carried almost unanimously.

Manlius, Marcus, consul 392 B.C.; took refuge in the Capitol when

Rome was taken by the Gauls in 390. The story went that when the barbarians tried to ascend the Capitoline hill, Manlius was roused from sleep by the cackling of sacred geese. Hurriedly collecting a body of men, he managed to drive back the enemy, who had just reached the summit, and for this heroic deed he was surnamed Capitolinus. In 385 B.C. he defended the cause of the plebeians, who were suffering from harsh treatment by their patrician creditors. In the following year he was charged by the patricians with aspiring to kingly power, and, being condemned to death by the people, was hurled from the Tarpeian rock. His house on the Capitoline was razed, and the members of the Manlia *gens* resolved that none of them should ever again bear the *praenomen* Marcus.

Mantinea (-eia), city of Arcadia, founded soon after the Persian wars by the merging of five villages. It was situated on the River Ophis, which, when the city was rebuilt in 370 B.C., was diverted so as to encircle the place instead of flowing through it as before. The history of Mantinea is largely one of intermittent conflict with its neighbour Tegea (q.v.). As a result of its treachery to the Achaean League, Aratus (q.v.) put to death its leading citizens, sold the rest into slavery and called the city Antigonea in honour of Antigonus Doson. The original name was restored by Hadrian in A.D. 133.

Mantinea was famous for three battles fought in the vicinity: (1) 418 B.C., when the Argives and Mantineans defeated the Spartans and their allies in the Peloponnesian war. (2) 362 B.C., when Epameinondas (q.v.) defeated the Spartans. (3) 207 B.C., when the forces of the Achaean League under Philopoemen (q.v.) defeated the Spartans under their tyrant Machanidas.

Mantua, town of Gallia Cisalpina (Transpadana), on the River Mincius. Virgil considered it his birth-place, although he was actually born in the neighbouring village of Andes.

Manumission (Lat. *manumissio*), in Roman law, the freeing of a slave. The usual form was *per vindictam*, in which the master turned the slave round, with the words 'liber esto', in presence of the praetor, that officer or his lictor (*see* Lictors) at the same time striking the slave with his rod. Manumission might also be effected by adoption, by will or by registration in the census (this last abandoned after the reign of Vespasian).

All the above were forms of *manumissio iusta* (valid manumission). Less valid (*manumissio minus iusta*) were a variety of acts which had come to be regarded as expressing an intention to manumit, e.g. pronouncing a slave free in presence of five friends, inviting him to dinner, etc.

Marathōn, a plain with village of the same name, on the north coast of Attica, 22 miles from Athens by one road and 26 by another. This plain, through which runs a small stream named Charadra, extends along the shore for about 6 miles, varying in breadth from 3 to 1½ miles. The surrounding arc of hills is terminated at either end by a marsh. Here was fought the celebrated battle between the Persians and the Athenians and Plataeans in 490 B.C. The tumulus raised over the 192 Athenian dead survives. *See also* Miltiades; Pheidippides. *See* G. B. Grundy, *The Great Persian War*, 1901.

Marcellus, Gaius Claudius: 1. Consul 50 B.C., brother of M. Claudius Marcellus (consul 51 B.C.). He was a member of the Pompeian party on the outbreak of civil strife; but he took no active part against Caesar during the remainder of the war, and led the successful appeal for his brother's pardon (46 B.C.).

2. First cousin of the preceding, consul in 49 B.C., when he accompanied Pompey to Greece; pardoned by Caesar after Pharsalus (48 B.C.).

Marcellus, Marcus Claudius: 1. Roman general, five times consul. In his first consulship (222 B.C.) he slew in battle with his own hand Britomartus or Viridomarus, King of the Insubrian Gauls, whose spoils (*see* SPOLIA OPIMA) he dedicated in the temple of Jupiter Feretrius on the Capitoline, the third and last time in Roman history that such an offering was made. During the second Punic war (211 B.C.) Marcellus captured Syracuse after a siege of two years (*see also* ARCHIMEDES). He fell in battle against Hannibal (208 B.C.).

2. Consul in 51 B.C., and a bitter enemy of Julius Caesar. Pardoned by the latter in 46 B.C.—for which act of clemency Cicero gave thanks in the extant speech *Pro Marcello*—he started back from Mytilene, where he had been living in voluntary exile, but was murdered at Peiraeus by one of his own attendants, P. Magius Chilo.

3. Son of C. Claudius Marcellus (consul 50 B.C.) and Octavia, sister of the emperor Augustus, born 42 B.C. In 25 B.C. Augustus, intending Marcellus as his heir, adopted him and gave him as wife his daughter Julia (*see* JULIA, 5). In 23 Marcellus was curule aedile, but died the same year at Baiae, supposedly poisoned by Livia Drusilla (q.v.). He is commemorated by Virgil in a famous passage (*Aen.* vi. 860–86) which the Middle Ages understood as prophetic of Christ.

Marcius, legendary Italian seer, whose oracular verses were 'discovered' in 213 B.C. and deposited in the Capitol together with the Sibylline Books (*see* SIBYL).

Marcomanni, 'men of the border', a Germanic tribe of the Suebic race, originally dwelt between the Rhine and the Danube. Under their chief Maroboduus (q.v.) they migrated into Bohemia and parts of Bavaria. Here they settled, after subduing the Boii (q.v.), and founded a kingdom which extended southward to the Danube. Later, with the Quadi and other tribes, they were engaged in war with Rome during the reign of Marcus Aurelius; and these hostilities continued until Commodus purchased peace (A.D. 180).

Marcus Aelius, Aurelius Antoninus, commonly called Marcus Aurelius, Roman emperor A.D. 161–80; born at Rome A.D. 121, son of Annius Verus. He received his early education from tutors, among them Herodes Atticus and M. Cornelius Fronto (qq.v.); but being attracted to Stoicism he placed himself at the age of twenty-five under Rusticus the Stoic. In 138 he was adopted by Antoninus Pius (q.v.), and married the latter's daughter Faustina (q.v.). Succeeding to the throne on Antoninus' death in 161, he took his adoptive brother L. Aelius Verus (q.v.) as partner in the empire. Soon afterwards Verus was dispatched to the East and for four years (162–5) campaigned with some success against Vologaeses III of Parthia; he died in 169, leaving Marcus sole emperor. Marcus himself was for several years engaged in war against the Marcomanni and Quadi (qq.v.). In 174 he won a decisive victory over the latter (*see* Gibbon, ch. xvi), and in the following year set out for the East, where Avidius Cassius (q.v.) had proclaimed himself emperor. Having pacified Syria, Marcus returned to Italy via Greece, where he was initiated into the Eleusinian Mysteries and gave handsome endowments to the schools of philosophy and rhetoric at Athens. After celebrating a triumph at Rome (176) he was obliged once more to take the field against the Marcomanni, and died at Sirmium or Vindobona in 180. We still possess his *Meditations*. *See* the edition with commentary and translation by A. S. L. Farquharson (1944), published in Everyman's Library. *See* A. S. L. Farquharson, *Marcus Aurelius: his Life and his World*, ed. D. A. Rees, 1952.

Mardonius (-os), Persian general and son-in-law of Darius I. In 492 B.C. he was sent to punish Athens and Eretria for their support of the Ionian revolt. The expedition, however, came to nothing; for his fleet was destroyed by a storm off Mt Athos, while his land forces were partly annihilated on the march by Thracian tribes. In 480 Mardonius urged Xerxes to undertake the invasion of Greece, which resulted in the Persian defeat at Salamis. He was left by the king to carry on the war by land, but was defeated and killed by the Greeks in 479 B.C.

Mareōtis, lake in the Nile delta; separated from the sea by a neck of land on which stood Alexandria (q.v.).

Marius, Gaius: 1. Roman general and statesman, born at Arpinum in 157 B.C. He served under Scipio Africanus at Numantia (134 B.C.), was tribune of the plebs in 119 and subsequently married Julia, aunt of Julius Caesar. By this time he had established himself as a leader of the popular party at Rome. In 107 he was consul and received command of the war against Jugurtha, in which he had already served on the staff of Q. Caecilius Metellus (109). The brilliance of his quaestor Sulla (q.v.) and the surrender of Jugurtha to the latter in 106 mark the beginning of that deadly rivalry between the two men which ended in civil war.

Marius's next task was that of military reform in the light of Caepio's defeat at Arausio (q.v.). His measures, which made the army a more efficient tactical weapon (*see* LEGION; ROMAN ARMY) and bound it more closely to its commander, were perhaps the most fruitful stage in Roman military history. Italy meanwhile was threatened by barbarians, mostly Cimbri and Teutones (qq.v.), and Marius alone was thought capable of saving the state. He was accordingly elected consul a second time, for 104 B.C. The menace was indeed postponed, but Marius was consul a third and fourth time (103 and 102). In this latter year he defeated the Teutones and their allies at Aquae Sextiae, and in 101, with his colleague Q. Lutatius Catulus, the Cimbri at Campi Raudii near Vercellae.

Marius was received back at Rome with unprecedented honours; but in order to secure the consulship a sixth time, he associated himself with two demagogues, Saturninus (q.v.) and Glaucia. He gained his object, was elected consul for 100 B.C., and in that capacity put down the insurrection of Saturninus and Glaucia. In 88, though advanced in years and full of honours, Marius was anxious to obtain

the command against Mithradates, and, through the good offices of
Sulpicius Rufus (q.v.), obtained a vote of the people conferring upon
him that command which the senate had already bestowed on Sulla.
Sulla managed to escape to his legions in Campania, and promptly
marched on Rome. Marius fled, and after wandering along the coast
of Latium he was at length taken prisoner in the marshes formed by
the River Liris near Minturnae. It is said that when a Cimbrian
soldier entered the prison to kill him, Marius exclaimed in a terrible
voice: 'Man, darest thou murder Gaius Marius?' Whereupon the
barbarian dropped his sword and rushed from the prison. The people
of Minturnae then took compassion on Marius, and placed him on
board a ship. He reached Africa safely, and landed at Carthage; but
he had scarcely set foot on shore when the Roman governor sent an
officer to bid him leave the country. 'Tell the praetor', Marius is said
to have replied, 'that you have seen Gaius Marius a fugitive, sitting
on the ruins of Carthage.'

Soon afterwards (87) Marius returned to Italy, where the popular
party under the consul L. Cornelius Cinna (q.v.) were making a new
bid for power. Cinna had been driven out of Rome, but he now
re-entered the city together with Marius. Their guards stabbed
everyone whom Marius did not salute, and the streets ran red with
the noblest blood of Rome. Without an election, Marius and Cinna
nominated themselves consuls for the ensuing year (86). But on the
eighteenth day of his seventh consulship Marius died of pleurisy.

2. Adoptive son of the preceding, born in 109; consul in 82 B.C.,
when he was defeated by L. Cornelius Sulla (q.v.) at Sacriportus near
Praeneste. After Sulla's victory at the Colline Gate Marius put an
end to his life.

Mark Antony, *see* ANTONIUS, MARCUS, 3.

Maroboduus, Latin form of the name Marbod borne by a Suebian
noble who was born *c.* 18 B.C. He was sent in boyhood with other
hostages to Rome, where he attracted the notice of Augustus and
received a liberal education. Soon after attaining manhood, he
returned to his own country, and there founded the kingdom of the
Marcomanni (q.v.). The other German tribes, however, became
suspicious, and he was eventually obliged to flee from his dominions
(A.D. 19). The emperor Tiberius allowed him to reside in Italy, and he
spent the remainder of his life at Ravenna, where he died in A.D. 37.

Marpessa (-é), mountain in the island of Paros, famous for its
marble. *See* PAROS.

Marrucini, tribe occupying a narrow strip of territory on the east
coast of Italy, along the right bank of the Aternus. They submitted to
Rome in 304 B.C. Their principal town was Teate.

Mars, together with Jupiter and Quirinus (qq.v.), one of the three
great tutelary gods of Rome. He had his *flamen* (q.v.). As god of war,
with the title *Gradivus*, he gave his name to the place set apart for
military exercises (Campus Martius) and was identified with the Greek
Ares (q.v.). *See also* SALII. But he was also a god of agriculture, and
was regarded as protector of cattle. The wolf and the woodpecker
were sacred to him, and he was the source of an ancient oracle (*see*
ORACLES). The most important temples of Mars at Rome were that

outside the Porta Capena, on the Via Appia; that in the Campus Martius, near the Circus Flaminius, built by D. Brutus Gallaecus (138 B.C.); and that of Mars Ultor in the Forum of Augustus, built by him to commemorate his vengeance for the murder of Julius Caesar, and described by Ovid (*Fasti*, v).

Marsi: 1. People of central Italy. Their chief town was Marruvium, on the eastern shore of Lacus Fucinus. At the south-west corner of the lake was the temple of Angitia, goddess of healing; and her worshippers, who professed acquaintance with medicinal herbs, earned for their country the reputation of a home of witchcraft. The Marsi became allies of Rome in 304; and instigated the Social War (q.v.) in 90 B.C.

2. A German tribe dwelling north-west of the Chatti (q.v.).

Marsyas (-suas), in Greek legend, a Phrygian satyr who found the flute discarded by Athena because the playing of it distorted her features. He thereupon challenged Apollo to a musical contest, on condition that the victor should do what he liked with the vanquished. The Muses decided in favour of Apollo, who bound Marsyas to a tree and flayed him alive. His blood was the source of the River Marsyas. *See* Ovid, *Metam.* vi. 382–99; Sir J. G. Frazer, *Adonis, Attis and Osiris*, ch. vi, 1906.

Martialis, Marcus Valerius, called in English **Martial** (*c.* A.D. 40–*c.* 104), Latin poet, born at Bilbilis in Spain. Coming to Rome under Nero in 64, he enjoyed the patronage of Titus and Domitian, and returned to Spain in 98. Of his works the following survive: thirty-three poems from the *Liber Spectaculorum* (published A.D. 80 to commemorate the opening of the Colosseum); two collections of short mottoes entitled *Xenia* and *Apophoreta* (published 84–5); and twelve books of epigrams (published 86–102). All these are included by modern editors in fourteen books with the general title *Epigrams*. Martials' fertility of imagination, ready wit, felicity of language and genuine affection for his friends are undeniable; but many of his poems are grossly obscene, both in thought and expression, as well as servile in flattery of Domitian. Martial throws much valuable light on Roman social life in the 1st century A.D. There are editions by L. Friedländer, 1886, M. Lindsay, 1903, and W. Gilbert, 1912. *See also* text and translation by W. C. A. Ker, 2 vols. (Loeb Library), 1919–20; A. G. Carrington, *Aspects of Martial's Epigrams*, 1960.

Masinissa, King of the Massyli, the easternmost tribe of Numidia (q.v.). On the outbreak of the second Punic war he supported Carthage, but later transferred his loyalty to Rome. He stood his ground against attacks by the Carthaginians and by his neighbour Syphax (q.v.) until the arrival in Africa of Scipio (204 B.C.). Then (203) he went over to the offensive, reduced Cirta, the capital of Syphax, and took him prisoner (*see also* SOPHONISBA). In 202 he commanded the cavalry of the Roman right wing at Zama, and on the conclusion of the war was rewarded with most of Syphax's territory. Except for a dispute with Carthage, which led to the third Punic war, he spent the remainder of his reign in peace, dying in 148 B.C. at the age of ninety, and leaving three legitimate sons: Micipsa, Gulussa and Mastanabal.

Massa, Baebius, Roman governor of Hispania Baetica, who was accused (A.D. 93) by the younger Pliny and Herennius Senecio of having plundered his province. He escaped punishment through the favour of Domitian, under whom he then became one of the most notorious court favourites and informers.

Massagetae (-gētai), general name given by Herodotus to all the barbarous tribes living east of the Caspian. It was, according to one account, on an expedition against the Massagetae that Cyrus the Great (q.v.) lost his life (*see* Herodotus, i. 204–16; iv. 11, 172).

Massalia, called in Latin **Massilia** (mod. Marseilles), founded by Greeks from Phocaea (q.v.) *c*. 600 B.C. It became one of the most important commercial cities of the ancient world. It sided with Rome in the Punic wars, largely with a view to the ruin of its commercial rival, Carthage. In the civil war (49 B.C.) it supported Pompey, but was besieged by a Caesarian force under Trebonius and forced to capitulate (*Bell. Civ.* ii. 1–16). From the time of Augustus it was included in the province of Gallia Narbonensis (*see* GALLIA).

Massicus, Mons, a mountain ridge of Italy, dividing the lower course of the Liris from Campania. It was famous for its wines; the celebrated Falernian came from its southern slopes.

Massilia, *see* MASSALIA.

Massiva, name of two members of the Numidian royal house.
1. Nephew of Masinissa.
2. Son of Gulussa (second son of Masinissa), assassinated at Rome by order of Jugurtha (q.v.) in 111 B.C.

Mastanabal, youngest of the three legitimate sons of Masinissa (q.v.). He was father of Hiempsal II (*see* HIEMPSAL, 2) and of an illegitimate son, Jugurtha (q.v.).

Matronalia, at Rome, the principal festival of Juno (q.v.), celebrated on 1st March.

Matuta or **Mater Matuta,** Roman female divinity identified with Leucothea (*see* ATHAMAS). According to Lucretius she was the goddess of dawn, but was more probably a goddess of childbirth.

Mauretania, a region of north-west Africa, bounded by the Mediterranean, the Atlas range and the Atlantic. The lower slopes of Atlas were well wooded and produced the ornamental wood called *citrum*, which was highly valued at Rome for tables.

The Romans first became acquainted with Mauretania during the Jugurthine war (110–106 B.C.), when it was ruled by Bocchus (q.v.). Half a century later it consisted of two kingdoms separated by the River Mulucha. Both supported Caesar in the civil war, but were given as a whole to Juba II of Numidia (q.v.) (*see* JUBA, 2) by Augustus in 25 B.C. Claudius formed it into two provinces, Mauretania Tingitana and Mauretania Caesariensis, with their respective capitals at Tingis and Caesarea Mauretaniae. Diocletian (q.v.) included Tingitana for administrative purposes in the diocese of Spain.

Mausolus (more correctly **Maussollus**), satrap and virtual ruler of Caria (377–353 B.C.). He took part in the revolt against Artaxerxes Mnemon, conquered much of Lydia, Ionia and several Greek islands, assisted the Rhodians in their war with Athens and removed the Carian capital from Mylasa to Halicarnassus (q.v.). He is best known from the tomb (Mausoleum) erected for him by his widow Artemisia.

The architects Satyrus and Pythis, and the sculptors Scopas, Leochares, Bryaxis and Timotheus finished the work after her death.

Maxentius, Marcus Aurelius Valerius, Roman emperor A.D. 306–12, son of Maximianus (q.v.). He was passed over in the division of the empire, following the abdication of his father and Diocletian (q.v.) in 305; but he seized Rome and was proclaimed emperor in 306. After the death of Galerius (311), Constantine the Great marched on Rome and defeated Maxentius at Saxa Rubra (312). Maxentius tried to escape into the city over the Milvian Bridge, but was drowned.

Maximianus, Marcus Aurelius Valerius, Roman emperor A.D. 286–305, originally a Pannonian soldier, was made by Diocletian his colleague in the empire, but was compelled to abdicate when Diocletian did so voluntarily, and went into retirement. When his son Maxentius (q.v.) assumed the imperial title in the following year (306), he returned to Rome; but being expelled from the city by Maxentius, he took refuge in Gaul with Constantine, who had married his daughter Fausta. It is generally believed that he was compelled by Constantine to commit suicide at Massilia (A.D. 310).

Maximinus, Gaius Julius Verus (commonly called **Maximinus Thrax**), Roman emperor A.D. 235–8, originally a Thracian shepherd. He was of gigantic size and enormous physical strength. Having received from Alexander Severus command of a new legion raised in Pannonia, he followed the emperor in his campaigns against the Germans on the Rhine. There he induced some of his companions to murder Alexander and his mother Mammaea (235). He was proclaimed emperor; but his cruelty and rapacity, which were the accompaniment of undeniable ability, created enemies in various parts of the empire. He was killed by his own troops while besieging Aquileia in A.D. 238.

Maximinus, Galerius Valerius, Roman emperor A.D. 308–14. Originally an Illyrian shepherd, his real name was Daia, and he is often called **Maximinus Daia.** Becoming a soldier he was raised by his uncle Galerius (q.v.) to the rank of Caesar, and made governor of Syria and Egypt in 305. In 308 he assumed the title of Augustus, and on the death of Galerius (311) succeeded to the provinces of Asia, and entered into a secret alliance with Maxentius (q.v.). Having invaded Thrace (313) in the absence of Licinius, he suffered an overwhelming defeat at Heraclea and fled. He died at Tarsus.

Maximus Tyrius (i.e. of Tyre), Greek rhetorician and Platonic philosopher of the late 2nd century A.D. There are extant forty-one of his dissertations on various aspects of Platonism, written in an easy and pleasing style, but more commendable for their form than for their content. The following examples will give some idea of their subject-matter: 'On Plato's Opinion respecting the Deity'; 'Whether we ought to return Injuries done to us'; 'Whether Prayers should be addressed to the Deity'. There is a French translation by Dounais (1910).

Meclosedum (mod. Melun), Gallic town on an island in the Sequana (Seine), about 30 miles south-east of Lutetia (q.v.). In 52 B.C. it was occupied by T. Labienus (q.v.) as a prelude to a projected attack on Lutetia.

Medea, *see* JASON AND MEDEA.

Media, a country forming the north-west part of what is now Iran.
Bounded north by the Araxes; west and south-west by the ranges of
Zagros, which divided it from the Tigris valley; east by the Para-
choatras and Caspian (mod. Elburz) ranges. Media, which had been a
satrapy of the Persian Empire since 549 B.C., entered classical history
in 330, when it was occupied by Alexander the Great and placed two
years later under a satrap named Atropates, an ex-general of the
defeated Persian army, whose daughter was subsequently (324)
married to Perdiccas. In the division of Alexander's territories
southern Media, with its capital Ecbatana, was assigned to Peithon,
a Macedonian, while the more northerly parts were left to Atropates
who formed them into an independent kingdom known as Atropatene
(q.v.). From Peithon southern Media (henceforward called simply
Media) passed to Antigonus and then (*c.* 310) to Seleucus I. Under the
Seleucids it was thoroughly hellenized (*see* RHAGAE), but was conquered *c.* 150 B.C. by Mithradates I of Parthia. Together with
Atropatene it became subject to the Sassanid monarchy of Persia
in A.D. 226.

Mediolanum (mod. Milan), city of Gallia Cisalpina (Transpadana),
founded by the Insubres (q.v.). Captured by the Romans in 222, it
rebelled during the Hannibalian war and was again reduced in 196
B.C. From the time of Diocletian it was the headquarters of the
praefectus praetorio and of the imperial vicar of Italy.

Medusa (-dousa), one of the Gorgons (*see* GORGON). *See also* AEGIS;
PERSEUS.

Megacles (-klēs), a member of the Alcmaeonid family (*see* ALCMAE-
ONIDAE); archon eponymous in 632 B.C., when Cylon (q.v.) attempted
his *coup d'état*, and was responsible for the murder of the suppliants.
See Thucydides, i. 126; Aristotle, *Constitution of Athens*, 1.

Megaera (-gaira), *see* ERINYES.

Megalopolis, city of Arcadia, situated on both banks of the River
Helisson 20 miles south-west of Tegea; birth-place of Philopoemen
and Polybius (qq.v.). Founded by Epameinondas (q.v.) in 369 B.C.
as a defence against Sparta and as headquarters of the Arcadian
League, its population was drawn from thirty-eight smaller townships. In 353 it was threatened by Sparta, and was saved by the
intervention of Thebes; but meanwhile it had also invoked Athenian
aid, an appeal which was the occasion of Demosthenes's speech *On
the Megalopolitans*. From this time Megalopolis was consistently
friendly towards Macedon, and after the death of Alexander was
governed by a succession of native tyrants until 234 B.C., when it
joined the Achaean League (q.v.).

The whole site was excavated in 1890–2, and found to have been
very accurately described by Pausanias (viii. 27). *See* Society for the
Promotion of Hellenic Studies, *Excavations at Megalopolis*, 1892.

Megara, a Greek city-state between Attica and Corinth, bounded
north and south by the Corinthian and Saronic gulfs respectively.
On the first of these gulfs was the port of Pegae, and on the second
that of Nisaea. With these facilities Megara soon rose to importance
as a commercial power and established numerous colonies, among

which were Megara Hyblaea (q.v.) in Sicily, Chalcedon and Byzantium (qq.v.) on the Thracian Bosporus, Astacus and Heraclea (qq.v.) in Bithynia. Her commercial pre-eminence, however, yielded to competition from Miletus, Athens, Corinth and Corcyra. In 459 Megara, being attacked by Corinth, sought help from Athens and received an Athenian garrison, which was massacred by the townsfolk in 445 B.C. Athens retaliated with an embargo on Megarian trade throughout her empire. After the Peloponnesian war Megara regained some of her former prosperity and was eventually admitted to the Achaean League (q.v.). *See* E. L. Highbarger, *The History of Ancient Megara*, 1927.

Megara Hyblaea, town of Sicily, 12 miles north-west of Syracuse, founded from Megara in 726 and in turn helped to found Selinus (q.v.) 651 or 628 B.C. Destroyed by Gelon *c.* 481, it was fortified by the Syracusans in 414 and captured by M. Claudius Marcellus in 214 B.C.

Megarians, *see* ERISTICS.

Mela, Pomponius, Latin geographer of the 1st century B.C., born at Tingentera in Spain, author of an extant work *De Situ Orbis*. It is in three books, and contains a very brief but often vivid description of the various parts of the world. *See* edition by C. Frick, 1880.

Melampus (-os), in Greek legend, son of Amythaon and brother of Bias. He was said to have introduced the worship of Dionysus into Greece and to have been the first to practise medicine. He was also reputed the first mortal to possess prophetic powers. *See also* PROETUS.

Melas, 'black', a river in the north-east of Sicily, flowing into the sea between Mylae and Naulochus through meadows in which the legendary oxen of the Sun were pastured.

Meleager (Meleagros), in Greek legend, son of Oeneus (q.v.) and one of the Argonauts (q.v.). Oeneus, King of Calydon, when sacrificing to the gods, overlooked Artemis, who took revenge by sending a huge boar to ravage the kingdom. Meleager consequently assembled a band of hunters from all over Greece and slew the monster. A quarrel over the distribution of the spoils developed into a war, during which Meleager killed his uncles, brothers of his mother Althaea. Althaea cursed her son, who forthwith declined to take any more part in the fighting until his city was in the direst straits. Then he resumed his arms, defeated the enemy and lived uneventfully until his death, which occurred some time before the Trojan war. Such is Homer's account. A later and more romantic version of the tale related that Meleager wished to give the spoils of the boar hunt to Atalanta (q.v.), who had taken part therein, and that he killed his mother's brothers who objected. However, when he was seven days old, his mother had heard the Moirae (Fates) declare that the boy would live so long as a log then burning on the hearth should be unconsumed. Althaea had extinguished the log and concealed it in a chest. Now, to avenge her brothers, she threw it on the fire and Meleager died. She afterwards committed suicide, while her daughters were so grief-stricken at Meleager's death that Artemis changed them into guinea-fowl (*meleagrides*).

Meleager (Meleagros) of Gadara, Greek poet of the late 2nd and early 1st century B.C. Born at Gadara in Decapolis, he was educated at Tyre, but spent the remainder of his life in the island of Cos. He compiled an anthology (q.v.) entitled *The Garland*, which includes about 134 of his own epigrams (*see also* LEONIDAS OF TARENTUM). *See* J. W. Mackail, *Select Epigrams from the Greek Anthology*, 3rd ed., 1911; F. A. Wright, *Meleager's Complete Poems* (translated), 1924.

Meliboea (-boia), town on the coast of Magnesia in Thessaly, the traditional home of Philoctetes (q.v.).

Melicertes (-kertēs), son of Athamas by Ino. *See* ATHAMAS.

Melita (mod. Malta), island in the Mediterranean, colonized by Phoenicians in the 8th or 7th century B.C. and became subject to Carthage in the 6th century. Owing to the heavy taxes imposed by Carthage to help meet her needs during the second Punic war, the island surrendered voluntarily to Rome and was granted the privileges of a *municipium* (q.v.). Malta produced a fine cloth in Roman times, but is more celebrated in Christian history as the scene of St Paul's shipwreck (Acts xxvii).

Melitēnē (mod. Malatya), town of eastern Cappadocia, on a small tributary of the Euphrates. Under Titus it was headquarters of Legio XII Fulminata. Trajan raised it to the rank of a city, and it became the capital of Armenia Minor.

Mēlos, island of the Sporades (q.v.), occupied in the 8th century B.C. by Dorians from Laconia, though there is evidence of a Bronze Age settlement. Some of its ships fought at Salamis (480 B.C.); but it did not join the Delian League (q.v.), and professed neutrality during the Peloponnesian war. In 416 B.C., however, it was attacked by an Athenian force: all the adult males were killed, the women and children reduced to slavery, and 500 Athenian colonists were settled there. Excavation has yielded a Roman theatre and many fine works of art, including the statue of Aphrodite now in the Louvre and known as the 'Venus of Milo'.

Melos was important for certain natural products: alum, Melian earth (used in the manufacture of pigments), but above all obsidian, of which it was the chief source for the whole Aegean area.

Memnōn, in Greek legend, son of Eos (Dawn) and Tithonus, King of the Æthiopians. He fought for his uncle, Priam of Troy, against the Greeks, but after heroic exploits was slain by Achilles. Memnon has been identified with the Egyptian pharaoh Amenhotep III, whose colossal statue near Thebes is still standing. It was supposed to give forth musical sounds at dawn when touched by the sun's rays. *See* Quintus Smyrnaeus, *Posthomerica*, ii; G. Rawlinson on Herodotus, iii. 254; Sir J. G. Frazer on Pausanias, i. 42; J. E. B. Mayor on Juvenal, xv. 5.

Menander (Gk Menandros), Athenian poet of the New Comedy; born 342, and drowned while swimming in the harbour of Peiraeus 292 B.C., Menander is said to have written over one hundred comedies: most of what has survived was discovered at Oxyrhynchus in the first decade of the present century, before which time he was known almost exclusively through Latin adaptations. The *corpus* of Menandrian fragments then consisted of portions of seven plays. In three cases it was possible to make out the plot in some detail, while in the case of one (*Epitrepontes*) as much as 700 lines had been found. *See* text and translation by F. G. Allinson in the Loeb Library; *see also* J. U. Powell and E. A. Barber, *New Chapters in Greek Literature*, 1st and 2nd series, 1921, 1929.

In 1958, however, the complete text of *Dyscolus* (Misanthrope) was discovered by Prof. Victor Martin among the Egyptian papyri in the private library of Martin Bodmer at Colgny, near Geneva. *See* the edition by E. Handley, 1965; translation (*The Bad-tempered Man or The Misanthrope*) by P. Vellacott, 1960.

Through his Roman disciples Menander has transmitted an abiding influence. It can be traced in Shakespeare and more clearly in Ben Jonson; it is powerful in the dramatists of the English Restoration and the Comédie Française, and it is still very apparent in the school of Goldsmith and Sheridan. Indeed Menander is the fountainhead of the whole modern comedy of manners.

Menapii, a people inhabiting the north of Gallia Belgica in the time of Caesar, against whom they joined the Belgic conspiracy in 57 B.C., and contributed a force of 7,000 men. Some years before Caesar's arrival in Gaul they had occupied both banks of the Rhine, near its mouth, but had been driven from the right bank by the Usipetes and Tencteri.

Mendē, an Eretrian colony on the Macedonian promontory of Pallene (*see* CHALCIDICE). It exported a good wine.

Menedemus (-dēmos), Greek philosopher of the late 4th and early 3rd century B.C.; a native of Eretria, which gave its name to his school. Having been in turn a tent-maker and a soldier, he is said to have met Phaedon (q.v.). He abandoned the military life and became a student of Phaedon, whose academy he subsequently transferred to Eretria. Having taken an active part in the affairs of his city, he fell into disfavour through his intrigues with Antigonus Gonatas, at whose court he is supposed to have starved himself to death (*c.* 276 B.C.).

Menelaus (-os), King of Sparta, brother of Agamemnon, husband of Helen (*see* ATREIDS), and father of Hermione (q.v.). The rape of Helen (q.v.) was the immediate cause of the Trojan War (q.v.), during which Menelaus took no very distinguished part. As soon as Troy was taken, Menelaus, with Odysseus, went to the house of Deiphobus (q.v.), recovered Helen and started almost at once for home. Owing to a succession of misfortunes the journey took him eight years, and might have taken longer had not Proteus (q.v.) revealed to him the means of appeasing the gods. Having returned to Sparta, Menelaus and Helen lived peacefully together until they were translated by Zeus to Elysium (q.v.). Their tombs were shown at Therapnae (q.v.), where they were worshipped jointly with the Dioscuri (q.v.).

Menippus (-os), Greek cynic philosopher and satirist of the mid 3rd century B.C., born at Gadara in Coele-Syria. Originally a slave, he set up as a money-lender and made a fortune; this, however, he lost, and committed suicide. His satires, written in a mixture of verse and prose, served as a model for those of M. Terentius Varro (q.v.), who called them *Saturae Menippeae*. Nothing of Menippus's own work has survived.

Menoeceus (Menoikeus), son of Creon and nephew of Jocasta. He committed suicide because Tiresias (q.v.) had declared that his death would bring victory to his city in the war of the Seven against Thebes (*see* THEBAN, LEGEND, 3). He must be distinguished from his grandfather, who bore the same name but was grandson of Pentheus (q.v.) and father of Jocasta.

Mentōr: 1. Friend of Odysseus and tutor of his son Telemachus (q.v.). His name has become proverbial for one who is considered an unfailing and reliable adviser. It was in the guise of Mentor that Athena often appeared to Telemachus.

2. Greek silver-chaser (*fl. c.* 360 B.C.), whose vases and cups were highly prized at Rome.

Mercenaries, War of the. At the end of the first Punic war (*see* CARTHAGE; PUNIC WARS) the Carthaginians wished to disband their forces, a large majority of whom were foreign mercenaries. But these mercenaries demanded their arrears of pay and were refused. They pillaged the suburbs of Carthage and invested the city itself. The siege was raised by Hamilcar Barca (q.v.), and the rebellious troops were destroyed in the defile of the Axe. This campaign against the mercenaries is the theme of Flaubert's *Salammbô*.

Mercurius (Eng. Mercury), Roman god of commerce and gain. A temple near the Circus Maximus was dedicated to him. His festival was celebrated on 25th May by the *mercuriales*, members of a college regulating the corn trade. Mercury was often, though not universally, identified with the Greek Hermes (q.v.), to whom in fact he bore only the slightest resemblance. His temple at Rome was between the Circus Maximus and the Aventine. A 21-in. bronze Mercury has been recovered from the site of an exceptionally large Roman temple near Camulodunum (Colchester).

Meropē: 1. Wife of Cresphontes.

2. Daughter of Atlas and wife of Sisyphus. One of the Pleiades (q.v.), she was identified with the faintest star of the cluster, being said to hide her light from shame at having married a mortal.

Mesēmbria, city of Thrace on the Pontus Euxinus, founded in the 7th century B.C. by colonists from Byzantium and Chalcedon. It is sometimes described as a colony of Megara, because the two former cities were themselves Megarian settlements.

Messala, Marcus Valerius Maximus Corvinus: 1. Consul 263 B.C., when he carried on war against the Carthaginians in Sicily, and received the *cognomen* Messala for his relief of Messana.

2. Fought on the republican side at the battle of Philippi (42 B.C.), but was afterwards pardoned by the triumvirs, and became one of the chief generals and closest friends of Augustus. He was consul 31, and governor of Aquitania 28–27 B.C. He died in A.D. 8. Messala was a patron of learning, and was himself an historian, a poet, a grammarian and an orator, but none of his works has survived. His friendship for Horace and his intimacy with Tibullus are well known. In the elegies of the latter poet the name of Messala frequently occurs.

Messalina, Valeria, third wife of the emperor Claudius and mother of Britannicus. Renowned for her unspeakable debauchery, she fell in love with young Gaius Silius, 'best and fairest of a patrician house', and obliged him to bring ruin upon himself by 'marrying' her in a public ceremony. This outrage, however, was the woman's own undoing: Narcissus (q.v.), the emperor's freedman and secretary, persuaded Claudius to have her put to death (A.D. 48). *See* Tacitus, *Annales*, xi. 12, 26 ff., 33–7; Juvenal, vi. 115–32; x. 329–45.

Messana (Gk Messēnē, formerly Zancle; mod. Messina), city on the east coast of Sicily, on the straits to which it gives its name; birthplace of Dichaearchus and Euhemerus (qq.v.). Zancle ('sickle', from the shape of its harbour) was settled early in the 8th century B.C. by colonists from Cumae and Chalcis. About 494 B.C. some Samian and Milesian refugees, who had come to Regium (q.v.) after the capture of Miletus (q.v.) by the Persians, assisted Anaxilas to obtain possession of Zancle, the name of which was now changed to Messene because Anaxilas was a native of Messene (q.v.) in Peloponnesus or of Messenian descent. In 397 B.C. the city was captured and destroyed by the Carthaginians, but was quickly retaken and rebuilt by Dionysius I of Syracuse. Nevertheless it supported Carthage against Agathocles (q.v.), after whose death it was seized (288 B.C.) by the Mamertines from southern Italy. These people were defeated by Hieron II (q.v.) of Syracuse in 270. Carthage came to their rescue and occupied the citadel; but in 264 the Mamertines invoked the aid of Rome against a renewed attack by Hiero, and the Romans took this opportunity to secure a long-desired foothold in Sicily. Thus the 'affair of the Mamertines' became the *casus belli* of the first Punic war (*see* PUNIC WARS), at the end of which Messana (such is the Latin form of 'Messene') was made a free and allied city. It came within the province of Sicily in 211 B.C.; supported Sextus Pompeius (q.v.) against Caesar; was sacked by Octavian's forces in 35 B.C.; but continued under the empire to flourish as a commercial port.

Messapii, a tribe inhabiting the 'heel' of Italy, which was called variously Messapia, Calabria and Iapygia. They inflicted a serious defeat on Tarentum in 473 B.C.

Messēnē, capital city of Messenia (q.v.), founded in 369 B.C. by the Theban and Argive armies under Epameinondas (q.v.), together with some Messenian exiles, with Mt Ithome as its acropolis. Pausanias describes the city in detail. There are impressive remains of the walls, the theatre, the stadium, the bouleuterion and the gateway of the agora. *See* Sir J. G. Frazer, *Pausanias's Description of Greece*, iii.

Messēnia or **Messēnē,** south-western district of Peloponnesus. Homer represents the western part of the country as ruled by Nestor (q.v.) from Pylos, the eastern part as subject to Menelaus (q.v.). On the conquest of Peloponnesus by the Dorians (q.v.), Messenia fell to Cresphontes. It was more fertile than Laconia, and the Spartans soon coveted the territory. There followed three 'Messenian wars'. The first was said to have lasted for about twenty years (743–724). Despite a gallant resistance on the part of their king Aristodemus, the Messenians were obliged to submit. After bearing the Spartan yoke for thirty-nine years, according to ancient historians, the second war (685–666) broke out, the Messenians taking arms under their king Aristomenes (q.v.; *see also* ITHOME). Once again the country was subjugated; most of the population emigrated, and those who stayed behind were reduced to the condition of helots (q.v.). In this state they remained until 464 B.C., when they and other helots, taking advantage of the devastation caused by an earthquake at Sparta, revolted. The result of this third Messenian war (463–456) was that the Messenians surrendered a third time; but they were allowed safe passage out of the country and were settled by the Athenians at Naupactus (456). After the overthrow of Sparta at Leuctra and the foundation of Messene (q.v.) the country remained independent until 146 B.C. when it became subject to Rome.

Metaneira, wife of Celeus and mother of Triptolemus (qq.v.).

Metapontum (Gk Metapontion), a Greek coastal city in Lucania, near the mouth of the River Bradanus about 24 miles from Tarentum; founded from Sybaris and Croton *c.* 700 B.C. Here Pythagoras was said to have died in 497 B.C. Taken by the Romans with other cities of Magna Graecia in the war against Pyrrhus, it revolted to Hannibal after Cannae (216) and the inhabitants followed his retreat in 207 B.C. The city soon fell into ruins.

Metaurus, river in Umbria, flowing into the Adriatic near Fanum Fortunae. On its banks Hasdrubal (*see* HASDRUBAL, 2) was defeated by the consuls M. Livius Salinator and C. Claudius Nero in 207 B.C.

Metellus, plebeian family of the *gens* Caecilia.

1. LUCIUS CAECILIUS METELLUS, consul in 251 B.C. when he defeated a large Carthaginian force led by Hasdrubal at Panormus in Sicily. Consul a second time in 247, he was afterwards pontifex maximus. The story that he lost his sight while rescuing the Palladium (q.v.) from a fire in the temple of Vesta (241 B.C.) is not well supported.

2. QUINTUS CAECILIUS METELLUS MACEDONICUS, grandson of the preceding, was praetor in 148 B.C., when he defeated the pretender Andriscus (q.v.) in Macedonia and supervised that country's organization as a Roman province. In 146, while engaged in a successful campaign against the Achaean League, he was superseded by L. Mummius (q.v.); but on his return to Italy he celebrated a triumph and received the surname Macedonicus. As consul in 143 B.C. he subdued the Celtiberi (q.v.). He built the temples of Jupiter Stator and Juno Regina at Rome. Died in 115 B.C.

3. QUINTUS CAECILIUS METELLUS NUMIDICUS, nephew of the preceding and one of the leaders of the aristocratic party. As consul in 109 B.C. he commanded successfully against Jugurtha (q.v.), but was superseded by Marius (q.v.) in 107 when he celebrated a triumph (q.v.) and received the added surname Numidicus. Censor in 100 B.C., he tried to remove from the senate L. Appuleius Saturninus (q.v.). The latter, inspired by Marius, passed an agrarian law which required from all senators an oath to observe its provisions. Metellus refused and went into exile. After the death of Saturninus he returned (99 B.C.), and died about eight years later.

4. QUINTUS CAECILIUS METELLUS PIUS, son of the preceding, called 'Pius' because of his devotion to his father when the latter was in exile. Praetor in 89 B.C. he was one of the commanders in the Social War (q.v.). He subsequently fought as one of Sulla's generals, and was consul with Sulla himself in 80 B.C. In the following year he went as

proconsul to Spain where he opposed Sertorius (q.v.) until 72. In 71 he returned to Rome, celebrated a triumph and became pontifex maximus. Died 64 B.C., when he was succeeded as pontifex maximus by Julius Caesar.

5. QUINTUS CAECILIUS METELLUS PIUS SCIPIO, adoptive son of the preceding, son of P. Scipio Nasica. Pompey, who had married his daughter Cornelia, had Metellus Scipio elected as his colleague in the consulship (52 B.C.), and it was Metellus who, in 50 B.C., proposed in the senate that Caesar should disband his army or be declared a public enemy. On the outbreak of civil war (49 B.C.) he was appointed governor of Syria, and in 48 commanded the Pompeian centre at Pharsalus. From there he crossed to Africa, but was defeated by Caesar at Thapsus (q.v.) in 46 and committed suicide.

6. QUINTUS CAECILIUS METELLUS CRETICUS, grandson of Macedonicus (No. 2 above). Consul in 69 B.C., he commanded in the war against Crete (q.v.), which was the headquarters of the Mediterranean pirates. He subdued the island in three years, celebrated a triumph and was given the surname Creticus.

7. LUCIUS CAECILIUS METELLUS, brother of the preceding, was praetor in 71 B.C., and in the following year succeeded Verres (q.v.) as governor of Sicily.

8. M. CAECILIUS METELLUS, first cousin of the preceding. As praetor in 69 B.C. he presided at the trial of Verres (q.v.).

Methōnē, town of Macedonia on the Thermaic Gulf, founded from Eretria. It was while besieging Methone that Philip II lost an eye (*see* ASTER OF AMPHIPOLIS).

Methymna (-umnē), second city of Lesbos (q.v.), celebrated for its wine; birth-place of Arion (q.v.). During the Peloponnesian war it remained faithful to Athens, even during the Lesbian revolt, and was sacked by the Spartans in 406 B.C.

Metic (Gk *metoikos*), resident alien in a Greek city-state. Though obliged to pay certain taxes, and though special privileges were sometimes granted to individuals, the metic generally had no citizen rights; he could neither vote nor hold office; nor could he transact legal business except through the medium of a patron (*see* PROSTATES). *See* M. Clerc, *Les Métiques Athéniens*, 1893; A. E. Zimmern, *The Greek Commonwealth*, 1931.

Mētis, in Greek mythology, the personification of Counsel, daughter of Oceanus and Tethys. Another legend makes her the first wife of Zeus, who, fearful lest she should bear a child wiser than herself, devoured her in the first month of her pregnancy. Later there sprang from his head, full grown, Athena (q.v.).

Metōn (*fl.* 432 B.C.), Athenian astronomer who is said by Diodorus Siculus (q.v.) to have discovered the 'Metonic' or lunar cycle of nineteen years. This, however, is doubtful, seeing that the first attested use of the period in Greece was in 342 B.C.

Metrodorus (-dōros): 1. Greek philosopher of the Atomistic school, a pupil of Democritus (q.v.). While professing to accept the latter's cosmological theories, he believed (or perhaps pulled a contemporary leg by pretending to believe) that the stars are formed from day to day by the sun's heat out of moisture in the air. Metrodorus was author of a work *On Nature*, which, according to Cicero (*Acad.* ii. 23, 73), opened with the frank admission that 'we know nothing, even whether or not we know', and followed the view of Protagoras (q.v.) that 'man is the measure of all things'.

2. Greek philosopher of the Epicurean school, born at Lampsacus in 330 B.C. Though he was one of the four principal exponents of Epicureanism, the surviving fragments of his work appear to confirm the judgment of Epicurus (q.v.) that he was not an original thinker. He died in 277 B.C.

Mevania (mod. Bevagna), town of Umbria on the River Tinea, celebrated for a breed of white oxen. According to some it was the birth-place of Propertius (q.v.).

Micipsa, King of Numidia 148–118 B.C., eldest son and successor of Masinissa (q.v.), and uncle of Jugurtha (q.v.).

Micon (-kōn), an Athenian painter and sculptor, *fl. c.* 460 B.C. He painted an 'Amazonomachy' in the Stoa Poikile (q.v.).

Midas, in Greek legend, son of Gordius (q.v.) and a king of Phrygia. Having placed Dionysus under obligation by his kindly treatment of Silenus (q.v.), he was promised by the god fulfilment of any one favour he chose to ask. Midas requested that all he touched might turn to gold; and so it did—even his food. He prayed relief from this embarrassing situation, and was ordered by Dionysus to bathe in the sources of the River Pactolus, near Tmolus. The king was saved, but the sands of Pactolus became gold-bearing (*see* PACTOLUS).

Another story related that Midas, chosen to umpire a musical contest between Apollo and Pan, decided in favour of the latter. Apollo thereupon changed his ears into those of an ass. Midas contrived to hide the disfigurement beneath his tall Phrygian cap; not, however, from his barber. The terrible secret so harassed this poor man that he dug a hole and whispered into it: 'King Midas has ass's ears.' He then filled up the hole, feeling much relieved. But alas, a reed grew on the spot, whose whispering betrayed the secret.

Mideia or **Midea** (mod. Dendra), hill town of Argolis, five and a half miles north-east of Argos; destroyed by the latter, probably at the same time as Tiryns, 468 B.C. Remains of a Mycenean city have been excavated.

Milanion (Meilaniōn), in Arcadian legend, the successful suitor of Atalanta (q.v.).

Miletus (-ētos), city of Asia Minor, near the mouth of the Maeander, famous for its woollen fabrics known as *Milesia vellera*. It belonged territorially to Caria but politically to Ionia (qq.v.), being the southernmost of the twelve cities of the Ionian confederacy. Its geographical situation, together with its four harbours, gave it commercial power; and by the middle of the 7th century B.C. it had founded or helped to found more than sixty cities on the shores of the Hellespont, the Propontis and the Euxine. Miletus was also the earliest home of Greek philosophy, birth-place of Thales, Anaximander and Anaximenes (qq.v.).

Miletus, with other Greek cities of Asia Minor, passed from Lydian to Persian overlordship when Darius Hystaspis overthrew the empire of Croesus (546 B.C.). It led the Ionian revolt at the suppression of which it was sacked by the Persian forces (494 B.C.; *see also* PHRY-NICUS, 1). Freed in 479, it joined the Delian League (q.v.), but revolted to Sparta in 412. In 334 B.C. it was besieged and almost destroyed by Alexander the Great, but recovered and retained some commercial importance. During the hellenistic and Roman periods its harbours were gradually silted up by the Maeander, and it yielded pride of place as a maritime city to Ephesus. There are considerable remains.

Millearium Aureum, 'golden milestone', a column erected by Augustus in the Forum at Rome. Sheathed in gilt bronze, it was inscribed with the names and distances of the principal towns situated on the highways which radiated from the thirty-seven gates of the city. A fragment survives.

Milo, Titus Annius, Roman politician, a native of Lanuvium. As tribune of the plebs in 57 B.C. he took an active part in the recall of Cicero from exile. In 53 he was a candidate for the consulship while P. Clodius (q.v.) stood for the praetorship. The two men were bitter enemies; each kept a gang of thugs who fought one another in the streets of Rome. At length, on 12th January 52 B.C., they met (it seems by accident) at Bovillae; an affray ensued between their followers, and Clodius was killed. At Rome such tumults followed that Pompey was appointed sole consul to restore order. Milo was brought to trial and defended by Cicero (*Pro Milone*), but he was convicted and went into exile at Massilia. He returned to Italy in 48 B.C. in order to support the revolutionary schemes of the praetor M. Caelius, but was taken and put to death at Cosa.

Milōn (6th century B.C.), Greek athlete, born at Croton in Magna Graecia. He was six times victor in wrestling at the Olympic games, and as often at the Pythian. Many stories were told of his enormous strength. Thus he was said to have carried a live ox on his shoulders a distance of 120 yards, to have killed it with a blow of his fist, and to have eaten all its flesh at a single meal. Another tradition stated that when he had grown old he was passing one day through a forest when he saw a tree whose trunk was split. Wishing to try his strength, he attempted to force the two prongs apart; but they closed on his hands, and he was devoured by wild beasts. The death of Milon is the subject of a remarkable statue by Pierre Puget in the Louvre.

Miltiadēs, Athenian general and statesman, son of Cimon, and nephew of another Miltiades, who had made himself tyrant of the Thracian Chersonnese. When the tyranny became vacant, Miltiades was sent out by Hippias (successor of Peisistratus) to take possession of the territory on behalf of Athens. He joined Dareios I (q.v.) on his Scythian expedition (513 B.C.), was left with other Greeks in charge of the bridge over the Danube, and afterwards claimed to have advocated its destruction before the Persian army could return (*see* HISTIAEUS). After the suppression of the Ionian revolt Miltiades fled to Athens (493), and when Greece was invaded (490) by the Persians under Datis and Artaphernes, Miltiades was chosen one of the ten generals (*strategoi*). Before Marathon, the opinions of these ten were equally divided, and it was Miltiades who induced the polemarch Callimachus to give his casting vote in favour of battle, and it was he who actually commanded the Athenian army on that most glorious occasion.

After the victory of Marathon, Miltiades persuaded the Athenians to entrust him with a fleet of seventy ships to be used at his discretion, and he used it for an attack on the island of Paros to gratify a private grudge. After receiving a dangerous wound in the leg, he was compelled to raise the siege and return to Athens, where he was impeached by Xanthippus for having deceived the people. His wound had turned gangrenous; he was carried into court on a couch, and the defence was conducted by his brother Tisagoras. Miltiades was condemned, but on the grounds of his great services to the state the supreme penalty was commuted to a fine of fifty talents. Unable to pay, he was thrown into prison, where he died soon afterwards (489). The fine was later paid by Callias, who had married his daughter Elpinike (*see also* CIMON). *See* H. Berve, *Miltiades*, 1937.

Mimnermus (-os), Greek elegiac poet of the 7th century B.C., a native of Colophon. He was the first to use elegiac verse as a vehicle of mourning and erotic sentiment. Only a few fragments (about eight lines in all) survive.

Minerva, Roman goddess of wisdom and good counsel, identified with the Greek Pallas Athena, worshipped with Jupiter and Juno in the Capitol. Her festival, *quinquatrus*, began on 19th March and lasted five days. A carved image of her, called the Palladium (q.v.), supposed to have been brought from Troy by Aeneas, was kept in the temple of Vesta. *See* A. Warde Fowler, *Roman Festivals*, 1908.

Minōs, in Greek mythology, King of Crete, son of Zeus by Europa, and brother of Rhadamanthus. Such was his wisdom and justice that after death he was appointed one of the judges in Hades (*Odyssey*, xi. 568). Only in Attic legend is he of evil repute, due perhaps to an old feud with Crete. He was husband of Pasiphaë (q.v.), and father of Androgeos, Ariadne and Phaedra (qq.v.). *See also* THESEUS. When Daedalus (q.v.) fled from Crete he was pursued by Minos, who, on reaching Sicily, was drowned in boiling water by the daughters of Cocalus (q.v.).

Minotaur, a mythical monster, offspring of Pasiphaë (q.v.) and a bull. He was part man, part bull, and was kept by Minos (q.v.) in a labyrinth at Knossos, where he was slain by Theseus (q.v.).

Minturnae, town of Latium, colonized by the Romans, together with Sinuessa, in 295 B.C. In the neighbourhood were marshes, formed by the River Liris, where Marius (q.v.) sought refuge and was taken prisoner. The forum and citadel have been excavated.

Minyae (Minuae), a legendary Greek people, originating in Thessaly, whence their eponymous hero Minyas (q.v.) migrated to Boeotia, and established the empire of the Minyae with its capital at Orchomenus (q.v.). They were also believed to have settled in the islands of Lemnos and Thera, as well as in the south of Elis (Triphylia).

Minyas, in Greek legend, a Thessalian, eponymous ancestor of the Minyae (q.v.). All but one of his daughters were turned into bats for having slighted the worship of Dionysus.

Misenum, port in Campania, about three miles south of Baiae (q.v.). Under the republic it was a villa resort; but in 31 B.C. M. Vipsanius Agrippa (q.v.) made it the chief naval base of the Mediterranean fleet, a position which it continued to hold under the empire.

Mithradates or **Mithridates**, name of many oriental kings in the hellenistic and Roman periods, by far the most celebrated of whom was Mithradates VII, surnamed the Great, of Pontus (q.v.) in Asia Minor. A man of great ability and unflagging energy, he is said to have learnt more than twenty languages. It is also related that when quite young and the continual object of hostile court intrigue, he studied the properties of venomous plants to such good effect that by repeatedly taking very small doses he rendered himself immune from poison.

Mithradates became king in 120 B.C., and at once set about strengthening and enlarging his dominions, until he was ready to pit his force against the might of Rome. In 88 B.C. he drove Ariobarzanes from the kingdom of Cappadocia and Nicomedes IV from that of Bithynia. By the winter of that year he was master of the Roman province of Asia, and proceeded to order a general massacre of Italians, in which no fewer than 80,000 persons are said to have died. Meanwhile Sulla (q.v.) had received command of the war. He crossed into Greece (87), and twice defeated Mithradates's general Archelaus in Boeotia (86), while the king himself was outmanœuvred by C. Flavius Fimbria in Asia. Mithradates now sued for peace, which was granted him by Sulla in 84 B.C. Hostilities were renewed in 83–82 B.C. through the unprovoked aggression of Murena (*see* MURENA, LUCIUS LICINIUS, 1), who was defeated. Sulla, however, intervened and peace was restored.

The third Mithradatic war (74–63 B.C.) was precipitated by the king's seizure of Bithynia, which had lately been bequeathed to the Roman people by Nicomedes IV, Philopator (q.v.). The Roman command was entrusted to L. Licinius Lucullus (q.v.), whose operations were entirely successful. In 73 he relieved Cyzicus, and during the next two years drove Mithradates from Pontus, compelling him to take refuge with his son-in-law Tigranes (q.v.), King of Armenia. Lucullus then marched into Armenia, defeated Tigranes in two battles (69 and 68) and occupied his capital, Tigranocerta. Unfortunately his troops mutinied; he could not follow up these victories, and was superseded first by M. Acilius Glabrio (67) and then by Pompey (66). Meanwhile Mithradates had regained Pontus; but he was overwhelmed by Pompey. Tigranes would not receive him; so he moved into Colchis and thence to Panticapaeum in Chersonesus Taurica (*see* BOSPORUS). From here he planned to march round the north and west coasts of the Euxine, and to invade Italy at the head of barbarian hordes. But disaffection was rife among his followers: before he could move, his own son Pharnaces rebelled, supported by the army and by the citizens of Panticapaeum. Mithradates committed suicide (63 B.C.).

Mithras or **Mithra,** an ancient Aryan god of light, whom the Zoroastrians conceived of as a champion of Ahura-Mazda in his eternal conflict with Ahriman, the prince of evil. His cult spread over most of Asia Minor, and, according to Plutarch, was introduced at Rome by Pompey's pirate captives in 68 B.C. Its shrines have been found wherever the Roman legions went. A temple of Mithras, with some beautiful statuary illustrative of the cult, was excavated in London in 1953, and is preserved there (*see* LONDINIUM). Mithras, naturally, was closely associated with Helios, the sun-god. He is often represented as a beautiful youth driving a sword into the neck of a prostrate bull which at the same time is being bitten by a scorpion, a crab and a dog, illustrative of some cosmic myth. Mithraism's most striking ceremony was the blood baptism called Taurobolium. What is extant of its ritual suggests the existence of an organized hierarchy and a worship assimilated to the Greek mysteries (see MYSTERIES). In the struggle of Paganism with Christianity Mithraism exercised a powerful attraction, being a pure and elevated religion, and though at first a form of sun worship, it became modified by syncretism. See F. Cumont, Textes et monuments figurés relatifs aux mystères de Mithras, 2 vols., 1896–9.

Mithridates, see MITHRADATES.

Mnemosyne (Mnēmosunē), 'memory', mother of the Muses (q.v.).

Mnesicles (Mnēsiklēs), Greek architect who designed the Propylaea (q.v.) at Athens.

Moesia, district of eastern Europe, bounded south by Thrace and Macedonia, west by Illyricum and Pannonia, north by the Danube and east by the Euxine. It thus corresponded roughly to modern Serbia and Bulgaria. The inhabitants were a Thracian people, who were finally subdued c. 25 B.C. by Roman forces under M. Licinius Crassus, grandson of the triumvir. The country was organized as a province of the empire shortly before the death of Augustus. Domitian divided it into two, Moesia Superior and Inferior, being the western and eastern halves respectively, divided by the River Cebrus. Moesia was invaded by the Goths in A.D. 250, and when Aurelian surrendered Dacia (q.v.) to the barbarians and moved its inhabitants south of the Danube, the central region of Moesia was called Dacia Aureliani. See Th. Mommsen, Provinces of the Roman Empire, 1886.

Moguntiacum (mod. Mainz), town on the left bank of the Rhine, originating in a fortified camp erected here by Drusus (see DRUSUS, NERO CLAUDIUS) c. 13 B.C. A small fort called 'castellum Mattiadorum' was built on the opposite bank, and connected with the camp by a bridge at the beginning of the 1st century A.D. A town grew up around the camp and became capital of Germania Superior (see GERMANIA).

Moirae (-ai), called in Latin **Parcae,** the Fates. They were three in number. Sometimes they appear as goddesses of fate in the strict sense, and are depicted with sceptres or staves, the symbol of dominion. More often, however, they are conceived as divinities allegorical of the duration of human life. In this capacity Lachesis assigns to a man his term, Clotho spins the thread of his existence and Atropos breaks that thread. See W. C. Greene, Moira, 1944.

Molōn, see APOLLONIUS, 2.

Molossi, a people of Epirus (q.v.), inhabiting a narrow strip of country along the west bank of the Arachthus as far as the Ambracian Gulf. C. 342 B.C. their ruler, a brother of Olympias (q.v.), was made King of Epirus and took the name Alexander (see ALEXANDER, (A) 1). Molossian hunting hounds were famous in antiquity.

Momus (Mōmos), in Greek mythology the personification of fault-finding, represented by Hesiod as a son of Nyx (Night). In an Aesopic fable he complains of a house that it has no wheels to facilitate movement from place to place, of a bull that its horns are above eye level and therefore out of sight when in use, and of a man that he has no window in his breast to afford a view of his most secret thoughts and feelings.

Mona, the island of Anglesey, off the north-west coast of Wales. Raided by Suetonius Paulinus *c.* A.D. 60, it was conquered about twenty years later by Agricola. There were copper mines in the island.

Moneta (whence Eng. 'mint', 'money'), in Roman mythology, a title of Juno (q.v.) as patron of state finances. The temple of Juno Moneta on the Capitoline hill at Rome contained the mint.

Monoeci Portus (mod. Monaco), port on the coast of Liguria, founded from Massalia. The name was apparently derived from a temple of Herakles Monoikos which was situated on the promontory, and later Latin writers often call the place Portus Herculis.

Monumentum Ancyranum. When the emperor Augustus, then in his 77th year, recorded the principal events of his reign on bronze tablets at Rome, the citizens of Ancyra (q.v.) had a copy made in both Latin and Greek, carved on marble blocks and placed in the temple of Rome and Augustus. This inscription, discovered in 1555, is known as the 'Monumentum Ancyranum'. Its unique interest lies in the fact of its giving us, in his own words, the dying statement of the empire's founder. The record is fourfold: (1) a short summary of the 'deeds done' (largely military) between 44 and 28 B.C.; (2) domestic administration and constitutional changes, together with such public acts as triumphs, thanksgivings, honours and titles given or bestowed; (3) financial matters, e.g. sums expended on public works (aqueducts, roads, temples, etc.), pensions and allowances to discharged soldiers, grants of corn to the citizens of Rome, and costs of gladiatorial and other shows; (4) mainly political and diplomatic. *See* the edition by J. Gagé, 1934.

Mopsus (-os), in Greek legend, name of two seers:

1. Son of Ampyx by the nymph Chloris. He was soothsayer of the Argonauts (q.v.), and died of snake-bite in Libya.

2. Son of Apollo and Manto, daughter of Tiresias. He contended in prophecy with Calchas (q.v.) at Claros and worsted him. Together with Amphilochus (q.v.) he founded Mallos in Cilicia; but a dispute arose between them, and they slew one another.

Morini, a Gallic people inhabiting coastal territory between the modern French department of Pas de Calais and the mouth of the Scheldt. They contributed 25,000 men to the Belgic rising against Caesar in 57 B.C.

Morpheus, in Greek mythology, son of Hypnos (q.v.) and bringer of dreams. The name means 'shaper', 'fashioner', 'moulder'.

Mors, *see* THANATOS.

Moschus (-khos), Greek bucolic poet, born at Syracuse and *fl. c.* 150 B.C. Some of his pieces have survived, notably a short epic entitled *Europa* and an epigram on *Love, the Runaway*. There is a text with translation in *The Greek Bucolic Poets* (Loeb Library), 1912, and a verse translation by A. S. Way, 1913.

Mothōnes, the sons of Spartiates (*see* SPARTA) by helot mothers (*see* HELOTS). They were free men who received the normal Spartan training, but lacked full citizen rights.

Mummius, Lucius, Roman general. As consul in 146 B.C. he ended the war with the Achaean League by the capture and destruction of Corinth (q.v.), for which he received the surname Achaicus. Socially an upstart, his plebeian origins are shown by his celebrated remark when ordering the removal of the Corinthian art treasures to Rome: 'If they are lost or damaged, you will have to replace them.' It has been suggested, however, that his abominable conduct in destroying and despoiling so great and glorious a city arose from pressure by a commercial group in the Roman senate.

Munda, town of Hispania Ulterior (*see* HISPANIA), probably situated on a hill just over five and a half miles west by north of modern Osuna. Here Caesar defeated the Pompeian forces on 17th March 45 B.C. See *De Bello Hispaniensi.*

Mundus: 1. Traditionally a pit marking the centre of Rome, dug by Romulus (q.v.) in the Comitium. Filled with earth and other offerings from the various districts from which his followers came, it was covered by an altar.

2. A ritual pit on an unknown site at Rome, supposed to give admission to the underworld and closed with a stone slab. It was opened three times a year to receive gifts in honour of the *di inferi.*

Municipium, a city or town subject to the authority of Rome, possessing Roman citizen rights, but governed by its own laws.

Munychia (Mounuchia), the smallest and most easterly of the three harbours of Athens. *See* ATHENS: *Peiraeus and the Long Walls.*

Murena, Lucius Licinius: 1. Left by Sulla as governor of Asia at the end of the first Mithradatic war (84 B.C.), his unprovoked aggression caused a revival of hostilities (83–82) in the course of which he was defeated. *See* MITHRADATES.

2. Son of the preceding. In 64 B.C. he and Cicero were elected consuls for the following year; but Murena was accused of bribery. The extant speech by Cicero (*Pro Murena*) secured his acquittal; he took office, and voted for the execution of the Catilinarian conspirators (*see* CATILINE; LENTULUS SURA).

Mus, Greek artist of the 5th century B.C. He engraved the battle of the Lapithae and Centaurs (qq.v.) on the shield carried by Pheidias's statue of Athena Promachos on the Acropolis at Athens.

Musa, Antonius, physician to the emperor Augustus, whom he treated with cold baths for gout—a revolutionary form of healing. Among his other patients were Agrippa, Maecenas, Virgil and Horace.

Musaeus (Mousaios), a semi-legendary personage, represented as one of the earliest Greek poets, whose verses had the authority of oracles. *See* ONOMACRITUS.

Muses (Gk Mousai; Lat. Musae), in mythology, the inspiring deities of song, daughters of Zeus and Mnemosyne, born in Pieria at the foot of Mt Olympus. They appear to have been originally three in number, but from Hesiod onwards are always represented as nine. The assignment of a different sphere of literature and science to each, with their respective symbols, dates from the late Roman period as follows:

(1) *Clio:* History; open scroll or chest of scrolls. (2) *Euterpe:* Lyric Poetry; flute. (3) *Thalia:* Comedy and Idyllic Poetry; comic mask, shepherd's staff or wreath of ivy. (4) *Melpomene:* Tragedy; tragic mask, staff of Heracles or sword. (5) *Terpsichore:* Choral Dance and Song; lyre and plectrum. (6) *Erato:* Erotic Poetry and Mime; lyre. (7) *Polyhymnia:* Hymn; no symbol, but pensive attitude. (8) *Urania:* Astronomy; staff pointing to globe. (9) *Calliope:* Epic; tablet and stylus.

The cult of the Muses was introduced from Thrace, first into Pieria, and thence to Parnassus, and Helicon (qq.v.). Sacrifices offered to them consisted of honey and libations of water or milk.

Museum (Mouseion), name originally applied to a temple of the Muses (q.v.), and at Athens to a small hill sacred to them, immediately south-west of the city wall. Later the name was used more generally of a literary or educational foundation, and particularly of that part of the palace at Alexandria (q.v.) where Ptolemy I, Soter, established the most outstanding scholars of the age (*c.* 280 B.C.). The Alexandrian Museum must be carefully distinguished from the library.

Mutina, town of Gallia Cisalpina (Cispadana), adjacent to but not coincident with the present city of Modena. Originally a town of the Boii (q.v.) it became subject to Rome *c.* 212 B.C. and was made a Roman colony (*see* COLONIA). M. Brutus held it against Pompey in 72, and D. Brutus against Mark Antony (*see* ANTONIUS, MARCUS, 3) in 44 B.C. In the following year Octavian defeated Antony before Mutina.

Mycale (Mukalē), mountain promontory of Caria, opposite the island of Samos. Here was a temple of Poseidon, headquarters of the Ionian League, and scene of its annual festival (Panionia). *See* IONIA. In 479 B.C. the Greek fleet under Leotychidas (q.v.) won a decisive naval victory over the Persians off Mycale. *See* PERSIAN WARS.

Mycenae (Mukēnai), one of the oldest cities of Greece, situated in Argolis about nine miles from Tiryns. Dating from the 3rd millennium B.C., it was one of the most important centres of the prehistoric Bronze Age civilization in mainland Greece, and may have been founded to protect the trade routes that passed overland to the Corinthian Gulf. Its culture must have exerted considerable influence upon that of the hellenic invaders of later centuries. But the history of Mycenae as represented by archaeological excavation lies outside the scope of this book. In legend it was the royal city of Agamemnon (q.v.). During the 5th century B.C. it was attacked by Argos, starved into surrender and finally ruined. *See* J. I. Manatt, *The Mycenaean Age,* 1899; A. J. B. Wace, *Mycenae,* 1949.

Mylae (Mulai), town on the north coast of Sicily, situated on a promontory off which Duilius (q.v.) defeated the Carthaginian fleet in 260 B.C., as did M. Vipsanius Agrippa (q.v.) that of Sextus Pompeius in 36 B.C. *See also* COLUMNA ROSTRATA.

Myrmidons (Murmidones), a legendary or semi-legendary people of Greece, originally inhabiting Aegina (q.v.), a part of whom followed Peleus (q.v.), father of Achilles (q.v.), to Phthiotis. In the *Iliad*

Achilles himself is King of the Myrmidons and their leader before
Troy.

Myron (Murōn), Greek sculptor, born at Eleutherae in Boeotia *c.*
480 B.C. He was a pupil of Ageladas, rival of Polycleitus (q.v.) and a
younger contemporary of Pheidias (q.v.). He worked mostly at
Athens. Copies of his 'Discobolus' and 'Marsyas' are at Rome. The
'Marsyas' was part of a group, 'Athena and Marsyas', of which a
copy was at Frankfurt before the Second World War. *See* E. A.
Gardner, *Six Greek Sculptors*, 1910.

Myrtilus (Murtilos), in Greek legend, son of Hermes and charioteer
of Oenomaus, King of Pisa. He was thrown into the sea by Pelops
(q.v.), and placed among the stars as Auriga.

Mysia (Mu-), district of north-west Asia Minor, bounded north-east
by Bithynia, north and west by the Propontis and Aegean Sea, south
by Lydia and Phrygia. The chief cities were Pergamum, Cyzicus,
Lampsacus, Abydos and Assos (qq.v.). The Mysians occur in the
Iliad as allies of Troy. In historical times the country was subject first
to the Lydian empire of Croesus, then to Persia, then to Alexander
and the Seleucids (q.v.) until after the defeat of Antiochus III in
190 B.C., when the Romans added it to the kingdom of Pergamum.
Finally, in 133 B.C., with the rest of that kingdom, it was included in
the Roman province of Asia.

Mysteries (Gk *Mustēria*) were secret cults practised by initiates
(*mustai*) in honour of certain gods, e.g. Dionysus (*see* ORPHISM),
Demeter and the Cabeiri (qq.v.). By far the most celebrated were the
Eleusinian, held in honour of Demeter at Eleusis (q.v.) in the month
Boedromion (*see* CHRONOLOGY). A procession along the Sacred Way
was followed the same evening by a performance of the solemn mystic
rites. So closely was the secret guarded that we know very little about
the ceremonial. Today the initiates might be accused of hypocrisy in
seeking ritual purification rather than moral perfection. But it must
be remembered that the mysteries kept alive the ideal of a more perfect life hereafter, and no doubt made their contribution to the idea
of union with the godhead, and thus to the specifically Christian ideal
of everlasting life. *See* P. Foucart, *Les Mystères d'Eleusis*, 1914;
M. P. Nilsson, *History of Greek Religion*, 2nd ed., 1949.

Mytilene (Mutilēnē), chief city of Lesbos (q.v.), situated on the
eastern side of the island, opposite the coast of Asia Minor. It was an
Aeolian settlement. Mytilene became a great naval power, and
founded colonies on the coasts of Mysia and Thrace. Early in the 7th
century B.C. a dispute as to the possession of one of these colonies,
Sigeum at the mouth of the Hellespont, led to a war with Athens,
which greatly weakened the power of Mytilene. The island became a
member of the Delian League (q.v.) after the Persian war, but in 428
it headed the Lesbian revolt. The entire male population was condemned to death, but immediately reprieved. Nevertheless more than
a thousand prisoners were put to death, the walls demolished and the
fleet confiscated (427 B.C.). The might of Mytilene was no more (*see*
Thucydides, iii. 1–50). It was made a free city by Pompey, thanks to
the good offices of his friend Theophanes, a native of the place.

N

Nabataei (-taioi), name given by Greek and Latin writers to an Arab people who occupied the territory afterwards known as Arabia Petraea (*see* ARABIA). As the Seleucid Empire declined they formed an independent kingdom, which eventually controlled all the borderland between Syria and Arabia from the Red Sea to the Euphrates. They sided with the Maccabees against the Seleucids, but the subsequent rivalry between them and the Judaean monarchs was largely responsible for Roman intervention in Palestine (65 B.C.). Petra (q.v.) was the Nabataean capital. *See also* ARETAS.

Nabis, tyrant of Sparta, noted for his cruelty. He succeeded Machanidas in 207 B.C., was defeated by Philopoemen and Flamininus (qq.v.) in 193, and was assassinated in the following year by some Aetolians.

Naevius, Gnaeus, Roman poet of the 3rd century B.C., important as having developed Roman low-life comedy, and as having invented historical drama. He produced his first play in 235 B.C., was later imprisoned for having attacked Scipio and the Metelli on the stage, but obtained his release by recanting. He was soon compelled to expiate a new offence by exile, and retired to Utica, where he died *c.* 201 B.C. Naevius was also the author of a poem on the first Punic war, the first Roman national epic, written in the old Saturnian metre. Only a few fragments of his works have survived. *See* E. H. Warmington, *Remains of Old Latin* (Loeb Library), vol. ii.

Naiads (Gk Naiades), nymphs (q.v.) of fresh water.

Naisus, Naïssus or **Naesus** (mod. Nish), town of Moesia Superior (*see* MOESIA), on an eastern tributary of the Margus; scene of the Gothic defeat by Claudius II in A.D. 269, and birth-place of Constantine the Great.

Napaeae (-paiai), nymphs (q.v.) of glens.

Narbo (mod. Narbonne) was originally the chief town of the Volcae Tectosages; subsequently capital of the Roman province Gallia Transalpina, and then, from the time of Augustus, of Gallia Narbonensis (*see* GALLIA). A Roman colony was established there in 118 B.C. (*see* REX, Q. MARCIUS, 2). As a port it soon rivalled Massilia. Narbo was birth-place of the emperors Carus, Carinus and Numerianus.

Narcissus (-kissos), in late Greek legend, son of the river-god Cephissus and Liriope. Having rejected the love of Echo (q.v.), he was caused by Nemesis to become enamoured of his own image reflected in the waters of a spring. He pined away (or threw himself in), and was changed into the flower that bears his name.

Narcissus (-kissos), Greek freedman and private secretary of the emperor Claudius (A.D. 41–54), who at his instigation put to death Messalina (q.v.). He amassed a huge fortune, and committed suicide by order of Agrippina the younger on the death of Claudius. *See* Tacitus, *Annals*, xi. 29 ff.

Narnia (mod. Narni), town of Umbria on the Via Flaminia (q.v.), birth-place of the emperor Nerva (q.v.); originally called Nequinum until its capture in 299 B.C. by the Romans, who planted a colony there. The town is situated on a lofty hill south of the River Nar, which is crossed, just below the town, by one of the finest bridges of antiquity.

Naucratis (-kratis), a Greek trading settlement in Egypt, founded from Miletus (q.v.) 640 B.C. It was situated on the western or Canopic mouth of the Nile, not far from Sais, and was celebrated for its pottery. The phil-hellene pharaoh Amasis (569–526 B.C.) did much to advance its prosperity, both by his gifts to the Greek shrines and by his making it the only place in Egypt where the Greeks might do business. Excavations carried out between 1884 and 1886 revealed the sites of many temples erected by representatives of Greek states and described by Herodotus.

Naumachia, a sea fight usually staged in the Roman amphitheatre, the arena of which was flooded for the occasion, or on an artificial lake. The combatants were prisoners of war or convicts, who often fought until one side was annihilated. In the celebrated *naumachia* staged by the emperor Claudius I on Lacus Fucinus (q.v.), no fewer than 100 ships and 19,000 men took part.

Naupactus (-ktos), modern Lepanto, a town of the Ozolian Locrians, having the best harbour on the north coast of the Corinthian Gulf. It was said to have been the place from which the Heraclidae and their Dorian allies crossed into Peloponnesus. After the Persian wars it became an Athenian possession, and there the Athenians settled the Messenians who were exiled after the third Messenian war (456 B.C.). *See* MESSENIA. During the Peloponnesian war Naupactus was an important naval base (*see* PHORMION). In 399 the Messenian settlers were expelled by the Spartans. Philip II of Macedon later restored the town to Athens.

Nauplius (-os), legendary king of Euboea. To revenge the death of his son Palamedes (q.v.), he watched for the Greek fleet returning from Troy, and by means of flares caused many of its ships to be wrecked on the promontory of Caphareus.

Nausicaa (-kaa), in Greek legend, daughter of Alcinoüs, King of the Phaeacians (q.v.) in Scheria. It was she who discovered Odysseus, when he was shipwrecked on the island, and brought him to her father's court. The episode is one of the finest things in Homer. See *Odyssey*, vi.

Navius, in Roman legend, an augur who opposed the project of Tarquinius Priscus to double the number of equestrian centuries. Tarquinius bade him: 'Tell me whether that of which I am now thinking can be done.' The king held out a whetstone and razor, whereupon Navius took them and cut the stone clean in half.

Naxos: 1. Island of the Cyclades, famous for its wine and a centre of the worship of Dionysus. Here too Dionysus was said to have found Ariadne after her desertion by Theseus. Captured by the Persians in 490, it contributed four ships to the fleet of Xerxes (480 B.C.), but these deserted to the Greeks at Salamis. After the Persian wars Naxos became a member of the Delian League (q.v.); but it revolted in 471, was captured by Athens and remained directly subject to her until after the Peloponnesian war.

2. Greek city of Sicily, founded from Chalcis in 735 B.C. In 403 B.C. it was destroyed by Dionysius I of Syracuse, but the refugees were brought together at Tauromenium (q.v.) in 358 B.C. *See also* HIERON, I.

Neapolis (mod. Naples), a Greek city of Campania. The original foundation from Cumae was made upon a site named Parthenope, on a fine natural acropolis (now called the hill of Pizzofalcone). Later some more settlers came, this time from Chalcis and Athens. These built themselves a 'new city', Neapolis, while the earlier town became known as Palaeopolis, 'old city'. In 328 B.C. Palaeopolis was besieged by the Romans; it was betrayed into their hands and forthwith vanished from history. Neapolis must have surrendered voluntarily, for it was admitted to the privileges of a *civitas foederata*.

Its powerful fortifications successfully defied Pyrrhus in 280 B.C. and later daunted Hannibal. Though sacked by Sulla in 82, it quickly recovered and continued to prosper with its own Greek culture and institutions under the empire. Neapolis was the birth-place of Statius and the home of Silius Italicus. Virgil wrote most of his *Georgics* there, and wished to be buried on the hill of Pausilypon; but the tomb now shown as his is in fact the *columbarium* of an unknown family.

Nearchus (-khos), an officer of Alexander the Great (q.v.). He led the Macedonian fleet from the Indus to the Persian Gulf (326–325 B.C.), and his account of the voyage is preserved by Arrianus (q.v.).

Nēleus. After his expulsion by Pelias (*see* JASON AND MEDEA) Neleus went to Pylos, of which he became king. All his twelve sons, except Nestor (q.v.), were slain by Heracles when the latter attacked Pylos.

Nemausus (mod. Nîmes), city of Gallia Narbonensis, established by Augustus as a *colonia* (q.v.) of military veterans. It was named after a sacred grove (*nemus*) in which the Volcae Arecomici used to hold their meetings before their subjugation by Rome in 121 B.C. Nemausus became one of the richest cities of Gaul; according to Strabo it was independent of the provincial governor.

The many fine Roman remains include an amphitheatre; the Maison Carrée, formerly a temple dedicated to Gaius and Lucius Caesar (*see* GAIUS CAESAR); baths; two gateways; and the magnificent Pont-du-Gard (*see* AQUEDUCTS).

Nemea, a valley in Argolis, where Heracles (q.v.) was said to have killed the Nemean Lion. There was here a grove and temple of Zeus, where the Nemean Games (q.v.) were celebrated. The site has been excavated.

Nemean Games, one of the four great athletic festivals of Greece, held in honour of Zeus at Nemea biennially from 516 B.C. (For legend of their institution *see* ARCHEMORUS). The records mention all the usual contests (*see* OLYMPIC GAMES), excepting the chariot race. The Nemean games were celebrated under the presidency of Cleonae, Argos and Corinth in turn; the prize was a wreath of wild parsley; and many of the victors are commemorated in the *Nemean Odes* of Pindar (q.v.). *See* E. N. Gardiner, *Greek Athletic Sports and Festivals*, 1910. *See also* PINDAR.

Nemesianus, Marcus Aurelius Olympius, Roman poet of the late 3rd century A.D., author of four *Eclogues* and an incomplete *Cynegetica* (on hunting). *See* text and translation by J. W. and A. M. Duff in *Minor Latin Poets* (Loeb Library).

Nemesis, Greek goddess who measured out to mortals happiness and misery, and visited with disaster those who were blessed with too many gifts of fortune. Such is her character in early Greek writers; later she was conceived as the deity who punished crime.

Nemetes, *see* TRIBOCI.

Nemorensis, Lacus (mod. Nemi), a lake in the Alban hills, a little to the east of Lacus Albanus. It was in the territory of Aricia (q.v.), and on its north-eastern shore was a sanctuary to Diana, whose worship, even under the empire, provided a unique relic of ancient barbarism. The ritual originally included human sacrifice. In historical times the priest was always a man of low degree (usually a runaway slave), who was called *Rex Nemorensis.* He obtained the office by killing his predecessor in single combat, and retained it until he was likewise slain (*see* J. G. Frazer, *The Golden Bough,* 1913–14). Remains of two floating palaces were discovered under water on the west side of the lake, one of them dating from the reign of Caligula.

Neodamōdes, emancipated helots (q.v.) and their descendants. They were employed chiefly in the army on foreign service.

Neoptolemus (-os) or **Pyrrhus** (Purrhos), alternative names of the son born to Achilles by Deidameia, daughter of Lycomedes (q.v.), King of Scyros. The first name means 'young warrior', the second 'fair haired'. Neoptolemus was brought up at Scyros, but was taken thence by Odysseus to Troy, where he was one of the warriors concealed in the wooden horse. On the fall of the city he killed Priam, and afterwards sacrificed Polyxena (q.v.) to the spirit of his father. At the distribution of the Trojan captives he received Andromache (q.v.), widow of Hector. Arrived home, Neoptolemus was said to have abandoned Phthia, his paternal kingdom, and to have settled in Epirus where he became ancestor of the Molossian kings. He married Hermione (q.v.), daughter of Menelaus and Helen, and afterwards died a violent death which is attributed by the ancient authorities to various causes (*see* ORESTES).

Nephelē, in Greek legend, wife of Athamas (q.v.), and mother of Phrixus (q.v.) and Helle.

Nepos, Cornelius, Roman historian and friend of Cicero, was probably a native of Verona, and died during the reign of Augustus. There is still extant a work *De Excellentibus Ducibus Exterarum Gentium,* which was part of a larger work *De Viris Illustribus*; also a life of Atticus and a fragment of a life of Cato the censor. *See* text and translation by J. C. Rolfe (Loeb Library).

Neptunus (Eng. Neptune), a Roman god of water, who became god of the sea only after his identification with the Greek Poseidon (q.v.). His temple stood in the Campus Martius. On his festival the people built bowers from the branches of trees, in which they feasted and drank.

Nereids (Gk Nērēides), *see* NYMPHS.

Nēreus, in Greek mythology, son of Pontus and Gē, and husband of

Doris, by whom he begat the nereids (*see* NYMPHS). He is described as the wise old man of the sea, in whose depths he lived. His territory was the Mediterranean, and more particularly the Aegean Sea. He was believed, like other marine deities, to have the gift of prophecy and to be able to change his shape.

Nero, Roman emperor A.D. 54–68, son of Cn. Domitius Ahenobarbus by Agrippina the younger, daughter of Germanicus. Born at Antium in A.D. 37, his original name was Lucius Domitius Ahenobarbus; but following his mother's marriage to her uncle, the emperor Claudius, he was adopted (A.D. 50) by the latter, and named Nero Claudius Caesar Drusus Germanicus. Soon after his adoption, being then sixteen years of age, Nero married (A.D. 53) Octavia, daughter of Claudius and Messalina (*see* OCTAVIA, 2). On the death of Claudius (A.D. 54), Agrippina secured the succession for her son to the exclusion of Britannicus (q.v.), who was poisoned by order of Nero in the following year. But despite this act of revolting brutality, the reign began auspiciously. His former tutors, the younger Seneca and Burrhus, managed to check his vicious propensities; and though Agrippina was murdered by her son in 59, she richly deserved her fate, to which Seneca himself was privy. But the mad streak in Nero now emerged in all its horror. In 62 Octavia (*see* POPPAEA SABINA) and Burrhus were put to death, and the emperor, fancying himself as poet and actor, visited Greece, and actually performed on the stage at Athens. The great fire of Rome in A.D. 64 was attributed by some ancient writers to the emperor himself. He rebuilt the city on an improved plan and with greater magnificence (including his own Golden House, on a site now partly occupied by the Colosseum). But the odium of the conflagration belonged in the public mind to himself, and he tried to place it elsewhere by a terrible persecution of the Christians. His abominable tyranny led in A.D. 65 to the conspiracy of Piso (*see* PISO, GAIUS CALPURNIUS, 3); but the plot was discovered, and many distinguished persons were executed or compelled to commit suicide, among them Piso himself, Seneca and the poet Lucan. Three years later the standard of revolt was raised by Julius Vindex, governor of Gallia Lugdunensis. When the news reached Rome Nero was quickly deserted. He fled to a house about four miles from the city, and put an end to his life as the soldiers sent to dispatch him rode up to the place (A.D. 68). *See* B. W. Henderson, *Life and Principate of the Emperor Nero,* 1903; J. Bishop, *Nero,* 1964.

Nero, Gaius Claudius, consul in 207 B.C., when he defeated and slew Hasdrubal, brother of Hannibal (q.v.) on the Metaurus.

Nero, Tiberius Claudius, husband of Livia Drusilla (q.v.), and father of the emperor Tiberius (q.v.). He died in 33 B.C.

Nerva, Marcus Cocceius, Roman emperor A.D. 96–8, born at Narnia (q.v.) in Umbria (A.D. 30). On the assassination of Domitian, Nerva was chosen to succeed him, and his administration at once restored order to the state. The informers were suppressed, and Nerva swore that he would put no senator to death. He kept that promise, even in face of a conspiracy against his life. His successor was Trajan (q.v.). *See* B. W. Henderson, *Five Roman Emperors,* 1927.

Nestor, King of Pylos (q.v.), the only one of the twelve sons of Neleus (q.v.) who was not slain by Heracles. He took part in the battle between the Lapithae and the Centaurs (qq.v.), and is mentioned as among the Argonauts (q.v.) and the Calydonian hunters (*see* MELEAGER). Although far advanced in age he accompanied the Greeks against Troy. Having ruled over three generations of men, he was renowned for his justice and knowledge of war, not to mention his astonishing garrulity. After the fall of Troy Nestor returned safely to Pylos.

Nicaea: 1. (mod. Nice), town on the coast of Liguria (q.v.), in the extreme south-west of Gallia Cisalpina (*see* GALLIA). It was founded from Massalia.

2. City of Bithynia, built by Antigonus *c.* 316 B.C. At first called Antigonea, its name was changed by Lysimachus in honour of his own wife. In A.D. 325 (20th May–25th July) it was the scene of a general council of the Church, convoked by Constantine, at which the Arian heresy was condemned.

Nicander (Nikandros), Greek poet, grammarian and priest of Apollo at Claros in Ionia, *fl.* 185–135 B.C. Two of his poems, *Theriaca* and *Alexipharmaca* (both medical) are extant. *See* MACER, AEMILIUS.

Nicias (Nikias), Athenian general during the Peloponnesian war. He first appears in 427 B.C., when he occupied the small island of Minoa, off Megara. In 425 he and two colleagues led an expedition into Corinthian territory, and then sailed on to fortify the peninsula of Methana in Argolis. Next year he was one of the commanders of a force which occupied the island of Cythera, and in 423 he was one of the signatories to a year's armistice with Sparta. Nicias, however, was an ardent advocate of peace, and in 421 he used his influence to conclude the ineffectual fifty-year treaty with Sparta called after him the Peace of Nicias. He used all his efforts to induce the Athenians to preserve this peace; but he was opposed by Alcibiades, and in 415 the Athenians dispatched the celebrated expedition to Sicily. Although Nicias disapproved of this decision, he was appointed one of its commanders; and his timidity and irresolution were among the principal causes of failure. Notwithstanding the reinforcements sent to his assistance under Demosthenes (*see* DEMOSTHENES, 1), the Athenians were utterly defeated, and both generals were taken prisoner and put to death (413 B.C.). *See* Thucydides, vi, vii.

Nicias (Nikias), Athenian artist of the late 4th century B.C. He painted for the sculptor Praxiteles.

Nicolaus (Nikolaos) of Damascus, Greek historian of the 1st century B.C., friend of Augustus and of Herod the Great. Fragments survive, including part of a biography of Augustus.

Nicomedes (Nikomēdēs), name of four kings of Bithynia (q.v.):

1. Reigned 278–250 B.C., eldest son and successor of Zipoetes; founded the city of Nicomedia (q.v.).

2. Surnamed Epiphanes, reigned 149–128 B.C., son and successor of Prusias II (q.v.), whom he dethroned and put to death. He was a staunch ally of Rome.

3. Surnamed Euergetes, reigned 128–94 B.C., son and successor of the preceding.

4. Surnamed Philopator, reigned 94–74 B.C. He was alleged to have

had unnatural relations with Julius Caesar. He assisted Rome against Mithradates (q.v.), and dying childless after a troubled reign bequeathed his kingdom to the Roman people. *See* T. Reinach, *Trois Royaumes de l'Asie Mineure*, 1888; T. Rice Holmes, *The Roman Republic*, 3 vols., 1923.

Nicomedia (Nikomēdia), city of Bithynia, at the head of the bay of Astacus in the Propontis. It was founded by Nicomedes I (q.v.) in 264 B.C., and was made chief city of the East by Diocletian. Its importance was due to its situation at the convergence of several trade routes from Asia, a factor of added consequence after the foundation of Constantinople. Hannibal (q.v.) died at Nicomedia, which was also the birth-place of Arrian.

Nicopolis, city founded by Octavian in 31 B.C. to commemorate his victory at Actium (q.v.); situated at the south-western extremity of Epirus, on the northern side of the entrance to the gulf of Ambracia. It was peopled with settlers drawn from many neighbouring towns. It became the capital of southern Epirus and Acarnania and enjoyed the right of sending five members to the Amphictyonic Council.

Niger, Gaius Pescennius, Roman general, acclaimed as emperor by the legions of the East after the death of Commodus (A.D. 193). In the following year he was defeated near Issus by Septimius Severus, taken prisoner and put to death.

Nikē, Greek goddess of victory, daughter of Pallas by Styx, and sister of Zelos (zeal), Kratos (strength) and Bia (force). Her name is perpetuated in the glorious winged 'Victory of Samothrace', now in the Louvre, and in the tiny temple of Nike Apteros (Wingless) on the Acropolis at Athens (*see* ATHENS: *Acropolis*). This edifice is described in a guide-book of about 1458 as 'a small school of musicians, founded by Pythagoras'! As F. L. Lucas remarks 'they must have been very small musicians'. ('The Literature of Greek Travel' in *The Greatest Problem and Other Essays*, 1960.)

Niobē, *see* AMPHION AND ZETHOS.

Nisyrus (Nisuros), an island off the coast of Caria. Its volcanic nature gave rise to a legend that Poseidon tore it from the neighbouring island of Cos to hurl at a giant named Polybotes.

Nola, city of Campania, subdued by the Romans in 313 B.C. Its capture by Sulla (q.v.) in 88 B.C. terminated the Social War (q.v.). Nola was stormed by Spartacus (q.v.) in 73 B.C., and became a Roman colony in the reign of Augustus, who died there.

Nomothetai, an Athenian court instituted *c.* 403 B.C. Its members were chosen from among the dicasts, and its principal duty was to approve or reject by a majority decision changes in the constitution voted by the Ecclesia (q.v.).

Noricum, a district south of the Danube, between Rhaetia and Pannonia. Its Celtic inhabitants, who had subdued an earlier Illyrian population, were ruled by native princes and traded with the Romans until 16 B.C. In that year they joined a Pannonian invasion of Istria (q.v.) and were defeated by the governor of Illyricum, Publius Silius. From this time it was called a province, though not organized as such; it remained a kingdom with the title *regnum Noricum* and was controlled by an imperial procurator. (*See* Th. Mommsen, *Provinces of* *the Roman Empire.*) The chief products of Noricum were iron, used in the manufacture of Roman weapons of war; wild nard, used for perfume; gold and salt.

Notos, in Greek mythology, personification of the south-west wind, son of Astraeus by Eos and brother of Boreas (q.v.). *See* AUSTER.

Noviodunum (mod. Soissons), town of Gallia Belgica, capital of the Suessiones. At the beginning of the empire it took the name Augusta Suessionum and became the second town of Gallia Belgica after Remi (formerly Durocortorum; mod. Rheims). It quickly developed into an important road centre.

Novius, Quintus (*fl.* 90 B.C.), Latin writer of *Atellanae fabulae* (q.v.), of which some fragments survive.

Numa Pompilius, legendary second king of Rome. He was a native of Cures, and was elected king in 714 B.C. His great wisdom was supposed, in defiance of chronology, to have been derived from Pythagoras. His piety was proverbial; he received from the nymph Egeria (q.v.) instruction in those forms of worship which he afterwards gave to the Roman people, and was revered by them as the author of their whole religious system. He was also the traditional builder of a covered passage north-east of the Forum, wrongly called the 'temple' of Janus (q.v.). He died in 671 B.C.

Numantia, a hill fortress in northern Spain in the upper valley of the Douro. It played an important part in the native resistance to the Roman conquest of the peninsula between 144 and 133 B.C. In the latter year, after an historic siege of fifteen months, it was forced into surrender by Scipio Aemilianus Africanus (q.v.). The magnitude of this task is shown by extensive excavations made between 1905 and 1910, which have revealed Scipio's lines of circumvallation (six miles) with seven camps. *See* A. Schulten, *Numantia,* 4 vols., 1914–31.

Numerianus, Marcus Aurelius, Roman emperor A.D. 283–4, younger son of Carus, and brother of Carinus (qq.v.) with whom he succeeded jointly to the throne. Eight months later he was murdered. Suspicion fell upon his father-in-law, the praetorian prefect Arrius (q.v.), who was slain by Diocletian.

Numidia, district of north Africa, which in the 3rd century B.C. consisted of all the territory eastwards from the River Mulucha to the Carthaginian border. The population was made up of two great tribes: the Massyli and the Massaesyli, dwelling east and west respectively of the River Ampsaga. During the second Punic war (218–201 B.C.) the former were governed by Masinissa, the latter by Syphax (qq.v.). Syphax allied himself with Carthage, Masinissa with Rome; with the result that, when the war was over, Rome confiscated the dominions of Syphax and appointed Masinissa to rule the whole of Numidia. On the defeat of Jugurtha (q.v.) in 106 B.C., it became virtually subject to Rome, who gave the territory west of the Ampsaga to the Mauretanian king Bocchus (q.v.) but allowed the descendants of Masinissa, Hiempsal II and Juba I (qq.v.), to govern the remainder, and bear the kingly title, until Juba's defeat by Caesar in 46 B.C. Eastern Numidia then became a short-lived Roman province called Africa Nova, but was restored to Juba II (q.v.) by Octavian in 30 B.C.

Five years later Juba surrendered it in return for Mauretania (including the former western half of Numidia) and it was incorporated in the province of Africa (q.v.). Septimius Severus detached it from Africa and placed it under an imperial procurator, an arrangement which lasted until Diocletian made it one of the seven provinces of the diocese of Africa.

Numitor, in Roman legend, King of Alba Longa and grandfather of Romulus (q.v.).

Nycteus (Nuk-), brother of Lycus and father of Antiope, *see* ANTIOPE, 2.

Nyctymene (Nuktēmenē), in Greek legend, daughter of Epopeus, King of Sicyon. Having been raped by her father, she hid herself in a forest and was changed by Athena into an owl.

Nymphs (Gk *Numphai*; Lat. *Nymphae*), female demigods with whom the ancients peopled all parts of nature, as follows: (1) *Oceanids,* daughters of Oceanus (q.v.), and nymphs of Ocean. (2) *Nereids,* daughters of Nereus (q.v.), and nymphs of the Aegean. (3) *Naiads,* nymphs of fresh water, whether of rivers, lakes, brooks or streams; many of them presided over springs believed to inspire those who drank their waters, and hence were thought themselves to be endowed with prophetic gift and powers of inspiration. (4) *Oreads,* nymphs of mountains and caves; also called after particular mountains which they inhabited. (5) *Napaeae,* nymphs of glens. (6) *Dryads* and *Hamadryads,* nymphs of trees, who were believed to die together with the trees which had been their abode.

The name 'nymphs' was also applied to a class of beings, distinct from the above, who were thought to be the maiden companions of certain goddesses, e.g. Artemis.

Nyx (Nux), in Greek mythology, personification of Night, called in Latin Nox. She was daughter of Chaos, wife of her brother Erebus, and mother of Aether (Air) and Hemera (Day). Her other two sons, Hypnos (Sleep) and Thanatos (Death) are often mentioned as having no father; others make them sons likewise of Erebus.

O

Oceanids (Gk Okeanides), daughters of Oceanus (q.v.) and nymphs (q.v.) of Ocean.

Oceanus (Ōkeanos), in Greek mythology, god of the river which was believed to encircle the earth. Homer (*Il.* xiv. 201) calls him father of the gods (cf. Virgil, *Georg.* iv. 382); but in most later writers he is son of Uranus and Gē, husband of Tethys, and father of all other river-gods as well as of the oceanids (*see* NYMPHS). With the advance of geographical knowledge the name Oceanus was given to the outer waters of the earth, particularly the Atlantic, as distinct from the Mediterranean, Euxine and other enclosed seas.

Octavia: 1. Sister of the emperor Augustus, married first to C. Claudius Marcellus, consul 50 B.C., and after his death (40 B.C.) to Mark Antony (*see* ANTONIUS, MARCUS, 3), who quickly abandoned her for Cleopatra. She died in 11 B.C. By her first husband she was mother of M. Claudius Marcellus (*see* MARCELLUS, MARCUS CLAUDIUS, 3) and two daughters. To Antony she bore two daughters, one of whom was the mother of the emperor Claudius, grandmother of Caligula and great-grandmother of Nero; the other, also named Antonia, was grandmother of the latter. *See* TABLES 1 and 2.

2. Daughter of the emperor Claudius by Messalina, and first wife of Nero, who divorced her in order to marry Poppaea Sabina (q.v.), and had her put to death in A.D. 62.

Octavianus, Gaius Julius Caesar, in English Octavian, name of the future emperor Augustus (q.v.) from his adoption by Caesar (44 B.C.).

Octavius, Gaius, original name of the emperor Augustus (q.v.). He was the son of C. Octavius by Atia, niece of Julius Caesar. *See also* preceding article.

Odaenathus or **Odenathus, Septimius,** an Arab prince, ruler of Palmyra (q.v.). Having checked the victorious Persians after the defeat and capture of Valerian (A.D. 260), he obliged the emperor Gallienus to bestow upon him the title of Augustus. He was assassinated in 267, some said with the connivance of his wife Zenobia (q.v.).

Odeum (Ōdeion), a building for musical performances. The three most famous were at Athens: (1) near the fountain of Enneakrounos, capable of holding 3,000 people; (2) the Odeum of Pericles, with pointed roof; (3) the great Odeum built by Herodes Atticus (A.D. 150) beneath the south-west corner of the Acropolis (*see* ATHENS).

Odrysae (Odrusai), a Thracian people dwelling in the plains of the Hebrus. In the 5th century B.C. their king, Sitalces, ruled over a great empire whose coastline ran from Abdera to the mouth of the Danube. Although Sitalces was an ally of Athens, his invasion of Macedonia with an enormous force in 429 B.C. was a cause of grave anxiety to the Greek city-states then engaged in the Peloponnesian war; but his subjects were inadequately organized for foreign wars, and his armies withdrew after eighty days. *See* Thucydides, ii. 95–101.

Odysseus (Odusseus), Lat. Ulysses or Ulixes, in Greek legend, son of Laertes and Anticleia, husband of Penelope, daughter of Icarius, and father by her of Telemachus. After some hesitation (*see* PALAMEDES) he sailed with the Greeks against Troy. His courage, cunning and eloquence, for which he was so greatly esteemed by the ancients, were a match for every conceivable situation during the ten-year siege. Among his principal exploits were the fight with Telamonian Ajax for the arms of Achilles and the carrying off of the Palladium (q.v.). But the most celebrated part of his story consists of his adventures after the destruction of Troy, which form the subject of Homer's *Odyssey*. After visiting the Cicones and Lotophagi, he sailed to the western coast of Sicily, where with twelve companions he entered the cave of the Cyclops Polyphemus. This giant devoured six of his companions, and kept Odysseus himself and the six others prisoners in his cave. Odysseus made the monster drunk and having with a burning pole deprived him of his one eye, succeeded in making his escape with his friends by concealing himself and them under the bodies of the sheep which the Cyclops let out of his cave. Odysseus next arrived at the island of Aeolus, and the god on his departure gave him a bag of winds, which were to carry him home; but his companions opened the bag, and the winds escaped, whereupon the ships were driven back to the island of Aeolus, who refused further assistance. After a visit to the city of the Laestrygones, his fate carried him to Aeaea, an island inhabited by the sorceress Circe (q.v.; *see also* TELEGONUS). Odysseus sent part of his people to explore the island, but they were changed by Circe into swine. By the advice of Circe he sailed across the River Oceanus, and having landed in the country of the Cimmerians, he entered Hades, and consulted Tiresias about the manner in which he might reach his native island. Odysseus then returned with his companions to Aeaea, when Circe again sent them a wind which carried them by the island of the Sirens. Odysseus, in order to escape their enticing songs, filled the ears of his companions with wax, and had himself fastened to the mast of his ship. In sailing between Scylla and Charybdis, the former monster carried off and devoured six of his companions. Having next landed on Thrinacia, his companions, contrary to the admonitions of Tiresias, killed some of the oxen of Helios; in consequence of which, when they put to sea, Zeus destroyed their ship by lightning, and all were drowned with the exception of Odysseus, who saved himself by means of the mast and planks, and after ten days reached the island of Ogygia, inhabited by the nymph Calypso. She received him with kindness, and desired him to marry her, promising immortality and eternal youth. But Odysseus, who had spent eight years with Calypso, longed for his home: and at the intercession of Athena, Hermes carried to Calypso the command of Zeus to let him go. The nymph obeyed, and taught him how to build a raft, on which he left the island. In eighteen days he came in sight of Scheria, the island of the Phaeacians, when Poseidon sent a storm, which cast him off the raft; but by the assistance of Leucothea (q.v.) and Athena he swam ashore. The exhausted hero slept on the shore until he was awakened by the voices of maidens. He found Nausicaa, the daughter of King Alcinoüs and Arete, who conducted him to her father's court. Here the minstrel Demodocus sang of the fall of Troy. This moved Odysseus to tears, and being questioned, he related his history. A ship was provided to convey him to Ithaca, from which he had been absent twenty years. During his absence his father Laertes, bowed down by grief and old age, had withdrawn into the country, his mother Anticleia had died of sorrow, his son Telemachus had grown up to manhood, and his wife Penelope had rejected the offers made to her by the importunate suitors from the neighbouring islands. In order that he might not be recognized, Athena metamorphosed Odysseus into a beggar. He was kindly received by Eumaeus, the swineherd, a faithful servant of his house, and recognized by the dog Argus (a most moving scene). While Odysseus sheltered with Eumaeus, Telemachus returned from Sparta and Pylos, whither he had gone to obtain information concerning his father. Odysseus revealed himself to his son, and a plan was evolved for dealing with the suitors. Penelope, with great difficulty, was made to promise her hand to him who should win at shooting with the bow of Odysseus. As none of the suitors was able to draw this bow, Odysseus himself took it up, and, directing his arrows against the suitors, slew them all. He then made himself known to Penelope, and went to see his father. Meanwhile news of the suitors' death got abroad, and their relatives rose in arms against Odysseus; but Athena, in guise of Mentor (*see* MENTOR, 1), brought about a reconciliation. *See* M. P. Nilsson, *Mycenaean Origin of Greek Mythology*, 1932; E. Bradford, *Ulysses Found*, 1964.

Oedipus (Oidipous), *see* THEBAN LEGEND.

Oeneus (Oi-), 'vintner', King of Calydon; husband of Althaea, father of Meleager (*see* MELEAGER), Tydeus, Gorge and Deianeira. Deprived of his kingdom by his nephews, he was subsequently avenged by his grandson Diomedes (*see* DIOMEDES, 2), son of Tydeus, who slew all but two of the usurpers and placed upon the throne Andraemon, husband of Gorge, because Oeneus himself was now too old to govern. Oeneus then accompanied Diomedes back to Argos, but was murdered there by his two surviving nephews.

Oenotropae (Oinotropai), the three daughters of Anius (q.v.). They received from Dionysus the power of producing at will any quantity of wine, corn and oil; and they supplied these necessaries to the Greeks before Troy during the first nine years of the siege.

Ogyges (Ōgugēs), in Greek legend, King of Thebes, in whose reign occurred a flood which submerged Boeotia and part of Attica.

Oileus, in Greek legend, King of the Opuntian Locrians, one of the Argonauts (q.v.) and father of the lesser Ajax.

Olbia, Greek city near the mouth of the River Hypanis (Bug), on the north coast of the Euxine. Founded from Miletus *c.* 645 B.C., it became during the following century an important centre of the grain trade.

Olympia (Olumpia), a plain in Elis (q.v.), bounded south by the Alpheus and west by the Cladeus; scene of the Olympic Games (q.v.). The most important site was the Altis, a grove sacred to Zeus, which, together with its immediate neighbourhood, was adorned with temples, statues and public buildings. Of these temples the most celebrated was the Olympieion, dedicated to Zeus Olympios, which housed the great chryselephantine statue of the god by Pheidias (q.v.). Extensive excavations have brought to light magnificent architectural and sculptural remains. *See* E. N. Gardiner, *Olympia, its History and Remains*, 1925.

Olympiad, period of four years between each celebration of the Olympic Games (q.v.); 776 B.C. was reputed to be the first year of the first Olympiad. Olympiads began to be reckoned from the victory of Coroebus (776 B.C.), the first victor in the games after their suspension for eighty-six years; but Timaeus of Sicily (264 B.C.) was the first writer who regularly arranged events according to the winners in each Olympiad. This practice was followed by Polybius, Diodorus Siculus, Dionysius of Halicarnassus (qq.v.) and others. For converting Olympiads into years B.C., multiply the number of Olympiads that have actually elapsed by 4, and deduct the number thus obtained from 780. For converting Olympiads into years A.D., go through the same process, but subtract 706 from the number obtained by multiplication. But since the games were celebrated about midsummer, and the Attic year began about the same time, it is necessary to reduce the year B.C. by one if an event happened in the second half of the year. The method of calculation by Olympiads was used only for literary purposes, and was never adopted in everyday life.

Olympias, sister of King Alexander I of Epirus, wife of Philip II of Macedon and mother of Alexander the Great. She withdrew from Macedonia when Philip married Cleopatra (337 B.C.), and it was commonly believed that she was privy to his assassination in 336 B.C. In 317 she put to death Alexander's half-brother, Philip Arrhidaeus, and the latter's wife Eurydice. Attacked by Cassander (q.v.), she took refuge in Pydna, and on its surrender was herself put to death (316 B.C.). *See* G. A. Macurdy, *Hellenistic Queens*, 1932.

Olympic Games, the chief national festival of the Greeks, held once every four years at Olympia (q.v.), and celebrated in honour of Zeus. They occupied five days, and consisted of two parts: the presentation of offerings and the contests. At first the contest consisted of a simple running match held in the stadium, but about 724 B.C. the *diaulos*, or double course, was introduced, in which the runners had to make a circuit of the goal and return to the starting-point. Later came the *dolichos*, or long race, and in 708 B.C. the *pentathlon* was introduced, a five-fold contest consisting of leaping, running, throwing the discus, wrestling and throwing the javelin. Wrestling and boxing, too, were combined in the *pankration* (648). In 680 chariot-racing in the hippodrome was introduced, and though this was twice as long as the stadium, it had to be traversed about ten times in both directions (at first with four horses, after 500 with mules, and after 408 with two horses). There were also races in armour, and those in which the horsemen had to leap from their horses and run beside them holding the bridles, besides competitions between heralds and trumpeters. The contests were open to all freemen of pure hellenic descent who had not incurred any personal disgrace; but all barbarians and slaves were excluded. (The Romans, not being reckoned barbarians, were allowed to take part.) Women too were excluded, and were not even allowed to watch the games, there being but one exception, the priestess of Demeter. Supervision of the contests belonged to the Hellanodici, who were appointed by popular election from the Eleans themselves. At the end of the contests a sacrifice was made by the victors wearing their crowns, and a banquet was held in the *prutaneion* of the Altis, during which a song of victory, composed by an eminent poet, was chanted by choral bands. Authors, poets, orators and artists also used the opportunity afforded by the assembling of so vast a crowd to make themselves known. The Olympic games were abolished in A.D. 394. *See* F. A. M. Webster, *The Evolution of Olympic Games*, 1914. (*See also* PINDAR.)

Olympus (Olumpos), name of numerous mountains in Greece and Asia Minor. The most famous was the high range (mod. Elympo) on the borders of Thessaly and Macedonia, separated from Mt Ossa by the vale of Tempe (q.v.). It was probably the sight of this impressive ridge, which rises to a height of 9,600 feet, that caused the Greeks to give the name Olympus to the supposed mountain home of their gods, though the latter was not, at any rate in earlier times, identified with any particular locality.

Olynthus (Olunthos), city of Chalcidice (q.v.), near the neck of the peninsula of Pallene. Subject to the Persians from the time of Darius I, to whom its possessors, a Thracian tribe known to the Greeks as Bottiaioi, had submitted *c.* 512 B.C., it was sacked by Artabazus (q.v.) in 379 and occupied by Greeks from the neighbouring city-states of that region. It then became a member of the Delian League (q.v.), but revolted from Athens (424 B.C.) and quickly established itself leader of a confederation of neighbouring cities, which in 357 B.C. included thirty-two states. In this latter year, on the outbreak of war between Philip II and the Greeks, Olynthus was allied with Macedon, but later sided with Athens and was razed to the ground by Philip in 348 B.C. *See also* DEMOSTHENES, 2. *See* A. B. West, *The History of the Chalcidic League*, 1919; D. M. Robinson, *Excavations at Olynthus*, 1929–33.

Onatas, Greek sculptor of the 5th century B.C. He renewed the image of the Black Demeter at Phigaleia (q.v.).

Onomacritus (-kritos), an Athenian who made a collection of oracular responses (*c.* 500 B.C.). Detected in interpolating an oracle attributed to Musaeus (q.v.), he was banished from Athens. *See* Herodotus, vii. 6.

Opheltēs, *see* ARCHEMORUS.

Opimius, Lucius, consul 121 B.C., when he took a leading part in the proceedings that led to the murder of C. Gracchus (q.v.). Convicted of having received a bribe from Jugurtha, he went into exile at Dyrrachium and died in poverty. The year of his consulship was remarkable for the autumnal heat, and its vintage was celebrated as *vinum Opimianum*.

Oppianus (-os), name of the authors of two extant Greek poems entitled respectively *Cynegetica* (on hunting) and *Halieutica* (on fishing). The author of the first was a native of Apamea or Pella in Syria, and *fl. c.* A.D. 180; the second was written by a native of Anazarba or Corycus in Cilicia, who lived in the early years of the

3rd century A.D. *See* text and translation of both poems by A. W. Mair (Loeb Library).

Oppius, Gaius: 1. Tribune of the plebs in 215 B.C., when he carried a law curtailing the luxury of Roman women.

2. Friend of Julius Caesar, to whom the latter, when Oppius was taken ill on a journey, once gave up the only bedroom in a rustic inn, sleeping himself in the open air (Suetonius, *Divus Julius*, 72). He served under Caesar in the African campaigns (46). During Caesar's absence on the Spanish campaign (46–45 B.C.), Oppius and L. Cornelius Balbus (q.v.) were two of the eight city prefects appointed by Caesar to manage affairs at Rome; they were also the most authoritative of this board, having the ultimate decision on all vital points.

Ops, Roman goddess of plenty and fertility, cult-partner of Saturnus (q.v.)

Optimates, name given to the senatorial or aristocratic party at Rome during the late 2nd and early 1st century B.C.

Opus (-os), town of Locris, legendary birth-place of Patroclus (q.v.). *See* LOCRI.

Oracles (Gk *manteia*; Lat. *oracula*). There are said to have been upwards of 250 oracular seats in the Greek world, curiously enough not one of them in Attica. The following (with name of deities or heroes associated therewith) were among the most popular: Branchidae (Apollo); Epidaurus (Asclepius); Dodona (Zeus); Lebadea (Trophonius); Ammonium (Zeus Ammon). *See* separate articles.

But by far the most celebrated of all Greek oracles was that of Apollo at Delphi (q.v.). We know Apollo only in the days of his decline, when he had sacrificed much of his authority by siding with the Persian invader. That was after he had founded what we may almost call a Church. In the 7th century B.C. Delphi was the seat of a gospel, and it was a gospel to which Greece was drawn to listen. Its 'good tidings' were very simple—the duty of self-control and recognition of human limitation. They are summed up in two sayings of two words each: '*Gnōthi seauton*' ('Know thyself') and '*Mēden agan*' ('No excess'). For several generations the Delphic oracle was the greatest spiritual power in Greece, not to mention its position as the centre of a worldwide intelligence service.

In Italy there were no oracles in which a god revealed his will through the mouth of an *inspired* individual. The Romans learnt the divine will from the Sibylline Books (*see* SIBYL), from augurs and from haruspices (qq.v.). The only Italian oracles known to us are those of Faunus and Fortuna, one ancient oracle of Mars and one of the dead at Avernus.

Orbilius Pupillus, Roman grammarian and schoolmaster, born at Beneventum in 113 and settled at Rome in 63 B.C. Among his pupils was Horace (q.v.), who calls him *plagosus*, 'flogger'.

Orcades (mod. Orkney and Shetland islands), visited by Agricola *c.* A.D. 80. *See* PYTHEAS.

Orchomenus (-khomenos): 1. City of Boeotia, situated on a hill not far from the confluence of the rivers Cephissus and Melas. Formerly the capital of a powerful mainland and maritime kingdom (*see* MINYAE), it had been overshadowed by Thebes (q.v.) at the beginning of the historical period. It was destroyed by the Thebans in 368 and again in 346, and although restored after each of these disasters it never recovered its prosperity. The Charites (q.v.) were worshipped at Orchomenus, as also was Dionysus. Excavations have brought to light considerable remains of the prehistoric city.

2. City of Arcadia, north-west of Mantinea (q.v.). Having exercised some authority over the whole of Arcadia during the 7th century B.C., it yielded pride of place first to Mantinea and then to Megalopolis (q.v.). In the 3rd century it was subject to the Aetolian League, to Sparta, to the Achaean League and finally (146 B.C.) to Rome.

Oreads (Gk *Ōreades*), nymphs (q.v.) of mountains.

Orestēs, in Greek legend, son of Agamemnon and Clytaemnestra. On the murder of his father, Orestes was saved from the same fate by his sister Electra, who caused him to be secretly removed to the court of Strophius, King of Phocis, who had married Agamemnon's sister Anaxibia. There he formed a close friendship with the king's son Pylades. When they had grown up the two friends went to Argos, where Orestes slew Clytaemnestra and Aegisthus.

For the dreadful crime of matricide Orestes was driven mad and pursued by the Erinyes (q.v.) until, on the advice of Apollo, he took refuge in the temple of Athena at Athens, when he was acquitted by the court of Areopagus, which had been appointed by the goddess to decide his fate. (*See* Aeschylus, *Choephori* and *Eumenides*; Euripides, *Orestes*.) According to another legend Apollo sent him to Chersonesus Taurica to fetch the statue of Artemis, an undertaking in which he was accompanied by Pylades (*see* IPHIGENEIA). After his return to Peloponnesus, he took possession of his father's kingdom and married Hermione, widow of Neoptolemus (q.v.), whom, according to some authors, he himself had slain.

Orion, in Greek legend, a Boeotian giant and hunter. Having come to Chios, he fell in love with Merope, the daughter of Oenopion; his treatment of the maiden so exasperated her father, that, with the assistance of Dionysus, he deprived the giant of his sight. Being informed by an oracle that he would recover his sight if he exposed his eyeballs to the rays of the rising sun, Orion found his way to the island of Lemnos, where Hephaestus gave him Cedalion as his guide, who led him to the east. After the recovery of his sight he lived as a hunter with Artemis. His death is related variously. According to some Orion was carried off by Eos (q.v.), who had fallen in love with him; but as this was displeasing to the gods, Artemis killed him with an arrow in Ortygia (Delos). (Cf. Homer, *Od*. v. 121–4.) According to others, he was beloved by Artemis; and Apollo, indignant at his sister's affection for him, asserted that she was unable to hit with her arrow a distant point which he showed her in the sea. She thereupon took aim, the arrow hit its mark, but the mark was the head of Orion, who was swimming there. A third account, which Horace follows, states that he offered violence to Artemis, and was killed by the goddess with one of her arrows. A fourth account states that he was stung to death by a scorpion. After his death he was placed among the stars, a fact acknowledged in Homer; and Orion is thus the subject of the earliest star myth. The constellation of Orion set at the commencement of November, at which time storms and rain were frequent; hence by Roman poets he is often called *imbrifer, nimbosus* or *aquosus*.

Orodes, King of Parthia in 53 B.C., when his general, Surenas, defeated M. Licinius Crassus (q.v.) at Carrhae. Soon after the defeat and death of his brother Pacorus (q.v.), he resigned the throne to his son Phraates (q.v.).

Oropus, coastal town on the border of Attica and Boeotia, with its port, Delphinium, about a mile to the north. Within its territory was the oracular shrine of Amphiaraüs (q.v.). In 156 B.C. it was destroyed by the Athenians. *See* CARNEADES.

Orpheus, legendary Greek poet, musician and founder of Orphism (q.v.); son of the Thracian king Oeagrus, husband of Eurydice and one of the Argonauts (q.v.).

Presented with the lyre by Apollo, and instructed by the Muses in its use, Orpheus enchanted not only men and beasts, but even trees and rocks. His wife having been killed by a snake (*see* ARISTAEUS), he descended into Hades in order to win her back. His music prevailed, and Eurydice was allowed to go upon condition that he should not look back until they had reached the upper world; but at the last moment anxiety overcame him: he turned his head, saw her following, and then beheld her snatched from him for ever. His grief led him to despise the Thracian women, who took revenge by tearing him to pieces under the influence of Bacchic frenzy. The Muses collected the fragments of his body, and buried them at Libethra near the foot of Mt Olympus. His head was thrown into the Hebrus, down which it was carried to the sea and thence to Lesbos (q.v.). His lyre was placed among the stars. Many poems ascribed to Orpheus were current in classical Greece; the extant verses bearing his name are forgeries, though they contain some genuine fragments of the later 'Orphic' poetry. *See* W. K. C. Guthrie, *Orpheus and Greek Religion*, 1935.

Orphism, a Greek mystical cult, the doctrines of which were contained in certain poems attributed to Orpheus (q.v.). It should be noted, however, that these poems are of late date, and it is, at best, only a matter of surmise how much of their doctrine dates back to the 6th or 7th century B.C. when Orphism is believed to have emerged. Orphism included several elements which are absent from the Homeric religion; and it is probable that, like all Greek mystical religions, the cult had its origin in pre-hellenic religion preserved in secret societies. The non-Homeric aspects included a sense of sin and the need of personal atonement; the idea of the suffering and death of a god-man; a belief in immortality following a cycle of transmigrations; and an asceticism derived from the Pythagoreans. The rites were purificatory and initiative; they turned about the central myth of Dionysus-Zagreus, which was as follows: Zeus begot by Persephone Dionysus and entrusted to him the government of the world. The Titans, prompted by jealous Hera, attempted to kill him. Dionysus, however, in an effort to escape, went through a series of metamorphoses, but was finally torn to pieces in the form of a bull. The Titans devoured his remains except the heart, which was rescued by Athena, delivered to Zeus, and eaten by him, who immediately begot by

Semele (q.v.) a new Dionysus. According to the Orphics Zeus destroyed the Titans with a thunderbolt, and from their ashes he made man, who thus has in him something of good (from the remains of Dionysus) and something of bad (from the evil Titans). To liberate the divine element was the duty of the initiate. In the classical period Orphism was regarded as a base superstition; but it revived and enjoyed considerable popularity in the Roman Empire. *See* W. K. C. Guthrie, *Orpheus and Greek Religion*, 1935. For the Orphic texts *see* E. Abel, *Orphica*, 1885; O. Kern, *Fragmenta Orphicorum*, 1922.

Orthia, surname of Artemis at Sparta. At the altar of Artemis Orthia boys underwent the ritual flogging called *diamastigōsis*. *See* IPHIGENEIA.

Ortygia (-tugia), the ancient name (1) of Delos, and (2) of an island off Syracuse (q.v.).

Osiris, Egyptian god, identified by Herodotus with Dionysus.

Osroëne, *see* EDESSA.

Ossa or **Phēmē**. Homer represents Ossa as the messenger of Zeus, who spreads rumours with the speed of a conflagration. He treats Pheme simply as a presage drawn from human utterances. Hesiod, however, speaks of Pheme as a goddess, and Sophocles calls her a daughter of Elpis (Hope). The corresponding Latin Fama was never more than a mere poetical figure.

Ossa, mountain in the north of Thessaly, connected with Pelion (q.v.) on the south-east, and divided from Olympus on the north-west by the vale of Tempe (q.v.). *See* ALOIDAE.

Ostia, town at the mouth of the left arm of the Tiber, and the port of Rome, from which it was distant 16 miles by land. Traditionally it was founded by Ancus Marcius (q.v.). Claudius I built an improved harbour (*Portus Ostiensis* or *Portus Augusti*) two miles to the northwest, and another (*Portus Trajani*) was built by Trajan (A.D. 103). Between 1907 and 1938 very remarkable excavations were carried out, and still continue. *See* R. Meiggs, *Roman Ostia*, 1960.

Ostracism (from Gk *ostrakon*, a potsherd), form of banishment practised at Athens, intended to prevent conspiracy against the constitution. It was introduced by Cleisthenes (508), first used in 488–487, and for the last time in 417 B.C. An annual vote of the Ecclesia (q.v.) was taken to decide whether or not ostracism should be applied that year (*see* Aristotle, *Constitution of Athens*, 22). If the vote was in favour, each citizen might inscribe on a potsherd the name of his intended victim. The ballot was secret, and a quorum of 6,000 votes was necessary to secure banishment. The penalty was ten years' exile, but without loss of property or civil rights. Only ten persons are known for certain to have been ostracized, and *ostraka* referring to each have been found. *See* J. Carcopino, *L'Ostracisme Athénien*, 1935.

Otho, Lucius Roscius, tribune of the plebs in 67 B.C., when he carried a law reserving for the equites (q.v.) the first fourteen rows in the theatre behind the *orchestra* where senators sat. The law was unpopular, and once occasioned a riot during the consulship of Cicero (63 B.C.).

Otho, Marcus Salvius, Roman emperor 15th January–16th April

A.D. 69, born in A.D. 32. As a young man he was one of Nero's companions in debauchery. In 58, however, the emperor took possession of his wife Poppaea Sabina (q.v.), and Otho was sent to govern Lusitania—which he did with great credit. On the accession of Galba (68), Otho returned to Rome and supported him in the hope of succeeding to the empire. But when Galba adopted Piso on 10th January 69, Otho formed a conspiracy, and was proclaimed emperor by the troops, who promptly assassinated Galba. Meanwhile, however, the legions of Germany had proclaimed Vitellius emperor at Colonia Agrippina (Cologne) and were marching on Rome. Otho hurried north and encountered them at Betriacum in northern Italy, where he was defeated. He escaped to Brixellum, and there committed suicide.

Otus (Ōtos), one of the Aloidae (q.v.).

Ovation (Lat. *ovatio*), lesser triumph (q.v.) awarded to a Roman general who had achieved minor success or success in a minor war. The senate did not head the procession; the general entered on foot or horseback instead of in a chariot; he was clad in the *toga praetexta* or ordinary magistrate's robe, instead of the *tunica palmata* and *toga picta*, and was crowned with myrtle instead of laurel. A sheep was sacrificed instead of an ox, hence the term (*ovis*=sheep).

Ovidius Naso, Publius, called in English **Ovid**, Latin poet, born at Sulmo 20th March 43 B.C., descendant of an ancient equestrian family. Having studied rhetoric under Arellius Fuscus and Porcius Latro, he completed his education at Athens, and afterwards travelled in Sicily and Asia with the poet Aemilius Macer (q.v.). He held legal appointments at Rome, but devoted most of his time to poetry. Ovid was twice married in early life, at the wish of his parents; but he divorced both wives and led a gay life. Later he married a third wife, to whom he seems to have been sincerely attached and who brought him a stepdaughter Perilla. After living many years in Rome, and enjoying the favour of Augustus, he was suddenly banished (A.D. 9) to Tomis (q.v.) on the Euxine. The pretext was his licentious poem *Ars Amatoria*, which had been published nearly ten years earlier. The real cause of Ovid's exile remains uncertain; it has been suggested that he was guilty of an intrigue with the emperor's granddaughter Julia (*see* JULIA, 6), who was banished in the same year. He sought relief in the composition of his *Tristia* and *Epistolae ex Ponto*, and learned the language of his hosts, the Getae. But he was never pardoned, and died at Tomis in A.D. 17. Besides the works mentioned above Ovid was the author of *Fasti*, *Metamorphoses*, *Heroides* and *Amores*. There is a complete edition with translations by J. H. Mozley *et al.*, 5 vols. (Loeb Library). *See* H. Fränkel, *Ovid, a Poet between two Worlds*, 1945; L. P. Wilkinson, *Ovid Recalled*, 1955, and *Ovid Surveyed*, 1962.

Oxyrhynchus (Oxurhunkhos), an Egyptian village near modern Fayum, now called Behnesa. Systematic exploration of the site began in 1895, and in the following year yielded large numbers of papyri. Many of these contained parts of hitherto lost works of Greek literature. Subsequent years produced other important finds, which have been published from time to time since 1898 by B. P. Grenfell and A. S. Hunt in *Oxyrhynchus Papyri*.

Pacorus, brother of the Parthian king Orodes (q.v.), who gave him command of the army on the defeat and death of Crassus (53 B.C.). Pacorus invaded Syria in 52 and 51, but was driven back in each year by C. Cassius Longinus. In 40 the Parthians again invaded Syria, under the command of Pacorus and Q. Labienus (q.v.), but were defeated (39) by Ventidius Bassus, a legate of Mark Antony. In 38 Pacorus once more invaded Syria, but was defeated and killed in battle.

Pactolus (Paktōlos), a small river of Lydia, rising in Mt Tmolus and flowing past Sardis into the Hermus. It seems to have been gold-bearing in historical times, and thus contributed to the great wealth of the Lydian kings. For the legend explaining this prosperity of Pactolus and its sands *see* MIDAS.

Pacuvius, Marcus, Latin tragic poet and nephew of Ennius (q.v.), born *c.* 220 B.C. at Brundisium. After spending much of his life at Rome, where he acquired a reputation as painter as well as poet, he returned to his native city, where he died in 130 B.C. The tragedies of Pacuvius owed much to their greater Greek counterparts; but they had the merit of being adaptations rather than mere translations. Fragments amounting to about 400 lines are extant. *See* text and translation by E. H. Warmington, *Remains of Old Latin* (Loeb Library), 1936.

Padus (mod. Po), river of Gallia Cisalpina. *See* ERIDANUS.

Paean (Paian), originally, in Greek mythology, name of the physician to the immortal gods. It was subsequently used in the more general sense of deliverer from evil, and was applied to Apollo. From Apollo itself it was transferred to songs dedicated to him and to other gods, and ultimately to a battle, victory or festive song.

Paeligni, a Sabine people of central Italy, bounded by the Marsi, Marrucini, Samnites and Frentani. They took part in the Social War (q.v.) and their chief town, Corfinium (q.v.), was destined by the allies to be the new capital of Italy.

Paeonia (Paiōnia), district of northern Macedonia (q.v.), extending eastwards from Illyria to the River Strymon. The Paeonians were made up of several tribes united under a king, and they were permitted to retain this form of government even after their subjugation by Philip II of Macedon. Their territory was ravaged by Brennus (q.v.) in 280. After the Roman conquest (168 B.C.), Paeonia east and west of the River Axius formed respectively the second and third districts of Macedonia, until the reign of Diocletian when Paeonia was united with Pelagonia to form a province within the prefecture of Illyricum (*see* ILLYRICUM, 2).

Paestum (Gk Poseidōnia) (mod. Pesto), city of Lucania, situated near the Sinus Paestanus (Gulf of Salerno), five miles south of the River Sīlarus. It was founded by Greeks from Sybaris *c.* 600 B.C.

Having become subject to the Lucanians, Poseidonia eventually (273 B.C.) came under Roman rule, when its name was altered to Paestum, and during the early empire it was well tilled and famous for its roses. Thereafter silting of the river made the place unhealthy, and it gradually declined. The splendid remains of temples dedicated to Poseidon (6th century B.C.), to Ceres (*c.* 530 B.C.) and (as was formerly but wrongly supposed) to Neptune (*c.* 420 B.C.) have long been familiar to travellers. Further excavations since the 1939–45 war have uncovered another well-preserved building, which gives an exact idea of the structure of a Greek temple. This site was found to contain a number of bronze vessels which provide evidence of the presence of skilled bronze workers in southern Italy in the 6th century B.C. The original three-mile circuit of walls is practically complete.

Palaemon (-aimōn), in Greek legend, a marine deity, formerly Melicertes. *See* ATHAMAS.

Palaemon, Quintus Remmius, Roman freedman of Greek origin, the most famous grammarian of the early 1st century A.D. His 'Grammar' is mentioned by Juvenal; Martial ridicules his excursions into poetry.

Palaestra (-aistra), *see* GYMNASIUM.

Palamēdēs, in Greek legend son of Nauplius (q.v.) by Clymene, and one of the Greek heroes who sailed against Troy. When Odysseus (q.v.) feigned idiocy, to avoid having to accompany the expedition, Palamedes discovered his deceit by placing the babe Telemachus (q.v.) in the track of his plough. Later, before Troy, Odysseus took his revenge. He bribed a slave of Palamedes to conceal beneath his master's bed a letter written in the name of Priam. This done, Odysseus charged Palamedes with treachery; a search was made, the letter was found and the victim was stoned to death.

Later writers describe Palamedes as a sage, and attribute to him the invention of lighthouses, measures, scales, the discus, dice, etc. He is also said to have added the letters *thēta, ksi, phi* and *khi* to the original alphabet of Cadmus.

Pales, a Roman divinity (variously male and female) of shepherds and herds. His (her) festival, the Palilia, was celebrated on 21st April, the date on which Rome was supposed to have been founded in 753 B.C.

Palici, in Greek mythology, Sicilian deities, twin sons of Zeus and the nymph Thalia. Their mother, terrified of Hera, prayed to be swallowed up by the earth. And so she was; but in due time these boys issued from the earth, through the gaseous Delli pools (mod. Lago Naftia) near Mt Aetna, in the neighbourhood of Palice, where they were worshipped.

Palladium (-on), an image of Pallas Athena, especially the legendary image preserved at Troy, upon whose safety depended the city's survival. It was said to have been stolen by Odysseus and Diomedes and to have been carried by the latter to Greece. According to some accounts Troy possessed two palladia, one of which was taken as related above, while the other was conveyed by Aeneas to Italy.

Pallas, a Greek slave of Antonia, mother of the emperor Claudius. He was manumitted, became financial secretary to the latter and amassed a huge fortune. It was Pallas who persuaded Claudius to marry Agrippina the younger (A.D. 49), and who abetted her in poisoning his master. He was put to death under Nero in A.D. 62.

Palmyra, Roman name for an ancient city called Tadmor which existed at least as early as the 2nd millennium B.C. it was situated in an oasis of the great Syrian desert, and its position on important trade routes brought it immense wealth (especially after the fall of Petra, q.v.) and introduced many Greek and Roman elements into its material culture. Palmyra recognized the overlordship of Rome not later than A.D. 15, but remained self-governing. The years 130–270 were those of its greatest prosperity, but the ambitious schemes of Odaenathus and Zenobia (qq.v.) led to its capture and loss of independence at the hands of Aurelian in 273. A revolt in the same year brought about its total destruction by the same emperor, and although he partially rebuilt it in 274, it never regained its importance. There are magnificent remains. *See* D. Robinson, *Baalbek; Palmyra*, 1946.

Pamphylia, district in southern Asia Minor, between Lycia and Cilicia, bounded north by the Taurus range. The principal cities were Attalia, Aspendus, Side and Perga (qq.v.). After being subject to the Lydian and Persian monarchies, Pamphylia came within the dominions of Alexander and then of the Seleucids. Following the defeat of Antiochus III, in 190 B.C., it was attached by Rome to the kingdom of Pergamum (q.v.). Later it was briefly included in the dominions of Amyntas, King of Galatia, but after his death was at various times part of the provinces of Galatia, Lycia or Cilicia.

Pan, Greek god of flocks and herds, usually called a son of Hermes (q.v.), was originally an Arcadian divinity. He was supposed to wander among the mountains and valleys of that country, either in the chase or leading a dance of nymphs to the accompaniment of the syrinx ('pipes of Pan'), which he had invented. His appearance was dreaded by travellers, whom he sometimes startled; whence sudden fright without visible cause was ascribed to him and called 'panic' fear. His cult reached Athens in 490 B.C., following a report that he had appeared to Pheidippides (q.v.) and promised his help in the forthcoming battle of Marathon (q.v.). There was, however, another side to his character. The word *pan*, in Greek, means 'all', and he came to be regarded as the personification of Nature or the Universe. It was probably in this capacity that he was one of the gods to whom Socrates prayed for beauty of soul. In works of art Pan is usually represented with horns, snub nose and goat's legs. He was identified by the Romans with their god Faunus (q.v.). *See* PAXOS.

Panaenus (Panainos), Athenian painter, *fl.* 448 B.C. He was a nephew and pupil of Pheidias, whom he assisted with the decoration of the temple of Zeus at Olympia. He was also one of the artists who adorned the Stoa Poikile (q.v.) at Athens.

Panaetius (-aitios), Greek Stoic philosopher of the 2nd century B.C., a native of Rhodes. Having lived some years at Rome, he succeeded Antipater of Tarsus as head of the Stoa, and died at Athens in 109 B.C. None of Panaetius's work survives, but the *De Officiis* of Cicero is in part an adaptation of his treatise on the theory of moral obligation.

Panathenaea (-thēnaia), annual Athenian festival in honour of

Athena, held in the late summer (August). Every fourth year it was celebrated with extraordinary splendour, and was called the greater Panathenaea, the intervening festivals being known as the lesser Panathenaea. The former included a magnificent procession which, starting from a point outside the walls, entered the city and ascended the Acropolis, to offer Athena the newly woven saffron robe (*peplos*). This procession is depicted on the frieze of the Parthenon (q.v.), now in the British Museum. Musical and athletic contests were also regular features of the festival, which was of legendary origin.

Pandareōs, in Greek legend, a native of Miletus, whose daughters were said to have been carried off by the Harpies (q.v.) and given to the Erinyes (q.v.) as servants.

Pandīŏn, name of two legendary kings of Athens:

1. Son of Erechtheus-Erichthonius (*see* ERECHTHEUS), father of Erechtheus, Procne and Philomela (*see* TEREUS).

2. Son of Cecrops. Driven from Athens, he fled to Megara, of which he later became king.

Pandōra, 'All Gifts', the Greek version of Eve. When Prometheus (q.v.) stole fire from heaven, Zeus ordered Hephaestus (q.v.) to fashion a woman who should bring misery on the race of men. Aphrodite endowed her with beauty, Hermes with boldness and cunning. The latter then escorted her to Epimetheus (q.v.), who made her his wife, forgetting the counsel of Prometheus to accept no gift from the gods. Pandora had brought with her a box containing every human ill. Epimetheus opened it and they all escaped, Hope alone remaining. (*See* Hesiod, *Works and Days*, 50 ff.) A later version of the story makes the box contain every blessing which would have been preserved for mankind had not Pandora raised the lid.

Paneas, *see* CAESAREA PHILIPPI.

Panionia, annual festival of the Ionian League. *See* IONIA; MYCALE.

Pankration, *see* OLYMPIC GAMES.

Pannonia, country of central Europe, bounded north and east by the Danube, west by Noricum, south by Dalmatia and Moesia. From the 4th century B.C. it was occupied by Celtic tribes, who subdued the original Illyrian population. In 35 B.C., having taken arms in support of the Dalmatians, they were defeated by Augustus, but were not finally subdued until 9 B.C., when Pannonia was included in Illyria (q.v.). In A.D. 7 it joined a great Illyrian revolt, after the extinction of which it was organized as a separate province in A.D. 10. The Pannonian legions mutinied on the death of Augustus (A.D. 14). *See* Tacitus, *Annales*, i. 8.

Panormus (-os), modern Palermo, ancient Phoenician city on the north-west coast of Sicily, afterwards subject to Carthage. In 254 B.C. it was taken by the Romans, who gave it municipal rights and freedom from taxation.

Pansa, Gaius Vibius, consul with Aulus Hirtius (q.v.) in 43 B.C., when he was killed at the battle of Mutina.

Pantheon, a temple in the Campus Martius at Rome, now a church (S. Maria della Rotunda). It was built by the emperor Hadrian on the site of an earlier temple dedicated to Mars and Venus by M. Vipsanius Agrippa (q.v.) during his third consulship (27 B.C.). The name is derived from a much later tradition that it was a temple 'of all the gods' (Gk *pantōn tōn theōn*). The Pantheon is a circular building, the largest of its kind in antiquity; it is surmounted by a dome (142 feet interior diameter; 148 feet from floor to summit) and is entered by a portico of sixteen Corinthian columns which may have formed part of Agrippa's edifice. *See* G. Boltrani, *Il Panteon*, 1893.

Panthous (-os), priest of Apollo at Troy and father of Euphorbus (*see* EUPHORBUS, 1). Pythagoras (q.v.) is sometimes called Panthoides, because he claimed that his soul had, in a previous existence, animated the body of Euphorbus.

Panticapaeum (-aion), Greek colony in Chersonesus Taurica (q.v.), founded from Miletus *c.* 550 B.C. Sepulchral mounds in the neighbourhood have yielded wonderful treasures. *See* M. Rostovtzeff, *Iranians and Greeks in South Russia*, 1922.

Panyasis (Panu-), Greek epic poet, a native of Halicarnassus and uncle of the historian Herodotus, put to death by the tyrant Lygdamis. *See* HERODOTUS.

Paphlagonia, district of Asia Minor, situated on the Euxine between Bithynia and Pontus. The most important town was Sinope (q.v.). Though subject successively to Lydia, Persia, Alexander and the Seleucids, it continued to be governed by native princes until it had been gradually incorporated in the kingdom of Pontus (*c.* 300–183 B.C.). After the fall of Mithradates the Great (63 B.C.), Pompey restored the inland parts to native rulers, but united the coastal regions to the province of Bithynia. Under the empire the whole of Paphlagonia, together with most of Pontus (q.v.), formed a single province with Bithynia; it was made a separate province by Constantine.

Paphos, name of two towns on the west coast of Cyprus, called 'Old Paphos' and 'New Paphos'. Old Paphos was traditionally founded by Cinyras, whose reputed descendants enjoyed royal privileges until 295, and the Paphian priesthood until 58 B.C. This priesthood was concerned with the worship of a nature-goddess; the Greeks identified her with Aphrodite (q.v.), whom they declared to have risen from the waves at Paphos. The sanctuary of the goddess, where she was worshipped under the form of a conical stone, was several times destroyed by earthquake, notably in 15 B.C., when it was rebuilt by Augustus, and the whole place gradually declined. New Paphos, already in the 3rd century B.C. an important commercial centre, eclipsed the old town. There are remains of the sanctuary, and (in New Paphos) of Roman buildings.

Papinianus, Aemilius, one of the greatest of Roman jurists. Praetorian prefect under Septimius Severus in A.D. 203, he was put to death by Caracalla (q.v.) in 212 for declining to excuse the murder of Geta. His legal writings consisted of two works: *Quaestiones* and *Responsa*, many parts of which are cited in Justinian's *Digest*. Papinian's reputation is illustrated by the Law of Citations (A.D. 426), which gave his opinion the force of law in any dispute where there was no majority on either side. *See* E. Costa, *Papiniano*, 1894–9.

Parcae, *see* MOIRAE.

Parian Marble, The, an inscription discovered in the island of Paros (q.v.) in 1627, now preserved partly at the Ashmolean, Oxford, and partly at Smyrna. In its perfect state it consisted of ninety-three lines recording events from the legendary king Cecrops (1580) to the archonship of Diognetus at Athens (263 B.C.). It deals with the establishment of festivals, births and deaths of poets, and suchlike, rather than with political and military events.

Paris, also called Alexander, in Greek legend the second son of Priam and Hecuba. Before his birth Hecuba dreamed that she had brought forth a firebrand, the flames of which spread over the whole city. Accordingly, as soon as the child was born, he was exposed on Mt Ida, but was brought up by a shepherd, who gave him the name of Paris. When he had grown up he distinguished himself as a defender of the flocks and shepherds, and was hence called Alexander, or the defender of men. He discovered his real origin, and was received by Priam as his son. He married Oenone, the daughter of the river-god Cebren, but he soon deserted her for Helen. The tale runs that when Peleus and Thetis solemnized their nuptials, all the gods were invited to the marriage with the exception of Eris, or Strife. Enraged at her exclusion, the goddess threw a golden apple among the guests, with the inscription, 'To the fairest'. Thereupon Hera, Aphrodite and Athena each claimed the apple for herself. Zeus ordered Hermes to take the goddesses to Mt Ida, and to entrust the decision of the dispute to the shepherd Paris. The goddesses accordingly appeared before him. Hera promised him the sovereignty of Asia, Athena renown in war, and Aphrodite the fairest of women for his wife. Paris decided in favour of Aphrodite, and gave her the golden apple. Under the protection of Aphrodite, Paris now sailed to Greece, and was hospitably received in the palace of Menelaus at Sparta. Here he succeeded in carrying off Helen, the wife of Menelaus, who was the most beautiful woman in the world. Hence arose the Trojan war. Paris fought with Menelaus before the walls of Troy, and was defeated, but was carried off by Aphrodite. He is said to have killed Achilles, either by one of his arrows or by treachery. On the capture of Troy, Paris was wounded by Philoctetes with one of the arrows of Heracles, and then returned to Oenone. But as she refused to heal the wound, Paris died. Oenone repented and put an end to her own life.

Paris, name of two famous *pantomimi* (ballet dancers) in imperial Rome. One was a favourite of Nero, but was executed by him as a rival (A.D. 67). The other was a favourite of Domitian, and was also put to death (A.D. 87).

Parisii, *see* LUTETIA.

Parmenidēs, Greek philosopher, born at Elea in southern Italy, *c.* 515 B.C. He wrote a poem *On Nature*, of which fragments survive, and marks one of the most important stages in the history of philosophy. In opposition to the earlier monists, Thales, Anaximander and Anaximenes (qq.v.), who maintained that the world had developed from a single element, Parmenides held that there is no change or multiplicity. His argument involved an analysis of the verb 'to be', which in turn drove later philosophers either to admit a plurality of original elements (as did Empedocles, Anaxagoras and Democritus), or, like Plato and Aristotle, to discover another and immaterial kind of being. *See* F. M. Cornford, *Plato and Parmenides*, 1939; J. Burnet, *Early Greek Philosophy*, 4th ed., 1945; H. Diels, *Die Fragmente der Vorsokratiker*, 6th ed., 1951.

Parmeniōn, a Macedonian general in the service of Philip II and Alexander the Great (q.v.). When Alexander crossed to Asia (334 B.C.) Parmenion was his second-in-command. His son Philotas (q.v.), however, was in 330 accused of conspiracy against Alexander's life. At this date Philotas was with Alexander in Drangiana, Parmenion in Media. The young man not only confessed his own guilt, but also involved his father. Whether or not Alexander really believed in the guilt of Parmenion, he caused him to be assassinated before he could receive news of his son's death.

Parnassus (-os), mountain range of Greece, extending south-east through Doris and Phocis, and terminating at the Corinthian Gulf between Cirrha and Anticyra. The name, however, was usually restricted to the most lofty part of the range, a few miles north of Delphi (q.v.), of which the two summits were called Tithorea and Lycoreia. Just above Delphi are two projecting cliffs, known as the Phaedriadae, from which flows the Castalian spring. Parnassus was sacred to Apollo and the Muses.

Paros, island of the Cyclades (q.v.) and birth-place of Archilochus (q.v.), was believed to have been colonized first from Arcadia and afterwards by Ionians from Athens. In the Persian wars it sided both with Darius and with Xerxes. After Marathon Miltiades attempted unsuccessfully to reduce the island, and on the final Persian defeat it was punished by Themistocles with a heavy fine. It then became a member of the Delian League. Later it belonged to the Ptolemies, and ultimately to Rome.

Paros was famous chiefly for its white semi-transparent marble, which was obtained from underground quarries in Mt Marpessa. Some ancient galleries are still to be seen. *See also* PARIAN MARBLE, THE.

Parrhasios (*fl.* 400 B.C.), Greek painter, contemporary and rival of Zeuxis (q.v.). He was a native of Ephesus, but spent most of his time in Athens, and is ranked among the greatest Attic artists; indeed he is said to have done for painting what Pheidias did for sculpture. His picture of the Athenian Demos is famous, and his study of Theseus afterwards adorned the Capitol at Rome.

Parthenius (-os), Greek grammarian and poet of the 1st century B.C.; a native of Nicaea, but lived for some time at Neapolis where he taught Virgil Greek. Fragments of his poems have been discovered in Egyptian papyri (*see* HERMOPOLIS; OXYRHYNCHUS). A prose collection of love stories by him has also survived; *see* text and translation by S. Gaselee (with Longus) in the Loeb Library.

Parthenius (-os), a mountain on the border of Argolis and Arcadia, where Telephus, son of Heracles, was said to have been suckled by a hind. Here also Pan was believed to have appeared to Pheidippides (q.v.).

Parthenon, the temple of Athena Parthenos ('Virgin') on the south side of the Acropolis at Athens. The most celebrated Doric temple of ancient Greece, and one of the finest pieces of architecture in the world, it was commenced in 447 and dedicated in 438; the sculptures were completed in 432 B.C. Its architects were Ictinus and Callicrates, but the whole of the work was carried out under the supervision of the sculptor Pheidias (q.v.), by whom the chryselephantine statue of the goddess, which stood in the *naos*, was executed. The Parthenon is octastyle (with eight columns in front) and pseudodipteral (with only one range of columns at the side). The number of columns along the flank is seventeen, counting those at the corners. The most notable feature in the architecture of the Parthenon is the delicacy of the refinements introduced to counteract various optical illusions. These are to be found everywhere, in the curves of the columns, stylobate, cornice, etc. The chief dimensions are as follows (outside measurements): length, 228 feet; width, 101 feet; height, 64 feet; length of *naos*, 98 feet; width of *naos*, 63 feet. The fine sculptures of the metopes, frieze, etc., were mostly removed to the British Museum by Lord Elgin in 1801–16. Those of the eastern pediment represented the birth of Athena; those of the western, the contest between Athena and Poseidon for possession of Attica. The metopes depicted various subjects of Attic legend, including the battle between the Lapithae and the Centaurs. On the frieze was shown the Panathenaic procession. *See* the official *Guide to the Department of Greek and Roman Antiquities in the British Museum*, which contains plans of the building; H. B. Walters, *The Art of the Greeks*, ch. vi, 31st ed., 1934.

Parthenopaeus (-paios), one of the Seven Against Thebes, *see* THEBAN LEGEND, 3

Parthenopē, ancient name of Neapolis (q.v.).

Parthia, a country of western Asia, situated south-east of the Caspian Sea, and corresponding to the northern portion of the modern Persian province of Khorassan. In the early 5th century it became subject to Arsacid Persia, and later to the Seleucids (q.v.). But *c.* 250 B.C. the satrap Pherecles was slain, and Arsaces, leader of the Parnians, a tribe of the Dahae, was proclaimed first king of Parthia; such is the official account, but Pherecles was more probably satrap of Pstaueue, to the north-west of Parthia. The empire thus started grew in importance, until after the time of its greatest power, under Mithradates I and II, it extended to the Euphrates, Caspian Sea, Indus and Indian Ocean. From the 1st century B.C. onwards Parthia was frequently at war with Rome (*see* ARTABANUS; ORODES; PACORUS; PHRAATES), and was at one time her ally and at another her vassal. The Parthian mounted archers were famous, and from their method of firing as they appeared to retreat comes the expression a 'Parthian shot'. In A.D. 226 the country was annexed to the newly established Persian empire of the Sassanids. The Latin poets of the Augustan age use the name Parthi, Persae and Medi indifferently. *See* M. A. R. Colledge, *The Parthians*, 1968.

Pasargadae, city of Persia, founded by Cyrus at the scene of his victory over Astyages (549 B.C.). Though supplanted by Persepolis (q.v.) in the reign of Darius I, the Persian monarchs continued to be invested there, and it contained a rich treasury, which was surrendered to Alexander the Great in 336 B.C. Outside the town (now a scanty heap of ruins) is the tomb of Cyrus, a seven-tiered structure surrounded by a colonnaded court.

Pasiphaē, in Greek legend, daughter of Helios by Perse, and wife of Minos. Concealed in a wooden cow made by Daedalus, she had intercourse with a bull and produced the Minotaur (q.v.).

Patavium (mod. Padua), city of Gallia Cisalpina, afterwards in Venetia (*see* VENETI, 2); birth-place of Livy, Q. Asconius Pedianus and Thrasea Paetus (qq.v.). By its commerce and manufactures (of which woollen stuffs were the most important) it enjoyed great opulence in the time of Augustus; but a century later it had begun to by outstripped by Mediolanum and Aquileia. *See* C. Foligna, *The Story of Padua*, 1910.

Paterculus, Gaius Velleius, Roman historian, born 19 B.C.; served under Tiberius (q.v.) in Germany during the reign of Augustus, and was still living in A.D. 31, when he dedicated his *Historiae Romanae* to M. Vinicius, consul in that year. This work is a brief compendium of Roman history from the destruction of Troy to A.D. 30. It is typical of the rhetorical style of the Silver Age of Latin Literature, but is also a valuable counterbalance to the furious attacks of Tacitus and Suetonius upon the emperor Tiberius. *See* the edition by F. Kritz, 1948; also text and translation by F. W. Shipley (Loeb Library), 1924.

Paterfamilias, *see* PATRIA POTESTAS.

Patrae (-ai), one of the twelve cities of Achaea (q.v.), traditionally founded by Eumelus with the name Aroe (ploughland). It was called Patrae because the ruling families of Achaea dwelt there. Augustus changed its name back to Aroe and established a military colony of veterans from the Tenth and Twelfth Legions.

Patria Potestas, the authority exercised in Roman law by the head of a family (*paterfamilias*) over all its members, including wife and daughters-in-law. Originally this authority extended even to the power of life and death; no one subject to it had any rights of any description whatsoever. But in course of time *patria potestas* was limited by custom and by law, especially under the influence of Christianity.

Patrician, a title of honour created by Constantine the Great, conferred on those who stood highest in the emperor's esteem, and even extended to foreign princes.

Patricians and Plebeians. From the earliest period of Roman history, the population of Rome was made up of two classes: (1) A dominant class with its own religious rites, legal privileges and a monopoly of sacerdotal and political functions. This was the patrician class, consisting doubtless of the primitive Roman families. (2) An inferior class which could not intermarry with the other, possessing different rites and subject to a different set of laws. This was the plebeian class, probably the descendants of conquered peoples transported to the city.

Having need of protection, the plebeians made themselves *clients* of, i.e. placed themselves in a position of dependence upon, the patricians; so that there frequently arose a social link between the two classes analogous to that which in the Middle Ages bound the vassal to his overlord.

The inequality of the two classes gave rise to bitter conflicts which rent the state until the plebeians managed to wring from the patricians civil and political rights. The main episodes in this struggle were the secession of the people to the Sacred Mount (q.v.), followed by the creation of tribunes of the people (*see* TRIBUNE); the agrarian law of Spurius Cassius (486 B.C.) (*see* AGRARIAN LAWS); the granting of *connubium*, i.e. the right of intermarriage (445); the opening to the plebs of all magistracies (*see* PHILO, QUINTUS PUBLILIUS) and even the senate (409–300 B.C.). *See also* COMITIA. The obtaining of equality of status, however, did not abolish the distinction of patrician and plebeian *gentes*; none but a member of a plebeian *gens* could stand for the tribunate. *See* CATILINA; CLODIUS.

Patroclus (-klos), in Greek legend, son of Menoetius of Opus in Locris by his wife Sthenele. Having involuntarily committed homicide while a boy, he was taken by his father for purification to Peleus (q.v.) at Phthia, where he formed a close friendship with Achilles (q.v.). He accompanied Achilles to the Trojan war; and when the hero withdrew from active service, leaving the Greeks hard-pressed, Patroclus obtained his permission to lead the Myrmidons. Achilles equipped him with his own arms and armour, and he drove back the Trojans to their walls, where he was slain by Hector. It was the determination to avenge the death of his friend that brought Achilles once more into the field.

Paulinus, Gaius Suetonius, Roman governor of Britain (q.v.) A.D. 59–62; consul in 66, and one of Otho's generals in the unsuccessful campaign against Vitellius (69).

Paullus, Lucius Aemilius, name of two Roman generals:

1. Consul in 219, and again in 216 B.C., when he fell in action at Cannae (q.v.). *See* VARRO, GAIUS TERENTIUS.

2. Consul for the first time in 182 B.C. During his second tenure of that office, in 168, he won a decisive victory at Pydna over Perseus (q.v.), King of Macedon, and was granted the title Macedonicus. He then made a regular tour of Greece, which was already becoming a land of historic ruins. Paulus died in 160 B.C.; and it was on the occasion of his funeral games that the *Adelphi* of Terence was first staged. His younger son was Scipio Africanus Minor (q.v.).

Pausanias: 1. Spartan general, son of Cleombrotus and nephew of Leonidas I. Some writers err in calling him king; he was only regent for Leonidas's infant son Pleistarchus. He commanded the victorious Greek army at Plataea (479 B.C.), and in the following year led an expedition which subdued most of Cyprus and captured Byzantium. His violence, however, and a certain arrogance which spoke of lofty ambition, disgusted the allies, particularly the Ionians and the newly liberated populations. One by one, therefore, the various city-states transferred to Athens the hegemony hitherto enjoyed by Sparta. Hence the Delian League (q.v.).

Complaints as to the conduct of Pausanias having reached Sparta, he was recalled (477) and censured for his private acts of oppression, but found not guilty on the more serious charge of collaboration with Persia. Despite this acquittal he was not sent out again in a public capacity; but he took a galley of Hermione on his own responsibility, and arrived as a private person in the Hellespont. He came ostensibly on voluntary service in the war, but really to carry on his intrigues with the Persian monarch, through whose good offices he hoped to become tyrant of all Hellas. When news of his proceedings in Asia was reported to the Spartan government, Pausanias was ordered to return. He did so, anxious to avoid suspicion and confident of being able to bribe his way out of any danger. The difficulty facing his accusers was the absence of tangible proof such as was required to substantiate a charge of treason against a member of the royal family. But at length a man who had been entrusted by Pausanias with a letter for the Persian king provided the necessary evidence. His suspicion having been aroused by the consideration that no previous messenger had returned, he counterfeited the writer's seal, opened the letter and found directions for his own death. He carried the letter to the ephors (q.v.), who trapped Pausanias into an oral admission of his guilt and prepared to arrest him. He escaped and took refuge, however, in the temple of the goddess of the Brazen House. But the ephors stripped off the roof of the small chamber in which he had hidden; and having thus exposed him to the weather, they made sure he would starve by barricading the door and setting a watch outside. When they found him on the point of death, they carried him outside in order to avoid pollution of the sanctuary, and he died immediately (470 B.C.). *See* Thucydides, i. 95, 128–34.

2. Young Macedonian nobleman who assassinated Philip II in 336 B.C., possibly with the connivance of Olympias. According to Aristotle (*Pol.* 1311^b), the king had allowed one Attalus and his circle to indulge their unnatural propensities at Pausanias's expense, and the murder was committed as an act of revenge.

3. Greek traveller and topographer, perhaps a native of Lydia, lived in the reigns of Antoninus Pius and Marcus Aurelius (138–80). His *Periēgēsis* (Itinerary) *of Greece* is in ten books as follows: (1) Attica and the Megarid; (2) Corinthia, Sicyonia, Phliasia and Argolis; (3) Laconia; (4) Messenia; (5 and 6) Elis; (7) Achaea; (8) Arcadia; (9) Boeotia; (10) Phocis. Its detailed information is of the greatest interest, and even in recent times it has proved of the utmost value in guiding the work of archaeologists. *See* the edition with translation and commentary by Sir J. G. Frazer, 6 vols., 1898; text and translation by W. H. S. Jones and R. Wycherley, 6 vols. (Loeb Library).

Pausōn, Greek painter, a native of Sicyon, *fl. c.* 360–330 B.C. He seems to have distinguished himself as a trick-painter. His 'Hermes', mentioned by Aristotle (*Metaph.* 1050^a 19), probably appeared to stand out from the surface in high relief; he is also said to have painted a picture of a horse running, which by being turned upside-down showed a horse rolling on its back. In another passage (*Pol.* 1340^a) Aristotle says that 'young people should be encouraged to look not at the works of Pauson, but at those of Polygnotus and any other painter or sculptor who depicts moral character'.

Pax, Latin name for the goddess of peace (*see* IRENE). Her temple at Rome, one of the most magnificent in the city, was built by the emperor Vespasian.

Paxos, island in the Ionian Sea, about eight miles south of Corcyra, and scene in Plutarch's *De defectu oraculorum* of a curious story about Pan: In the reign of Tiberius (A.D. 14–37) the pilot of a ship bound for Italy heard off Paxos some words that proclaimed the death of the pagan world. The pilot's name was Tammuz, and as he coasted past here in the still night a voice called out to him: 'Tammuz! Tammuz! Great Pan is dead.'

Peculium. Those subject to *patria potestas* (q.v.) were incapable under Roman law of owning property. But the *paterfamilias* sometimes gave his son (and even a slave) as allowance known as *peculium*, which he could administer freely, though he was not the legal owner. Augustus provided that, *patria potestas* notwithstanding, whatever the son acquired during military service (*peculium castrense*) was his own property, and the principle was extended by later emperors.

Pedianus, Quintus Asconius (*c.* 9 B.C.–*c.* A.D. 76), Latin grammarian, born at Patavium. He wrote a commentary, of which considerable fragments have survived, on the speeches of Cicero. *See* the edition by A. C. Clark, 1907.

Pegasus (Pēgasos), in Greek mythology, a winged horse, sprang from the blood of Medusa (q.v.) when Perseus (q.v.) cut off her head. Pegasus bore Perseus to the rescue of Andromeda, and carried Bellerophon (q.v.) in his fight with the Chimaera, after which he was placed among the stars. He was also considered as the symbol of poetic genius, and was said to have brought forth with a stroke of his hoof the fountain Hippocrene on Mt Helicon (qq.v.).

Peiraeus (Peiraieus), *see* ATHENS, *Peiraeus and the Long Walls.*

Peisistratids (Gk Peisistratidai), name given to Hippias and Hipparchus as sons and successors of Peisistratus (q.v.).

Peisistratus (-os), tyrant of Athens 560–555, 551–545 and 535–527 B.C. He was son of Hippocrates, and his mother is said to have been first cousin of Solon's mother. When Solon (q.v.) withdrew from Athens after reorganizing the constitution, three conflicting parties soon emerged, called after the districts where their lands were situate. The party of the Coast, led by the Alcmaeonid Megacles, appeared to be striving after a moderate form of government; that of the Plain, under Lycurgus, wished for an oligarchy. But the party of the Highlands was led by Peisistratus, who had the reputation of an extreme democrat. When Peisistratus saw that the time was ripe, he appeared in the Agora, his mules and his own person exhibiting recent wounds, and pretended only just to have escaped assassination by his political opponents as he was riding into the country. The people took his word for it, and passed a measure assigning him a bodyguard of fifty men. With these he turned on the people and seized the Acropolis 560 B.C. But in 555 the parties of Megacles and Lycurgus combined to expel him before his power was firmly rooted.

At the end of another four years, however, Megacles found himself embroiled with Lycurgus, and therefore approached Peisistratus with an offer of his daughter's hand in marriage. Peisistratus agreed; but there were faces to be saved, and the exile was brought back to Athens by means of an almost childish ruse. Megacles announced that Athena herself was bringing back Peisistratus. He then found a woman of great stature and beauty named Phye, dressed her up to resemble the goddess, and introduced her to the city riding in a chariot with Peisistratus. The crowds were duly impressed and welcomed him with acclamation (551 B.C.).

Again, however, his government was short-lived. Refusing to treat Megacles's daughter as his wife, he was faced with a coalition of the other parties and fled the country (545), first to Rhaicelus in Macedonia, and then to the neighbourhood of Mt Pangaeus in Thrace. In this latter place he made a fortune, with which he was able to raise a band of mercenaries and re-establish the tyranny by force of arms. He was not again disturbed, and died at Athens in 527 B.C.

The administration of Peisistratus was more like that of a constitutional monarch than of a tyrant. He governed in such a way as to foster peace and contentment among all classes, and his reign was afterwards considered a golden age, especially under the harsher regime of his sons. Peisistratus was also a munificent patron of literature and the arts, and he developed the industrial life of Athens. To him we owe the first written text of the *Iliad* and *Odyssey*, which but for his care would most likely now exist only in fragments.

Peisistratus was succeeded in the tyranny by his two sons, Hippias and Hipparchus. They took over the government jointly; but Hippias was *de facto* ruler, owing to his natural statesmanship and shrewd disposition. Hipparchus inherited his father's literary tastes, and several distinguished poets, e.g. Simonides of Ceos and Anacreon, lived under his patronage at the Athenian court. After the assassination of Hipparchus (*see* HARMODIUS AND ARISTOGEITON) the tyranny of Hippias became much more severe. The vengeance he exacted for his brother's death, in the shape of numerous executions and banishments, brought him into hatred and contempt, which in turn embittered him still further. Discontent reached a head in 510 B.C.: Hippias and all his family were expelled with the help of King Cleomenes I of Sparta. He went to the Persian court, and accompanied the Persian expedition which ended in the battle of Marathon (490 B.C.). According to some accounts he fell in action. Others, with more probability, say that he died at Lemnos on the return journey.

Pelasgi (**-oi**), name used by ancient writers to describe the prehellenic population of Greece. The term Pelasgic was applied to any survival from prehistoric times.

Pēleus, son of Aeacus (q.v.), King of the Myrmidons in Aegina (qq.v.). Having, with his brother Telamon (q.v.), murdered his half-brother Phocus, he was expelled by Aeacus and went to Phthiotis in Thessaly, together with some of the Myrmidons, who recognized him as their king. Here he was purified from the guilt of murder by the king, Eurytion, who gave him his daughter in marriage and a third part of his kingdom. Peleus accompanied Eurytion to the Calydonian hunt (*see* MELEAGER); but having accidentally killed his father-in-law, he again became a wanderer and took refuge in Iolcus, whose king, Acastus (q.v.), purified him. During the funeral games celebrated for Pelias (*see* JASON AND MEDEA), Acastus's wife Hippolyte (or Astydameia) fell in love with Peleus, and when he refused her advances she accused him to her husband of having attempted to dishonour her. Shortly afterwards, while Acastus and Peleus were hunting on Mt Pelion, and the latter had fallen asleep, Acastus took his sword and left him alone. He was rescued from death through wild beasts (or the Centaurs) by Hermes (or Chiron); after which he returned to Iolcus, where he slew both Acastus and Hippolyte. Meanwhile, on Mt Pelion, he had covered the nereid Thetis (q.v.), by whom he became the father of Achilles (q.v.). Too old to accompany Achilles in the Trojan war, Peleus survived his illustrious son.

Pelias, *see* JASON AND MEDEA.

Pēlion, mountain in the north of Thessaly, connected with Ossa (q.v.) on the north-west. On its summit was a temple dedicated to Zeus Actaeus, and its wooded slopes provided the timber from which the Argo (*see* ARGONAUTS) was built. *See* ALOIDAE.

Pella, city of Macedonia, capital of Philip II and birth-place of Alexander the Great. Situated midway between Thessalonica and Edessa, the site was rediscovered in 1957. Excavation still continues. See *The Times,* 9th May and 13th September 1957.

Pēlopia, daughter of Thyestes and mother of Aegisthus, *see* ATREIDS, LEGEND OF THE.

Pelopidas, Theban general and friend of Epameinondas. He took a leading part in driving the Spartans from Thebes (*see* ARCHIAS), shared in the victory of Leuctra, and was killed in the hour of victory over Alexander of Pherae at Cynoscephalae (364 B.C.).

Peloponnesian War, name given to the conflict between Athens and Sparta, with their respective allies. It lasted from 431 to 404 B.C. and ended with the defeat of Athens. A number of secondary occurrences, e.g. Athenian intervention in a quarrel between Corinth and Corcyra (qq.v.), precipitated its outbreak; but the real cause was the hatred inspired among the mainland, Dorian and oligarchical states (of which Sparta was the chief) by the commercial prosperity of Athens, which rested upon her control of an empire (*see* DELIAN LEAGUE) composed principally of maritime, Ionian and democratic states.

The Peloponnesian war falls naturally into three periods. From 431 to 421 the belligerents ravaged one another's territory without any decisive result. This first period closes with the Peace of Nicias, which guaranteed a fifty years' truce, but which proved to be no peace at all and was formally violated in 416 by the Athenian decision to send an expedition to Sicily (*see* SYRACUSE). The second period ends with the annihilation of the Athenian armament in 413. In the third period, 412–404, the Athenians were victorious at Miletus, Cyzicus and Arginusae, but the Spartans, helped by Persian gold, took Lampsacus, inflicted an overwhelming defeat upon the last Athenian naval squadron at Aegospotami (405), and in the following year installed at Athens the violent and reactionary government of the Thirty. The main source of information for the first twenty years of the war (i.e. to 411 B.C.) is Thucydides (q.v.). *See* AGIS; ALCIBIADES; BRASIDAS; CLEON; CONON; DEMOSTHENES, I; GYLIPPUS; HERMAE; MELOS; NICIAS; PERICLES; PHORMION. *See also* B. W. Henderson, *The Great War between Athens and Sparta,* 1927; G. B. Grundy, *Thucydides and the History of his Age,* 1948.

Peloponnesus (-nēsos), 'island of Pelops', that part of Hellas which lies south of the isthmus of Corinth. The name occurs first in the Homeric *Hymn to Apollo*. On the east and south are three great gulfs, the Argolic, Laconian and Messenian. The ancients compared the shape of the country to the leaf of a plane-tree; its medieval name, Morea, which first occurs in the 12th century, derives from its supposed resemblance to the mulberry leaf. Peloponnesus was divided into six districts: Achaea, Elis, Messenia, Laconia, Argolis and Arcadia (qq.v.).

Traditional accounts represent Peloponnesus as inhabited at the time of the Trojan war by Ionians in Achaea, by Achaeans in Argolis, Laconia, Elis and Messenia, and by the aboriginal Pelasgi (q.v.). The same accounts tell us that eighty years after the Trojan war Peloponnesus was invaded by the Dorians (q.v.) who established themselves in Argolis, Laconia and Messenia; that some of the Achaean population remained as subjects of the Dorians (*see* HELOTS); and that the remainder shifted to the north, expelled the Ionians and settled in that part of the country known in classical times as Achaea (q.v.). From the 7th to the 4th century B.C. the entire peninsula was dominated by Sparta (q.v.). *See also* ACHAEAN LEAGUE. After 146 B.C. it formed part of the Roman province of Achaea.

Pelops, in Greek legend, son of Tantalus (q.v.). His father once invited the gods to dinner, slew Pelops and served up his flesh to table. The immortals, however, were not deceived, excepting Demeter (q.v.), who was so absorbed in grief for her lost daughter Persephone (q.v.) that she ate a shoulder. Hermes was ordered by Zeus to put the remaining limbs into a boiling cauldron, and thus restored Pelops to life. The missing shoulder was replaced by one of ivory. When Pelops grew up he was expelled from Lydia and went to Elis. Here King Oenomaus of Pisa was offering the hand of his daughter Hippodameia to anyone who could beat him in a chariot race; the reason being that an oracle had told him he would be killed by his son-in-law, and his horses were the swiftest on earth. Pelops therefore bribed Myrtilus, the king's charioteer, to remove the linchpin from his master's car, in return for half the kingdom. In consequence, during the race, Oenomaus was flung from his chariot and killed. Pelops succeeded to the throne, and married Hippodameia, but he would not keep faith with Myrtilus. One day as they were driving along a cliff top he threw him into the sea, and Myrtilus, as he sank, cursed the whole race of Pelops. For the sons of Pelops *see* ATREIDS. Pelops gave his name to Peloponnesus ('Isle of Pelops'). He appears to have died a peaceful death (but *see* TANTALUS), and was worshipped at Olympia. The curse took effect on his descendants.

Peltasts (Gk *Peltastai*). Greek light infantry, wearing no body armour but carrying large shields, short swords and spears, seem to have been introduced from Thrace during the 5th century B.C. Early in the following century this force was remodelled by Iphicrates (q.v.), who equipped them with quilted tunics and leather leggings; substituted for the shield a small round targe (*peltē*, whence their name); and also lengthened the sword and spear. This model became the standard in all Greek armies, but light infantry ceased to be employed when the Macedonian phalanx became the principal arm of warfare. *See* H. W. Parke, *Greek Mercenary Soldiers*, 1933.

Penates, in Roman religion, originally deities of the threshold, but subsequently guardians of the home along with the *Lares* (q.v.).

Pēnelopē, daughter of Icarius and Periboea, and wife of Odysseus (q.v.), to whom she bore Telemachus (q.v.). During the long absence of Odysseus, Penelope was wooed by persistent suitors, but put them off with the excuse that she had to weave a robe for Laertes, her father-in-law, while she undid by night her work of the day. Odysseus returned in time to save her and kill these parasites. She is the type of wifely faithfulness.

Pentapolis, 'Five Cities', a name for any group of five cities, but applied more particularly to those of Cyrenaica: Cyrene, Berenice, Arsinoë, Ptolemais and Apollonia.

Pentathlon, *see* OLYMPIC GAMES.

Pentelicus (Gk Pentelikon oros; mod. Mendeli), mountain of Attica, famous for its white marble. This was obtained from quarries on the southern slopes; it was first worked on a large scale after the Persian wars and formed the material of all the chief monuments of Athens.

Penthesileia, in Greek legend, daughter of Ares by Otrera, and Queen of the Amazons. After the death of Hector she came to the assistance of the Trojans, but was slain by Achilles. A later story adds that Achilles, while mourning over her body, was mocked by Thersites, whom he promptly slew.

Pentheus, son of Echion (one of the 'Sparti'; *see* CADMUS) by Agave, daughter of Cadmus, succeeded the latter as King of Thebes. He resisted the introduction of the worship of Dionysus (q.v.), a story which doubtless reflects an historical opposition on the part of many Greek princes to the spread of those orgiastic rites. By way of revenge the god drove him mad, his palace was hurled to the ground, and he himself was torn to pieces on Mt Cithaeron by his wife and two of her sisters, Ino and Autonoë, who in their frenzy believed him to be a wild beast. *See* Euripides, *Bacchae.*

Perdiccas (-dikkas): (A) Name of three Macedonian kings:

1. A native of Argos in the 8th century B.C.; with two of his brothers he conquered a large part of Macedonia and founded the Macedonian dynasty.

2. Reigned *c.* 454–413 B.C. During the Peloponnesian war he allied himself first with the Athenians and then with the Spartans, betraying both parties.

3. Reigned 364–359 B.C., brother of Philip II (q.v.). Aided by the Athenian Iphicrates he overthrew the regent Ptolemy. Later he made war against the Athenians, and fell in battle against the Illyrians.

(B) One of the most famous generals of Alexander the Great. He became chief minister of Alexander's successor, Philip Arrhidaeus; but his rivals, Antipater, Antigonus, Craterus and Ptolemy, conspired against him. While marching against Ptolemy he was murdered at Memphis by his own soldiers (321 B.C.).

Perdix, in Greek legend, nephew of Daedalus (q.v.) and inventor of the saw, chisel and compasses. Daedalus became jealous of the young man's skill, and threw him down from the temple of Athena on the Acropolis at Athens. A later version of the story states that as he fell the goddess changed him into a partridge.

Perga, city of Pamphylia (q.v.), on the River Cestus eight miles from the coast; birth-place of the mathematician Apollonius. It was the chief centre of the worship of a local nature-goddess, represented as a human-headed cone and identified by the Greeks with Artemis (q.v.), but is now more famous as the starting-point of St Paul's first missionary journey.

Pergamum (-on), city of Mysia in Asia Minor; capital of the kingdom of Pergamum and afterwards of the Roman province of Asia. Said to have been founded by Aeolian Greeks, it is first mentioned in Xenophon's *Anabasis*, but was a place of some importance as early as 420 B.C. After the death of Alexander the Great, Lysimachus (q.v.) became master of the city, but was ousted in 283 B.C. by Philetaerus, governor of the fortress. Philetaerus died in 263, bequeathing his small principality to his nephew Eumenes I, who died in 241 and was succeeded by his cousin Attalus I. Attalus and his son Eumenes II allied themselves closely with Rome, as a result of which their territory was progressively enlarged, and on the death of Eumenes in 159 the Pergamene kingdom included almost the whole of western Asia Minor. Attalus III died in 133 B.C. and left his dominions to Rome; they were formed into the province of Asia, excepting Great Phrygia which was given to Mithradates of Pontus. Pergamum was the birthplace of Galen (q.v.), and the home of a celebrated school of sculpture which was largely influenced by Lysippus and Scopas (qq.v.). *See* ARISTONICUS; ATTALUS; EUMENES (B). *See also* E. V. Hansen, *The Attalids of Pergamum*, 1947.

Periander (Gk Periandros), tyrant of Corinth 627–581 B.C., son of Cypselus (q.v.) and one of the Seven Sages of Greece. His government during the latter part of his reign was severe, but he greatly enhanced the prosperity of Corinth and proved himself a brilliant soldier. A famous story illustrates his rather dry sagacity. Thrasybulus, tyrant of Miletus, sent to ask the advice of Periander upon some problem of government. The messenger found him in a cornfield: by way of answer Periander spoke never a word, but merely levelled the surface of the field by lopping off the outstanding ears. The messenger, quite bewildered, returned to Miletus and told his master what had happened. Thrasybulus, however, understood that he must get rid of the outstanding men in his own state.

Pericles (-klēs), Athenian statesman, born *c.* 490 B.C., son of Xanthippus and Agariste. His father commanded the Athenian squadron at the battle of Mycale (479). Pericles received his higher education under the sophist and musician Damon, and the philosopher Anaxagoras (q.v.), who became his closest friend. By 469 Pericles was regarded as leader of the democratic party in opposition to Cimon (q.v.). In 461, through the medium of his friend Ephialtes, he carried a measure to restrict the powers of the Areopagus, and secured the ostracism (q.v.) of Cimon. Pericles likewise enjoyed the confidence of his fellow citizens as a military commander; and his most outstanding successes in this capacity were the recovery of Euboea (446) and the reduction of Samos (440). After the death of Cimon (449) the aristocratic party was led by Thucydides, son of Melisias; but on the ostracism of Thucydides, in 443, Pericles was left without a rival. He spent the years 440–432 beautifying Athens (q.v.) with public buildings. Meanwhile his enemies did their best to destroy his reputation; but failing in this, they attacked him through his friends. Pheidias, Anaxagoras and Pericles's mistress Aspasia were all denounced. The great sculptor went into exile after a trumped-up charge of impiety; the philosopher, because of his unorthodoxy, was ordered to pay a heavy fine and to leave Athens; Aspasia also was accused of blasphemy, and was saved only through the eloquence of her lover.

On the outbreak of the Peloponnesian war (431 B.C.), which Pericles had long foreseen, he urged the Athenians to rely wholly upon their sea-power; and their neglect of that advice led to ultimate disaster. At the end of the first year's campaign Pericles delivered the celebrated funeral oration, which forms perhaps the most memorable statement of Athenian values and aspirations. In the summer of 430 plague broke out at Athens, carrying off his two sons, Xanthippus and Paralus, and most of his intimate friends, besides demoralizing the people. Pericles himself died in the following year (429 B.C.). Renowned for his dignified bearing and splendid eloquence, he was also a man of unimpeachable honour and courage. Under his leadership Athens attained the zenith of her artistic glory, of her imperial greatness and of her commercial prosperity. *See* Thucydides, bks i and ii; A. R. Burn, *Pericles and Athens*, 1949.

Perillus (-os), inventor of the brazen bull of Phalaris (q.v.).

Perinthus (-os), a Thracian town on the Propontis, was colonized from Samos *c.* 559 B.C. It was afterwards called Heraclea Perinthus, and in 340 B.C. resisted an attack by Philip II of Macedon.

Perperna, Marcus, name of two Roman soldiers:

1 Consul 130 B.C., when he defeated Aristonicus (q.v.) who had laid claim to the Pergamene kingdom bequeathed by Attalus III to Rome.

2. Grandson of the preceding. A supporter of the Marian party during the civil wars, he afterwards (77 B.C.) went to Spain and fought under Sertorius (q.v.), of whose assassination he was the principal agent (72 B.C.). In the same year Perperna was defeated and put to death by Pompey.

Persē, daughter of Oceanus and Tethys, mother by Helios (q.v.) of Perses, husband of Asteria (q.v.).

Persephonē, in Greek mythology, daughter of Zeus and Demeter, called in Latin Proserpina. For her legend *see* DEMETER. She was worshipped in Attica under the name Korē, 'Maid'.

Persepolis, Greek name for the official capital of the Persian Empire, 40 miles east of Shiraz. It superseded Pasargadae (q.v.) in the reign of Darius I. The vast palace, with its treasury and splendid works of art, was built on an artificial terrace. It was partly destroyed in 331 B.C. by Alexander the Great. There are considerable remains. Eight miles to the north-east are the rock-hewn tombs of Darius I, Xerxes I, Artaxerxes I and Darius II. Those of Artaxerxes II, Artaxerxes III and (probably) Darius III are immediately behind the palace. Persepolis was afterwards capital of the Seleucid province of Persis, and, from the 3rd century A.D., of the Sassanid Empire. *See* E. F. S. Schmidt, *The Treasury of Persepolis*, 1939.

Persēs, son of Helios by Perse (q.v.), brother of Circe and Pasiphae (qq.v.), and father of Hecate by Asteria (q.v.).

Perseus. Lynceus, mythical son of Aegyptus and husband of Hypermestra (see DANAÜS), was succeeded as King of Argos by his son Abas, who in turn begat twins, Acrisius and Proetus (q.v.).

Acrisius followed his father on the throne of Argos and had a daughter named Danaë; but since he had been warned by an oracle that she would bear a son who would kill him, he shut her up in an apartment of bronze (stone according to some versions). Zeus, however, transformed himself into a shower of gold, penetrated the roof of Danaë's prison and became by her the father of Perseus.

As soon as Acrisius learned that Danaë had given birth to a son he put them both into a chest and set them adrift in the Aegean. But Zeus caused the chest to come ashore at Seriphos (q.v.), where Dictys, a fisherman, found Danaë and her son, and took them to King Polydectes. In course of time Polydectes fell in love with Danaë, and wishing to get rid of Perseus, who had now grown up, sent him to fetch the head of Medusa (q.v.). Guided by Athena and Hermes, Perseus went first to the Graeae (q.v.), took from them their one eye and one tooth, and would not restore them until they had showed him the way to the nymphs who possessed the winged sandals, the magic wallet and the helmet of Pluto (see TITANS) which rendered its wearer invisible. Having received these from the nymphs, together with a sickle from Hermes and a mirror from Athena, Perseus rose into the air and reached the abode of the Gorgons. Finding them asleep, he cut off Medusa's head (see PEGASUS) with the sickle—watching her in the mirror, for a direct sight of the monster would have turned him to stone—and put it into the wallet which he carried on his back. The helmet rendered him invisible as he fled, pursued by the other Gorgons.

On the way home Perseus rescued and married Andromeda (q.v.), and, according to some versions, used the Gorgon's head to turn Atlas (q.v.) to stone. Arrived at Seriphos, he found that Danaë had taken refuge from Polydectes in a temple. He therefore went to the palace, where he petrified the king and his guests. Then, having presented the head to Athena (see AEGIS), he proceeded to Argos accompanied by Danaë and Andromeda. Acrisius, hearing of all this and remembering the oracle, escaped to Larisa in Thessaly, whither Perseus also went in disguise, meaning to persuade him to return. But on arrival he took part in some games, and accidentally killed Acrisius with the discus. Then, leaving the kingdom of Argos to Megapenthes, son of Proetus, he received in exchange the throne of Tiryns (q.v.). See J. M. Woodward, *Perseus: A Study in Greek Art and Legend*, 1937.

Perseus, last king of Macedonia, son of Philip V (see PHILIP, 3), whom he succeeded in 179 B.C. at the age of thirty-three. In 171 Rome's third Macedonian war broke out, and lasted until 168, when Perseus was defeated at the battle of Pydna by the consul L. Aemilius Paulus (see PAULUS, LUCIUS AEMILIUS, 2). He adorned the triumph of his conqueror, but ended his days in honourable captivity at Alba Fucens.

Persian Wars, The, an intermittent conflict between the Achaemenid

empire of Persia and the Greek city-states (490–449 B.C.). The
initial attack by Dareios I (q.v.), in 490, was provoked by Athenian
assistance rendered to the Ionian revolt (see IONIA). It ended with the
Greek victory at Marathon (q.v.; see also MILTIADES) in the same
year.

The second Persian war began in 480, when Xerxes (q.v.), successor
of Dareios, invaded Greece and burned Athens. His forces, however,
were defeated at the naval battle of Salamis (q.v.; see also ARTEMIS-
IUM; THEMISTOCLES), and again at Plataea and Mycale (qq.v.) in 479.

In 468 the Greeks counter-attacked, and won a victory on the
Eurymedon (q.v.). The struggle was renewed in 450; but in the
following year the Persians agreed to the Peace of Cimon (see CIMON),
whereby their armies were forbidden to approach the Greek cities of
Asia Minor, and their fleets were banned from Greek waters. See
G. B. Grundy, The Great Persian War, 1901.

Persis (mod. Persia), the Greek name for a country bounded south-
west by the Persian Gulf, and which was the original nucleus of the
Persian Empire. It was so called from the name of its inhabitants, the
Parsa, which the Ionian Greeks of Asia Minor pronounced as Persai.
At the beginning of the 6th century B.C. the population consisted of a
number of tribes subject to the overlordship of Media. In 549 B.C.
the king of one of these tribes, Cyrus the Great, overthrew the empire
of the Medes and became master of western Asia. The third Persian
king, Darius I, established an empire which, on the death of his
successor Cambyses II, extended from Thrace and Cyrenaica on the
west to the Indus on the east, and from the Euxine, the Caucasus, the
Caspian, the Oxus and Jaxartes on the north to Aethiopia, Arabia and
the Red Sea on the south. For a summary of Persian history, so far
as it enters directly into that of Greece and Rome, see ARTAXERXES;
CAMBYSES; CYRUS; DAREIOS; SASSANIDAE; XERXES. See also P. R.
Sykes, History of Persia, 1930.

Persius Flaccus, Aulus, Roman satirist, born of a wealthy equestrian
family at Volaterrae, 4th December A.D. 34. His father died when he
was only six years old; but his mother devoted much care to his
education, first at Volaterrae, and then removing him in his twelfth
year to Rome. There he went through the usual course of instruction
for youths in his position, attending the lectures first of the grammarian Remmius Palaemon, and afterwards those of the rhetorician
Virginius Flavus. At the age of sixteen he was placed under the Stoic
philosopher L. Annaeus Cornutus (q.v.). Though living in a small
domestic circle with his mother, sister and aunt, he was admitted to
the best literary society of the time: Caesius Bassus, Thrasea Paetus
(whose wife Arria was his kinswoman) and Lucan (qq.v.) were among
his friends. He died on 24th November A.D. 62, leaving the six extant
Satires (unrevised) to Cornutus. The latter made a few corrections
and then left the editing of them to Bassus. See modern editions by
J. Conington and H. Nettleship, 1893; S. G. Owen (with Juvenal),
1907; G. G. Ramsay (with Juvenal and prose translation, Loeb
Library), 1918. There is a complete verse translation by W. Gifford
(1821), revised by J. Warrington, in Everyman's Library, 1954. See
also J. Wight Duff, Roman Satire, 1937.

Pertinax, Helvius, Roman emperor 1st January–28th March A.D. 193. At the age of sixty-seven he was reluctantly persuaded to accept the purple on the death of Commodus. But having attempted to check the licence of the praetorian guards he was murdered by them, and the empire put up for auction. *See* DIDIUS SALVIUS JULIANUS, MARCUS.

Perusia (mod. Perugia), originally one of the twelve cities of the Etruscan confederacy. Here L. Antonius took refuge late in the year 41 B.C. and was besieged by Octavian. Famine obliged the city to capitulate in the following spring; but one of its citizens having set fire to his own house, the flames spread, and the whole place, excepting the Etruscan walls and two temples, was burned to the ground. It was rebuilt almost at once. *See* W. Heywood, *History of Perugia,* 1910.

Pervigilium Veneris, title of an anonymous Latin poem (quatrains of trochaic tetrameters), describing the awakening of the world by the goddess of spring. It has been attributed to Florus in the 2nd century A.D.; but other authorities place it as much as two hundred years later, and assign it to Tiberianus. *See* edition by Sir Cecil Clementi, 1936, and verse translation by A. S. Way.

Pessinus (-ous), a Phrygian city in Asia Minor, and principal sanctuary of the Great Mother of the Gods (q.v.) under the name Dindymene or Agdistis, whose priests were also rulers of the neighbourhood. At some date before 164 B.C. Pessinus became subject to Gallic invaders and was thenceforward reckoned part of Galatia (q.v.).

Petra, capital of the Nabataei (q.v.), and afterwards (A.D. 106) of Arabia Petraea, situated in the dry bed of the Wadi Musa, on an ancient caravan route, about 115 miles south-west of Amman; remarkable for the reds, browns, purples and ivory of its sandstone. It lies in a steep-sided basin, and contains over 750 tombs and tomb-temples, their façades cut from the living rock, constructed chiefly between 100 B.C. and A.D. 100. There is an amphitheatre (*c.* 1st century A.D.) among the remains of the Roman city. With the exploitation of Palmyra (q.v.) as a caravan centre, the importance of Petra declined; but its prosperity was suddenly terminated during the reign of Alexander Severus (A.D. 222–35), probably as the result of a large-scale desert raid connected with the rising power of Sassanid Persia. By the end of the 3rd century it was largely abandoned. Petra was rediscovered in 1812 by J. L. Burkhardt. *See* Sir A. Kennedy, *Petra,* 1925; M. A. Murray, *Petra,* 1939.

Petreius, Marcus, Roman soldier; first mentioned in 62 B.C., when he defeated Catiline (q.v.). In 49 he was one of Pompey's three lieutenants in Spain, and together with his colleague L. Afranius (q.v.), was defeated by Caesar in the campaign of Ilerda. Their lives were spared, but their army was disbanded, and Petreius makes his next appearance in the African war. After the battle of Thapsus he and King Juba I of Numidia fled to one of the latter's estates, where they agreed to seek death honourably in mutual combat. Juba was slain; and Petreius, who could expect no mercy even from Caesar, chose to perish by the sword of his slave. *See* T. Rice Holmes, *The Roman Republic,* vol. iii, 1923.

Petronius, Gaius, a companion of Nero, 'managing director' of his entertainment (*arbiter elegantiae*). His influence roused the jealousy of Tigellinus (q.v.): being accused of treason, he committed suicide by opening his veins (A.D. 66). *See* Tacitus, *Annales*, xvi. 18, 19.

It is not absolutely certain, though it is generally agreed, that he was the author of a partly extant work entitled *Petronii Arbitri Satyricon*, a comic romance, often licentious but keenly satirical, the most complete surviving fragment being the celebrated 'Cena Trimalchionis'. The *Satyricon* is a mine of information upon contemporary Latin slang, surpassed only by the *graffiti* of Pompeii. *See* W. D. Lowe's edition and translation, 1905.

Peucini, *see* BASTARNAE.

Phaeacians (Gk Phaiakes), a legendary people in the island of Scheria (*see* ALCINOÜS; NAUSICAA), immortalized in *Odyssey* vi. They lived in undisturbed happiness and peace, had ships that needed no guidance, but became types of gluttony and luxury. *See* A. C. Merriam, *Phaecians of Homer*, 1880; L. Cottrell, *The Bull of Minos*, 1955.

Phaedon (Phaidōn), a native of Elis in Peloponnesus, sold as a slave at Athens. He obtained his freedom, became a disciple of Socrates, and was present at his death, as described in the magnificent dialogue of Plato which bears Phaedon's name. He then returned to Elis, where he founded a school of philosophy. *See* MENEDEMUS.

Phaedra (Phai-), in Greek legend, daughter of Minos and wife of Theseus, who falsely accused her stepson Hippolytus (q.v.). Overcome with remorse she strangled herself.

Phaedrus (Phaidros), Latin fabulist, born in Thrace or Macedonia *c*. 30 B.C. He came to Rome as a slave in the household of Augustus, where he learned Latin and received from the emperor his freedom. His fables, which form part of the traditional Aesopian canon, are ninety-seven in number. *See* the edition by J. B. Postgate (Oxford Classical Texts), 1920.

Phaëthōn, 'the shining', used as an epithet or surname of Helios (the Sun), but more commonly of a son of Helios by Clymene, who requested his father to allow him to drive the chariot of the sun across the heavens for one day. Helios yielded, but the youth being too weak to check the horses, they rushed out of their track, and came so near the earth as almost to set it on fire. Thereupon Zeus killed him with a flash of lightning, and hurled him down into the River Eridanus (q.v.). Later it was said that Phaëthon's sisters, who had harnessed the horses to the chariot, were changed into pine-trees and their tears into amber.

Phalanx, name given to the formation of the heavy infantry of Greek armies. It consisted of a series of parallel columns of men standing close one behind the other, and capable of penetrating and resisting almost any other formation. The Spartan phalanx was the original, and consisted of soldiers standing from four to eight men deep. The Macedonian phalanx, the last of this formation, was sixteen men deep, the soldiers being armed with swords and 13-foot pikes. They were flanked by light infantry and cavalry. The Romans defeated the phalanx by a combination of missile attacks and harassing tactics.

Phalaris, tyrant of Acragas (Agrigentum) in Sicily 570–554 B.C.; perished in an outbreak of popular fury. He is celebrated particularly for the brazen bull in which he burned alive the victims of his cruelty, having tried it out for the first time on its inventor, Perillus. The epistles bearing his name were shown by Bentley (*Dissertation*, 1699) to be forgeries of the 2nd century B.C.

Pharmakoi, human 'medicines'. In primitive times, at the festival Thargelia (q.v.) at Athens, two human beings were slain and burnt, and their ashes cast into the sea. This rite, non-Greek in origin, was regarded as a purification or 'medicine' of the city. It has been suggested that the *pharmakos* was originally a messenger representative of a whole people, carrying at his death their petition to the god for deliverance from calamity (cf. the Jewish scapegoat). As manners became softened, a dough figure was substituted for the human sacrifice. *See* J. C. Lawson, *Modern Greek Folklore and Ancient Greek Religion*, 1910.

Pharnabazus (-os), Persian satrap of the Hellespont and Phrygia, who aided the Spartans during the last years of the Peloponnesian war. He is believed to have been responsible for the death of Alcibiades (q.v.).

Pharnaces: 1. King of Pontus (q.v.) *c.* 185–169 B.C., grandfather of Mithradates VII the Great.

2. Son of Mithradates above-mentioned (*see* MITHRADATES). Having obliged his father to commit suicide (63 B.C.), he was rewarded by Pompey with the kingdom of Bosporus. While Rome was distracted by civil war (49–48 B.C.), Pharnaces decided to enlarge his dominions. He overran Lesser Armenia and Cappadocia; and when Domitius Calvinus intervened on behalf of Deiotarus (q.v.), he was defeated by Pharnaces at Nicopolis (48 B.C.). Pharnaces then invaded Pontus (q.v.), stormed many of the towns, plundered both Roman and native residents and castrated all the Roman youths whose beauty recommended them to his lust. In 47 B.C., however, he was decisively beaten by Julius Caesar at Zela (q.v.), deprived of his territories and put to death later in the year by Asander, whom he had left as regent.

Pharos, a long low island offshore from Alexandria (q.v.). It was connected with the city by a mole, called the Heptastadion, or Seven Furlongs, which formed the western side of the Great Harbour and severed it from a smaller port, the harbour of Eunostos; but ships could pass from harbour to harbour through two arches, one at either end of the mole. At the extreme north-eastern tip of the island stood the great lighthouse which took its name from the island, transmitted that name to similar structures, and was among the Seven Wonders of the World. The lighthouse was built of white limestone by Ptolemy II, Philadelphus (285–246 B.C.). It consisted of a square tower 60 metres high, above which rose a smaller octagonal structure of 30 metres, surmounted by one of cylindrical form, which was smaller still. The total height, from sea level to the top of the statue which stood upon the apex, was about 360 feet. The Pharos was destroyed in the 14th century by successive earthquakes. *See* H. Thiersch, *Pharos*, 1909.

Pharsalus (-os), town of Thessaly which is often, though wrongly, supposed to have given its name to the battle in which Caesar defeated Pompey (9th August 48 B.C.). The action was fought, it is now generally agreed, on the north bank of the River Enipeus, near Palaepharsalus which lay about seven miles north-west of Pharsalus, on the south bank of the river.

Phayllus (Phaullos), one of the Phocian leaders in the Sacred war (352 B.C.). He carried off from Delphi what was claimed to be the necklace of Harmonia (q.v.), and gave it to his mistress. After she had worn it for some time, her son went mad and set fire to the house, where she perished.

Phēgeus, King of Psophis, *see* ALCMAEON.

Pheidias or **Phidias** (*c.* 500–*c.* 417 B.C.), Greek sculptor, born at Athens, son of Charmides; studied under the Argive Ageladas, or, according to another authority, under Hegias of Athens. He was entrusted by Pericles (q.v.) with general superintendence over the erection of those public buildings with which the great statesman adorned his native city, in particular the Propylaea and the Parthenon (qq.v.). Pheidias and his school were responsible for the sculptures of the Parthenon. The master himself made the gold and ivory statue of Athena, which was completed and installed in the *naos* of the temple 438 B.C. Six years later he was accused of having stolen some of the gold; but this charge was at once refuted, as Pericles had advised him to apply the precious metal in such a way that it could be detached and weighed. Thereupon Pheidias was charged with impiety in having introduced his own and Pericles's image into the shield of the goddess. He was found guilty and went into exile, where he died. Other works by Pheidias were the colossal bronze Athena Promachos on the Acropolis at Athens, the Lemnian Athena, a gilt Athena at Plataea, and the great chryselephantine Zeus at Olympia. Pheidias was considered by ancient critics as the greatest of sculptors, and the impression of supreme eminence remains, although no single extant masterpiece can be certainly credited to him. *See* C. Waldstein, *On the Art of Phidias*, 1885, and general works on Greek sculpture.

Pheidippidēs, an Athenian courier, sent to Sparta in 490 B.C. to announce the Persian invasion and demand help. He reached his destination on the second day after leaving Athens, having covered a distance of about 150 miles (*see* PAN). After the battle of Marathon he set out for Athens with news of the Greek victory, but collapsed and died on arrival. The Marathon race had no place in the ancient Olympic Games (q.v.). When it was instituted in 1896 it was based on the distance (26 miles approx.) between Marathon (q.v.) and Athens.

Phēmē, *see* OSSA.

Pherecydes (-kudēs): 1. Greek philosopher, a native of Syros, *fl. c.* 544 B.C. Pythagoras is said to have learned from him the doctrine of metempsychosis, or transmigration of souls.

2. Greek logographer, a native of Athens, contemporary with Herodotus.

Phidias, *see* PHEIDIAS.

Phigaleia, city of Arcadia with temples of Artemis and Dionysus. It was also the home of two strange cults, doubtless of pre-hellenic origin: that of Eurynome, a fish-tailed goddess, and that of Black Demeter whose image had a horse's head (*see* ONATAS). *See also* BASSAE.

Philadelphia (mod. Amman), city of the Decapolis (q.v.), of which it became a member in 63 B.C. It was originally called Rabbath-Ammon, but was renamed in honour of Ptolemy II, Philadelphus (283-246 B.C.). From A.D. 106 it was one of the chief cities of the Roman province Arabia Petraea.

Philammōn, legendary Greek poet and musician, son of Apollo by Chione (daughter of Daedalion), and father of Thamyris (q.v.) by the nymph Argiope.

Philēmōn, Greek poet of the New Comedy, born at Soli in Cilicia 361 B.C., but went to Athens at an early age and was granted Athenian citizenship. He began writing for the stage in 330 and died in 262 B.C. The *Mercator, Trinummus* and *Mostellaria* of Plautus (q.v.) are Latin adaptations of Philemon.

Philēmōn and Baucis (-kis), in Greek mythology, a Phrygian couple whose names are symbolic of conjugal love. When Zeus and Hermes visited Phrygia, only Philemon and Baucis welcomed them, though they were unaware of the gods' identity. Zeus, having flooded the whole land, changed the cottage of Philemon and Baucis into a temple; the couple asked to be appointed its ministers and that they might die together. Their prayer was granted: when they reached extreme old age Philemon was transformed into an oak, Baucis into a lime.

Philētas of Cos (3rd-2nd century B.C.), Greek elegiac poet and grammarian of the Alexandrian school. He was tutor to Ptolemy II, Philadelphus (*see also* THEOCRITUS), and wrote a commentary on Homer. Fragments of his poems survive. *See* G. Kuchenmüller, *Philetae Coi Reliquiae,* 1928.

Philip (Gk Philippos), name of five kings of Macedon, of whom the following are most famous:

1. Commonly called Philip II, or simply Philip of Macedon, born 382 B.C. On the death of his brother, Perdiccas III, he acted as guardian of and regent for the latter's infant son Amyntas. After a few months, however, he assumed the royal title and authority (359 B.C.). His first measures were military and economic reforms, which he saw to be essential preliminaries to the fulfilment of his ambitions. He next resolved to obtain possession of the Greek cities on the Macedonian coast. Amphipolis, Pydna, Potidaea, Methone, and finally Olynthus fell successively into his hands. Demosthenes (q.v.), in the 'Olynthiac' and 'Philippic' orations, vainly endeavoured to rouse Athens to a sense of her peril and that of all the Greek states. In 346 Philip subdued the Phocians (*see* SACRED WARS) and was rewarded with their place in the Amphictyonic Council. The Athenians at last awoke; when Philip marched through Thermopylae to punish Amphissa, they determined to oppose him, and on the advice of Demosthenes made an alliance with Thebes. But their united army was routed by Philip at Chaeronea (338 B.C.), and Greek independence was no more. A congress of the Greek states was then held at Corinth. It was decided to make war on Persia, and Philip was appointed to command the

forces of the national confederacy. But he was murdered at a festival held to celebrate the marriage of his daughter with Alexander of Epirus (336 B.C.). The assassin was Pausanias (*see* PAUSANIAS, 2), but Philip's wife Olympias (q.v.) was believed to have encouraged the young man. Philip II was succeeded by Alexander the Great (q.v.), his son by Olympias. *See* D. G. Hogarth, *Philip and Alexander of Macedon*, 1897.

2. Surnamed Arrhidaeus (Arrhidaios), sometimes called Philip III, son of the preceding by Philinna, a dancing-girl from Larisa, and half-brother of Alexander the Great. Though a congenital idiot, he was recognized as king jointly with Alexander (*see* ALEXANDER 4) on the death of Alexander the Great (323 B.C.), and next year married Eurydice. Arrhidaeus and his wife were put to death by order of Olympias (317 B.C.).

3. Known as Philip V, son of the Antigonid king Demetrius II, whom he succeeded in 221 B.C. During the first three years of his reign he made war on the Aetolian League, at the request of Aratus (q.v.) and the Achaean confederacy. Soon afterwards he caused Aratus to be poisoned. But the most fateful events of his reign were two wars with Rome (215–205 and 200–197 B.C.). The second of these wars ended with the defeat of Philip by the consul Flamininus (q.v.) at Cynoscephalae, but he was allowed to keep his throne. Philip was led by the false accusations of Perseus (q.v.) to put to death his elder son Demetrius; but discovering the victim's innocence, he died a prey to remorse (179 B.C.), and was succeeded by Perseus. For a fascinating account of these two Macedonian wars and of Philip's end, *see* Livy xxi–xxx.

Philippi, city of Macedonia. Originally called Crenides, it was renamed after Philip II of Macedon, who fortified it in order to control the neighbouring gold mines. Philippi is chiefly famous as the scene of Octavian's victory over Brutus and Cassius (42 B.C.), and as the place where St Paul first preached the Gospel in Europe (A.D. 53). *See* S. Casson, *Macedonia, Thrace and Illyria*, 1926.

Philippus, Marcus Julius, commonly called 'Philip the Arabian', Roman emperor A.D. 244–9. An Arabian by birth, he rose to high rank in the Roman army and obtained the throne by the assassination of the third Gordian (*see* GORDIANUS). He was killed near Verona, either in battle against Decius (q.v.) or by his own soldiers. His son, who was named likewise and to whom he had given the rank of Augustus in 247, perished at the same time.

Philistus (-os), Greek historian of Sicily, a native of Syracuse, born *c*. 440 B.C. He assisted Dionysius I (q.v.) to power, but afterwards incurred his displeasure and was banished. Recalled by Dionysius II (q.v.) in 366, he brought about the expulsion of Dion (q.v.); but on the latter's return Philistus committed suicide after a naval defeat (356 B.C.). His history of Sicily (*Sikelika*) was written during his exile; only fragments have survived. *See* C. Müller, *Fragmenta Historicorum Graecorum*, vol. i, 1841.

Philo, Quintus Publilius, Roman general in the Samnite wars. He was the first plebeian dictator (339 B.C.), in which year also he carried a law whereby the censorship became open to the plebeians. He was the first plebeian praetor (337), and twice again held the consulship (327 and 320 B.C.).

Philo Judaeus ('the Jew'), Graeco-Jewish philosopher, exegete and apologist, born at Alexandria *c.* 15 B.C. Though a Jew by birth, his studies were mainly in Greek philosophy. He was especially familiar with the writings of Plato, upon whose language his own is closely modelled; and it is for his attempt to reconcile Platonic philosophy with the Mosaic revelation that he is principally famed. Philo adapted the pantheistic form of the Logos as taught by the Stoics, drawing a sharper distinction between the Logos and the world; and his influence is manifest in such scriptural books as Wisdom, St John's Gospel and Hebrews. The only event in Philo's life to which it is possible to assign a date is his membership of the embassy to Caligula (q.v.) to protest against the threatened desecration of the temple (A.D. 40). The best edition of his collected works is that of L. Cohn and P. Wendland, 8 vols., 1930. There is also a text with translation by F. H. Colson and G. H. Whitaker, 10 vols. (Loeb Library), 1929–50, together with two supplementary volumes (translation only) in the same series by R. Marcus. *See* E. R. Goodenough, *By Light, Light : the Mystic Gospel of Hellenistic Judaism*, 1935; *The Politics of Philo Judaeus*, 1938; *An Introduction to Philo Judaeus*, 1940.

Philoctetes (-ktētēs), in Greek mythology, a famous archer, to whom Heracles (q.v.) bequeathed his poisoned arrows. On the voyage to Troy, while staying in the island of Chryse, Philoctetes was bitten in the foot by a snake, or wounded by one of his own arrows. The wound produced such an intolerable stench that he was abandoned by his people on the solitary coast of Lemnos (q.v.). Here he remained until the tenth year of the war, when he was fetched by Odysseus and Diomedes after an oracle had declared that Troy could not be taken without the arrows of Heracles. On arrival before Troy he was healed by Asclepius, or by the latter's sons Machaon and Podalirus. *See* Sophocles, *Philoctetes*.

Philodemus (-dēmos), of Gadara, Epicurean philosopher and epigrammatic poet of the mid 1st century B.C. Fragments of his works have been found, with many other Epicurean writings, in a villa at Herculaneum (q.v.).

Philomēla, daughter of Pandion, King of Athens, and sister of Procne. *See* TEREUS.

Philōn, Athenian architect of the 4th century B.C., built the portico of the great temple at Eleusis.

Philopoemen (-poimēn), Greek general and statesman, born at Megalopolis in Arcadia 253 B.C. He distinguished himself at the battle of Sellasia (222 B.C.), in which Antigonus Doson and the Achaean League (q.v.) defeated Cleomenes III of Sparta. In 208 he was elected general of the league; in 207 and 193 respectively he overthrew the Spartan tyrants Machanidas and Nabis. He filled this office eight times with honour to himself and advantage to his country. In 183 B.C., while marching against the Messenians, who had revolted from the league, he was made prisoner, carried to Messene, and compelled to drink poison. Philopoemen was one of the few great men produced by Hellas in her decline : indeed he has been called 'the last of the Greeks'.

Philostratus (-os), Greek rhetorician and biographer, died between A.D. 224 and 229. A native of Lemnos, he taught for some while at Athens, and eventually came to Rome in the train of the empress Julia Domna, at whose request he wrote the *Life of Apollonius of Tyana.* Other works certainly by Philostratus are *Lives of the Sophists* and the first collection of *Imagines* (descriptions of pictures). *See* text and translation of these works by F. C. Conybeare, W. C. Wright and A. Fairbanks, 4 vols. (Loeb Library), 1912–31.

Philōtas, son of Parmenion (q.v.). Though a close friend of Alexander the Great (q.v.), he was accused in 330 B.C. of conspiracy against the monarch's life. There was no proof, but a confession was wrung from him by torture, and he was stoned to death.

Philoxenos: 1. Greek dithyrambic poet, born in the island of Cythera 436 B.C. He spent part of his life at Syracuse, where he lived at the court of Dionysius the elder, and died in 380 B.C. Only a few fragments of his work survive. *See* text and translation by J. M. Edmonds in *Lyra Graeca*, 3 vols. (Loeb Library), 1922.

2. Greek painter of Eretria in Euboea, *fl.* 316 B.C., remarkable for the speed with which he worked. His greatest work was a picture of a battle (? Gaugamela) between Alexander the Great and the Persian king Darius III, Codomannus, painted by order of Cassander.

Phineus, legendary king of Salmydessus in Thrace, a famous soothsayer. Having revealed some secret of the gods, he was blinded, and then tormented by the Harpies (q.v.). When the Argonauts (q.v.) called at Salmydessus Phineus was delivered from the Harpies by Zetes (q.v.) and Calais. For a totally different story *see* ZETES.

Phintias, *see* DAMON.

Phlegethōn, one of the rivers of the underworld, flowing not with water but with flame.

Phocaea (Phōkaia), the northernmost of the Ionian cities on the west coast of Asia Minor, celebrated as a great maritime state and especially as the mother city of Massilia (q.v.). It took part in the Ionian revolt (499 B.C.), but thereafter lapsed into insignificance.

Phocion (Phōkiōn), Athenian general and statesman, born *c.* 402 B.C. Though an opponent of Demosthenes, advocating peace with Philip, he was always influenced by upright motives; and as a commander in the field he never allowed his political beliefs to affect his duty as a soldier. Phocion was celebrated as an extempore orator of the first rank. An aristocrat to the bone, he entertained splendid contempt for the mob and their tastes. One day, when their plaudits interrupted him on the *bema*, he asked: 'Have I said something ridiculous?' In 318 B.C. Cassander's general Nicanor seized Peiraeus; Phocion was suspected of having advised this step, and took refuge with Alexander Aegus (q.v.). But he was surrendered to the Athenians by Polysperchon (q.v.) and condemned to drink the hemlock (317 B.C.).

Phocis (Phōkis), country of central Greece, bounded north by Opuntian Locris, east by Boeotia, south by the Corinthian Gulf, west by Doris and Ozolian Locris. It is traversed by the range of Parnassus and the valley of the Cephissus. The most important place in Phocis was the sanctuary of Delphi (q.v.), which was controlled by the

Phocians until 590 B.C. (*see also* CRISSA AND CIRRHA). In that year an alliance of Greek states won independence for Delphi, but allowed the Phocians two votes in the Amphictyonic Council. They made no attempt to check the Persians at Thermopylae in 480, and actually sided with them at Plataea in 479. From then until 346 B.C. the history of Phocis is mainly that of the Sacred Wars (q.v.). The first step to recovery from the disasters brought about by the last of these was to rebuild the cities (339 B.C.); but Phocis and other Greek states were overwhelmed by Philip II of Macedon at Chaeronea (q.v.) in 338. The Phocians took part in the Lamian War (q.v.) in 323. Thereafter they were subject to Macedon, to the Aetolian League, and finally as part of the province of Achaea to Rome.

Phoebe (Phoibē), a female Titan (*see* TITANS), wife of Coeus, mother of Leto and Asteria (qq.v.). Later authors give the name to the moon, and hence to Artemis and Diana (qq.v.).

Phoebus, *see* APOLLO.

Phoenicia, coastal territory of Syria, lying between the Mediterranean Sea and the Libanus range. In Homer, as in the Old Testament, the Phoenicians, who inhabited the commercial seaboard towns of Canaan, are called Sidonians. Herodotus says that they were originally settled on the 'Red Sea' (by which he means the Persian Gulf) and migrated to Syria. Ethnically they were a branch of the Canaanites. As to the age of the Phoenician towns we have no sure information; but one thing is clear, namely that in the 15th century B.C. the island city of Tyre (q.v.) was not only existent but powerful. The most remarkable aspect of Phoenician history is the extraordinary development of commerce and colonization: the whole Mediterranean coastland and many of the islands were dotted with Phoenician trading stations, of which the most famous was Carthage (q.v.); and a splendid picture of Tyrian commerce is given in the book of Ezekiel (xxvii). The Phoenicians, being essentially traders, were also the greatest navigators of their time. Their country, after many vicissitudes, and partial conquests by the Assyrians and Persians, was absorbed into the empire of Alexander the Great. It belonged to the Seleucids from 197 until 64 B.C., when it was included in the Roman province of Syria (q.v.). *See* A. R. Burns, *Minoans, Philistines and Greeks*, 1930; D. B. Harden, *The Phoenicians*, 1962.

Phoenix (Phoi-), in Greek legend, son of Amyntor and Cleobule. His father took a mistress, whom Cleobule persuaded Phoenix to seduce. Cursed by Amyntor, he took refuge in Phthia and was welcomed by Peleus, who made him King of the Dolopes, and entrusted him with the education of his son Achilles.

Phoenix (Phoi-), fabulous sacred bird of Egypt, which according to the people of Heliopolis visited them once every 500 years on the death of its father. The story, as told by Herodotus, who did not believe it, was that the phoenix came from the Arabian desert, bearing its father embalmed in a ball of myrrh, and buried him in the temple of the sun. It was said to resemble an eagle in size and shape, but had red and gold plumage. According to another story the bird placed itself on the burning altar at Heliopolis, and from the ashes there flew a young phoenix, freshly feathered. Pliny's version is that it built for itself a nest in which to die, and that a new bird sprang from the corpse. There was never more than one phoenix at a time.

Pholus (-os), one of the Centaurs (q.v.). Heracles, while hunting the Erymanthian boar (*see* TWELVE LABOURS OF HERACLES, 4), came to the grotto of Pholus who had received from Dionysus a cask of excellent wine. Against the wishes of his host, Heracles broached it, and the delicious fragrance attracted the other Centaurs, who besieged the grotto. Heracles drove them off, and they fled to the house of Chiron (q.v.); but in his pursuit he accidentally slew Pholus with his poisoned arrows.

Phormiōn, Athenian admiral. He appears first as one of the commanders in the expedition against Samos (440 B.C.), and eight years later was sent to besiege Potidaea. In the winter of 430 B.C. he was given command of a naval squadron which made its base at Naupactus, and in the following summer won two brilliant victories over the Peloponnesian fleet in the gulf of Corinth (*see* Thucydides, ii. 82–92).

Phosphoros (Lat. Lucifer), in Greek mythology, the morning star, son of Astraeus or Cephalus.

Phraates, King of Parthia *c.* 38 B.C.–*c.* A.D. 4, the fourth of that name. He was son and successor of Orodes (q.v.). In 20 B.C., when his throne was unstable and his infant son had been kidnapped, he was obliged by the diplomacy of Augustus to restore the standards which had been captured at Carrhae (53 B.C.); and this event was celebrated at Rome with great rejoicing, as herald of a new period of Roman greatness. Phraates was poisoned by his wife, assisted by that son for whose return he had sought the intervention of Augustus.

Phrixus (-os), son of Athamas (q.v.) by Nephele and brother of Helle. In consequence of the intrigues of Ino, his father's concubine, brother and sister were to be sacrificed to Zeus. Nephele, however, rescued her two children, who rode away through the air on a golden-fleeced ram, the gift of Hermes. Between Sigeum and the Chersonesus Thracica, Helle fell into the sea, which was called after her Hellespont. Phrixus duly arrived in Colchis (q.v.), whose king, Aeëtes (*see also* JASON AND MEDEA), gave him his daughter Chalciope in marriage. Phrixus, having sacrificed the ram to Zeus, gave its fleece to Aeëtes, who fastened it to an oak-tree in the grove of Ares, guarded day and night by a dragon. *See* ARGONAUTS.

Phrygia (Phru-), a district of Asia Minor. The Phrygians are mentioned by Homer as living on the banks of the Sangarius, where later writers speak of the powerful kingdom of Gordius and Midas (qq.v.). They appear to have been of Thracian origin, and to have been driven by successive migrations of other Thracian peoples (Thyni, Bithyni, Mysians, Teucrians) farther inland. They were not, however, entirely displaced from the shores of the Hellespont and Propontis, where they continued side by side with the Greek colonies, and where their name was preserved in that of 'Phrygia Minor' throughout subsequent changes. Phrygia was subject in turn to the Lydian empire of Croesus, to the Persians, to Alexander the Great and to the Seleucids; but under the last the north-eastern territory, adjacent to Paphlagonia and the River Halys, was conquered by the Gauls and formed the western part of Galatia. The Romans gave Phrygia to Eumenes II of Pergamum (q.v.). In 133 B.C. it became part of the province of Asia. In imperial times it was bounded on the west by Mysia, Lydia and Caria; on the south by Lycia and Pisidia; on the east by Lycaonia (which was sometimes reckoned as part of Phrygia) and Galatia; on the north by Bithynia.

Phrygia was important in the early cultural development of Greece. The earliest Greek music, especially for the flute, was borrowed in part, through the Asiatic colonies, from Phrygia, which was also the chief centre of the worship of Cybele (q.v.).

Phryne (Phrunē), Athenian courtesan of the mid 4th century B.C., daughter of Epicles. She was born at Thespiae in Boeotia. Hypereides the orator, Apelles the painter and Praxiteles the sculptor (qq.v.) are said to have been among her lovers. She is believed to have been the model for the 'Aphrodite Anadyomene' of Apelles, and for the Cnidian 'Aphrodite' of Praxiteles.

Phrynichus (Phrunikhos): 1. Athenian tragic poet, probably a disciple of Thespis, produced his first play in 511 B.C. He was the first to use female masks. Herodotus relates that when his *Capture of Miletus* was exhibited (492), the audience was moved to tears, that the author was fined 1,000 drachmae, and that a law was passed forbidding it ever to be shown again. His last work (*Phoenician Women*) was staged in 476 B.C. *See* A. Nauck, *Tragicorum Graecorum Fragmenta*, 1926.

2. Athenian poet of the Old Comedy, *fl.* 430 B.C., when his first play was produced. Aristophanes attacks him in *The Frogs* for his use of low buffoonery. Titles of five of his comedies are known.

3. Greek sophist and grammarian of the late 2nd century A.D. His *Selection of Attic Words and Phrases* has survived. *See* W. G. Rutherford, *The New Phrynicus*, 1881.

Phthiōtis, a district of Thessaly (q.v.) and legendary home of Achilles.

Picenum, district of Italy between the Appenines and the Adriatic, bounded north by the Senones and south by the Vestini. Augustus made it the fifth region of Italy (*see* ITALIA). It was enlarged by Constantine to include the north-eastern portion of Umbria, which had been known since the end of the 2nd century A.D. as Flaminia.

Picti, originally a people inhabiting modern Scotland and parts of northern Ireland. By the end of the 3rd century A.D. the name had come to be used exclusively of the people of northern and central Scotland. The old theory that the word was derived from their custom of painting bodies is now discredited; it is believed to be a Latin version of a native name.

Pindar (Gk Pindaros), Greek poet, born at Cynoscephalae in Boeotia 518 B.C. In his youth he was defeated in a poetical contest by Corinna (q.v.), who is said to have warned him to sow his mythological detail 'by the handful, not by the sackful'. His earliest extant poem (*Pythian*, x) dates from 498, and during the next forty years he became a famous figure throughout the Greek world, from Sicily to Rhodes, from Macedon to Cyrene. His works were collected in seventeen books, and included hymns, paeans, dithyrambs, processional songs, maiden songs, hyporchemata, encomia, dirges and epinicians. These last, in four books, have survived complete. They celebrate victories gained in the Olympian, Pythian, Nemean and Isthmian games. Of his other poetry we have only fragments, augmented since 1900 by papyri from Oxyrhynchus and Hermopolis. Pindar's power lies not in his ideas, which are often naïve and muddled, but rather in an amazing splendour of language, rhythm and imagery, which has made his work impossible to translate and fatal to imitate. This praiser of athletes was indeed one of the most purely aesthetic writers there have ever been. The only value of his moralizing, for the modern reader, lies in a grace and magnificence of phrase and symbol such as few poets have attained. The last complete editions of the *Odes* are those of C. M. Bowra (1947) and L. R. Farnell (with translation and commentary, 1930). *See* Sir M. Bowra, *Pindar*, 1964.

Pirithoüs (-thoös), in Greek legend, King of the Lapithae, son of Ixion. It was during the marriage feast of Pirithoüs and Hippodameia that the bride was abducted by the drunken Centaur Eurution, an event which resulted in the fight between the Lapithae and Centaurs, and which was a favourite subject with sculptors of the classical period. In this fight Pirithoüs was helped by his friend Theseus (q.v.), and after Hippodameia's death the two men decided each to wed a daughter of Zeus (for Theseus's part of the bargain *see* DIOSCURI; THESEUS), and Pirithoüs chose Persephone ! Theseus would not desert his friend in this dangerous enterprise, and together they made their way to Hades. Here they were seized by Pluto and fastened to a rock. Theseus was delivered by Heracles, but Pirithoüs remained for ever in torment.

Pisae : 1. (Peisai), chief town of Pisatis, a district of Elis (q.v.), situated north of the River Alpheus, a little east of Olympia with which the poets often identified it. The history of Pisa is that of its long struggle with the Eleans for the presidency of the Olympic Games (q.v.). The conflict was ended in 572 B.C. by the conquest and destruction of Pisa by the Eleans.

2. (Mod. Pisa), city of Etruria on the River Arnus, traditionally founded by the companions of Nestor (natives of 1 above), who had been driven upon the coast of Italy on their return from Troy. Situated on the Via Aemilia, it was important as a frontier fortress against the Ligurians. The neighbouring forests produced timber for ship-building.

Pisidia, district of Asia Minor, bounded north by Phrygia, east by Lycaonia, Isauria and Cilicia, south by Pamphylia, west by Lycia. It was inhabited by a race of lawless brigands, whose depredations afforded the pretext upon which Cyrus the younger (*see* CYRUS, 2) raised the army intended for the overthrow of his brother, Artaxerxes Mnemon (401 B.C.). They opposed the march of Alexander, and maintained their independence until about 5 B.C., when they became subject to Rome, though continuing to be governed by native rulers.

Piso, Gaius Calpurnius, leader of the conspiracy against Nero (q.v.) in A.D. 65. On discovery he committed suicide.

Piso, Gnaeus Calpurnius, consul in 7 B.C., and subsequently governor first of Spain, then of Africa. In A.D. 17 Tiberius appointed him

governor of Syria with secret instructions to thwart Germanicus
(q.v.). Popular indignation at the death of Germanicus obliged
Tiberius to order an investigation. Piso committed suicide (A.D. 20),
though it was rumoured that Tiberius, fearing incriminating dis-
closures, had put him to death. The case was prosecuted against
Piso's wife, Plancina; the influence of Livia secured her acquittal, but
the charge was revived in A.D. 33, and she too committed suicide.

Piso, Lucius Calpurnius, surnamed *Frugi* (Worthy). As tribune of
the plebs in 149 B.C. he carried the *Lex Calpurnia repetundarum,*
which began the system of establishing regular courts for the trial of
particular offences in place of the old system of appointing special
tribunals for each case. As praetor in 136, and consul in 133, he fought
against the slaves in Sicily (*see* SERVILE WARS). Piso was also the
author of annals, of which some fragments survive. *See* H. Peter,
Historicorum romanorum reliquiae, vol. i, 1870.

Piso Caesoninus, Lucius Calpurnius: 1. Consul in 112 B.C. In 107 he
served under L. Cassius Longinus in Gaul, and fell in battle against
the Tigurini.

2. Consul 58 B.C., when he and his colleague, Aulus Gabinius, supported the proceedings of Clodius which led to the exile of Cicero. He
was governor of Macedonia from 56 until the beginning of 55, when he
was recalled, probably on account of a violent attack made upon him
by Cicero in the speech *De provinciis consularibus.* Accused of extortion, he addressed the senate in his defence, and Cicero replied with
the speech *In Pisonem.* The case was never brought to trial; Piso was
the father of Caesar's wife Calpurnia, and Cicero dared proceed no
further.

Pistoriae (mod. Pistoia), town of Etruria, near which Catiline was
defeated and slain in 62 B.C.

Pithēkoussa, Greek name for the island of Aenaria (q.v.).

Pittacus (-kos), Greek soldier and statesman, one of the Seven
Sages of Greece, born at Mytilene (q.v.) in Lesbos *c.* 650 B.C. In 606
he commanded in the war with Athens for possession of Sigeum. At
about this time the supreme power at Mytilene was disputed by a
succession of tyrants, and the aristocratical party was driven into
exile. In 589 these exiles, headed by Antimenides and the poet
Alcaeus (q.v.), attempted to return by force of arms. Pittacus was
chosen dictator (*asumnētēs*) to oppose them, and held the office for ten
years until he had restored order. Among the most curious of his laws
was one which doubled the penalty for an offence committed when
drunk. He died in 570 B.C.

Placentia (mod. Piacenza), town of Gallia Cisalpina (Cispadana),
founded as a Roman colony in 218 B.C., at the same time as Cremona
(q.v.). Destroyed by the Gauls in 200 B.C., it was restored soon afterwards by the Romans and became an important road centre.

Plataea (Gk Plataiai), city of Boeotia. In 519 B.C. Athens secured
the independence of Plataea in face of encroachment by Thebes, and
thereby won the undying gratitude of her people. Consequently, when
the Persians invaded Attica in 490 B.C., Plataea sent her entire levy of
1,000 men to support the Athenians, and it fought at Marathon.
Again in 480 the Plataeans took an active part in opposition to

Xerxes. In the following year they helped to defeat the Persian army of Mardonius and thus assured the freedom of Hellas (*see* PERSIAN WARS). To commemorate this great victory the territory of Plataea was declared inviolate; but in 429 Thebes persuaded Sparta to attack the city, which was obliged to capitulate after a siege of two years (427 B.C.). Plataea was then razed to the ground; the survivors were granted residence with limited citizenship at Athens, and in 421 were settled in the territory of Scione. Driven out by Lysander in 404, they returned to Athens and remained there until Plataea was rebuilt by the Spartans as a check upon the growing power of Thebes. Plataea was again destroyed by the Thebans in 373, when the population were once more allowed Athenian citizenship. It was finally restored by Philip II of Macedon and Alexander the Great.

Plato (Gk Platōn), Greek philosopher, son of Ariston and Perictione, was born at Athens 428–427 B.C. His father boasted descent from Codrus, his mother from the archon Dropides (644). After the death of Socrates (399), he is said to have resided for a time with Eucleides of Megara (q.v.), and then to have travelled in Greece, Egypt and Italy. About 387 B.C. he returned to Athens and founded the Academy (q.v.), over which he presided for the remainder of his life, except for two visits to Sicily. The first of these was in 367, when, following the death of Dionysius I (q.v.) of Syracuse, he was invited by the tyrant's brother-in-law Dion (q.v.) to educate the new ruler, Dionysius II (q.v.). The scheme failed, but Plato was called upon once more (361–360), this time, and again unsuccessfully, to compose the differences between Dionysius and Dion. He then resumed his work at the Academy, and died in 348–347 B.C.

The following are the genuine works of Plato, all of them (except the *Apology*) in dialogue form: *Hippias Major* and *Minor*, *Ion*, *Menexenus*, *Charmides*, *Laches*, *Lysis*, *Cratylus*, *Euthydemus*, *Gorgias*, *Meno*, *Protagoras*, *Euthyphro*, *Apology*, *Crito*, *Phaedo*, *Symposium*, *Phaedrus*, *Republic*, *Parmenides*, *Theaetetus*, *Sophist*, *Statesman*, *Philebus*, *Timaeus*, *Laws* and *Epinomis*. There have also survived a number of *Epistles* of which Nos. 1 and 12 are certainly spurious, 7 and 8 certainly authentic and the remainder probably so. Plato's will is preserved by Diogenes Laërtius (iii. 41–3).

It is impossible in a volume of this scope and design to provide even an adequate summary of the content and richness of Plato's thought, which has had—and still has—untold influence upon human thought and therefore upon human history. It traverses the fields of metaphysics, epistemology, ethics and politics, and is written in a style unsurpassed for purity and elegance in the whole domain of Greek prose. His central contribution to philosophy is the theory of 'Forms' or 'Ideas', according to which reality, the object of knowledge, consists not in particular and transient phenomena, but in the 'Forms' or 'Ideas', which are the pure types of each class of things, with the Form of the Good at their summit. Closely bound up with this theory are two others, namely that the soul is immortal and that knowledge is recollection. This is to say that the soul, being immortal, has long since learned all truth by contemplation of the Forms, and therefore needs in this life only to be reminded by sense experience of what it has forgotten. The foregoing theory is developed mainly in *Phaedo* and *Republic*. The two great 'moral' dialogues are *Gorgias* and *Protagoras*, while *Sophist* and *Statesman* are the foundations respectively of all subsequent logic and constitutionalism.

The Aldine edition of Plato's complete works was published at Venice in 1513, that of H. Stephanus and J. Serranus at Paris in 1578, and that of J. Burnet at Oxford in 1899–1907. There are numerous editions of separate works. The complete English translation of the *Dialogues* by Benjamin Jowett (3rd ed., 1892) contains introductions that are models of fine criticism; but the work itself contains numerous errors, and his commentaries have been largely superseded. Translations of separate dialogues are plentiful. *See* W. Pater, *Plato and Platonism*, 1893; T. Gomperz, *Great Thinkers*, vols. ii and iii (trans.), 1905; E. Barker, *Greek Historical Theory*, 1918; P. E. More, *The Religion of Plato*, 1921; A. E. Taylor, *Plato, the Man and His Work*, 1926; F. M. Cornford, *Plato's Theory of Knowledge*, 1935; R. Demos, *The Philosophy of Plato*, 1939; J. Wild, *Plato's Theory of Man*, 1946; G. C. Field, *The Philosophy of Plato*, 1949; Sir David Ross, *Plato's Theory of Ideas*, 1951.

Plautius, Aulus, Roman soldier and administrator. He was governor of Pannonia in A.D. 43, when Claudius placed him in command of the expedition to Britain (q.v.). He was recalled in 47 and allowed an ovation (*see* OVATION).

Plautus, Titus Maccius (*c.* 254–184 B.C.), Roman comic poet, born at Sassina in Umbria. Leaving his native place, he settled in Rome, earned a little money which he promptly lost, and took to writing plays. He was then probably about thirty years of age. The extant plays, all of them free adaptations of Greek models of the New Comedy, are as follows: *Amphitruo, Asinaria, Aulularia, Bacchides, Captivi, Casina, Cistellaria, Curculio, Epidicus, Menaechmi, Mercator, Miles Gloriosus* (*c.* 205 B.C.), *Mostellaria, Persa, Poenulus, Pseudolus, Rudens* (192 B.C.), *Stichus* (200 B.C.), *Trinummus, Truculentus.* Thirty-five other titles are known, and fragments of the *Vidularia* have survived.

Plautus had a perfect command of language and metre. He enjoyed unrivalled popularity, though critics of the Augustan age frowned upon him just as, later, Addison frowned upon Spenser; but since the Renaissance he has been acknowledged as one of the greatest of ancient playwrights, and he has exercised much influence upon the later European stage. *See* the complete text edited by W. M. Lindsay, 1904–5. There is a text with prose translation by P. Nixon in the Loeb Library, 4 vols., 1918–38. *See also* G. Michaut, *Plaute*, 1920.

Pleiades, in Greek mythology, daughters of Atlas (q.v.) by Pleïone, and sisters of the Hyades (q.v.). Their names were Alcyone, Asterope, Celaene, Electra, Maia, Merope (q.v.) and Taÿgete. They and their mother were pursued by Orion (q.v.) through the woods of Boeotia for five years, until Zeus changed them all into stars. The constellation was called by Latin poets Vergiliae.

Plinius Caecilius Secundus, Gaius, called in English **Pliny the Younger,** Latin orator and author, born A.D. 61 at Novum Comum in Gallia Transpadana. His father's name was Caecilius Clio, and his mother was Plinia, sister of Pliny the Elder (*see* next article); but Clio died while Pliny was still a child, and he was adopted by his uncle. He studied rhetoric under Quintilian (q.v.), and became an advocate (80); was admitted to the senate (*c.* 81), served as military tribune in Syria (*c.* 82), and after holding various other offices was finally consul under Trajan (100), and subsequently governor of Bithynia (111), where he remained rather less than two years. He died *c.* 113. Pliny's extant works are (1) a fulsome *Panegyric* on Trajan, and (2) ten books of *Letters*, among which is one describing in detail his uncle's death, and the famous epistle to Trajan about treatment of the Christians in his province. *See* the complete editions by C. R. Kukula, 1912, and M. Schuster, 1933. There is also a text of the *Letters* (with Melmoth's translation revised by the editor, W. M. L. Hutchinson) in the Loeb Library.

Plinius Secundus, Gaius, called in English **Pliny,** or **Pliny the Elder,** Latin author, born probably at Novum Comum (mod. Como) in Gallia Transpadana, A.D. 23. Having seen military service in Africa, and commanded a troop of cavalry (46), he settled at Rome, in 52. His scientific studies, pursued relentlessly during the remainder of his life, won him fame as the most learned man of his age. Pliny was procurator in Spain (*c.* 68–72), held high office under Vespasian, and was in command of the fleet at Misenum under Titus. His curiosity and sense of duty led to his death by suffocation at Stabiae, in the great eruption of Vesuvius (A.D. 79), whither he had sailed from his headquarters, partly to observe the awful phenomena, and partly to see if he could help some friends living in the neighbourhood. Of all his writings (history, tactics, grammar, etc.) only the *Historia Naturalis* has survived. It is a not always accurate encyclopaedic work in thirty-seven books on science, art, natural history and allied subjects, with digressions on human inventions and institutions. The style varies, but is vigorous if sometimes obscure as a result of brevity. *See* edition (with commentary) by J. Sillig, 8 vols., 1851–8. There is also a text and translation by H. Rackham and W. H. S. Jones, 10 vols (Loeb Library). *See* J. O. Thomson, *History of Ancient Geography*, 1948.

Pliny, *see* PLINIUS.

Plotina, Pompeia, wife of the emperor Trajan, upon whose advice he adopted Hadrian (q.v.).

Plotinus (Plōteinos), Greek philosopher, founder of Neoplatonism, born at Lycopolis, in Egypt, A.D. 205. At the age of twenty-eight he first attended the lectures of Ammonius Saccas. Later (242) he accompanied the emperor Gordian III to Mesopotamia and the East, and in 244 established a school at Rome. About 262 he retired to Campania, where he died in A.D. 270. His writings were edited by his disciple Porphyrius (q.v.) in six groups, each containing nine books, and hence known as the *Enneads* (Gk *ennea* = 9).

Plotinus is an idealist pure and simple. God is a spirit, and all that can be attributed to Him are goodness and unity. From Him emanates Intellect (*Nous*), whence proceeds the world-soul, from which again emanate various forces (including the human soul), whence finally comes matter. Man's work is to return to union with God by eliminating from his life the unreal and material, and the final step towards this union is ecstasy. The best edition of the *Enneads* is that by P. Henry and F. R. Schwyzer, 1951. There is an English translation by S. Mackenna and B. S. Page, 5 vols., 1926–30. *See also* W. R. Inge, *The Philosophy of Plotinus*, 3rd ed., 1929; A. H. Armstrong, *Architecture of the Intelligible Universe in the Philosophy of Plotinus*, 1940.

Plutarch (Gk Ploutarkhos), Greek miscellaneous writer, philosopher and moralist, and biographer, born at Chaeronea in Boeotia *c.* A.D. 46. He lectured on philosophy at Rome during the reign of Domitian, winning the friendship of many eminent men, and holding office under Trajan and Hadrian. He returned to his native city, where he served both as magistrate and as priest, and died at an unknown date after A.D. 120.

Plutarch's *Parallel Lives* of Greeks and Romans, upon which his fame chiefly rests, consists of forty-six lives arranged in pairs for comparison (e.g. Theseus and Romulus; Alexander and Caesar), and four separate lives. The interest of these biographies is mainly ethical, not historical; but they remain among the great books of the world, and their influence has been vast. *See* text and translation by B. Perrin, 11 volumes (Loeb Library), 1914–26. *See also* the famous translation by Sir T. North, 1579, republished 1928–30; that of Dryden, revised by A. H. Clough is in Everyman's Library.

The other writings of Plutarch, above sixty in number are placed under the general title *Moralia*, or ethical works. Their merit consists in the soundness of his views on the ordinary events of human life. *See* edition and translation by F. C. Babbitt, H. N. Fowler and W. Helmhold, 14 vols. (Loeb Library), 1927 ff. Two works included in the *Moralia* are the *Greek Questions* and *Roman Questions*, which give many interesting details of folklore. The first has been translated by W. R. Halliday (1928), the second by H. J. Rose, with an important preface (1924).

Pluto (Ploutō), 'giver of wealth', a euphemistic name for Hades (q.v.).

Plutus (Ploutos), personification of the earth's abundant increase. Popularly he was conceived as the blind distributor of wealth.

Pluvius, title of Jupiter (q.v.) as 'sender of rain'.

Pnyx (Pnux), original meeting-place of the Ecclesia (q.v.) at Athens. *See* ATHENS: *Peiraeus and the Long Walls*.

Podalirus (-os), son of Asclepius (q.v.) and brother of Machaon.

Pola, coastal town of Istria, traditionally founded by Colchians in pursuit of Medea (*see* JASON AND MEDEA). It was captured by the Romans in 178 B.C., destroyed by Augustus for having sided with Pompey, and rebuilt as Pietas Iulia. The Roman remains include a huge amphitheatre, of which the outer walls are intact.

Polemōn: 1. Greek philosopher (*c.* 351–273 B.C.), born at Athens. He was said to have been converted from a profligate's life by a discourse on temperance by Xenocrates (q.v.), whom he succeeded as head of the Academy (q.v.).

2. Son of Zeno, a rhetorician of Laodicea. In 39 B.C. he was appointed by Mark Antony to govern part of Cilicia, and subsequently

obtained in exchange the kingdom of Pontus (q.v.). Although he opposed Octavian at Actium, he afterwards profited by the emperor's clemency, and was confirmed in his kingdom. About 16 B.C. he was entrusted by M. Vipsanius Agrippa with the reduction of the kingdom of Bosporus (q.v.), which was afterwards included in his dominions. He fell in an expedition against the barbarian Aspurgi, and was succeeded by his wife Pythodoris. His son, also named Polemon, was appointed (A.D. 39) by Caligula, King of Bosporus and Pontus, the throne being then vacant. In 64 he was induced by Nero to abdicate, and Pontus became a Roman province.

Polias, title of Athena as 'protectress of the city' of Athens.

Pollio, Gaius Asinius, Roman orator, poet and historian, born 76 B.C. During the civil war he fought under Caesar, and after the latter's death supported the triumvirs. He was appointed to settle the disbanded soldiers on the lands commandeered for them (41 B.C.), and was consul in the following year, when Virgil addressed the fourth Eclogue to him. As legate of Antony in 39, he defeated the Parthini, taking the Dalmatian town of Salonae; and it was during this Illyrian campaign that Virgil addressed to him another of the Eclogues. Pollio now retired from public life, devoting himself to literature and to the patronage of letters (Horace, Virgil and others) until his death in 5 B.C.; he was also the first person to establish a public library at Rome. His most brilliant attainments were in the field of oratory, but he wrote a history of the civil war in seventeen books, and also a number of tragedies. Nothing of his work survives.

Pollio, Trebellius (*fl. c.* A.D. 300), Latin historian, one of the six *Scriptores Historiae Augustae* (q.v.).

Pollio, Vedius, a wealthy Roman, friend of the emperor Augustus, to whom he bequeathed a large part of his property. He built a famous villa at Pausilypon, near Neapolis, where he was said to feed live slaves to his lampreys.

Pollux, Latin name for Polydeuces, one of the Dioscuri (q.v.).

Polyaenus (Poluainos), Greek rhetorician of the mid 2nd century A.D., born in Macedonia. He served in the Roman army, and later entered political life. His work, *Stratēgēmata*, on stratagems of war, was translated by R. Shepherd, 1793.

Polybius (Polubios), Greek historian of Rome, son of Lycortas, born at Megalopolis in Arcadia *c.* 204 B.C. After the Roman conquest of Macedonia (168 B.C.), Polybius was taken to Rome as one of 1,000 Achaean hostages for the good conduct of their countrymen, who had failed to assist Aemilius Paulus against Perseus. These men were distributed among the Etruscan towns; but through the influence of Paulus himself, Polybius was treated with exceptional leniency and was permitted to settle at Rome. There he enjoyed the patronage of Paulus's son, Scipio Africanus Minor, who gave him access to the public records. He accompanied Scipio to Carthage in the third Punic war, and was present at the destruction of that city (146 B.C.). Immediately afterwards he hurried to Greece, and helped to alleviate her misfortunes after the fall of Corinth in the same year. He died in 122 B.C. The *History* of Polybius, one of the most valuable relics of antiquity, covered the period from 221 to 144 B.C. The first five books are extant, but of the rest only fragments and abstracts have survived. *See* edition and translation by W. R. Paton, 6 vols. (Loeb Library), 1922–7. *See also* J. B. Bury, *Ancient Greek Historians*, 1909.

Polybus (Polubos), legendary king of Corinth. *See* THEBAN LEGEND, 2.

Polycleitus (Polukleitos), Greek sculptor of the mid 5th century B.C., a native of Argos; may have studied under Ageladas. Copies of several of his works have survived, notably the 'Doryphoros' (youth with javelin) and the 'Wounded Amazon'. *See* A. Mahler, *Polykletus und seine Schule*, 1902; E. A. Gardner, *Six Greek Sculptors*, 1910.

Polycrates (Polukratēs), Greek tyrant of Samos (q.v.), friend and patron of Anacreon (q.v.). He began his rule in 535 B.C., collected a powerful fleet, mastered the Aegean, and by means of ubiquitous piracy amassed a large fortune. A story is told that, in order to avoid the enmity of the gods, he threw into the sea his most valuable possession, a ring of exceptional beauty. This ring, however, was discovered in the maw of a fish which had been presented to him. Not long afterwards Polycrates was lured to the mainland by Oroetes, satrap of Sardis, and crucified (522 B.C.). *See* Herodotus, iii. 39 ff.

Polydectes (Poludectēs): 1. King of Seriphos, *see* PERSEUS.

2. Spartan king, brother of Lycurgus (*see* LYCURGUS, 1).

Polydeuces (Poludeukes; called Pollux in Latin), one of the Dioscuri (q.v.).

Polydorus (Poludōros): 1. Youngest son of Priam and Hecuba. According to Homer he was slain by Achilles. Other writers give a different account. Shortly before the fall of Troy, they relate, Priam entrusted Polydorus and a large sum of money to Polymestor, King of the Thracian Chersonnese, who, on learning of the fate of Troy, murdered Polydorus, secured the money and threw the boy's body into the sea. Hecuba (q.v.), discovering the fate of her child, slew both the sons of Polymestor and put out his eyes. Yet another tradition represents Polydorus as entrusted to his sister Iliona, wife of Polymestor. She brought him up as her own son, persuading others that Deiphilus (or Deipylus), whom she had born to Polymestor, was in fact Polydorus. Instigated by the Greeks, Polymestor slew Deiphilus in mistake for Polydorus; whereupon the latter persuaded his sister to put Polymestor to death.

2. King of Thebes. He was son of Cadmus, father of Labdacus and great-grandfather of Oedipus. *See* THEBAN LEGEND, 1.

3. Rhodian sculptor of the 1st century A.D. *See* AGESANDER.

Polygnotus (Polugnōtos), Greek painter, born in the island of Thasos about 500 B.C. He came to Athens about 462, where he enjoyed the friendship of Cimon and was honoured with the citizenship. At Athens he executed mural paintings of the 'Sack of Troy' in the Stoa Poikile (q.v.) and of the 'Rape of the Leucippidae' in the shrine of the Dioscuri. His most famous works, however, were another 'Sack of Troy' and 'Odysseus in the Underworld' at Delphi. Polygnotus excelled in the delineation of character in the human face, and this characteristic work receives unqualified praise from Aristotle and other ancient critics. *See* H. F. Walters, *The Art of the Greeks*, 31st ed., 1934.

Polynices (Polunikēs), son of Oedipus by Jocasta, *see* THEBAN
LEGEND.

Polyphemus (Poluphēmos), son of Poseidon, and one of the Cyclopes
(q.v.). *See also* ACIS; ODYSSEUS.

Polysperchon (Polusperkhōn), an officer of Alexander the Great.
Antipater on his death-bed (319 B.C.) appointed Polysperchon to
succeed him as regent of Macedonia, assigning to his own son Cassander (q.v.) the subordinate station of chiliarch. Polysperchon
fought against Cassander, who abandoned Peloponnesus to him.

Polystratus (Polustratos), Epicurean philosopher of the late 3rd
century B.C., who succeeded Hermarchus as head of the school.
Two works by him were discovered in the ruins of Herculaneum (q.v.),
and are now in the Museum at Naples.

Polyxena (Polu-), daughter of Priam and Hecuba. The shade of
Achilles appeared to the returning Greeks on the shores of Thracian
Chersonnese and demanded the sacrifice of Polyxena, who had fallen
to the share of Neoptolemus, and she was accordingly put to death on
the hero's tomb.

Polyxo (Poluxō), wife of Tlepolemus (q.v.).

Pomona, ancient Italian goddess of orchards and gardens. At Rome
she had a special priest, the *flamen Pomonalis*, and a sacred grove
near Ostia.

Pompeia: 1. Daughter of Q. Pompeius Rufus (consul 88 B.C.) by
Mucia, daughter of Sulla. Married to Julius Caesar (as his second wife)
in 67 B.C., she was divorced by him six years later after the affair of
Bona Dea (q.v.).

2. Daughter of Pompey the Great by his third wife, Mucia, was
married to Faustus Sulla, son of the dictator.

3. Daughter of Sextus Pompeius (son of Pompey the Great) by
Scribonia (q.v.). She was betrothed in 39 B.C. to M. Marcellus, son of
C. Marcellus by Octavian's sister Octavia; but the marriage did not
take place.

Pompeii, city of Campania at the foot of Mt Vesuvius, two miles
from the shore of the Bay of Naples. It was not originally a Greek
colony; according to Strabo it was occupied first by Oscans, afterwards by Etruscans and lastly by Samnites. During the Social War
(q.v.) it was besieged by Sulla; after which it was granted the Roman
franchise, but received a military colony (80 B.C.), which quickly
romanized the population. Towards the end of the republican period
it became a favourite villa resort of Roman nobles, among whom was
Cicero. In A.D. 63 Pompeii was partly destroyed by an earthquake,
and was still in process of reconstruction when the entire city was
overwhelmed by the tremendous eruption of Vesuvius, 24th August
A.D. 79, along with Herculaneum and Stabiae (qq.v.). The lava did not
reach Pompeii, which was buried, however, to a depth of about 20 feet
by cinders and small volcanic stones. A soil was gradually formed,
and in time the site was utterly forgotten; it was not rediscovered
until 1748. In 1763 systematic exavations were begun. Since 1861 the
Italian Government has carried forward the work on a system devised
by G. Fiorelli, and the greater part of the whole town has now been
unearthed.

The chief buildings of interest are the great amphitheatre to seat 20,000 persons, one of the finest in existence; the forum, with public buildings on all sides; the paved way to the forum, which latter was for pedestrians only and adorned with many statues; the temples of Jupiter, of Apollo, of Isis, of Zeus Meilichios, of Vespasian and Fortuna Augusta, and the Doric temple which stands in the so-called Triangular Forum with a large and small theatre adjoining; and three separate baths, with complete apparatus for hot and cold water, etc. Adjoining the theatres were the barracks of the gladiators (q.v.), where objects of personal use were discovered just as they were left on the day of destruction. The streets with their shops and houses have now been revealed, and among the most interesting of these are the House of the Vettii, the House of the Faun, and the Mansion of Sallust, etc. In the Street of Abundance, one of the wine-sellers' shops contained all the vessels and pots and pans for daily use in good preservation. The private buildings are of great interest because of the light they throw on the domestic side of Greek and Roman life at that period.

Of the numerous objects of art found, many are very beautiful, though inferior to those found at Herculaneum; some of the green bronze statuettes are of exceptional workmanship, among them the dancing Faun and that called the youthful Bacchus or Narcissus. Many of the mural paintings and fresco works are of high artistic excellence. The mosaics especially call for attention. The most complete and beautiful was found in the House of the Faun, representing Alexander at the battle of Issus, and now in the museum at Naples, where nearly all the movable artistic objects have been placed. Great care has been taken to restore the remains of the upper storeys, with their balconies and pillared openings, and these assist largely in giving a true picture of the house-planning and architecture of the time. The volcanic matter that buried the city and suffocated the people as they tried to escape preserved the very forms of the men and women, whose bodies were practically moulded into the mixture of ash and cinders that later formed a plaster to perpetuate the very costumes and attitudes in which the people died.

The House of the Vettii has been restored as far as possible to show the actual conditions in which the wealthier classes of Pompeii lived at that time. Excavations in 1921 on the north-eastern side disclosed, among the more interesting objects, several fine paintings, including a large one of the twelve custodians or *penates* (q.v.) of Pompeii; a house with the remains of a balcony on the first floor; a bar or *thermopolium* (for sale of hot drinks); and two beautiful porticoes, almost intact, and a pergola above four shops. These pictures were discovered at the *compita*, i.e. street-crossings, which were held sacred and generally marked with sacred pictures and an altar. Below one such *compitum* was found an altar of masonry, built into the wall, on which were still preserved the ashes of the last sacrifice offered before the fatal hour. The bar is interesting for its many terra-cotta amphorae found still fixed in the ground, and for its furnace situated at the end of the counter. Above the furnace was found a cauldron in which remained some liquid placed there on the day of the catastrophe. This

bar was no doubt much frequented; for on its walls were found many
election manifestoes, one being on behalf of a man named Lollius, and
between each letter of his name were smaller letters announcing that
he was a *duumvir* who looked after the streets and sacred buildings.
In the entrance to one of the four shops were found the remains of a
little staircase leading up to the pergola.

Another well-preserved building has a fine crypto-portico of three
long corridors facing on to a garden. The walls of these corridors still
retained their decorations, which take the form of imitation encrusted
marble slabs dating from the 2nd century B.C. During excavations in
1941 some 465 inscriptions, figures and sketches on the columns of the
palaestra were discovered. At the same place the excavators found the
skeleton of eighty-five people killed or buried while fleeing for safety.
Near these remains were also found a case containing surgical instruments for eye operations, several of them in a very good state of
preservation.

During the Second World War severe damage was done by allied
aircraft, whose occupants pleaded that they thought to have detected
enemy troops among the ruins! Excavations during the 1956–7 season
concentrated on an area close to the Porta Nocera. Here were found
the remains of a tavern, with (near by) a statue of a gladiator believed
to have been the tavern's sign, the first of its kind unearthed at
Pompeii. *See* R. C. Carrington, *Pompeii*, 1936; E. C. Corti, *The Destruction and Resurrection of Pompeii and Herculaneum* (trans.), 1951.

Pompeius Magnus, Gnaeus: 1. Called in English **Pompey the Great,**
or simply **Pompey,** Roman general and statesman, born 106 B.C., son
of Cn. Pompeius Strabo (*see* POMPEIUS STRABO). He fought under his
father in the Social war (89 B.C.), and distinguished himself as one
of Sulla's lieutenants (83–82). In 81 he fought a successful campaign
against the Marian leaders in Africa, and was honoured by Sulla on
his return with the surname *Magnus* ('the Great'). Pompey continued
faithful to the aristocracy after Sulla's death (78), and supported the
consul Q. Lutatius Catulus in resisting the attempts of his colleague,
M. Aemilius Lepidus, to repeal the Sullan constitution. From 76 to 71
he was in Spain, helping to crush the rebellion of Sertorius (q.v.); and
on his way back to Rome he mopped up the remnants of Spartacus's
army (*see* SPARTACUS). In 70 he was consul with M. Licinius Crassus
(q.v.), and it was at this time that his sympathies veered from the
aristocratic to the popular party. Three years later the *Lex Gabinia*
(*see* GABINIUS, AULUS) gave him command of a war against the
Mediterranean pirates (*see* CILICIA), whom he swept from the sea in the
amazingly short period of three months. In 66 the *Lex Manilia* (*see*
MANILIUS, GAIUS) entrusted him with command of the third Mithradatic war (*see* MITHRADATES). After the defeat of Mithradates (64), he
formed Syria into a Roman province, intervened in the affairs of
Judaea, and captured Jerusalem (63).

Pompey then returned to Rome, and celebrated a triumph (q.v.) on
30th September 60 B.C. The senate's refusal to ratify his Asian settlement, or to provide land for his disbanded veterans, led him to form
the first triumvirate with Caesar (q.v.) and Crassus. To cement this
union Caesar gave him his daughter Julia in marriage (59). Pompey

and Crassus were again consuls in 55; but Caesar's subsequent victories in Gaul were fatal to Pompey's supremacy at home, and their alliance became merely nominal. The death of Julia in 54 further loosened the bonds, and Pompey, seeing that he must sooner or later clash with Caesar, stayed in the neighbourhood of Rome instead of going to Spain which had been assigned as his province and which he entrusted to legates (see AFRANIUS; PETREIUS; VARRO, MARCUS TERENTIUS). The last ties were broken by the death of Crassus at Carrhae (53). Pompey now aimed at dictatorship, and by encouraging civil strife (see MILO) secured his appointment as sole consul (52). Soon afterwards he became reconciled with the aristocracy, who thenceforward regarded him as their leader. In 49 civil war broke out (see CAESAR, GAIUS JULIUS). The decisive battle of Pharsalus (9th August 48) ended the career of Pompey. He fled to Egypt, but while landing was stabbed to death by order of the ministers of Ptolemy XII (29th September 48 B.C.). See Sir Charles Oman, Seven Roman Statesmen, 1902.

2. Elder son of the preceding by his first wife, Mucia; principal leader of the Pompeian party in the Spanish war (45 B.C.). He was defeated by Caesar at Munda in that year, escaped, but was caught and put to death soon afterwards.

Pompeius Magnus, Sextus, younger son of Pompey the Great by his first wife Mucia. Together with his brother Gnaeus he fought against Caesar at Munda, and escaped with his life. After Caesar's death (44 B.C.) he obtained a large fleet and occupied Sicily. He was eventually beaten by M. Vipsanius Agrippa (q.v.; see also AUGUSTUS) in 36, and was taken and put to death in Asia (35 B.C.).

Pompeius Rufus, Quintus, consul with Sulla (q.v.) in 88 B.C. He was directed to take over the army then serving under Cn. Pompeius Strabo in southern Italy; but Strabo, unwilling to surrender his command, had him assassinated.

Pompeius Strabo, Gnaeus, father of Pompey the Great. As consul in 89 B.C. he fought with success in the Social War (q.v.), and continued his campaigns as proconsul in southern Italy in the following year, when he ordered the assassination of Q. Pompeius Rufus (see preceding article) and was soon afterwards killed by lightning. His avarice and cruelty caused him to be hated by his soldiers.

Pompeius Trogus, see JUSTINUS, 1.

Pompey the Great, see POMPEIUS MAGNUS, GNAEUS, 1.

Pomponia: 1. Sister of T. Pomponius Atticus, was married in 69 B.C. to Q. Cicero, brother of the orator. He divorced her, after an unhappy life, in 45 or 44 B.C.

2. Daughter of T. Pomponius Atticus, was married to M. Vipsanius Agrippa. Her daughter, Vipsania Agrippina (q.v.), was married to the future emperor Tiberius.

Pomponius, Sextus, Roman jurist who lived in the reigns of Antoninus Pius and M. Aurelius. He is frequently quoted in the Digest.

Pomponius Atticus, Titus (109–32 B.C.), Roman eques, patron of art and literature. His original name was T. Pomponius, until his adoption by his maternal uncle Q. Caecilius (who left him 10 million sesterces), after which he was officially styled Q. Caecilius Pomponianus. Atticus was a nickname bestowed upon him by his friends because of his long residence at Athens, where he settled *c*. 88 B.C. He returned to Rome ten years or so later, kept aloof from politics, and was thus able to live on intimate terms with distinguished men of all parties. His closest friend, however, was Cicero, whose correspondence with him (68–43 B.C.) forms one of the most important relics of antiquity. His death was brought about by voluntary starvation when he found himself attacked by an incurable disease. By his wife Pilia, whom he married in 56 B.C., Atticus was the father of Pomponia, wife to M. Vipsanius Agrippa (q.v.). *See* G. Boissier, *Cicero and his Friends* (trans.), 1897.

Pomptinae Paludes (Pomptine Marshes), a marshy plain on the coast of Latium between Velletri and Terracina. As early as 312 B.C. the censor Appius Claudius tried to drain this district when constructing the Via Appia (q.v.). Augustus made further efforts, and a canal was dug alongside the road, so that travellers might avoid the noxious vapours and the footpads who abounded in the neighbourhood. None of the ancient or medieval attempts at drainage was entirely successful, and reclamation of the area was effected only by the Fascist government of Italy.

Pomptine Marshes, *see* POMPTINAE PALUDES.

Pontius Pilatus, an equestrian, appointed procurator of Judaea by Tiberius in A.D. 26. Under him Jesus Christ was crucified (*c*. 33). Recalled in 36 after endless quarrels with the Jews, and riots culminating in the brutal suppression of a Samaritan rising, he is reported by Eusebius (4th century A.D.) to have committed suicide at Vienna (mod. Vienne) in Gaul. Coptic tradition says he was martyred as a Christian, and he is revered as a saint by the Æthiopian Church. Authorities for Pilate's life are the New Testament, Eusebius, Josephus and Philo Judaeus. His name occurs on a stone discovered (1961) among the ruins of Caesarea Palestinae. *See* M. Radin, *The Trial of Jesus Christ*, 1931.

Pontus (-os), the north-easternmost district of Asia Minor, along the coast of the Euxine. About 301 B.C. a Persian satrap named Mithradates, who had been left by Alexander to govern the region, made himself independent and established a kingdom which was greatly extended by Mithradates the Great (q.v.). The principal towns were Amasia, Amisus, Cerasus, Comana, Trapezus and Zela (qq.v.). After the defeat of Mithradates by Pompey, in 63 B.C., the western part of Pontus, from Heraclea to Amisus, was joined to Bithynia (q.v.) to form a double province called 'Pontus and Bithynia'—the province governed by Pliny the Younger (q.v.). The remainder was granted *c*. 35 B.C. to Polemon (*see* POLEMON, 2), but was made a Roman province in A.D. 64. *See* PAPHLAGONIA.

Popilia, Via, name of two Italian highways. The first, built either in 159 B.C. by the censor M. Popilius Laenas or in 132 B.C. by the consul P. Popilius, ran from Capua to Rhegium (321 miles) through the interior. The second, constructed in 181 B.C. and remade by the consul P. Popilius in 132 B.C., ran from Ariminum to Aquileia (178 miles).

Poppaea Sabina, daughter of Titus Ollius, called herself after her maternal grandfather, Poppaeus Sabinus (consul A.D. 9). She was married first to Rufus Crispinus, and secondly to M. Salvius Otho (q.v.), one of the companions of Nero. The latter soon fell in love with her, and sent Otho to govern the province of Lusitania (A.D. 58). Poppaea now became the acknowledged mistress of Nero, over whom she exercised absolute sway. Anxious to marry the emperor, she persuaded him first to murder his mother, Agrippina the younger (A.D. 59), who was opposed to the union, and then to divorce and subsequently put to death his innocent wife Octavia (A.D. 62). In 65, while pregnant, she died from a kick given her by Nero.

Populonia, city of Etruria, dating from at least the 9th century B.C. It was situated on a lofty hill which sinks abruptly to the sea and forms a peninsula. In the neighbourhood were tin and copper mines; the inhabitants also worked the iron mines of Ilva (q.v.), and supplied iron to Scipio in 205 B.C. It was destroyed by Sulla during the civil wars, and never recovered its prosperity. Remains include part of the walls and numerous tombs dating from the 9th to the 3rd century B.C. In the time of Strabo (q.v.) there was a look-out tower for the shoals of tunny-fish, and a mosaic with a design of fishes has been excavated.

Porcia, daughter of M. Porcius Cato 'Uticencis' (q.v.), was married first to M. Calpurnius Bibulus (q.v.) and afterwards to M. Junius Brutus (see BRUTUS, 2). She was said to have induced her husband, on the night before the Ides of March, to reveal to her the conspiracy against Caesar's life, and to have wounded herself in the thigh as proof that she could be entrusted with the secret. She died in 43 B.C.

Porphyrius (-phurios), Greek Neoplatonist philosopher, born in Palestine A.D. 233. After studying at Athens under Longinus (q.v.), he settled at Rome and became a pupil of Plotinus (q.v.), whose writings he edited and whose life he wrote. This latter work has survived, together with an important treatise *On Abstinence*. Of his polemic against the Christian religion we have only fragments; the work itself was publicly destroyed in 448. See J. Bidez, *Vie de Porphyre*, 1913.

Porsena or Porsenna, Lars, in Roman legend, king of the Etruscan town of Clusium, marched against Rome to restore Tarquinius Superbus (see TARQUINIUS, LUCIUS, 2). He occupied the Janiculum hill, but was prevented by Cocles (q.v.) from entering the city, to which he then laid siege. When the Romans had been reduced to famine, Gaius Mucius (see SCAEVOLA, GAIUS MUCIUS) entered the Etruscan camp with the intention of killing Porsena, but he accidentally slew the royal secretary instead. Seized and threatened with torture, he thrust his right hand into a fire, and there let it burn, in order to show how little he minded pain. Astonished at his courage, the king bade him depart; but Mucius, out of gratitude, advised him to make peace with Rome, 'since 300 noble youths have sworn to take your life, and I was the first upon whom the lot fell'. Porsena did as he was counselled.

Portunus or Portumnus, an early Roman god of gates and doors (Lat. *porta*). He was gradually transformed into a protector of harbours (Lat. *portus*) and was identified with the Greek Palaemon (see ATHAMAS). He had a temple near Ostia, where his festival was celebrated on 17th August. At Rome, what is now thought to be the temple of Portunus was long known as the temple of Vesta, a circular building on the left bank of the Tiber near the foot of the Aventine. Here the god was served by a special priest, the *flamen Portunalis*.

Porus (-os), Greek form of the name Paurava, an Indian king who ruled over territory east of the River Hydaspes. Defeated by Alexander the Great on the banks of the Hydaspes in 326 B.C., he was allowed to retain his kingdom, which the conqueror enlarged. He was assassinated between 321 and 315 B.C. *See* Arrian, *Anabasis*, v. 18, 19; Plutarch, *Alexander*, 60.

Poseidōn, Greek god, most probably of pure hellenic origin, consort of Earth, and hence lord of earthquakes and of the fresh-water streams that fertilize the soil. After his original worshippers entered Greece his dominion was extended to the sea, with which he is principally associated in classical mythology. Here he is described as a son of Cronus and Rhea, and brother of Zeus. His palace was in the depths of the sea, off Aegae (q.v.) in Euboea, where he kept his horses with golden manes and brazen hoofs. He married Amphitrite.

Poseidon, however, was also a god of horses, and may have originally been worshipped in horse form. The reason for this is uncertain; but it has been suggested, with much probability, that it may have been due to the horse-breeding interests of the Thessalian plains where his cult in all likelihood began. He was accordingly believed to have taught men the art of horsemanship, and to have been the originator of horse races, of which he was the special patron. In Attic legend, it was said that when Poseidon contended with Athena for the office of tutelary deity of Athens, he created the first horse, while Athena produced the olive.

Other legends represent Poseidon as having built the walls of Troy for Laomedon. But the *Iliad* shows him as favouring the Greeks during the Trojan war; his hostility towards Odysseus, as described in the *Odyssey*, arose from the hero's slaying of Polyphemus (q.v.). Sacred to Poseidon, besides the horse, were the dolphin and the pine-tree. Sacrifices offered to him generally consisted of black or white bulls, but also included wild boars and rams. The Isthmian Games (q.v.) were celebrated in his honour. His symbol was the trident. *See* NEPTUNE.

Poseidōnia, *see* PAESTUM.

Poseidōnios, Greek Stoic philosopher, born at Apamea, in Syria, *c.* 135 B.C. He studied at Athens under Panaetius (q.v.), and taught at Rhodes, where Cicero (q.v.) was among his hearers. He settled at Rome in 51 B.C. and died five years later. Poseidonios was a man of immense and varied learning. He may be compared with Aristotle; for as the latter sums up the achievement of the classical period, so Poseidonios epitomized the hellenistic culture and transmitted it to the men of the Renaissance. Only a few fragments of his works have been preserved.

Posidippus (-os), *fl.* 280 B.C., Greek poet of the New Comedy, of which he was the last and one of the most distinguished representatives. Seventeen titles and some fragments of his forty plays have survived. He was much imitated by Roman writers, and is believed by some to have been the author of a play from which the *Menaechmi* of Plautus was adapted. There is a fine statue of Posidippus in the Vatican.

Postumia, Via, an Italian highway constructed in 148 B.C. by the consul Spurius Postumius Albinus. It ran from Genua to Betriacum via Dertona, Placentia and Cremona (qq.v.). From Cremona one branch went to Aquileia via Mantua and Altinum, another to Verona and the Brenner. The Via Postumia was of great strategic importance, for it alone made possible the occupation of Liguria.

Postumus, Roman soldier who assumed the imperial title in Gaul, A.D. 258. He reigned until 268, when he was murdered by his own troops. *See* THIRTY TYRANTS, 2.

Potidaea (-daia), town at the northern end of Pallene in Chalcidice, founded from Corinth. After the Persian wars it became a tributary ally of Athens, but having revolted in 432 B.C., it was captured in 429 after a siege of two years and resettled from Athens (*see* Thucydides, ii. 70). In 356 B.C. the town was taken and destroyed by Philip II of Macedon, but on its ruins Cassander (q.v.) built a new city called Cassandreia.

Praefectus : 1. In republican times the title of a Roman cavalry commander (*praefectus equitum*); under the empire an officer of equestrian rank who gradually superseded the senatorial *legatus* as commander of a legion (q.v.), also sometimes the commander of an auxiliary unit of infantry or cavalry.

2. *Praefectus Praetorio,* commander of the Praetorian Guard (q.v.). After the abolition of the guard by Constantine (A.D. 312), the term was used of those who governed the largest divisions of the empire (praefectures).

3. *Praefectus Urbi,* originally an official who in early times represented the kings and afterwards the consuls when they were absent from Rome. Under the empire it was applied to the commander of the *cohortes urbanae* who were responsible for public order in Rome. *See* ROMAN ARMY.

4. *Praefectus Vigilum,* commander of the Vigiles, a body created by Augustus to act as a night-watch, fire brigade, etc.

5. *Praefectus Annonae,* an officer responsible for management of the corn supply.

6. *Praefectus Aerarii,* official in charge of the *aerarium* (q.v.).

Praeneste (mod. Palestrina), city and villa resort of Latium, 23 miles east of Rome by the Via Praenestina. It was famous for its nuts, its roses, its pleasant climate, but chiefly for its temple of Fortuna (q.v.). Praeneste, which dates from the 7th or 8th century B.C. at latest, was founded, according to tradition, by Telegonus (q.v.). Following a long, intermittent struggle with Rome, which ended in 338 B.C., Praeneste was an allied city until after the Social War (q.v.), when it received the Roman franchise. In 82 B.C. the younger Marius was besieged here by Sulla's troops; the city was captured and a military colony established in the neighbourhood.

Praetor, originally a title designating a Roman consul as leader of an army. After 366 B.C. it was applied to the annually elected curule magistrate who administered justice and was subordinate to the consuls. The office was open to plebeians by 337 B.C. (*see* PHILO, QUINTUS PUBLILIUS). By 246 B.C. there were two praetors, *urbanus* and *peregrinus*, the first concerned with the decision of suits between citizens, and the second with cases between two aliens or between an alien and a citizen. From 241 B.C. praetors were occasionally appointed to govern provinces. Later, however, they came to be entrusted with this work immediately after their year of office, and were then called *propraetores*. The number of judicial praetors was increased to eight and sixteen by Sulla and Caesar respectively; Augustus reduced it to twelve, but it rose again under Nerva to eighteen. Praetors were attended by lictors (q.v.). Under the empire one of their chief functions was management of public games.

Praetorian Guard (Lat. Praetoriani), Roman imperial bodyguard, instituted by Augustus (2 B.C.). It consisted of nine (later ten) cohorts of about 1,000 men each, horse and foot, commanded by a prefect (*see* PRAEFECTUS, 2). They had higher rank and pay than the legions, and their term of service was sixteen years. The praetorians came to possess an almost acknowledged right to choose the new emperor. These cohorts, which were stationed in Rome, occupied the famous Praetorian Camp, in the north-west corner of the city (*see* SEJANUS), from the reign of Tiberius onward. They were abolished by Constantine (A.D. 312). The name *praetoria cohors* had been applied under the republic to select troops attendant on the general of an army.

Praetorium, originally the headquarters of a Roman camp. Later, in the provinces, the term was applied to the governor's official residence, to villas, and sometimes to wayside inns.

Pratinas, Athenian tragic poet, an elder contemporary of Aeschylus. He also wrote dithyrambs, and introduced satyric plays as entertainment distinct from their normal function as appendages to the tragic trilogy. Among the surviving fragments of Pratinas's work is part of a choral ode of the kind known as 'hyporchemata'. *See* Athenaeus, xiv. 617.

Praxias (*fl.* 448 B.C.), Athenian sculptor whose work looks back to the more archaic school of Calamis (q.v.). He worked on the pediments of the temple of Apollo at Delphi.

Praxiteles (*fl. c.* 350 B.C.), Athenian sculptor. His chief works have perished, including the 'Aphrodite' of Cnidus, for which Phryne (q.v.) was probably his model. This was ranked in antiquity next to the 'Zeus' of Pheidias at Olympia. It was destroyed by fire in A.D. 475, but a copy exists in the Vatican. Other works were a 'Satyr', 'Eros of Thespiae' and 'Apollo Sauroctonos'. His 'Hermes', a most important monument of 4th-century art, was found in the Heraeum at Olympia (1877). *See* Pliny, *Hist. Nat.* xxxiv and xxxvii; A. Furtwängler, *Masterpieces of Greek Sculpture* (trans), 1895; W. Klein, *Praxiteles*, 1898; K. Schefold, in *Pio Arte*, 1945.

Priam (Gk Priamos), in Greek legend, King of Troy during the Trojan war. He was son of Laomedon, married first Arisba, and secondly Hecuba who, according to Homer, bore him nineteen of his fifty children. In the early years of his reign Priam helped the Phrygians in their war against the Amazons; but when the Greeks laid siege to Troy he was already an old man, and took no active part in the war. Once only he ventured on to the field of battle, and that was to conclude an agreement for the single combat between Paris and

Menelaus. After the death of Hector (q.v.), Priam ransomed the body of his son at an interview with Achilles (*Iliad* xxiv). On the capture of Troy he was slain by the latter's son Neoptolemus.

Priapus (-os), in Greek mythology, son of Dionysus and Aphrodite. A god of fruitfulness in general, he was worshipped as protector of flocks, of bees, of the vine and of garden produce. He was represented by the phallus alone, or as a human deformity with enlarged genitals. The original home of his cult was Lampsacus on the Hellespont.

Priēnē, one of the twelve cities of the Ionian federation. Situated in the foothills of Mt Mycale, six miles north of the River Maeander, it was once on the coast, but is now some miles inland. Having prospered under Bias, one of the Seven Sages of Greece, in the mid 6th century B.C., it was afterwards subject to the kingdoms of Lydia and Persia. Its fortunes declined after the death of Alexander, but revived with the advent of Roman power in Asia Minor. There are magnificent remains of this admirably planned city, which was rebuilt in the 4th and 3rd centuries B.C. and occupied a series of terraces enclosed by a wall. *See* H. Schrader, *Priene*, 1904; T. Fyfe, *Hellenistic Architecture*, 1936.

Primus, Marcus Antonius, a general of Vespasian, who defeated the army of Vitellius at Betriacum (q.v.) in A.D. 69. He is remarkable as having led a stormy life in an age of violence yet surviving into a peaceful old age.

Probus, Marcus Aurelius, Roman emperor, A.D. 276–82. He was appointed by the emperor Tacitus governor of the east, and, upon the death of Tacitus, the purple was forced on him by the armies of Syria. The downfall of Florianus (q.v.) removed his only rival. During his reign he completed the walls of Aurelian at Rome (q.v.), and gained many brilliant victories over the barbarians on the frontiers of Gaul and Illyricum, but was killed in a mutiny of his own troops. His successor was Carus (q.v.).

Probus, Marcus Valerius, Roman grammarian and critic of the 1st century A.D. Nothing survives of his work except part of the *De notis*, which is probably a section of a larger work. It contains a list of abbreviations used in legal and historial documents. Other works have been wrongly attributed to Probus, though his opinions may be represented in the commentary on Virgil's *Bucolics* and *Georgics* which has come down to us under his name.

Procne (Proknē), daughter of Pandion, King of Athens, and sister of Philomela. *See* TEREUS.

Procris (-kris), daughter of Erechteus, King of Athens, and wife of Cephalus (q.v.).

Procrustes (-krustēs), in Greek legend, a robber who dwelt near Eleusis; also called **Damastēs** or **Polypemon** (Polupēmōn). Having tied his captives to a bed, he would stretch their limbs if they were shorter than its frame, or chop off an appropriate length of leg if they were too tall. He was slain by Theseus (q.v.).

Proculus, Roman jurist of the 1st century A.D., gave his name to the legal school (Proculian), said to have been founded by M. Antistius Labeo (q.v.).

Proculus, Julius, a legendary senator of Rome, to whom Romulus was supposed to have appeared after death with instructions that the people should worship him under the name Quirinus (q.v.).

Proetus (Proitos), son of Abas, King of Argos, grandson of Lynceus and twin brother of Acrisius (*see* PERSEUS). In a dispute between the brothers for the kingdom of Argos, Proetus was worsted. He fled to Iobates, King of Lycia (*see* BELLEROPHON), whose daughter Antea or Sthenoboea he married. With the help of Iobates he returned to Argos and obtained from Acrisius a share in the kingdom.

Proetus had three daughters who, when they reached the age of maturity, were stricken with madness, either because they had slighted the worship of Dionysus or because they had presumed their beauty to be equal with that of Hera. The frenzy spread throughout the female population of Argos until Proetus agreed to divide his share of the kingdom (or the whole kingdom if Acrisius was already dead) with Melampus (q.v.) and Bias, upon the former promising to cure the women of their madness. According to Ovid, Proetus expelled Acrisius from Argos, and was turned to stone by Perseus with the head of Medusa.

Promētheus, 'Forethought', in Greek mythology, son of the Titan Iapetus, father of Deucalion, and brother of Atlas and Epimetheus (qq.v.). He stole fire from heaven for man, and warned Epimetheus against receiving any gift from the gods (*see* PANDORA). He was the earliest teacher and benefactor of mankind. Zeus punished his presumption by chaining him to a mountain in the Caucasus, where an eagle devoured his liver, which was daily renewed; but he was eventually set free by Heracles. *See* Aeschylus, *Prometheus Bound*. *See also* CHIRON.

Pronuba, title of Juno as patroness of marriage.

Propertius, Sextus Aurelius, Latin elegiac poet, born of a well-to-do family at Asisium (mod. Assisi) in Umbria *c.* 50 B.C. After the battle of Philippi (42) his patrimony was confiscated, but he received a good education and afterwards settled at Rome. Here he became deeply attached to 'Cynthia', a courtesan from Tibur; but nothing is known of his life after her death, though he is believed to have died *c.* 16 B.C.

Propertius enjoyed the patronage of Maecenas (q.v.), while his friends included Tibullus, Ovid and Horace. Although the four books of his extant poems contain work of unequal quality, no Roman poet, except Catullus, so forcibly described the passion of love. Most of the poems are concerned with Cynthia, but the fourth book deals with Roman legend and history. A student of his Greek and Latin predecessors, he was influenced also by Virgil, Horace and other contemporaries; but his own influence upon these last, especially upon Ovid, is likewise manifest. *See* the edition by H. E. Butler and E. A. Barber, 1933; text with translation by H. E. Butler (Loeb Library), 1912. *See also* W. Y. Sellar, *Horace and the Elegiac Poets*, 1892.

Propylaea (Propulaia), a monumental entrance gateway to a Greek temple or sacred precinct. The most famous is that of the Acropolis at Athens (q.v.), designed by the architect Mnesicles and built of Pentelic marble between 437 and 433 B.C. A hall in its north wing was adorned with murals by famous artists.

Prostatēs, word used at Athens to denote one who in his own person supplied the legal status which was wanting to resident aliens, but without which they could not act in a legal capacity. *See* METICS.

Prōtagoras (*c.* 485–*c.* 415 B.C.), Greek sophist, born at Abdera in Thrace. He was the first to call himself a sophist and to teach for pay. According to Plato, he professed to teach not science or scholarship, but conduct. Protagoras is most famous for the opening sentence of his (lost) work entitled *Truth*, 'Man is the measure of all things', which fairly sums up his teaching that there are no absolute standards of truth. The statement is the object of an elaborate refutation by Aristotle (*Metaphysics*, iii. 5, 6). *See* D. Loenen, *Protagoras and the Greek Community*; K. Freeman, *Companion to the Pre-Socratic Philosophers*, 1946. *See also* Plato's dialogue *Protagoras*.

Protesilaus (Prōtesilaos), a Thessalian hero, son of Iphicles by Astyoche, and husband of Laodameia. He was first of the Greeks to spring ashore on Trojan soil, although he knew it meant instant death. Laodameia prayed that he might be allowed to return to earth for three hours; her request was granted, and when the time was up she returned with him to the underworld. Another version relates that on the death of her husband she conceived a morbid love for his image; that her father, Acastus, made a bonfire of this object; and that Laodameia joined it in the flames.

Prōteus, in Greek mythology, a marine demi-god, son or subject of Poseidon, whose flocks (the seals) he tended. He possessed the gift of prophecy, but courage and resourcefulness were needed to wring the truth from him. Each day at noon he rose from the sea and slept in the shade of rocks. There it was necessary to lay hold of him; but he immediately assumed every possible shape in quick succession, and only if the inquirer hung on would he resume his normal form and prophesy. For one of the most celebrated of such occasions *see* ARISTAEUS.

Prōtogenēs (*fl.* 330–300 B.C.), Greek painter, born at Caunus in Caria, but spent most of his time in Rhodes. Apelles (q.v.) is said to have admired his work, but to have considered him too imitative of nature. His masterpiece, 'Ialysus', a picture of the founder of Rhodes, took him seven years to paint.

Provocatio, term of Roman law originally signifying a criminal appeal. Towards the end of the 2nd century A.D. it came to be used synonymously with *appellatio*, a civil appeal, and hence to mean any recourse to a superior tribunal.

Provinces of the Roman Empire, *see* ACHAEA; AFRICA; ARABIA PETRAEA; ARMENIA; ASIA; BITHYNIA; BRITAIN; CAPPADOCIA; CILICIA; COMMAGENE; CORSICA; CRETE; CYPRUS; CYRENAICA; DACIA; EGYPT; EPIRUS; GALATIA; GALLIA; GERMANIA; HISPANIA; ILLYRICUM; MACEDONIA; MAURETANIA; MESOPOTAMIA; MOESIA; NORICUM; NUMIDIA; PAMPHYLIA; PANNONIA; RHAETIA; SARDINIA; SICILY; SYRIA; THRACE; VINDELICIA.

Proxenoi, diplomatic representatives of Greek city-states; but, unlike modern ambassadors, they were members of the state in which the interests of another (or of its individual members) were to be represented. Thus the orator Demosthenes acted as proxenos of Thebes at Athens. The position was often hereditary.

Prusias (Prou-): 1. King of Bithynia (q.v.) from 228 to 180 B.C.; son and successor of Zielas. Under him Bithynia enjoyed great prosperity, and it was to his court that Hannibal (q.v.) fled for refuge in 190 B.C.

2. Son and successor of the preceding, reigned from 180 to 149 B.C. He warred against Attalus II of Pergamum, with whom the Romans obliged him to make peace in 154 B.C. He was dethroned and put to death by his son Nicomedes II (q.v.).

Prytaneis (Pru-), *see* BOULE.

Pseudo-Longinus (1st century A.D.), an otherwise unknown Greek author of a treatise *On the Sublime*, formerly attributed to the rhetorician Longinus (q.v.) of Emesa. The work, which quotes numerous writers, including *Genesis*, is acknowledged as one of the great masterpieces of literary criticism. *See* edition, commentary and translation by W. Rhys Roberts, 1903. There is a translation by H. L. Havell in Everyman's Library.

Psyche (Psukhē), hellenistic personification of the human soul. According to legend, she was the eldest of a king's three daughters, and her beauty roused the jealousy of Aphrodite. The goddess ordered Cupid to inspire Psyche with love for the most contemptible of all men, but he himself became enamoured of her. Unseen and unknown, he visited her every night, and left her as soon as day began to dawn. But her jealous sisters persuaded her that under cover of darkness she might be cohabiting with some dreadful monster. Accordingly one night, while Cupid lay asleep, she approached him with a lamp, and beheld the most beautiful of the gods. A drop of hot oil falling from the lamp on to his shoulder awakened him; he rebuked her for her mistrust and fled. Psyche's happiness was gone: she wandered from temple to temple in search of her lover, and at length reached the palace of Aphrodite, who detained her and set her to perform the hardest tasks. Psyche would have perished had not Cupid, who still loved her, invisibly aided her. With his help she survived the perils of her labours, overcame the hatred of Aphrodite, attained immortality and was united with Cupid for ever. The story is told in the *Golden Ass* of Apuleius (q.v.), and is translated in Pater's *Marius the Epicurean*. *See also* E. Rohde, *Psyche*, 1907.

Ptolemaeus, Claudius, Greek astronomer and geographer of the 2nd century A.D. He was certainly observing at Alexandria in A.D. 139, and was still alive in 161. His principal extant works are the *Syntaxis* (commonly called *Almagest*) and the *Geography*. The first, written about A.D. 150, gives definitive form to the astronomy of Hipparchus (q.v.), and was absolutely authoritative until the time of Copernicus (1473–1543). The second is the most important work on ancient mathematical geography which we possess. *See* Heiberg's edition of the astronomical works, 1899–1907, and that of the *Geography* by P. J. Fischer, 1932. *See also* T. G. Rylands, *Geography of Ptolemy*, 1893.

Ptolemaïs, name of two towns, one in Syria and another in Cyrenaica (q.v.).

Ptolemy (Gk Ptolemaios), dynasty of Macedonian kings who ruled in Egypt from 323 to 30 B.C. The founder, *Ptolemy I, Soter* (323–283

B.C.), was the son of Lagus, one of Alexander the Great's most trusted generals. Egypt was his share of Alexander's conquests. He assumed the kingly title in 305 B.C. He commenced the great library and museum at Alexandria, where, under his patronage, Euclid taught mathematics; it was through him that the worship of Serapis (q.v.) was introduced. His name Soter (Saviour) was earned by the assistance he gave to the Rhodians when they were besieged by Demetrius (304). *Ptolemy II*, posthumously called Philadelphus (283–246 B.C.), was famous chiefly for his splendid court and general delight in luxury, and his encouragement of commerce. His first wife was Arsinoë I, daughter of Lysimachus. After repudiating her he married his sister, the beautiful Arsinoë II, widow of Lysimachus, and deified her at her death. Philadelphus built the Pharos (q.v.) at Alexandria. He delighted in the library and encouraged all intellectual pursuits. *Ptolemy III* (Euergetes I) (246–221 B.C.), son of Philadelphus by his first wife, married Berenice, daughter of Magas, King of Cyrene. He invaded the Seleucid kingdom as far as Babylonia, while his fleet was victorious as far as Thrace. He left many monuments in Egypt, among them the unfinished temple of Edgu. *Ptolemy IV*, called Philopator (221–203 B.C.), son of the preceding. He married his sister Arsinoë III. He was a debauchee, and started the decline of his kingdom. *Ptolemy V*, called Epiphanes (203–181 B.C.), son of the preceding, was only five years old when he became king. He married Cleopatra, daughter of Antiochus III. His reign was chiefly remarkable for the cruelty employed in suppressing native rebellions. *Ptolemy VI, Philometor* (181–145 B.C.), and *Ptolemy VII* (later nicknamed Physkon, 'Puffer', from his bloated appearance, died 116), sons of Ptolemy V, came to the throne jointly and quarrelled continuously, Philometor being the better of the two. Rome intervened in their quarrels and Philometor's war with the Seleucids, Physkon eventually retiring to Cyrene until his brother's death, when he returned, murdered Philometor's son, and married the mother (his sister) and her daughter, also called Cleopatra. Physkon left Cyrene to an illegitimate son, and Egypt with Cyprus to Cleopatra (Kokkē) and his two sons by her, *Ptolemy VIII*, Soter II (nicknamed Lathyras, 'Chickpea'), and *Ptolemy IX*, Alexander (*d.* 88). There followed a long period of domestic strife, the brothers ruling alternately in Egypt and Cyprus, until Alexander was killed in a rising, having melted down the golden sarcophagus of Alexander the Great to pay his mercenaries; after this Lathyrus ruled until 80 B.C. *Ptolemy X*, Alexander II (*d.* 80 B.C.), son of Ptolemy IX, entered Alexandria with the support of Rome, married his stepmother Berenice III, assassinated her, and was at once killed by the mob. He was the last of the legitimate line. *Ptolemy XI*, known as Aulētēs, 'the flute-player' (80–51 B.C.), an illegitimate son of Ptolemy VIII, was then chosen by the Alexandrians. He spent most of his reign trying to buy the support of influential Romans; and was at last recognized in 55, when he was restored after three years' exile. He left Egypt to his children, Cleopatra (q.v.) aged seventeen, and her brother *Ptolemy XII* (51–47 B.C.), whose ministers assassinated Pompey (48), and who perished in the war with Caesar, when his younger brother, *Ptolemy XIII*, was associated with Cleopatra and soon poisoned.

Caesarion, Cleopatra's son by Julius Caesar, was known as *Ptolemy XIV*. He was murdered by Octavian, 30 B.C. *See* J. Mahaffy, *The Empire of the Ptolemies*, 1895; E. Bevan, *A History of Egypt under the Ptolemaic Dynasty*, 1927.

Publicani, Roman business men who bid every *lustrum* (five years) at a public auction, held in Rome by the newly appointed censors, for the right either of collecting the taxes due to the state treasury from the lands of Italy and the provinces, or of contracting for the execution of public works. Often the *publicani* formed joint-stock companies (*societates publicanorum*). Drawn from the equestrian ranks (*see* EQUITES), they rapidly acquired great political influence as the capitalistic class, their enormous wealth being amassed often by gross extortion and embezzlement; hence the derogatory 'publicans and sinners' of the New Testament.

Publilius Syrus, Latin mimeographer of the 1st century B.C. Originally a slave, he was brought to Rome *c.* 45 B.C. An extant compilation entitled *Publilii Syri Sententiae* is believed to contain many of his lines. *See* the edition by R. A. Bickford-Smith, 1895. There is a text and translation by J. W. and A. M. Duff in *Minor Latin Poets* (Loeb Library), 1934.

Punic Wars, name given to the conflict between Rome and Carthage (q.v.), which ended in the latter's ruin after three prolonged and ferocious wars. The principal cause of the Punic wars was the Roman ambition to obtain possession of Sicily (q.v.), which was dominated by Carthage.

The first of these wars (264–241 B.C.) was centred upon Sicily. It ended with the reduction of most of the island to the status of a Roman province, after the Roman victory of the Aegates (q.v.) in 241 B.C. *See also* DUILIUS; HIERON, 2; MESSANA.

The second war (218–201 B.C.) was almost entirely the work of Hannibal (q.v.). It ended with his defeat at Zama (202) by P. Cornelius Scipio (*see* SCIPIO AFRICANUS MAJOR) and the acceptance by Carthage in the following year of a humiliating peace. *See also* CANNAE; TICINUS; TRASIMENUS; TREBIA.

The third war (149–146 B.C.) was short and decisive. Carthage, at Hannibal's instigation, had gradually rebuilt its fortifications, and Rome found a pretext for war when the Carthaginians attacked the Numidian king Masinissa (q.v.). Carthage was taken by a Roman army under the command of Scipio Africanus the younger (*see* SCIPIO AEMILIANUS AFRICANUS) and razed to the ground. *See also* CATO, MARCUS PORCIUS.

Pupienus Maximus, Marcus Clodius, elected by the senate joint emperor with Decimus Caelius Balbinus in succession to the Gordians (*see* GORDIANUS) in A.D. 238. Both were slain by the Praetorian Guard (q.v.) at Rome in the same year.

Purgotelēs, official engraver of signet rings to Alexander the Great.

Puteoli (mod. Pozzuoli), coastal town of Campania, situated on a narrow hill on the eastern side of the Bay of Puteoli, six miles west of Neapolis. Founded, with the name Dichaearchia, by Samians from Cumae *c.* 520 B.C., it was held by a Roman garrison against Hannibal in 214; received a Roman colony (194), which was afterwards enlarged by Vespasian; and appears to have enjoyed a large measure of self-government. Puteoli was a station of the imperial post, with sailors of the fleet at Misenum acting as couriers. But it was chiefly famous, from the late 2nd century B.C. onwards as a great commercial port, highly organized and with all the characteristics of such places in every age and clime. The excellent harbour was protected by an artificial mole, to which Caligula attached a pontoon bridge extending as far as Baiae two miles away.

It was to Puteoli that Sulla retired in 79 B.C., and here St Paul first set foot on Italian soil in A.D. 61 (Acts xxviii. 13). The remains of Hadrian, who died at Baiae, were interred here before their removal to Rome, and in his memory Antoninus Pius built a temple on the site of a house once owned by Cicero. Two amphitheatres have been excavated. The larger was erected during or soon after the reign of Vespasian; in the smaller Nero fought in games given in honour of the Armenian king Tiridates. Other remains include those of the mole, a market hall, two aqueducts, baths and reservoirs. See C. Dubois, *Pouzzoles Antiques*, 1907.

Pyanepsia (Pu-), an Athenian festival in honour of Apollo, celebrated on the 7th of the month Pyanepsion (October). Two offerings were made to the god, the first of which was a mess of pulse. The other, called 'eiresiōnē', was a branch of olive or laurel, bound with purple or white wool and decked with fruit, pasties and miniature jars of honey, oil and wine. This object was carried in procession to the temple of Apollo, where a boy whose parents were both living hung it on the gate; it remained there for the ensuing year. Similar branches were hung on the doors of private houses. The text of a chant sung during the procession and also called 'eiresiōnē' is preserved in Plutarch's *Theseus*, 22. See J. R. Farnell, *Cults of the Greek States*, vol. iv, 286.

Pydna (Pudna), town of Macedonia in the district of Pieria, famous for the victory won by L. Aemilius Paulus over Perseus, the last Macedonian king, in 168 B.C. See GALLUS, GAIUS SULPICIUS.

Pygmaei (Pugmaioi), men the height of a *pugmē*, i.e. 13½ inches. They are mentioned first by Homer (*Il.* iii. 5), who represents them as dwelling in the far south, in a land whither cranes fly from the northern winter. Later writers and many vase-painters tell of battles between the pygmies and the cranes. According to Herodotus (ii. 52) the pygmies dwelt in the region of what is probably to be identified with the Niger, and Ctesias describes a race of men only 27 inches high in central India. Aristotle locates the pygmies near the sources of the Nile, and Pliny mentions dwarf races in both Africa and Asia. Judging by physical features depicted on Greek vases, as well as in Egyptian sculptures of the 3rd millennium B.C., it is clear that these writers were referring to the forbears of the modern Negrillos and Negritos in Africa and Asia respectively.

Pygmalion (Pugmaliōn), in Greek legend, King of Cyprus. He fell in love with the ivory image of a maiden which he himself had made, and prayed Aphrodite to give it life. The goddess did so, and Pygmalion married the damsel, by whom he became father of Paphus.

Pylades (Puladēs), legendary son of the Phocian king Strophius and friend of Orestes (q.v.), whose sister Electra (*see* ELECTRA, 3) he subsequently married.

Pylos (Pulos), name of three towns on the west coast of Peloponnesus. The most famous was in Messenia, at the northern entrance of what is now called the Bay of Navarino, the largest and safest harbour in Greece. This harbour was protected by the small island of Sphacteria, which stretches for a distance of about 1¾ miles, leaving only a narrow entrance at each end. The place became memorable in the Peloponnesian war, when the Athenians built a fort on the promontory of Coryphasium, a little south of the ancient town and just inside the northern entrance to the harbour (425 B.C.). Spartan attempts to dislodge the Athenians proved unavailing, and the eventual capture by Cleon of the Spartan force which had been landed on Sphacteria was one of the most important events in the whole war. Since 1939, when it was first discovered, American archaeologists have excavated near Pylos a huge Mycenaean palace of the 15th century B.C. Professor Blegen of Cincinnati University, in charge of operations, has called it the 'Palace of Nestor', on the grounds that this magnificent building could have belonged only to a ruler of the wealth, power and fame ascribed by Homer to Nestor (q.v.) of Pylos. See *The Times*, 10th August and 5th November 1957.

Pyramus and Thisbe, the hero and heroine of a love story, represented by Ovid (*Metam.* iv. 55–465) as of Babylonian origin. Forbidden by their parents to marry, the lovers used to talk through a chink in the wall between their houses. They determined to elope, and appointed a mulberry-tree near the tomb of Ninus as their meetingplace. Thisbe was first on the scene; but she was scared by the roar of a lion, and ran off, dropping her veil. Along came the lion, which had just devoured an ox, tore the veil to pieces with its bloody jaws and went on its way. Pyramus then arrived, and, thinking that Thisbe had been eaten by the lion, stabbed himself. Thisbe returned, found her lover dying and took her own life. Hence the dark colour of the mulberry, which had hitherto been white.

Pyrgi (Purgoi, i.e. 'towers'), town on the south-west coast of Etruria, nine miles north-west of Caere. It possessed a temple of Leucothea (q.v.). In 1964 tablets were discovered which may, it is hoped, solve the mystery of the Etruscan language.

Pyrrhon (Purrhōn), Greek philosopher, founder of the Sceptic or Pyrrhonian school, born *c.* 360 B.C., a native of Elis in Peloponnesus. He is said to have been poor, to have begun life as a painter, and to have been drawn to philosophical speculation by the works of Democritus. He then attended the lectures of Bryson, disciple of Stilpon, attached himself to Anaxarchus, and with him accompanied the expedition of Alexander the Great (334 B.C.). He taught that man cannot attain to truth; all organic beings are subject to continuous renewal, so that one is able to know nothing but appearances. Among men, one meets at every step error, contradiction and illusion; so that the search for truth has no solid bases: to any proposition one can oppose a contrary and equally probable proposition. The wise man, therefore, does not pass judgments. He follows appearances without proclaiming them true, and endeavours in the moral field to attain to a sort of negative happiness, *ataraxia* (freedom from trouble), the only kind to which man can pretend. Pyrrhon died in 270 B.C., and left no writings, except a (lost) poem addressed to Alexander. His philosophical system was first reduced to writing by his disciple Timon. *See* E. Zeller, *Stoics, Epicureans and Sceptics* (trans.), 1892; L. Robin, *Pyrrho et la scepticisme grec*, 1944.

Pyrrhus (Purrhos), King of Epirus, born 319 B.C. He claimed descent from Achilles's son Neoptolemus (q.v.), who was also called Pyrrhus and was reputed ancestor of the Molossi (q.v.). Driven from his kingdom at the instigation of Cassander (q.v.) in 302, he was present at Ipsus (301), and in 295 was assisted by Ptolemy I to regain his throne. Pyrrhus aspired to emulate Alexander the Great, and tried to win the throne of Macedon; but though he acquired considerable territory in Macedonia, his brother-in-law Demetrius Poliorcetes was chosen king. War broke out between them (291); Demetrius was forced to flee (288). but Pyrrhus was soon superseded by the Macedonian Lysimachus (q.v.) in 287. His next famous exploit was aiding the Tarentines (*see* TARENTUM) against Rome (280). His defeat of the consul Laevinus at Heraclea was marked by such heavy losses as to beget the phrase 'Pyrrhic victory'. Pyrrhus could not prevail on the Roman senate to make peace, and, after defeating another Roman army at Asculum (279), he went to Sicily to aid the Greeks against Carthage. On returning to Italy in 275, he was crushed at Beneventum by the consul M. Curius Dentatus, and forced to withdraw to Epirus. He again made himself master of Macedonia in 273, but was killed next year in a riot at Argos, by a tile flung by a woman from a roof top.

Pythagoras (Pu-), Greek philosopher, born at Samos, but emigrated *c.* 531 B.C. to Croton in Magna Graecia, and there established a religious society whose aim was to liberate the soul from corruption of the body by study and the practice of asceticism. A conspiracy of his enemies, however, obliged Pythagoras to withdraw to Metapontum, where he died (497).

The mass of legend which even in ancient times gathered round the name of Pythagoras is wholly fanciful. Pythagoras wrote nothing, though various works, including the 'Pythagoras theorem' of Euclid, were attributed to him. From casual references in later writers it is learned that his central belief was the doctrine of metempsychosis, or transmigration of souls (*see* PHERECYDES). Thus the way of life, or religion, taught by Pythagoras was a combination of asceticism and the investigation of nature. Pythagoras discovered the numerical ratios which determine the principal musical intervals, and his school was thus led to interpret the world in terms of number. *See* W. Jaeger, *Theology of the Early Greek Philosophers*, 1947; J. Burnet, *Early Greek Philosophy*, 4th ed., 1948; J. E. Raven, *Pythagoras and Eleatics*, 1948.

Pytheas (Pu-), Greek navigator and astronomer, probably a contemporary of Alexander the Great. He was a native of Massalia, whence he sailed to the west and north of Europe, visiting Britain and sailing along its eastern coast for a considerable distance. He was credited with having visited 'Thule' (the Orkneys and Shetlands);

but this view is no longer accepted, and it is believed that his knowledge of these islands was derived merely from hearsay. He was also
said to have made another voyage, from Gades (Cadiz) to the Tanais
(Don). He is traditionally supposed to have been the first to connect
the spring tides with the phases of the moon, and it is certain that
he made astronomical observations for determining latitudes. Only
fragments of his *Oceanus* and *Periplus* are extant. *See* edition by M.
Fuhr, 1834–5. *See also* M. Cary and E. Warmington, *Ancient Explorers*,
1929; G. E. Broche, *Pythéas le Massiliote*, 1936.

Pythian Games, one of the four great hellenic athletic festivals,
celebrated at Delphi (Pytho) in honour of Apollo. Superintended by
the Amphictyonic Council after 586 B.C., these games were held in
August–September in the third year of each Olympiad (q.v.). *See also*
PINDAR.

Pythis (Pu-), Greek architect of the 4th century B.C. He worked
mostly in the Ionic style, in which he constructed the temple of
Athena Polias at Priene (founded by Alexander the Great). He was
also responsible for the great marble quadriga which crowned the
Mausoleum at Halicarnassus.

Python (Puthōn), in Greek legend, a female serpent which was
killed by Apollo at Delphi. It was generally said to have been produced from slime left by the flood in the time of Deucalion (q.v.); and
there can be little doubt that the legend refers to the existence of an
oracle of Earth at Delphi before the advent of Apollo. (*See* J. R.
Farnell, *Cults of the Greek States*, iii. 9; iv. 180.) It was in commemoration of his victory over the serpent that Delphic Apollo instituted the
Pythian games and was called Pythias, while his oracular priestess of
Delphi was called the Pythia.

Q

Quadi, a Germanic people of Suebic race, dwelling in the south-east of Germany; bounded west by the Marcomanni and south by the Pannonians. Taken under the protection of Rome in the reign of Tiberius, they later joined the Marcomanni and other tribes in a long war against the empire. They were defeated by Marcus Aurelius in A.D. 174, and disappear from history towards the end of the 4th century.

Quadrigarius, Quintus Claudius, Roman historian and one of Livy's main sources, *fl.* 100–78 B.C. His work, of which fragments survive, covered the period 390 B.C. to the time of Sulla.

Quaestor, name common to two distinct classes of Roman officials:

1. The criminal *quaestores*, or, as Maine styles them, Roman commissioners, were the body to whom the *Comitia* (q.v.) delegated its criminal jurisdiction. Maine thinks that in the earliest times a *quaestio* (commission) of this sort was appointed only to try a particular offender, like the *quaestores parricidii* who tried all cases of parricide and murder, though later commissions were appointed periodically without waiting for occasion to arise. Finally, when a *quaestio perpetua* (permanent commission) was appointed, Roman criminal jurisprudence had attained to a developed classification of crimes and a regular criminal tribunal. *Quaestores parricidii* disappear after 366 B.C. when their functions were transferred to *triumviri capitales* (q.v.).

2. The *quaestores classici* were officials charged with superintendence of the public treasury. A special body, the military quaestors, accompanied consuls and provincial governors to the field, took charge of the military chest, and supervised pay, provisions and booty. *See also* PRAEFECTUS, 6.

Quattuorviri, Roman municipal magistrates corresponding to the two pairs of colonial Duumviri (q.v.).

Quintilianus, Marcus Fabius, known in English as **Quintilian,** Latin rhetorician and critic, born at Calagurris in Spain *c.* A.D. 40; educated at Rome, which he left early in Nero's reign. Returning with Galba in 68, he quickly achieved fame and wealth as a teacher, and in 88, or soon afterwards, was entrusted with the education of Domitian's grand-nephew, together with the consular title and insignia. He was also the first public instructor to receive a regular state salary from the fund endowed for that purpose by Vespasian.

The principal and sole surviving work of Quintilian is the *Institutio Oratoria,* an exhaustive treatise in twelve books on the education of an orator. His style is good, his taste impeccable, while his moral tone is in striking contrast with the general degradation of his age. The best edition is that of L. Radermacher (1907–35).

Quintillus, Quintus Aurelius, brother of the emperor Claudius 'Gothicus', upon whose death in A.D. 270 he was proclaimed emperor by the troops at Aquileia. But the army at Sirmium, where Claudius had died, chose Aurelian (q.v.); whereupon Quintillus was deserted and committed suicide.

Quintus Calaber (Calabar or Smyrnaeus), Greek poet, *fl.* 3rd–4th century A.D., a native of Smyrna; called Calaber because his epic, *Paralipomena Homeri*, or *Posthomerica* (continuing the Trojan war from Hector's death to the return of the Greeks), was discovered at Otranto in Calabria in the 15th century. His materials were derived mainly from the cyclic poets. *See* edition by A. Zimmerman, 1881, translated by A. S. Way, 1931. *See also* G. W. Paschal, *A Study of Quintus of Smyrna*, 1904; M. W. Mansur, *The Treatment of Homeric Characters by Quintus of Smyrna*, 1940.

Quirinus, *see* ROMULUS.

Quirites, name of the Roman people in their civic capacity. It is connected with Quirinus, an ancient Sabine deity (*see* ROMULUS).

R

Rabirius, Gaius, Roman senator, accused in 63 by T. Labienus (q.v.) of having put to death the tribune L. Appuleius Saturninus (q.v.) in 100 B.C. The accusation was inspired by Caesar, who wished to deter the senate from using armed force against the popular party. The *duumviri perduellionis* (an obsolete court) appointed to try the case were Caesar himself and his relative Lucius Caesar. Rabirius was convicted; but the senate ruled the process invalid, and a new trial was ordered to be held before the people. On this occasion Rabirius was defended by Cicero (*Pro Rabirio*), but before a decision could be reached the meeting was broken up by the praetor Q. Metellus Celer.

C. Rabirius Postumus, nephew of the above, was appointed (55 B.C.) Treasurer of the Household by Ptolemy XI, Auletes (*see* PTOLEMY: *Ptolemy XI*); but his attempts to recover the enormous sums he had advanced to Ptolemy were so oppressive that he was arrested and imprisoned. Rabirius escaped and returned to Rome. Here he was put on trial and defended by Cicero, who secured his acquittal.

Raetia, *see* RHAETIA.

Ravenna, town of Gallia Cisalpina (Cispadana), situated in a marshy district on the River Bedesis. It was said to have been founded by Thessalians, who later handed it over to Umbrian settlers. It became subject to Rome after the conquest of the Boii in 191 B.C. Ravenna was of little or no importance until Augustus made its port, Classis, a naval station. The town lacked a good water supply, but this was remedied by Trajan, who built an aqueduct nearly 20 miles in length. *See* E. Hutton, *The Story of Ravenna*, 1926.

Reate (mod. Rieti), Sabine town on the Velinus, a small tributary of the Tiber. The fertility of its neighbourhood is mentioned by Cicero and by Virgil.

Regillus, Lacus, a lake in Latium, now dried but probably occupying the depression called today Pantano Secco. It is memorable for the victory said to have been gained on its shores by the Romans under Postumius Albinus over the Latins in 496 B.C. The victors had employed Greek cavalry, to whose twin patrons, the Dioscuri (q.v.), the first temple of Castor and Pollux was erected in the Forum Romanum, 434 B.C.

Regium (Gk Rhēgion; mod. Reggio di Calabria), Greek town in the territory of the Bruttii, on the eastern side of the strait separating Italy from Sicily. It was founded in 743 B.C. by a joint colony from Chalcis in Euboea and Messenia. About 494 B.C. it became subject to Anaxilas, leader of the Messenian element, who in 488 got possession of Messana (q.v.) in Sicily. Regium was in alliance with Athens from 433 until 415, when it chose to remain neutral at the time of the disastrous Athenian expedition. It was at war with Dionysius I of

Syracuse from 399 until 387, when it was captured and destroyed, but soon regained its prosperity. The Regians having applied to Rome for assistance on the invasion of Italy by Pyrrhus (q.v.) in 280 B.C., the Romans placed in the town a garrison of 4,000 men levied from the Latin colonies of Campania. In the following year these troops revolted, massacred the male population and held the town until they were overcome and put to death by the consul Genucius (270). Thereafter Regium remained consistently loyal to Rome, and maintained, even under the empire, its Greek culture and institutions.

Regulus, Marcus Atilius, Roman general. As consul in 267 B.C. he conquered the Sallentini, took the town of Brundisium and was granted a triumph. In 256 (ninth year of the first Punic war) he was consul a second time, when he and his colleague defeated the Carthaginian fleet off Ecnomus and landed with a large force in Africa. The other consul was recalled, Regulus being left to finish off the war. After sustaining a severe defeat at Adys near Carthage, the enemy sued for peace; but Regulus was prepared to grant it only upon terms so unacceptable that they decided to fight on. In 255 Regulus was overwhelmed and taken prisoner by a Carthaginian army under the Spartan general Xanthippus. So much may be taken as historical. The account which follows rests upon no compelling evidence and is very likely to have been invented in order to justify the ill treatment of Carthaginian prisoners at Rome.

Regulus was said to have remained in captivity until 250 B.C., when the Carthaginians, after their defeat at Panormus by L. Caecilius Metellus in the previous year, sent him to Rome on parole to negotiate peace or an exchange of prisoners. He persuaded the senate to reject both proposals and, returning to Carthage, was tortured to death. When the news of his death reached Rome two of the noblest Carthaginian prisoners suffered a like death. As a result of this story Regulus came to be looked upon as the model of Roman honour and endurance.

Remi, a people of Gallia Belgica. Their immediate neighbours were the Nervii, Veromandui and Suessiones on the north and west, the Catuvellauni and Mediomatrici on the south and south-east, and the Treveri on the north-east. Their capital was Durocortorum (mod. Rheims). The Remi distinguished themselves in 57 B.C. by allying themselves with Caesar when the other Belgic tribes combined against him. See *Bell. Gall.* ii. 3, 4.

Remus, twin brother of Romulus (q.v.).

Rex, Quintus Marcius: 1. Praetor at Rome in 144 B.C., when he built the aqueduct called Aqua Marcia.

2. Consul in 118 B.C., when he founded the Roman colony at Narbo (q.v.) in Gaul.

3. Consul in 68 B.C., and governor of Cilicia in the following year. In 63 B.C. he was outside Rome, hoping to secure a triumph, when the conspiracy of Catiline was brought to light, and he was dispatched to Faesulae to watch the movements of Catiline's general Mallius.

Rhadamanthus (-os), son of Zeus by Europa, and brother of Minos, King of Crete. According to Homer he dwelt in the Elysian fields (*Od.* iv. 564); but later legends represent him as meriting, by the absolute integrity of his life, to be appointed one of the judges in the lower world, together with Aeacus and Minos.

Rhaetia or **Raetia,** a province of the Roman Empire; originally bounded west by the Helvetii, east by Noricum, north by Vindelicia, south by Gallia Cisalpina. It was a very mountainous country. The inhabitants (mainly Celtic) were said to have followed an earlier Etruscan population. They remained independent until their subjugation by Tiberius and Drusus in 13 B.C., when the province was formed. Towards the end of the 1st century, however, Rhaetia was enlarged by Vindelicia, whence Tacitus (*Germania,* 41) speaks of Augusta Vindelicorum (Augsburg) as a colony of the province of Rhaetia. Under Diocletian Rhaetia was divided into two provinces, Prima and Secunda, corresponding to the original province and Vindelicia respectively. *See* Th. Mommsen, *Provinces of the Roman Empire* (trans.), 1886.

Rhagae (-ai), city of Media, at the foot of the mountains which border the southern shores of the Caspian. Having been destroyed by an earthquake, it was restored by Seleucus Nicator and called Europos. Again destroyed, during the Parthian revolt from Antiochus II, it was restored a second time by Arsaces (q.v.), who renamed it Arsacia.

Rhea, in Greek mythology, one of the Titans (q.v.) and mother of Zeus, later identified by the Greeks of Asia Minor with Cybele (*see* GREAT MOTHER OF THE GODS). The Romans, who identified Cronus with their god Saturnus (q.v.), likewise identified Rhea with Ops (q.v.).

Rhea Sylvia or **Ilia,** in Roman legend mother of Romulus and Remus (*see* ROMULUS). Her father, King Numitor of Alba Longa, was dethroned by his brother Amulius, who forced Rhea Sylvia to become a vestal virgin, and, when she bore twin sons, had her drowned in the Tiber. She became a goddess and the wife of Anio.

Rhesus (Rhēsos), son of the Thracian king Eïoneus. He went to the assistance of Priam in the Trojan war, an oracle having declared that Troy would never be taken if the snow-white horses of Rhesus once drank from the River Xanthus and ate the grass of the surrounding plain. But as soon as Rhesus entered Trojan territory he was slain by Odysseus and Diomedes, who carried off his horses.

Rhianos (*fl.* 230 B.C.), Alexandrian poet and grammarian, born in Crete. His most famous poem was the *Messeniaca* dealing with the second Messenian war and the exploits of Aristomenes (q.v.). This, however, together with all the rest of his work except eleven epigrams, has perished. Rhianos also contributed as a grammarian to Homeric studies. *See* C. Mayhoff, *De Rhiani Studiis Homericis,* 1870.

Rhodes (Gk Rhodos; Lat. Rhodus), easternmost island of the Aegean, about 12 miles off the southern coast of Caria. There are mythological accounts of its origins; but at the beginning of the historical period it was peopled by Dorians, whose three cities, Lindus, Ialysus and Camirus, together with Cos, Cnidus and Halicarnassus (qq.v.), formed the Dorian Hexapolis in the south-west corner of Asia Minor. The three cities soon became a great maritime confederacy and founded numerous colonies. Nothing is known of the island's history during the Persian wars. At the outbreak of the

Peloponnesian war it was a member of the Delian League, but in 412 B.C. it joined the Spartan alliance and became the main base of the Spartan fleet. In 408 the capital city, Rhodes, was built to the designs of Hippodamus and further enhanced the island's commercial importance. During the first six decades of the 4th century B.C. Rhodes was controlled successively by Sparta, Athens, Halicarnassus and Persia. In 332 it submitted to Alexander the Great, but after his death it expelled the Macedonian garrison. In the wars that followed between the Diadochi, the Rhodians allied themselves with Ptolemy, and in 304 their capital endured a memorable siege by Demetrius Poliorcetes (q.v.), who at length abandoned his attempt and, as a mark of his esteem for their valour, presented the city with the engines he had used against them, from the sale of which they defrayed the cost of the Colossus (q.v.). Rhodes supported the Romans against Philip V of Macedon and Antiochus III of Syria. The alliance with Rome was interrupted by a short-lived espousal of the cause of Perseus (q.v.). After his defeat, in 168 B.C., the island was punished by the loss of some territory on the mainland, but recovered the favour of Rome by the naval assistance it rendered during the Mithradatic wars. The Rhodian fleet assisted Pompey against the pirates and later against Caesar; but after Pompey's death a squadron of their ships fought with Caesar at Alexandria. Rhodes was deprived of its independence by Claudius, and its prosperity received a final blow from an earthquake in A.D. 155.

In addition to political and commercial eminence, the island long enjoyed great cultural prestige. Birth-place of Panaetius and home of Poseidonios, Apollonius Rhodius, Chares and Protogenes (qq.v.), it also possessed a famous rhetorical school, among whose leading lights was Apollonius 'Molon' (q.v.). *See* C. Torr, *Rhodes in Ancient Times*, 1885.

Rhodopis (*fl. c.* 600 B.C.), Greek courtesan. Charaxus, Sappho's brother, saw her at Naucratis in Egypt, where she was a slave living with her master Xanthus; he fell desperately in love with her, and, to his sister's indignation, paid a great sum to purchase her liberty.

Rhoecus (Rhoikos), Samian sculptor of the 6th century B.C. He and his son Theodorus were noted for their work in bronze, and they, with another son, Telecles, made a statue of the Pythian Apollo for Samos. Rhoecus was also the sculptor of a marble 'Artemis' in the great temple of that goddess at Ephesus, and he built the temple of Hera at Samos.

Rhoxolani, a Sarmatian tribe first mentioned as having been defeated by Diophantus, general of Mithradates, King of Pontus, *c.* 100 B.C. They suffered the same fate at the hands of the Romans in A.D. 60, on the lower Danube, and again in the reign of Marcus Aurelius.

Robigo or Robigus, a Latin deity who was supposed to protect cornfields from blight and too great heat. His festival, known as the Robigalia, was celebrated on 25th April and was said to have been instituted by Numa.

Roman Army. The backbone of the Roman Army was, and remained far into the 3rd century A.D., the legion (q.v.). Attached to the legion were units of auxiliary horse and foot, recruited outside Italy and commanded by *praefecti* (*see* PRAEFECTUS, 1), some of whom were native officers. The cavalry was mainly from Gaul, Germany and Spain; the infantry were light-armed troops, e.g. Balearic slingers and Cretan archers. This organization remained substantially the same until the time of Diocletian (A.D. 284), except that Augustus incorporated a single *vexillum* of 120 horsemen into each legion, for use as dispatch riders and mounted orderlies. Besides the legions he also raised the Praetorian Guard (q.v.). Internal security was provided by *cohortes urbanae* (*see* PRAEFECTUS, 3), who were stationed both at Rome and in larger provincial cities.

Under the early emperors there was no great military power inimical to Rome, and therefore no need for a field army. Apart from the praetorians and the *vigiles*, the only function of the army was frontier defence against tribal raids. These were kept in check by the legions concentrated at strategic points behind the actual fortified frontier (*limes*), which was manned by auxiliaries (*see* AUXILIA). Augustus greatly expanded and reorganized these latter troops. They were formed into cohorts of infantry and *alae* of cavalry. While the praetorian and urban cohorts were each 1,000 strong, and the legionary cohort 600, an auxiliary cohort might contain ten centuries each of 100 men, or only five centuries of the same size. *Alae* could likewise be either 500 or 1,000 strong; they were divided into *vexilla*. There were also mixed cohorts of one *vexillum* of horse and four centuries of foot, and mixed *alae peditatae* of one century and three *vexilla*, or twice that number in the same proportion. There were also marines (*classici*) forming cohorts on the auxiliary model. The term *vexillatio* was originally applied to a fighting unit, but subsequently to a draft of reinforcements or to a working party responsible for maintaining a stretch of road or sector of fortification. Under the later empire, however, barbarians began to serve Rome under their own leaders, and both *vexillationes* and *cunei* were probably only vague names for native war bands. After the reign of Diocletian such bodies came to preponderate in the Roman Army; and the legion, whose infantry strength had been somewhat reduced by the introduction of field engines (*tormenta*; *ballistae*) which were served by detachments drawn from within the legion, was further reduced in strength, though the number of legions (33) remained the same.

Rome (Lat. Roma), capital of the Roman republic, and afterwards of the empire; traditionally founded by Romulus (q.v.) in 753 B.C., but in fact originating from the coalescence of a number of hill-top settlements formed by Latins, a branch of the Indo-European peoples who came to Italy from across the Alps towards the end of the second millennium B.C. Rome was not the only Latin agglomeration of this kind; but its predominance was assured by its geographical situation within easy reach of the sea (*see* OSTIA) and as centre of the peninsula, by its command of the Tiber ford, and by its consequent control of an important salt route between the mouth of the river and the Apennines. This article is concerned with the city as such, not with the history of its people, which eventually embraced that of the whole world then known.

The first city, whose nucleus was the Palatine, included also the Capitoline and Quirinal hills. It rapidly increased. The addition of the Aventine was attributed to Ancus Marcius (who was also said to have built a fort on the Janiculum, beyond the Tiber, and linked it to the city by the Pons Sublicius), and of the Viminal and Esquiline to Servius Tullius, who, traditionally, built the *agger*, an earthwork between those two hills. After the sack of Rome by the Gauls (390 B.C.) the city was hurriedly rebuilt, on no regular plan and with narrow crooked streets; it was surrounded by the so-called Servian wall (seven miles in circumference) in 378 B.C. As a result of the huge access of wealth after the defeat of Antiochus III and of Perseus (197 and 168 B.C.) Rome began to be adorned with many public buildings and grand private houses. It was embellished still further under Augustus (*see* AGRIPPA, MARCUS VIPSANIUS). He used to boast that he had found a city of brick and had left it of marble, and he divided it for administrative purposes into fourteen *regiones* which included both the Servian city and all the more recent suburbs. Still, the main features remained unaltered; the narrow streets with the mean and crowded dwellings of the masses formed a striking and disagreeable contrast to the new temples and palaces. The great fire in A.D. 64 (*see* NERO) destroyed about two-thirds of the city; Nero availed himself of this opportunity to indulge his passion for building, and Rome now assumed a more regular appearance.

As already indicated, Rome had long since extended far beyond the limits of the old 'Servian' wall, which had also become useless as a means of defence. The emperor Aurelian accordingly began (A.D. 271) a new and greatly enlarged circuit, which was completed by his successor Probus. For the line both of the Servian and of the Aurelian wall and their gates *see* maps in *Everyman's Classical Atlas*, edited by Professor J. O. Thomson, 1961.

1. *Bridges*. Of the ten bridges which crossed the Tiber at Rome by the end of the 3rd century A.D., the oldest was the *Pons Sublicius*, traditionally built by Ancus Marcius. It was built of wood (whence its name, from *sublices*, wooden piles), and though several times carried away by flood, it was always reconstructed from the same material. The central arches of the modern Ponte Sant' Angelo date from the reign of Hadrian, who built the bridge (Pons Aelius) to connect the city with his mausoleum. The Pons Fabricius (1st century B.C.) and the much later *Pons Cestius* link the city with the Insula Tiberina and the latter with the opposite bank respectively; they are called now Ponte Quattro Capi and Ponte S. Bartolommeo. The famous *Pons Mulvius* or *Milvius* (*see* MAXENTIUS), built by the censor M. Aemilius Scaurus in 109 B.C., is now represented by the Ponte Molle, north of the *Pons Aelius*.

2. *Fora*. These open, paved spaces, surrounded by public buildings, were five in number: (*a*) The *Forum Romanum*, or simply 'the Forum', was an irregular quadrangle lying between the foot of the Capitoline and the Velian ridge opposite the north-eastern end of the Palatine. Here was the *comitium*, meeting-place of the *comitia curiata* (*see* COMITIA), and the Rostra (q.v.). The Forum has been fully excavated, and is one of the most historic sites in the western world. (*b*) The

Forum Julium, built by Julius Caesar, was close to the north-eastern end of the Forum Romanum (behind the present church of S. Martino); to the rear of it lay (*c*) the *Forum Augusti*, built by the emperor Augustus. North of the Forum Romanum was (*d*) Vespasian's *Forum Pacis*; between it and the fora of Julius and Augustus, and giving access to all three, lay (*e*) the *Forum Nervae*, built by the emperor in fulfilment of a plan conceived by his predecessor Domitian. (*f*) Trajan's *Forum Traiani*, designed by the architect Apollodorus, lay between the Forum Augusti and the Campus Martius. It was the most splendid of all the fora, and considerable remains of it still exist. There were also a number of market-places known as fora: *Boarium* (cattle), *Clitorium* (vegetables), etc.

3. The *Campus Martius* was an open space north-west of the Servian wall. Originally used for military exercises, and meeting-place of the *comitia centuriata* (*see* COMITIA), it was afterwards the site of many public buildings, mostly for exercise and entertainment. *See also* SCELERATUS CAMPUS.

4. *Districts*. The most famous of these were *Subura*, in the valley between the Esquiline, Quirinal and Viminal hills, one of the most densely populated quarters of the city with many shops and brothels; *Carinae*, on the south-west area of the Esquiline (where S. Pietro in Vincoli now stands), an exclusive residential quarter (Pompey, Cicero and others); *Argiletum*, probably at the southern extremity of the Quirinal, a centre of the book trade; *Lautumiae*, where was a celebrated prison of that name.

5. *Temples*. There are said to have been 400 temples at Rome, among which the following are celebrated: *Jupiter Optimus Maximus* (*see* CAPITOLIUM); *Saturnus* (q.v.) and *Concordia* (q.v.), both on the Capitoline slope overlooking the Forum Romanum; *Juno Moneta* (*see* JUNO), on the Capitoline; *Jupiter Stator*, near the arch of Titus on the Via Sacra, which ran on the north side of the Palatine and past the Forum Romanum; *Mars Ultor* (*see* MARS) in the Forum Augusti; *Vespasian and Titus*, in the Forum near the temple of Concord; *Peace*, in the *Forum Pacis* (see *Fora* above); *Apollo*, on the Palatine, surrounded by a portico which housed the Palatine Library; *Pantheon* (q.v.).

6. *Circuses*. The *Circus Maximus*, traditionally built by Tarquinius Priscus, lay between the Palatine and the Aventine. It was successively enlarged by Caesar, Augustus, Domitian, and Trajan, under the last of whom it seated 200,000 spectators. The *Circus Flaminius*, in the southern part of the Campus Martius, was built in 220 B.C. by the censor C. Flaminius (q.v.), but soon became too small and was seldom used. The *Circus Gaii et Neronis* lay somewhat to the south of the crypts of modern St Peter's, and was the scene of the first martyrdoms at Rome (A.D. 63).

7. *Theatres*. There were no theatres in early Roman times; they began to be built in the 1st century B.C., and even then they were only temporary wooden structures. The first permanent stone theatre was constructed by Pompey (55 B.C.). It stood in the Campus Martius, north-east of the Circus Flaminius, and seated about 10,000 spectators. Ruins can be seen near the Palazzo Pio, not far from the

Campo dei Fiore. South-east of Pompey's theatre was another
dedicated by Cornelius Balbus (13 B.C.), and to the west again the
great theatre of Marcellus. This latter was begun by Julius Caesar,
and dedicated (13 B.C.) by Augustus, in memory of his nephew
Marcellus. It seated between 10,000 and 14,000 spectators. Its
remains, near the Piazza Montanara, are still used from time to time.
Amphitheatres, used mainly for gladiatorial shows, date likewise from
the late 1st century B.C. By far the grandest and most famous is the
Colosseum (q.v.).

8. *Baths* (*see* THERMAE) were among the most magnificent buildings
of imperial Rome. Extensive remains can be seen of the *Baths of
Titus*, on the Esquiline; of the *Baths of Caracalla* (completed by
Elagabalus and Alexander Severus), south-west of the Basilica of St
John Lateran; and of the *Baths of Diocletian*, the most extensive of
all, on the Viminal, near the church of S. Maria degli Angeli.

9. *Other monuments* which have survived whole or in part include
the following: *Basilica Ulpia*, in the Forum Traiani, and *Porticus
Octaviae* (built by Augustus) in the Campus Martius. The *Arch of
Titus*, on the Via Sacra, was erected in honour of Titus after his con-
quest of Judaea (A.D. 70), but was not finished until after his death.
Its sculptures show the spoils from the temple carried in triumphal
procession. *The Arch of Constantine*, between the Palatine and the
Coelian hills, was erected to commemorate Constantine's victory over
Maxentius (A.D. 312). It is profusely ornamented, largely with bas-
reliefs taken from one of the arches built during the reign of Trajan.
The *Cloaca Maxima*, a huge drain, was used to carry off the water
brought down from the adjacent hills into the valley of the Forum.
It empties into the Tiber nearly opposite the Insula Tiberina, and was
attributed by the ancients to Tarquinius Superbus; but the earliest
existing remains cannot be dated earlier than 33 B.C. The *Mausoleum
of Hadrian*, now called Castel Sant' Angelo, was begun by Hadrian in
the gardens of Domitia on the right bank of the Tiber. It was finished
and dedicated by Antoninus Pius in A.D. 140. Here were buried
Hadrian, Antoninus Pius, Lucius Verus, Commodus, and probably
also Septimius Severus, Geta and Caracalla. In the Forum Traiani
stands the *Column of Trajan*, in which that emperor's ashes were
deposited. Rising to a height of 117 feet, it was originally crowned
with a statue of Trajan, now replaced with one of St Peter. Round the
cylinder runs a spiral of bas-reliefs, representing scenes from the
emperor's Dacian wars. The inscription on the pedestal is a marvel of
calligraphy. The *Column of Marcus Aurelius*, in the Piazza Colonna,
was raised by the senate to commemorate the victories of Marcus over
the Marcomanni and other Germanic tribes. It is an imitation of
Trajan's Column, and has similar bas-reliefs illustrative of the
emperor's wars. *See also* AQUEDUCTS. *See* E. Hutton, *Rome*, 1909;
H. Stuart-Jones, *Classical Rome*, 1911; E. V. Lucas, *A Wanderer in
Rome*, 1926; G. Lugli, *I Monumenti Antichi di Roma e suburbio*,
1930–40, and *Roma Antica, il centro Monumentale*, 1946; T. Ashby
and S. Platner, *Topographical Dictionary of Ancient Rome*, 1949;
H. V. Morton, *A Traveller in Rome*, 1957.

Romulus, legendary founder of Rome, son of Mars and Rhea

Sylvia (qq.v.), and twin brother of Remus. Their uncle Amulius ordered them to be drowned together with their mother; but they were miraculously saved, and were reared by a she-wolf, finally receiving protection from the herdsman Faustulus and his wife. On reaching manhood they expelled the usurper, Amulius, and restored their grandfather Numitor to the throne of Alba. They then asked his permission to build a city on the Tiber, but quarrelled over its site and name. Romulus killed Remus for laughing at his walls on the Palatine (753 B.C.). He made the Capitol an asylum for refugees and adventurers, and provided wives for his citizens by the 'rape of the Sabines'. The resulting war ended in the joint rule of Tatius, King of the Sabini (q.v.), and Romulus. Later Romulus ruled alone, was carried up to heaven and worshipped as the god Quirinus by the Romans. This deity was in origin a Sabine god, probably of war (whence his close association with Mars, who bore the name Quirinus as one of his titles). Roman tradition connected a *niger lapis* (black stone) with the tomb of Romulus. This stone was unearthed in 1899 near the church of St Hadrian by G. Boni, but was shown to mark no tomb. *See* S. B. Platner, *A Topographical Dictionary of Ancient Rome*, 1949.

Roscius, Sextus, a native of Ameria (q.v.), who was charged with parricide in 81 B.C. and successfully defended by Cicero (*Pro Roscio Amerino*). The case was the first criminal trial in which Cicero took part, and one of the major causes to be heard by Sulla's restored senate.

Roscius Gallus, Quintus (*c.* 126–62 B.C.), Roman comic actor; originally a slave, born at Solonium near Lanuvium. His great histrionic powers were acquired, or at any rate developed, by careful study of the leading forensic orators, particularly Hortensius (q.v.). Cicero was his friend and was not above taking lessons from him. This is remarkable enough when we recall that the actor's profession was held in contempt; but there was more to come. Q. Lutatius Catulus wrote a short poem in his honour, and Sulla presented him with a golden ring, the badge of the equestrian order. Like his contemporary Clodius Aesopus (q.v.), he made a huge fortune and retired some time before his death. In 76 he was sued for 50,000 sesterces by one C. Fannius Chaerea and was defended by Cicero (*Pro Roscio Comoedo*).

Rosetta Stone, The, *see* BOLBITINE.

Rostra, a platform at Rome, from which orators addressed the people. It stood between the Forum and the Comitium, and was so called because it was adorned with the prows (*rostra*) of warships captured from Antium (q.v.) in 338 B.C.

Rotomagus (mod. Rouen), Roman name for the Gallic town of Ratuma or Ratumacos, on the River Sequana (Seine). In the time of Caesar and under the early empire it was the chief town of the Veliocasses, and towards the end of the 3rd century A.D. was made the centre of Gallia Lugdunensis Secunda.

Roxana, daughter of the Bactrian king Oxyartes. She fell into the hands of Alexander the Great after his capture of a hill fort in Sogdiana, 327 B.C. Alexander married her, and soon after his death she gave birth to a son, Alexander IV. This child was recognized by the Macedonian generals as joint king with Philip Arrhidaeus (q.v.).

She came to Europe with her child, placed herself under the protection of Olympias (q.v.) and took refuge with her in Pydna. In 316 Pydna was taken by Cassander; Olympias was put to death; Roxana and her son were imprisoned at Amphipolis and murdered by order of Cassander in 310 or 309 B.C.

Rubicon, small river falling into the Adriatic. Under the Roman republic it formed the boundary between Italy and Cisalpine Gaul. Its upper course is represented today by the Rugone, and its lower by the Firmicino, which the Rugone once joined 12 miles north-west of Ariminum. As the boundary aforesaid, its crossing by Caesar in 49 B.C. constituted an act of war against Pompey and the senate.

Rufus, Lucius Varius (*c.* 74–14 B.C.), Roman poet, author of a play *Thyestes*, which is stated by Quintilian (*Inst. Orat.* x. i. 98) to have been in the same class as the greatest of Greek tragedies. He is praised both by Horace and by Virgil (q.v.), and together with Plotius Tucca he prepared the *Aeneid* for publication. Virgil is said to have imitated or appropriated some lines of his epic poem *De Morte.* For the surviving fragments *see* E. Bährens, *Fragmenta Poetarum Romanorum,* 1886.

Rufus, Publius Rutilius, Roman statesman and orator. He was military tribune under Scipio at the siege of Numantia (q.v.), praetor in 111, consul in 105 and legatus in 94 under Q. Mucius Scaevola, governor of Asia. In this last capacity he was so firm in resisting the oppression of the *publicani* (q.v.) that he became an object of fear and hatred to the whole abominable class of tax collectors. On his return to Rome he was accused of malversation (*de repetundis*), found guilty upon no shred of evidence and driven into exile (92 B.C.).

Rupilius, Publius, Roman politician. As consul in 132 B.C. with Popilius Laenas he proceeded with the utmost severity against the supporters of Tiberius Sempronius Gracchus (*see* GRACCHUS, 2). In the same year he went to Sicily and suppressed a revolt of slaves. (*See* SERVILE WARS.) As governor of the Sicilian province in 131 he assisted ten commissioners appointed by the senate to draw up the *leges Rupiliae,* regulations for the island's government. In 123 B.C. he was condemned for his treatment of the Gracchans, and died soon afterwards.

Rusellae, city of Etruria, on the Via Aurelia (q.v.); one of the twelve members of the Etruscan confederation. It was taken by the Romans in 294 B.C.; supplied corn and timber to Scipio's fleet in 205. There are remains of the walls.

Rusticus, Lucius Junius, a friend of Thrasea Paetus (q.v.). He was put to death by Domitian for having written a panegyric on Paetus.

Rutuli, a people of Italy, inhabiting Ardea (q.v.) and the surrounding district on the coast of Latium.

Rutupiae (mod. Richborough), a Roman fortress and station, often mentioned by Latin authors as a port of arrival in Britain, and in particular by Juvenal (iv. 141) for its oysters. The site lies on the River Stour, just north of Sandwich; it has been scientifically excavated, and is one of the show-places of Roman Britain. Its importance began with the invasion of Claudius (A.D. 43), and the defensive ditches of the base camp have been located, as have the granaries and other wooden buildings of the supply depot which followed the Claudian camp. About A.D. 85 the camp area was cleared to make room for a magnificent marble-cased building, probably to mark the final conquest of the island under Domitian; the cruciform foundations can still be seen. The most prominent feature of the site is the great stone walls and ditches of the Fort of the Saxon Shore (late 3rd century). See *Society of Antiquaries Research Reports, Richborough, I, II* and *III*, 1926–32.

S

Sabazius (-os), a Thracian or Phrygian nature-god whose worship was connected with that of Cybele and Attis (qq.v.). During the 5th century B.C. this cult reached Greece, where he was often identified with Dionysus. According to Valerius Maximus (q.v.) he was also worshipped by the Jews; but this statement is doubtless due to a confusion of his name with the Hebrew *sabaoth* (Lord God *of Hosts*). The cult of Sabazius was popular during the 2nd century A.D. at Rome, where his rites were known at Sacra Savadia.

Sabina, grand-niece of Trajan and wife of the emperor Hadrian (q.v.), to whom she was married *c*. A.D. 100. She died probably in A.D. 136.

Sabini, one of the oldest peoples of central Italy. Their territory was bounded north by Picenum, west by Umbria and Etruria, south by Latium, east by Samnium. They were not finally subdued by Rome until 290 B.C. (*see* DENTATUS), although elements of their race went to compose the Roman people. This last fact is reflected in a celebrated legend according to which the wives and daughters of the Sabines were carried off by the subjects of Romulus (q.v.) during a festival. Their menfolk marched against the ravishers, but as the two sides were about to join battle the Sabine women, holding their infants, rushed between the opponents. Peace was made, and a portion of the Sabines united with the Romans to form one people. From the rest descended the Samnites (*see* SAMNIUM).

Sabinus, Flavius, brother of the emperor Vespasian, governed Moesia for seven years in the reign of Claudius and held the office of *praefectus urbi* during the last eleven years of Nero's reign. Dismissed by Galba, he was reinstated by Otho who was anxious to conciliate Vespasian. When Vespasian advanced upon the capital Sabinus took refuge in the Capitol, where he was attacked by the troops of Vitellius. The Capitol was burned, Sabinus was taken prisoner and murdered by the soldiers in presence of Vitellius who tried in vain to save his life.

Sabinus, Julius, a chieftain of the Batavi (q.v.) and husband of Eponina. Together with Civilis and Classicus he led the Gallic revolt in A.D. 70 (*see* VESPASIAN). After their defeat by Cerealis, Sabinus and Eponina hid for nine years in the depths of a cave. They were eventually betrayed, and delivered to Vespasian, who ordered the execution of Sabinus. Eponina, unwilling to survive her husband, insulted the emperor and was put to death, A.D. 78.

Sabinus, Masurius, a distinguished jurist in the reign of Tiberius, after whom the Sabinian school of jurisprudence was named to distinguish it from the Proculian (*see* CAPITO).

Sabratha, coastal city of north Africa, 48 miles west of Tripoli, originally a Punic settlement; later a Roman *municipium* which in the early second century A.D. attained colonial status. Its prosperity was based on the export of olive oil (for which Roman Africa was famous) and on a trans-Saharan trade in gold, ivory, ostrich feathers and slaves. Excavations have revealed a fine imperial city with basilica, forum, temples, churches, baths, shops, houses decorated with mosaic floors and walls, and a large amphitheatre. The Sabratenses maintained a shipping office at Ostia (q.v.). Apuleius (q.v.) was tried by a court sitting at Sabratha.

Sacra, Via, the 'Sacred Way', principal street of Rome. It ran from the valley between the Caeilian and Esquiline hills to the Capitol by way of the Forum Romanum.

Sacramentum, the Roman military oath of allegiance. The term was also used in law of moneys paid into court by the parties to an impending action.

Sacred Mount, The, a hill near Rome to which the plebeians seceded in 493 and 448 B.C. in order to escape the tyranny of the patricians. It was after the first of these secessions that the office of tribune of the plebs (*see* TRIBUNE) was instituted.

Sacred Wars, in Greek history, name given to several armed conflicts between two or more states, and caused by some violation of the sanctity of Delphi (*see* AMPHICTYONIC LEAGUE). By far the most important, often called 'the Sacred War', was the last (355–346 B.C.). In 595 B.C., after the destruction of Crissa (q.v.) and Cirrha, the rich Crissaean plain was declared by the Amphictyonic Council sacred to Delphic Apollo, and its cultivation forbidden for all time. In 358 B.C. the citizens of Amphissa defied this ancient statute and brought it under plough. The council, on a motion of its Theban delegates, imposed a heavy fine on the Phocians; and upon their refusal to pay the whole of Phocian territory was declared forfeit to the god. The Phocians seized the treasury at Delphi; war broke out and most of the Greek states became involved. The long indecisive conflict did nothing but exhaust the belligerents, until at last the Amphictyons invited Philip II of Macedon to intervene. He invaded Phocis, razed all its cities (except Abae), and was rewarded with the two votes held hitherto by Phocis in the Amphictyonic Council.

Sacriportus, small town of Latium (site unknown), near which Sulla defeated the younger Marius (*see* MARIUS, GAIUS, 2) in 82 B.C.

Saguntum (mod. Sagunto), Greek city of Iberia, founded from Zacynthus (q.v.); afterwards in the Roman province of Hispania Ulterior (*see* HISPANIA), on the road between Carthago Nova and Castulo. Its capture by Hannibal (q.v.), after a terrible siege, in 219 B.C., was the *casus belli* of the second Punic war.

Salacia, Roman goddess of spring water. When Neptunus (q.v.) was identified with Poseidon, she in turn was identified with the latter's wife Amphitrite (q.v.).

Salamis: 1. Island off the west coast of Attica, from which it is separated by a narrow channel. Its greatest length in any direction is 10 miles, and it forms the southern boundary of the Bay of Eleusis. It appears to have been colonized from Aegina, and according to Homer it was the abode of Telamon (q.v.), who took refuge there after the murder of his half-brother, became king of the island and, together with his sons Ajax and Teucer (qq.v.), accompanied the Greeks to Troy with twelve Salaminian ships.

Salamis was an independent state until about 620 B.C., when it was seized by the Megarians, only to be wrested from them some twenty years later by the Athenians under Solon (q.v.). In 480 B.C. its waters were the scene of that famous naval victory of the Greeks over the Persians which broke the power of Xerxes and ensured the freedom of the West (*see* PERSIAN WARS). In 318 B.C. the island surrendered voluntarily to Cassander (q.v.); but in 232 the Macedonian garrison was withdrawn through the intervention of Aratus (q.v.). Athens then evicted the inhabitants and substituted a cleruchy (q.v.).

The original Aeginetan settlement, the old city of Salamis, lay on the southern side of the island; but this was afterwards abandoned and a new city of the same name built on the east coast, opposite Attica, on a small bay now called Ambelaki.

2. City on the east coast of Cyprus (q.v.), traditionally founded by Teucer (q.v.). It revolted three times from the Persians, in 500, 386 and 352 B.C. In 306 Demetrius Poliorcetes defeated Ptolemy I in a naval action off Salamis. The city flourished under both Ptolemaic and Roman rule. Having suffered greatly in the Jewish uprising of A.D. 116–17 and from a series of earthquakes, it was rebuilt in the year of Constantine's death (337) by his son Constantius II. The Christian community was established by Sts Paul and Barnabas in A.D. 45–6.

Salaria, Via, highway of Italy, running for a distance of 151 miles from Rome through Fidenae, Reate and Asculum to Castrum Truentinum on the Adriatic. The name was due to the fact that the first part of its course coincided with the route by which the Sabines came to fetch salt from marshes near the mouth of the Tiber. There are considerable remains.

Salii, ' dancers ', a priesthood at Rome, divided into two colleges of twelve members each, the Salii Palatini and the Salii Collini, connected respectively with the worship of Mars and Quirinus. During the festivals of Mars (Quinquatrus and Armilustrium) in March and October, wearing an ancient form of armour and singing hymns, they went in procession carrying the ancilia (*see* ANCILE) and performing a ritual dance. The whole ceremony was probably a survival of war magic. *See* W. Warde Fowler, *Roman Festivals*, 1908.

Sallustius Crispus, Gaius, called in English **Sallust,** Roman historian, was born at Amiternum into a distinguished plebeian family, 86 B.C. As tribune of the plebs in 51 he took an active part in opposing T. Annius Milo (q.v.). Two years later he was expelled from the senate by the censors, probably because he belonged to Caesar's party; but in 49 Caesar appointed him quaestor and restored him to his seat. In 47, as praetor-elect, he nearly lost his life when trying to quell a mutiny of some of Caesar's legions in Campania. He accompanied Caesar to the African war (46), and was appointed by him governor of Numidia, in which capacity he is said to have enriched himself by unjust means. Great wealth he certainly enjoyed, as was shown by the splendid gardens (*Horti Sallustiani*) which he laid out on the Quirinal. On his return from Africa he retired into private life, passed quietly through the troubled period after Caesar's death and died at Rome in 34 B.C.

It was probably during these years of retirement that Sallust wrote his account of Catiline's conspiracy (*Bellum Catilinarium*) and of the war against Jugurtha (*Bellum Jugurthinum*), together with the five books of *Histories*. Of this last work only fragments have survived; it covered the period 78–67 B.C. and was a continuation of Sisenna (q.v.). Two other works have been wrongly attributed to Sallust: *Duae epistolae de republica ordinanda* and *Declamatio in Ciceronem*. Both appear to be the work of a rhetorician of the 1st century A.D. *See* the edition with translation (*Bell. Cat.*; *Bell. Jug.*) by J. C. Rolfe (Loeb Library), 1921, and general works on Latin literature.

Salmōneus, in Greek legend, son of the Thessalian king Aeolus, and brother of Sisyphus and Athamas (qq.v.). He was said to have emigrated to Elis and to have built the town of Salmone. Deeming himself equal to Zeus, he ordered sacrifices to be offered to himself, and even imitated the thunder and lightning of Zeus. But the Father of Gods slew him and destroyed his town.

Salona, town of Dalmatia, in the neighbourhood of which Diocletian was born. It was made a Roman colony in 78 B.C. and became one of the chief ports of the Adriatic. Four miles to the south-west was the great palace built by Diocletian, to which he retired after his abdication. The ground plan of this enormous edifice resembled that of a Roman camp. It covered an area of 99 acres, and in the 7th century formed the nucleus of a separate town now called Split (Italian Spalato). Many features of the palace were converted to or incorporated in medieval buildings, a fact which has greatly facilitated archaeological research. Remains include walls with gates, the massive arcades lining the two main streets, the temple of Jupiter (now the cathedral) and that of Aesculapius (now a baptistery).

Salus, a Roman goddess of safety, whence she was soon regarded as patroness or personification of the public welfare (*Salus publica* or *Romana*). In this capacity she was honoured at Rome with a temple on the Quirinal hill, which had been vowed to her in 302 B.C. by the censor C. Junius Bubulcus and which was afterwards decorated with paintings by C. Fabius Pictor (q.v.). Her festival was on 30th April, when she was worshipped together with Pax, Concordia and Janus. She soon came to represent prosperity in general, and in the 3rd century B.C. was identified with Hygieia (q.v.), the Greek goddess of health.

Salvius Julianus, one of the greatest of Roman jurists. Born near Hadrumetum, in north Africa, *c.* A.D. 100, his reputation was already great when he was commanded by Hadrian to revise the praetorian edict. Under that emperor and his successor Salvius held many public offices. He died *c.* 169, having written several legal works which are quoted extensively in Justinian's *Digest*. *See* A. Guarino, *Salvius Julianus*, 1946.

Salyes (-ues), Sallyes, Salyi or **Salluvii**, a Ligurian people dwelling on the south coast of Gaul between the Rhône and the Maritime Alps. They were troublesome neighbours of Massilia, which had been friendly towards Rome since the second Punic war and which appealed to her for assistance in 124 B.C. War broke out (*see* FLACCUS, MARCUS VALERIUS), and two years later (122) the Salyes were subdued by C. Sextius Calvinus. Their chief town was destroyed, and the colony of Aquae Sextiae founded near by.

Samaria, city of central Palestine, does not enter classical history until 331 B.C., when it was taken by Alexander the Great and became a hellenistic city. It suffered likewise during the wars of the Diadochi (q.v.). Severely damaged while resisting John Hyrcanus II, it was rebuilt by Pompey, restored by Gabinius and adorned with many fine buildings by Herod the Great, who fortified it and made it his capital with the name Sebaste. See *Harvard Excavations at Samaria, 1908–10,* 1924.

Samian Ware, a kind of red glazed pottery produced in Gaul and Germany in Roman imperial times. The name is misleading: the article was not a product of Samos, but has been so called owing to the misinterpretation of a passage in Pliny's *Historia Naturalis* (xxxv. 16 sqq.).

Samnite Wars, *see* SAMNIUM.

Samnites, *see* SAMNIUM.

Samnium, district of Italy, adjoining Apulia, Campania and Latium. Its inhabitants were called by the Romans Samnites. *See* SABINI. In the 4th century B.C. their invasion of Capuan territory led to continual wars with Rome; the first in 343, the second in 327–304, during which Rome suffered the disaster of the Caudine Forks (*see* CAUDIUM). She recovered Campania, however, and after having taken the chief Samnite town, made peace in 304. War broke out again in 298, when the Samnites allied with the Gauls and Etruscans. They were defeated at Sentinum (q.v.) in 295 (*see* FABIUS MAXIMUS, QUINTUS, 1), and in 290 submitted to Rome (*see* DENTATUS). They fought for their independence in the Social war (90 B.C.). They also joined Marius against Sulla, but at the Colline Gate were crushed by the latter, who ravaged and depopulated Samnium (82 B.C.).

Samos, island in the Aegean, about a mile from the west coast of Asia Minor. Colonized in the 11th century B.C. by Ionians mainly from Epidaurus. Four hundred years later it had become one of the chief commercial centres of the Greek world, trading particularly with Chalcis, Corinth and Cyrene, and thus incurring the permanent enmity of Miletus. In 535 B.C. the Samian oligarchy was overthrown, and the island became subject to Polycrates (q.v.), under whom it reached the zenith of its power and prosperity. At this period the Samians were trading with Egypt and obtained from Amasis the privilege of a separate temple at Naucratis (q.v.). After the death of Polycrates (522) Samos was conquered by the Persians and remained subject to them until after the battle of Mycale (479), when it regained its independence and joined the Delian League as a privileged member. It seceded in 440, but was reduced by an Athenian fleet under Pericles, after a nine-month siege, and degraded to the position of a tributary. A democracy was established, and Samos remained loyal to Athens throughout the Peloponnesian war, towards the end of which it was granted the Athenian franchise. The oligarchy was restored by Lysander after the fall of Athens (404) and Samos became the chief Spartan naval base. In 394, however, the Spartan fleet withdrew; the Samians declared their independence and restored the democracy. Subjected to Persia by the Peace of Antalcidas (387), it was recovered in 366 by the Athenians, who expelled the inhabitants in 352 and occupied it with a cleruchy (q.v.) until 324. The history of Samos is confused from this date until 189 B.C., when the Romans gave it to Eumenes II of Pergamum. As part of his kingdom it passed to Rome in 133 B.C. Having supported Aristonicus in 132 and Mithradates in 88 B.C., it was deprived of its autonomy, but this was restored between the reigns of Augustus and Vespasian.

Samos was the birth-place of Pythagoras (q.v.) and one of the chief centres of Ionian culture. It produced the sculptors Rhoecus and Pythagoras of Regium, the painter Agatharchus, and its pottery was famous throughout the ancient world in the 6th century B.C.

The capital, also called Samos, lay on the south-eastern side of the island, rising in the form of an amphitheatre from the shore to the ridge beyond. This latter, called Astypalaea, is crowned by the wall of Polycrates, who also employed Eupalinus (q.v.) to drive a tunnel through it to form an aqueduct (*see* AQUEDUCTS). The foundations of the Heraeum, designed by Rhoecus, have been excavated.

Samosata (mod. Samsat), capital of Commagene (q.v.), situated on the right bank of the Euphrates, north-west of Edessa. It was the birth-place of Lucian (q.v.).

Samothrace (-kē), island in the northern Aegean. It rises to a height of more than 5,000 feet, and Homer represents Poseidon as surveying the plain of Troy from its summit (*Il.* xiii. 12). It was the principal seat of the worship of the Cabeiri (q.v.), and remains of their sanctuary can be seen. The famous statue of Victory, which is now in the Louvre, was erected by Demetrius Poliorcetes *c.* 305 B.C. It was discovered in 1863, and the broken right hand in 1950. Samothrace always remained autonomous in both Greek and Roman times.

Sancus or **Semo Sancus**, a Sabine deity whom the Romans subsequently identified with Hercules and with Dius Fidius (*see* FIDIUS). He presided over oaths, represented good faith in social life and had a temple on the Quirinal hill at Rome.

Sannyrion (-uriōn), Athenian comic poet (*fl.* 407 B.C.) whose excessive leanness is ridiculed by Aristophanes.

Sapor, Latin form of the Persian name Shapur borne by three Sassanid kings of Persia. *Sapor I* reigned from A.D. 240 to 273. After defeating the Roman emperor Valerian (260), he conquered Syria, destroyed Antioch, seized the passes of Taurus, laid Tarsus in ashes and took Caesarea in Cappadocia. His further progress was stopped by Odaenathus and Zenobia (qq.v.).

Sapor II and *III* reigned respectively from 311 to 380, and from 385 to 390.

Sapphō, Greek lyric poetess of the Lesbian school; born *c.* 612 B.C., probably at Mytilene, where she was later head of a female literary society. She married Cercylas, to whom she bore a daughter, Cleis, and was a friend of Alcaeus (q.v.). Legend notwithstanding, the date, place and manner of her death are alike unknown. She wrote in a great variety of metres, including the Sapphic which is named after her, and surviving fragments reveal that deep personal feeling which won the unbounded admiration of ancient critics. The lyrics of Sappho consisted originally of nine books; considerable portions of I, II and IV have come down to us, together with smaller fragments of V. These have been edited by E. Lobel, *Sapphous mele*, 1925, and by J. M. Edmonds in *Lyra Graeca* (with translation) in the Loeb Library, 1922. *See also* verse translation by A. S. Way. *See* D. M. Robinson, *Sappho and her Influence*, 1924; A. Weigall, *Sappho of Lesbos*, 1932.

Sarcophagus (Sarkophagos; from *sarx*, flesh, *phagein*, to eat), name given originally to a coffin made of a stone which was said to possess caustic properties so strong that they consumed the body within forty days; thence to any sepulchral chest of no matter what material. Numerous examples have survived, ranging from the Egyptian to the Byzantine period. The most famous of all is the 'Sarcophagus of Alexander', discovered at Sidon in 1887 and now in the Museum of Antiquities at Constantinople. This magnificent work of art is so called not because it once contained the body of Alexander the Great, but because the subjects sculptured in relief upon its sides represent scenes from his life. The style is Attic and suggests the influence of Scopas (q.v.). The general effect is enhanced by its beautiful colouring. *See* P. Gardiner, *Grammar of Greek Art*, pp. 94, 113.

Sardinia (Gk Sardōn), island of the Mediterranean, was occupied by Carthaginians between 500 and 480 B.C., though it was known to the Greeks at least as early as the first of these dates. After the first Punic war, in 235 B.C., Rome took advantage of the war of the Mercenaries (q.v.), with which Carthage was then preoccupied, to take posession of Sardinia. It was formed into a Roman province, to which Corsica (q.v.) was added in 227, but separated therefrom under Nero in A.D. 67. More than a century passed before Sardinia was completely subjugated, and even then it continued to be noted for the brigandage of its people. It was, however, one of the chief sources of the Roman corn supply, and also produced silver and salt. Carales (q.v.) was the principal town. Among the island's flora was a poisonous plant known as *Sardinia herba*. The fatal convulsions caused by eating it distorted the mouth so that the victim appeared to be laughing; whence some have derived the word 'sardonic'.

Sardis or **Sardes** (Sardeis), city of Asia Minor and capital of the Lydian kingdom, at the downfall of which (546 B.C.) it resisted all the attacks of Cyrus and was taken only by surprise. Under the Persian and Seleucid empires Sardis was the residence of a satrap. The rise of Pergamum diminished its importance; but in Roman times, as part of the province of Asia, it was an assize town. In the reign of Tiberius (A.D. 17) it was destroyed by an earthquake, but was rebuilt with the emperor's aid. The chief cult of pagan Sardis was that of Cybele (q.v.), the remains of whose temple have been excavated. Christianity was introduced at an early date, and the Church of Sardis is one of the seven addressed by St John in the Apocalypse. See W. M. Ramsey, *Letters of the Seven Churches*, 1904; *American Journal of Archaeology*, 1911–27.

Sarmatae (-ai), *see* SAUROMATAE.

Sarmatia, name first used by Pomponius Mela in the 1st century A.D. to denote that part of Europe and Asia which extended from the Vistula to the Volga, bounded south-west and south by Pannonia, Dacia, the Euxine and the Caucasus, north by the Baltic.

Sarpēdōn, in Greek legend, son of Zeus and Europa, and brother of Minos and Rhadamanthus. Involved in a quarrel with Minos, he took refuge with Cilix in Cilicia, and assisted him against the Lycians. Later he became King of Lycia, and Zeus granted him the privilege of living for three generations. He also assisted Troy against the Greeks, but was slain by Patroclus (q.v.).

Sassanidae, a Persian dynasty which ruled from its foundation by Ardashir (q.v.) I in A.D. 226 until its destruction by the Arabs in 637. *See* SAPOR.

Sassina (mod. Sarsina), town of Umbria on the River Sapis, 16 miles south of Caesina. Subdued by the Romans in 267 B.C., the Sassinates were numbered among her allies in 225. Here Plautus (q.v.) was born *c.* 254 B.C.

Saturnalia, a Roman festival of Saturnus (q.v.), originally celebrated on 19th December, but afterwards extended to a period of seven days. It arose, no doubt, from rites connected with the winter sowing, but in historical times was a season of popular merry-making. Among the principal features of the Saturnalia were the suspension of all business, the closing of schools, the postponment of executions and (when possible) of military operations, the temporary licence given to slaves, the exchange of gifts (wax candles and clay dolls) with the greeting ' Io Saturnalia! ' and the right to gamble with dice which was forbidden at other times.

Saturninus: 1. One of the Thirty Tyrants (*see* THIRTY TYRANTS, 2). An erstwhile friend and trusted general of Valerian, he was disgusted by the profligacy of Gallienus (q.v.) and accepted the imperial title from his troops; but the latter were unwilling to support his stern discipline, and put him to death.

2. A Gallic officer appointed by Aurelian commander on the eastern frontier. During the reign of Probus (q.v.) he was proclaimed emperor by the troops at Alexandria, but was eventually overpowered and slain.

Saturninus, Lucius Appuleius, Roman politician and demagogue. Quaestor in 104 B.C., he joined the popular party later that year, and was tribune of the plebs in 103. In this capacity he ingratiated himself with Marius by proposing an agrarian law in favour of the latter's veterans, and took various steps to curry popular favour. Then, in 101, when Marius returned from defeating the Cimbri, Saturninus and C. Servilius Glaucia joined hands to serve as Marius's political agents and to further their own ends. Accordingly, as the fruit of bribery and murder, the year 100 B.C. found Marius consul for the sixth time, Saturninus tribune for the second and Glaucia praetor. A new and controversial agrarian law introduced by Saturninus led to the exile of his chief enemy, Q. Metellus Numidicus (*see* METELLUS, 3). Soon afterwards Saturninus was elected tribune a third time; but there was a struggle for the consulship of 99 B.C. between Glaucia and the senatorial candidate C. Memmius (q.v.). As the latter seemed likely to win, Saturninus and Glaucia hired a gang of ruffians who beat him to death openly in the *comitia*. This last outrage produced a reaction against Saturninus and his supporters. The senate declared them public enemies and ordered the consuls to put them down by force.

Marius, though his ardour had already cooled, was reluctant to take such stern measures against his former friends and supporters, but he had no choice. Driven from the Forum, Saturninus and Glaucia, with the quaestor Saufeius, took refuge in the Capitol; but members of the opposite party cut the pipes supplying water to the Capitol. They therefore surrendered to Marius, who placed them for security in the Curia Hostilia; but their enemies tore off the roof and pelted them to death with the tiles.

Saturnus (Eng. Saturn), a Roman god of sowing or of seed corn. It is not improbable that he was derived from Etruria, being perhaps an Etruscan divinity corresponding to the Greek Cronus, with whom he was subsequently (and otherwise for no apparent reason) identified. In this capacity he was considered to be the father of Jupiter, Neptune, Pluto and Juno. His original cult partner was Lua, goddess of destruction in various forms; but she gave way to Ops, cult partner of Consus (q.v.), who had become identified with Rhea (q.v.). Legend represented Saturn as a mythical king of Italy, who introduced social order and the arts of civilization, and whose reign was a golden age. The temple of Saturn at Rome, at the foot of the *clivus Capitolinus*, contained the Republican treasury, was an occasional meeting-place of the senate, and housed a statue of the god. This statue was worshipped with Greek forms; like other Greek and barbarian cult images, too, its feet were tied with woollen bands, except during the festival of Saturnalia.

Satyrs (Gk Saturoi), in Greek legend, creatures of the woods and mountains, half man, half beast, indolent and lascivious, closely connected with Dionysus. They represent the vital powers of nature. The older ones were known as Sileni (*see* SILENUS), the younger as Satyrisci. They had men's bodies but goat's ears, horns, hoofs and tails. Later writers confused them with the Italian *fauni*. Christian art used them as images of the devils with whom it sometimes identified the pagan gods.

Satyrus (-turos), Greek peripatetic philosopher and historian, lived at Alexandria in the reign of Ptolemy IV, Philopator (221–204 B.C.). Of his collection of biographies only a small fragment survives, namely four pages of the *Life of Euripides*. This takes the form of a dialogue; it was discovered at Oxyrhynchus (q.v.) in 1911.

Sauromatae or **Sarmatae**, commonly supposed to be two forms of a name used respectively by earlier Greek and by later Greek and Roman writers with reference to a people akin to the Scythians (*see* SCYTHIA). They are located by Herodotus east of the River Tanaïs (Don), and appear to have supplanted the Scythians proper in south Russia by the 3rd century B.C. Their principal tribes were the Rhoxolani, Iazyges and Alani (qq.v.). *See*, however, M. Rostovzeff's *Iranians and Greeks in South Russia* (1922) for the view that the Sauromatae and Sarmatae were not the same people.

Saxa, Decidius, a native of Celtiberia who, having served with the Roman army under Caesar, accompanied Mark Antony to the east and was made by him governor of Syria. Here he was defeated and slain by the Parthians under Quintus Labienus (q.v.) in 46 B.C.

Saxa Rubra, a post station on the Via Flaminia, nine miles north of

Rome, so named from the local cliffs of red tufa. Here, in A.D. 312, Constantine defeated Maxentius in an action usually called after the Milvian Bridge at Rome because Maxentius and many of his fleeing troops were killed while attempting to cross it.

Saxones, a Teutonic people first mentioned by Ptolemy (*c.* A.D. 150) as inhabiting Chersonesus Cimbrica (mod. Holstein) and three adjacent islands. During the classical period they make only a brief appearance, in A.D. 286, as pirates in the North Sea.

Scaevola, Gaius Mucius, a young noble of Roman legend, originally named Gaius Mucius. The surname, meaning 'left handed', arose from the loss of his right hand as described in the article Porsena (q.v.).

Scaevola, Publius Mucius, an expert on the Roman pontifical law; tribune of the plebs 141 B.C., praetor 136, consul 133. In 131 he succeeded his brother Mucianus as pontifex maximus.

Scaevola, Quintus Mucius: 1. Called 'the Augur', tribune of the plebs in 128 B.C., plebeian aedile in 125, praetor and governor of Asia 121–120. On his return to Rome he was tried but acquitted on a charge of extortion, and was consul in 117 B.C. Scaevola was also a distinguished jurist; he was still living in 88, when Cicero, having assumed the *toga virilis*, was among the young men who attended his receptions and conferences, in order to profit by his learning and refinement, and thus to complete his education. None of Scaevola's writings has survived. He is one of the speakers in Cicero's *De Oratore*, *De Amicitia* and *De Republica*.

2. Son of P. Mucius Scaevola (q.v.). He too was an expert jurist, and Cicero attended him, as he had attended the Augur, after the latter's death (? 87 B.C.). Scaevola was tribune of the plebs in 106 B.C., curule aedile in 104 and consul with L. Licinius Crassus in 95. In the following year he was governor of Asia, and won the esteem of that province. Later he was elected pontifex maximus, and died in the Sullan proscription of 82 B.C. His work on the *Jus Civile* in eighteen books (the first of its kind) is lost.

Scamandrius (Skamandrios), *see* ASTYANAX.

Scapte Hyle (Skaptē Hulē), small town on the coast of Thrace, opposite the island of Thasos, in a gold-mining district. Here Thucydides (q.v.) arranged the materials of his history.

Scapula, Publius Ostorius, Roman general, governor of Britain A.D. 47–52. He defeated the Silures, took prisoner their king Caratacus and sent him in chains to Rome. *See* Tacitus, *Annales*, xii. 31–9.

Scaurus, Mamercus Aemilius, Roman orator and poet, *see* SCAURUS, MARCUS AEMILIUS, 3.

Scaurus, Marcus Aemilius: 1. Roman magistrate and general (*c.* 163–88 B.C.): curule aedile 123; consul 115 B.C., when he warred successfully against Alpine tribes, repaired the Milvian bridge and constructed the second Via Aemilia (q.v.). In 111 he accompanied the consul L. Calpurnius Bestia as one of his legates—Opimius (q.v.) was another—in the war against Jugurtha. They took bribes from the Numidian king to obtain from him a favourable peace, and were prosecuted on an indictment brought forward by C. Mamilius, tribune of the plebs. Scaurus contrived to have himself appointed one of the prosecutors, and thus secured himself though unable to save his accomplices. He was censor with M. Livius Drusus in 109 and *consul suffectus* in 107 B.C. Scaurus had some reputation as an orator, and was a moderate supporter of the aristocratical party.

2. Eldest son of the preceding. He served as Pompey's quaestor during the third Mithradatic war, and was sent by him to settle the dispute between Hyrcanus and Aristobulus, but his decision in favour of the latter was quickly overruled. He was curule aedile in 58 B.C., when he celebrated the public games with extraordinary magnificence. In 56 he was praetor, and in the following year governor of Sardinia. Returning to Rome in 54, he was accused of extortion (*de repetundis*). Though manifestly guilty, his defence by Cicero, Hortensius and others secured his acquittal. Two years later, under Pompey's new law, he was accused of illegal practices when canvassing for the consulship (*ambitus*), found guilty and exiled.

3. Brother of the preceding. His mother was Mucia, former wife of Pompey, so that he was half-brother of Sextus Pompeius. He accompanied the latter into Asia after the defeat of his fleet off Sicily, but betrayed him to Mark Anthony, by whose orders Sextus was put to death in 35 B.C. His son, Mamercus Aemilius Scaurus, was a distinguished orator and poet. Accused of treason (*majestas*) under Tiberius, he committed suicide, A.D. 34

Sceleratus Campus, a piece of ground just inside the 'Servian' wall at Rome, near the Porta Collina, where vestals who broke their vow of chastity were entombed alive.

Scenitae (Skēnitae), general name used by the Greeks for the Bedouin tribes of Arabia Deserta.

Scholia, marginal and other notes written by ancient (and for the most part anonymous) grammarians and commentators on the manuscripts of classical texts.

Scipio, Publius Cornelius, Roman general in the second Punic war; consul in 218 B.C., when he was defeated by Hannibal (q.v.) on the Ticinus in Cisalpine Gaul, and narrowly escaped death. He retreated beyond the Padus, first to Placentia, and then to the Trebia, where he was joined by his colleague Tiberius Sempronius Longus. The Roman army was again defeated. In the following year (217), his *imperium* having been prolonged, he joined his brother Gnaeus in Hither Spain, and together they enjoyed some success; but in 211 they crossed the Iberus, and were both defeated and slain. Scipio's son was Scipio Africanus Major (q.v.).

Scipio, Quintus Caecilius Pius, *see* METELLUS, 5.

Scipio Aemilianus Africanus, Publius Cornelius, Roman general, often called 'Minor' to distinguish him from the conqueror of Hannibal (*see* next article). Born *c.* 185 B.C., he was the younger son of Lucius Aemilius Paulus, the victor of Pydna, and was adopted by P. Cornelius Scipio, son of the elder Africanus. He served with great distinction as military tribune in Spain (151 B.C.). On the outbreak of the third Punic war (149) he went to Africa, again as military tribune, and won yet greater renown. Returning to Rome in 148 he stood for office as aedile for the following year, but was elected consul, though still under age. Africa was assigned as his province (147). Carthage fell to his arms in the spring of 146, and later that year he celebrated a triumph at Rome. He was censor in 142. Consul a second time in 134, he was sent to Spain, and in the following year captured Numantia (q.v.). Meanwhile, however, the tribune Tiberius Sempronius Gracchus (q.v.) had been assassinated. Scipio was married to his sister Sempronia; but he had no sympathy with the Gracchan programme of reform, and on his return to the capital (129 B.C.) he took the lead in opposition to the popular party. One morning he was found dead in his room, almost certainly murdered, and Cicero names Carbo as the assassin. *See* K. Bilz, *Die Politik des Publius Cornelius Scipio Aemilianus*, 1935.

Scipio Africanus Major, Publius Cornelius, Roman general, son of P. Cornelius Scipio (q.v.); born 234 B.C. He is first mentioned at the battle of the Ticinus (218), where he saved his father's life. He fought as a military tribune at Cannae (216), and was one of the few Roman officers who survived that field. He was chosen with Appius Claudius to command the remnants of the beaten army, which had taken refuge in Canusium; and it was his courage and presence of mind which prevented the Roman nobility from leaving Italy. After this his popularity was such that he was elected aedile for 121, although he had not reached the legal age. In 211, after the death of his father and uncle, he was given command of the army in Spain, where, in his first campaign (209) he took Carthago Nova, and during the next three years he drove the Carthaginians from the peninsula. Returning to Rome in 206, he was elected consul for the following year, despite the fact that he had not yet held the office of praetor (*see* CURSUS HONORUM). He was anxious to carry the war into Hannibal's own homeland, and obtained a fleet and army for that purpose. After wintering in Sicily and completing his preparations, he crossed to Africa in 204. He defeated a Carthaginian army which was supported by Syphax (q.v.), and Hannibal was recalled from Italy. The second Punic war was brought to a close by Scipio's great victory over Hannibal at Zama, 19th October 202 B.C. Carthage had no alternative but submission, and the final treaty was concluded in the following year. Scipio returned to Rome in 201, celebrated his triumph and received the surname Africanus (he is called 'Major' by later historians to distinguish him from his grandson by adoption; *see* preceding article). He was censor in 199, consul a second time in 194. In 190 he served as *legatus* under his brother Lucius in the war against Antiochus III (q.v.). Years later (184 B.C.) he was accused of having accepted bribes from Antiochus and of embezzlement. The case was never brought to trial; but Scipio withdrew to his private estate at Liternum, and never returned to Rome. The year of his death is uncertain, but it probably occurred in 183 B.C. *See* B. H. Liddell Hart, *A Greater than Napoleon : Scipio Africanus*, 1926; R. M. Hayward, *Studies on Scipio Africanus Major*, 1933.

Sciron (Skeirōn), a legendary robber infested the borders of Attica and Megaris. He not only robbed the travellers who passed through that country, but compelled them on the Scironian rock to wash his feet, and kicked them into the sea while they were thus employed. At the foot of the rock was a tortoise which devoured the bodies of his victims. Sciron was slain by Theseus.

Scopas (Sk-), Greek sculptor of the early to mid 4th century B.C., a native of Paros. A contemporary of Lysippus and Praxiteles (qq.v.), he was distinguished from them by a greater intensity of emotion. His work is associated with the Mausoleum at Halicarnassus and the temple of Athena Alea at Tegea, of which he was architect. *See* K. A. Neuegebauer, *Studien über Skopas*, 1913.

Scordisci, a Celtic tribe occupying the southern part of Lower Pannonia between the rivers Savus, Dravus and Danubius. They assisted Perseus of Macedonia against the Romans, who continued to have trouble with them after that country had become a Roman province. Conquered by M. Cosconius in Thrace (135 B.C.), they in turn defeated and slew Sextus Pompeius, grandfather of Pompey the Great, near Stobi (118 B.C.). Four years later they annihilated a Roman army under C. Porcius Cato, but were themselves defeated by Q. Minucius Rufus in 107, and finally subdued in 88 B.C. by L. Cornelius Scipio Asiaticus, who drove them across the Danube.

Scotti, name which, from about A.D. 250, gradually replaced the older name Hiberni (or Iverni) for the inhabitants of Ireland (*see* HIBERNIA), who had begun to make raids upon Roman Britain.

Scribonia, sister of L. Scribonius Libo, father-in-law of Sextus Pompeius. She had already been twice married and borne children when, in 40 B.C., she was married to Octavian, the future emperor Augustus. This union was effected on the advice of Maecenas (q.v.), as it was feared that Sextus Pompeius might join with Antony to crush Octavian. Almost at once, however, the latter renewed his alliance with Antony, and with a view to marrying Livia (*see* LIVIA, 2), he divorced Scribonia on the very day that she bore him his daughter Julia (*see* JULIA, 5). Scribonia long survived this insult, and in A.D. 2 chose to accompany Julia into exile on the island of Pandataria.

Scriptores Historiae Augustae, name given jointly to six writers who compiled mostly unreliable biographies of the Roman emperors from Hadrian to Numerianus (A.D. 117–284). They wrote almost certainly under Julian the Apostate, and their names are these: Aelius Spartianus, Julius Capitolinus, Aeilius Lampridius, Vulcatius Gallicanus, Trebellius Pollio and Flavius Vopsicus. *See* text and translation by D. Magie (Loeb Library), 1922–32.

Scylax (Sku-), Greek historian, a native of Caryanda in Caria. He was sent by Darius Hystaspis to explore the Indus. His course is unknown; but Herodotus (iv. 44) states that he reached the sea and sailed west through the Indian Ocean to the Red Sea. Scylax wrote an account of his journey, and a *Periplus* bearing his name is extant. This, however, cannot be the work of Scylax; it was probably written *c.* 350 B.C. and is wholly concerned with the Mediterranean. *See* the edition by C. Müller in *Geographici Graeci minores*, I.

Scylla (Skulla) and **Charybdis** (Kharub-), two rocks in the Straits of Messina. In the one on the Italian side there was a cave, the home of Scylla, a monster having twelve feet, six long necks each terminating in a head with three rows of teeth, twelve legs, and barking like a dog. The much lower rock on the Sicilian side supported a huge fig-tree, beneath which dwelt Charybdis, who thrice a day swallowed the sea and thrice threw it up again. Scylla devoured six companions of

Odysseus (*Od*. xii. 73–110). The legend represents the hazard of navigation in those waters. In later accounts Scylla is slain by Heracles for stealing some of the oxen of Geryon, but restored to life by Phorcys, a sea-god. Virgil (*Aen*. vi. 286) speaks of Scyllas in the plural, and calls them 'double-shaped'.

Scyros (Skuros), island in the Aegean, off the coast of Thessaly. Several legends connected it with Achilles (q.v.), who had a sanctuary on the island. The best known of these tells how the hero's mother, Thetis, sent him to live there disguised as a girl among the daughters of Lycomedes (q.v.). Scyros was occupied by Philip II and remained subject to Macedon until 196 B.C., when the Romans restored it to its previous owners, the Athenians. It was sacked by the Goths and other Barbarians in A.D. 269.

Scythia (Sku-), name applied to different regions at different periods. Herodotus represents it as comprising the south-eastern parts of Europe between the Carpathian mountains and the River Tanaïs (Don). The Scythians were a nomad people. They lived in covered wagons, which Aeschylus describes as 'lofty houses of wicker-work on well-wheeled chariots'. They kept large troops of horses, and were skilled cavalrymen and archers; hence, as Darius I found when he invaded their country (512 B.C.), it was almost impossible for an army to operate against them. They retreated, wagons and all, before the enemy, harassing him with their light cavalry, and leaving exposure in their barren steppes to do the rest.

Some modification in their habits had, however, taken place before Herodotus described them. The fertility of the plains north of the Euxine, together with the influence of Greek settlements at the mouth of the Borysthenes (Dnieper) and along the coast, had led the inhabitants of this part of Scythia to settle down as agriculturists, and had brought them into commercial and social relations with Greek culture.

In later times the Scythians were overpowered by the Sarmatians (*see* SAUROMATAE), who gave their name to the whole country. Writers in Roman imperial times use the name Scythia to describe the greater part of northern Asia. *See* E. H. Minns, *Scythians and Greeks*, 1913; G. Borovka, *Scythian Art*, 1928.

Segesta (Gk **Egesta** or **Aegesta**), called by Virgil **Acesta**, town of the Elymi in north-western Sicily (q.v.), near the coast between Panormus and Drepanum. For its legendary foundation *see* ACESTES. From the early 6th century B.C. onwards it was engaged in frequent boundary disputes with Selinus (q.v.). One such quarrel, which also involved rights of marriage, caused Segesta to appeal for help to Athens, an event which the latter put forward as one of several excuses for the Sicilian expedition in 415 B.C. After the Athenian disaster at Syracuse (413), Segesta looked to Carthage. When Carthaginian supremacy was established in the western half of the island (409) the city became a dependent ally of Carthage and so remained (except for a brief interval when it was occupied by Agathocles, q.v.) until it sided with Rome early in the first Punic war. Remains are few, but the Roman theatre is well preserved.

Segovia, town of Hispania Tarraconensis, notable for the wonderful

Roman aqueduct dating from the reign of Trajan. It is still in use, and brings water to the city from a distance of 12 miles. In the last 847 yards of its journey it crosses the valley on a line of double-tiered superimposed arches, built of rough-hewn granite blocks laid without lime or cement.

Segusio (mod. Susa), town of northern Liguria, capital of Cottii Regnum (q.v.). Here Cottius (q.v.) erected a triumphal arch in honour of Augustus, which still stands. There are also remains of the walls with a double-arched gate. Segusio was captured by Constantine in A.D. 312 on his march against Maxentius.

Sejanus, Lucius Aelius, minister of the emperor Tiberius, was born at Vulsinii in Etruria. Son of Seïus Strabo, commander of the praetorian guards in A.D. 14, he succeeded to that office when his father was appointed governor of Egypt. He concentrated the praetorians in a camp on the Viminal hill and thus made himself to all intents and purposes ruler of the city. He gained such ascendancy over Tiberius that the latter made him his confidant and gave him a free hand. Having dominated the emperor for several years Sejanus formed the design of winning the purple for himself. With this end in view he sought popularity with the troops, then arranged the poisoning of Drusus, son of Tiberius by his first wife Vipsania (A.D. 23). The murder was carried out by Drusus's own wife Livilla (*see* LIVIA 3), whom Sejanus had seduced. After Tiberius had withdrawn to Capreae (A.D. 26), Sejanus had full scope for his machinations. The death of the emperor's mother Livia in A.D. 29 was followed by the banishment to Pandataria of Agrippina the Elder (q.v.) with her sons Drusus and Nero.

Tiberius at last began to suspect the designs of his minister, and sent Sertorius Macro to Rome with a commission to take command of the praetorian cohorts. Macro, after assuring himself of the troops, and depriving Sejanus of his usual bodyguard, produced a letter from Tiberius ('*verbosa et grandis epistula*', as Juvenal calls it) in which the emperor expressed his mistrust of Sejanus. The senate decreed his death: he was strangled, and his body, mangled by the mob, was eventually thrown into the Tiber. Many of his friends perished at the same time, among whom were his son and daughter (A.D. 31). *See* Tacitus, *Annales*, iv. v; Dio Cassius, lvii, lviii; Juvenal, x. 65–86.

Selēnē, Greek goddess of the moon, later identified with Artemis (q.v.). In mythology she was a daughter of Hyperion, and sister of Helios (Sun) and Eos (Dawn). The Romans called her Luna, identified her with Diana (q.v.) and built her a temple between the Aventine and the Circus Maximus.

Seleucia (-keia), name of several hellenistic cities. The most important were the following.

1. *Seleucia ad Tigrin*, founded by Seleucus I, Nicator, in 312 B.C.; situated on the right bank of the Tigris, a little north of its junction with the Royal Canal and opposite to the future site of Ctesiphon (q.v.), which subsequently eclipsed it as the capital of western Asia. Seleucia is said to have been built in the form of a spreadeagle. It was peopled by Macedonians, Greeks, Jews and Syrians. Even after the rise of Ctesiphon it remained a place of considerable importance; in

the reign of Titus it had, according to Pliny, a population of 600,000, which had been reduced to half that number in A.D. 164 when the city was burned by Avidius Cassius.

2. *Seleucia Pieria*, founded by Seleucus I, Nicator, in 300 B.C.; situated on the border of Syria and Cilicia, four miles north of the mouth of the Orontes, where it served as the port of Antioch. In the war with Egypt following the murder of Antiochus II, Seleucia surrendered to Ptolemy III (246), but was recovered by Antiochus III in 219 B.C. In 109 or 108 B.C., during the internecine war of Antiochus VIII and IX, Seleucia declared itself an independent city, and was recognized as such by Rome in A.D. 70. Among the most interesting remains is a deep rock-hewn road leading from the city to the sea.

3. *Seleucia Tracheotis* (mod. Selefke) or *Trachea*, founded by Seleucus I, Nicator, in 300 B.C.; situated on the right bank of the River Calycadnus about four miles from its mouth. It had an oracle of Apollo and annual games in honour of Olympian Zeus.

Seleucidae, the Seleucids, name of a dynasty founded by Seleucus I, Nicator, after the death of Alexander the Great. It reigned from 312 until 65 B.C. *See* ANTIOCHUS; DEMETRIUS (B); SELEUCUS. *See* E. R. Bevan, *The House of Seleucus*, 1902.

Seleucus (-loukos), name of six kings of Syria (*see* SELEUCIDAE).

1. *Seleucus I, Nicator*, founder of the Syrian monarchy, son of Antiochus, a Macedonian of distinction among the officers of Philip II, and was born *c.* 358. He accompanied Alexander on his expedition to Asia. After the death of Alexander (323) he espoused the side of Perdiccas, whom he accompanied on his expedition against Egypt; but he took a leading part in the mutiny of the soldiers, which ended in the death of Perdiccas (321). In the second partition of the provinces which followed, Seleucus obtained the important satrapy of Babylonia; but it is not till his recovery of Babylon from Antigonus, in 312, that the Syrian monarchy is reckoned to commence. He conquered Susiana and Media, and extended his power over all the eastern provinces which had formed part of the empire of Alexander, from the Euphrates to the banks of the Oxus and the Indus. In 306 Seleucus formally assumed the regal title and diadem. Having leagued himself with Ptolemy I, Lysimachus and Cassander against Antigonus, he obtained, by the defeat and death of that monarch at Ipsus (301), a great part of Asia Minor, as well as the whole of Syria, from the Euphrates to the Mediterranean. Seleucus in 293 consigned the government of all the provinces beyond the Euphrates to his son Antiochus, upon whom he bestowed the title of king, as well as the hand of his own youthful wife, Stratonice, for whom the prince had conceived a violent attachment. In 285, with the assistance of Ptolemy and Lysimachus, he defeated and captured Demetrius I, Poliorcetes, King of Macedonia, who had invaded Asia Minor. For some time jealousies had existed between Seleucus and Lysimachus (q.v.). Seleucus crossed the Hellespont to take possession of the throne of Macedonia, which had been left vacant by the death of Lysimachus (281); but he had advanced no farther than Lysimachia, when he was assassinated by Ptolemy Ceraunus, to whom, a younger son of his old friend and ally, he had extended a friendly protection. His death took

place in the beginning of 280, and in the thirty-second year of his reign; he was in his seventy-eighth year. Seleucus appears to have carried out, with great energy and perseverance, the projects originally formed by Alexander himself for the hellenization of his Asiatic empire; and we find him founding, in almost every province, Greek or Macedonian colonies, which became so many centres of civilization and refinement.

2. *Seleucus II, Callinicus*, son and successor (246 B.C.) of Antiochus II by his first wife Laodice. The first measure of his administration, or rather that of his mother, was to put to death his stepmother, Berenice, together with her infant son. To avenge his sister, Ptolemy Euergetes, King of Egypt, invaded the dominions of Seleucus, and not only made himself master of Antioch and the whole of Syria, but carried his arms unopposed beyond the Euphrates and the Tigris. When Ptolemy had been recalled to his own dominions by domestic disturbances, Seleucus recovered possession of the greater part of the provinces which he had lost. He next became involved in a dangerous war with his brother, Antiochus Hierax, and afterwards undertook an expedition to the east, with a view to reducing the revolted provinces of Parthia and Bactria. He was, however, defeated by Arsaces, King of Parthia, in a great battle which was long after celebrated by the Parthians as the foundation of their independence. Seleucus appears to have been engaged in an expedition for the recovery of his provinces in Asia Minor, which had been seized by Attalus I of Pergamum, when he was accidentally killed by a fall from his horse (226 B.C.).

3. *Seleucus III, Ceraunus*, eldest son and successor of the preceding, was assassinated by two of his officers after a reign of only three years (223 B.C.).

4. *Seleucus IV, Philopator*, son and successor (187 B.C.) of Antiochus III the Great. After a feeble reign he was assassinated by one of his own ministers (175 B.C.).

5. *Seleucus V*, eldest son of Demetrius II, Nicator, assumed the crown on the death of his father in 126 B.C. He was assassinated by order of his own mother, Cleopatra, in the following year.

6. *Seleucus VI, Epiphanes*, eldest son of Antiochus VIII, Grypus. On the death of his father, in 96 B.C., he ascended the throne, and in the following year defeated and killed his uncle Antiochus IX, Cyzicenus, but was soon afterwards defeated by the latter's son, Antiochus X, Eusebes, and expelled from the kingdom. He took refuge in Mopsuestia (Cilicia), but in consequence of his tyrannical behaviour was burned to death by the inhabitants (93).

Selinus (-ous), city on the south coast of Sicily, situated on a hill whose southern portion overlooks the sea and formed the acropolis. Founded jointly by Megara Hyblaea and the parent city of Megara in Greece in 651 or 628 B.C., it was named, as was the river to the west of it, after the wild celery that grew there in abundance. Its quarrels with Segesta (q.v.) led to Athenian intervention in 415 B.C., and the debacle at Syracuse seemed to have assured the victory of Selinus. In 409, however, the city was taken and destroyed by the Carthaginians. A handful of refugees under Hermocrates returned in the following year and rebuilt the walls; but Hermocrates was killed in

407, and Selinus continued to exist as a mere village until the removal of its inhabitants to Lilybaeum in 250 B.C.

Remains include those of a fort (408 B.C.) on the neck of the acropolis, and of walls. In the south-east corner of the acropolis excavations have revealed five temples, the dedications of which are unknown. Outside the walls are ruins of three huge temples, standing on a hill east of the city. The largest of these was dedicated to Apollo and another to Hera. West of the river are ruins of the temple of Demeter Malophoros. All these buildings appear to have been destroyed by earthquake.

Sella Curulis, chair of office used by the 'curule' or higher magistrates (consuls, praetors and aediles) at Rome, and afterwards by the emperors. Made of (or inlaid with) ivory, it had curved legs but no back, and could be folded. The epithet *curulis* is derived from *currus*, a chariot, and it is believed that the chair was originally set up in the magistrate's chariot.

Semelē, daughter of Cadmus (q.v.), was with child by Zeus. The jealous Hera appeared to her disguised as her old nurse Beroë, and induced her to ask the god to visit her in the same splendour as his own spouse was used to behold. Zeus unwillingly complied, for he had sworn to grant her whatever she desired. He revealed himself to her amid thunder and lightning. Semele was consumed by the flames; but Zeus saved the child (none other than Dionysus), sewed him into his thigh and thus preserved him till he reached maturity. *See* DIONYSUS. Semele was afterwards conducted from the underworld to Olympus, where she became immortal under the name of Thyone.

Semnones, a German tribe of the Suebic group (*see* SUEBI), dwelling below the junction of the Saale and the Elbe. In A.D. 17, together with the Langobardi, they revolted against Maroboduus (q.v.).

Sēmōnides, *see* SIMONIDES OF AMORGOS.

Senate (Lat. Senatus, from *senes*, elders), the great council of the Roman republic, corresponding in dignity, though not exactly in functions, to the Boule (q.v.) at Athens and the Gerousia at Sparta. The senate consisted originally of 100 members, increased later to 300, by Sulla to 600, by Julius Caesar to 900, but finally reduced by Augustus to the number of 600. Senior magistrates were *ex officio* members, and the minimum age seems to have been twenty-six. From about 443 B.C. vacancies were filled once every five years by the censors (q.v.), who could also remove members for scandalous conduct.

The senate exercised general supervision of public welfare; it managed foreign relations, superintended the state religion, ordered levies of troops, and regulated taxation and state expenditure. Under the empire it was completely subject to the will of the sovereign.

Meetings were originally held in the Curia Hostilia, on the north side of the Comitium in the Forum. About 50 B.C. the site was given up for a temple of Fortune, and a new senate-house, the Curia Pompeia, was built in the Campus. Here Caesar was murdered. Another meeting-place was the Curia Julia, at the south-east corner of the Forum Julii, built by Caesar; sometimes, however, the senate assembled in one or other of the following temples: Castor and Pollux, Bellona, Jupiter Stator, Quirinus. *See* P. Williams, *Le Sénat de la république romaine,* 1885; C. Lécrivain, *Le Sénat romain depuis Dioclétien,* 1888; M. Hammond, *The Augustan Principate,* 1933.

Seneca, Lucius Annaeus, Latin Stoic philosopher, son of M. Annaeus Seneca (q.v.), born at Corduba *c.* 4 B.C. He was brought to Rome when still a child, and early devoted himself to the study of rhetoric. Later he acquired a reputation at the Bar, aroused the jealousy of Caligula, and in the first year of Claudius (A.D. 41) was banished to Corsica on account of intimacy with the emperor's niece Julia. He was recalled in 49 through the influence of Agrippina, who had married Claudius, and was appointed tutor to her son, the future emperor Nero (q.v.). On the accession of Nero (54) Seneca's authority increased, and he shared the administration of affairs with Burrhus (q.v.), the praetorian prefect. His restraining hand, however, soon made him irksome to Nero, whose cupidity too was excited by the wealth of his minister. He withdrew from public life, but was eventually implicated in the conspiracy of Piso (A.D. 65), and committed suicide, together with his wife Pompeia Paulina.

Seneca's fame rests upon his writings. They have been variously estimated by critics, but all agree as to their clear and forcible style. They consist of ten *Dialogues,* one hundred and twenty-four *Moral Letters* to Lucilius, the *Apocolocyntosis* (Pumpkinification) *of Claudius,* a group of *Moral Essays* which include the 'De Beneficiis' and 'Naturales Quaestiones', and nine *Tragedies. See* the complete edition by F. Haase, 1898. There is a text and translation of all, except the *Dialogues,* by R. M. Gummere, W. H. D. Rouse, J. W. Basore and F. J. Miller, 9 vols. (Loeb Library). Of the *Tragedies* there is a verse translation by E. I. Harris, 1904. *See* Sir S. Dill, *Roman Society from Nero to Marcus Aurelius,* 1904; F. L. Lucas, *Seneca and Elizabethan Tragedy,* 1952.

Seneca, Marcus Annaeus, Latin rhetorician, born at Corduba in Spain *c.* 55 B.C. He visited Rome in the early years of Augustus, but returned to Spain and married Helvia, by whom he had three sons: L. Annaeus Seneca (*see* preceding article), L. Annaeus Mela (father of the poet Lucan) and M. Annaeus Novatus. He subsequently paid another visit to Rome, and died there *c.* A.D. 41. His extant writings consist of a book of *Suasoriae* (extracts from celebrated rhetoricians on standard school themes), and five of ten books of *Controversiae* (imaginary legal cases). Books iii–v, vii, and viii have survived only in a later epitome. The works have been edited by H. Borneque, 1902, and the *Suasoriae* (with translation) by W. A. Edward, 1928. *See* H. Borneque, *Les Déclamations et les déclamateurs d'après Sénèque le père,* 1902; S. F. Bonner, *Roman Declamation,* 1949.

Senones, a powerful people of Gallia Celtica, who in Caesar's time inhabited the modern departments of Seine-et-Marne, Loiret and Yonne. They fought against Caesar for two years (53–51 B.C.) and thereafter disappear from Gallic history. Their chief town was Agedincum (mod. Sens), afterwards a member of Gallia Lugdunensis. In 400 B.C. a branch of the Senones crossed the Alps (*see* CELTAE) and settled on the east coast of Italy between Ariminum and Ancona, in the so-called Ager Gallicus (q.v.). In 391 B.C. the Senones invaded Etruria and besieged Clusium, whose inhabitants appealed to Rome.

The resulting war led to the Roman defeat on the Allia (390) and the capture of Rome. The Senones were finally subdued and expelled from Italy by P. Cornelius Dolabella in 283 B.C.

Sentinum, town of Umbria, near the River Aesis. In its neighbourhood was fought the battle (295 B.C.) which ended in the defeat of the Samnites and Gauls by the Romans (*see* SAMNIUM). Sentinum was captured and destroyed by the forces of Octavian in 41 B.C., but it revived under the empire.

Sequani, a people of Gallia Celtica, who inhabited what is now Franche-Comté and a part of Burgundy, with Vesontio (mod. Besançon) as their capital. In 71 B.C. they had invited Ariovistus (q.v.) to help them and their allies the Arverni against the Aedui. But Ariovistus proceeded to deprive them of a third of their territory, and was threatening to take still more, when the Sequani appealed to Caesar (58 B.C.). He put an end to the encroachments of Ariovistus; but he also obliged the Sequani to disgorge what they had taken from the Aedui, and it was this action which caused them to join the revolt of Vercingetorix (q.v.) in 52 B.C. Under Augustus their territory, then called Sequania, formed part of Gallia Belgica; Diocletian enlarged it by adding Helvetia and part of Germania Superior, and called the whole Provincia Maxima Sequanorum.

Serapis, a late Egyptian divinity, derived from the dead and Osirified Apis bull of Memphis. Serapis was chosen by Ptolemy I to be the deity of both his Greek and Egyptian subjects. Worshipped in Greek with statue and temple in Greek style at Alexandria, Serapis became the official deity of the kingdom. After the Roman conquest (30 B.C.) the cult spread all over the empire.

Serenus, Sammonicus, Roman physician and polymath, one of the most learned men of his age, was murdered at a banquet to which he had been invited by the emperor Caracalla (A.D. 212). His son, who bore the same name and was tutor to the younger Gordian, inherited from his father a library of 60,000 volumes. It is not known which of them wrote *De medicina praeceptis*, a long didactic poem on popular remedies and magical formulae culled from various sources, which ends with an interesting account of the celebrated antidote against poison used by Mithradates the Great of Pontus. *See* the edition by E. Bährens in *Poetae Latini minores*, iii.

Sēres, from Greek *sēr* (silkworm), name given by ancient writers to the Chinese when approached by land. The Roman historian Ammianus Marcellinus (late 4th century A.D.) refers to the Great Wall of China as *Aggeres Serium. See* SINAE.

Seriphos, island of the Aegean, connected in Greek mythology with the legend of Perseus (q.v.). Its copper mines were worked as early as the 2nd millennium B.C., and it was subsequently colonized by Ionians from Athens. One of the few islands to refuse submission to Xerxes, it eventually became subject to Rome and was used by the emperors as a place of banishment.

Sertorius, Quintus, Roman soldier, born at Nursia *c.* 121 B.C. He served under Marius (q.v.) in the war against the Teutones (102), and it was said that before the battle of Aquae Sextiae he disguised himself and went into the enemy's camp as a spy. In 98 he served as military tribune in Spain under T. Didius. He was quaestor in 91, by which date he had lost an eye in battle. In 87 Sertorius was one of the commanders under Marius and Cinna when they entered Rome, but he disapproved of the massacres which followed. In 83 he was praetor; but on Sulla's return to Italy in that year, Sertorius went to Spain, and thence into Mauretania, where he defeated Paccianus, one of Sulla's generals. Sertorius was now committed to rebellion against the Sullan regime, an absolute monarchy in all but name. He returned to Spain, and placed himself at the head of the Lusitanian revolt. His wise rule and military skill won him great popularity and widespread support. In 77 B.C. he was joined by a number of Romans, among them Perperna with fifty-three cohorts; he was able to establish a regular state within the state, and to withstand the efforts of every general sent against him, including Pompey. In 72 B.C., however, he was assassinated by Perperna and some other Roman officers, who had become jealous of his authority, and the flames of rebellion were firmly extinguished. *See* A. Schulten, *Sertorius*, 1926.

Servile Wars. The first two were fought in Sicily, where at two periods (136–132 and 104–99 B.C.) the slaves rose in formidable insurrections against Rome. Torture, starvation and injustice were suffered from overseers, who, at the bidding of the landowners, forced them to toil in chained gangs. The consul Rupilius crushed the first revolt, of which Eunus, a Syrian juggler, was leader, by capturing the two strongholds of Enna and Tauromenium. The second and more formidable came to an end after Tryphon's death and Athenio's defeat in battle. For the third servile war *see* SPARTACUS.

Servilia, Roman matron, daughter of Q. Servilius Caepio by Livia, sister of M. Livius Drusus (tribune of the plebs 91 B.C.). She was thus half-sister to Cato Uticensis. Servilia was married first to M. Junius Brutus, to whom she bore M. Junius Brutus, the murderer of Caesar; but she was known to have been on terms of intimacy with Caesar, who was rumoured to be in fact the father of her son. She was married secondly to D. Junius Silanus (consul 62 B.C.), by whom she was the mother of M. Junius Silanus, who served as Caesar's legate in Gaul (53 B.C.). Servilia had a sister of the same name, who was the second wife of L. Licinius Lucullus (consul 74 B.C.).

Sestertius, *see* COINAGE.

Setia (mod. Sezze), town of the Volsci overlooking the Pomptine marshes. It became a Latin colony in 382 B.C., was captured by Sulla in 82 B.C., and under the empire was famous for its wine, which Augustus preferred to the Falernian. There are remains of the walls and of some Roman villas.

Seven Sages of Greece, The, famous Greek legislators, tyrants and others, who lived between 620 and 550 B.C. Each was noted for a wise maxim as follows: Cleobulus of Rhodes—'*Moderation is the chief good*'; Periander of Corinth—'*Forethought in all things*'; Pittacus of Mytilene—'*Know your opportunity*'; Bias of Priene—'*Too many workers spoil the work*'; Thales of Miletus—'*Suretyship brings ruin*'; Chilon of Sparta—'*Know thyself*'; Solon of Athens—'*Nothing to excess*'.

Severus, Flavius Valerius, Roman emperor A.D. 306–7. He succeeded

Constantius Chlorus in 306, and was soon afterwards sent against Maxentius (q.v.), who had assumed the imperial title at Rome. Severus was defeated and taken prisoner, and compelled to commit suicide at Rome in the following year.

Severus, Lucius Septimius, Roman emperor A.D. 193–211, born at Leptis Magna (q.v.) in north Africa A.D. 146. After holding various commands under Marcus Aurelius and Commodus, he was appointed commander-in-chief of the army in Pannonia and Illyria. These troops proclaimed him emperor on the death of Pertinax (q.v.), and he at once marched on Rome (*see* DIDIUS JULIANUS). Having obtained possession of the throne, Severus turned his arms against Pescennius Niger, who had been saluted emperor by the legions of the east. Niger was defeated near Issus, and put to death soon afterwards (194). Severus next laid siege to Byzantium (q.v.), which was not taken until 196; but in the meantime he made a successful punitive raid against the Arabs east of the Euphrates (195). After the fall of Byzantium, the emperor returned to Rome, but set out again almost at once for Gaul, to deal with Albinus (q.v.). The latter was defeated and killed near Lugdunum in 197, and Severus was undisputed master of the Roman world. Between 199 and 202 he was in the east, repelling an invasion of the Parthians who had overrrun Mesopotamia. Returning to Rome in the latter year, he immediately inaugurated a persecution of his Christian subjects. This, however, does not appear to have been prolonged, and during the next five years or so he proved himself a patron of letters and did much to restore and improve the imperial city. Earlier in life he had married a Syrian princess known to history as Julia Domna. This lady had brought with her from the east her sister Julia Maesa, and her nieces Julia Saemias and Julia Mammaea. They were all highly intelligent; but they were devotees of mysticism and esotericism, and it was through them that the oriental flood finally submerged the Latin soul.

In 208 the state of Britain (q.v.) called Severus to that province, together with his two sons Caracalla and Geta. He did not return: after nearly three years of successful campaigning and reform he died at Eburacum (York) on 4th February A.D. 211. *See* M. Platnauer, *The Life and Reign of the Emperor Septimius Severus*, 1918.

Severus, Marcus Aurelius Alexander, commonly called Alexander Severus, Roman emperor A.D. 222–35. He was son of Gessius Marcianus and Julia Mammaea, niece of the empress Julia Domna. He was born in Phoenicia on 1st October A.D. 205, adopted and given the rank of Caesar by his first cousin, the emperor Elagabalus (q.v.) in 221, and succeeded him on 11th March in the following year. The first years of his reign were peaceful; they were devoted to attempts at reform, and are particularly notable for the emperor's interest in and goodwill towards Christianity. Eventually Alexander became involved in war with Artaxerxes, founder of the Sassanid dynasty of Persia. He won an indecisive victory in 232, but was unable to follow up his advantage, owing to disturbances on the Gallo-German frontier. He therefore returned to Rome and celebrated a triumph in 233. In 235 the Germans were devastating Gaul, and Alexander started for the Rhine. But having made himself unacceptable in military quarters by his attempts to curtail the political power of the army, he was waylaid near Moguntiacum (Mainz) by a band of mutinous soldiers and put to death. *See* W. Thiele, *De Severo Alexandro Imperatore*; H. Daniel-Rops, *The Church of Apostles and Martyrs* (trans.), 1960.

Sextus Empiricus, Greek philosopher of the late 2nd century A.D., the principal and most impartial historian of scepticism. Three of his works are extant, remarkable for their learning and acumen: *Outlines of Pyrrhonism*; *Against the Dogmatists*; *Against Schoolmasters*. *See* the edition and translation by R. G. Bury, 4 vols. (Loeb Library).

Sibyl (Lat. Sibylla), the name of certain priestesses of Apollo, who prophesied under his direct inspiration. The most famous, the Cumaean Sibyl (*see* CUMAE), guided Aeneas to Hades (Virgil, *Aen.* vi). She sold the Sibylline Books to Tarquinius Priscus, offering him first nine books, then six and finally three for the same price. These were preserved in the Capitol (q.v.), and might be consulted only by order of the senate. The Sibylline Books were destroyed in the fire which burned the Capitol in 83 B.C. A new collection was assembled and was preserved until A.D. 405. During that time additions were made from Jewish and Christian sources. *See* H. Diels, *The Sibylline Oracles* (translated by M. S. Terry), 1890.

Sicani (Sikanoi), a people who, with the Elymi (q.v.), were the oldest inhabitants of Sicily. Originally they occupied nearly the whole of the island, but were gradually driven by the Siculi (q.v.) into the centre and the north and north-west. Among the cities founded by the Sicani was Hyccara (q.v.).

Siceli, *see* SICULI.

Sicily (Gk Sikelia; Lat. Sicilia), island of the Mediterranean, only two miles at its nearest point from Italy. It was sometimes called by the poets Trinacria, on account of its roughly triangular shape, and identified with Homer's Thrinacia. The fertile soil produced wheat in such abundance that Sicily came, under Greek influence, to be held sacred to Demeter (q.v.; *see also* HENNA), and was later the chief source of Roman corn supplies before the conquest of Africa. Other valuable products were wine, saffron, honey (*see* HYBLA), almonds and fruit.

The earliest recorded inhabitants were the Elymi and Sicani (qq.v.), who were driven by the Siculi (q.v.) or Siceli into the central and western parts of the island. The first settlers from overseas were Phoenicians, who established a number of trading stations; but they too were gradually confined to the north-west by the advent of Greek colonists, who came to be called *Siceliotae* to distinguish them from the native Siceli. *See* AGRIGENTUM; CAMARINA; CATINA; GELA; HIMERA; LEONTINI; MEGARA HYBLAEA; MESSANA; NAXOS; SELINUS; SYRACUSE.

In 409–408 B.C. the Carthaginians, who had long been overlords of the few remaining Phoenician settlements in Sicily, established a firm foothold there by the destruction of Selinus and Himera. Their capture of Acragas (Agrigentum) in 405 made them masters of the western part of the island, and they soon came into conflict with Syracuse and other Greek city-states. *See* AGATHOCLES; DIONYSIUS; GELON; HIERON; TIMOLEON.

At the close of the first Punic war (241 B.C.), the Carthaginians were obliged to evacuate Sicily, the western half of which was made a Roman province while the eastern half continued under the rule of Hieron II of Syracuse as an ally of Rome. But after the revolt of Syracuse during the second Punic war and its capture by M. Claudius Marcellus (211 B.C.), the whole island was included in the province of Sicily and administered by a praetor.

Sicily was the first Roman territory to be cultivated by slave-gangs, and the cruel treatment of these unfortunates, together with the general lawlessness then rife, gave rise to two slave revolts. The first of these lasted from 136 to 132, the second from 104 to 99 B.C. *See* SERVILE WARS; VERRES. The later history of Roman Sicily is uneventful. *See* E. A. Freeman, *History of Sicily*, 4 vols., 1890–4.

Siculi or **Siceli** (Sikeloi), a people who, coming from central Italy in prehistoric times, entered Sicily (which derived its name from them) and drove the Sicani (q.v.) from the eastern half of the island. Their principal towns were Agyrium, Centuripae, Henna and the three named Hybla (qq.v.). The agricultural pursuits of the Siculi, and the volcanic nature of the island, led them to worship gods of the under-world.

Sicyon (-kuōn), city in northern Peloponnesus between Corinth and Achaea, about two miles from the Corinthian Gulf. Its territory, though small, was fertile, producing olives and fruit; there were also valuable fisheries. Sicyon is represented by Homer as a dependency of Argos. After the Dorian invasion of Peloponnesus the population consisted of three Dorian tribes, an Ionian tribe representative of the original inhabitants, and a class of serfs. Sicyon's virtual independence, however, was established by the emergence in 665 B.C. of a tyranny which lasted for one hundred years and which was thoroughly anti-Dorian. Dorian supremacy was restored at the end of the 6th century, and thenceforward Sicyon was largely dominated by Sparta or Corinth. A new succession of tyrants followed one another from 369 until 251 B.C., when the city was freed (*see* ARATUS) and made a member of the Achaean League (q.v.). The glory of Sicyon is to be found rather in the field of art. The school of painting established by Eupompus had among its students Pamphilus and Apelles, and a long line of sculptors, beginning with Canachus, reached its climax in Lysippus. *See* C. Skalet, *Ancient Sicyon*, 1928.

Sidē, coastal city of Pamphylia, about 12 miles east of the mouth of the Eurymedon, founded from Cyme in Aeolis. Here was a temple of Athena, who is represented on the city's coins holding a pomegranate (Gk *sidē*). The harbour was one of the chief bases of the Cilician pirates in the 1st century B.C. There are extensive remains, which include a large theatre.

Sidōn, maritime and commercial city of Phoenicia, praised in the Homeric poems for the skill of its craftsmen. It does not enter Greek history until 480 B.C., when the ships of Sidon were the best in the whole Persian fleet and her king ranked next to Xerxes himself in the council of war. Sidon submitted without resistance to Alexander the Great, and was thereafter subject in turn to the Seleucids, the Ptolemies and the Romans. Under these last it was lavishly adorned by Herod the Great. Christianity obtained an early footing in this ancient city. It was visited by St Paul (who had friends there) on his way to Rome, and its bishop attended the Council of Nicaea in 325.

Sigeum (Sigeion), promontory of the Troad, in Mysia at the southern extremity of the Hellespont. Here Homer places the Greek camp in the Trojan war. Here too was a town of the same name, founded from Mytilene in Lesbos (*see* MYTILENE).

Signia (mod. Segni), town of Latium on the east side of the Volscian mountains, about 35 miles south-east of Rome. Its foundation was attributed to Tarquinius Superbus, and fresh colonists were sent there in 495 B.C. It was famous for its wine, its pears and a paving material called *opus Signinum*. There are remains of the city walls.

Silaniōn, Athenian sculptor of the 4th century B.C., a contemporary of Lysippus. His bronze 'Sappho' at Syracuse is praised by Cicero.

Silenus (-lēnos), in Greek mythology, son of Hermes or Pan, an aged woodland deity or satyr (*see* SATYRS), with a reputation for song, prophecy, drunkenness and lechery. With other aged satyrs (collectively called *Silēnoi*), he was the companion of Dionysus, and always carried a wine-skin. He is represented commonly as a jovial old man, bald and puck-nosed, fat and round, phallic and intoxicated. Unable to trust his own legs, he is generally shown riding on an ass or supported by other satyrs. When he was in a drunken sleep, mortals might compel him to prophesy by surrounding him with chains of flowers.

Silius Italicus, Tiberius Catius Asconius (*c.* A.D. 25–*c.* 101), Latin epic poet; consul in 68 and governor of Asia in 77. He was the author of *Punica*, on the second Punic war, which was rediscovered by Poggio Bracciolini in 1416; it is by common consent the longest and worst poem in the whole range of Latin literature. Silius starved himself to death rather than suffer the pains of an incurable disease. There is an edition and translation by J. D. Duff, 2 vols. (Loeb Library), 1934. *See* H. E. Butler, *Post-Augustan Poetry*, 1909.

Silures, a British tribe inhabiting territory which corresponds roughly to the modern counties of Monmouth, Brecon and Glamorgan. They opposed the Roman conquest (*see* BRITAIN), but resistance was overcome by Ostorius Scapula (q.v.) and his successors. The legionary fortress of Isca (q.v.) was established in their territory and by A.D. 78 they were completely subdued. Their chief town was Venta Silurum (mod. Caerwent), about six miles west of Chepstow, where extensive excavations have been made.

Silvanus, an old Italian deity, originally of uncultivated fields and forests, especially as protector of their boundaries. Later his patronage was extended to cattle, and he was identified with Pan and Faunus (qq.v.). A marble statue of Silvanus, believed to date from the 2nd century A.D., has recently been unearthed beside the Via Appia. It was found near the site which from earlier discoveries is thought to have been the meeting-place of a private society of devotees, who used to offer sacrifices to Silvanus and regale themselves with good food.

Simōnides (more correctly **Sēmōnides**) **of Amorgos** (*fl.* 664 B.C.), Greek iambic poet, born at Samos and founded a colony on the island of Amorgos. About thirty fragments of his poems remain, including one on the 'Pedigree of Women'. *See* T. Bergk, *Poëtae lyrici Graeci*, 1877–82, and edition by P. Malusa, 1900.

Simōnides of Ceos (*c.* 556–468 B.C.), Greek lyric poet, born at Iulis in Ceos. Having visited the tyrant Hipparchus at Athens, he stayed for a time in Thessaly, and returned to Athens at the beginning of the Persian wars, moving to the court of Hieron I at Syracuse *c.* 476 B.C. The most famous of Simonides's surviving fragments is the epitaph on the Spartan dead at Thermopylae. *See* J. M. Edmonds, *Lyra Graeca* (with translation), 1922; C. M. Bowra, *Greek Lyric Poetry*, 1936.

Sinae (-ai), name used by ancient writers for the Chinese when approached by sea from India. *See* SERES.

Sinis, in Greek legend, a bandit who infested the isthmus of Corinth. He used to kill those whom he had robbed by fastening the victims' arms to two fir-trees which he had bent, and then letting them spring up again. He himself was torn apart in this way by Theseus.

Sinōn, in Greek legend, a relative of Odysseus, whom he accompanied to Troy. He allowed himself to be taken prisoner, and persuaded the Trojans to admit the wooden horse.

Sinōpē, Greek city on the Euxine, situated on the western headland of the great bay of which the delta of the Halys forms the eastern. Founded in 630 B.C. from Miletus, it became the greatest commercial city on the Euxine, being the terminus of a caravan route from the Euphrates. Among its exports was red sulphate of arsenic from Cappadocia, commonly called Sinopic red earth. In the 5th century B.C. Sinope received a colony from Athens; during the next hundred years it extended its sway over a large area, and its fleet dominated the eastern half of the Euxine. In 183 B.C., however, it was captured by Pharnaces I of Pontus and became capital of the Pontic kingdom. Mithradates the Great had brought it to the highest prosperity and material splendour when it was taken by Lucullus (q.v.) and nearly burned down (70 B.C.). Julius Caesar established a Roman colony at Sinope shortly before his death; but the port was already yielding pride of place to Ephesus, which was more favourably situated for Roman shipping, and by the time of Constantine it ranked second to Amisus (q.v.). Sinope was the birth-place of Diogenes the Cynic (q.v.), of the comic poet Diphilus (q.v.) and of the historian Baton. *See* D. Robinson, *Ancient Sinope*, 1906.

Sinuessa (mod. Rocca di Mandragone), coastal town on the border of Latium and Campania, on the Via Appia. Colonized by the Romans, together with Minturnae, in 295 B.C., it possessed a good harbour and was a place of commercial importance.

Siphnos (mod. Siphanto), island of the Cyclades, colonized by Ionians from Athens. Possessing mines of gold and silver, it was regarded in the time of Herodotus as the richest of the islands. It refused tribute to Xerxes, and one of its ships fought with the Greek fleet at Salamis. The moral reputation of the islanders was such that the word *Siphniazein*, 'to behave like a Siphnian', was used as a term of reproach.

Sirens (Gk Sirēnes), nymphs whose songs irresistibly lured sailors to destruction. Odysseus (q.v.) plugged his men's ears with wax and had

himself tied to the mast, and so passed them in safety (*Od.* xii).
When the Argonauts sailed by, the Sirens began to sing, but in vain,
for Orpheus was on board, and outsang them; whereupon they threw
themselves into the sea and became rocks. *See* SURRENTUM.

Sirenusae, three small uninhabited islands off the promontory of
Misenum, one of the traditional abodes of the Sirens (q.v.). Virgil
calls them 'Sirenum Scopuli' (*Aen.* v. 864).

Sirmio, promontory on the southern shore of the Lacus Benacus
(mod. Lago di Garda) in Gallia Cisalpina (Transpadana). Here
Catullus had a villa to which one of the most beautiful of his poems is
addressed.

Sisenna, Lucius Cornelius, Roman annalist. He was a *legatus* of
Pompey in the war against the pirates (67 B.C.), but died the same
year in Crete at the age of about fifty-two. Sisenna translated the
Milesian Tales of Aristeides, and wrote annals of his own times.
Neither of these works has survived, but it is known that the lost
Histories of Sallust (q.v.) were a continuation of Sisenna's *Annals.*

Sisygambis (Sisu-), Greek form of the name borne by the mother of
Darius III, Codomannus, last king of Persia. After the battle of Issus
(333 B.C.) she fell into the hands of Alexander the Great (q.v.),
together with her daughter-in-law and granddaughters. All these
ladies were treated with courtesy and kindness, and it is said that
when Alexander died Sisygambis starved herself to death.

Sisyphus (Sisuphos), legendary son of Aeolus and brother of
Athamas (q.v.). His wife was Merope (*see* MEROPE, 2), daughter of
Atlas, by whom he was father of Glaucus (*see* GLAUCUS, 1). He was
said to have built Corinth and become its first king. In this capacity
he promoted navigation and commerce, but was fraudulent and
avaricious (*Il.* vi. 153). He was punished in Hades by being for
ever obliged to roll uphill a marble block which always rolled down
again just as it was reaching the top (*Od.* xi. 593).

Sitalces (-kēs), *see* ODRYSAE.

Sittius, Publius, a native of Nuceria in Campania, went in 64 B.C. to
Spain. Here he raised a band of free-lances, and in the following year
crossed to Africa, where he pursued the career of a soldier of fortune.
Towards the end of 47 B.C., soon after the arrival of Caesar for the
African war, Sittius formed an alliance with Bocchus, King of
eastern Mauretania, one of Caesar's partisans. Then, by storming
Cirta and ravaging its neighbourhood, he both enriched himself and
established a claim to Caesar's gratitude; for this sudden attack
prevented the Numidian king Juba II from reinforcing Metellus
Scipio. After the victory of Thapsus (46), Caesar rewarded Sittius
and Bocchus for this and other services with the grant of Western
Numidia, which had belonged to a friend of Juba. Sittius was afterwards assassinated by Arabio, a son of Juba.

Skolia, short lyric poems sung by the Greeks after dinner. They
were in high favour at Athens, and several specimens, notably those
of Bacchylides (q.v.), are extant.

Smyrna (Smurna), city of Asia Minor, said to have existed before
the arrival of Greek colonists, when it was occupied by Aeolic settlers
from Lesbos and Cyme. It then became the frontier city between

Aeolis on the north and Ionia on the south; but, being more easily accessible from the south, it gradually received many settlers from Ionian Colophon, lost its Aeolic character, passed into the possession of Colophon and thence into the Ionic confederation (c. 690 B.C.).

The geographical situation of Smyrna quickly raised it to a position of great power and prosperity, but it was captured by Alyattes III of Lydia (609–560) and ceased for three hundred years to be a Greek city. The scheme to restore it as such, which had been devised by Alexander, was carried out by Antigonus; he built a new city on a nearby though different site, which was enlarged and embellished by Lysimachus. Smyrna was included in the territories given by Rome to Eumenes II of Pergamum, and afterwards belonged to the Roman province of Asia. It was one of the seven cities which claimed to be the birth-place of Homer, whose temple, the Homereion, stood on the banks of the River Meles. Christianity was introduced at an early date, thanks to the presence of a large Jewish colony, and Bishop Polycarp was martyred in A.D. 155. *See* C. J. Cadoux, *Ancient Smyrna*, 1938.

Social War, a two-year conflict caused by the persistent refusal of Rome to extend her franchise to her Latin allies ; began (*see* MASRI) in 90 B.C., following the assassination of M. Livius Drusus (q.v.). All central and southern Italy, excepting some isolated Latin colonies (*see* COLONIA), flew to arms; the machinery of a new Italian state was planned, and Corfinium (q.v.), renamed Italica, was to be its capital.

The first year's campaigns were on the whole disastrous for Rome; but towards the end of that year and early in 89 some partial concessions did much to satisfy the requirements of the allies, who gradually lost interest in the struggle. By the end of 89 only the Lucanians and Samnites were in open revolt, which was quelled by some brilliant operations on the part of L. Cornelius Sulla (q.v.). He finally brought the war to a close by the capture of Nola (q.v.) in 88 B.C.

Socrates (Sōkratēs), Greek philosopher, born at Athens 469 B.C., the son of well-to-do parents, Sophroniscus and Phaenarete. He left no writings, so that our information about him depends upon the record of others. Socrates grew to manhood while Athens was at the height of her glory. About 450 he seems to have become interested in the Ionian philosophy recently introduced at Athens by Anaxagoras (q.v.), and he attached himself to Archaelaus, the latter's successor. It seems that this early interest in physical science led to disillusionment, and Socrates determined to strike out on his own. In doing so he was undoubtedly influenced by Pythagorean teaching; at any rate, by 439 he enjoyed a widespread reputation for wisdom. He is next found serving as a hoplite in the army at Potidaea (430), Delium (424) and Amphipolis (422), where he won renown for his courage and powers of endurance. About 423 he was burlesqued in the *Connus* of Ameipsias and the more celebrated *Clouds* of Aristophanes; and it is certain that the causes of this not always good-natured satire were Socrates's new asceticism and novel doctrines about the soul. In 406 he allowed himself to be elected to the Boule (q.v.), where, despite popular clamour, he refused to lend his voice to the condemnation of the victorious admirals after Arginusae. Following the expulsion of the Thirty Tyrants and the restoration of the democracy (late summer 404 B.C.) Socrates was charged with impiety (*asebeia*) and corruption of youth. The latter indictment amounted to his encouragement of the young to criticize the existing order. He was found guilty by a narrow majority, but by his attitude after the verdict he so enraged his judges that he was sentenced to death. The execution was delayed for thirty days, during the Delian festival, and in that time Socrates refused to avail himself of plans made for his escape. He drank the hemlock in the spring of 399 B.C. His last hours are described in Plato's *Phaedo*; the account is reckoned as one of the great masterpieces of European literature.

The value of Socrates's contribution to philosophy is much disputed. Some attribute directly to him much of the doctrine of his disciple Plato; but this view is rejected by most scholars, and indeed Socrates himself denied that he had any set of positive doctrines to teach. Nevertheless it may safely be maintained that Socrates founded the spiritual view of knowledge and conduct. He defined the soul as that in man which has knowledge, and also ignorance, good and bad. Thus for the first time intelligence is distinguished from sensation, and the soul identified with the normal consciousness or character of man. Moreover Socrates declared the immortality of the soul. It was but a step from this discovery to the doctrine that goodness is knowledge (*epistēmē*). The Socratic method of 'examination in arguments' (*skepsis en logois*) or 'Socratic irony' was in itself not new; it had already been employed by Zeno of Elaea against the Pythogorean geometry. What was new was its application by Socrates to questions of ethics and aesthetics. Socrates believed that he had a divine mission to convict men of sin (i.e. ignorance) by question and answer, examining systematically the fundamental assumptions from which discussions of conduct and morality arose, and insisting on a strict definition of terms. In this method Socrates may be regarded as the forerunner of formal logic. *See* G. C. Field, *Plato and his Contemporaries*, 1930; A. K. Rogers, *The Socratic Problem*, 1933; Sir R. W. Livingstone, *Portrait of Socrates*, 1940; L. Nelson, *Socratic Method and Critical Philosophy* (translated), 1949.

Sol, *see* HELIOS.

Soli (-oi): 1. City on the coast of Cilicia, said to have been founded by a joint colony from Argos in Greece and Lindus in Rhodes. It is not mentioned earlier than the 4th century B.C., but by that time its wealth was such that Alexander was able to fine it 200 talents. During the Mithradatic war it was destroyed by Tigranes, but was afterwards rebuilt by Pompey (q.v.), who settled there many of the pirates whom he had taken prisoner in 67 B.C. and called the city Pompeiopolis. Soli was the birth-place of the Stoic philosopher Chrysippus and of the poets Aratus and Philemon (qq.v.).

2. City on the north coast of Cyprus, traditionally founded by Acamas (q.v.) immediately after the Trojan war. During the classical period it was of no political importance, but possessed valuable copper mines.

Solinus, Gaius Julius (3rd century A.D.), Roman compiler, was the author of a geographical work entitled *Collectanea Rerum Memorabilium*, commonly known by its second title, *Polyhistor*. Solinus was so obviously indebted to Pliny's *Natural History*, a debt which he nowhere acknowledges, that he has been called 'Pliny's Ape'. *See* edition by J. Mommsen, 1895.

Solōn, Athenian legislator, born *c.* 639 B.C. His father Execestides claimed descent from Codrus, and his mother was a cousin of the mother of Peisistratus. Execestides had been prodigal of his resources, and Solon in his youth made a livelihood as a foreign trader. He early distinguished himself, too, by his poetical abilities. His first effusions were in a light and amatory strain, which afterwards gave way to the more earnest purpose of inculcating sage advice (gnomic poetry). So widely indeed did his reputation spread, that he was ranked as one of the Seven Sages. The occasion which first brought Solon prominently into politics was the contest between Athens and Megara respecting the possession of Salamis. Indignant at the dishonourable renunciation of their claims by the Athenians, he feigned madness, rushed into the agora, and there recited a short elegiac poem of 100 lines, in which he called upon the Athenians to retrieve their disgrace and reconquer the 'lovely island'. The pusillanimous law was rescinded; war was declared, and Solon himself appointed to conduct it. The Megarians were driven out of the island, but a tedious conflict ensued, which was finally settled by the arbitration of Sparta. Both parties appealed, in support of their claim, to the authority of Homer; and it was currently believed in antiquity that Solon had surreptitiously inserted the line (*Il.* ii. 558) which speaks of Ajax as ranging his ships with the Athenians. The Spartans decided in favour of Athens, *c.* 596 B.C. Solon himself, probably, was one of those who received grants of land in Salamis, and this may account for his being termed a Salaminian. Soon after these events (*c.* 595) he promoted hostilities on behalf of Delphi against Crissa (q.v.), and was the mover of the decree of the Amphictyons by which the first Sacred war was declared.

It was about the time of the outbreak of this war, that, in consequence of the distracted state of Attica, which was rent by civil commotions, Solon was called upon by all parties to mediate between them and alleviate the miseries that prevailed. He was chosen archon 594, and with that office was invested with unlimited power. His principal measures were the cancellation of existing debts, and the prohibition of making loans on the security of the borrower's person; the encouragement of trade by a revision of the Athenian coinage; and the impulse given to industry by the offer of citizenship to immigrant craftsmen. These measures procured for Solon such confidence and popularity that he was charged with the task of remodelling the constitution. He repealed all the laws of Dracon except those relating to bloodshed, and introduced reforms by a new distribution of the different classes of citizens, by enlarging the functions of the Ecclesia, or popular assembly, and by instituting the Boule (q.v.) of 400 members, afterwards increased by Cleisthenes to 500.

These, together with other laws of Solon, were set up at first in the Acropolis, afterwards in the Prytanᴗum. He also made some rectification of the calendar, and then absented himself from Athens for ten years. He visited Egypt, and from there proceeded to Cyprus. He is further said to have visited Lydia; and his interview with Croesus is celebrated. During the absence of Solon the old dissensions were renewed, and shortly after his arrival at Athens the power was seized by Peisistratus. The tyrant is said to have paid considerable court to Solon, and on various occasions to have solicited his advice, which Solon did not withhold. Solon probably died *c.* 559, two years after the overthrow of the constitution, at the age of eighty. Of his poems considerable fragments remain, which are of great interest as historical documents. They do not indicate any great degree of imaginative power, but their style is vigorous and simple. *See* K. Freeman, *The Work and Life of Solon* (with translation of the poems), 1926.

Somnus, *see* HYPNOS.

Sophists (Gk Sophistai), originally teachers of rhetoric and the art of disputation. They were not a school or sect, but a class of popular lecturers who aimed at imparting universal culture. The name implied an element of professional skill over and above the wisdom denoted by its literal meaning. Thus Pythagoras and Socrates were sometimes called sophists by their contemporaries. After 450 B.C. the term covered anyone who taught for pay, and because of the repugnance felt for this practice by men such as Plato it began to acquire a derogatory meaning. The subject of their teaching really amounted to 'how to get on in life', whether by the 'virtue' of Protagoras, the oratory of Gorgias, or the memory-training of Hippias. For this reason a sophist came to mean one who merely pretends to knowledge, or who attempts to make the worse appear the better cause. Under the Roman Empire, until the final triumph of Christianity, the name sophist was confined to teachers of rhetoric, which was fast becoming a literary exercise practised for its own sake. *See* W. Jaeger, *Paideia* (trans.), 1939; K. Freeman, *Companion to the Pre-Socratic Philosophers*, 1946; T. A. Sinclair, *History of Greek Political Thought*, 1932.

Sophocles (-klēs), Athenian tragic poet, born at Colonus 496 B.C. He early excelled in both music and gymnastic, being chosen at the age of sixteen to lead the chorus at a victory celebration after Salamis (480). He won the tragic prize for the first time, with *Triptolemus*, in 468. In 440 he was one of the ten *strategoi* (q.v.) appointed to conduct the Samian war. A story is told that in his last years his son Iophon asked the court to declare Sophocles *non compos mentis*. By way of reply the aged dramatist read a passage from *Oedipus Coloneus*, which had been lately written but not yet produced; and the judges immediately dismissed the suit. He died in 406 B.C.

Sophocles made three notable innovations in the drama. (1) He raised the number of the chorus from twelve to fifteen, but gave it a less direct share in the action than heretofore. (2) He introduced a third actor. (3) He produced trilogies the members of which were unconnected in subject. Only seven of his 123 plays are extant: *Ajax* (before 440), *Antigone* (440), *Electra* (between 440 and 412), *Oedipus Tyrannus* (*c.* 431), *Trachiniae* (between 420 and 415), *Philoctetes* (409), *Oedipus Coloneus* (posthumous, 401). Besides these we possess more than 1,100 fragments, including 400 lines of the satyric drama

Ichneutae found in a papyrus at Oxyrhynchus in 1907. *See* text with commentary by R. C. Jebb, 7 vols., 1884–96; Oxford Text and Fragments by A. C. Pearson, 1924 and 1917 respectively. *Ichneutae* has been edited (with translation) by R. J. Walker, 1919. There is a verse translation of the tragedies by Sir G. Young in Everyman's Library. *See also* T. B. L. Webster, *An Introduction to Sophocles*, 1936; Sir C. M. Bowra, *Sophoclean Tragedy*, 1944; F. R. Earp, *The Style of Sophocles*, 1944; F. J. Letters, *The Life and Work of Sophocles*, 1953; H. Kitto, *Sophocles*, 1958.

Sophonisba, daughter of the Carthaginian general Hasdrubal, son of Gisco. She had been betrothed by her father to the Numidian prince Masinissa (q.v.); but later Hasdrubal gave her in marriage to Syphax (q.v.), being anxious to win his support in the second Punic war. At the capture of Cirta by Masinissa (203 B.C.), Sophonisba fell into the hands of the conqueror, who was so struck with her beauty that he resolved to marry her himself. Their nuptials were celebrated without delay; but the Roman commander, Scipio Africanus Major (anxious that she should not exercise upon Masinissa the anti-Roman influence to which Syphax had been subject), refused to ratify the arrangement, and demanded the immediate surrender of the lady. Not daring to defy this order Masinissa spared her the humiliation of captivity by sending her a cup of poison, which she drank without hesitation.

Sophrōn (*fl.* 460–420 B.C.), Greek writer of mime, the first to reduce this primitive style of drama to literary form. He was a native of Syracuse, and his work is said to have been introduced at Athens by Plato. A substantial fragment of Sophron was found in a papyrus at Oxyrhynchus.

Sora, town of the Volsci overlooking the valley of the Liris. The Romans captured it in 345, 314 and 305 B.C., but did not finally control it until 303 when a colony was established. Augustus colonized it with soldiers of Legio IV, Sorana, which had been mainly recruited there. Sora was the birth-place of the Decii, Atilius Regulus and L. Mummius.

Soracte, a mountain in Etruria, about 24 miles from Rome, whence its highest summit (2,267 feet) is visible (*see* Horace, *Odes*, i. 9). The 'mountain' is actually an isolated ridge of limestone from which there is a most magnificent view. On the summit was a temple of Apollo, with whom the Romans identified a Sabine deity called Soranus.

Soranus (Sōranos), Greek physician, born at Ephesus. He practised at Alexandria, and afterwards at Rome during the reigns of Trajan and Hadrian (A.D. 98–138). Several of his works are extant, notably a gynaecological treatise in four books.

Sosigenes (Sōsigenēs), Greek astronomer and mathematician of the 1st century B.C. He was employed by Julius Caesar to reform the calendar (*see* JULIAN CALENDAR). It appears from Pliny (*Hist. Nat.* ii. 8) that he taught the motion of Mercury round the sun. Sosigenes was tutor to Alexander of Aphrodisias (q.v.). He is said to have been the author of other treatises; but all that remains of his work consists of extracts from his *Revolving Spheres*, preserved in the 6th-century commentary by Simplicius on Aristotle's *De caelo*.

Sosii, two brothers who ran a booksellers' business at Rome in the time of Horace.

Sositheus (Sō-), Greek tragic poet of the early 3rd century B.C.; said to have been born at Syracuse, to have lived mainly at Alexandria Troas (*see* ALEXANDRIA, 3), but to have spent some time at Athens, where he was hissed off the stage for an attack upon the Stoic philosopher Cleanthes (q.v.). Sositheus is also said to have restored the satyric drama. He was author of a pastoral play, fragments of which are extant.

Sosius, Gaius, one of Mark Antony's lieutenants in the East, by whose order he placed Herod the Great upon the throne of Judaea (39 B.C.).

Sōtadēs (3rd century B.C.), Greek satirist, born at Maronea in Thrace (according to others in Crete), but lived at Alexandria under Ptolemy II, Philadelphus. He was leader of a group of poets writing obscene satirical verses, in Ionic dialect and in the sotadic metre named after him. It is related that Sotades was imprisoned for a satire on Ptolemy, that he escaped, but was recaptured, placed in a leaden box and hurled into the sea. A few fragments of his work have survived.

Sparta or Lacedaemon, Greek city and capital of Laconia (q.v.), situated in a plain on the right bank of the Eurotas, about 20 miles from the sea. Archaeological excavations have shown that Sparta was an important centre of Aegean civilization in the 2nd millennium B.C. On the Dorian conquest of Peloponnesus (*c.* 1000 B.C.) the Achaean inhabitants were reduced to slavery, they and their descendants being known thenceforward as Helots (q.v.); while the provincial population and surrounding villages became tributary to Sparta, and became known as Perioeci, in whose hands were trade and industry. Neither of these classes had political rights, so that the state was dominated by a ruling body consisting of less than 30,000 persons, forming an exclusively warrior caste called Spartiates. There were two kings, ruling jointly and with limited powers, and a council of elders (the *Gerousia*) consisting of thirty members, including the kings. A board of five Ephors, elected annually, presided over this council and submitted its measures to the popular assembly (*Apella*), of which all Spartiates over the age of thirty were members.

The reduction of Messenia (q.v.) led to an increase in the number of Helots, who, with the Perioeci, seem to have amounted to about 600,000. By 490 B.C. the Spartan hegemony extended over Elis, Arcadia, Argolis, Sicyon and Corinth; and Sparta was unanimously assigned the chief command on the outbreak of the Persian war in that year. After the final defeat of the Persians at Plataea (479), the conduct of Pausanias (q.v.) alienated many of the Greek states, who attached themselves to Athens. But Sparta regained her supremacy at the end of the Peloponnesian war (404). She was herself defeated by the Thebans under Epameinondas (q.v.) at Leuctra (371), and the liberation of Messenia two years later completed her humiliation. After the Macedonian conquest of Greece (338), Sparta retained sufficient independence to refuse participation in the Asiatic campaigns of Alexander (334–323); but her power continued to decline. Agis III

(244–241) attempted in vain to restore the institutions of Lycurgus (q.v.). Cleomenes III (235–222) was more successful, but following his defeat at Sellasia in the latter year, Sparta was obliged to join the Achaean League, and in 146 B.C. became part of the Roman province of Achaea. See F. Ollier, *Le Mirage spartiate*, 1933; K. Chrimes, *Ancient Sparta*, 1949; H. Michell, *Sparta*, 1952; G. L. Huxley, *Early Sparta*, 1962. For archaeological excavations *see* the *Annual of the British School at Athens*, Nos. xii–xv and xxvi–xxx.

Spartacus, by birth a Thracian, was originally a shepherd. Later he served in the Roman army, but deserted and placed himself at the head of a brigand troop. Taken prisoner on one of his predatory expeditions he was sold to a trainer of gladiators. In 73 B.C. Spartacus belonged to a company owned by one Lentulus at Capua and destined for the games at Rome. He persuaded his fellows to make a bid for freedom, and about seventy of them broke out of their barracks and took refuge in the crater of Vesuvius. Chosen as their leader, he was soon joined by a number of runaway slaves. Having defeated two Roman forces, their numbers had risen by the year's end to 90,000, and they were in possession of most of southern Italy. In 72 they defeated both consuls, and made their way to the foot of the Alps. The slaves, however, would go no further. Spartacus was obliged to retrace his steps, and was defeated and slain on the River Silarus by the praetor M. Licinius Crassus (71 B.C.). Those of his followers who were captured were crucified, and the remaining fugitives were liquidated by Pompey on his way home from Spain.

Spes, a goddess personifying hope. She was worshipped at Rome in a temple in the Forum Holitorium, built during the first Punic war in consequence of a vow made by the consul A. Atilius Calatinus (q.v.).

Speusippus (-os), Greek philosopher, born at Athens *c.* 407 B.C., a son of Eurymedon by Potone, sister of Plato. Educated first in the school of Isocrates, he joined the Academy on its foundation, and accompanied Plato to Sicily in 361. He succeeded Plato as head of the Academy in 347, and held this position until his own death in 339 B.C.

Sphacteria (Sphaktēria), island of the Ionian Sea, opposite Pylos (q.v.). Here Cleon shut up a small Spartan force in 425 B.C.

Sphinx, 'strangler', a female monster, said variously to have been daughter of Orthus and Chimaera, of Typhon and Echidna (qq.v.), of Typhon and Chimaera. For her visitation of Thebes *see* THEBAN LEGEND, 2.

The Egyptian sphinx is half lion and half woman. The Greeks thought of her as the winged body of a lion having the form of a woman from the breast upwards. *See* R. C. Jebb's appendix to his edition of Sophocles's *Oedipus Tyrannus*.

Spolia opima, 'spoils of honour', arms taken on the field of battle by a victorious Roman general personally from the commander-in-chief of a vanquished army. The spoils thus obtained were dedicated to Jupiter Feretrius. Roman history (or legend) affords only three examples of *spolia opima*: (1) those won by Romulus from King Acro of the Caenenses; (2) those won by A. Cornelius Cossus from Tolumnus (q.v.), King of Veii; (3) those won by M. Claudius Marcellus (*see* MARCELLUS, 1) from Viromanduus, King of the Insubres.

Sporades (-eis), 'Scattered', a group of Aegean islands between Crete and Asia Minor. They were so called to distinguish them from the Cyclades (q.v.), which encircle Delos. The list varies, but includes Patmos, Thera and Cos (qq.v.).

Stabiae (mod. Castellamare di Stabia), coastal town of Campania, between Pompeii and Surrentum. It was captured and destroyed by Sulla in 89 B.C., during the Social war; but it was rebuilt and continued to flourish until the great eruption of Vesuvius in A.D. 79, when it was overwhelmed, together with Pompeii and Herculaneum (qq.v.). *See also* PLINY THE ELDER.

Stadium (Stadion; Eng. Stade), a standard Greek measure of length. The course of the foot-race at Olympia was exactly one stade in length; whence the word came to be applied first to the race itself and then (as today) to the place where it was run. The distance was equal to 600 Greek *orguiai*, or 625 Roman *pedes* (125 *passus*); and since the Roman mile contained eight stadia, the stadium was equivalent to 606 feet 9 inches English. *See* E. N. Gardner, *Athletics of the Ancient World*, 1930.

Stateira, sister and wife of the Persian king Darius III, Codomannus. Together with her daughters (*see* BARSINE, 2) and her mother-in-law, Sisygambis (q.v.), she was taken prisoner by Alexander after the battle of Issus (333). They were all treated with respect, but Stateira died shortly before the battle of Gaugemala (331 B.C.).

Statius, Publius Papinius (*c.* A.D. 61–96), the most outstanding Latin poet of the Silver Age, born at Neapolis in Campania, son of a poet and grammarian who was tutor to the emperor Domitian. As a youth he was many times winner of poetic contests at Neapolis, and three times at Alba. In 94, however, he failed in his expectations of victory at the Capitoline games at Rome, and withdrew to his birthplace with Claudia, his wife.

Statius is at his best in a collection of miscellaneous poems entitled *Silvae*. He was also the author of *Thebaïs*, an epic poem on the expedition of the Seven Against Thebes. Of the *Achilleïs*, another epic, only a fragment has survived. Despite many good things, the epics are wearisome to us. Juvenal, however, affords evidence of Statius's popularity, and names the *Thebaïs* in particular (vii. 82–6). The latter work was a great favourite in the Middle Ages; it was imitated by Chaucer in *Troilus and Criseyde*. There is a translation of the *Silvae*, with critical introduction, by D. A. Slater (1908), and an edition with translation of the complete works by J. H. Mozley (Loeb Library).

Stentōr, herald of the Greeks before Troy. His voice was as loud as that of fifty men together (*Il.* v. 785).

Steropēs, one of the Cyclopes in the legend of the Titans (q.v.).

Stesichorus (Stēsikhoros), Greek lyric poet, born at Himera in Sicily *c.* 640 B.C. He stands with Alcman (q.v.) at the head of the Dorian school of choral poetry; and is described by pseudo-Longinus as 'most like Homer'. Stesichorus is remarkable as having employed a lyric metre for epic subjects. He died *c.* 555 B.C. Only about thirty short fragments of his work have survived.

Sthenelus (-os): 1. Son of Perseus (q.v.) and Andromeda; King of Mycenae and father by Nicippe of Eurystheus (q.v.).

2. Son of Androgeos (q.v.). He accompanied Heracles from Paros on his expedition against the Amazons, and was appointed by Heracles, together with his brother Alcaeus, joint ruler of Thasos.

3. Son of Capaneus (q.v.).

4. A tragic poet attacked by Aristophanes in *The Wasps*.

Sthenoboea (-boia), *see* ANTEA.

Stilo Praeconinus, Lucius Aelius (*c.* 154–74 B.C.), Roman philologist, born at Lanuvium. A member of the equestrian order and with strong aristocratic leanings, he nevertheless took no part in politics, but spent his life quietly at Rome writing and teaching. Among his pupils were Varro and Cicero. Small fragments of his works (e.g. on the hymns of the Salii) have survived, though some modern scholars credit him with an extant rhetorical treatise entitled *Ad Herennium*.

Stoa, the Greek word for a portico or covered colonnade. It was in the Stoa Poikile (q.v.) at Athens that Zeno of Citium lectured; whence his followers were called Stoics, and their school 'the Stoa'.

Stoa Poikilē, a covered colonnade on the north side of the Agora at Athens. It was restored by Cimon in the 5th century B.C. and adorned with frescoes by Polygnotus and Panaenus. *See also* previous article.

Strabo (Gk Strabōn), Greek geographer, a native of Amasia in Pontus, was born *c.* 63 B.C. He appears to have visited Rome as a young man, and afterwards travelled extensively, though without seeing all the places he mentions. He died after A.D. 21. The *Historical Memoirs* of Strabo, now lost, were a continuation of Polybius. His *Geography* has come down to us intact, except for the seventh book, of which we have only an epitome. The materials were collected mainly in the library at Alexandria, but probably with some later reference to Agrippa's map in the Porticus Vipsaniae at Rome. They were arranged according to the principles of geography as established by Eratosthenes, and are enriched by the author's own historical notices. Of the seventeen books which form the *Geography* of Strabo, the first two are introductory; Nos. 3–10 deal with Europe; No. 11 with the main divisions of Asia; Nos. 12–14 with Asia Minor; No. 15 with India and Persia; No. 16 with Mesopotamia, Syria and Arabia; No. 17 with Egypt and Africa. *See* the edition with translation by H. L. Jones, 8 vols. (Loeb Library), 1922–8.

Stratēgoi, the Athenian army council, consisting of ten generals elected annually and at first commanding in rotation. In the time of Aristotle (325 B.C.) one *strategos* commanded the heavy infantry, one looked after home defences, two those of Peiraeus, while one acted as superintendent of symmories (groups) of wealthy citizens who defrayed extraordinary charges in time of war. The other five were detailed for a variety of duties as need arose.

Stratōn, Greek philosopher of the 3rd century B.C., born at Lampsacus in Mysia. After residing for some while at the court of Ptolemy II, Philadelphus, he succeeded Theophrastus (q.v.) as head of the Peripatetic school. Straton's interest lay chiefly in the field of natural science, whence he was surnamed Physicus. He died in 269 B.C. and was succeeded in turn by Lycon (q.v.).

Stratonice (-kē), daughter of Demetrius Poliorcetes by Phile, daughter of Antipater. In 300 B.C., at the age of seventeen, she was married to Seleucus I, Nicator, and lived in harmony with the old king for some years. Then it was discovered that her stepson Antiochus (the future Antiochus I, Soter) was in love with her, and Seleucus, to save the life of his son, which was said to be endangered by the violence of his passion, gave Stratonice to him as his bride.

Strophades (-eis), two islands in the Ionian Sea, off the coast of Messenia. Virgil names them as the abode of the Harpies (q.v.).

Strophius (-os), legendary king of Phocis, husband of Agamemnon's sister Anaxibia, father of Pylades (q.v.).

Stymphalides (Stumphalides), the Stymphalian birds. *See* TWELVE LABOURS OF HERACLES, 6.

Stymphalus (Stumphalos), town in north-eastern Arcadia on a mountain of the same name, immediately north of Lake Stymphalis (mod. Zaraka). On an island in this lake dwelt the Stymphalides.

Styx (Stux), 'hateful', a river of Peloponnesus, rising in the mountains near Nonacris, in northern Arcadia, and falling 600 feet sheer down a rock into a wild ravine. From this point it was supposed to flow round the underworld (*see* CHARON). When the gods swore by Styx they dared not break the oath, under pain of a year's unconsciousness and nine years' exile. To mortal oath-breakers, its waters (which, as in the case of the immortals, were drunk at the time of swearing) were deadly poison. The tradition probably originated in a form of trial by ordeal.

The nymph of this river was said to dwell at the entrance to Hades, in a grotto supported by silver columns. She was the mother of Zelos (zeal), Nike (victory), Bia (force) and Kratos (strength).

Sublaqueum (mod. Subiaco), town of Latium, on the River Anio, about 40 miles east of Rome. Its name was derived from its situation below three artificial lakes which were constructed to supply an aqueduct. On the lowest of these lakes, called Simbruina stagna, Nero built a villa, in the ruins of which was discovered the headless statue of a kneeling youth now in the Museo della Terme at Rome.

Sublicius, Pons, oldest of the bridges across the Tiber at Rome, traditionally founded by Ancus Marcius (q.v.). It was built of wood (*sublicae*: piles), and though often destroyed by flood it was always rebuilt of the same material. Its site was that of an ancient ford near the Insula Tiberina.

Subura or **Suburra,** a densely populated district of Rome. It lay in the valley between the Esquiline, Quirinal and Viminal hills, and contained numerous shops and brothels.

Suebi or **Suevi,** name given by the Romans to a group of people inhabiting central Germany, the chief of whom were the Marcomanni, Quadi, Hermanduri, Semnones and Langobardi. Tacitus, however, uses the name to include all the tribes in the basin of the Elbe, together with all those to the north and east thereof. Others, writing between the 2nd and the 4th century A.D., apply it almost exclusively to the Quadi.

Suessa (mod. Sessa) **Aurunca,** town of Campania, birth-place of the satirist Lucilius (q.v.); founded in 337 B.C. to take the place of

Aurunca or Ausona, the capital of the Aurunci (q.v.), which is believed to have been situated on the south-western rim of an extinct volcano now called Rocca Monfina. Suessa Aurunca received a Latin colony in 313 B.C., when it was first called by this name. There are considerable remains of an amphitheatre, of a gymnasium (under the church of S. Benedetto) and of a brickwork bridge.

Suessula, town of Campania at the entrance to the Caudine pass (*see* CAUDIUM), on the Via Popilia. There are remains of a Roman theatre. Somewhat to the east, M. Claudius Marcellus fortified a camp to serve as an outpost against Hannibal during the latter's occupation of Capua.

Suetonius Tranquillus, Gaius, Roman historian, born towards the end of the 1st century A.D. Son of a tribune of the Thirteenth Legion, he started his adult life as a teacher of rhetoric and an advocate. He was a friend of the younger Pliny, accompanied him to Bithynia (111) and afterwards exchanged many letters with him. It was indeed at Pliny's request that Trajan granted Suetonius the *ius trium liberorum*, although he had not the three sons necessary to qualify him for that privilege. Later, as secretary (*magister epistolarum*) to Hadrian, he had access to the imperial archives, upon which to draw in the preparation of his historical works; but he was dismissed in consequence of uncourtly behaviour towards the empress during Hadrian's absence in Britain. The date of his death is unknown.

Suetonius was the author of *Lives of the Caesars*, which, though not a general history, is an important source of our knowledge of the period. It deals (always with an ear to gossip) with the first twelve Caesars, Julius to Domitian. The language is straightforward, without ornament, but the chronological order is not observed. Parts of his *De viris illustribus* have also survived: these are the lives of Terence and Horace, fragments of those of Lucan and the elder Pliny, and most of the section on grammarians and rhetoricians. Lost works are an encyclopaedic miscellany entitled *Prata*, and treatises on the *Roman Year, Roman Institutions and Customs, Greek Children's Games, Roman Public Spectacles, The Kings* and *Cicero's Republic.* The surviving works have been edited by C. G. Baumgarten-Crusius (with commentary), 1816; C. L. Roth, 1886; J. C. Rolfe, 2 vols., with translation (Loeb Library), 1914. Philemon Holland's translation of the Lives (1606) is a classic in its own right; *see also* the rendering by Robert Graves (Penguin Books), 1959. There are also editions of separate lives, notably that of Julius (with historical introduction) by H. E. Butler and M. Cary, 1927.

Suevi, *see* SUEBI.

Sugambri, a German tribe dwelling between the rivers Sieg and Lippe. In the winter of 54–53 B.C. they crossed the Rhine and made the celebrated attack on Q. Cicero's camp at Atuatuca (*Bell. Gall.* vi, 35–40).

Sulla, Faustus Cornelius, son of L. Cornelius Sulla the dictator, born shortly before 88 B.C. Having served in Asia under Pompey, he married the latter's daughter Pompeia and sided with him in the civil war. He was present at the battle of Pharsalus (48 B.C.), and subsequently joined the leaders of his party in Africa. After Thapsus (46),

he was arrested by P. Sittius (q.v.) while attempting to escape into
Mauretania with his wife and children. They were taken to Caesar's
camp at Zama. A few days later Sulla was murdered in a tumult of
soldiers; but Caesar pardoned Pompeia and her children, and allowed
them to keep their property.

Sulla, Lucius Cornelius, surnamed Felix, Roman general and
statesman, was born in 138 B.C. One of his ancestors, P. Cornelius
Rufinus, was twice consul during the Samnite wars; and his great-
grandfather, P. Cornelius Sulla, was praetor in 212 B.C., when he presided over the first celebration of the Ludi Apollinares. Although his
father left him only a small property, Sulla received a good education,
and appears early to have imbibed the love of art and literature which
went hand in hand throughout his career with sensual vices.

He was quaestor in 107 under Marius (q.v.) in the Jugurthine war;
and it was to him that Jugurtha (q.v.) surrendered, an event which
marked the beginning of his rivalry with Marius. He continued,
however, to serve under Marius against the Cimbri and Teutones
from 104 until 102, when Marius's undisguised jealousy drove him to
take a command under Q. Lutatius Catulus (q.v.) with whom he
fought at Campi Raudii in the following year. In 93 he was praetor,
and in 92 was sent as propraetor to Cilicia with orders from the senate
to restore Ariobarzanes to the throne of Cappadocia, from which he
had been driven by Mithradates. This task fulfilled, he received a
Parthian embassy asking alliance with the republic, and returned in
91 to Rome.

Sulla's ability and reputation had led the aristocratic party to look
to him as their leader, and thus political animosity was added to
professional jealousy and personal hatred on the part of Marius. At
this stage, however, the outbreak of the Social war hushed all private
quarrels. Both men took an active part in hostilities against the
common foe; nevertheless, whereas Marius was now advancing in
years, Sulla gained some brilliant victories, notably his defeat of the
Samnites and capture of their chief town Bovianum. Sulla was consul
in 88, and ended the war by taking Nola. Meanwhile he had obtained
by lot command in the Mithradatic war. For the events which
followed—his flight from Rome and his return to the city at the head
of his legions—see MARIUS. Sulla remained at Rome until his year of
office had expired, and then set out to oppose Mithradates at the
beginning of 87. During the next four years he won a series of amazing
victories, and collected plunder beyond the dreams of avarice, at very
small cost to himself. Having sacked Athens (86), and cleared the
enemy from Greece, he crossed the Hellespont in 84 and in the same
year concluded peace with Mithradates.

Sulla now prepared to return to Italy, where the Marian party had
regained the upper hand (see CINNA; MARIUS). Leaving his legate, L.
Licinius Murena, as governor of Asia, and taking with him, among
other booty, the library of Apellicon (q.v.), he set out and landed at
Brundisium in the spring of 83. By promises and bribery he won over
or neutralized most of the forces which his enemies could bring against
him, leaving a few Samnites alone in arms. In 82 the struggle was
brought to a close, first by the defeat of the younger Marius at

Sacriportus near Praeneste, and then by the great victory over the Samnites under Pontius Telesinus before the Colline Gate at Rome.

Sulla was now absolute master of Rome and Italy; he resolved to take revenge upon his enemies and to extirpate the popular party. The steps he took are known to history as the 'Sullan proscription'. He was given the office of dictator and drew up a list (*proscriptio*) of men who were declared to be outlaws and enemies of the state. The reign of terror spread to the whole peninsula; fresh lists appeared; no one was safe, for Sulla gratified his friends by including in these fatal documents their personal enemies, or those whose property was coveted by his adherents. At the beginning of 81 he celebrated a magnificent triumph for his victories in the Mithradatic war, and devoted the following year to the carrying of his constitutional and administrative reforms. These were in effect a restoration of the senate to its old legislative and executive supremacy. Believing he could ensure the stability of his regime by the constant threat of arms, he established military colonies throughout the length and breadth of Italy. His personal safety was in the hands of a bodyguard created for this purpose by the emancipation of slaves who had belonged to persons proscribed by him. They were known as Cornelii after their patron, and are said to have numbered as many as ten thousand.

Quite suddenly, while at the very height of his power, Sulla resigned the dictatorship and withdrew into private life at Puteoli (79). Here, amid the beauties of Nature in her every aspect, he devoted such time as the imperious flesh allowed to the charms of literature and the preparation of his memoirs (now lost but used by Plutarch). Sulla died in 78 at the age of sixty. The immediate cause of death was rupture of a blood-vessel, but his dissolute way of life had already made him victim to the disease now called pediculosis. His reforms were unsuited to the times; they scarcely survived him, except for the *quaestiones perpetuae* (permanent tribunals), which formed the basis of all future criminal justice. See Life by Plutarch; C. W. Oman, *Seven Roman Statesmen*, 1902.

Sulla, Publius Cornelius, nephew of L. Cornelius Sulla the dictator. He and P. Autronius Paetus were elected consuls for the year 65 B.C.; but neither took office, as they were accused of bribery by L. Manlius Torquatus and condemned. It was currently believed that Sulla and his brother Servius were privy to both Catiline's conspiracies. In the civil war he supported Caesar, served under him as legate in Greece and commanded the right wing at Pharsalus. He died in 45 B.C.

Sulmo (mod. Sulmona), town in the country of the Sabines, birthplace of Ovid and famous for its ironsmiths.

Sulpicia, name of two Roman poetesses. The first lived under Augustus and was the author of six artless love poems of great beauty, addressed to one Cerinthus, which are preserved among the works of Tibullus (iv. 7–12). The second lived during the reign of Domitian and wrote verses full of wifely devotion towards her husband Calonus, but none has survived.

Sulpicius Rufus, Publius (*c.* 121–88 B.C.), Roman politician. He was quaestor in 93, and in 89 served as legate to the consul Cn. Pompeius Strabo during the Social war. In 88, as tribune of the plebs, he deserted the aristocrats in favour of Marius and the popular party. He then proceeded to introduce a franchise bill, which, despite senatorial opposition, was forced through by violence and followed in due course by the appointment of Marius to command in the first Mithradatic war. Sulla (q.v.) thereupon marched on Rome; Marius and Sulpicius Rufus fled, but the latter was caught hiding in a villa at Laurentum and put to death.

Sulpicius Rufus, Servius, a friend of and about the same age as Cicero, who considered him one of the noblest characters, one of the best jurists, and quite the finest orator of that time. He espoused the cause of Caesar during the civil war, and was appointed by him governor of Achaea (46 or 45 B.C.). In 43 B.C. he was sent by the senate on a mission to Antony, who was besieging Brutus in Mutina, and died of sickness in Antony's camp.

Summanus, 'highest', an ancient Etruscan deity, adopted by the Romans as god of the nocturnal sky. His temple at Rome, near the Circus Maximus, was built in 278 B.C., and his feast was celebrated on 20th June. He was one of the Consentes Dii (q.v.).

Sunium (Sounion), the most southerly promontory of Attica, rising to some 300 feet above the sea. Here was a temple of Poseidon, built of white marble in the time of Pericles on the site of an earlier shrine. It served as a landmark for shipping, and its thirteen remaining columns still present a beautiful sight from the sea. A few hundred yards to the north-east was a temple of Athena.

Surenas, a Parthian general who defeated and slew M. Licinius Crassus at Carrhae in 53 B.C.

Surrentum (mod. Sorrento), town of Campania, on the promontory which forms the southern limit of the Sinus Cumanus (Bay of Naples). Famous for its wine, fish and red Campanian vases, it also possessed the only known temple in the Greek world dedicated to the Sirens (q.v.). The walls and original lay-out of the town can still be traced, and there are remains of an enormous Roman reservoir once supplied by subterranean aqueducts.

Susarion (Sousariōn), Greek comic poet of the 6th century B.C. He was said to have brought the old Megarian comedy to Icaria, in Attica, the most ancient seat of the worship of Dionysus, c. 570 B.C.

Sutrium (mod. Sutri), town of Etruria, on the Via Cassia. It fell into Roman hands after the destruction of Veii (396 B.C.), and its strategic importance as one of the 'keys of Etruria' (Livy) gave rise to the proverb 'Sutrium ire' used by Plautus of one who goes on important business. South of the town is the rock-hewn church of Madonna del Parto, once a Mithraeum (see MITHRAS), and remains of an amphi-theatre.

Sybaris (Su-), city of Magna Graecia, on the Gulf of Tarentum, between the rivers Sybaris and Crathis (mod. Coscile and Crati), which in ancient times had separate mouths but now join three miles from the sea. Founded c. 720 B.C. by Achaeans and Troezenians, it attained in the 6th century unparalleled wealth and splendour, and became a byword for effeminate luxury. Internal dissensions resulted in a number of citizens taking refuge at Croton. The Crotoniats were soon at war with Sybaris, which they razed to the ground in 510, and diverted the River Cràthis over its ruins. The site was identified by electronic instruments in 1963.

Symplegades (Sumplēgadai), two legendary islands which were supposed to clash together (*sumplēssein*) and crush any ship that tried to pass between them. Eventually the Argonauts (q.v.) managed to get through, and thereafter the islands remained fixed. They were identified with the Cyaneae Insulae at the entrance to the Hellespont.

Symposium (Sumposion), a Greek word meaning literally a drinking party. At Athens, however, drinking was not the predominant element; music, table games and, above all, conversation were the principal attractions. *See* Plato's *Symposium*.

Syphax, King of the Massaesyli, the westernmost tribe of Numidia (q.v.). Defeated and taken prisoner by Masinissa (q.v.) in 203 B.C., he was sent by Scipio to Rome, and died there soon afterwards. *See also* SOPHONISBA.

Syracuse (Gk Surakousai; Lat. Syracusae; mod. Siracusa), city of Sicily, founded by Corinthian and other Dorian colonists in 734 B.C. Archaeological research, however, has shown that the island of Ortygia off the mainland was inhabited before the Greeks settled there. The town of Syracuse was originally confined to the island, which is about two miles in circumference. At the time of its greatest prosperity it had two harbours. The Great Harbour, still called *Porto Maggiore*, is a bay about five miles in circumference formed by the island Ortygia and the promontory Plemmyrium. The Small Harbour, also called Laeceius, lying between Ortygia and Achradina, was capacious enough to receive a large fleet of ships. There were several stone quarries (*lautumiae*) in Syracuse, in which the Athenian prisoners were confined (413 B.C.). (Thucydides, vii; Plutarch, *Life of Nicias*.) The modern city of Syracuse is limited to the island. Of the ruins of the ancient town the most important are those of the great theatre, and of an amphitheatre of the Roman period. The government of Syracuse was originally an aristocracy, and afterwards a democracy, till Gelon made himself tyrant in 485 B.C. Under his rule and that of his brother Hieron, Syracuse became prosperous. Hieron died in 467, and was succeeded by his brother Thrasybulus: but the cruelty of the latter provoked a revolt which led to his deposition and the establishment of a democracy. The next most important event in the history of Syracuse was the siege of the city by the Athenians, which ended in the total destruction of the great Athenian armament in 413. The democracy continued till 405, when the elder Dionysius (q.v.) became tyrant. After a prosperous reign he was succeeded in 367 by his son, the younger Dionysius, who was expelled by Timoleon in 343. A republican government was established, but it did not last, and in 317 Syracuse fell under the sway of Agathocles. This tyrant died in 289, and the city being distracted by factions, the Syracusans conferred the power upon Hieron II, with the title of king, in 270. Hieron cultivated friendly relations with the Romans; but on his death in 216, at the age of ninety-two, his grandson Hieronymus, who succeeded him, espoused the side of the Carthaginians. A Roman army under Marcellus was sent against Syracuse, and after a siege of two years the city was taken in 211 B.C. From this time Syracuse became a town of the Roman province of Sicily. *See* E. A. Freeman, *History of Sicily*, 1890-4).

Syria, originally known as Aram ('the highlands'); general name for the country north and north-east of Palestine. In a wider sense the word was used for the whole tract of country bounded by the Tigris on the east, Mediterranean on the west, Arabian Desert on the south and the mountains of Armenia on the north. At the beginning of the Hebrew monarchy Syria was divided into petty kingdoms, which were generally at war with Israel. As the great Assyrian kingdom waxed, Syria waned, and Damascus was destroyed by Tiglath Pileser, King of Assyria, who conquered all Syria (middle of 8th century B.C.). After having been a part successively of the Assyrian, Babylonian, Persian and Macedonian empires, Syria once more became powerful under the rule of Seleucus Nicator (312 B.C.), with Antioch for its capital. Its strength was increased by Antiochus the Great; it was then that Palestine became a Syrian province. In 64 B.C., after the destruction of the kingdom of Syria (*see* TIGRANES), Syria was added by Pompey to the possessions of the republic, and became a Roman province; as such it is mentioned in the New Testament. Much later Zenobia attempted to make Syria the seat of empire. The Roman emperors defended Syria from Persian attacks; but the country was not finally disposed of till the great Arabian invasion and conquest in the 7th century A.D. *See* E. S. Bouchier, *Syria as a Roman Province*, 1916; H. R. Hall, *Ancient History of the Near East*, 11th ed., 1950; P. K. Hitta, *History of Syria*, 1951.

Syria Dea, the 'Syrian goddess' of Hierapolis, otherwise known as Atargatis or Astarte, whose Greek counterpart was Aphrodite (q.v.). She was a goddess of generation or fecundity; her rites, which were celebrated by men dressed as women, and which are described by Lucian, spread to Greece and Italy. In the 3rd century A.D. the cult of these goddesses was favoured at Rome by the empress Julia Domna, her sister and her nieces; it was introduced even into the palace of the Caesars by Elagabalus.

Syrinx (Suringx), Greek name for the pan-pipes. A legend told how an Arcadian nymph, pursued by Pan, fled into the River Ladon, where, at her own request, she was transformed into a reed (*suringx*), of which Pan made his pipes.

T

Tabularium, a building at the west end of the Forum at Rome, along the side of the Capitoline hill. Dating from 78 B.C., it housed the national archives (*see* ACTA; ACTA DIURNA; ACTA SENATUS).

Tacitus, Marcus Claudius, Roman emperor 25th September A.D. 275 until March 276. He was seventy years of age at the time of his election, and accepted the purple with great reluctance; but he amply sustained the high character which he had borne before his elevation. He died at Tyana in Cappadocia.

Tacitus, Publius Cornelius (*c.* A.D. 55–*c.* 120), Roman historian. In 78 he married the daughter of Cn. Julius Agricola (q.v.), who became governor of Britain in the same year. Tacitus was praetor in 88, and assisted as a *quindecimvir* at the *Ludi Saeculares*; he was consul suffectus in A.D. 97–8, and governor of Asia 112–13. At this point our information fails. Among Pliny's letters are eleven addressed to Tacitus, who was his intimate friend. The extant works are as follows: *Dialoguus de Oratoribus,* a treatise on the decline of rhetoric; *Agricola,* a portrait of his father-in-law; *Germania,* a valuable ethnographical work: *Historiae,* a history of the empire from Galba to Domitian (68–96) in twelve or fourteen books, of which only i–iv and part of v remain; and *Annales,* a history of the empire from the death of Augustus to that of Nero, of which books vii–x and parts of v, xi and xvi are lost.

Though Tacitus did not, perhaps, quite attain his ideal of writing without prejudice, he remains the most reliable witness for the period covered by his works. His style is unique—rapid and condensed, combining great force with biting epigram, and often rising to unsurpassed heights of sonority and splendour. His power derives largely from his knowledge of the human heart and its motives, and for this study he found abundant material in the history of the emperors. The best edition is that of C. D. Fisher and H. Furneaux (Oxford Classical Texts). There are translations of the *Histories* by G. G. Ramsay, 1915; of the *Annales* by A. T. Church and W. J. Brodribb, 1921; of *Agricola* and *Germania* by H. Mattingley, 1948; and of the *Dialogues* by Sir W. Peterson (Loeb Library). *See* G. W. Mendell, *Tacitus,* 1958.

Taenarum (Tainaron), now called Cape Matapan, a promontory of Laconia and most southerly point of Peloponnesus. Here stood a temple of Poseidon which afforded inviolable sanctuary, and in the neighbourhood were valuable marble quarries. A cave in the vicinity was said to be that through which Heracles dragged Cerberus from the underworld. *See* TWELVE LABOURS OF HERACLES, 12.

Tages, an Etruscan deity. His legend tells how a man was ploughing a field near Tarquinii when a creature of boyish appearance sprang from the furrow. The ploughman's shouts assembled all the folk of Etruria, whom the lad then instructed in the art of divination (*see*
491

HARUSPICES), and suddenly disappeared. His words were said to have been transmitted by word of mouth, until they were eventually written down to form the Twelve Books of Tages, a manual of Etruscan love. *See* Cicero, *De Divinatione*, ii. 23.

Talaus (-os), legendary king of Argos, father of Adrastus (q.v.).

Talos, a bronze giant in Crete. He was guardian of that island, and among his devices for keeping it free from strangers was to make himself red hot and embrace the unwelcome guest. *See* Sir J. G. Frazer's note on Pausanias, i. 21, sec. 4.

Talthybius (-thubios), herald of Agamemnon at Troy. In historical times he was worshipped as a hero at Sparta and Argos.

Tanagra, town of Boeotia. Situated close to the Attic border, it was exposed to attack by the Athenians, but the latter were themselves defeated here in 457 B.C. by a Spartan force on its way back from Doris (Thucydides, i. 107, 108). The statuettes recovered from the site of Tanagra are characteristic of the best Greek work in terra-cotta; they date from between 350 and 200 B.C.

Tantalus (-os), legendary king of Sipylus in Lydia, father of Pelops and Niobe. He was a son of Zeus by the nymph Pluto, but was punished everlastingly for a sin of which several variants are given. According to Pindar it was the murder of his son Pelops (q.v.). Diodorus Siculus relates that he was admitted to the table of the gods, but revealed to mankind their secrets. Pindar also makes him steal nectar and ambrosia from heaven on behalf of men; and there are yet other versions. The form of his punishment, as described by Homer, was as follows. He stood up to his neck in water which flowed from him whenever he tried to drink; and over his head hung fruit which was blown out of reach by the wind every time he attempted to grasp it (hence the English word 'tantalize'). For the fruit, Euripides (*Orestes*, 5) substitutes a rock which was ever ready to fall and crush him.

Tarentum (mod. Taranto), city of Magna Graecia, situated in fertile country on the west coast of the Calabrian peninsula. It was colonized by Lacedaemonians under Phalanthus in 708 B.C., and became the most flourishing city of that region. The inhabitants were notorious for their love of luxury, and in the second half of the 4th century B.C. they were attacked by the Lucanians and other Italian peoples of the neighbourhood. The Spartan Archidamus (338) and King Alexander I of Epirus (*c.* 330 B.C.) both came to their assistance, but both were killed in action. About fifty years later the Tarentines were so misguided as to attack some Roman ships, and to insult the ambassadors who came to demand reparation. War was declared by Rome (*see* PYRRHUS), and the city was ultimately captured in 272 B.C. It revolted to Hannibal in 213, but was retaken in 209. From that date its prosperity declined, but it was still a place of some importance under Augustus.

Tarpeia, in Roman legend, daughter of Spurius Tarpeius who was commander of the Capitol during the war with the Sabines resulting from the rape of the Sabine women. Tarpeia offered to betray the Capitol to the besiegers if they would give her what they wore on their left arms, meaning their bracelets. The agreement was made, and

Tarpeia opened one of the gates. The Sabines, however, obeyed the letter of their undertaking by crushing her to death with their shields. The Tarpeian rock was a place for the execution of traitors; but it is unlikely that the tradition arose to account for this fact. More probably Tarpeia was a local deity in whose cult a heap of shields played some part and suggested the manner of her death, which in turn gave rise to the story of her crime.

Tarquinii, city of Etruria, the traditional home of the Tarquins (*see* next article). It was subsequently a Roman colony and municipium. Etruscan painted tombs have been excavated. *See* M. Pallottino, *Tarquinii*, 1937.

Tarquinius, Lucius, name of two legendary Etruscan kings of Rome:

1. Called by Livy 'Priscus'. Demaratus, a Corinthian nobleman, settled at Tarquinii in Etruria and married an Etruscan lady, Tanaquil, who bore him two sons, Lucumo and Aruns. Lucumo, the elder, inherited his father's property; but despite his wealth and social rank he was excluded from public life as an alien. Dissatisfied with this state of affairs, he set out for Rome, riding in a chariot with his wife and accompanied by a large train of followers. When they reached the Janiculum an eagle appeared and seized Lucumo's cap, carried it high into the air, then swooped down and replaced it on his head. Tanaquil, expert in Etruscan divination, interpreted the event as an omen of the most favourable kind, and she was not mistaken. The stranger was welcomed, admitted to citizenship, took the names Lucius Tarquinius, and was eventually chosen to succeed Ancus Marcius (q.v.). His exploits in war included the subjugation of both Latins and Sabines; the latter people ceded to him the town of Collatia, where he placed a garrison commanded by his nephew Egerius, who called himself Tarquinius Collatinus. Tarquinius was also said to have made constitutional changes, and to have erected many public buildings and other works. He was murdered after a reign of thirty-eight years (616–578 B.C.) by the sons of Ancus Marcius, and was succeeded by Servius Tullius (q.v.). *See* KINGS OF ROME.

2. Called by Livy 'Superbus', son of the preceding, obtained the throne by murdering Servius Tullius (q.v.) in 534 B.C. According to the legend he abolished the rights conferred on the plebeians, and put to death or exiled all whom he mistrusted or whose wealth he coveted. Nevertheless he enhanced the power and prosperity of Rome, and made her head of the Latin confederacy. He defeated the Volsci, took the wealthy city of Suessa Pometia and used its spoils to build the Capitol (*see* CAPITOLIUM), which had been vowed by his father and in the vaults of which he deposited the Sibylline Books (*see* SIBYL). The glory of Tarquin was crowned by the capture of Gabii, but owing to an outrage committed by his son Sextus (*see* next article) he was expelled and the monarchy abolished (510 B.C.). While Sextus fled to Gabii, Tarquin and his two younger sons went to Caere. There they enlisted the support of Veii and Tarquinii, and subsequently of Clusium (*see* PORSENA). None, however, could overpower the new republic. Finally Tarquinius had recourse to his son-in-law, Octavius Mamilius (q.v.) of Tusculum, at whose instigation the Latin states combined against Rome, but were defeated at the battle of Lake

Regillus (*see* REGILLUS, LACUS). Tarquin submitted to his fate and died at Dumae.

The fame of Tarquin's story makes it all the more necessary to emphasize that the tale is mere fiction, and represents only a short-lived Etruscan supremacy in Latium. The details narrated above are no more than the stock-in-trade of ballad writers.

Tarquinius, Sextus, in the legendary history of Rome, son of L. Tarquinius Superbus (*see* TARQUINIUS, LUCIUS, 2). When his father failed to take Gabii at the first assault, Sextus resorted to a stratagem. Pretending to have been ill-treated by his father, he appeared at Gabii covered with the marks of scourging. The citizens entrusted him with the command of their army; he thus reduced the place to submission, and received it from the elder Tarquin as his principality. His next step proved the undoing of his house: by raping Lucretia (q.v.), wife of his cousin Collatinus, he caused the expulsion of the Tarquin family from Rome. Sextus withdrew to Gabii, where he was murdered soon afterwards by the friends of those whom he had put to death when he first obtained possession of the city.

Tarraco (mod. Tarragona), ancient city on the east coast of Spain. Augustus, who wintered here after his Cantabrian campaign (25 B.C.), made it the capital of Hispania Tarraconensis, and founded a Roman colony. There are remains of walls (6th century B.C.), and many Roman relics, including an amphitheatre and an aqueduct.

Tarsus (-os), now called Tersous, the birth-place of St Paul, an ancient city of Cilicia (q.v.), on the River Cydnus which flowed through it. It seems to have been founded by Ionian Greeks before the mid 9th century B.C., and its future importance was due to the fertility of its neighbourhood, to its possession of an excellent harbour and to its command of the road leading across the Taurus range through the Cilician Gates. Though Greek by origin, its geographical situation made it even in the 2nd century A.D. more Phoenician than Greek in character. Subject in turn to native princes, to Persia, to Alexander the Great and to the Seleucids, it was made autonomous by Antiochus IV, Epiphanes, in 171 B.C. Under the Romans Tarsus was one of the greatest and wealthiest cities of the East. Here, in 42 B.C., Antony met Cleopatra; in A.D. 72 it was made capital of the Roman province of Cilicia; and Augustus granted it immunity from taxes through the influence of the emperor's former tutor Athenodorus Cananites (q.v.), who was a native of Tarsus and taught at its university.

Tartarus (-os), in Greek mythology, a place as far below Hades (q.v.) as heaven is above the earth, reserved for the rebellious Titans (q.v.). Later poets, however, use the name as synonymous with Hades.

Tartessus, a Phoenician settlement on the south coast of Spain, probably the Tarshish of Scripture. In 170 B.C. it was colonized by 4,000 Roman soldiers and renamed Carteia. Some ancient writers apply the name Tartessis to the whole southern part of the country west of Fretum Gaditanum (Straits of Gibraltar).

Tauri (-oi), inhabitants of Chersonesus Taurica (mod. Crimea). According to legend they sacrificed strangers to a goddess whom the Greeks identified with Artemis (q.v.). *See* IPHIGENEIA.

Tauris, *see* CHERSONESUS TAURICA.

Tauromenium (mod. Taormina), city on the east coast of Sicily, 27 miles south-west of Messana and within sight of Mt Aetna. It was founded by Greeks *c.* 398 B.C. Ruins include a Greek theatre rebuilt by the Romans, and several Roman buildings.

Taÿgetus (Taügetos), mountain range of Laconia (q.v.) running southwards from the Arcadian mountains to Taenarum (Cape Matapan). The range was well watered, and its forests supplied abundant game. Its mineral wealth consisted of iron and marble (*see* TAENARUM).

Tecmessa (Tek-), in Greek legend, daughter of the Phrygian king Teleutas, whose territory was ravaged by the Greeks during a predatory expedition from Troy. Tecmessa was made captive and given to Telamonian Ajax, by whom she was the mother of Eurysaces.

Tegea, town of Arcadia; named after a legendary founder, Tegeates, son of Lycaon. It was long subject to the hegemony of Sparta, but became independent with other Arcadian towns after the Spartan defeat at Leuctra (371 B.C.). Tegea possessed a famous temple of Athena (394 B.C.). Extensive excavations have been made.

Telamōn, son of Aeacus and brother of Peleus (qq.v.). Having assisted Peleus to slay their half-brother Phocus, he fled from Aegina to Salamis, where he married Glauce, daughter of the island's king, Cychreus, whom he succeeded. He married secondly Periboea, daughter of Alcathoüs (q.v.), by whom he was the father of Ajax (*see* AJAX, I). He also took part in the Calydonian hunt (*see* MELEAGER) and was one of the Argonauts (q.v.). Accompanying Heracles (q.v.) in his expedition against Laomedon of Troy, he was first to enter the city. Heracles rewarded him with the gift of Laomedon's sister Hesione (q.v.), who bore him a son Teucer (q.v.).

Telegonus (Tēlegonos), son of Odysseus (q.v.) by Circe. Sent by her to find Odysseus, he landed in Ithaca, but was attacked by his father and Telemachus, who imagined him a pirate. Having slain Odysseus, not knowing who he was, he conveyed the body to Circe for burial, and later married the widowed Penelope.

Telemachus (Tēlemakhos), son of Odysseus (q.v.) and Penelope, a child when his father set out for Troy. After about twenty years he set sail in search of news of him, visiting Pylos and Sparta, and returning to Ithaca in time to help his father in the celebrated massacre of the suitors.

Telephus (Tēlephos), in Greek legend, a son of Heracles. He became King of Mysia, and attempted to oppose the Greeks when they landed in Asia on the way to Troy. Wounded by Achilles and informed by an oracle that none could cure the wound but he who had inflicted it, Telephus went to the Greek camp, where another oracle had proclaimed that none but Telephus could show the way to Troy. Achilles therefore healed his wound with rust from the spear that had caused it, and Telephus provided details of the road.

Tempē, valley in northern Thessaly (q.v.), famous for its beautiful scenery, to which there are many references in ancient literature. It was the legendary scene of Apollo's purification after the slaying of Python, and of Daphne's metamorphosis.

Ten Thousand, Expedition of The, an army originally composed partly of large levies of native troops in the Persian satrapies of Asia Minor, but mainly of Greek mercenaries collected by Cyrus, younger son of Darius II of Persia, who hoped to win the crown from his elder brother Artaxerxes II. At the battle of Cunaxa (401 B.C.) the Greeks routed their opponents, but Cyrus was killed. The native levies at once dispersed, and the Greek mercenaries found themselves isolated in Mesopotamia. Their officers were killed by a trick of the enemy. The men chose new officers, among them Xenophon (q.v.), the historian of the expedition, and fought their way north into the Armenian mountains. Ultimately they reached the Euxine at Trapezus. The journey caused a great sensation throughout the Greek world, and, by revealing the weakness of Persia, did much to pave the way for Alexander's undertaking. *See* TISSAPHERNES.

Tencteri and Usipetes, German tribes inhabiting the basins of the Lahn and the Ruhr respectively. In 55 B.C. they invaded Gaul and were annihilated by Caesar (*Bell. Gall.* iv. 1, 7–9, 11–15).

Tenedos, Aegean island off the coast of Troas. In legend it was the place to which the Greeks withdrew their fleet, to make the Trojans think they had departed. During the Persian war (480) it was used by Xerxes as a naval base, and afterwards joined the Delian League (q.v.). It was surrendered to Persia by the Peace of Antalcidas (386 B.C.), and was not liberated until the Asian conquests of Alexander.

Tentyra (mod. Dendera), city of Egypt and principal seat of the worship of Hathor, the cow-goddess of love and joy, whom the Greeks identified with Aphrodite. The temple of Hathor, begun under the later Ptolemies, was completed by Augustus; the two stone gateways in the enclosure wall were built by Domitian. Tentyra has been immortalized by the 15th satire of Juvenal, which concerns a religious riot between the Tentyrites and the inhabitants of Ombos, about 15 miles away.

Terence, *see* TERENTIUS.

Terentia, first wife of Cicero, to whom she bore the younger Marcus and a daughter Tullia. Her firmness of character was of great service to her vacillating husband at some critical periods of his life, but he divorced her in 47 B.C. She is said to have died at the age of 103.

Terentius Afer, Publius, called in English **Terence,** Latin comic poet, born *c.* 195 B.C. at Carthage, probably of Libyan stock. Brought to Rome as a slave by P. Terentius Lucanus, he received a good education and was afterwards manumitted. He died in 159 B.C. Six of his plays are extant: *Andria* (166 B.C.), *Hecyra* (165), *Heautontimoroumenos* (163), *Eunuchus* (162), *Phormio* (162) and *Adelphi,* which was first performed at the funeral games of L. Aemilius Paulus (160). Four of these are adaptations from Menander, two from Apollodorus. Supreme in point of both style and dramatic skill, Terence influenced many later writers, including Molière. The best edition is that of R. Kauer and W. M. Lindsay, 1926. There is a prose translation by J. Sargeaunt in the Loeb Library. *See* G. Norwood, *Terence,* 1923; W. Beare, *The Roman Stage,* 1950.

Tēreus, in Greek legend, son of King Ares of Daulis in Phocis. He married Procne, daughter of Pandion, King of Athens, who bore him a son, Itys. Wishing to marry her sister Philomela, he concealed Procne in the country, and told Philomela she was dead; then, having married Philomela, he cut out her tongue. Philomela, however, soon learned the truth and made it known to her sister by a few words woven into a garment. Procne thereupon slew Itys and served up his flesh to Tereus. The sisters fled, Tereus pursuing with an axe. Before they were overtaken they appealed to the gods for help, and their prayer was heard: Procne became a nightingale, Philomela a swallow, Tereus a hoopoo. Ovid (*Metam.* vi. 565) reverses the roles of Procne and Philomela. Some writers make Procne the swallow, Philomela the nightingale, Tereus a hawk.

Terminus, Roman god of boundaries and frontiers. His cult was supposed to have been introduced by Numa, who made everyone mark the boundaries of his land with stones consecrated to Jupiter, and offer yearly sacrifices at these stones. The festival, *Terminalia*, was celebrated on 23rd February.

Terpander (-dros), Greek musician and lyric poet of the mid 7th century B.C., born at Antissa in Lesbos (q.v.). He has been called the father of Greek lyric poetry, but no genuine fragment of his work survives.

Terpsichore (-khorē), muse of choral dance and song. *See* Muses.

Terra sigillata, Latin name for the medicinal earth of Lemnos (q.v.).

Testudo, 'tortoise', Roman military term for the massed overlapping shields covering troops as they advanced to the assault of a town. It denoted also a frame covered with skins or clay, used to protect the battering-ram (*aries*).

Tethys (Tēthus), in Greek mythology, daughter of Uranus and Gē (*see* TITANS), and wife of Oceanus (q.v.), to whom she bore the Oceanids (*see* NYMPHS) and the river-gods. She was also the teacher of Hera.

Tetricus, Gaius Esuvius, last of the so-called Thirty Tyrants (q.v.) who sprang up during the reigns of Valerian and Gallienus. He ruled in Gaul from A.D. 270 to 274, when he was defeated by Aurelian at Chalons.

Teucer (Teukros). Son of Telamon by Hesione (qq.v.), was the best archer among the Greeks before Troy and founded the town of Salamis (*see* SALAMIS, 2) in Cyprus.

Teuthras, legendary king of Mysia; father of Thespius, who had fifty daughters called by Ovid *Teuthrantia turba*.

Teutones or **Teutoni**, a Germanic tribe first mentioned by Pytheas (q.v.) as living on the coast of what was afterwards called Holstein. They migrated and wandered with the Cimbri (q.v.) from 102 B.C. until their annihilation by Marius (q.v.) at the battle of Aquae Sextiae (102 B.C.).

Thaïs, Athenian courtesan who accompanied Alexander the Great to Asia (334 B.C.). After his death she attached herself to Ptolemy, and bore him two sons and a daughter: Leontiscus, Lagus and Irene.

Thalēs (*fl.* 600 B.C.), Ionian philosopher and one of the Seven Sages of Greece, born at Miletus *c.* 636 and died *c.* 546. He taught that water, or moisture, was the one element from which all things evolved. He appears to have owed much to Egyptian and Mesopotamian influences. Thales is regarded as founder of abstract geometry, of the strict deductive form as shown in Euclid's collections; he is said to have shown how to calculate the distance of a ship at sea, and the heights of objects. In astronomy he was credited by ancient authorities with prediction of the total solar eclipse identified by many modern astronomers with that of 28th May 585 B.C.; he is said to have noted the Lesser Bear and to have shown its superiority for the purposes of navigation. *See* Sir T. Heath, *Greek Astronomy*, 1932.

Thamugadi (mod. Timgad), city of Numidia in a rich agricultural district, about 20 miles east of Lambaesis (q.v.). Founded in A.D. 100 by the emperor Trajan, it enjoyed its greatest prosperity in the reigns of Septimius Severus and Caracalla (193–217), but afterwards declined. The state of the ruins, which have been fully excavated, is surpassed only by that of Leptis Magna (q.v.). *See* A. Ballu, *Les Ruines de Timgad*, 1902.

Thamyris (-muris), legendary Thracian bard, son of Philammon (q.v.). He challenged the Muses to a trial of skill, and was struck blind and dumb for his presumption. He was represented in art with a broken lyre.

Thanatos (Lat. Mors), in Greek mythology, personification of death; son of Nyx and brother of Hypnos (qq.v.).

Thapsus, city of north Africa, celebrated for Caesar's victory over the Pompeians under Cato, Metellus Scipio and King Juba II in late May 46 B.C.

Thargēlia, chief Athenian festival of Apollo, celebrated on 6th and 7th of the month Thargelion (May–June). Human sacrifice (*see* PHARMAKOI) was offered in early times. *See* Jane Harrison, *Prolegomena*, 1922.

Thasos, island in the northern Aegean, off the coast of Thrace. It was early occupied by Phoenicians on account of its gold mines, but was subsequently (708 B.C.) colonized by Parian settlers, among whom was the poet Archilochus (q.v.). The Thasians once possessed considerable territory on the coast of Thrace, and were one of the richest and most powerful communities in that area. Subjugated by Persia, they regained their freedom in 479 B.C., and joined the Delian League. They revolted, however, in 465 and were not subdued until they had endured a three-year siege. A second revolt, in 411, was more successful; but the island was restored to Athens by Thrasybulus in 409 B.C. Thasos was the birth-place of Polygnotus.

Theanō: 1. Daughter of Cisseus, sister of Hecuba and wife of Antenor (qq.v.).

2. Female member of the Pythagorean school, supposed to have been the wife (or daughter) of Pythagoras.

Theatre (Gk *Theatron*; Lat. *Theatrum*). The religious origins of Greek drama made it essentially a popular art, so that the theatre in which it was presented had to provide for the accommodation (standing and later seating) of a very large audience. In the earliest theatres these requirements were met by a suitable hillside with a level circular space (*orkhēstra*) at its foot, in the centre of which an altar was erected. The primitive Greek theatre thus assumed its shape, having seats in a slightly extended semicircle (the *theatron* or auditorium) around the orchestra. At Athens, about 465 B.C., the orchestra was moved 50 feet forward, and on the farther side a small wooden hut (*skēnē*) was built as a dressing-room for the actors. It had a long front wall with projecting wings towards either end, between which a stage was probably raised a foot or so above the level of the orchestra. This stage was possibly backed with a row of columns (*proskēnion*, proscenium), originally also of wood, behind which was the wall pierced by doors for the actors' entrances and exits.

By the 3rd and 2nd centuries B.C., the chorus had practically disappeared from tragedy; and although choral odes were still retained in comedy, they had become separate interludes. The *skēnē* was generally two-storeyed, with a row of columns some to 10 feet in front, the space between filled in with painted boards, and on top a platform on which the actors performed. Immediately behind and above this was the proscenium, which usually had three doors. By Graeco-Roman times the stage front and the background had been altered. The proscenium was more elaborate and dominated the theatre with its columns, doors and architectural embellishments. Spectacular scenic effects were eagerly sought. The *paraskēnia* now formed part of the theatre's structure. Low platforms carrying scenic effects could be pushed on to the stage through the doors; semicircular and triangular turntables painted with tragic, comic and satyric designs; a hook-and-pulley device for lowering and raising gods from and to the heavens; trap-doors in the orchestra, through which ghosts and other spirits could appear; means of producing lightning, thunder, fires, etc. —all these are either recorded or to be inferred from a study of the plays.

Stage costume was highly stylized. Certain conventions fully established by Aeschylus's day remained unchanged until Roman times. Although the earlier tragedies had usually been set in the legendary era, the tragic actor's dress was always that of the 5th century B.C.

The Roman theatre differed from the Greek, first, in having nothing to do with religion, and secondly, in being built on level instead of sloping ground, possibly for the sake of a more imposing architectural exterior. The auditorium was an exact semicircle around the orchestra space, the farther half occupied by the stage, the front half being used sometimes for additional seating accommodation and sometimes for gladiatorial or other spectacular displays, when it could be railed off from the audience. The stage doors in the front wall (*hyposcenium*) and steps down to the orchestra were usual. This wall was no longer plain, but decorated in keeping with the embellishment of the *frons scoenae* at the back of the stage, from which a roof stretched over it. Awnings over the auditorium were also provided.

Greek tragedy and comedy introduced to Rome quickly degenerated into dance and satirical mime, and the status of the Roman actor never approached the dignity of that of his Greek predecessor. In the original Greek drama the poet himself would play the leading part and train the chorus. Actors were originally amateurs; but later companies of actors were formed with their own guild, and were held in high esteem. In Rome the custom of maintaining troupes of actors,

mostly slaves, and the introduction of women to the stage, made the
profession generally and deservedly despised. *See* A. F. Haigh, *The
Attic Theatre* (revised by A. W. Pickard, Cambridge), 1907. *See also*
AESCHYLUS; ARISTOPHANES; EURIPIDES; SOPHOCLES; THESPIS.

  Theban Legend, The : 1. Cadmus (q.v.) had by his wife Harmonia
four daughters, Semele and Ino (qq.v.), Agave and Autonoë (*see*
PENTHEUS), and a son named Polydorus. The latter succeeded
Pentheus as third king of Thebes. He was father of Labdacus, who
was succeeded by his son Laius. Laius married Jocasta, great-grand-
daughter of Pentheus and sister of Creon (*see* below), by whom he had
an only son.

  2. This child, immediately after birth, was exposed on Mt Cithaeron with his feet pierced and tied together, because Laius had
been told by an oracle that he would die by the hand of his own son.
The baby was found by a shepherd in the employ of King Polybus of
Corinth, and named Oedipus from his swollen feet. Polybus reared
him as his own child; but when Oedipus had grown up he was told by
the oracle at Delphi that he would slay his father and marry his
mother. Thinking that Polybus was his father, he would not return to
Corinth; but on the road between Delphi and Daulis he met Laius,
whom he slew in a scuffle without knowing who he was. Meanwhile the
Sphinx (q.v.) had appeared in the neighbourhood of Thebes. Seated
on a rock, she put a riddle to every passer-by: 'What goes on four
feet in the morning, on two feet at noon, and on three feet in the
evening?' Those who could not answer correctly were slain by the
monster. In this terrible predicament the Thebans now swore that
whoever delivered the country of the Sphinx should obtain the kingdom and Jocasta as his wife. Along came Oedipus from Delphi and
solved the riddle. The being in question, said he, is Man, who in
infancy goes on all fours, in his prime on two feet, and in old age
supported by a staff. The Sphinx straightway threw herself down
from the rock; Oedipus was hailed as King of Thebes and married
Jocasta—his own mother, by whom he begot Eteocles, Polynices,
Antigone and Ismene. Thebes was then visited by a plague. The oracle
directed that the murderer of Laius should be expelled, and the seer
Tiresias (q.v.) told Oedipus that he was the guilty man. Jocasta
immediately hanged herself; Oedipus, in horror, tore out his own eyes
and wandered from Thebes accompanied by his daughter Antigone.
At last he found a place of refuge at Colonus (q.v.), where the
Eumenides (q.v.) removed him from the earth. *See* Sophocles,
Oedipus the King and *Oedipus at Colonus*. Antigone returned to
Thebes.

  3. After the flight of Oedipus, his sons Eteocles and Polynices
succeeded as joint sovereigns. But disputes arose between them, and
it was agreed that each should govern in alternate years, the other
withdrawing from Thebes while not in office. Polynices accordingly
withdrew; but when Eteocles's first year of kingship was ended he
would not allow his brother to return. Polynices appealed to Adrastus
(*see* ADRASTUS, 1), King of Argos. Adrastus organized the expedition
known as the 'Seven Against Thebes', although the prophet Amphiaraüs (q.v.), his brother-in-law, had foretold it would end disastrously.

Eteocles and Polynices slew one another in single combat, and five of the other chiefs—Tydeus, Amphiaraüs, Capaneus (qq.v.), Hippomedon and Parthenopaeus—were killed (*see* MENOECEUS). Adrastus alone escaped. *See* Aeschylus, *The Seven Against Thebes*.

4. Creon now succeeded to the throne of Thebes. His first act was to forbid the burial of Polynices, and he sentenced Antigone to death for disobeying this order. She was immured in a subterranean cavern, where she took her own life, together with her lover, Haemon, son of Creon.

5. Ten years after these events Adrastus persuaded the descendants (Gk *epigonoi*) of the Seven to undertake another expedition against Thebes. In this 'War of the Epigoni' Thebes was captured and razed to the ground. The only one of the Epigoni who fell was Aegialeus, whose father, Adrastus, died of grief and was buried at Megara on his way home to Argos.

Thebes (Gk Thēbai), city of Boeotia and birth-place of Pindar (q.v.). Its situation was well defended, since it was situated in a plain surrounded by mountains, and no place is more celebrated in Greek legend (*see* THEBAN LEGEND). Here the alphabet was introduced from Phoenicia; here was the birth-place of Dionysus and Heracles; here too lived Tiresias and Amphion. It was also the scene of Oedipus's dreadful fate and of the war of the 'Seven against Thebes' as well as of the expedition of the Epigoni. The first historical trace of the city dates from the Boeotian conquest (*c.* 1100 B.C.), when Thebes became head of a confederacy. She became the closest ally of Sparta, and was the most bitter enemy of Athens during the Peloponnesian war (431–404 B.C.); but she made an anti-Spartan alliance with Athens in 394 B.C. In 382 B.C. the citadel (*Cadmeia*) was occupied by Spartan troops; but its recovery by Theban exiles in 378 led to war with Sparta. After the battle of Leuctra (371 B.C.), Thebes enjoyed for a while the hegemony of Greece (*see* EPAMEINONDAS); but the hegemony was lost in 362. In 338 B.C. Thebes was induced by the eloquence of Demosthenes to unite with Athens against Macedon; but their united army was defeated by Philip at Chaeronea in 338. In 335 B.C. Thebes attempted to resist the arms of Alexander the Great (q.v.), when she was captured and razed by Alexander, excepting the temples and the house of Pindar; 6,000 of her inhabitants were killed, and 30,000 sold into slavery. The city was rebuilt by Cassander and the Athenians in 316 B.C. In 290 it was taken by Demetrius Poliorcetes, and thereafter declined rapidly. The final blow was administered by Sulla (q.v.), who gave half of its territory to Delphi. Excavations have been made. (See *Annual of the British School at Athens*, xvii, xxix ff.)

Themis, in Greek mythology, daughter of Uranus and Gē, and mother by Zeus of the Horae and Moirae. In Homer she personifies the order established by law, custom and equity, and convenes the assembly of the gods.

Themistocles (-klēs), Athenian soldier and statesman, born *c.* 528 B.C. His political eminence began in 483, when he helped to secure the ostracism of Aristeides. Then, foreseeing the likelihood of another Persian attack, he persuaded the Athenians to employ the revenues from their silver mines at Laurium (q.v.) in building 100 triremes, and to move the naval base from Phalerum to Peiraeus. When Xerxes began his invasion (480), Themistocles was appointed commander of the Athenian fleet, in which capacity he was responsible for the evacuation of the city and for the final victory of Salamis. He next induced his fellow citizens to build the Long Walls, and to abolish the *metoikon*, a tax on aliens, removal of which encouraged many foreign traders and craftsmen to settle at Athens. But his arrogance soon caused his popularity to decline: he was accused (perhaps justly) of peculation, and ostracized (471). He settled at Argos, but not long afterwards evidence was found that seemed to implicate him in the conspiracy of Pausanias, and envoys were dispatched from Athens to apprehend him (468). Themistocles, however, learning what was afoot, escaped first to Corcyra, then to Epirus, whence he made his way to the coast of Asia Minor. Having spent a year learning the Persian language and customs, he was welcomed by Artaxerxes I, who provided him with handsome maintenance. He took up residence at Magnesia, promising to do the king good service, but died before he could fulfil that undertaking (457 B.C.).

Theocritus (-kritos), Greek pastoral poet, born at Syracuse *c.* 310 B.C., son of Praxagoras and Philinna. Having studied under Philetas in Cos, he visited Alexandria and obtained the patronage of Ptolemy II, Philadelphus, in praise of whom he wrote the 14th, 15th and 17th Idylls. Theocritus was the creator of bucolic poetry: his Idylls, of which thirty have survived, are of a dramatic and mimetic character, and are pictures of everyday life in Sicily. *See* editions by U. von Wilamowitz-Moellendorff, 1910, and A. S. F. Gow (with translation and commentary), 2nd ed., 1952.

Theognis (late 6th century B.C.), Greek elegiac poet, a native of Megara. He is the reputed author of a collection of political verses strongly aristocratic in temper. *See* the edition with commentary by T. Hudson-Williams, 1910. *See also* C. M. Bowra, *Early Greek Elegists*, 1938.

Theophrastus (-os): 1. Greek philosopher, born at Eresus in Lesbos *c.* 370 B.C. He was for some time a pupil at the Academy (q.v.); but after Plato's death (347) he joined Aristotle (q.v.) at Assos, and succeeded him as head of the Lyceum in 322 B.C. From that time until his death (*c.* 286 B.C.) he laboured with much success to consolidate and expand the teaching of his master. His surviving works include the *History of Plants* and *Causes of Plants*, edited and translated by A. F. Hort, 2 vols. (Loeb Library), 1916; *Metaphysics*, edited and translated by W. D. Ross and F. H. Forbes, 1929; and *Ethical Characters*, a most entertaining collection of typical 'bad hats', edited and translated by J. M. Edmonds (Loeb Library), 1929. The fullest account of Theophrastus and his work is O. Regenbogen's article in Pauly-Wissowa's *Realencyclopädie*, supp. vol. vii, 1950. *See also* E. Zeller, *Aristotle and the Earlier Peripatetics*, 1897.

2. *See* TYRANNION.

Thera, island of the Cyclades (q.v.), from which Cyrene (q.v.) was founded.

Thēramenēs, Athenian politician, a member of the oligarchical government known as the Four Hundred (411 B.C.), which he subsequently helped to depose. In 404 he was one of the Thirty Tyrants (q.v.); but when he attempted to curb their excesses he was accused of treason by Critias, one of his colleagues, and put to death. His turncoat methods led to his being nicknamed *Kothornos* (the actor's 'buskin', which fitted either foot).

Therapnae (-ai), town of Laconia, on the Eurotas, a little above Sparta. It was celebrated as the mythical birth-place of the Dioscuri (q.v.), and also as possessing the tomb of Menelaus and Helen, who were in historical times the objects of a cult jointly with the Dioscuri. The temple was excavated in 1909–10.

Thermae, later Roman name for public baths. In republican times such buildings were called *balnea,* and were quite modest both in size and in the amenities they offered. The imperial *thermae* were enormous structures, comprising not only baths of various kinds, but often libraries, gymnasia, theatres, etc., also. The *tepidarium* was a warm room, with no bath, in which the bather usually spent some while before undressing. The apartment for undressing was the *apodyterium*; the *frigidarium* contained a cold bath, and the *calidarium* warm baths. Heating was done by hypocaust. The principal surviving ruins of *thermae* at Rome are of those built by Caracalla and by Diocletian (*see* ROME: *Baths*), the latter of which was converted by Michelangelo into the church of S. Maria degli Angeli. Others were erected by Agrippa (25–12 B.C.) and by the emperors Nero, Titus, Trajan, etc. Outside Rome there are remains of *thermae* at Pompeii in Italy, at Bath (Aquae Sulis) and Wroxeter (Viriconium) in England, near the Musée de Cluny at Paris, and elsewhere.

Thermopylae (-pulai), often called simply Pylae, a pass leading from Thessaly into Locris, celebrated on account of its heroic defence by Leonidas (q.v.) against the Persians in 480 B.C.

Thērōn, tyrant of Acragas (*see* AGRIGENTUM), *c.* 488–472 B.C. In 482, or thereabouts, he added Himera to his dominions, and two years later assisted Gelon of Syracuse to defeat the Carthaginians under Hamilcar. Under Theron, Acragas attained the zenith of its prosperity; he was a generous patron of art and literature, and his successes at the Olympic Games (q.v.) are celebrated by Pindar. He was succeeded by his son Thrasydaeus, under whom the glory of Acragas quickly diminished.

Thersitēs, a deformed, uncouth and bombastic individual among the Greeks at Troy (*Il.* ii. 121 ff.). According to later poets he was slain by Achilles (*see* PENTHESILEA).

Thēseus, legendary hero of Attica, son of Aegeus (q.v.), King of Athens, and of Aethra, daughter of King Pittheus of Troezen. Brought up at Troezen, when he reached maturity he took his father's sword and sandals, and went to Athens. Acknowledged by Aegeus as his heir, after slaying the Marathonian bull, Theseus went of his own accord as one of the seven youths and seven maidens whom the Athenians had to send every year to Crete, to be devoured by the Minotaur (q.v.; *see also* ANDROGEOS). In Crete, Ariadne (q.v.), the daughter of Minos, fell in love with Theseus, and gave him a sword with which he slew the Minotaur and a clue of thread by means of which he found his way out of the labyrinth. Theseus then sailed away, taking Ariadne, but he abandoned her in the island of Naxos. Approaching Athens, he forgot to hoist the white sail (black was used for these mournful voyages), which was to have been the signal of his success; and Aegeus, watching, thought his son had perished, and threw himself into the sea. Theseus was now King of Athens. He fought the Amazons (q.v.) and carried off their queen Antiope (or Hippolyte), who bore him a son Hippolytus (q.v.). He was also one of the Argonauts (q.v.); hunted the Calydonian boar (*see* MELEAGER); helped Adrastus (q.v.) to recover the bodies of the slain at Thebes; with Pirithoüs (q.v.) abducted the young Helen (q.v.) from Sparta and hid her at Aphidnae (whence she was rescued by the Dioscuri, q.v.), and tried to abduct Proserpina from Hades. Meanwhile Menestheus roused the people against Theseus, who, unable to re-establish his authority, retired to Scyros, where he was treacherously hurled to death from a cliff by King Lycomedes. Theseus was afterwards said to have appeared at Marathon and assisted the Athenians (490 B.C.). Bacchylides and Euripides seem to misrepresent the legend by calling Theseus a son of Poseidon; but the fact is that Aegeus and Poseidon were originally identical. *See* L. Cottrell, *The Bull of Minos*, 1955.

Thesmophoria, annual Greek festival in honour of Demeter. At Athens it lasted for five days in the month Pyanepsion (early November), only women of Attic birth and stainless character participating. It was a corn festival, and the occasion of a singularly disgusting rite. At the festival of Scirophoria, four months earlier, pigs were hurled into subterranean caverns; their rotting remains were brought out at the Thesmophoria, and mixed with seed-corn on an altar. The institution of this festival was variously ascribed to Triptolemus Orpheus and the Danaids.

Thespiae (-ai), city of Boeotia, near the foot of Mt Helicon. The Thebans dismantled its walls in 423, and razed it to the ground in 372 B.C. Thespiae possessed a famous statue of Eros by Praxiteles.

Thespis (6th century B.C.), called the father of Greek tragedy, born at Icarius, one of the Attic demes. He was the first to introduce an actor into what had been hitherto a merely choral performance in honour of Dionysus. This individual took various parts in the same piece under the several disguises provided by linen masks. *See* A. W. Pickard-Cambridge, *Dithyramb, Tragedy and Comedy*, 1927.

Thespius (-os), son of Teuthras (q.v.).

Thessalonica (-kē), the modern Salonika, a city of Macedonia, originally called Therma and situated at the north-eastern extremity of the Thermaic Gulf. Occupied by the Athenians in 432 B.C., it was soon afterwards restored to Perdiccas (*see* PERDICCAS (A), 2). Its importance was greatly increased by Cassander (315 B.C.), who renamed it after his wife, a sister of Alexander the Great. It was visited (Acts xvii) by St Paul, who afterwards (between A.D. 51 and 53) addressed from Corinth his two epistles to the Thessalonians.

Thessaly (Gk Thessalia), the largest division of Greece, a large plain watered by the River Peneus and its tributaries. About 70 miles wide, it is shut in on every side by mountain barriers, broken only at the north-east corner by the valley and defile of Tempe, which separates Ossa from Olympus. There were two other districts included under the general name of Thessaly: one, called Magnesia, being a long strip of country extending along the Aegean coast from Tempe to the Pagasaean Gulf, and the other a long narrow vale at the extreme south of the country, lying between Mts Othrys and Oeta. Thessaly proper was divided in very early times into four districts or tetrarchies, a division which still subsisted during the Peloponnesian war. These districts were (1) Hestiaeotis, in the north-west; (2) Pelasgiotis, in the east; (3) Thessaliotis, in the south-west; (4) Phthiotis, in the south-east. It is in this last district that Homer places Phthia and Hellas proper, and the dominions of Achilles. Besides these, there were four other districts, viz.: (5) Magnesia; (6) Dolopia, a small district bounded east by Phthiotis, north by Thessaliotis, west by Athamania and south by Oetaea; (7) Oetaea, a district in the upper valley of the Spercheus; and (8) Malis.

The Thessalians were a Thesprotian tribe, and invaded the western part of the country, afterwards called Thessaliotis, whence they spread over the rest of the country. Government in the various cities became oligarchical, power being chiefly in the hands of a few great families descended from the ancient kings. Of these, two of the most powerful were the Aleuadae and the Scopadae. The Thessalians never became of much importance in Greek history. In 344 B.C. Philip completely subjected Thessaly to Macedon. The victory of Flamininus (q.v.) at Cynoscephalae (197 B.C.) again gave the Thessalians a semblance of independence under the Romans, but the country was eventually included in the province of Macedonia.

Thetis, Greek sea-goddess, daughter of Nereus and Doris, and mother of Achilles. Poseidon and Zeus sued for her hand; but when Themis declared that Thetis's son would outshine his father, both gods withdrew. Others said that Thetis rejected Zeus because she had been brought up by Hera, and that the god, in revenge, decreed that she should wed a mortal. At length she was married against her will to Peleus (q.v.). *See also* ERIS.

Thirty Tyrants: 1. Sometimes called simply 'The Thirty', an oligarchical government of thirty members imposed on the Athenians after the capture of their city by Lysander in 404 B.C. They distinguished themselves by their monstrous cruelty (*see* Aristotle, *Ath. Con.* 35–8), but were defeated later in the year by the returning exiles under Thrasybulus (q.v.), and deposed.

2. Name given to the Roman generals who assumed the purple in various provinces of the empire during the reigns of Valerian and Gallienus (A.D. 254–368).

Thoas: 1. King of Calydon, son of Andraemon and Gorge. *See* OENEUS.

2. King of Lemnos, son of Dionysus by Ariadne, husband of Myrina and father of Hypsipyle (q.v.).

3. King of Tauris, where Iphigeneia (q.v.) was carried by Artemis.

Thrace (Gk Thrakia), originally a vast tract of country bounded on the north by the Danube, on the south by the Propontis and Aegean, on the east by the Euxine, and on the west by the River Strymon and

the easternmost of the Illyrian tribes. It was divided into two parts by
Mt Haemus (the Balkan), running from west to east and separating
the plain of the lower Danube from the rivers which fall into the
Aegean. At a later time the name was applied to a more limited area,
the western boundary being drawn at Mt Rhodope, the northern at
Mt Haemus.

Thrace in its widest extent was peopled in the time of Herodotus
and Thucydides by various tribes. The earliest Greek poets and other
cultural pioneers (e.g. Orpheus, Linus, Musaeus, Eumolpus) are
represented as coming from Thrace, which indeed received Greek
colonies at an early date. The first really historical fact respecting
the Thracians is their subjugation by Megabazus, the general of
Darius (c. 512 B.C.). After the Persians had been driven out of Europe
by the Greeks, the Thracians recovered their independence; and at
the beginning of the Peloponnesian war (431 B.C.) almost all the
Thracian tribes were united under the dominion of Sitalces, King
of the Odrysae (q.v.). Sitalces fell in battle against the Triballi in 424,
and was succeeded by his nephew Seuthes, who raised his kingdom to
a height of power and prosperity which it had never previously
attained. Philip II of Macedon reduced the greater part of Thrace;
and after the death of Alexander (323) the rest of the country fell to
the share of Lysimachus (q.v.). It subsequently formed part of the
dominions of the Antigonid kings of Macedonia. It became a separate
province of the Roman Empire in A.D. 45. *See* S. Casson, *Macedonia,
Thrace and Illyria*, 1926.

Thrasea Paetus, Publius Clodius, Roman senator and Stoic philosopher of the 1st century A.D., born probably at Patavium soon after
the death of Augustus. He wrote an account of the younger Cato,
upon whom he modelled his own life. His independent character, and
the freedom with which he expressed his views, made him odious to
Nero, by whose order the senate condemned him to death, and he
committed suicide (A.D. 66). *See* Tacitus, *Annales*, xiv-xvi

Thrasybulus (Thrasuboulos), son of Lycus. Athenian statesman.
He took an active part in overthrowing the government of the Four
Hundred in 411 B.C., was banished by the Thirty Tyrants (q.v.), but
returned to expel them and to restore the democracy in 404. In 390 he
commanded the Athenian fleet in the Aegean, and recovered much
territory for Athens before his murder by the inhabitants of Aspendus
in Pamphylia (388 B.C.).

Thucydides (Thoukudidēs): 1. Athenian statesman who led the
aristocratic party against Pericles (q.v.). He was ostracized in 443 B.C.

2. Greek historian, born at Halimus in Attica c. 464 B.C., son of
Olorus and Hegesipyle. He is said to have been instructed in oratory
by Antiphon and in philosophy by Anaxagoras. He owned gold mines
in that part of Thrace which is opposite to the island of Thasos, and
there he was a person of the greatest consequence. In 424 B.C. he
commanded an Athenian squadron of seven ships at Thasos, but
having failed in an attempt to save Amphipolis, he became an exile in
Thrace, probably to avoid worse punishment. He spent twenty years
in exile, returning to Athens in 404 B.C., when a general amnesty was
granted on the restoration of democracy. According to some accounts

he was assassinated at Athens, or possibly in Thrace; according to others he died at Thasos, and his remains were carried to Athens. At all events his death cannot be placed later than 401 B.C.

The Peloponnesian war forms the subject of the *History* of Thucydides. Though he was engaged in collecting materials during the whole of the war, he does not appear to have reduced them to literary form until after his return from exile, since he alludes in many places to the conclusion of the war (i. 13; v. 26). He did not, however, live to complete it; the eighth book ends abruptly in the middle of the year 411 B.C., seven years before the termination of the conflict. The purpose of Thucydides was to give such a faithful representation of the past as would serve as a guide for the future (i. 22). His understanding of human character was profound, and his painstaking accuracy and careful attention to chronology are remarkable. His claim to strict impartiality is nowadays disputed. His style is marked by great strength and energy, but he is often obscure, particularly in the speeches. *See* the Oxford text edited by H. Stuart Jones and J. Powell, 1942; text and translation by C. F. Smith, 4 vols. (Loeb Library). *See also* A. W. Gomme, *A Historical Commentary on Thucydides*, 1945; G. B. Grundy, *Thucydides and the History of his Age*, 2nd ed., 2 vols., 1948; J. de Romilly, *Thucydides and Athenian Imperialism*, 1962.

Thule (Thoulē), name given by the ancients to the most northerly part of Europe known to them. According to Pliny it was an island in the northern ocean discovered by Pytheas (q.v.), six days' sail from the Orcades. Müllenhoff plausibly identifies it with the Shetlands. *Thoule* appears to be a Greek form of the Gothic *Tiel* or *Tiule*, 'remotest land'.

Thurii (Thourioi), Greek city in Lucania (q.v.), near the site of Sybaris (q.v.). It was founded in 443 B.C. by colonists from various parts of Greece, among them the historian Herodotus and the orator Lysias. Thurii became one of the most important towns in southern Italy.

Thyestes (Thuestēs), son of Pelops, brother of Agamemnon and father of Aegisthus by his own daughter Pelopia, *see* ATREIDS, LEGEND OF THE.

Tiber (Lat. Tiberis; mod. Tevere), river of central Italy, on which stands the city of Rome; length 245 miles. It rises from two springs in the Apennines, near Arretium, and flows in a south-westerly direction, separating Etruria from Umbria, the country of the Sabines and Latium. After about 110 miles it receives the Nar (mod. Nera), the Anio (Aniene) joining it some three miles above Rome. At Rome the Tiber is about 300 feet wide, and from 12 to 18 feet deep. In ancient times it often overflowed its banks and did much damage to the lower parts of the city. Its waters are a muddy yellow, whence the phrase used by Latin poets: *flavus Tiberis*.

Tiberianus, Latin poet of the 4th century A.D. The *Pervigilium Veneris* (q.v.) has been attributed to him. *See* the edition and translation of his known works by J. W. and A. M. Duff in *Minor Latin Poets* (Loeb Library).

Tiberius Claudius Nero, usually called simply Tiberius. Roman emperor A.D. 14–37, son of Tiberius Claudius Nero and Livia, after-wards wife of Augustus. Tiberius was born on 16th November 42 B.C.; he was carefully educated, and became well acquainted with both Greek and Latin literature. At the age of twenty-two he was sent by Augustus on a diplomatic mission to Armenia, and in 13 B.C. he was consul with P. Quintilius Varus (q.v.). Three years before this, Tiberius, with his brother Nero Claudius Drusus, had been entrusted with the defence of the northern frontiers, and during the years 12–9 B.C. he fought successful campaigns against the Dalmatians and Pannonians. After the death of Drusus in the latter year, Tiberius took command in Germany, and remained there until 6 B.C., when he was granted the *tribunitia potestas* for five years and retired with the emperor's permission to Rhodes. This sudden withdrawal from public affairs at the age of thirty-six was dictated by domestic unhappiness. Tiberius was married to Vipsania Agrippina (q.v.), to whom he was deeply attached and who had borne him a son, Drusus. But in 12 B.C., or soon afterwards, Augustus compelled him to divorce Vipsania and marry the emperor's own daughter Julia. This woman (*see* JULIA, 5) was a notorious adulteress, and Tiberius desired to escape from her at any cost. Her detestable life caused her father to banish her in 2 B.C., but Tiberius did not return until A.D. 2. Two years later he was adopted by Augustus and given command of the armies in northern Germany. Excepting occasional brief visits to the capital he remained there for seven years. On the death of Augustus (A.D. 14) he hurried home, and the skilful management of his mother Livia (q.v.) secured the throne for him without opposition. Tiberius was a suspicious character, and he began his reign by putting to death Postumus Agrippa, the surviving grandson of Augustus. Then he proceeded to make his rule absolute. Tacitus admits that from A.D. 14 to 23 Tiberius governed with justice and moderation (*Annales*, i–iii), but ascribes his departure from Rome to a desire to give full vent to his sensual inclinations in privacy. Whether or not this be true, it is certain that Tiberius had long hated Rome; and in 26 he left it, never to return. He went first to Campania on the pretext of dedicating temples, but in the next year he moved to the island of Capreae (q.v.) off the Campanian coast. Meanwhile his minister Sejanus (q.v.), in whose hands the government of the state had long rested, was plotting to obtain for himself nothing less than the imperial throne. Tiberius awoke to the situation in A.D. 31, and had him put to death. Six years passed, the emperor occupying himself with none knew what, though rumour was always busy. Then, one night he happened to sleep on the mainland, in the villa of Lucullus at Misenum, and next morning (16th March A.D. 37) he was found dead, smothered, it was said, by order of Macro, the praetorian prefect. The character of Tiberius has been much disputed. Tacitus and Suetonius paint it in the darkest colours, but it has been defended by many historians from Merivale onwards. *See* F. B. March, *The Reign of Tiberius*, 1931; R. S. Rogers, *Studies in the Reign of Tiberius*, 1943.

Tibullus, Albius (*c.* 54–19 B.C.), Latin elegiac poet, member of an equestrian family whose estate was at Pedum, between Tibur and Praeneste. In 28 B.C. he accompanied his patron, Messala, who went out as governor of Aquitania, and later started for the east; but he was taken ill at Corcyra, and had to return. His poetry, addressed to two mistresses named Delia and Nemesis, has little ardour, but is notable for its quiet tenderness and spirit of self-abnegation; on the other hand, his bucolic elegies are among the most charming things in the whole range of Latin poetry. Horace was warmly attached to him. *See* edition by J. P. Postgate, 1915, and translation by A. S. Way, 1936. *See also* W. Y. Sellar, *Horace and the Elegiac Poets*, 1892.

Tibur (mod. Tivoli), town of Latium, 15 miles north-east of Rome, standing 800 feet above sea level on the Anio, at a point where the river forms a series of beautiful cascades, now sadly diminished by the greed of an electric power station. In Horace's day Tibur was a resort of wealthy Romans; ruins still exist of fine villas, in particular of a magnificent one built by Hadrian. There are also remains of mausolea, aqueducts and a temple of Vesta. Zenobia (q.v.) resided at Tibur after gracing the triumph of Aurelian.

Ticinus (mod. Ticino), river of Gallia Cisalpina, upon the banks of which Hannibal gained his first victory over the Romans, 218 B.C. (*see* SCIPIO, PUBLIUS CORNELIUS).

Tigellinus, Tofonius, son of a native of Agrigentum, minister to Nero's worst passions, and of all his favourites the most obnoxious to the Roman people. On the accession of Otho (A.D. 68) he was compelled to take his own life. *See* Tacitus, *Annals*, xiv, xv; *Histories*, i.

Tigranes, Graeco-Latin form of the name Dikran, borne by several kings of Armenia, one of whom flourished as early as 550 B.C., and was a friend of Cyrus the Great of Persia, helping him to overthrow the Median Empire. The best known, however, reigned from about 96 to 55 B.C. He was the son-in-law of Mithradates the Great of Pontus (*see* MITHRADATES), and in 83 he made himself master of the Seleucid Empire from the Euphrates to the sea, founding the city of Tigranocerta. He first supported Mithradates against the Romans (76), but was defeated by Lucullus (69–68) and by Pompey (66).

Tilphusium (Tilphousion), a town in Boeotia on a mountain of the same name, south of Lake Copaïs between Coronea and Haliartus. Here was a spring sacred to Apollo, after drinking whose waters Tiresias (q.v.) was said to have died.

Timaeus (-maios): 1. Supposed philosopher of the Pythagorean school; invented on the strength of Plato's *Timaeus* and credited with a treatise *On the Soul of the Universe*, which deals with the same subjects as part of Plato's dialogue.

2. Greek historian (*c.* 346–*c.* 250 B.C.), son of Andromachus, tyrant of Tauromenium in Sicily. Banished from Sicily by Agathocles, he lived in exile at Athens for fifty years. He was the author of a work (now lost) on the history of Sicily to 264 B.C.

Timgad, *see* THAMUGADI.

Timoleōn (4th century B.C.), Corinthian patriot. Born of noble family, he spent his life in the cause of liberty, and as a youth murdered his own brother Timophanes, whose ambitions were directed to the establishment of tyranny. In 346 B.C. the Greek cities of Sicily applied to Corinth for aid against the Carthaginians, and Timoleon was sent with a small force. He took Syracuse, and set about the establishment of democratic governments in all the Sicilian colonies. Meanwhile the Carthaginians landed at Lilybaeum with a large army. Timoleon was not able to collect more than 12,000 men, but with these he won a victory on the Crimissus (339). A treaty was concluded in the following year, fixing the River Halycus as boundary between the Greek and Carthaginian spheres in Sicily. Timoleon continued his work of democratization, though he himself was *de facto* ruler of the island. The flourishing state of Sicily at the time of his death (date unknown) shows how beneficial was his influence. *See* H. A. Holden's introduction to Plutarch's *Life of Timoleon*, 1889.

Timōn the Misanthrope, an Athenian who lived in the second half of the 5th century B.C. On account of ingratitude and disappointments he believed himself to have suffered, he withdrew from the society of all but his friend Alcibiades. He is the central figure of Shakespeare's *Timon of Athens*.

Timotheus (-os): 1. Musician and poet of the late Athenian dithyramb, born at Miletus in 446 and died in 357 B.C. Athenian audiences were at first offended by his bold innovations in the theatre; but Euripides encouraged him, and was justified by the immense popularity which Timotheus afterwards enjoyed. These innovations included intricate forms of musical expression, a more liberal use than hitherto customary of instrumental music without vocal accompaniment, and the addition of an eleventh string to the cithara. An Egyptian papyrus was discovered in 1902 containing 250 lines of a *nome* by Timotheus—the *Persae*, to which Euripides is known to have written a prologue. A *nome* was originally a slow and stately piece for solo voice and cithara. The metre of the *Persae*, however, is very free. *See* text by U. von Wilamowitz-Moellendorff, 1903.

2. Greek sculptor of the school of Scopas (q.v.). He worked on the Mausoleum at Halicarnassus (q.v.), and some of his sculptures from the temple of Asclepius at Epidaurus have survived.

Tirēsias, a blind soothsayer of Thebes who plays so prominent a part in the legendary history of Greece that there are few outstanding events with which he is not in some way connected.

In the war of the Seven against Thebes (*see* THEBAN LEGEND, 3) he predicted that Thebes would be victorious if Menoeceus (q.v.) would sacrifice his life. After the defeat of Thebes in the War of the Epigoni (*see* THEBAN LEGEND, 5) he advised the citizens to begin negotiations for peace and to take the opportunity which would thus be afforded them to escape. He himself fled with them (or was carried off as a captive); but on the road he drank from the spring Tilphusa (*see* TILPHUSIUM) and died. Tiresias was believed to retain his powers as a seer even in the underworld (*Od.* xi. 90–151).

Tiridates: 1. King of Armenia, which he conquered with the help of his brother Vologaeses I of Parthia. In A.D. 63 he was obliged by the victories of Corbulo (q.v.) to abdicate and accept his crown anew at the hands of Nero.

2. King of Armenia, on the throne of which he was placed by Diocletian in A.D. 286. He was constantly at war with the Persians, and died a Christian in A.D. 314.

Tiro, Marcus Tullius, freedman, secretary and friend of Cicero. He was himself an author of no mean repute, and notices of his works have been preserved by ancient writers. After Cicero's death (43 B.C.), Tiro bought a farm in the neighbourhood of Puteoli, and is said to have been aged more than one hundred at his death. He is commonly believed to have invented the first system of Latin shorthand.

Tiryns (-runs), town of Argolis on a site which was occupied as early as the 3rd millennium B.C., and one of the most important centres of Mycenaean culture in prehistoric times. In classical legend it was founded by Proetus, brother of Acrisius, who built the massive walls with the aid of the Cyclopes. He was succeeded by Perseus; and it was here that Heracles was brought up. In historical times Tiryns with Mycenae sent an army to Plataea (479), but was destroyed by Argos in 468 B.C. Important excavations of the prehistoric city were made between 1884 and 1927.

Tisiphonē, *see* ERINYES.

Tissaphernes, Persian satrap of Lower Asia in 413 B.C. during the Peloponnesian war. He pretended to support the Spartan cause, but gave no active help, his real policy being to exhaust both belligerents by a continuance of hostilities. In this he was thwarted by the arrival in Asia Minor of Cyrus the younger, who gave the Spartans effective aid (407 B.C.). At the battle of Cunaxa (401) Tissaphernes was one of the four generals commanding the army of Artaxerxes, and his troops were the only part of the left wing not routed by the Greeks (*see* TEN THOUSAND, EXPEDITION OF THE). When the latter began their retreat Tissaphernes offered to conduct them to safety, but he had their generals arrested and put to death. As a reward for his services he was invested by Artaxerxes with the territories formerly governed by Cyrus. This led to a war with Sparta, in which Tissaphernes was defeated by Agesilaus near Sardis, and he was put to death in 395 B.C. through the influence of Parysatis, mother of the king.

Titans, fabulous beings in Greek mythology. Uranus and Gē (qq.v.) had eighteen children: (*a*) the three Hecatoncheires ('hundred-handed' monsters), named Aegaeon or Briareus, Gyas or Gyes or Gyges, and Cottus; (*b*) three Cyclopes (q.v.), named Arges, Steropes and Brontes; (*c*) six sons and six daughters called Titans, the most important of whom were Cronus and Rhea (qq.v.).

Uranus cast the Hecatoncheires and Cyclopes into Tartarus (q.v.), and Rhea, indignant, persuaded the Titans to rise against their father. She gave Cronus a sickle, with which he emasculated Uranus and threw his genitals into the sea. From the blood that fell upon the earth sprang the Gigantes (q.v.; *see also* ERINYES), and from the foam thus generated in the sea rose Aphrodite (q.v.). The Titans then deposed Uranus, freed their brothers and made Cronus their king.

Cronus then flung the Hecatoncheires and Cyclopes back into Tartarus and married his sister Rhea. But he had been warned by his parents that one of his own children would dethrone him; so he swallowed each of them at birth: Hestia, Demeter, Hera, Pluto and Poseidon (qq.v.). Rhea, therefore, when pregnant with Zeus (q.v.), went to Crete, bore her child in the Dictaean cave, left him in the care of the Curetes (q.v.) and gave Cronus a stone wrapped in a cloth, which he swallowed in the belief that it was his son.

When Zeus grew up he employed Metis (q.v.) to give Cronus a potion that caused him to vomit up the children he had swallowed. Together with his brothers and sisters Zeus now began his struggle with the ruling Titans. It lasted ten years, until Gē promised victory to Zeus if he would deliver the Hecatoncheires and Cyclopes from Tartarus. He did so, and overcame the Titans with the help of the Cyclopes, who provided him with the thunderbolt, Pluto with a helmet and Poseidon with a trident. The Titans themselves were then thrust into Tartarus and the Hecatoncheires set to guard them.

The name Titans was often given to those divine or semi-divine beings who were descended from the Titans, e.g. Prometheus, Hecate, Latona, Helios and Selene (qq.v.).

Tithonus (-thōnos), in Greek legend, son of Laomedon and brother of Priam. On account of his beauty he was loved by Eos, who obtained for him from Zeus the gift of immortality. Not, however, having eternal youth, he grew hideously old, and Eos turned him into a grasshopper.

Titus Flavius Sabinus Vespasianus, Roman emperor, A.D. 79–81, commonly called by his praenomen Titus, was the son of Vespasian and Flavia Domitilla. He was born on 30th December A.D. 39. When a young man he served as military tribune in Britain and in Germany. After having been quaestor, he had the command of a legion, and served under his father in the Jewish wars. Vespasian returned to Italy, after he had been proclaimed emperor on 1st July A.D. 69; but Titus remained in Palestine to prosecute the siege of Jerusalem, which was concluded by the capture of the place, on 8th September 70. Titus returned to Italy in the following year (71), and triumphed at Rome with his father. He also received the title of Caesar and became the associate of Vespasian in the government. His conduct at this time gave no good promise, and his attachment to Berenice, the sister of Agrippa II, made him unpopular, but he sent her away from Rome after he became emperor. Titus succeeded his father in 79. Throughout his reign he displayed a sincere desire for the happiness of the people. He assumed the office of pontifex maximus after the death of his father, with the purpose, as he declared, of keeping his hands free from blood, a resolution which he kept. The first year of his reign is memorable for the eruption of Vesuvius. Titus endeavoured to repair the ravages of this; and he was also at great care and expense in repairing the damage done by a fire at Rome, which lasted three days and nights. He completed the Colosseum (q.v.), and erected the baths which were called by his name. He died on 13th September A.D. 81, and there were suspicions that he was poisoned by his brother, Domitian.

Tityus (-tuos), in Greek legend, a giant of Euboea. For offering violence to Artemis (or to Leto) he was killed by Apollo (or by Zeus) and cast into Tartarus, where two vultures perpetually devoured his liver.

Tlepolemus (Tlēpolemos), son of Heracles by Astyoche, daughter of Phylas, or by Astydamia, daughter of Amyntor. He was King of Argos, but after slaying his uncle Licymnius, he fled with his wife

Polyxo (see HELENA) and settled in Rhodes. He joined the Greeks against Troy with nine ships, and was slain by Sarpedon.

Toga, the formal dress of a Roman citizen in town, and obligatory on public occasions. It was made of white wool. Laid flat, it resembled a semicircle with the straight side bent outwards to form an obtuse angle. It measured lengthwise about three times, in width about twice, the wearer's own height. The method of donning the toga was as follows: It was made into thick folds lengthwise and cast over the left shoulder so that one-third of the total length hung down in front: the remainder was passed behind, under the left arm, and thence over the left shoulder. The left arm being now almost covered, the part lying across the back was spread to cover the right shoulder, and the front was arranged in a series of folds, forming a pocket (*sinus*). Curule magistrates and boys wore the *toga praetexta*, i.e. with a purple border; on attaining manhood the *toga virilis*, without the border, was assumed. The *toga picta* (embroidered) was worn by a general at his triumph; the *toga pulla* (of dark stuff) by mourners and persons impeached (q.v.). After Augustus the emperors commonly wore a purple toga. *See* L. Wilson, *The Roman Toga*, 1924.

Tolumnus, in early Roman history, King of Veii, to whom Fidenae revolted in 438 B.C., and at whose instigation the inhabitants of Fidenae slew four Roman ambassadors. In the war which followed Tolumnius was killed in single combat by Cornelius Cossus (*see* SPOLIA OPIMA).

Tomis (mod. Kustendje, or Constanza), town of Thrace, situated on the western shore of the Euxine. Colonized by Greeks from Miletus (*c*. 600 B.C.), it was afterwards famous as the place of Ovid's banishment.

Torquatus, Aulus Manlius, a friend of Cicero, presided at the trial of Milo (q.v.) in 52 B.C. He sided with Pompey in the civil war, and was living in exile at Athens in 45 B.C.

Torquatus, Lucius Manlius: 1. Consul with Lucius Aurelius Cotta in 65 B.C. He helped to suppress Catiline's conspiracy (63) and supported Cicero during his exile (58–57).

2. Son of the preceding, praetor 50–49 B.C., when he opposed Caesar on the outbreak of civil war. Obliged to surrender Oricum, he was taken prisoner, but released. He fought again in Africa, but was taken prisoner by Sittius and put to death after Thapsus (46 B.C.).

Torquatus, Titus Manlius: 1. Originally named Titus Manlius Imperiosus. While serving against the Gauls in 361 B.C. he earned the family name Torquatus by taking a necklace (*torques*) from the body of a huge Gaul slain by him in single combat. He was dictator 353 and 349, and consul 347, 344 and 340. On the last of these occasions he and his colleague, P. Decius Mus, defeated the Latins near Mt Vesuvius. Before battle the consuls ordered that none should engage in single combat, on pain of death. Torquatus's son disobeyed, and was executed by order of his father. *See* Livy, viii. 3–12; Cicero, *De officiis*, iii. 31.

2. Consul 235 B.C., when he conquered Sardinia; censor 231, and consul a second time in 224. In 216 he opposed the ransom of Romans taken prisoner at Cannae, and was dictator in 210 B.C.

Trachea, *see* SELEUCIA, 3.

Trachis (-khis), Greek town at the head of the Maliac Gulf, important as commanding the main road from Thessaly into Greece proper. It was famous in legend as the one-time home of Heracles (q.v.).

Traianus, Marcus Ulpius, called in English **Trajan**, Roman emperor A.D. 98–117, born at Italica in Spain A.D. 53. After a distinguished military career in the east and in Germany, he was consul in 91. In 97 he was adopted by Nerva (q.v.) whom he succeeded in the following year. In 101 he set out for his first Dacian campaign (*see* DACIA), and celebrated a triumph and assumed the title Dacicus in 103. The second campaign opened in 104, and was entirely successful: the Dacian king Decebalus committed suicide (106), his capital Sarmizegethusa became the Roman colony of Ulpia Traiana, and Dacia itself was made a Roman province. The celebrations in honour of these victories lasted at Rome for 123 days. About this time also Arabia Petraea was made a Roman province. In 114 Trajan once again moved eastwards, to deal with the Parthians, who had invaded Armenia. He spent the winter of that year at Antioch; two campaigns (115–16) sufficed for the conquest of most of the Parthian Empire, and the province of Mesopotamia was formed. Trajan then descended the Tigris to the Persian Gulf, but was obliged to return to Ctesiphon by news of a fresh revolt. In 117 he fell sick, set out for Rome, but died on the way at Selinus in Cilicia. Trajan's wife was Pompeia Plotina: they had no children, and she had persuaded him to adopt Hadrian as his successor. The emperor himself is acknowledged as one of the truly great men of antiquity. His ability as a soldier and administrator was altogether outstanding; his purpose at all times and in all circumstances was the welfare of his subjects; and he was an inspiration to those who dealt with him: strong, hard-working, simple in his mode of life but of majestic appearance. His public benefactions included several important roads, a number of libraries (notably the Bibliotheca Ulpia at Rome), baths on the Esquiline, and above all the magnificent Forum Traianum between the Capitoline and Quirinal hills (*see* ROME: *Fora*). Amid the ruins of this last stands a column, once the repository of his ashes (*see* ROME: *Other Monuments*). *See* B. W. Henderson, *Five Roman Emperors*, 1927.

Trapezos (mod. Trabzon), city on the north-east coast of Asia Minor, founded *c.* 600 B.C. by Greek settlers from Sinope. It was at Trapezos that the army led by Xenophon first reached the sea (*see* TEN THOUSAND, EXPEDITION OF THE). In later times the city belonged successively to Armenia Minor and Pontus. Pompey made it a free city; under Trajan it became capital of Cappadocian Pontus. Hadrian built a new harbour, and Trapezus grew in importance as a commercial centre.

Trasimenus, Lacus (mod. Lago Trasimeno), a lake in Etruria, upon the shores of which Hannibal (q.v.) defeated the Romans under C. Flaminius (217 B.C.).

Trebia (mod. Trebbia), a small river in Gallia Cisalpina, upon the banks of which Hannibal (q.v.) followed up his victory on the Ticinus (q.v.) by defeating the consuls P. Cornelius Scipio and Sempronius Longus (218 B.C.).

Trebonius, Gaius, tribune of the plebs in 55 B.C. when he carried a law assigning the two Spains and Syria to Pompey and Crassus respectively, and confirming Caesar's command in Gaul and Illyrium for another five years. From 54 to 50 he was one of Caesar's *legati* in Gaul, and did good service there. In 49 he was entrusted by Caesar with the siege of Massilia, and late in the following year he superseded Q. Cassius as governor of Further Spain. He was consul in the last three months of 45, and was then assigned the province of Asia. Despite the numerous benefits he had received from Caesar, he took part in the conspiracy against his life. He then went to his province; but in the following year (43) he was surprised at Smyrna by Dolabella (q.v.) who slew him in his bed.

Tresviri or **Triumviri,** *see* TRIUMVIRATE.

Triboci, Nemetes and **Vangiones,** name of three German tribes inhabiting the Rhine basin between Strasburg and Mainz. Some of them fought under Ariovistus against Caesar in 58 B.C.

Tribune (Lat. Tribunus), name given to certain Roman magistrates and other officials. Of these the most important were the *tribuni plebis,* tribunes of the plebs, whose office dated from 493, following the secession of the plebeians to the Sacred Mount. At first their power (*tribunitia potestas*) was small, and they were only two in number (raised to ten *c.* 449 B.C.). But soon they became formidable and not only preserved the rights of the people, but could summon assemblies, propose laws, stop the deliberations of the senate, and even veto its decrees and those of all other magistrates. Their consent was also necessary for the effectiveness of *senatus consulta,* and they could even imprison a consul if he acted so as to disturb the peace of Rome. Again, their persons were sacrosanct. Their authority was restricted by Sulla; but their privileges were restored by Pompey and Cotta. Augustus accepted the office for himself, and it was conferred upon successive emperors (often before their accession) until the reign of Constantine, who abolished it altogether. Under the republic the office could be held only by those who belonged to a plebeian *gens. See* G. Niccolini, *Il tribunato della plebe,* 1932.

Other officials called tribunes were (1) *tribuni militum* (*see* LEGION; ROMAN ARMY); (2) *tribuni cohortium praetoriarum,* officers of the Praetorian Guard (q.v.), under the praetorian prefect (*see* PRAEFECTUS); (3) *tribuni aerarii,* who kept the military chest, abolished by Caesar, but revived by Augustus who added to their number; (4) *tribuni voluptatum,* who had charge of popular entertainments.

Triptolemus (-os), in Greek legend, son of Celeus (q.v.) and Metaneira. A favourite of Demeter, he invented the plough and agriculture, and was consequently the earliest pioneer of civilization. He was a central figure in the Eleusinian Mysteries. *See also* THESMOPHORIA.

Trireme, Greek warship, held by some to have been of Phoenician if not of Egyptian origin. It was a light undecked craft about 120 feet long with a beam of some 20 feet; was fitted with two masts, except when in action; and normally carried 200 men, of whom 170 were rowers, ten marines and twenty seamen. The bow was armed with a strong beak and other projections for ramming, and reinforced with a cross-beam. The trireme's speed was probably 4 or 5 knots. The arrangement of oars has long been the subject of much discussion; but the theory that there were three distinct banks one above the other is now commonly rejected in favour of forward-sloping benches, each occupied by three men with one oar apiece. The gradual strengthening of the bow, which enabled triremes to meet a head-on collision, led to the construction of heavier quadriremes and quinquiremes with relatively greater oar-power; and these had become the standard warships in hellenistic times. *See* C. Torr, *Ancient Ships*, 1894; W. W. Tarn, 'The Greek Warship' in *Journal of Hellenic Studies*, 1905; F. Brewster, 'The Arrangement of Oars in the Trireme', *Harvard Studies*, 1933.

Triton, legendary son of Poseidon and Amphitrite, represented as human to the waist and dolphin below, usually blowing a shell to calm the seas. Sometimes Poseidon is said to be attended by a whole escort of Tritons.

Triumph (Lat. Triumphus), highest honour accorded to a victorious Roman general. Only a dictator, consul or praetor holding the *imperium* was entitled to the distinction, and then only after major success in true warfare, not rebellion or civil war. The honour, with necessary expenses, was granted by the senate. The celebration took the form of a procession to the Capitol through gaily decorated streets. The cortège was headed by the senate; next came trumpeters, then the spoils and trophies and the crowns presented to the victor by provincial cities. These were followed by the sacrificial victims, captives, lictors, musicians and priests. Immediately behind came the triumphal car, gilded, garlanded and drawn by white horses; in this stood the general, his face painted red and wearing the *toga picta* over the *tunica palmata*, the latter embroidered with palms, the former with golden stars. An ivory sceptre was carried in the left hand, a branch of bay in the right. Over his head a slave held a golden crown. The soldiers, singing bawdy songs, brought up the rear. Solemn sacrifice was offered in the Capitol, and the city gave itself over to merry-making. When the senate refused to authorize a triumph, the general might undertake one on his own account to the temple of Jupiter Latiaris, or he might be granted an ovation (q.v.). Under the empire only the emperor could celebrate a triumph, for all honours of war belonged to him, no matter by whom earned. *See* R. Payne, *The Roman Triumph*, 1962.

Triumvirate, name given to two famous associations of three Roman statesmen, who made themselves supreme during the last six decades of republican history and are called triumvirs (*triumviri*). The first triumvirate was formed in 60 B.C. by Caesar, Pompey and Crassus, the second by Octavian, Mark Antony and Lepidus in 43 B.C.

The name *triumviri* or *tresviri* was also applied to boards of three ordinary magistrates, or sometimes extraordinary commissioners, appointed to execute some public office. Thus *triumviri capitales* were appointed *c.* 292 B.C. to help preserve public order and administer the criminal law in capital cases.

Troas or **The Troad**, *see* TROY.

Troezen (Troizēn), city of Argolis, a short distance from the southeast coast, where it possessed a good harbour called Pogon, opposite the island of Calaurea. It was the birth-place of Theseus (q.v.).

Trojan War, *see* TROY.

Tros, *see* TROY.

Troy, Ilion or **The Troad,** city and district of Asia Minor, forming the north-west of Mysia. The district, usually known as 'Troas' or 'The Troad', was bounded west and north-west by the Aegean and the Hellespont, east by a ridge of Mt Ida, south by the Gulf of Adramyttium, its coastline extending from Lectum promontory, on the south, to the River Rhodius below Abydos on the north.

In classical legend the earliest king of the country was Teucer, after whom the Trojans are called Teucri or Teucrians. His daughter married Dardanus (q.v.), a neighbouring chieftain, hence Dardanidae is another name for Trojans. They were probably descended from Thracian emigrants. Dardanus was grandfather of Tros, whose son Ilus founded Ilion or the city of Troy, the largest and strongest settlement in the Troad. The next king was Laomedon (q.v.), who was succeeded by his son Priam (q.v.), in whose reign the famous siege of Troy (the Trojan war) by the Greeks took place, to avenge the rape of Helen (q.v.) by Priam's son Paris (q.v.). This siege lasted nearly ten years, and ended with the sack and capture of Troy by the stratagem of the wooden horse, traditionally 1184 B.C. The story is told in Homer's *Iliad* and part in the second book of Virgil's *Aeneid*. Once considered purely legendary, it is now commonly regarded as historical in its main outlines, the rape of Helen, perhaps, representing some act of piracy. Among the principal Greek heroes of the siege were Achilles, Agamemnon, Menelaus and Odysseus (qq.v.); and among the Trojans, Hector, Paris and Aeneas (qq.v.).

A small city on the site in Alexander's day was in ruins by Strabo's time. The site of ancient Troy is marked by the Hissarlik mound. The excavations carried on here by Schliemann (1870–90) and Dörpfeld (1893–4) brought to light much valuable information. Remains of some nine different cities were found, buried one beneath another, the earliest dating from about 3000 to 2560 B.C. Probably the beginning of the seventh phase in the history of the city was the Homeric Troy. There are traces of two great settlements (1000–1st century B.C.), and of a new Ilion (1st century B.C. to A.D. 500). *See* Herodotus, v. 95, vii. 75; Strabo xiii; J. B. Lechevalier, *Voyage de la Troade*, 1802; H. Schliemann, *Ilios*, 1880, and *Troja*, 1883; C. W. Blegen, 'Excavations at Troy' in the *American Journal of Archaeology*, 1932–9.

Tullia, daughter of Cicero and Terentia, born *c.* 79 B.C.; married first during her father's consulship (63) to C. Calpurnius Piso, who died 58–57; secondly to Furius Crassipes, by whom she was divorced soon afterwards; thirdly (50) to P. Cornelius Dolabella. This last marriage was unhappy; it was ended by divorce in 46, and early in the following year Tullia gave birth to her second child (a son) by Dolabella. As soon as she had recovered she accompanied her father to Tusculum, where she died (February 45 B.C.). Cicero was inconsolable.

Tullius, Servius (578–534 B.C.), sixth king of Rome. The account of the early life and death of Servius Tullius cannot be regarded as a real historical narrative. His mother, Ocrisia, was one of the captives taken at Corniculum, and became a female slave of Tanaquil, wife of

Tarquinius Priscus. He was born in the king's palace, and was brought up as the king's son, since Tanaquil by her powers of divination had foreseen the greatness of the child; and Tarquinius gave him his daughter in marriage, and entrusted him with the government. The sons of Ancus Marcius, fearing lest he should deprive them of the throne which they claimed as their inheritance, procured the assassination of Tarquinius; but Tanaquil, by a stratagem, preserved the royal power for Servius. Three important events are assigned to his reign by tradition. First, he gave a new constitution to the Roman state. This constitution, which is in fact a later invention, gave the plebs political independence, and assigned to property that influence in the state which had previously belonged to birth exclusively. Secondly, he extended the pomoerium, or hallowed boundary of the city, and completed the city by incorporating with it the Quirinal, Viminal and Esquiline hills. Thirdly, he established an alliance with the Latins, by which Rome and the cities of Latium became the members of one league. By his constitution Servius incurred the hostility of the patricians, who conspired with L. Tarquinius to deprive him of his life. According to the legend, Tullia, one of the daughters of Servius, an ambitious woman, who had paved the way for her marriage with L. Tarquinius by the murder of her former husband, Aruns, and of her sister, the former wife of Tarquinius, was one of the prime movers in this conspiracy. At her instigation Tarquinius entered the Forum arrayed in the kingly robes, seated himself in the royal chair in the senate-house, and ordered the senators to be summoned to him as their king. Servius hastened to the senate-house, and ordered Tarquinius to come down from the throne. Tarquinius seized the old man and flung him down the stone steps. Covered with blood, the king hastened home; but he was overtaken by the servants of Tarquinius and murdered. Tullia drove to the senate-house and greeted her husband as king; but her joy struck even him with horror. He bade her go home; and as she was returning, her charioteer pulled up and pointed out the corpse of her father. She commanded him to drive on: the blood of her father spurted over the carriage and on her dress; and from that day forward the street bore the name of the *Vicus Sceleratus*, or Wicked Street.

Tullus Hostilius, legendary third king of Rome 670–630 B.C. He is said to have forced Alba to acknowledge the supremacy of Rome, but later to have destroyed that city and settled its population on the Caelian hill. He subsequently vanquished the Sabines, but Jupiter at length avenged the destruction of Alba by slaying Tullus and all his house.

Turnus, in Roman legend, King of the Rutuli when Aeneas (q.v.) arrived in Italy. He made war upon Aeneas because Latinus (q.v.) had married his daughter Lavinia to the Trojan hero, whereas she had been promised to Turnus. The war ended with Turnus's death at the hands of Aeneas (*see* VIRGIL, *Aeneid*).

Tusculum (mod. Frascati), town of Latium, about 15 miles southeast of Rome, founded traditionally by Telegonus, son of Odysseus and Circe. Its proximity to Rome, its healthy climate and its beautiful situation made it a favourite summer residence of wealthy Romans.

Cicero had a famous villa here, where he wrote the *Tusculan Disputa-tions*. Tusculum was also the birth-place of the elder Cato. *See* G. McCracken, *Short History of Ancient Tusculum*, 1939.

Twelve Labours of Heracles. As explained in the article HERACLES, the hero was ordered by the Delphic oracle to serve Eurystheus, King of Tiryns, as atonement for the murder of his own sons and nephews. Eurystheus imposed upon him twelve superhuman tasks, which are known as the Twelve Labours of Heracles. Homer mentions only the twelfth; the remainder are derived from later writers and are usually arranged as follows:

1. *The fight with the Nemean lion.* The valley of Nemea, between Cleonae and Phlius, was inhabited by a monstrous lion, the offspring of Typhon and Echidna. Eurystheus ordered Heracles to bring him the skin of this monster. After using in vain his club and arrows against the lion, he strangled it with his own hands.

2. *Fight against the Lernean hydra.* This monster, like the lion, was the offspring of Typhon and Echidna, and was brought up by Hera. It ravaged the country of Lerne, near Argos, and dwelt in a swamp near the well of Amymone. It had nine heads, of which the middle one was immortal. Heracles struck off its heads with his club; but in the place of each head he cut off, two new ones grew. However, with the assistance of his faithful servant Iolaus, he burned away the heads of the hydra, and buried the ninth, or immortal one, under a rock. Having thus conquered the monster, he poisoned his arrows with its bile, whence the wounds inflicted by them became incurable.

3. *Capture of the Arcadian stag.* This animal had golden antlers and brazen feet. Heracles was ordered to bring the animal alive to Eurystheus. He pursued it in vain for a year; at length he wounded it with an arrow, caught it and carried it away on his shoulders.

4. *Destruction of the Erymanthian boar.* This animal, which Heracles was also ordered to bring alive to Eurystheus, had descended from Mt Erymanthus into Psophis. Heracles chased it through the deep snow, and having thus worn it out, he caught it in a net, and carried it to Eurystheus. Other traditions place the hunt of the Erymanthian boar in Thessaly. *See also* CHIRON; PHOLUS.

5. *Cleansing of the stables of Augeas.* Eurystheus imposed upon Heracles the task of cleansing in one day the stalls of Augeas, King of Elis. Augeas had a herd of 3,000 oxen, whose stalls had not been cleansed for thirty years. Heracles, without mentioning the command of Eurystheus, went to Augeas, and offered to cleanse his stalls in one day if he would give him the tenth part of his cattle. Augeas agreed to the terms; and Heracles, after taking Phyleus, the son of Augeas, as his witness, turned the rivers Alpheus and Peneus through the stalls, which were thus cleansed in a single day. But Augeas, who learned that Heracles had undertaken the work by the command of Eurystheus, refused to give him the reward. His son Phyleus then bore witness against his father, who exiled him from Elis. At a later time Heracles invaded Elis, and killed Augeas and his sons.

6. *Destruction of the Stymphalian birds.* These voracious birds had been brought up by Ares. They had brazen claws, wings and beaks, used their feathers as arrows and ate human flesh. They dwelt on a

lake near Stymphalus in Arcadia, from which Heracles was ordered by
Eurystheus to expel them. When Heracles undertook the task,
Athena provided him with a brazen rattle, by the noise of which he
startled the birds; and, as they attempted to fly away, he killed them
with his arrows.

7. *Capture of the Cretan bull.* The bull had been sent out of the sea
by Poseidon, that Minos might offer it in sacrifice. But he was so
charmed with the beauty of the animal, that he kept it and sacrificed
another in its stead. Poseidon punished Minos by driving the bull
mad, and Heracles was ordered by Eurystheus to catch it. He brought
it home on his shoulders, but then set it free again. The bull roamed
through Greece, and at last came to Marathon, where we meet it again
in the stories of Theseus (q.v.).

8. *Capture of the mares of the Thracian Diomedes.* Diomedes, King
of the Bistones in Thrace, fed his horses with human flesh. Eurystheus
ordered Heracles to bring him these animals. With a few companions,
he seized them, and led them to the sea coast. But here he was overtaken by the Bistones. During the fight he entrusted the mares to his
friend Abderus, who was devoured by them. Heracles defeated the
Bistones, killed Diomedes, whose body he threw to the mares, built
the town of Abdera in honour of his unfortunate friend, and then
returned to Eurystheus with the mares, which had become tame after
eating the flesh of their master. The mares were afterwards set free,
and destroyed on Mt Olympus by wild beasts.

9. *Seizure of the girdle of the queen of the Amazons.* Hippolyte,
Queen of the Amazons, possessed a girdle which she had received from
Ares. Admete, the daughter of Eurystheus, wished to obtain this
girdle, and Heracles was sent to fetch it. After various adventures in
Europe and Asia, he at length reached the country of the Amazons.
Hippolyte at first received him kindly, and promised him her girdle;
but Hera having excited the Amazons against him, a contest ensued,
in which Heracles killed their queen. *See* THESEUS. He then took her
girdle. On his way home he landed in Troas, where he rescued Hesione
(q.v.) from the monster sent against her by Poseidon; in return for
which service her father, Laomedon (q.v.), promised him the horses
he had received from Zeus as compensation for Ganymede. But, as
Laomedon did not keep his word, Heracles on leaving threatened
to make war against Troy, a threat which he afterwards fulfilled.

10. *Capture of the oxen of Geryon in Erythia.* Geryon, a monster
with three bodies, lived in the fabulous island of Erythia (the ' red-
dish '), so called because it lay in the west, under the rays of the setting
sun. This island was originally placed off the coast of Epirus, but was
afterwards identified with either Gades or the Balearic Islands. The
oxen of Geryon were guarded by the giant Eurytion and the two-
headed dog Orthus; and Heracles was commanded by Eurystheus to
fetch them. After traversing various countries, he reached at length
the frontiers of Libya and Europe, where he erected two pillars (Calpe
and Abyla) on the two sides of the straits of Gibraltar, which were
hence called the Pillars of Hercules. Being annoyed by the heat of the
sun, Heracles shot at Helios (the Sun), who so much admired his

boldness that he presented him with a golden cup or boat, in which he sailed to Erythia. He there slew Eurytion and his dog, as well as Geryon, and sailed with his booty to Tartessus, where he returned the golden cup to Helios. On his way home he passed through Gaul, Italy, Illyricum and Thrace. Many attempts were made to deprive him of the oxen, but he at length brought them in safety to Eurystheus, who sacrificed them to Hera.

11. *Fetching the golden apples of the Hesperides.* This was particularly difficult, since Heracles did not know where to find them. They were the apples which Hera had received at her wedding from Gē (the Earth), and which she had entrusted to the keeping of the Hesperides (q.v.) and the dragon Ladon, on Mt Atlas. On arriving at Mt Atlas, Heracles sent Atlas to fetch the apples, and in the meantime bore the weight of heaven for him. Atlas returned with the apples, but declined to resume the burden. Heracles, however, contrived by a stratagem to get the apples, and hastened away. On his return Eurystheus made him a present of the apples; but Heracles dedicated them to Athena, who restored them to their former place. Some traditions add that Heracles killed the dragon Ladon.

12. *Bringing Cerberus from the lower world.* This was the most difficult of the twelve labours of Heracles. He descended into Hades, near Taenarum in Laconia, accompanied by Hermes and Athena. There he delivered Theseus from his torments, and obtained permission from Pluto to carry Cerberus to the upper world, provided he could do so without force of arms. Heracles managed to seize the monster and carry it off; then, having shown it to Eurytheus, he returned it to the shades.

Twelve Tables, Law of the (Lex Duodecim Tabularum). The legal history of the Roman Republic begins with the Twelve Tables. It was, strictly, the first and only Roman code; and its importance lies in the fact that it substituted a public written body of laws, easily accessible and binding on all citizens, for an unwritten usage, knowledge of which was confined to a few. Till the close of the republican period this code was looked upon as a great legal charter, and in early times it was learned by heart in schools as a 'text-book inspired by fate'.

The Law, published *c.* 450 B.C. (*see* DECEMVIRI), was engraved on bronze tablets and fixed to the rostra which stood in front of the senate-house. We do not possess any part of the text in its original form: probably this important witness to the national progress was destroyed in the Gallic invasion (390 B.C.). Only detached fragments have survived, but they constitute about one-third of the entire code and suffice to indicate its character. A few specimens will illustrate their laconic brevity: (1) One who has confessed a debt, or against whom judgment has been given, shall be allowed thirty days in which to pay it. (2) Whenever a contract or conveyance is made, as it is specified so let it be binding. (3) If a patron defrauds his client let him be accursed. Cicero tells us that among the few offences punishable with death was *occantatio* or *malum carmen*, 'evil song', i.e. a charm intended to hurt (*see* FESCENNINI VERSUS).

Ancient law, among the Romans, was rather a matter of religious

and ancestral custom than a definite expression of the national con-
science on questions of abstract right or wrong. Law, as we understand it, was but the consolidation of custom.

For Latin text of fragments *see* H. J. S. Maine, *Ancient Law*, 1861;
L. Schoell, *Legis Duodecim Tabularum: Reliquiae*, 1866; H. F.
Jolowicz, *Historical Introduction to the Study of Roman Law*, 1932;
W. A. Hunter, *Introduction to Roman Law*, 1950.

Tydeus (Tu-), son of Oeneus (q.v.), King of Calydon. Obliged to
leave home on account of homicide, he fled to Adrastus (*see* ADRASTUS,
1). at Argos, who purified him and gave him his daughter Deipyle in
marriage, by whom he became the father of Diomedes (*see* DIOMEDES,
2). Tydeus was one of the Seven against Thebes (*see* THEBAN LEGEND,
3), and the manner of his death is particularly horrid. Wounded by
Melanippus, he lay helpless on the ground when Athena came with a
remedy from Zeus. But before he could take it, along came Amphiaraüs, who detested him, with the newly severed head of Melanippus.
Tydeus split this open and ate the brain, while Athena, in disgust,
left him to die.

Tyndareus (Tundareos), in Greek legend, son of the Spartan king
Oebalus. He and his brother Icarius were driven from Sparta by
their stepbrother Hippocoön; Tyndareus went to Aetolia, where he
married Leda, and was later restored to the throne of Sparta by
Heracles. He was the father or putative father of the Dioscuri, Helen
and Clytaemnestra (qq.v.).

Typhon (Tuphōn) or **Typhoeus** (Tuphoios), in Greek legend, a
hundred-headed monster buried by Zeus in Tartarus under Mt
Aetna, or, according to Homer, under the country of the Arimi, in a
place lashed with lightning. Typhon was the youngest son of Tartarus
and Gē, and father by Echidna of the dog Orthus, Cerberus, the
Lernaean Hydra, the Chimaera and the Sphinx; also, in some
accounts, of the dangerous winds and of the Harpies.

Tyrannion (Turanniōn), nickname of Theophrastus, a Greek
grammarian of Amisus in Pontus. Taken prisoner by Lucullus,
he was brought to Rome (72 B.C.) and given to L. Licinius, who
manumitted him. He set up as a teacher, and was also employed to arrange the library of Apellicon, which had been brought
to Rome by Sulla (q.v.). Cicero speaks highly of his learning and
ability.

Tyrant (Gk Turannos), Greek name for a man who availed himself
of popular discontent to overthrow the existing government and
make himself supreme. When a tyrant did not abuse his power, the
people often fared better under a 'benevolent despot', while a tyranny
often encouraged new developments in the state. Such tyrannies
arose most commonly in the 7th and 6th centuries B.C., and many of
the tyrants of that period have won a high reputation by the impetus
they gave to trade and commerce, and by their encouragement of the
arts. The dislike of monarchs in general, however, led men to associate
the name of tyrant with the idea of a cruel and arbitrary ruler, and its
modern meaning is also largely due to the ultra-constitutionalists of
the 4th century B.C. at Athens, to whom the democracy of Pericles
was the ideal of government. *See* P. N. Ure, *The Origin of Tyranny,*

1922. *See also* AGATHOCLES; DIONYSIUS; GELON; PERIANDER; POLY-
CRATES; THERON.

Tyre (Gk Turos; Lat. Tyrus; mod. Sur), ancient town of Syria, built
partly on an island and said to have been founded in the 15th century
B.C. It was the principal seaport of the Phoenicians, and as such
known to the Greeks. It was originally a colony of Sidon, divided
between the mainland and the island, which were linked by a causeway. As an island fortress Tyre withstood many sieges, but was sacked
by Alexander (332 B.C.) and did not recover. It was, however, a
flourishing port under the early Roman emperors.

Tyrtaeus (Turtaios), Greek poet of the 7th century B.C., probably a
Spartan (legends about his Athenian origin should be ignored). He
wrote military and elegiac poems, of which fragments have survived.
See C. M. Bowra, *Early Greek Elegists*, 1938; E Diehl, *Anthologia
Lyrica Graeca*, 1949.

U

Ubii, a German tribe inhabiting the Rhine basin in the neighbourhood of Cologne. In 55 B.C. Caesar crossed the Rhine, entered their territory and received hostages from them.

Ulpianus, Domitius, Roman jurist, born *c.* A.D. 170 at Tyre. Under Alexander Severus he held the offices of *libellorum magister, praefectus annonae, praefectus praetorio* and was the emperor's chief adviser. In 228 he was murdered by soldiers, who broke into the palace at night and slew him in presence of Alexander and the latter's mother (Julia Mammaea). About one-third of Justinian's *Digest* consists of extracts from his writings.

Umbria, district of Italy, bounded north by Gallia Cisalpina, east by the Adriatic, south by the Sabines, west by the Tiber. The Umbrians joined first with Etruria and Samnium (qq.v.) against Rome, but became allies of Rome after 295 B.C. The principal towns were Ariminum, Fanum Fortunae, Mevania, and Narnia (qq.v.). Augustus made Umbria the sixth Region of Italy (*see* ITALIA).

Urania (Ou-), the muse of Astronomy. *See* MUSES.

Uranus (Ouranos), 'Heaven', in Greek mythology husband of Gē (Earth) and father of the Titans (q.v.).

Usipetes, *see* TENCTERI.

Utica, city of north Africa, 25 miles north-west of Carthage. It was founded by Phoenicians *c.* 1100 B.C., and after the destruction of Carthage (146 B.C.) rose to be the first city of Africa and capital of the Roman province. Utica was later immortalized as the scene of Cato's suicide after Thapsus (46 B.C.).

Uxellodunum (mod. Puy d'Issolu), Gallic stronghold in the territory of the Cadurci, besieged and captured by Caesar in 51 B.C. (*see Bell. Gall.* viii, 33–44).

V

Vadimonis, Lacus (mod. Lago di Bassano), lake in Etruria, famous for its sulphurous waters and floating islands. Here the Romans won two victories over the Etruscans (310 and 283 B.C.).

Valerianus, Publius Licinius, Roman emperor A.D. 253–60, general and faithful supporter of Gallus (q.v.), after whose death he was proclaimed emperor by the troops. He took his son Gallienus as colleague, and, leaving him in charge of affairs in Europe, set out for the East to crush the Persian Sapor I (257). After some success he was entrapped by Sapor (260) and kept prisoner until his death. *See* Gibbon, *Decline and Fall*, ch. x.

Valerius Maximus, Roman historian of the early 1st century A.D. His *Factorum et Dictorum Memorabilium Libri IX*, dedicated to the emperor Tiberius, is interesting as a specimen of the transition from classical to 'silver' Latin. It records many curious events not to be found elsewhere, but its statements must often be accepted with caution. *See* edition by C. Kempf, 1888. There is a translation by W. Speed (1678).

Vandali, a Germano-Slavic people dwelling between the Oder and the Vistula. During the reign of Aurelian, Vandal troops were employed in the Roman army. Under Constantine many of this people setted in Pannonia.

Vangiones, *see* TRIBOCI.

Varius Rufus, Lucius, Roman poet, a friend of Virgil and Horace. The latter places him foremost among epic poets, and Quintilian declares that his *Thyestes* would stand comparison with the masterpieces of Greek tragedy. Nothing of his work has survived.

Varro, Gaius Terentius, Roman general. Of low birth and ultrademocratic opinions, he was chosen (216 B.C.), despite opposition from the senate, to oppose Hannibal. His fellow consul was L. Aemilius Paulus, a leader of the aristocratic party, and they were together defeated at Cannae (q.v.), which was fought against Paulus's advice. Varro was one of the few who escaped, and was subsequently made responsible for the disaster. His conduct after the battle, however, in organizing precautionary measures, won high praise. He was ambassador to Philip V of Macedon in 203, and to Syphax of Numidia in 200 B.C.

Varro, Marcus Terentius (116–27 B.C.), Latin antiquary, born at Reate. He fought against Caesar in the civil war, but was allowed by the second triumvirate (q.v.) to retire into private life (*c.* 42 B.C.). Varro is known to have written about seventy works on antiquarian subjects, and 150 Menippean satires; but, apart from numerous fragments, we possess only *De Re Rustica* and six of the twenty-five books of *De Lingua Latina*. A good deal of information derived from his *Antiquitates Rerum Humanarum et Divinarum* has been preserved by Aulus Gellius, Macrobius and St Augustine (*De Civitate Dei*). *See* the edition of *De Re Rustica* by G. Goetz, 1922, and of *De Lingua Latina* (v–x) by F. Schoell and G. Goetz, 1910. Both these works have been edited with translations in the Loeb Library, the former by W. D. Hooper and H. D. Ash (1934), and the latter by R. G. Kent (1938).

Varus, Publius Quintilius, consul in 13 B.C., and afterwards governor of Syria, when he acquired enormous wealth. About A.D. 7 he was given command of forces in Germany, but in A.D. 9 he was defeated by Arminius (q.v.) with the loss of three entire legions in the Saltus Teutoburgensis, between the upper Ems and Weser. Varus committed suicide, and Rome lost all her territory east of the Rhine. When news of the disaster reached Rome the city was thrown into consternation, and for long afterwards the aged Augustus was heard crying on sleepless nights: 'Varus, Varus! Give me back my legions!'

Veii, ancient city of Etruria, about 12 miles north-west of Rome. It was engaged in hostilities with Rome during a long period: we have records of no fewer than fourteen distinct wars between the two peoples before its destruction by Camillus (q.v.), after a ten-year siege, in 396 B.C.

Velleius Paterculus, *see* PATERCULUS.

Veneti: 1. Gallic tribe who dwelt in what is now the Morbihan department of France. Essentially sea-traders and with a prosperous agriculture, they carried on a considerable trade with Britain. They resisted Caesar, but were defeated in a naval battle (56 B.C.). Under the empire their trade declined.

2. People who dwelt in the area round the headwaters of the Adriatic, to which they had migrated about the mid 10th century B.C. At that time they were an Illyrian-speaking people. Civilized and peaceful, they preferred commerce to war, were prominent in the amber trade and famous for their horse-breeding. Friendly towards Rome, they fought for her against the Gauls and against Hannibal. Later they became subject to Rome, were romanized before the end of the republic, and under Augustus their territory (Venetia) became part of the tenth region of Italy (*see* ITALIA). They enjoyed prosperity until the end of the 2nd century A.D.; but later they were attacked in turn by the Alemanni (286), the Goths (*c.* 400) and the Huns (452). After this last attack many of them took refuge in the islands off their coast, on which Venice now stands.

Venta Belgarum (mod. Winchester), an important road centre, and the commercial and administrative capital of a district in Roman Britain. Many Roman finds are in the city museum, and remains of Roman buildings were discovered during excavations in 1953 and 1954.

Ventidius, Publius, Roman general, at first gained a livelihood by jobbing mules and carriages. Caesar, however, employed him in Gaul and during the civil war. After Caesar's death he supported Mark Antony, and was consul suffectus in 43 B.C. In 39 Antony sent him to Syria, where he won two brilliant victories over the Parthians, and in 38 B.C. he was granted a triumph (q.v.).

Venus, an Italian goddess, perhaps of garden fertility. Her cult seems to have been established at Rome in quite early times. Later she was identified with the Greek Aphrodite (q.v.), and this gave her various new attributes. At the beginning of the second Punic war the worship of Venus Erycina was introduced from Sicily. In the year 114 B.C., on account of corruption, especially among the Vestals, a temple was built to Venus Verticordia (the goddess who turns the human heart). After the close of the Samnite wars, Fabius Gurges founded the worship of Venus Obsequens and Postvorta; Scipio Africanus the younger that of Venus Genetrix, in which he was afterwards followed by Caesar, who added that of Venus Victrix. The worship of Venus was promoted by Caesar, who traced his descent from Aeneas, supposed to be the son of Mars and Venus. In her honour he erected a splendid temple; and in A.D. 135 Hadrian erected to her a still more majestic shrine. The month of April, as the beginning of spring, was sacred to Venus.

Venusia (mod. Venosa), town of Apulia, on the River Aufidus, celebrated as the birth-place of Horace.

Vercingetorix, chieftain of the Arverni in Transalpine Gaul. He led a revolt against the Romans, but was delivered to Caesar on the surrender of Alesia (52 B.C.) and sent to Rome. After adorning Caesar's triumph in 46 B.C. he was put to death. *See* life by M. A. Leblond, 1937–8.

Vergilius Maro, Publius, called in English **Virgil** (70–19 B.C.), Latin poet, born 15th October near Mantua in Cisalpine Gaul. He was educated at Cremona and Mediolanum, and assumed the *toga virilis* at the former place in 55. It is said that he subsequently studied Greek under Parthenius (q.v.) at Neapolis. He was also instructed by Syron, an Epicurean, probably at Rome. After completing his education, Virgil seems to have retired to his paternal farm. He probably became acquainted with Maecenas (q.v.) soon after completing his *Eclogues* (c. 37). His most finished work, the *Georgics*, was undertaken at the suggestion of Maecenas (iii. 41), and was published in 30. He probably began the *Aeneid* at about this time. In 19 he went to Greece, and caught a fever one burning day amid the ruins of Megara. Returning to Italy, he died soon after landing at Brundisium on 22nd September. He was buried near the road between Neapolis and Puteoli, and the *Aeneid*, which he desired to be burnt, was published by his executors on the order of Augustus. Virgil never married, and had made few friends; but those few included the emperor, Maecenas and Horace, and the latter has left a memorial of his affection (*Odes*, I. iii. 6; *Satires* I. v. 40). The best complete edition of Virgil's works is that by J. Conington (1883–98). There are numerous editions of separate works and translations of the same; *see* particularly Michael Oakley's version of the *Aeneid* in Everyman's Library (1957), that of the *Georgics* by C. Day Lewis (1940) and that of the *Eclogues* by Dryden (1697). *See also* T. Frank, *Virgil*, 1927; C. Bailey, *Religion in Virgil*, 1935; R. W. Cruttwell, *Virgil's Mind at Work*, 1946.

Verres, Gaius, quaestor to Cn. Papirius Carbo in 84 B.C., but later an adherent of Sulla. After serving as *legatus* of Cn. Cornelius Dolabella in Cilicia, he was praetor in 74, and from 73 to 70 B.C. governor of Sicily, which he impoverished by his extortions. On his return to Rome Cicero undertook to prosecute him at the request of the islanders, to whom he had promised his good offices when Lilybaean quaestor in 75. Supported by the aristocracy, Verres entrusted his defence to Hortensius, who attempted to have Q. Caecilius Niger substituted as prosecutor. Cicero successfully countered this move with the speech *Divinatio in Q. Caecilium*; he was allowed 110 days in which to collect his evidence, but was fully prepared within fifty. Hortensius hoped to prolong the trial until 69, when he himself would be consul. Cicero therefore abandoned all thought of eloquence; merely introducing his case with the first oration *in Verrem* (the rest were written for publication), he rested his hopes on the weight of testimony alone. Hortensius was unprepared with counter-evidence, and after the first day's hearing threw up the case. Verres fled, and was condemned in his absence. He retired to Massilia, but retained so much of his loot that he was eventually proscribed by the triumvirs (43 B.C.).

Verrius, Flaccus, Marcus, Roman grammarian in the reign of Augustus, author of a kind of dictionary of the Latin language (*see* FESTUS, SEXTUS POMPEIUS).

Vertumnus, Italian deity of Etruscan origin. The Romans connected Vertumnus with all occurrences to which the verb *verto* applies, such as the change of seasons, purchase and sale, the return of rivers to their proper beds, etc. The god was connected chiefly with the transformation of plants and their progress from blossom to fruit. Hence the story, that when Vertumnus was in love with Pomona he assumed all possible forms, until at last he gained his end by metamorphosing himself into a beautiful youth. Gardeners offered to him the first produce of their gardens. The people celebrated a festival to Vertumnus on 13th August, under the name of the Vortumnalia, denoting the transition from high summer to the more mellow season of fruits. For literary references to Vertumnus, *see* especially Varro, *De Lingua Latina*, v. 46, and Propertius, iv. 2.

Verulamium, a Belgic settlement immediately west of St Albans, Herts, England (*see* BRITAIN) founded at the end of the 1st century B.C. Under Claudius a new town was built in the valley below and created a *municipium* (q.v.). It was sacked by the Iceni under Boudicca (q.v.) in A.D. 61, but a new town of some 150 acres was subsequently laid out. There was a further development *c.* A.D. 137. It decayed much in the 3rd century, but towards 290 suffered a temporary reinstatement, only to waste again. The excavations in 1930 and the years following threw much light on the Roman occupation of south-east Britain. See *Society of Antiquaries Research Report*, No. xi, 1936; R. L. P. Jowett, *A Guide to St Albans and Verulamium*, 1948.

Verus, Lucius Aelius, Roman emperor jointly with Marcus Aurelius, his brother by adoption, from A.D. 161 to 169. *See* MARCUS AURELIUS.

Vespasianus, Titus Flavius Sabinus, called in English **Vespasian,** Roman emperor A.D. 69–79, born at Reate in A.D. 9, son of a tax collector. After serving in Thrace, Crete and Cyrene, he took command of a legion in Germany in the first year of Claudius, and held the same rank during the invasion of Britain (q.v.) where he subdued Vectis (Isle of Wight). Nero disliked him intensely, but could not dispense with his services, and therefore gave him command of the

Jewish war (A.D. 66). In this capacity he greatly enhanced his reputation, and when war broke out between Otho and Vitellius, he was proclaimed emperor at Alexandria (1st July A.D. 69), and soon afterwards by all the legions of the East. His general Antonius Primus defeated the forces of Vitellius in December of that year, and was quickly followed by Vespasian himself, who was soon firmly established on the throne.

By his wife, Flavia Domitilla, Vespasian had two sons, Titus and Domitian (qq.v.). The former had been left to complete the Jewish war, and now (71) Titus returned to celebrate a triumph with his father. See also CIVILIS. Vespasian died on 24th June A.D. 79. See B. W. Henderson, *Five Roman Emperors*, 1927; C. Longford, *Vespasian and some of his Contemporaries*, 1928.

Vesper, see HESPERUS.

Vesta, Roman goddess of the hearth, closely associated with the Penates (q.v.) and identified with the Greek Hestia (q.v.). From Lavinium, whither Aeneas had brought from Troy the sacred fire as well as the Penates, her cult was traditionally introduced to Rome by Numa, who was believed to have built her central shrine in the Forum between the Palatine and Capitoline hills. Here her fires were kept always burning by the Vestals (q.v.). Her festival, the Vestalia, was celebrated on 8th June.

Vestals, the six priestesses of Vesta (q.v.), in her temple at Rome. They were chosen by lot from twenty maidens, of free and worthy parentage, nominated by the pontifex maximus. They officiated for at least thirty years, ten years of learning and initiation, ten of actual ministration and ten teaching the neophytes. Violation of the vow of chastity was punishable by death in the form of burial alive, and retribution followed if they let the sacred fires go out.

Vesuvius, volcano in Campania, nine miles south-east of Neapolis. There are no records of any eruption in the pre-Christian era, but the ancients were aware of its volcanic nature from the igneous appearance of its rocks. The first recorded eruption is that of 24th August A.D. 79, which overwhelmed the cities of Pompeii, Herculaneum and Stabiae (qq.v.).

Vetulonia, one of the twelve cities of the Etruscan confederacy, whence the Romans were said to have derived the insignia of their magistrates, as well as the use of brazen trumpets in war. Its site has been discovered near a village called Magliano about nine miles from the sea, between the rivers now called Osa and Albegna.

Victoria, Roman goddess of victory, identified with Greek Nike (q.v.). Her temple was on the Palatine.

Vindelicia. The Roman province of Rhaetia (q.v.) was divided by Diocletian (A.D. 284–305) into two: Rhaetia Prima (south) and Rhaetia Secunda (north), the latter of which names was gradually supplanted by that of Vindelicia. This new province lay between Gaul, Rhaetia Prima, Noricum and Germany.

Vindobona (mod. Wien; Eng. Vienna), Roman garrison town of Pannonia, on the Danube, built on an earlier Celtic site. It was the chief station of the Danube squadron, and headquarters of a legion. Marcus Aurelius is said to have died there.

Vipsania Agrippina, daughter of M. Vipsanius Agrippa by his first wife, Pomponia. She was married to the future emperor Tiberius (q.v.), and bore him a son Drusus. After Tiberius had been compelled by Augustus to divorce her, she was married to Gallus Saloninus (q.v.).

Virbius, *see* DIANA.

Virgil, *see* VERGILIUS MARO.

Virginia, in Roman legend, a maiden who was killed by her father when forced to yield her to the lust of Appius Claudius the decemvir. Her death caused the overthrow of the decemvirate (450 B.C.). *See* DECEMVIRI.

Viriathus, a Lusitanian rebel leader. He successfully defied one Roman army after another from 150 until 141 B.C., when the Roman general, Fabius Servilianus, concluded a peace with him. Servilius Caepio, who succeeded to the command in the following year, renewed the war, and soon afterwards procured the assassination of Viriathus by bribing three of his friends (140 B.C.).

Viroconium (mod. Wroxeter), town of the Roman province of Britain (q.v.), covering an area of about 170 acres. It was founded about A.D. 48 as a legionary camp (or possibly fortress), and it so continued until under Agricola (q.v.) the Fourteenth and Twentieth Legions were transferred to Chester. The town was partly destroyed by fire *c.* A.D. 300, and was rebuilt on a smaller scale. Extensive excavations were carried out between 1912 and 1937: parts of the forum and basilica, as well as of the great *thermae* (q.v.), can be seen. See *Research Reports of the Society of Antiquaries, Wroxeter,* 1, 2, 3, 1913–16; *Archaeologia,* vol. 88 (1938), 175.

Virtus, Roman personification of manly valour, associated in cult with Honos (q.v.).

Vitellius, Aulus, Roman emperor 2nd January–22nd December A.D. 69, son of Lucius Vitellius (consul A.D. 34). Though he had some knowledge of letters, his vices had made him acceptable to Caligula, Claudius and Nero; and surprise was caused when Galba chose such a man to command the legions of Lower Germany, for he had no military talent. However, he was proclaimed emperor by the troops at Colonia Agrippinensis (Cologne); his generals, Fabius Valens and Caecina Alienus, marched into Italy, defeated Otho's forces at Betriacum, and thus secured the throne for their master. He displayed some moderation, but continued his gluttonous habits. In July Vespasian (q.v.) was proclaimed at Alexandria; Caecina was defeated by his general Antonius Primus, who marched on Rome and put Vitellius to death.

Vitruvius Pollio, Marcus (1st century B.C.), Roman architect and writer. He appears to have served as a military engineer under Julius Caesar in Africa (46 B.C.), and was advanced in years when he dedicated to Augustus his celebrated work *De Re Architectura,* a treatise on architecture and building construction, to which we owe much of our knowledge of Roman building methods and of Greek buildings which have perished since his day. A copy of this work was discovered in the 15th century, printed and translated into several languages. *See* the edition with translation by F. Granger, 2 vols. (Loeb Library), and translation by J. R. Morgan, 1914.

Volaterrae (mod. Volterra), one of the twelve cities of the Etruscan confederacy, and called by the Etruscans Velathri. Its dominions extended eastwards to Arretium, westward to the Mediterranean, and southward to its colony Populonia. Its influence was due mainly to its ports, Luna and Populonia. There are remains of walls (4th century B.C.), and, in the museum at Florence, some finds from tombs of five centuries earlier.

Volsci, an Italian people of eastern Latium, akin to the Oscans and Umbrians, dwelling on both sides of the River Liris down to the Tyrrhenian Sea. They were at war with Rome in the 5th and 4th centuries B.C. and often allies of the Aequi, but were subdued (338) and enjoyed Roman citizenship by 304 B.C.

Volsinii, one of the twelve cities of the Etruscan confederacy, and called by the Etruscans Velsina. It was situated on a lofty hill at the north-eastern extremity of the lake called after it Lacus Volsiniensis (mod. Lago di Bolsena). The city was at war with Rome in the 4th and 3rd centuries B.C., but seems to have been finally subdued by 280 B.C., when it was razed to the ground and its inhabitants compelled to settle on a less defensible site in the plain, that of modern Bolsena, where Sejanus (q.v.) was born.

Volumnia, wife of Coriolanus (q.v.).

Vulcan (Lat. Vulcanus), Roman god of fire, called also Mulciber (averter of fire). An area with altar (called Vulcanale) was dedicated to him on the north side of the Forum. His most ancient festival was the Fornacalia, held in his honour as god of furnaces. More important, however, was the Vulcanalia on 23rd August. Vulcan was identified with the Greek Hephaestus (q.v.).

W

Wine (Gk *oinos*; Lat. *vinum*). It was almost a universal custom among the Greeks to dilute their wine with water. Possibly they were no great connoisseurs, as the Romans were, and it is almost certain that their wines were less choice than the Italian vintages. There were red, white and yellow types, most of them cheap; the most noted of all was the Chian, but Lesbos, Cnidos, Thasos and Rhodes all produced good quality wines. Among Italian wines, Caecuban, Formian and Setinian were ranked among the best; next to these Falernian (a heady drink); and in a lower class Alban and Massic. The commonest of all was Vaticanum. Other brands often mentioned were the Sabine and the wine of Cales (both from Campania). *See* Athenaeus, *Deipnosophistae*, i–x; Columella, *De Re Rustica*, xii; C. Seltman, *Wine in the Ancient World*, 1957. *See also* OPIMIUS, LUCIUS.

X

Xanthippē, wife of Socrates, allegedly a shrew.

Xanthippus (-os), son of Ariphon and father of Pericles (q.v.). He succeeded Themistocles (q.v.) as commander of the Athenian fleet in 479, and commanded it at the battle of Mycale in that year.

Xanthus (-os), city of Lycia. It stood on the west bank of a river of the same name. Twice in the course of its history it sustained sieges which terminated in the self-destruction of the inhabitants with their property, first against the Persians under Harpagus (*c.* 546 B.C.), and afterwards against the Romans under Brutus (43 B.C.). The city was never restored after its destruction on the second occasion. It was rich in temples, tombs and monuments (*see* HARPIES).

Xenocrates (-kratēs), Greek philosopher, born at Calchedon 396 B.C. He became a member of the Academy (q.v.), and accompanied Plato (q.v.) on one of his visits to Syracuse. After Plato's death he spent some time with Aristotle (q.v.) at Assos; returned to Athens, whence he was sent on embassies to both Philip II of Macedon and Antipater; and succeeded Speusippus (q.v.) as head of the Academy in 339, a post which he held until his death in 314 B.C. None of his writings has survived, but his teaching is discussed by Aristotle and Theophrastus, and Panaetius and Cicero held him in high esteem.

Xenophanēs (*fl.* 540–500 B.C.), Greek poet and first philosopher-theologian. He was born at Colophon in Ionia, but settled in Sicily, where he wrote *Satires* and several elegiac poems, of which fragments remain. Xenophanes held that the world was evolved from a mixture of earth and water, and that it will gradually be dissolved again by moisture, after which the process will be resumed. He believed the heavenly bodies to be clouds set on fire, that the sun is renewed after every sunset and every eclipse, that there are many suns and moons according to the regions, divisions and zones of the earth, and that the earth is both flat and infinite in extent. He maintained the existence of one God who controls the universe by thought alone. *See* T. Bergk, *Lyrici Graeci*, 1900; Sir T. Heath, *Greek Astronomy*, 1932; J. Burnet, *Early Greek Philosophy*, 4th ed., 1943; J. E. Raven, *Pythagoreans and Eleatics*, 1948.

Xenophōn (*c.* 430–*c.* 356 B.C.), Greek historian and Athenian general, born at Athens. He was a friend and disciple of Socrates. In 401 Xenophon entered the service of the Persian prince Cyrus the Younger (q.v.), who was preparing to dispute the throne with his sovereign and brother Artaxerxes II, Mnemon (*see* TEN THOUSAND, EXPEDITION OF THE). The Greek officers were treacherously killed after the battle of Cunaxa, and Xenophon, with great courage and skill, led the retreat from the Tigris to Trapezus on the Euxine. A history of the expedition is given in his *Anabasis*. He enlisted his soldiers in the service of Sparta (399); and in the latter year or very soon afterwards he was banished from Athens, either on account of his Spartan sympathies or because of his friendship with Socrates. In 396 he joined the Spartan army, fought under King Agesilaus at Coroneia (394), and was rewarded with an estate at Scillus. Following the renewal of alliance between Athens and Sparta (371), the decree of banishment against Xenophon was repealed (369), but he is said to have spent the remainder of his life at Corinth. Besides the *Anabasis*, he wrote a life of Agesilaus; *Hellenica*, a history of Greece from 411 to 362 B.C.; *Memorabilia, Apologia, Oeconomicus* and *Symposium*, all of which are expositions of the teachings of Socrates and attempts to vindicate his old teacher and friend; *Hiero*, a dialogue on tyranny; *Cyropaedia*, a political romance; *On Horsemanship*; *Hipparchicus*, on the powers and responsibilities of a cavalry officer; *Cynegeticus*, on hunting; *The Lacedaemonian Constitution*; and *Athenian Revenues*. The complete works have been edited by E. C. Marchant, 5 vols., 1900–19, and translated by H. G. Dakyns, 1890–4. There are numerous editions and translations of separate works and groups of works. *See* H. Richards, *Xenophon and Others*, 1907.

Xerxēs, King of Persia 485–465 B.C., born *c*. 519 B.C., son of Darius I and Atossa, daughter of Cyrus the Great. Prior to his accession Xerxes had been twelve years Viceroy at Babylon. After ascending the throne he suppressed revolts there and in Egypt. He then set out against Greece at the head of a vast army, which he led across the Hellespont on a bridge of boats (480). Another great feat was the construction of a canal through Mt Athos. He marched south without meeting resistance, until he reached Thermopylae, where he defeated Leonidas (q.v.). Xerxes then marched through Phocis and Boeotia and at length reached Athens, while his fleet, battered by storm and action, arrived in the Bay of Phalerum. He destroyed Athens, and then decided to risk a naval battle with the Greeks, but his mighty armament was defeated and dispersed at Artemisium and Salamis (480). Fearful now for his own safety, he left Mardonius (q.v.) with a large army to complete the subjugation of Greece and, with the rest of his forces, retreated homewards, entering Sardis at the end of the year. In 479 Mardonius was defeated at Plataea by the Greeks, and at the same time the Persians were also defeated off Mycale in Ionia. Finally, the Greeks gained another victory on the banks of the Eurymedon (466), as a result of which the Persians lost all their western possessions outside Asia Minor. Xerxes was assassinated by Artabanus in 465.

Xuthus (-os), in Greek legend, son of Hellen (q.v.) by the nymph Orseis. He married Creusa, daughter of Erechtheus II of Athens, after whose death he was chosen to arbitrate upon the succession and adjudged the kingdom to Cecrops (q.v.). He was consequently expelled by the other sons of Erechtheus and settled at Aegialus in Peloponnesus. *See* Ion.

Z

Zacynthus (-kunthos), island in the Ionian Sea, now called Zante, off the coast of Elis. Colonized by Achaeans from Peloponnesus, it later formed part of the Athenian Empire.

Zama, town of Numidia, in north Africa, 70 miles south-west of Carthage, the scene of Scipio's victory over Hannibal (202 B.C.), which ended the second Punic war.

Zancle (Zanklē), see MESSANA.

Zela, city in the south of Pontus, celebrated as the scene of Caesar's victory over Pharnaces (q.v.) in 47 B.C. The words ' *Veni, vidi, vici* ', so famous in connection with this battle, were *not*, as is commonly supposed, a laconic dispatch to the senate. They were displayed (? on a picture) at Caesar's Pontic triumph in 46 B.C.

Zeno (Gk Zēnōn) **of Elaea**, in southern Italy, Greek philosopher of the early 5th century B.C. He was a favourite disciple of Parmenides (q.v.), whose doctrine of 'The One' he upheld in a series of famous paradoxes (*see* Plato, *Parmenides*). Aristotle called him the founder of dialectic. *See* H. D. P. Lee, *Zeno of Elea* (with translation of surviving fragments), 1936.

Zeno (Gk Zēnōn) **of Citium** in Cyprus, Greek philosopher and founder of the Stoic school, born 335 B.C., probably half Semitic. He came to Athens at the age of about twenty, and attached himself to the cynic Crates. Later he studied under Stilpo, Diodorus Cronus and Philo of the Megarian school, then went to the Academics, Xenocrates and Polemo, and (*c.* 300) opened a school of his own in the Stoa Poikile (q.v.), whence his disciples were called Stoics. He died in 263 B.C., and was given a public funeral in the Cerameicus. *See* A. C. Pearson, *The Fragments of Zeno and Cleanthes*, 1891; E. Bevan, *Stoics and Sceptics*, 1913; M. Pohlenz, *Die Stoa*, 1949.

Zenobia, Queen of Palmyra (q.v.). After the death of her husband Odaenethus (q.v.), whom, according to some accounts, she assassinated (A.D. 267), she assumed the diadem as regent for her sons (*see* LONGINUS). Not content, however, with the independence conceded by Gallienus and tolerated by Claudius II, she sought to include all Syria, Asia and Egypt in her dominions, and to make good her self-assumed title Queen of the East. She was defeated by Aurelian (q.v.), taken prisoner on the capture of Palmyra (273), and carried to Rome, where she adorned the triumph of her conqueror (274). Her life was spared, and she spent the remainder of her life at Tibur, together with her sons.

Zenodotus (Zēnodotos), Greek grammarian and critic, a native of Ephesus. He was superintendent of the library at Alexandria in the reign of Ptolemy II, Philadelphus (283–246 B.C.), who employed him, together with Alexander the Aetolian and Lycophron the Chalcidian, to collect and revise the works of all the Greek poets.

Zephyrus (-phuros), personification of the west wind, son of Astraeus by Eos and brother of Boreas (q.v.), Eurus and Notus. By the harpy Podarge (*see* HARPIES) he begat Xanthus and Balius, two horses belonging to Achilles; but by Chloris he was father of Carpus (Gk *karpos* = fruit).

Zētēs and Calais (Kal-), sons of Boreas (q.v.). Their sister Cleopatra was married to Phineus, King of Salmydessus (q.v.), who imprisoned her, together with her sons, at the instigation of his second wife. Here she was found by Zetes and Calais when they came to Salmydessus with the Argonauts (q.v.). They freed her and her sons, deposed Phineus in favour of the latter and sent his second wife back to her own country, Scythia. Other versions relate that Zetes and Calais delivered Phineus from the Harpies, or that they perished in pursuit of the latter, or, again, that they were slain by Heracles near the island of Tenos.

Zēthos, twin brother of Amphion and father of Itylus, *see* AMPHION AND ZETHOS.

Zeus, the greatest of the Olympian gods, was in origin the chief deity of the hellenic invaders of Greece, the personification of the bright sky and perhaps of the sky in another mood as sender of fertilizing rain. He was soon identified with the principal chthonian deity of pre-hellenic Crete, and from this source as well as from the Homeric poems there arose, by a natural process, a wealth of legend. In classical mythology Zeus was a son of Cronus and Rhea, a brother of Poseidon, Hades, Hestia, Demeter, Hera, and was also married to his sister, Hera. When Zeus and his brothers overthrew Cronus (*see* TITANS), and distributed among themselves the government of the world by lot, Poseidon obtained the sea, Hades the lower world and Zeus the heavens and the upper regions, but the earth became common to all. According to the Homeric account Zeus dwelt on Mt Olympus (q.v.). He is called the father of gods and men, the most powerful among the immortals. He is the supreme ruler, who with his counsel manages everything; the founder of kingly power, and of law and order, whence Dike, Themis and Nemesis are his assistants. Everything good, as well as bad, comes from Zeus; he assigns good or evil to mortals; and Fate itself was subordinate to him. He is armed with thunder and lightning, and the shaking of his aegis (q.v.) produces storm and tempest: a number of epithets of Zeus, in the Homeric poems, describe him as the thunderer, the gatherer of clouds and the like. By Hera he had two sons, Ares and Hephaestus, and one daughter, Hebe. Cronus swallowed his children immediately after their birth; but when Rhea was pregnant with Zeus, she applied to Uranus and Gē to save the life of the child. Uranus and Gē therefore sent Rhea to Lyctos, in Crete, requesting her to bring up her child there. Rhea accordingly concealed Zeus in a cave of Mt Aegaeon, and gave Cronus a stone wrapped up in cloth, which he swallowed in the belief that it was his son. Other traditions state that Zeus was born and brought up on Mt Dicte or Ida (also the Trojan Ida), Ithome in Messenia, Thebes in Boeotia, Aegion in Achaia, or Olenos in Aetolia. According to the common account, however, Zeus grew up in Crete. In the meantime Cronus, by a device of Metis, was made to bring up

the children he had swallowed, and first of all the stone, which was afterwards set up by Zeus at Delphi. Zeus now overthrew Cronus (*see* TITANS), and obtained the dominion of the world, and chose Metis for his wife. When she was pregnant with Athena, he took the child out of her body and concealed it in his head, on the advice of Uranus and Gē, who told him that thereby he would retain the supremacy of the world. For if Metis had given birth to a son, this son would have acquired the sovereignty. After this Zeus became the father of the Horae and Moirae by his second wife Themis; of the Charites or Graces by Eurynome; of Persephone by Demeter; of the Muses by Mnemosyne; of Apollo and Artemis by Leto; and of Hebe, Ares and Ilithyia by Hera. Athena was born out of the head of Zeus; while Hera, on the other hand, gave birth to Hephaestus without the co-operation of Zeus. The family of the Cronidae accordingly embraces the twelve great gods of Olympus (q.v.): Zeus (the head of them all), Poseidon, Apollo, Ares, Hermes, Hephaestus, Hestia, Demeter, Hera, Athena, Aphrodite and Artemis. The Romans identified their Jupiter (q.v.) with the Greek Zeus. The Greek and Latin poets give to Zeus or Jupiter an immense number of epithets and surnames. The eagle, the oak and the summits of mountains were sacred to him, and his sacrifices consisted of goats, bulls and cows. His attributes are the sceptre, eagle, thunderbolt and a figure of Victory in his hand, and sometimes also a cornucopia. The Olympian Zeus sometimes wears a wreath of olive, and the Dodonaean Zeus a wreath of oak leaves. In works of art Zeus is generally represented as the omnipotent father and king of gods and men, according to the idea which had been embodied in the statue of the Olympian Zeus by Pheidias. Respecting the Roman god *see* JUPITER. *See* A. B. Cook, *Zeus*, 3 vols., 1914–40; Sir J. G. Frazer, *The Golden Bough*, 3rd ed., 10 vols., 1911–19; W. K. C. Guthrie, *The Greeks and their Gods*, 1950; C. Seltman, *The Twelve Olympians*, 1952.

Zeuxis (*fl.* 425–400 B.C.), Greek painter. He belonged to the Ionic school of art, and apparently drew his inspiration from Apollodorus. His rivalry with Parrhasius is the subject of anecdote. His reputed masterpiece was a picture of Helen, which he painted for Crotona, combining in the figure the beauties of five maidens of that city. That realistic imitation was valued in his time is suggested by the story of the birds pecking his painted grapes.